I0729707

The Organic Line

The Organic Line

Toward a Topology of Modernism

Irene V. Small

ZONE BOOKS · NEW YORK

2024

ZONE BOOKS
633 Vanderbilt Street
Brooklyn, NY 11218

Printed in the United States of America.

Distributed by Princeton University Press,
Princeton, New Jersey, and Woodstock, United Kingdom

This publication is made possible in part by the Barr Ferree Foundation Fund for Publications, Department of Art and Archaeology, Princeton University.

Library of Congress Cataloging-in-Publication Data
Names: Small, Irene, author.
Title: The organic line : toward a topology of modernism / Irene V. Small.
Description: New York : Zone Books, 2024. | Includes bibliographical
    references and index. | Summary: "This book mobilizes the Brazilian
    artist Lygia Clark's notion of the organic line — an interval of space
    between material elements — as a conceptual instrument for reimagining
    the field of modernism as a topological surface capable of formation
    and deformation through critical description and artistic practice alike"
    — Provided by publisher.
Identifiers: LCCN 2023049664 (print) | LCCN 2023049665 (ebook) |
    ISBN 9781890951993 (hardback) | ISBN 9781890951955 (ebook)
Subjects: LCSH: Modernism (Art). | Art criticism. | Clark, Lygia, 1920–1988
    — Aesthetics.
Classification: LCC N6490.S5653 2024 (print) | LCC N6490 (ebook) |
    DDC 709.04 — dc23/eng/20231204
LC record available at https://lccn.loc.gov/2023049664
LC ebook record available at https://lccn.loc.gov/2023049665

Contents

Introduction: On Weak Links and Plagiotropic Relations   9

I   *Circling the Square: Discovery against Invention*   77

II   *Not/Making/Marks: On the Side of Composition*   153

III   *Inhabiting Networks, Subjecting Space*   241

Coda: Of Mutant Coordinates and Living Things   325

Acknowledgments   349

Notes   355

Index   445

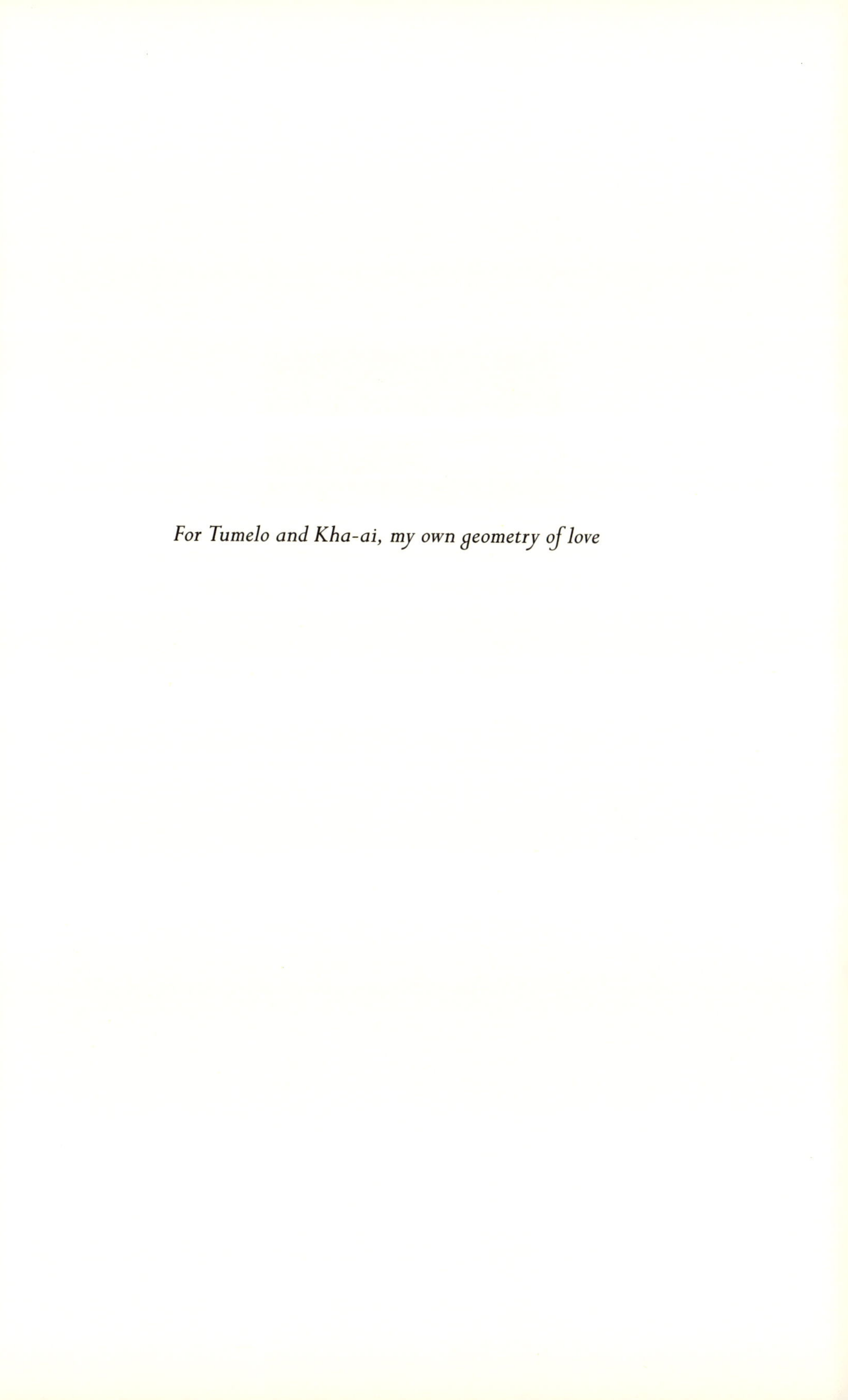

For Tumelo and Kha-ai, my own geometry of love

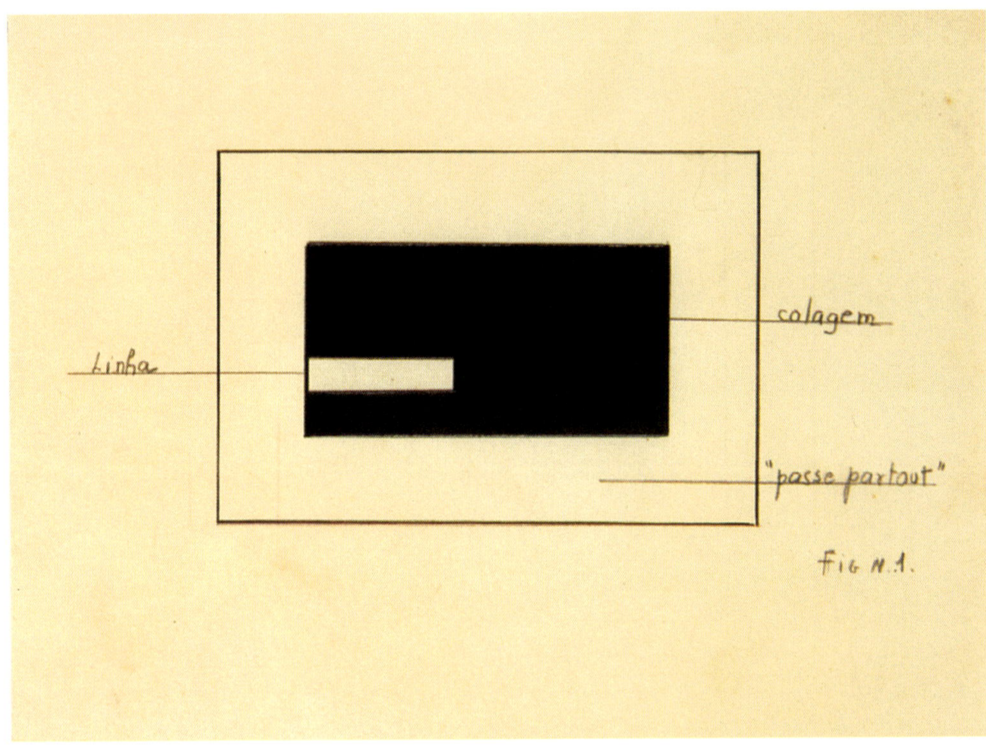

Figure I.1. Lygia Clark, *Estudo para Quebra da moldura* (Study for Breaking the frame), 1954. Courtesy of Associação Cultural "O Mundo de Lygia Clark." Photo: Marcelo Ribeiro Alvares Corrêa.

On Weak Links and

Plagiotropic Relations

The organic line is a line of space that lies between.

In 1954, the Brazilian artist Lygia Clark observed that when she abutted a work's framing mat, or *passe-partout*, with a collage element of the same color, a line of space appeared between them (fig. I.1). She observed that the line was liminal, contingent, and that it was found, not made. In a series of paintings that year, Clark deployed this line to "break the frame" of the painting support. The line of space entered the composition, while the painting moved out to envelop the frame. Clark soon connected this "undrawn line" to the lines of space that appear between doors and lintels, windows and frames, and tiles on the floor.[1] She named it "the organic line" and began to use it as a structuring element in her work. It played a significant role in her painterly and sculptural investigations of the late 1950s and 1960s, as well as in her subsequent explorations of social and therapeutic practice. For while the organic line initially manifested as a graphic phenomenon internal to the work and its conventions of display, its actualized, spatial character just as firmly secured it to an experiential realm beyond the work itself.

In this book, I argue that the organic line allows us to reconfigure the field of modernist art as a flexible and topological surface, porous to what has exceeded its purview and capable of formation and deformation through critical description and artistic practice alike. The organic line thus has far-reaching consequences for articulating the relations between modern and contemporary art, the canon and the so-called periphery, and formal innovation and the politics of making. On the occasion of Clark's 2014 retrospective at the Museum of Modern Art, New York, cocurator Luis Pérez-Oramas argued that the organic line transforms the "archaeology of painting" embedded in her work, signaling its archetypal character vis-à-vis the history of art.[2] In a 2006 essay, the artist Ricardo Basbaum proposed that Clark's organic line offers a paradigm of "between," rather than "beyond," thereby suspending schemas of linear development that undergird modernist thought.[3] His essay builds on sustained engagement by the psychoanalyst Suely Rolnik with Clark's later notion of an embodied and porous subjectivity.[4] The conceptual force of the organic line is activated by, indeed demands, "concrete engagement," Basbaum argues.[5] In part, this book is an answer to that call. But it recognizes that "concrete engagement" also requires an interrogation of method and scope (fig. I.2).

We might begin with the observation that while Clark's organic line has been familiar to Brazilian artists and critics since the 1950s, it remains relatively obscure within a broader history of art. For several decades, scholars have invoked alternative, synchronous, and multiple modernisms in order to complicate the notion of modernity as a Western phenomenon that spreads to the so-called periphery, erasing local expressions of difference in its wake. Yet as a scholarly subfield, modernist art history regularly insists on the comprehensive import of certain artistic articulations — the collage, the readymade, the grid, the monochrome, to name a few — that have had, in relation to this scholarly field, what might be described as a structuring force.[6] Such phenomena are often described with the language of invention: Pablo Picasso's and Georges Braque's *papiers collés* revolutionized the pictorial surface; Kazimir Malevich's *Black Square* blasted open the possibilities of abstraction; Marcel Duchamp's nomination of industrial commodities transformed

Figure I.2. Lygia Clark, *Quebra da moldura* (Breaking the frame), 1954. Courtesy of Associação Cultural "O Mundo de Lygia Clark." Photo: Marcelo Ribeiro Alvares Corrêa.

art into a conceptual act. As Mikhail Bakhtin argued of speech acts, such articulations are dialogic and always shared between artist and audience within a given historical context.[7] Moreover, precedents for such practices almost always exist. The grids of urban planning, woven cloth, and account books were what media theorists call "cultural techniques" long before modernist artists aesthetically represented their operations as art.[8] The modernist difference lies in "laying bare the device," as Viktor Shklovsky argued.[9] As the title of Shklovsky's 1917/1919 essay "Art as Technique" begins to suggest, the distinction between art techniques and cultural techniques is highly significant within the historiography of modernism. And while the former often strategically rework the latter (the readymade internalizing the shop display; photomontage recasting the protocols of advertising, the postcard, and the family album), it is the artistic intervention that modernist art history holds dear. The concept of the avant-garde proposes that to lay bare the device first is a historical innovation. That such devices are disseminated through the vehicle of influence consolidates notions of authorship and intentionality. And that this circulation occurs across widely divergent contexts suggests that artistic techniques approximate a quasi-universal language that can be adapted and reactivated toward distinct, yet self-consciously modernist ends.

In several aspects, the organic line resembles the artistic devices described above. Like phenomena such as the grid or the monochrome, it preexists and supersedes its deployment as a specifically modernist expression. Spatial intervals play both instrumental and incidental roles in our physical environments and artistic practices. There is no construction without a seam. "A prime axiom for artistic practice," as Gottfried Semper incisively put it, the seam allows for the aesthetic acknowledgment that composite entities are necessarily joined.[10] Its "binding and linking" quality thus inheres in the pure mechanics of technics and the primal symbolism of art alike.[11] In his influential 1949 thesis, the Brazilian critic Mário Pedrosa remarked on the value of the void in Asian aesthetics, from the hollowness of a vase to the emptied pictorial zones of paintings that result in differing velocities of attention.[12] Likewise, a long tradition of panel and pendant painting in Western art has harnessed the gaps between images toward symbolic and aesthetic ends.[13] As Wendy Ikemoto has noted, such doubled works activate spatial intervals in order to thematize "their own interpictoriality."[14] But when Clark called attention to preexisting intervals of space liminal to works of art and architecture and named them organic lines, she foregrounded the spatial and conceptual qualities of the interval itself. In this sense, her observation was a defined and historically punctual event. And although such lines have existed in relation to countless other works and quotidian phenomena, Clark's second-order observation transformed them into a conceptual object in their own right.

The organic line is a unique phenomenon in other ways, as well. Unlike virtually any other line in the history of art, the organic line is not a positive entity, by which I mean an entity conceived — or *perceived* — as self-evident content or form. A point, followed by a line, is the minimal condition to establish figure against ground. As such, lines are often equated with cognitive and epistemological distinction. As Catherine de Zegher writes, "If, for the linguists, naming with the word was the act of consciousness through which we begin to know, for the artists the rendering of form in drawing transformed perception into naming, and so was the process through which they came to know. Cognition thus proceeds from creation, with line as indicator of cognitive process."[15] Whether scratched in stone or drawn in pencil, lines delineate, construct, and register, operations intimately associated with action and the activity of differentiating. As Aleksandr Rodchenko wrote in 1921, "The line is the path of passing through, movement, collision, edge, attachment, joining, sectioning" (fig. I.3).[16] Even when transposed into what Eric de Bruyn has evocatively termed "political geometries," line is understood as a vector of force, whether disciplinary or emancipatory in character.[17] In *A Thousand Plateaus: Capitalism*

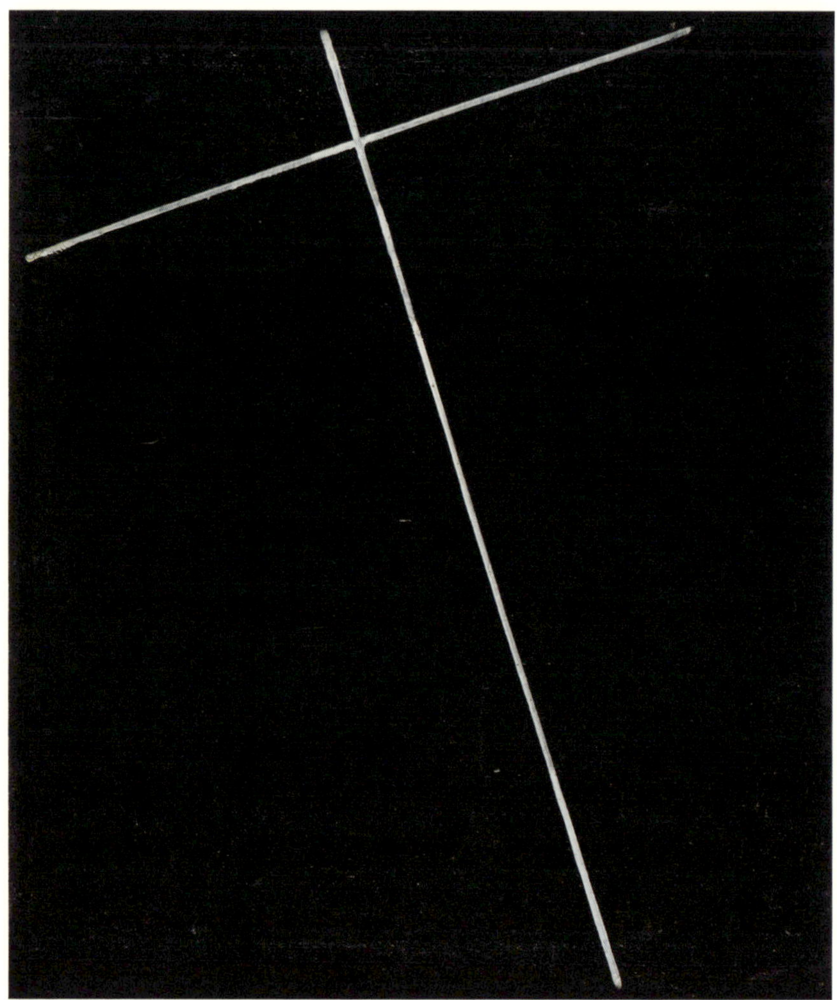

Figure I.3. Alexander Rodchenko, *Line. No. 128*, 1919. Oil on canvas, 62 × 53 cm. The Pushkin State Museum of Fine Arts, Moscow. © 2023 Estate of Alexander Rodchenko/UPRAVIS, Moscow/ARS, NY

and Schizophrenia, Gilles Deleuze and Félix Guattari juxtapose lines of rigid and supple segmentarity with "lines of flight" that "blast the two segmentary series apart," causing systems to leak and malfunction, like a hole in a pipe. Among other sources, the philosophers were inspired by the fugitive thought of George Jackson's prison writings and the *lignes d'erre* (errant or wander lines) Fernand Deligny traced in the movements of nonverbal autistic children.[18] Unlike Jackson's dynamic "line of escape," Deligny's "arachnean" itineraries resist production in favor of mappings of desire and convergence. But they, too, forge a network that circumvents existing inscriptions of power. As Deleuze and Guattari write, "There is nothing more active than a line of flight."[19]

As a line of space between features—a fissure that is observed, rather than made—the organic line is ontologically distinct from these technical, artistic, and philosophical articulations. In his 1925/1953 *Pedagogical Sketchbook*, Paul Klee describes a nonagential line that brings us somewhat closer to its operations. Here, Klee contrasts active lines that move "freely, without a goal," with medial lines that delineate "planar effects" and finally with passive lines, which result from the "activation" of such planar shapes.[20] In an accompanying illustration, Klee diagrams the "conjugations" of active, medial, and passive lines, providing linguistic equivalents apropos of a man who cuts down a tree: *I fell, I fall, I am being felled* (fig. I.4). But the organic line corresponds to none of these formulations. It is not a degree of agency in relation to a line: it is the space between the tree and the ax. Indeed, it is this *nothingness* that otherwise escapes legibility that invites metaphoric elaboration. Once recognized as actual, relational, and substantive, the interval of space appears to become a living, organic entity: a breath, a blade, a trace of air; a gutter and furrow; a void that irrigates and cleaves; a crevice and cleft that differentiates matter and ruptures the plane.

Although several of these metaphors convey demarcation, the organic line is unusual in the history of art, if not distinct, in that it is a line devoid of a mark. Of course, sight lines and perspectival

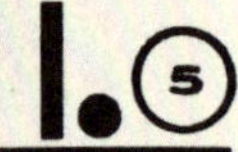

THREE CONJUGATIONS:

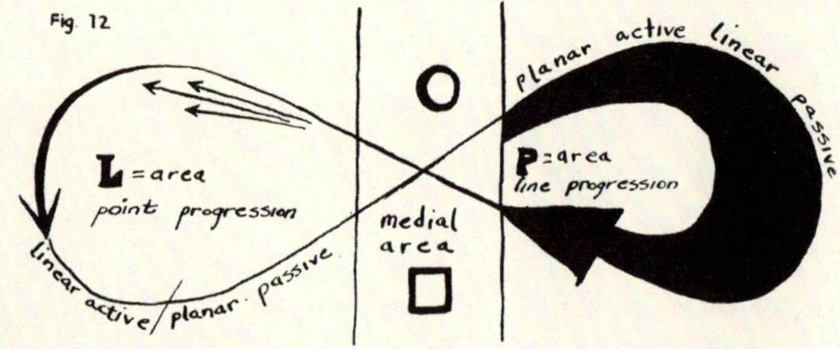

Semantic explanation
of the terms active, medial, and passive:

active: I fell (the man fells a tree with his ax).
medial: I fall (the tree falls under the ax stroke of the man).
passive: I am being felled (the tree lies felled).

21

Figure I.4. Paul Klee, from *Pedagogic Sketchbooks* (New York: Frederick A. Praeger, 1953), p. 21.

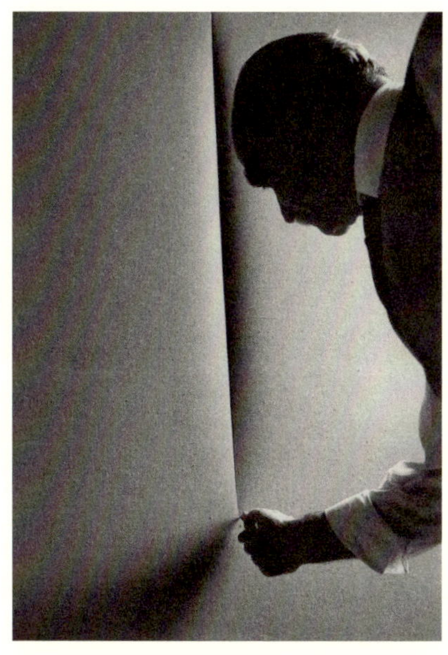

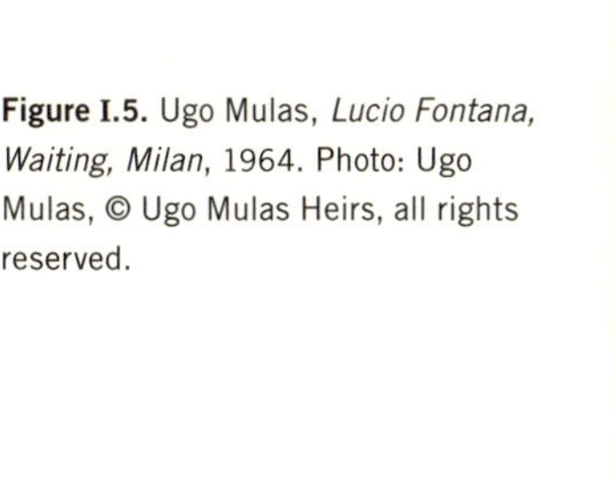

Figure I.5. Ugo Mulas, *Lucio Fontana, Waiting, Milan*, 1964. Photo: Ugo Mulas, © Ugo Mulas Heirs, all rights reserved.

lines are also lines without marks. But the organic line is not primarily or solely a concept or a projection. As a liminal, indexical phenomenon, the organic line activates — and is activated by — the material and temporal behavior of its contiguous borders.[21] The line of space that it concretizes is thus a thick void: thick in the sense that it is neither pure emptiness nor a virtual abstraction, but a dimensional, responsive, and actualized entity. The organic line cannot exist without flanking objects or surfaces. It is not a form that delimits its own boundaries so much as a shape that gets filled in. In this sense, one could provisionally define the organic line as *space materialized within a relation of material dependence.* By conceptually concretizing this space, the organic line recovers the paradoxical materiality of the cavity itself. The voids that riddle Lucio Fontana's *Tagli* (Cuts) series, begun in 1958, are likewise materializations of space (fig. I.5). Yet as registers of the gesture of cutting, they remain marks in an ontological sense. Photographs of

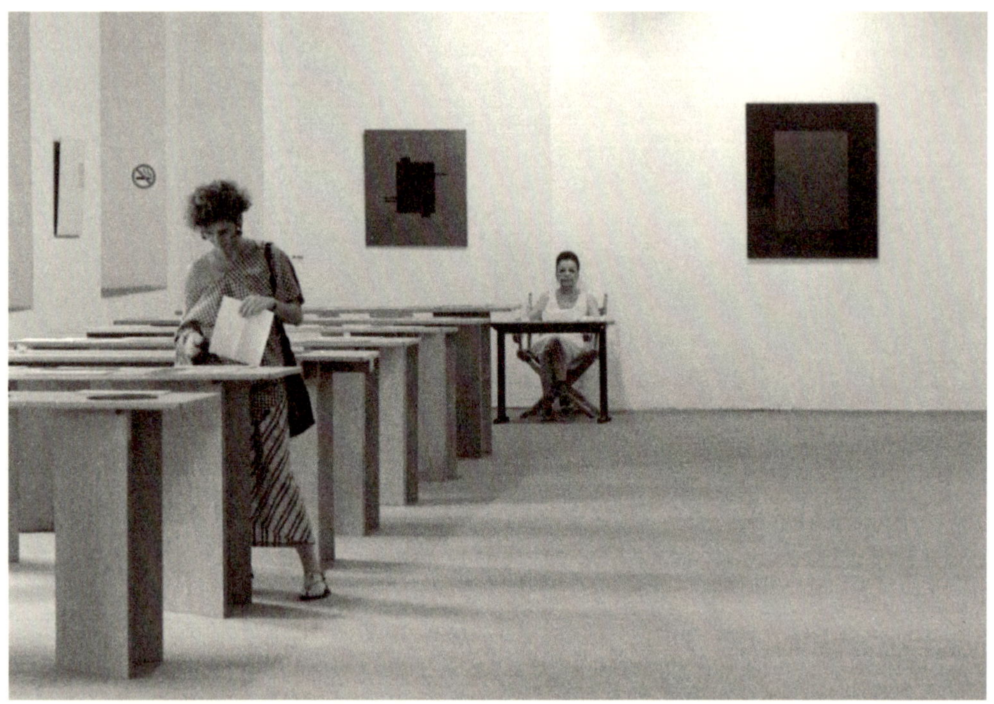

Figure I.6. Lygia Clark with *Quebra da moldura*
(Breaking the frame) paintings, 1954. Paço
Imperial, Rio de Janeiro, 1986. Courtesy of
Associação Cultural "O Mundo de Lygia Clark."

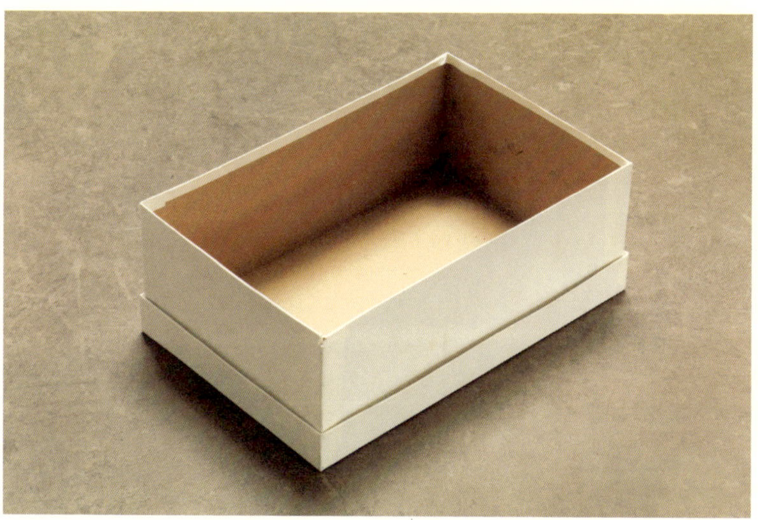

Figure I.7. Gabriel Orozco, *Empty Shoe Box*, 1993. Shoe box, 12.4 × 33 × 21.6 cm. © Gabriel Orozco. Image © The Museum of Modern Art / Licensed by SCALA / Art Resource, NY.

Fontana dramatize this moment, the artist piercing the canvas and recreating a spectacle of heroic, expressive, even violent action.[22] By contrast, the signal image of Clark with the organic line might be her seated alongside her *Quebra da moldura* (Breaking the frame) paintings and looking out toward the viewer. For it is the *viewer* who must perceive the organic line in order for it to count (fig. I.6).

Perceiving the organic line unleashes its conceptual potential as a device, and if we approach other works with this framework, we can begin to see its analytic force. Moving forward in time, take, for example, Gabriel Orozco's placement of a shoebox on the floor as his contribution to the Venice Biennale of 1993 (fig. I.7).[23] For Orozco, who had encountered Clark's work during his travels in Brazil, it was crucial to preserve the slender plane of space that exists between the box and the surface upon which it rested.[24] Rendering this space *thick*, Orozco figured forth an organic line. But by insisting on the continuity of this space and that around

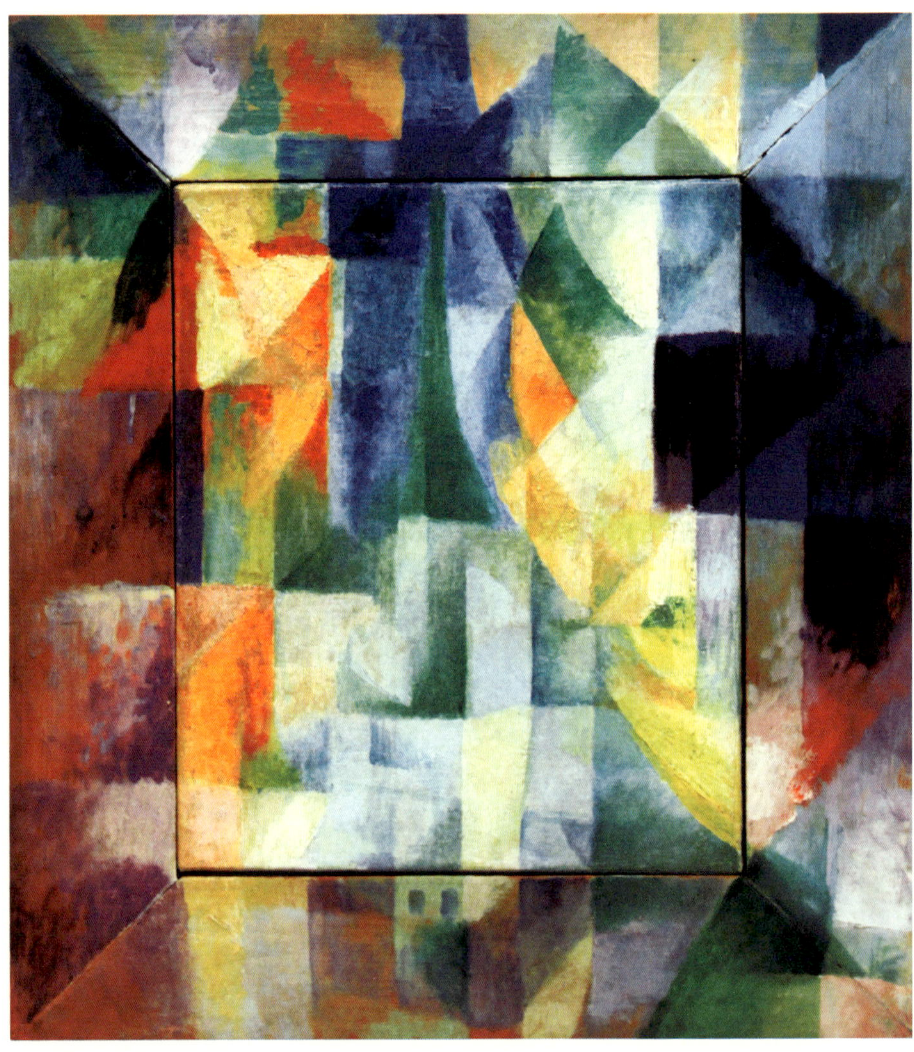

Figure I.8. Robert Delaunay, *Simultaneous Windows onto the City (1st part, 2nd Motif, 1st Replica)*, 1912. Oil and spruce wood on canvas, 40×46 cm. Hamburger Kunsthalle.

and within the box, Orozco displaced the form of the sculpture from the empty container to the volume of space that filled it. As he mused: "To occupy an empty space with another empty space."[25] While the shoe box demarcates this spatial form's interior edge, the plane of space beneath the box gestures to its exterior limit: that limit where a form (of space) disaggregates into a medium (of space), or full space once again becomes empty. It is now the *shoe box* that functions as the organic line of this sculpture, dividing medium from form and work from frame. From this perspective, Orozco's intervention lies less in his recuperation of the category of sculpture than in the way he slots sculpture into the liminal interval described by Clark's organic line.

The organic line can be retroactively located, as well. Consider Robert Delaunay's *Simultaneous Windows onto the City (1st part, 2nd Motif, 1st Replica)*, 1912, exhibited at the 1953 São Paulo Bienal, in which Clark also participated (fig. I.8). Instead of battling the traditional association of painting with the pictorial illusion of the window, Delaunay converted this convention into a site of perceptual investigation, extending his composition across both canvas and frame. Delaunay aligned his pictorial grid with the work's architecture in several instances. But in others, he disregarded the distinction between canvas and wood, stretching a swatch of blue over the miter (the diagonal joint of the frame) or elongating shapes so that they spanned the gap between the two elements. Such microadjustments result in a "double reinforcement and dissolution of the frame," as Gordon Hughes has put it, frustrating assumptions of how we look *through* a window or *onto* a surface.[26] This torquing of convention is intensified by Delaunay's actual frame, which is beveled so that it recesses from the canvas toward the wall, rather than the reverse. This convexity refuses the spatial recession and representational fragmentation inscribed within the Western tradition of the framed picture. And yet the parceled surface that flows across the frame flattens this material dimensionality, so much so, in fact, that it is all but impossible to detect in reproduction. For some observers,

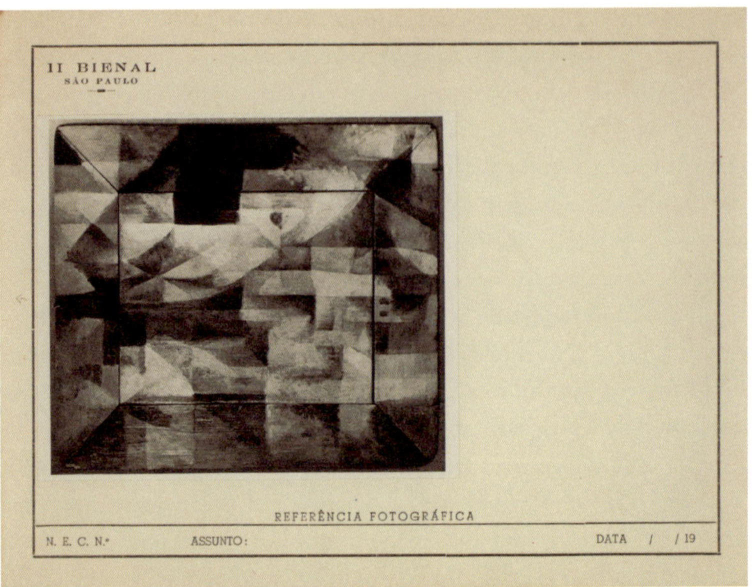

Figure I.9. Robert Delaunay, *Simultaneous Windows onto the City (1st part, 2nd Motif, 1st Replica)*, 1912. Exhibited as *As janelas* (The windows) at the Second São Paulo Bienal, 1953. Courtesy of Fundação Bienal de São Paulo/Arquivo Histórico Wanda Svevo.

Delaunay's chromatic faceting surmounted the work's physicality altogether. As the Argentine critic Jorge Romero Brest wrote of the work in 1952, "every plane acquires its physiognomy by means of color, and not by line-limit [*línea-límite*] that disappears along the gradient."[27]

Would Clark have agreed to Brest's assessment when she saw Delaunay's work, exhibited as *As janelas* (The windows, fig. I.9) in 1953? Or did a horizon of aesthetic possibility attune her eye to the *emergence* of the "line-limit" between work and frame, rather than its disappearance? We know that such a revelation did not occur (or was not pursued) by Delaunay; he returned to the convention of the pictorially autonomous canvas in his subsequent explorations. Clark went the other way. When invited to participate in Brazil's annual modern art salon in Rio de Janeiro in 1954, she contributed

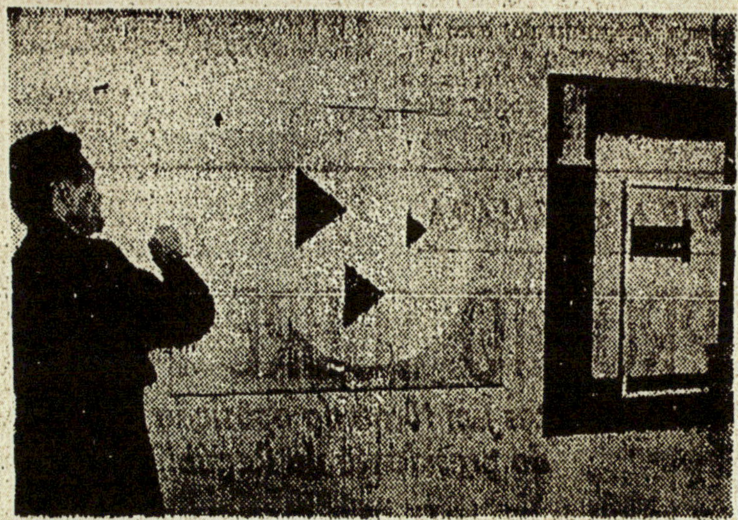

Prossegue alcançando intensa visitação o III Salão Nacional de Arte Moderna, este ano transformado em Salão Prêto e Branco. Aberto até o dia 29 do corrente, a mostra oficial do país abriga tôdas as tendências da arte dos nossos dias. No clichê vemos o pintor Aloizio Carvão — um dos artistas revelados pelo Museu de Arte Moderna do Rio — quando cuidava do trabalho que apresentou no certame. Ao lado a "moldura" enviada por Ligia Clark. O salão está situado no Ministério da Educação e Cultura

Figure I.10. Lygia Clark, *Quadro objeto* (Painting object), 1954 (*right*), at the Salão Preto e Branco (Black and White Salon). Published in *Correio da Manhã*, June 2, 1954. Courtesy of Associação Cultural "O Mundo de Lygia Clark."

a so-called *Quadro objeto* (Painting object) consisting of little more than two frames mounted on a wall (fig. I.10).[28] A newspaper photograph of the lost work shows that Clark attached a stretcher or thin white frame to a larger, thicker black frame so that the smaller structure incurs upon its counterpart along the lower edge. She also appended a rectangular white tab to the black frame and a similar black tab onto the blank wall. The piece thus operates at three, if not four physical strata, including the slice of space that hovers beneath the smaller frame above the wall. In laying bare the nuts and bolts of making — aspects she had depicted in early paintings of canvas easels, stretchers, and frames — Clark's idiosyncratic painting-object constitutes a radical intervention within a modernist genealogy that has investigated the pictoriality of the plane vis-à-vis its material architecture. By the time she participated in the Twenty-Seventh Venice Biennale as part of the Brazilian representation later that year, the organic line had appeared.

Yet the absorption of the organic line within an overarching narrative of the modernist device is not a clean-cut affair. The particular salon at which Clark exhibited her *Quadro objeto* was known as the Salão Preto e Branco (Black and White Salon), and here, if we begin to scratch the surface, the universalizing tendencies of this narrative begin to fall apart. The salon gained its moniker because the participating artists submitted works entirely composed in black and white. This withdrawal of color was a protest of the high tariffs the Brazilian government had recently imposed on imported artists' paints in an attempt to jump-start domestic industry.[29] Such economic policies were symptomatic of postwar strategies intended to correct structural dependencies produced and intensified during the early modern, colonial, and industrial eras in Latin America, Asia, and Africa. Without a functional domestic industry for artists' paints, however, the Brazilian government's tariffs effectively deprived artists of their tools for material practice and intellectual work. As I have elaborated elsewhere, the protest at the Salão Preto e Branco and its aftereffects were deliberate disruptions of the developmentalist mandate and the asymmetrical geopolitics of modernization.[30] Clark's own decision to lay bare the apparatus of art was thus as political as it was aesthetic and inextricable from the *longue durée* of modernity's fraught relation to colonial extraction and trade as a means for the circulation and accumulation of power.

In fact, while the history of art typically pegs modernism's inauguration to the artistic provocations that accompanied European industrialization at the end of the nineteenth century, anticolonial and decolonial theorists such as Sylvia Wynter and Aníbal Quijano have insisted that modernity and coloniality are cognate principles that stretch back to the era of encounter, when racialized schemas of knowledge and expropriation first took hold.[31] Within art history, it has become increasingly common to term this period "early modern" and to comprehend the florescence of European fifteenth-century and sixteenth-century art as conditioned as much by this expansionist drive as by the reimagined relation to a Greco-Roman past. But perhaps the more radical implication of the decolonial perspective is to conceive of twentieth-century modernism as forming not a rupture with the immediate past, but a complex continuity with this longer history of epistemic, economic, and ontological dispossession. To this extent, revisiting and reimagining Hal Foster's formative analysis of the neo-avant-garde, *all* modernist phenomena — the neo-avant-garde, but also the historical avant-garde, *modernismo*, high modernism, late modernism, even postmodernism — could be understood as deferred actions of working through — with greater and lesser clarity — the traumatic imbrication of coloniality and modernity.[32]

Repurposing such a theory willfully redirects its articulated specificity. Yet the mere exercise of a shift in temporal scale elucidates what we know in other terms to be true. What was primitivism's catalytic destruction of Western representational conventions if not a distorted mirror of Europe's rapacious relation to Africa? What was the Brazilian modernist embrace of *antropofagia* if not an appropriative defense for remapping the relations of internal and external colonialism? The point is not that such modernist phenomena amount to *only* these relations or that coloniality is the secret meaning of modern art. Rather, it is that coloniality is fully entangled with modernity in ways that both the modernist rhetoric of universal formal invention and the additive logic of multiple or comparative modernisms tend to obscure.[33] To absorb the organic line into the former would be to ignore the asymmetry that continues to structure the historiography of modern art. Merely to contextualize it as an instance of the latter would be to catastrophically localize its import. Setting aside both, I want to argue that the organic line's paradigm of interstitiality offers insights at the elemental level of techniques and descriptions. In other words, it bears on what modernism says at all.

———

In *The Signature of All Things: On Method*, the philosopher Giorgio Agamben describes a paradigm as a "singular object that, standing equally for all others of the same class, defines the intelligibility of the group."[34] A paradigm does not operate by means of deduction or induction, he argues, but by analogy. In other words, it does not proceed from particular to universal or vice versa, but "from singularity to singularity" establishing "a force field traversed by polar tensions" that iterate and exemplify the paradigm in turn.[35] The organic line is such a paradigm. Clark's paintings, studies, and maquettes that concern the organic line are not. Thus, while Clark's works — as singularities — are necessary to excavate the paradigm embedded within them, they are not wholly sufficient for its explanation, nor do they comprehensively constitute its point of origin.

Indeed, the organic line's very status as a spatial hiatus, interruption, or breach encourages us to "dispel the chimeras of origin," as Michel Foucault memorably wrote, so endemic to art history's narratives of modernist invention.[36] As I have already begun to intimate, Clark herself was deeply familiar with the historical avant-garde and had ample exposure to the work of artists such as Delaunay, Picasso, and Piet Mondrian, particularly through the São Paulo biennials of the early to mid-1950s (fig. I.11).[37] The organic line demonstrates a robust dialogue with such artists' propositions and to this extent was articulated in what could be called the "major" language of European modernism, a language that was considered universal — at least initially — even by Clark herself. Yet the organic

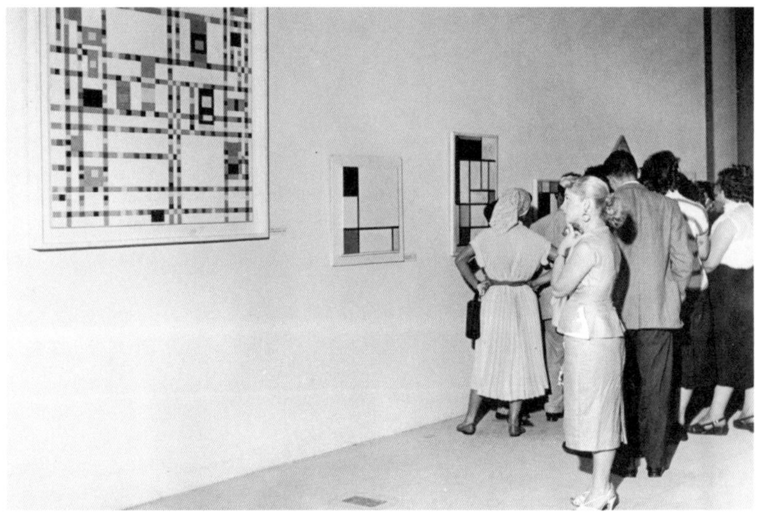

Figure I.11. Sala Especial de Mondrian, Second São Paulo Bienal, 1953. Courtesy of Fundação Bienal de São Paulo / Arquivo Histórico Wanda Svevo.

line's creative action *upon* this language continues to be informed by an exteriority indicative of Clark's position as a woman from the so-called marginal context of Brazil. Although her work was exhibited in her lifetime in traditional artistic centers such as Paris, London, New York, and Venice, there is little history of sustained reception and public engagement in these locations, even as important exceptions include the British critic Guy Brett, the Filipino artist David Medalla, and the French critic Jean Clay (fig. I.12).[38] While major histories of modern art tend to track what literary critic Harold Bloom termed "strong misreadings" of influence and intervention — think here of Vladimir Tatlin's response to Picasso's *Guitar* in his corner constructions or Jasper Johns's galvanizing reaction to Duchamp's readymades — Clark's organic line remains stubbornly, if generatively, in a minor vein. As Brandon Joseph writes, glossing Deleuze and Guattari's influential theorization, the major is "what can be made to serve an idea, category, or constant against which,

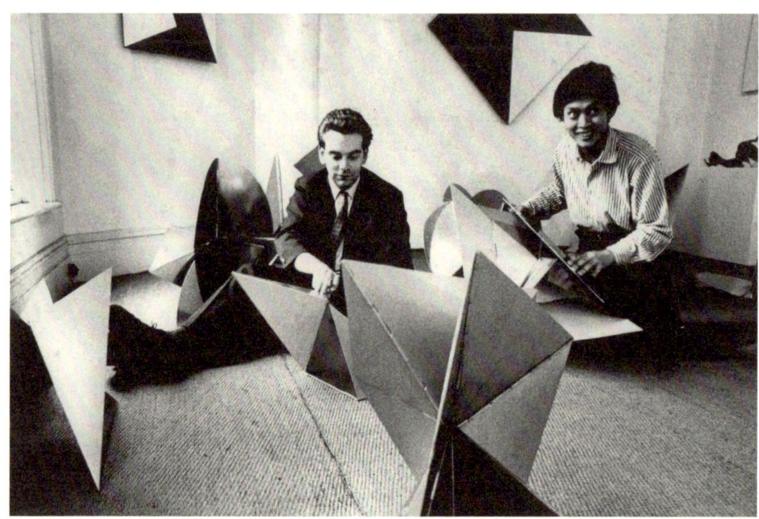

Figure I.12. Guy Brett and David Medalla with *Bichos* at Lygia Clark's solo exhibition, Signals Gallery, London, 1965. Courtesy of Associação Cultural "O Mundo de Lygia Clark."

whether explicitly or implicitly, other phenomena are measured."[39] The major is what produces the canon as a disciplinary history. In this sense, although Clark had ample artistic interlocuters in Brazil, particularly during Neoconcretism and its outgrowths in the late 1950s and 1960s, it is also significant that in her later years, she chose to set aside her institutional affiliation with art altogether.[40]

Donald Judd's typically terse review of Clark's 1963 exhibition of her manipulable *Bichos* in New York is symptomatic of the exteriority of her work to canonical histories of modern art. The entirety of the review reads as follows: "This sheet-metal sculpture is made of hinged segments and rectangles which adjust to various positions. The idea is clever. The style is ordinary capable Constructivism. Lygia Clark works and is well known in Brazil."[41] Written two years before his seminal essay "Specific Objects," Judd appears unaware or uninterested that the *Bichos* sprung from an intense interrogation of the relations between painting and sculpture by Brazilian artists such as Clark, Oiticica, and Lygia Pape. These debates, which resulted in the critic Ferreira Gullar's 1959 formulation of the Neoconcrete "non-object," provide an unacknowledged and chronologically anterior counterpart to the exploration of similar concerns in the mid-1960s development of Minimalism in the United States.[42] Yet as the curator Paulo Herkenhoff argued in 2001, the geopolitics of dominant art history cannot assimilate Neoconcretism as anything but a latecomer to a preexisting canon. Highlighting formal comparisons between works by Pape, Frank Stella, and Robert Morris, Herkenhoff observes that while nobody would suggest that the Pape had influenced the North American artists, "had the situation been reversed, Pape would have been considered derivative" of Stella and Morris (figs. I.13–I.14). "This tendency," he wrote, "seems to be prevailing law of modern art historicism."[43] Faced with the same resonance during a recent Pape retrospective in New York, one critic chalked up the similarity to formal zeitgeist. "Following Stella's famous dictum, it doesn't seem wrong to imagine that, at least in the years around 1960, what you saw was, in fact, what you saw. Or, to put it another way, pseudomorphism were us."[44]

Suffice it to say that both the "prevailing law of modern art historicism" and "pseudomorphism were us" are deeply unsatisfying art-historical options, as are their defensive inverse, namely, that Pape, not Stella, was the *true* pioneer or that the vastly different intellectual and aesthetic contexts of their works preclude their comparison. One strategy for obviating such analytic dead ends is to shift the axis of comparison, as the literary scholar Pedro Erber productively did in *Breaching the Frame: The Rise of Contemporary Art in Brazil and Japan* (2015). Here, Erber focuses on protagonists "working at the margins of the global art scene" to develop a notion of contemporaneity that sets aside the episteme of center and periphery and its associated symptoms of centrifugal spread, derivation, belatedness, and unidirectional translation.[45] In its place, following the Polish art historian Piotr Piotrowski, Erber advocates a "horizontal" history of modern art that proceeds from a "fundamentally

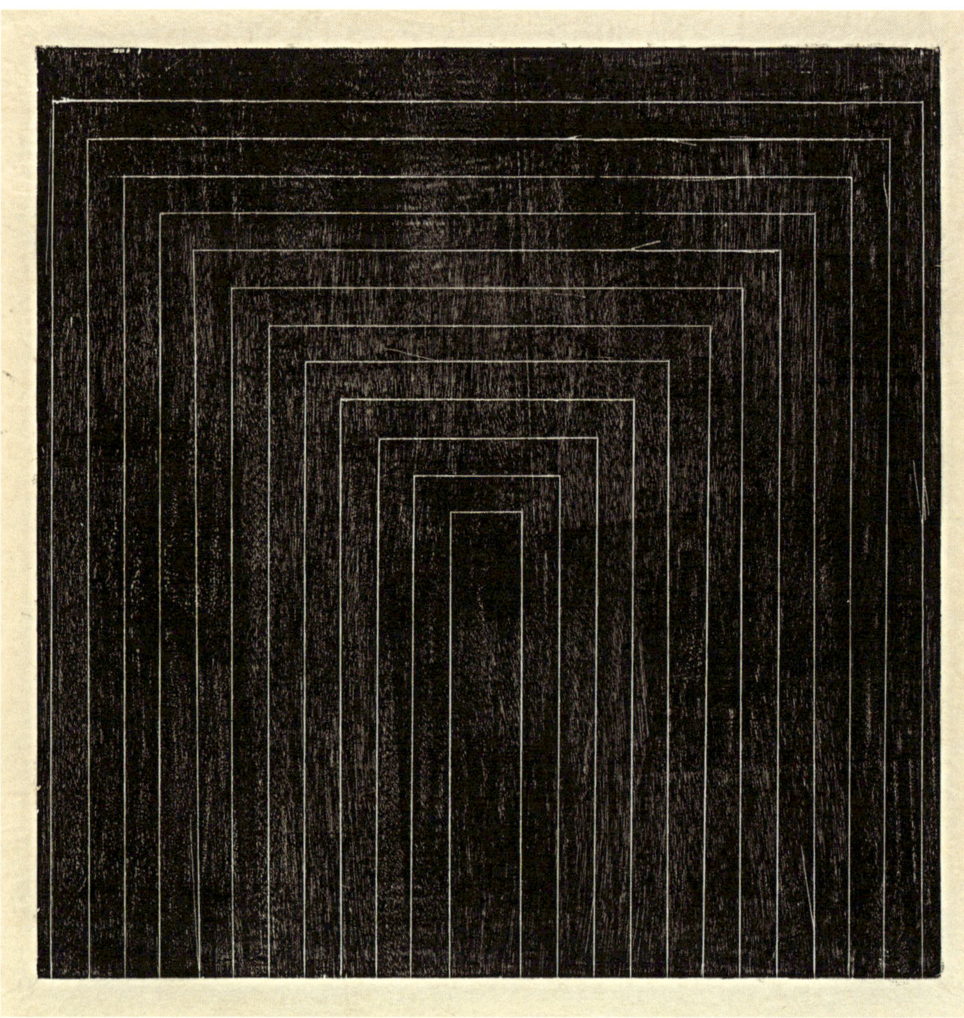

Figure I.13. Lygia Pape, *Untitled*, from the series *Tecelares* (Weavings), 1956. Woodcut on Japanese paper, 50×50 cm. © Projeto Lygia Pape.

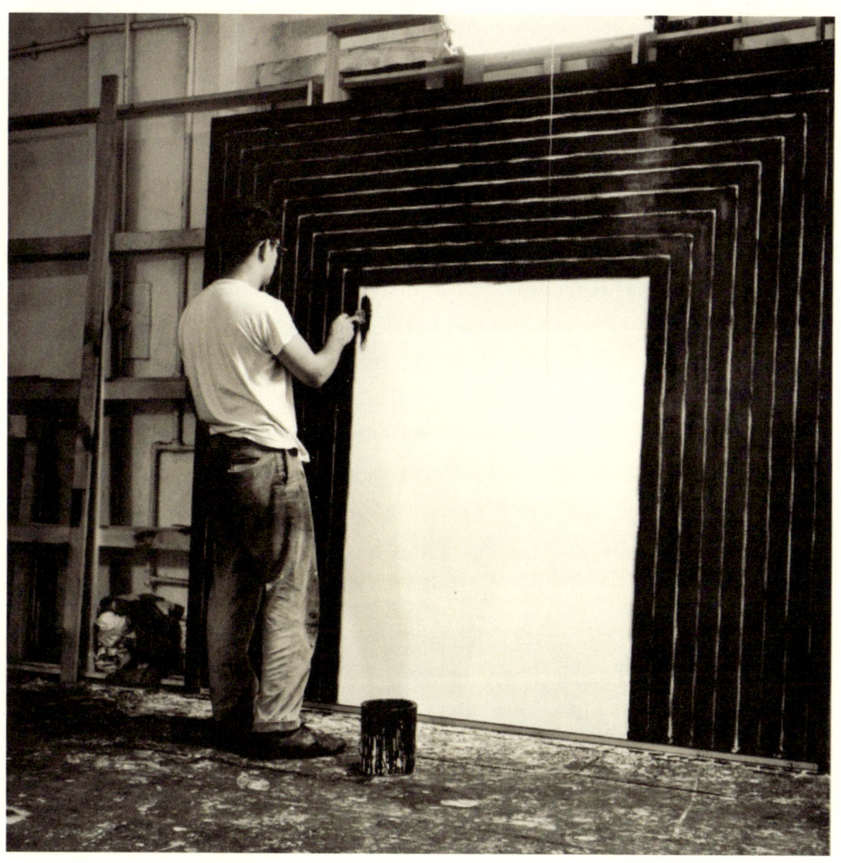

Figure I.14. Hollis Frampton, *Frank Stella Painting "Getty Tomb,"* 1959. © Estate of Hollis Frampton. Photograph courtesy of the Addison Gallery of American Art, Philips Academy, Andover, MA/ Art Resource, NY.

decentered perspective."[46] And yet "bracketing the center," as Erber describes this strategy, can have methodological and political pitfalls of its own. One is that it fails to account for the dynamics of power that constitute the center as an *operative* fiction, one that generated real vectors of influence from Europe to Brazil in these years. Both Clark and Oiticica, for example, had passionate responses to avant-garde artists such as Mondrian and Malevich. In 1959, Clark penned a love letter of sorts to the deceased Mondrian, drawing marked distinctions between his ethos and her own: "They say you detested nature — is this true? Because today I felt this transcendence through nature at night, in love." But Clark also expressed her searing loneliness, noting that "today you are more alive for me" than members of her immediate circle.[47] Beyond such expressed affinities, a second and perhaps more enduring danger in bracketing the center is that it precludes the possibility that so-called peripheral practices might have a reciprocal action upon "universal modernism," such that the mythical coherency of the center itself is disturbed. This book situates itself within this possibility of disruption.

Received histories of making condition patterns of viewing. But as a corollary, reorientations of making — and not making — have the possibility of radically *revisibilizing* the objects we view.[48] Returning to a comparison between Pape and Stella, we can note that Pape, who certainly knew of the organic line, explored and *differentiated* the implications of its interstitial space by way of the serial capacities of the woodcut (fig. 1.15).[49] In Pape's prints, the artist translates the preexisting organic lines of the block's wooden grain into the active mark-making of her metal gouge. This gouging process creates an absence upon the surface of the wooden matrix, which allows a new kind of organic line to reappear in the form of the unprinted blank lines in the final print. In other words, an interval between matter becomes the model for how to mobilize

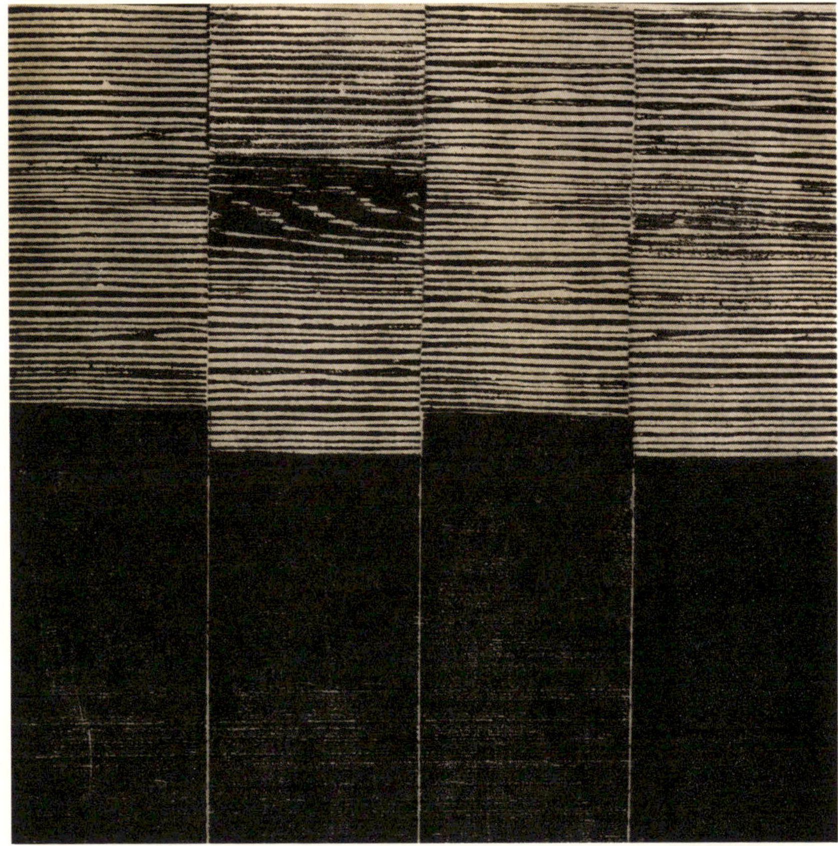

Figure I.15. Lygia Pape, *Untitled*, from the series *Tecelares* (Weavings), 1959. Woodcut. Composition and sheet: 24.4 × 24.8 cm. The Museum of Modern Art. Gift of Patricia Phelps de Cisneros through the Latin American and Caribbean Fund, 595.2013. Image courtesy of Colección Patricia Phelps de Cisneros. © 2023 Projeto Lygia Pape.

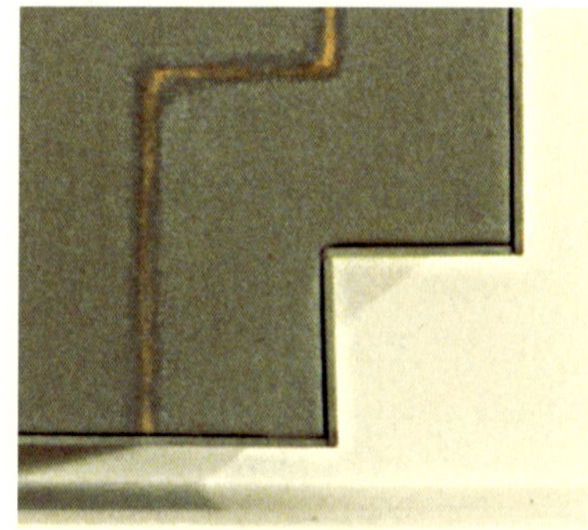

Figures I.16a–b. Frank Stella, *Kingsbury Run*, from the *Aluminum Series*, 1960. © 2023 Frank Stella/Artists Rights Society (ARS), New York.

an apparatus of making that occludes its own mark. The generative and recursive character of Pape's printmaking is thus rooted not in a coincidence of medium and mark, but medium and the pursuit of rendering visible what *resists* being made.

Stella's painting is likewise characterized by unmade lines, namely, the residual "breathing spaces," as he described them, of empty canvas that lie between his stripes of paint.[50] Yet the reception of Stella's painting has occurred almost entirely within the discourse of medium specificity in the United States, wherein the advance of the painterly medium depended on the relation between the artist's mark and the delimitation of the painterly plane.[51] Even when the sculptor Carl Andre developed his polemical reading of Stella's paintings as objects, his analogy was between Stella's brushstrokes and his own "pass of a saw."[52] Likewise, when Michael Fried described Stella's paintings in terms of their "deductive structure," he referred to the relation between the work's pictorial motif and its "framing edge."[53] Yet details of Stella's paintings demonstrate that Fried's notion of "framing edge" suppresses the gap between the exterior limit of the canvas and the interior limit of the frame (figs. I.16a–b). In short, attending to the organic line that lies between them reveals that both "delimitation" (within the discourse on medium specificity) and "objecthood" (within the polemics of Minimalism) are dramatically less secure.[54] The organic line reveals that any delimitation is not a singular limit, but an interface or threshold. In this sense, the unacknowledged organic lines between the painting and frame of Stella's works lead us not only toward the "breathing spaces" that constitute the interior intervals of the canvas, but to a sequence of marks and nonmarks that proceed outward. This sequence turns the corner of Stella's painted frames — themselves the same width as his painted strokes — in order to arrive at the liminal space between the work and the wall, the wall itself, and finally the space of the gallery.[55] The new demarcation of the gallery as an operation of marked and unmarked spaces provides an unexpected twist to the old problem of pictorial autonomy. Finally, as an interval, absence, and profoundly topological entity, the organic line demonstrates that both objects and mediums are not self-evident facts so much as temporalized configurations whose legibility depends upon shifting ecologies of discourse, sociality, and space.[56]

Clark's organic line is nothing if not a weak link: a void, a caesura that conjugates by virtue of its own lack. But this is as true of its spatial character as it is of its historiographic quandary. Artists and critics within Clark's intellectual circuit in Rio de Janeiro quickly recognized the paradigmatic character of the organic line and engaged its ramifications. Oiticica wrote of the line's formal impact in terms of the furrows of his architectural models and spatial reliefs. He also described the organic line's catalyzation of space as "situating [Clark] in relation to Mondrian as Cubism stands in relation to Cézanne."[57] Noting a constellation of artists including Delaunay, Malevich, Tatlin, Sophie Taeuber-Arp, and Wassily Kandinsky, Oiticica argued, "The importance of [Clark's] work is not a relative one within this panorama—it is universal, the missing landmark of that development."[58] Already in 1960, in other words, Oiticica recognized a certain absenting and genealogical displacement of the organic line. But his observation ended up being anticipatory, as well: beyond Brazil, we can trace only partial genealogies and pseudomorphic resonances for the organic line, rather than influence, reception, strong misreadings, and the like.[59] At the level of historiography, the organic line has no place in the directional flow of MoMA's notorious 1936 chart of abstraction or within the networked space of its 2012 cartography of invention (figs. I.17 and I.18).[60] One can concede that the chronological frames of such visualizations preclude (or mediate against) Clark's inclusion. But even the dialogue between Clark and her Argentine and Uruguayan counterparts who experimented with shaped canvases and irregular frames in the 1940s is muted, at best.[61] As I detail in Chapter 1, by the time Tomás Maldonado, a leading theorist of this group, exhibited in Brazil in 1953, he had already returned to the orthogonal picture plane and advanced a version of Concrete art defined by the precepts of the Swiss artist Max Bill.

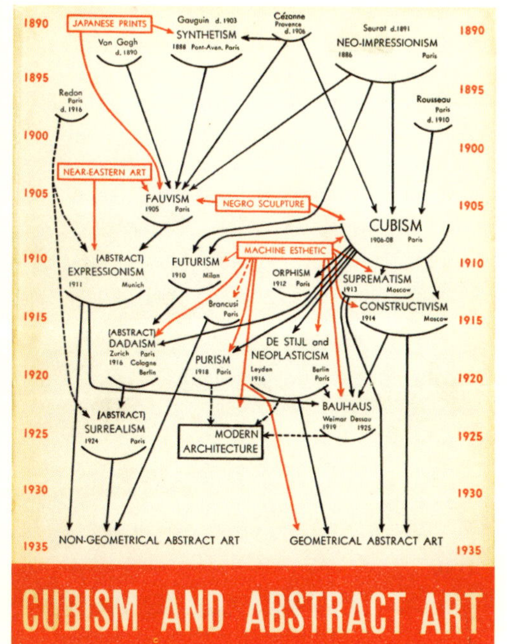

Figure I.17. Dust jacket with chart prepared by Alfred H. Barr, Jr., of the exhibition catalogue *Cubism and Abstract Art*, by Alfred H. Barr, Jr., 1936. Offset, printed in color, 25.7 × 19.7 cm. The Museum of Modern Art Library, New York. Digital image © The Museum of Modern Art / Licensed by SCALA / Art Resource, NY.

Figure I.18. Interactive diagram created for the exhibition *Inventing Abstraction: 1910–1925*, December 23, 2012 through April 15, 2013, The Museum of Modern Art, New York. Digital image © The Museum of Modern Art / Licensed by SCALA / Art Resource, NY.

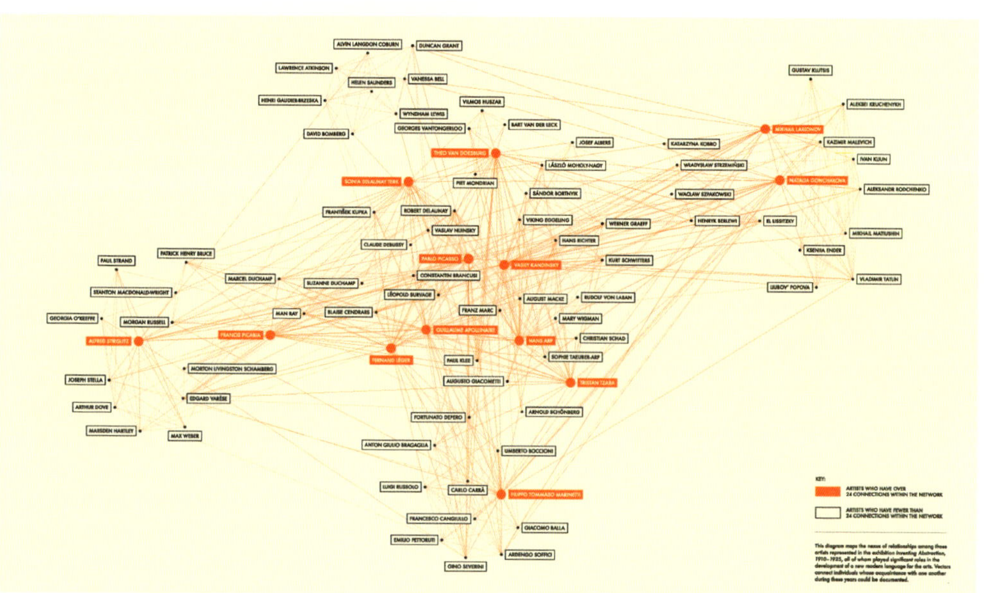

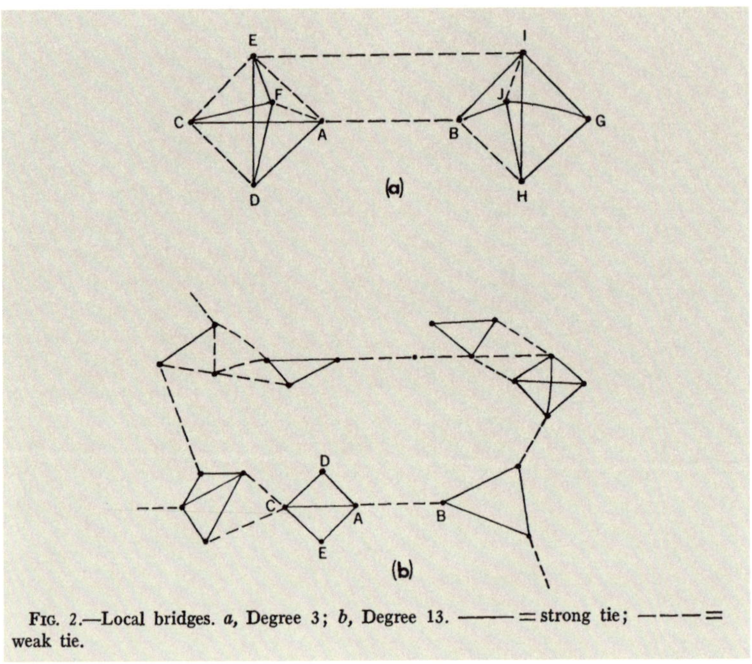

Figure I.19. Mark Granovetter, "The Strength of Weak Ties," *American Journal of Sociology* 78.6 (May 1973), pp. 1360–80.

To this degree, the organic line is a symptom of missed connections, fragmented networks, and artistic utterances unheard because they are separated in time and space. Not surprisingly, these conditions are deeply familiar to any artist or art historian working within the so-called margins, be that a geopolitical, sociocultural, or archival space. For such actors, assembling weak links has long been a practice of necessity, if also a site of ingenuity.

Yet weak links have their own powers of elucidation and effect, an agency, we might say, in the minor key. In 1973, the sociologist Mark Granovetter described the behavior of strong and weak ties within social networks (fig. I.19).[62] While dated from the perspective of today's media landscape, at least two elements of Granovetter's

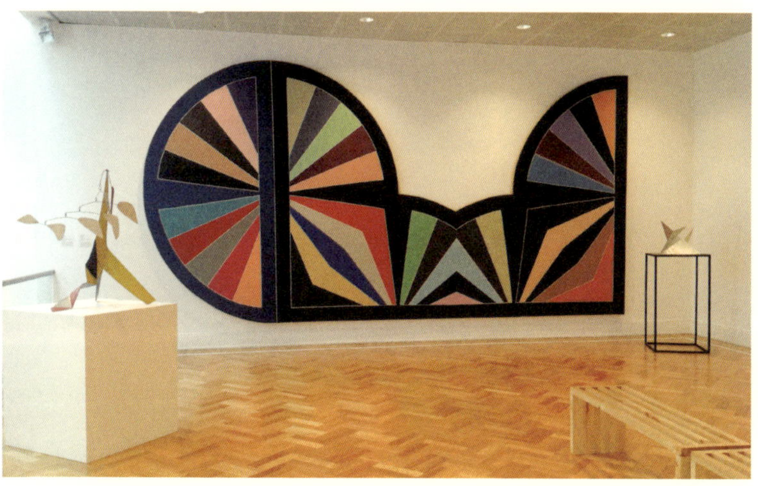

Figure I.20. Museo de la Solidaridad Salvador Allende showing works by Frank Stella, *Isfahan III*, 1968 (*center*), and Lygia Clark, *Bicho*, ca. 1960–64 (*right*), donated in 1972. Photo: Irene V. Small. Courtesy of Associação Cultural "O Mundo de Lygia Clark." © 2023 Frank Stella/Artists Rights Society (ARS), New York.

analysis deserve attention here. The first is the "cohesive power of weak ties."[63] Rumors, for example, diffuse more widely among weak connections than they do within strong. For this reason, the "overall fragmentation" of a given group (or here, a historical and historiographic phenomenon) is not inconsistent with its cohesion at the level of possible effects.[64] The second insight is that weak ties are a means of moving between different scales of analysis. Through them, we can bind "micro-level interactions to macro-level patterns."[65] To this end, I want to suggest that the organic line is not merely a delimited art-historical phenomenon that deserves archival exposition, although it is this, as well. It is a means by which to rethink the shape, dimensionality, and texture of the field of modernism itself. In other words, I want to treat the weak link as a *method*, rather than a requisite means.

While Stella and Clark never knew each other, for instance, their works are now joined in the galleries of the Museo de la Solidaridad Salvador Allende in Santiago de Chile (fig. I.20). As a permanent

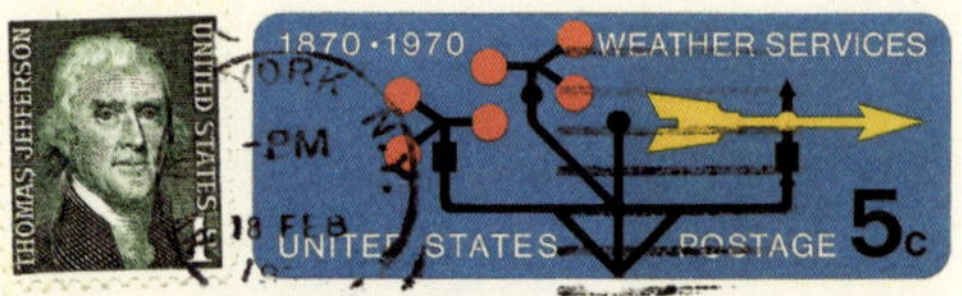

Figure I.21. Front and back of postcard from Carl Andre to Dore Ashton, New York, February 18, 1972. Museo de a Solidaridad Salvador Allende, MSSA Archive, cod. E-DA007.

museum, these galleries first opened to the public in 2005. Yet the idea for the museum was the initiative of the critic Mário Pedrosa, one of Clark's closest interlocuters, in 1971. At this time, Pedrosa, a Marxist and participant in the Fourth International, was living in exile in Santiago due to the right-wing military dictatorship that had seized power in Brazil in 1964. His idea was to form a first-rate collection of modern and contemporary art by means of donations from international artists. These donations would be gestures of political solidarity with Allende, whose experiment with democratic socialism offered a third way out of Cold War binaries. Stella and Clark donated their works at Pedrosa's request in 1972, a year before Allende's government was cut short by a CIA-sponsored coup. For a brief moment prior to that political trauma, Pedrosa's initiative offered an alternative and explicitly political vision of what an international modern art networked from the South could be.[66]

The New York–based critic Dore Ashton was Pedrosa's liaison to the United States, and she procured commitments from artists including Sol LeWitt, Philip Guston, Hans Haacke, and Carl Andre, among others. Pedrosa also worked with the Swiss curator Harald Szeemann and the Japanese curator Tadao Ogura, whom he met at the Second Indian Triennale in New Delhi in 1971. This is also where Pedrosa met Andre, who was exhibiting alongside the US artists Sam Gilliam, Eva Hesse, Robert Ryman, Richard Serra, and others (fig. I.21). Of note here is that the actual history of canonical figures such as Andre, and less canonical figures (at least in the United States), such as Bruce Onobrakpeya, who was part of the Nigerian representation, is far more global than canonical art history itself. Clark's first solo show, held in Paris in 1952, was the initiative of the Iraqi modern artist and critic Jamil Hamoudi, one of the pioneers of the *Hurufiyya* movement, which drew from the plasticity and cultural specificity of Arabic calligraphy to dynamize styles of geometric abstraction practiced in the West (fig. I.22). Hamoudi, who had moved to Paris in 1947, was pursuing research on the abstract origins of ancient Iraqi art alongside his

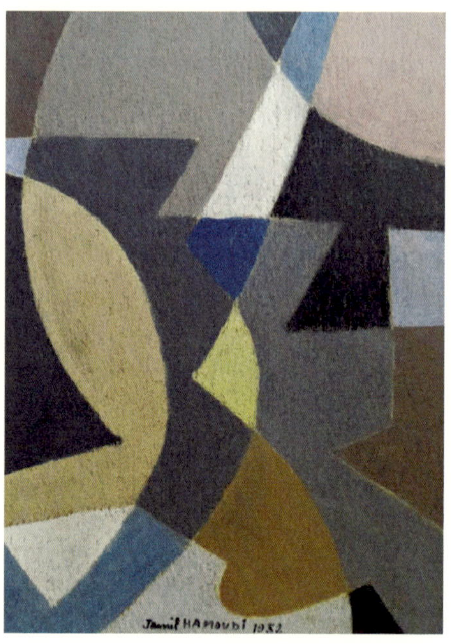

Figure I.22. Jamil Hamoudi, *Meditation*, 1952. Pastel on board, 25 × 20 cm. Barjeel Art Foundation.

contemporary practice.[67] He likewise exhibited alongside artists such as Hans Arp, Ellsworth Kelly, Carmen Herrera, and Barbara Hepworth at the Salon des Réalités Nouvelles.[68] In Rio de Janeiro, meanwhile, just as Clark was leaving to study in Paris in 1950, associates of the Teatro Experimental do Negro (Black Experimental Theater) led by Abdias Nascimento formulated the idea of a Museu de Arte Negra (Museum of Black Art), first realized as a temporary exhibition only in 1968. Working against the myth of racial democracy as well as the ghettoization of Afro-Brazilian culture within an unacknowledged *linha de côr* (color line), Nascimento and colleagues such as Guerreiro Ramos observed that such a museum logically would include not only works by Afro-descendent artists, but those influenced by Black culture and aesthetics such as Picasso and Henri Matisse. Clark was one of several Brazilian artists to donate a work to that collection.[69]

One of the imperatives of a global history of art is to excavate these kinds of cartographies and the expansive, transgressive, and nonnormative histories of modernism they imagined. But in the effort to reestablish the global complexity of art history, we also need to seek methods for recovering and narrating links that are fragile and vulnerable and that often entail, if not failure, certain opacities and intervals that pertain to institutionality, canonicity, and constraint, among other terms. Both the Museo de la Solidaridad Salvador Allende and the India Triennale were ambitious attempts to generate transnational networks from points outside the Euro-American axis, even as they were not premised on this axis's exclusion.[70] Both likewise sought to decouple their imagined network from one propelled by commodity circuits.[71] Nancy Adajania has described the India Triennale as an instance of "globalism before 'globalization,'" both in its orientation toward a cultural geopolitics of nonalignment and in terms of the internationally inflected leftism of its founder, the writer and critic Mulk Raj Anand.[72] Yet the first Triennale proved highly controversial in the Indian art world and foundered for much of the next two decades.[73] The Museo de la Solidaridad, meanwhile, was a victim of the 1973 coup, with both Pedrosa and the idea of the museum going into exile. In this sense, the very process of *instituting* such institutions registers a porosity and vulnerability indicative of their conditions of emergence. Pedrosa's museum never gained a physical home in his lifetime. As of this writing, Abdias Nascimento's Museu de Arte Negra has yet to do so.

This is not to suggest that weak links are not powerful. They can be. Pedrosa's museum in exile became the model for a similar initiative called International Art Exhibition for Palestine in 1978, where and when the question of a diasporic museum was ever more urgent (fig. I.23).[74] My point is that if we simply attempt to suture weak links together to strengthen their connectivity, we lose the ability to think seriously about the geopolitical, socioeconomic, and historiographic fractures that *structure* the singularity of these connections,

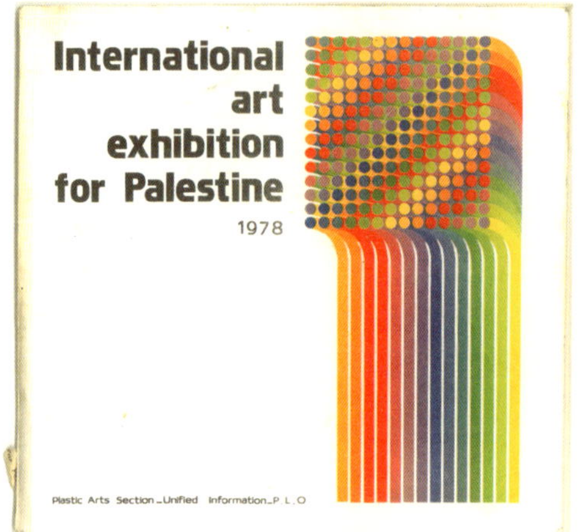

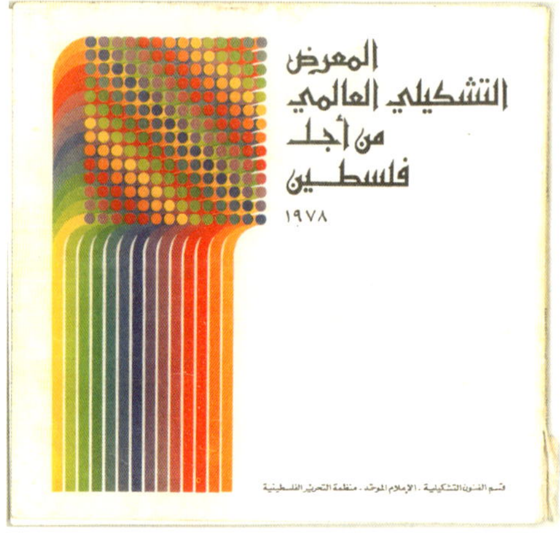

Figure I.23. Brochure for the International Art Exhibition for Palestine, Beirut, 1978, featuring *Volume Virtuel 19* (1974), by Julio Le Parc. Image courtesy of Kristine Khouri and Rasha Salti. © 2023 Artists Rights Society (ARS), New York / ADAGP, Paris.

or missed connections, in the first place. It is not enough to trace the network, in other words. We must also attend to what the network elides. To this extent, the lines that link Stella and Clark in the galleries of the Museo de la Solidaridad Salvador Allende are not positivities so much as ruptures and disjunctions that signal the multitude of paths not taken — or that were not possible — within a dominant history of modern art. Such fissures are part and parcel of the geopolitics of modernity, understood in its most devastatingly expansive sense as an apparatus for the unequal distribution and circulation of capital and power. Precisely for this reason, however, such fissures also offer intimations for how to rearticulate the legacy of modernism from a contemporary and even decolonial point of view. Mobilizing these works to appear in a single physical space, as Pedrosa sought to, but also comprehending them cotemporally, as we might today, are both projects of a contemporary history of modernist art in an expanded sense. But such weak links demand that we attend to the contingency of their connections and refuse to subsume their particularity within a triumphant, flattened project of global art or even a progressive, but defanged comparative art history that inadvertently leaves the center in place.

In light of these methodological and historiographic challenges, I want to suggest that the organic line allows us to conceptualize modernist art not as a Euclidian space marked by centers and peripheries, vertical traditions, and horizontal circumventions, but as a topological field of interactive, destabilizing tensions. Topological spaces emerge from metric spaces, but they dispense with elements such as fixed distances in favor of flexible continuities that bend, curve, and distend. In Clark's *Quebra da moldura (p x b) versão 1* (Breaking the frame [b x w] version 1, 1954), one can measure and compare the length of the black tabs that cluster around the edges of the canvas, noting that they index the width of the frame (fig. I.24). Yet a closer examination along the tabs' edges reveals that they also turn the corner of the canvas and frame, extending across the work's vertical thickness to its verso (fig. I.25). The organic line, as the space that lies between these elements, calls attention to how two dimensions are converted into three. But the organic line also exceeds this metric space. Not only does it flow along the chasm between canvas and frame, it overflows this channel and connects to the space beyond the work itself. It is topological par excellence, even as an emptiness, or more accurately, *as a shape of empty space.*

Topological figures and their transformations complicate (if not extinguish) notions of inside and out, stable orientation, center and periphery. As diagrams from mathematics textbooks contemporaneous with Clark's discovery aptly illustrate, topology allows triangular prisms to torque, circles to be stretched into irregular shapes, closed spheres to transform into elephants or pears, single-sided

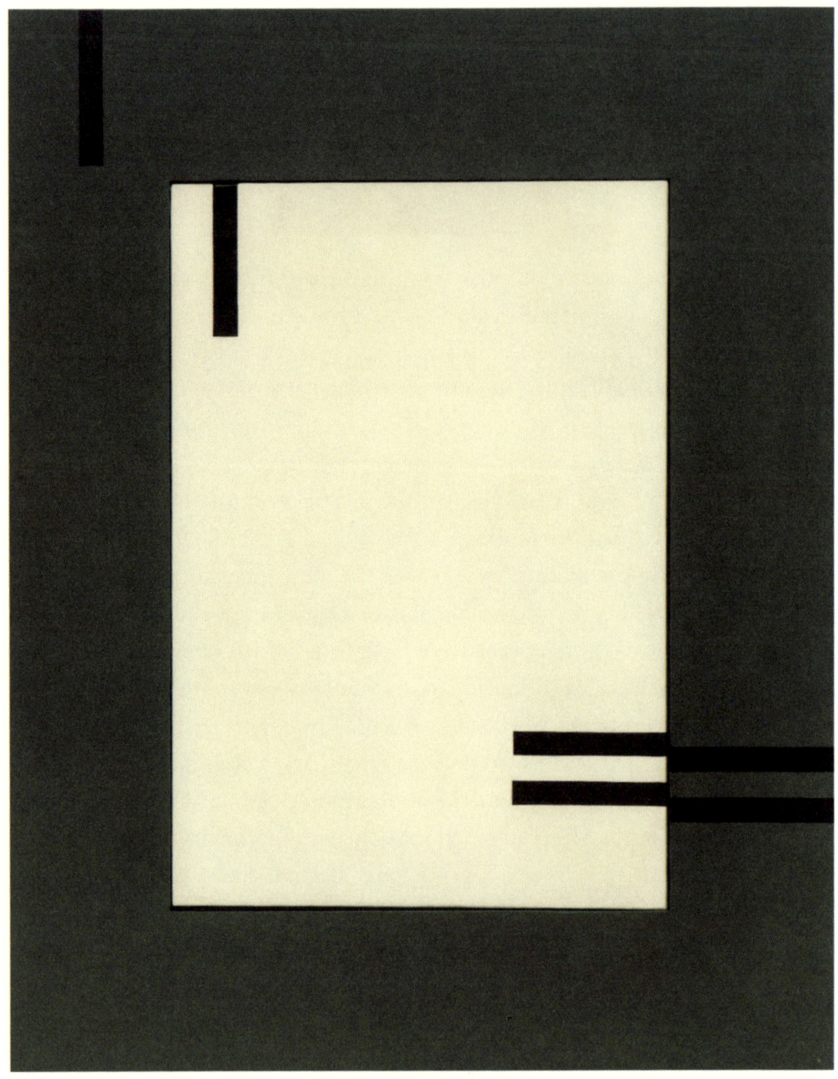

Figure I.24. Lygia Clark, *Quebra da moldura (p x b)
versão 1* (Breaking the frame [b x w] version 1),
1954. Enamel on wood, 110 × 88 cm. Photo:
Marcelo Ribeiro Alvares Corrêa. Courtesy of
Associação Cultural "O Mundo de Lygia Clark."

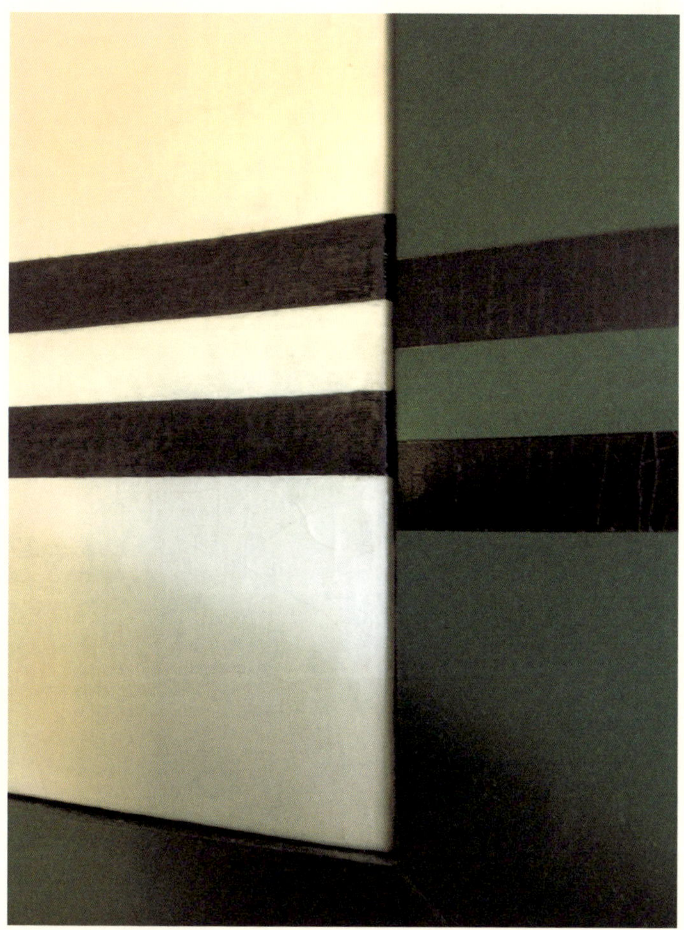

Figure I.25. Lygia Clark, *Quebra da moldura (p x b)
versão 1* (Breaking the frame [b x w] version 1),
1954 (detail). Enamel on wood, 110×88 cm.
Photo: Marcelo Ribeiro Alvares Corrêa. Courtesy
of Associação Cultural "O Mundo de Lygia Clark."

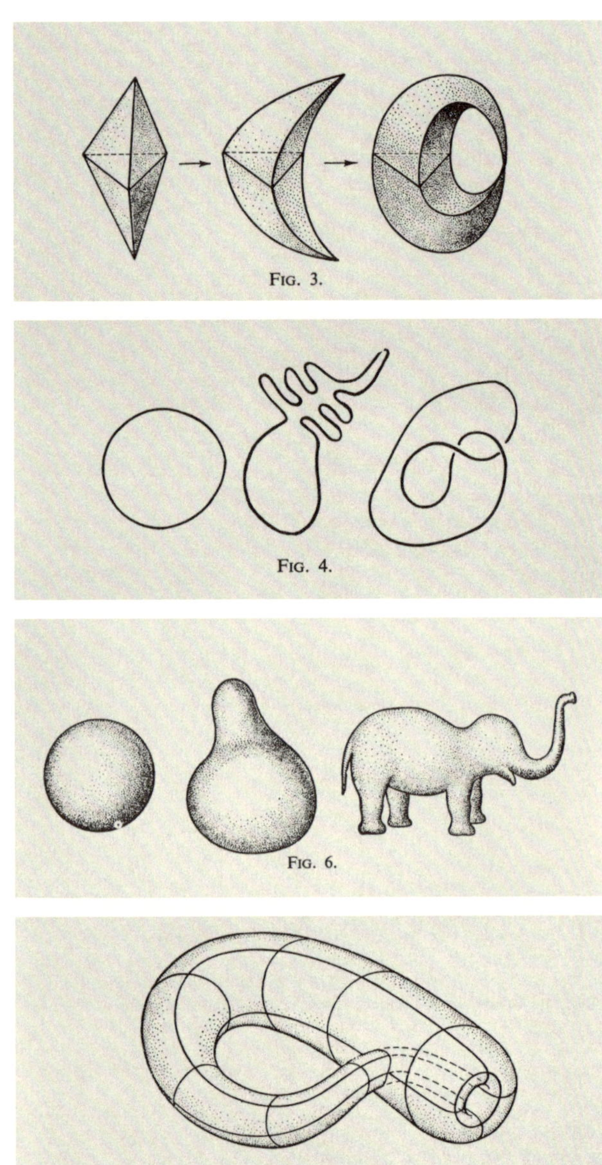

Figure I.26. Diagrams showing topological transformations and Klein bottle. From A. D. Aleksandrov, A. N. Kolmogorov, and M. A. Lavrent'ev, *Mathematics: Its Content, Methods, and Meaning*, trans. S. H. Gould and T. Bartha, 3 vols. (1953; Cambridge, MA: MIT Press, 1963), vol. 3, pp. 194, 196, 199.

surfaces such as the Klein bottle to enact spatial recursion (fig. I.26).[75] Clark herself wrote of demolishing orientation and antagonistic concepts such as "above and below, right and left ... good and evil" in a 1960 text, "The Death of the Plane."[76] To analogize modernist art to a topological space is thus to trouble the putative opposition between singular and plural modernities.[77] It is to conceive of the field of modernism not as a historical progression, a zero-sum equation, or an endlessly expanding territory, but as a mobile surface whose shape and volume shifts as a result of deformations.

Here, I understand deformations as a result of both artistic practices and historiographic analyses, in each case conditioned by the position or site from which they proceed. Some of these interventions transform the surface in a singular manner, creating new points of contact. But sometimes change occurs as a result of a multitude of minute pressures that together effect what the mathematician René Thom called a "catastrophe": a radical and qualitative change in the system's behavior.[78] Although catastrophe theory arose from mathematical modeling, Thom insisted that it is better comprehended as a "body of ideas" or "state of mind" with far wider epistemological purchase. My recourse to its terminology is a way of defamiliarizing the perceived canonicity — or "structural stability," as Thom would have it — of modernism in order to foreground its "unstable, threshold-like" qualities.[79] Comprehending modernist art as a field of existing and future deformations allows us to move away from an emphasis on the field's identity (and consequently its inclusions and exclusions) in favor of its temporalized enactment and transformations.

In calling attention to, indeed *catalyzing*, the radically disruptive capacity of such pressures on this field, my approach diverges from related formulations of "weak networks" and "weak modernism" articulated within literary criticism.[80] For thinkers associated with this turn, the epistemological value of weakness is an antidote to the "strong theory" of the Marxist and psychoanalytic interpretive traditions. Attending to scattered, nonhierarchical relations without an ordering principle of a "single morphology," as Wai Chee

Dimock puts it, sets aside the totalizing reach of the "hermeneutics of suspicion" in favor of a reparative approach to particularity, contingency, and relationality.[81] Building from the insights of affect studies, such "weak theory" does not seek to account for overarching or distant phenomena, but for what is proximate and close at hand.[82] My approach shares deep affinities with this focalization on fragilities, gaps, and lateral relations within the archive. It likewise approaches latency not as hidden content to be revealed so much as a strategy for noticing what is already there (or was already missing).[83] But I understand the heuristic of the weak link precisely, if paradoxically, as a *strong theory*, wherein lacunae and missed connections have the ability to reshape the morphology of modernism as such. In this, I resist an ableist inflection of "weak" as feeble or inadequate, and instead posit the weak link as a means of descriptive and epistemological efficacy, one that allows for distinct dispositions of modernism to emerge into view.

It follows that we might describe the surface of the modernist field and its transformations in terms of positive and negative relationalities, strong and weak links, each of which arise and recede in greater focus and complexity depending on the position and directionality of our observation. Any field of artistic production is characterized by lines of explicit, robust, and intentional connection that one can and should trace in time and space. It is a historical fact that Max Bill's 1949 sculpture *Tripartite Unity* had significant influence on Brazilian artists associated with Concretism in the early to mid-1950s and that subsequent works associated with Neoconcretism and its outgrowths—such as Clark's *Caminhando* (Walking), 1963—constitute a "strong misreading," as Yve-Alain Bois has put it, of Bill's version of the Möbius strip (figs. I.27 and I.28).[84] Clark herself recounts that it was Bill who introduced her to the topological form of the Möbius loop, and the history of Brazilian Concretism and Neoconcretism is frequently narrated within this Bloomian schema of catalyzing influence and dynamic response.[85] Works such as Clark's *Obras Moles* (Soft works) (1964) are premised on topological

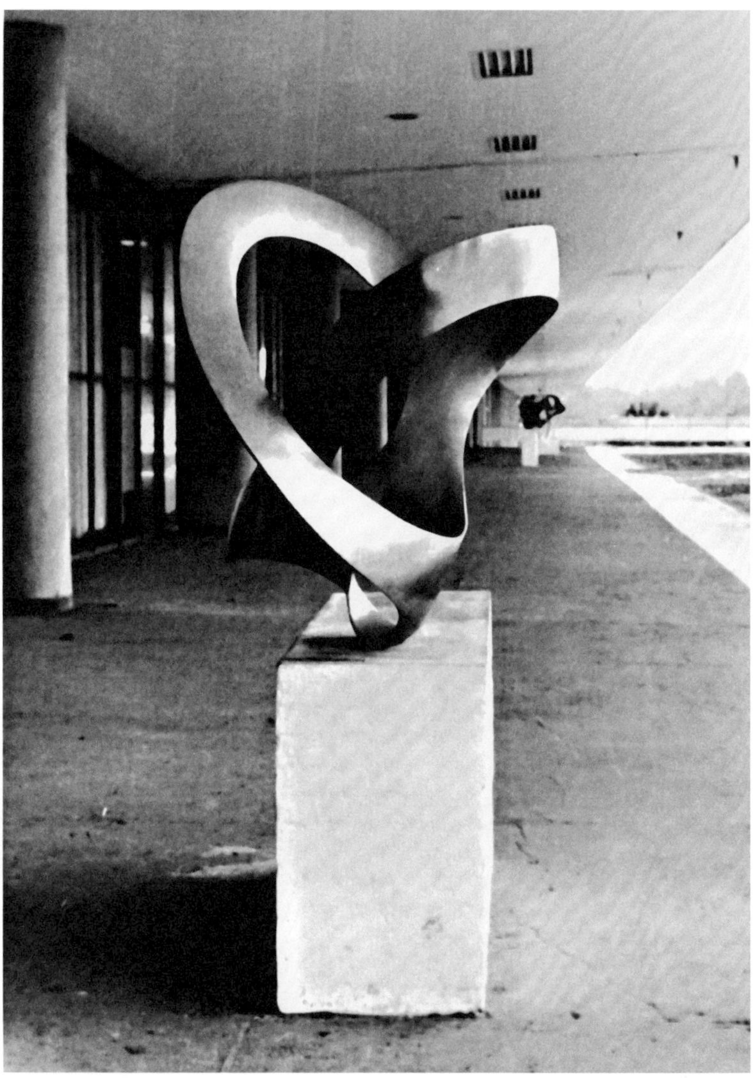

Figure I.27. Max Bill, *Unidade tripartida*
(Tripartite unity), 1948–49. Stainless steel,
114×88.3×98.2 cm. Image: Fundação
Bienal de São Paulo, Arquivo Histórico Wanda
Svevo. © 2023 Artists Rights Society (ARS),
New York/ProLitteris, Zurich.

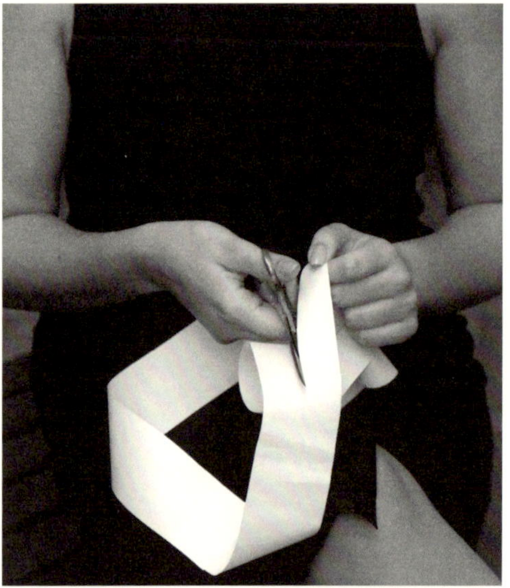

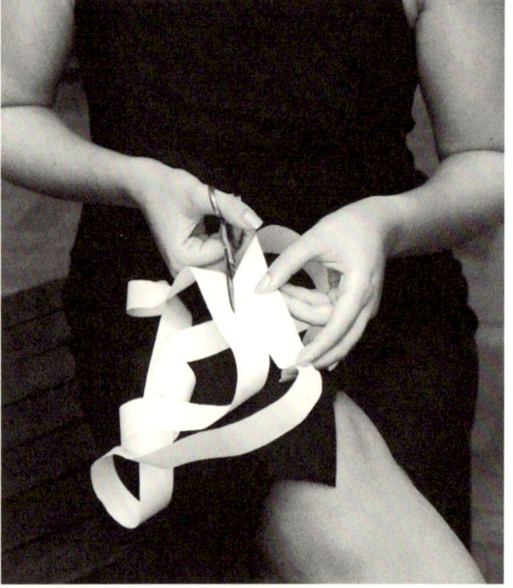

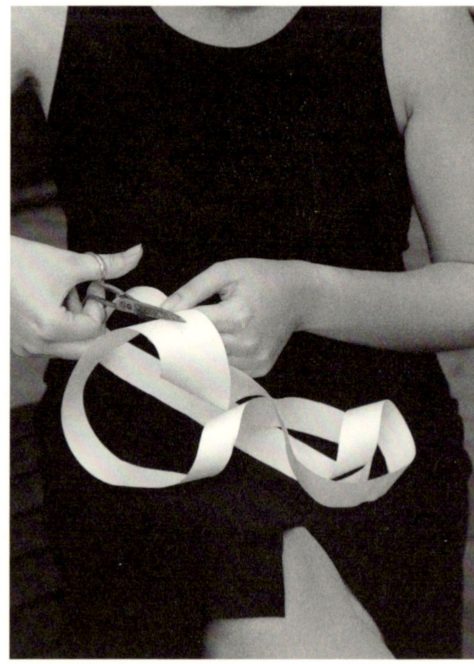

Figure I.28. Lygia Clark, *Caminhando* (Walking), 1963. Photo: Virna Santolia. Courtesy of Associação Cultural "O Mundo de Lygia Clark."

surfaces (see cover and fig. C.7). Clark indelibly described her dialogue with Oiticica by means of a topological metaphor, as well, suggesting that their work and relationship approximated the interior and exterior of a glove.[86] In pursuing topology as a thematic in this study, I therefore follow the interests of Clark and many of her fellow artists.[87] Insofar as Jacques Lacan began to explore the Möbius strip as a model for the psyche beginning in 1962, Clark's mobilization of surface and puncture in her 1963 *Caminhando* can be seen to recast Bill's rationalist and scientific formulation of topology into one engaging the Lacanian "pulsational circuit, a trajectory between subject and object," as Tania Rivera has put it.[88]

Yet it is also true that Clark was living in Paris when Bill held his influential 1951 retrospective in Brazil and that her initial point of reference for Concretism was more likely informed by the organic formulations of Hans Arp, rather than Bill's rationalist theorems. Moreover, as Adrian Anagnost has speculated, Clark's recourse to topological thinking circa 1954, the year she discovered the organic line, might be found in an essay Pedrosa began to write that same year, which mentioned Bill, but by means of the psychologist Jean Piaget's analysis of children's play.[89] While I explore further connections between Arp and Clark in Chapter 2, the archive does not support a relation of *influence* between these two artists and in fact suggests that we might be misguided to define their connection in this way. Such convergences pose a series of questions: What is lost when the history of art traffics only in strong ties? Conversely, how do we elaborate a field shaped by weak links? Can conceptualizing a scalar movement *between* singularities, as Agamben writes of the paradigm, illuminate the irreducible density of a given articulation alongside the inevitable abstraction of its theorization?

As the Arp-Clark example suggests, even when lines can be drawn within an art-historical field, they are often speculative, fragile, and suggestive of dormant or latent potentialities. Such relationalities may participate in heterogeneous or anachronic temporalities.[90] Sometimes connections do not appear at all. Moreover,

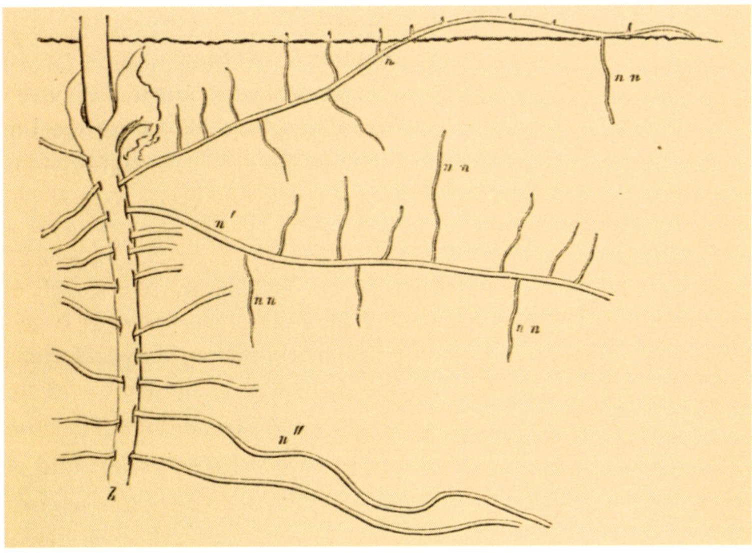

Figure I.29. Plagiotropic growth, illustrated in Julius von Sachs, *Lectures on the Physiology of Plants* (Oxford: Clarendon Press of Oxford University Press, 1882), p. 704.

connections are not always rectilinear or direct, but rather, drawing from a botanical term, *plagiotropic*, meaning slanting, transversal, to the side (fig. I.29). In two brief passages from a 1981 text that accompanied his translation of Goethe's tragedy *Faust*, the Brazilian poet and theorist Haroldo de Campos wrote of "what one might call a plagiotropic movement of literature," drawing etymologically from the Greek *plágios*, meaning "oblique," as in the "lateral branching of certain plants."[91] Here de Campos argues that translation is not the transposition of stable content from one language to another, but a transformation, as in the generation of a *canto paralelo*, or parallel poem. De Campos named this approach to translation *transcriação*, or transcreation. But he understood it to refer to literary practice more broadly, as writers "usurp," "convert," and "twist" their precursors "askew."[92] Setting aside the Bloomian inflection of these actions, what we can take from the plagiotropic is a form of oblique relationality that deflects the overdetermination of influence even as it indexes its history of orientation and change.

Here we might distinguish the conceptual implications of the plagiotropic from the related philosophical figure of the rhizome. Rhizomes, too, are plagiotropic in their root structure, because they refer to a subterranean form of lateral propagation. Because each offshoot can both join and continue independently from the rest, the rhizome has become an indispensable figure of multiplicity, horizontality, and the collapse of hierarchical positions. As Deleuze and Guattari put it, "Principles of connection and heterogeneity: any point of a rhizome can be connected to anything other, and must be."[93] But the plagiotropic is *differently* limber insofar as it does not describe an inherent quality of a plant or other entity, but rather the orienting behavior, or tropism, of its elements. The orthotropic growth of branches, for example, angles directly toward a stimulus, such as light, while plagiotropic manifestations are oblique in relation to such stimuli. In contrast to the rhizome, the emphasis is therefore on positionality (in a lateral sense), rather than proliferation (in an equivalent sense). Such relationality, likewise, is neither predetermined nor teleological: certain plants may oscillate between orthotropic and plagiotropic growth over the course of their lifetime or as a result of shifting external conditions. In the language of botanists, "The architecture of a plant depends on the nature and on the relative arrangement of each of its parts; it is, at any given time, the expression of an equilibrium between endogenous growth processes and exogenous constraints exerted by the environment."[94] Moreover, while "the rhizome is made only of lines," as Deleuze and Guattari write, the very obliqueness of the plagiotropic points us to the relations *between* lines, in other words, to the organic lines that lie within and beyond.

In fact, the interstitiality of a connection that is spaced, rather than continuous, is a preliminary way to understand the "organicity" of the organic line. An organism lives and changes by means of its internal systems, but also that entity's interface with an external ecosystem of factors, including other organisms as well as elements such as light, water, and air. Similarly, an artistic or material entity that contains an organic line is both held together and apart by its adjunctive and disjunctive action, and it is this double movement that gives the entity dynamism, one could even say life.

Clark's understanding of the plane as a textile illuminates the weak link as a fragile form of connection and the plagiotropic as a means of describing particular *kinds* of connection that manifest oblique or lateral relations. In 1953, a survey of Mondrian's work at the Second São Paulo Bienal ultimately led Clark to conceptualize the painterly surface as a woven, topological entity, one in which the very negativity of space was conceived as constructive matter.[95] In a 1959 letter, Clark noted the nucleic expansion of Mondrian's compositions of the teens, the plus-and-minus works that reached toward the canvas's edge, the inauguration of horizontal and vertical vectors, and the process of the *despojamento* ("stripping down" or "laying bare") of the painterly surface in the artist's late works (fig. I.30).[96] Clark also made two important distinctions between her then-recent experiments and Mondian's later phases. Rather than resorting to "repetition," as Mondrian did, Clark wrote, "I 'virtually' invert the surface itself, working with its limit, which I call the 'thread of space.'" Here it appears that Clark understood Mondrian's introduction of doubled and colored lines as intensifying the "lines of construction" from which a surface is built up, or for that matter, destroyed. For Clark, Mondrian's later work treated the plane like a virtual textile made of overlapping horizontal and vertical filaments. However, rather than approaching this surface *pictorially* and atomizing it via repetition, she treated her own surfaces *materially*, thereby revealing the thickness of the line's edge in space, and conversely, the thickness of space *as a line* (fig. I.31).

In her 1959 letter, Clark drew a second distinction in relation to her *Unidades* of 1958, which consist of black squares in which the organic line is transformed into a recessed white border or "light line" (fig. I.32). *Unidades* translates as both "units" and "unities," and

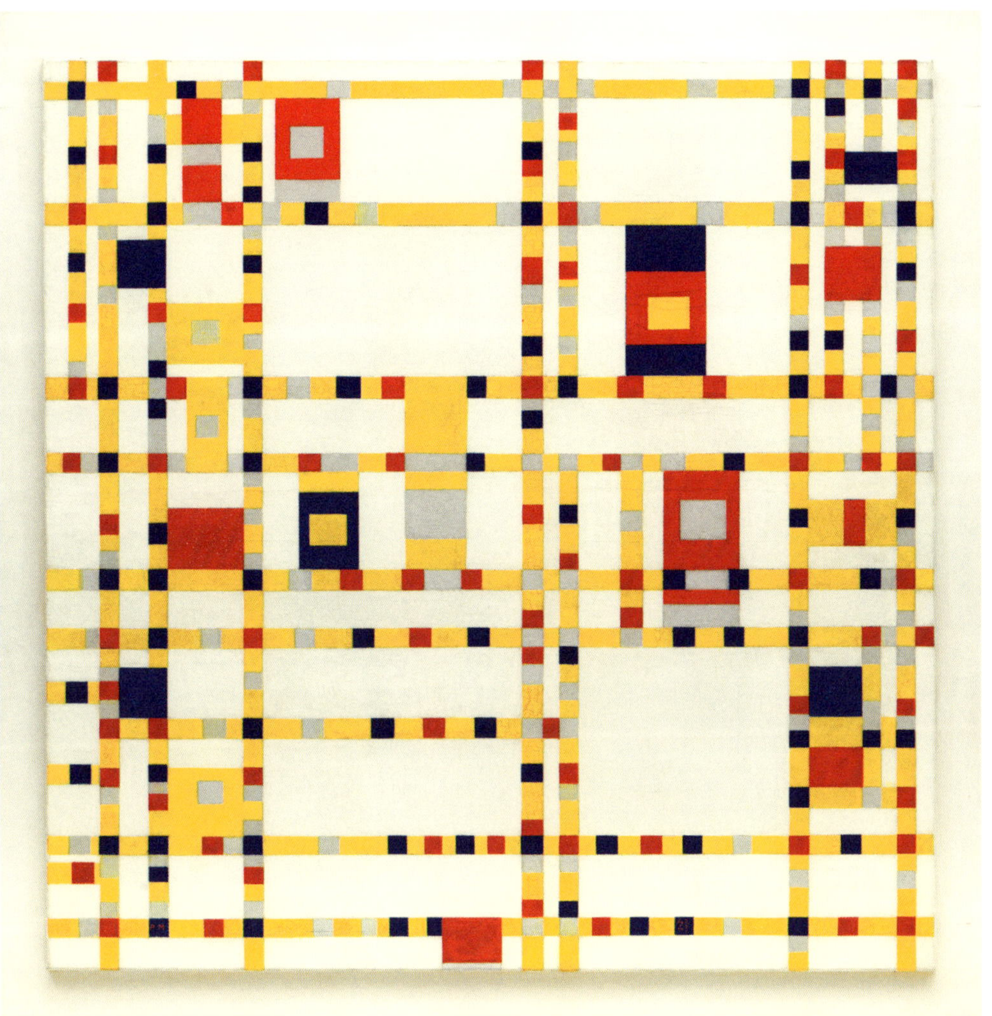

Figure I.30. Piet Mondrian, *Broadway Boogie Woogie*, 1942–43. Oil on canvas, 127 × 127 cm. Given anonymously. Digital image © The Museum of Modern Art / Licensed by SCALA / Art Resource, NY.

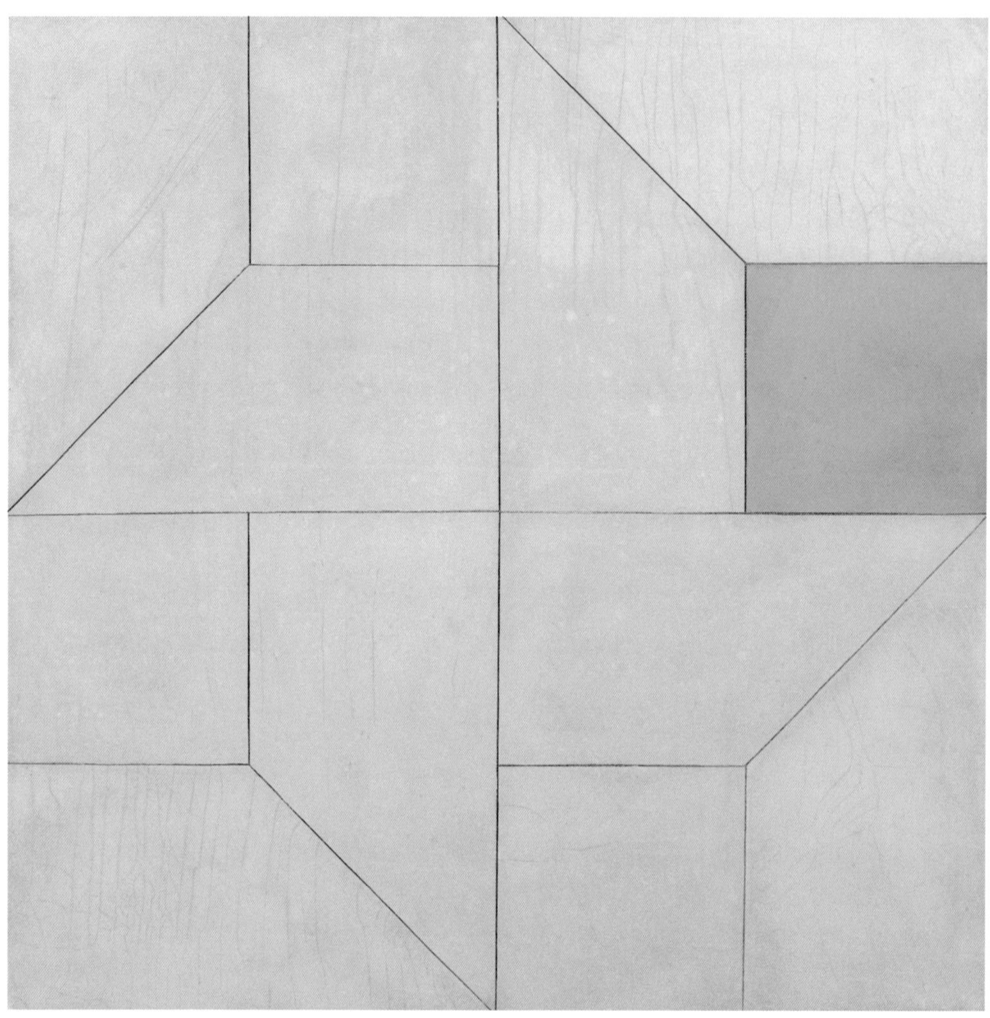

Figure I.31. Lygia Clark, *Planos em superfície modulada no. 3* (Planes in modulated surface no. 3), 1957. Industrial paint on wood, 75.8×75.8 cm. Photo: Jaime Teixeira Acioli. Courtesy of Associação Cultural "O Mundo de Lygia Clark."

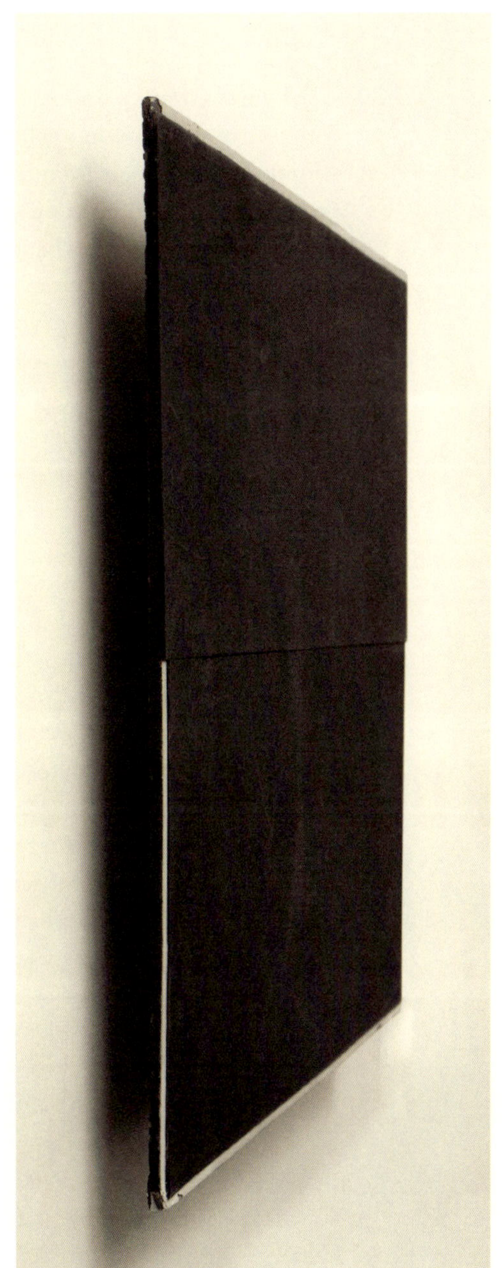

Figure I.32. Lygia Clark, *Unidade* (Unit), 1959. Photo: Sergio Roberto Guerini. Courtesy of Associação Cultural "O Mundo de Lygia Clark."

Clark invoked this paradoxical inflection of numeric singularity and integrative cohesion in explicating how her strategy departed from Mondrian's. Whereas Mondrian "subdivides" the surface beginning from its "very border," Clark wrote, "I add these elements [surface and border] and obtain the inverse: 'modulated space' is born from this sum and the surface is the logical consequence of the sum of the units."[97] In other words, while Mondrian commenced from the totality of the surface as a preexisting pictorial entity and subdivided it from edge to edge, Clark *arrived* at the surface as the additive result of surface, edge, and void. In short, surface is the composite unity of heterogeneous units: a space "modulated" according to its material topology. In his classic Renaissance treatise *De pictura*, Leon Battista Alberti similarly described a surface as an amalgamate, rather than continuous entity. "If more lines stick together like close threads in a cloth, they will make a surface," he wrote.[98] Whereas Alberti's formulation expresses a minimal condition for a surface in terms of the proximity and quantity of threads, Clark dispensed with the notion that a surface would necessarily consist of positive matter. Her interest was not that threads form a surface, but that threads *and space* form a surface and that the quality of line once synonymous with threads might apply to space itself.

In July of 1954, the Museu de Arte Moderna do Rio de Janeiro hosted an exhibition and lecture by the French tapestry artist Jean Lurçat, just months after Clark contributed her *Quadro objeto* to the Salão Preto e Branco and sent her first organic line paintings, as yet unnamed, to the Venice Biennale. Clark retained an article about the Lurçat exhibition in her archives, suggestive that in the wake of her firsthand exposure to Mondrian, textiles were becoming a model for thinking through her burgeoning concept of the organic line.[99] In her first public exposition of the phenomenon in 1956, Clark referred to the seams of clothing as an instance of how one might mobilize the organic line, repeating the example in a 1958 interview.[100] To this end, the organic line emerges as a means for comprehending the porosity of a surface (like a tapestry, it is woven and thus penetrated

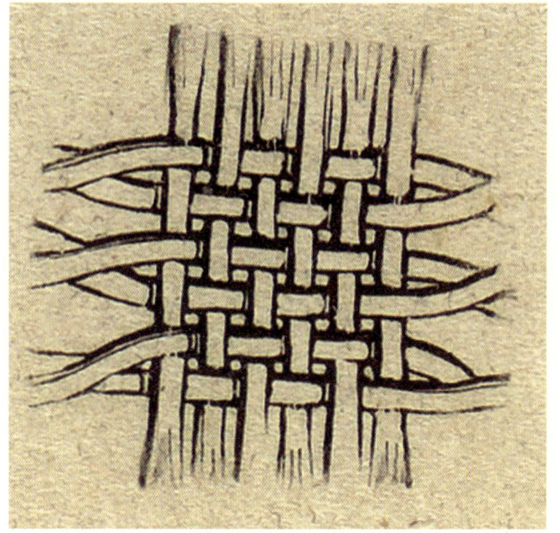

Figure I.33. From Gottfried Semper, *Der Stil in den technischen und tektonischen Künsten; oder, Praktische Aesthetik: Ein Handbuch für Techniker, Künstler und Kunstfreunde*, 2 vols. (Munich: F. Bruckmann, 1878–79), vol. 1, p. 174.

by space), as well as this surface's extensibility, since the organic line, conceived as a seam, allows discrete segments to be bound together, thereby modulating the whole. This model of the textile, moreover, allows us to pinpoint how the irreducible otherness of a spatial interstice paradoxically facilitates the reflexive enactment of the textile's material embodiment. After all, the grid that constitutes a tapestry or woven cloth is not separable from it support. It is not a grid *upon* a surface. The surface *is* the grid (fig. I.33).[101] But this grid is equally and necessarily constituted by a web of intersecting threads (that graphic configuration we colloquially designate a "grid"), as well as the space interleaved *between* them. Disengaging line from space allows for a grid's transportability, but only at the level of representation. The recursive enactment of a given pattern, by contrast, depends on both the alterity and literal presence of space.

Returning to the topological model of modernism, we can newly conceive of a field of modernist art whose mobile shape is formed by such a perforated textile. Across its surface, one can trace strong threads of connection and weak links of spatial hiatus, recognizing that both types of relationality are agential and shift the shape of the surface in their own right. Insofar as any materiality that traverses this surface requires corresponding spatial fissures for the reflexive enactment of its legibility, modernism might be conceived as fundamentally *constituted* by its interstices: in other words, by what at any given time is illegible to the existing representation of modernism itself. Perhaps this is an obvious point. As Partha Mitter has noted, the universalist presumptions of modernism can be located in Enlightenment thinking that has long been critiqued by protagonists within and beyond its bounds.[102] Several decades earlier, Griselda Pollock posited feminism as a structuring difference in the canon itself.[103] By seeking not to decenter modernism or augment its canon, but rather to reconceive of modernism's connective tissue as *always already* porous and riven, I want to elaborate an approach that eludes the fiction of ever-expanding visibility, incorporation, correction, or even dissolution. Instead, I want to advocate for preserving modernism's theoretical purchase, but as a mechanism for articulating incommensurability and elision alongside what is presumed to be actual and manifest.

———

I noted earlier that Clark's exteriority to the major language of European modernism was symptomatic of her position as a woman working in the so-called peripheral context of Brazil. To bring this introduction to a close, I want to underscore that for Clark, this exteriority was a fulcrum for thinking about practice, as well. As I explore in Chapter 1, Clark repeatedly characterized her artistic process through metaphors of ovulation, pregnancy, and parturition, commencing with the action of the organic line upon the orthogonal support. But she also articulated her difference from other models of artistic authorship through idiosyncratic corporeal and biological metaphors that both accentuated female reproductive processes and disrupted their legibility and distribution across bodies, species, behaviors, and effects.

In a 1969 letter to Pedrosa, she wrote of finding "my portrait" in a documentary about a scorpion, whose extreme solitude is conveyed by the "horrifying and beautiful" process of its molting, which Clark likened to an infinitesimally slow birth from the carapace of its prior skin.[104] Clark also commented on the female scorpion's lethargy after she lays her eggs, impervious to the movements of her offspring across her body once they hatch. In this recounting, "birth" stretches across self-production and progeneration, each solitary and self-differentiating in their own way. Clark subsequently observed that while most artists "vomit themselves out in a process of great extroversion," her own practice was to "swallow ever more in a process of introversion" in order to then "ovulate" in a "lamentably dramatic" manner, "one egg at a time."[105] She further noted that this ovulatory process had nothing to do with "invention," but rather "generation." "I only know that being fertilized and ovulating is my manner of holding on to the world." In this process, she added, "I am alone."[106]

Clark's description is fascinating. Not only does it invert the sequence of human biological reproduction — in her process, she is fertilized and *then* ovulates — she describes the catalyzing contact as between herself and the world, wherein she swallows elements of that world and then retreats into herself, a topological figure if there ever was one. Western culture has long analogized artistic insight to a seminal spark of creative genius, wherein the male artist appropriates the female reproductive capacity of gestation and birth while retaining the causal agency of conception.[107] (Here we only have to recall the etymological link between "seminal" and "semen.") This is precisely the trope of "invention" Clark dismisses, characterizing it as both "vomiting" and "extroversion." By contrast, she offers up "ovulation" and "generation" as the relevant processes for her art. I want to press on the implications of this shift in emphasis to these distinctly female-imaged principles, for her formulations compel us to imagine temporal alternatives to the patrilineal drive for origins that has long structured the history of art.

First, Clark's idiosyncratic description of ovulation and fertilization as a form of anchorage in the world offers a compelling way to rethink the autonomy or cohesiveness of the work of art or even a historiographic field such as modernism itself. Clark, we recall, imagines swallowing elements of the world (in Portuguese, *engolir*, which also conjures gulping and engulfing) and then retreating into herself before releasing "one egg at time." The egg that is released thus contains both an exteriority and the interface or threshold by which that exteriority is then incorporated as an *interior* content or form. In order to recover the conditions of possibility for a work or field of artistic articulation, it follows that we must move beyond an archaeology of intentions or influence to perform a corresponding topological operation in reverse. In other words, how can we comprehend the *exteriority* that has been deposited or absorbed within any putative origin?

Second, by disengaging generation from invention, Clark's articulation invites us to comprehend both artistic and historiographic processes as catalyzing, propulsive, and multiplicative — in short, *engendering* — rather than as defined narrowly by production or the proprietary capture of artistic or intellectual territory. For Clark, this process was akin to that of cellular mitosis: "From one to two, to three and then more, one thing always comes from another and it is an extremely intimate communication, from pore to pore, hair to hair, sweat to sweat."[108] There is no doubt that for Clark, this process of division and multiplication was embedded in her personal experience of artistic revelation, crisis, approximation, and growth. The organic line features centrally within this trajectory. As Clark wrote in her artist's book, *Livro-obra* (Book-work), "All of this research of mine began [in 1954] when I discovered the line that appears when two flat surfaces of the same color are laid touching" (fig. I.34).[109] She further commented in 1986 that "since 1954 until the moment in which I stopped working, it was always a direct line, without any breaks."[110] Since the late 1980s, several compelling accounts of Clark's artistic evolution have been written that elaborate this course of

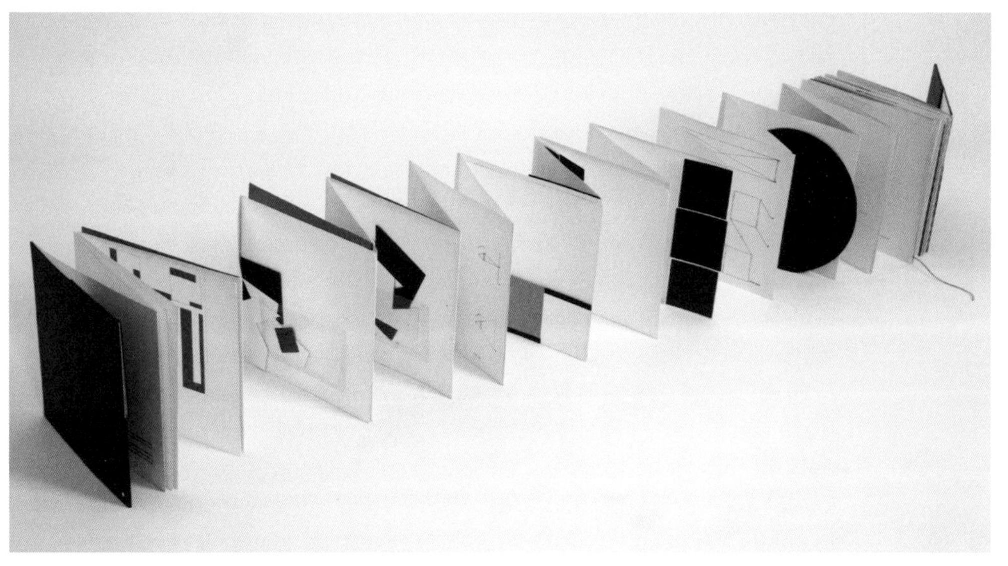

Figure I.34. Lygia Clark, *Livro-obra* (Book-work), 1964, 1983. One volume of a multivolume artist's book; one volume for each letter of the Portuguese alphabet. Paper, plastic, cardboard, and string, 31×21×4 cm. Courtesy of Associação Cultural "O Mundo de Lygia Clark."

experimentation, including foundational texts by Maria Alice Milliet, Ricardo Nascimento Fabbrini, and Paulo Herkenhoff.[111] Within Anglophone art history, Clark's work likewise features in a growing body of literature on Neoconcretism and Latin American abstraction that provides important historical context and analysis of this radical trajectory.[112] And yet in tracing a linear development from plane and object to space, corporeality, and psyche, Clark's own narrative—and many that follow from it—often inscribe a directionality and teleology strangely antithetical to the negative and interstitial character of the organic line itself.

To foreground the organic line as a phenomenon that *exceeds* Clark's work is thus to open an aperture in the artist's historiography, rather than to hew narrowly to her biography or immediate historical context.[113] To do so allows us to linger within the particularity of the organic line, as well as to move laterally — apropos of the generative cellular process Clark invoked — opening out to other artists, chronologies, operations, and effects. These lateral and plagiotropic relations do not so much claim new ground within modernist art as shift its points of articulation, revealing a series of lacunae innate to that field. The observation of such lacunae takes place from the present: Clark's present, when she observed the line, but also our own, as we draw the organic line into legibility and *use* it today. After all, the organic line is radically open to — and dependent upon — the actuality of encounter in ways that other elements of an artwork are not. Its constitutive empty space preexists the work and lasts beyond its making. Yet the organic line is recognized only in the present tense. In this sense, the organic line does not demand a new history of modernism so much as a *contemporary* art history of modernist art that unfolds in multiple temporal registers.

Indeed, by prioritizing the cyclical character of ovulation, rather than the inaugural punctuality of conception or birth, Clark's metaphor opens out to operations of latency, dormancy, and delay. This is a third implication that we might draw from Clark's description. Much like the organic line, a concept, work, artist, or convergence of making may not be sufficiently recognized or articulated in its time. This visibility — or lack thereof — is not infrequently correlated to the imbrication of modernity and coloniality I noted earlier. These relations, too, have a temporal dimension. To channel George Kubler's description of artistic sequences, an entrance of an artist or particular work may be too early or too late.[114] Rather than concentrate on *felicitous* timing, however, an art history informed by Clarkian ovulation enacts transversal movements that recover and reactivate phenomena as well as catalyze new possibilities for strong and weak connections that stretch into the now.

Reproductive metaphors have often been conscripted for the articulation of generational relations in which father/parent begets son/child within a vertical chain of influence.[115] But ovulation exists within a dizzying set of overlapping temporalities that exceed linear causality and invite us to comprehend generation disengaged from the telos of (re)production. Even before we consider the possibilities for suspending, transferring, stimulating, and extending ovulatory processes that are now medically available (but were beyond the horizon of Clark's time), ovulation compels us to think in multiple tenses in order to grasp finitude alongside cyclicity, dynamic impotentiality together with activation and expiration, futurity nested within contingency, discontinuity, and unknowability. When we consider that a mother gestating a female fetus carries within her not only the complexity of her own ovulatory history and futures, but that of her child, whose millions of eggs are both formed and largely *lost* during gestation, we can newly appreciate the proliferating temporalities of Clark's pronouncement, "I am 'the before and the after' since in me the future is present."[116]

Perhaps I am stretching the metaphor thin. One of Clark's late interviews, however, intimates that resonances between art-historical and biological processes were close at hand. Here, Clark humorously describes a wooden construction that was likely the impetus for Ferreira Gullar's 1959 term "non-object" through recourse to anachronic biological reproduction. As she quipped, her work was a "Cubist sculpture outside the Cubist era.... As if I had had a child with the face of the great-great-grandfather.... More than a daughter, a great-granddaughter of Cubism. Because a work of Cubism came out of me and the fact is Cubism didn't have great sculptors.... I would be the first great Cubist sculptor."[117] Within the vertiginous temporalities of this remark, genders and generations invert and oscillate as Clark situates her sculpture — an already lost work, itself something of a dead-end in her own practice — as the impossible culmination of a speculative art-historical genealogy.

To think with such deviant narratives requires temporal and geopolitical deformations that transform the historical legacy of modernism. Inevitably, these shifts draw modernist art in the arena of the so-called global contemporary. This field — variously comprehended as a network of artistic and curatorial practices, a set of critical and scholarly discourses, and a market phenomenon—has an ambivalent and unresolved relationship to its modernist precedents.[118] It often treats contemporary practice as a synchronic field and prioritizes sheer geographic scope at the expense of historical tethering. Such a flattened image of the global may offer the illusion of dismantling hierarchies, but it largely leaves canonical histories—and the structures of power from which they issue—in place. By limning the organic line's paradigm of interstitiality as a historical phenomenon, method, and tool, this book seeks to reconstellate the manifold roots of the contemporary.[119] In so doing, it comprehends modernism as neither a static construct nor a fixed limit, but as a series of dynamic and reciprocal edges. From the standpoint of topology, after all, edges are merely surfaces that change shape with greater or lesser acuity. The organic line situates us *alongside* this topological feature and directs our attention to how the surface shifts as a result.

Clark placed signal importance on the discovery of the organic line in her narration of her artistic practice. She also rehearsed various accounts of this discovery, first and most publicly in a 1956 lecture at the Escola Nacional de Arquitetura at the Universidade de Minas Gerais in her home state of Belo Horizonte, Brazil. In this lecture, she introduced "lines that I may call 'organic'" as pertaining to the "functional lines of doors, seams of materials and cloths, etc. in order to modulate a whole surface."[120] She noted that she had researched the line vis-à-vis her own paintings and existing architecture, further investigating its properties by way of precut plywood segments she manipulated to create "modulated surfaces."[121] In a 1957 typescript text intended for a newspaper article, Clark began to consolidate a narrative about her discovery and subsequent investigation. As she relayed there:

> All of my research began in 1954, with the observation of a line that appeared between a collage and a *passe-partout* when the color was the same and dis-

appeared when there were two contrasting colors. I began to explore the line, still making paintings with a canvas and frame, in which my preoccupation was in bursting open the nucleus of the canvas (the picture), bringing this same color onto the frame. The very thickness of the frame now began to enter as a plastic element (at certain points it was painted in relation to the formal composition of the painting itself). I stopped working on this research for two years, as I didn't know how to utilize this liberated space. In 1956, I found the relation between this line (which was not graphic) and the lines of juncture between doors, the casements of windows, and the materials of which floorboards are composed. I began to call it "the organic line," because it was real, existing in itself.[122]

Clark repeated this account of her discovery, with minor variations and elaborations, in numerous interviews and texts in subsequent years, often signaling the organic line's paradigmatic quality by setting off the term in quotes or italics.[123] She also formalized the narrative in *Livro-obra*, written and mocked up in 1964 and published as an edition in 1983, in which the reader is invited to experiment with cardboard elements that perform the appearance of the organic line (fig. I.35). Her narrative thus quickly became the kernel of subsequent critical and art historical accounts of the organic line, including my own at the outset of this introduction.

Within the historiography of Brazilian art, too, the organic line is nothing short of an inauguration: the irruption of real space within pictorial representation that would lead to the emergence of the Neoconcrete movement in the late 1950s and its participatory outgrowths in the 1960s and beyond. As Herkenhoff writes of the organic line, "the air that penetrates it is the same air that I breathe" and thus "solicits my body."[124] Because Neoconcrete works intensified this spatial engagement and activation of the viewer, phenomenology was a key point of reference for period critics such as Gullar, who were in turn informed by Pedrosa's research into Gestalt theory and the "affective nature of form in the work of art," as the older critic titled his 1949 thesis.[125] While Pedrosa's study provided

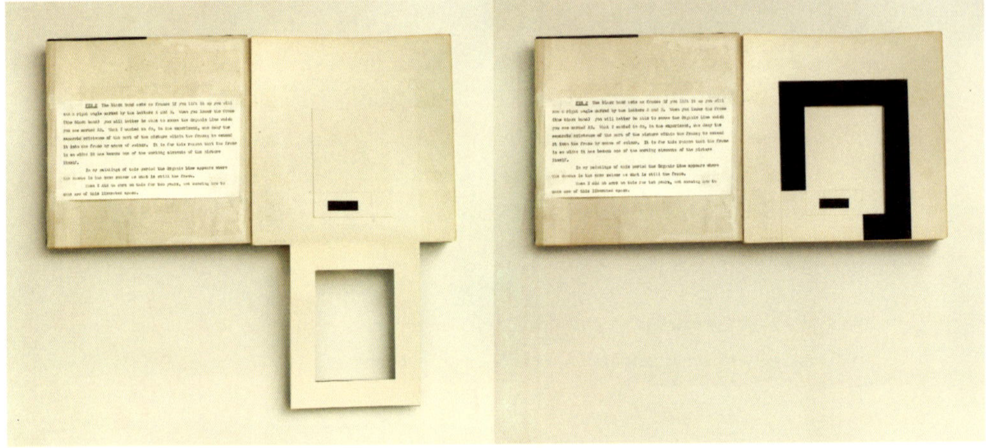

Figure I.35. Lygia Clark, original maquette for *Livro-obra* (Book-work), 1964–65. Mixed media on paper, 21.9 × 21.9 × 3.8 cm. Private collection, New York. Courtesy of Associação Cultural "O Mundo de Lygia Clark."

the foundation for Brazilian artists and thinkers to consider the vitality of perceptual processes, phenomenology offered a language of embodiment and subjective experience. These twinned philosophies have oriented subsequent scholarship on Neoconcretism, and compellingly so. As a channel of space open to the environment and that implicates the viewer in its living, actualized nature, the organic line is an indispensable point of departure for this narrative. Yet even as this orientation troubles both Gestalt relations and the affective boundaries of the viewer and the work of art (Gullar famously described the Neoconcrete work as a "quasi-corpus"), it frequently leaves the category of the human subject — and its presumed universality — intact.[126] This subject feels, touches, reciprocates, expresses, and in so doing, affirms its humanity against any reduction to mechanistic and rationalistic protocols.

But what if the human is not an a priori category, but a supposition, and thus also a space of contestation and experimentation?

Clark intimated as much in a 1965 interview when she remarked, "For me, making art was first a means to elaborate myself as a human being."[127] If we attend to the propositional nature of her observation, we can begin to glimpse art as a form of investigation by which the human is an emergent and unstable phenomenon: a question rather than a given fact. To this degree, Clark's insistence on a language of female difference — "art comes from the belly, not the head," she offered in another interview — disturbs the presumptive interchangeability of "Man" with the abstract category of the human as such.[128] Art is thus a means of continuing the practice of "elaboration," in Clark's words, or of conjuring the "hybridly human," as Sylvia Wynter would later put it.[129]

Clark was certainly not a feminist in any contemporaneous sense of the word. Her identification with the scorpion as a figure of solitude reflects a constitutive detachment, if not antipathy, to collective affiliation or action. Anecdotes abound of her allergic reaction to period designations such as "feminist" or "body art."[130] As Rolnik has observed, the "self" that Clark pursued in her later therapeutic practice was "processual, flexible, and impersonal" — an entity that is "birthed and rebirthed between the body and the world" — and thus the antithesis of the stable subjectivity presumed by identitarian politics, whether disciplinary or liberatory in impulse.[131] Yet if one were to ask if the unruly cluster of associations, metaphors, and materialities proximate to notions of "woman" or "the feminine" was generative to Clark, the answer would be a resounding *yes*.[132] To comprehend Clark's work in a feminist vein thus requires a conceptual queering of feminism itself in the sense proposed by such theorists as Eve Sedgwick, Paul Preciado, and Elizabeth Freeman, wherein cartographies of identity and linear history give way to practices of temporal anachronism, multiplicity, and transformation.[133] It is in precisely this sense that the organic line enacts the requisite voids of Sedgwick's queerness as "the open mesh of possibilities, gaps, overlaps, dissonances and resonances, lapses and excess of meaning when the constituent elements of anyone's gender, of anyone's sexuality aren't made (or *can't be* made) to signify monolithically."[134]

"Theoretically there would be no such thing as woman," Luce Irigaray memorably wrote. "The best that can be said is that she does *not exist yet*. Something of her a-specificity might be found in the *betweens* that occur in being, or beings. These *gaps* reopen the question of the 'void.'"[135] To depart from the historiography of the organic line as an inaugural rupture in order to concentrate on its status as a hiatus is to remain within this caesura. It is to allow its emptiness to reorient how we see, but also how we might set aside the epistemology of origin in favor of Clark's idiosyncratic process of porous fertilization, ovulation, and delay. For this reason, in the chapters that follow, I resist the tendency to chart a linear development that either culminates in or narrowly proceeds from Clark's discovery in favor of fleshing out multiplicities that pertain to the organic line's conditions of possibility and conceptual application. These are multiplicities that exceed the artist's oeuvre and move backward and forward in time. Thus, I attend carefully to the organic line's historical punctuality and engage with its archival specificity. But I also treat the organic line speculatively, as a theoretical track of investigation with broader ramifications for modern and contemporary art and their historiography.

For this reason, the book is a paramonograph, rather than a Clark study per se, by which I mean an investigation that probes elements of an artist's work not for their internal cohesion within the artist's trajectory, but for their applicability beyond this trajectory as such.[136] In this sense, I do not seek to encompass or account for the complexity of Clark's oeuvre, but to reveal the organic line as an instrument: *to show how it works*. As such, the book entails a double movement toward and away from "the canon" as it presently manifests. After all, a historical corpus of artistic techniques and enunciations is a toolbox for practice before (and long after) it is a disciplinary construct. (This is why artists, rightly, never give up their heroes, but are also constitutionally receptive to encountering unfamiliar work.) By demonstrating the archival and speculative potential of the organic line, I hope to suggest how the construct of the canon might give way to a more reflexive imbrication of the commons and undercommons as unstable, shifting, and interlaced phenomena that lend themselves to contestation, care, and use.[137] This book is an experiment in imagining the possibilities of their coconstitutive shapes.

In the first chapter, "Circling the Square: Discovery against Invention," I tackle the question of narrative and its role in the recounting of abstract art. Here I attempt to think through three discoveries: avant-garde artist Kazimir Malevich's arrival at *Black Square*, the so-called "zero of form" in 1915; Clark's nomination and narration of the organic line in her 1954 painting *Descoberta da linha orgânica* (Discovery of the organic line), which pictorially cites *Black Square*; and the 2015 revelation that Malevich's painting contains an inscription, "Battle of negroes...," which suggests that aesthetic and racial ontologies of b(B)lackness were linked from the start. I argue that Clark's *Descoberta da linha orgânica* mobilizes pictorial narration in order to enact a process of discovery in the real time of the viewer's observation while throwing into relief the unstable oscillation between abstraction and figuration at the core of the modernist rupture with representational art. Constellating Clark and Malevich alongside historical figures such as El Lissitzky and Tomás Maldonado, as well as contemporary artists and collectives such as Frente 3 de Fevereiro and Adam Pendleton, I suggest how the multitemporal and real-time tenses of the contemporary might allow us to recover, *dis-cover*, a paradigm of discovery against invention, thereby rearticulating the aesthetic and political stakes of the modernist inheritance for the present.

The second chapter, "Not/Making/Marks: On the Side of Composition," concerns the gesture of the mark that undergirds artistic practice at its elemental level and various efforts to reimagine or resist this gesture in modernist art. Here I investigate the ways marks, planes, and compositional processes become analogues for subjects and subjectivities, including in experiments with art therapy in the

Brazilian psychiatric institution Engenho de Dentro in the late 1940s and Clark's later therapeutic practice and formulations of autocure. While contemporaneous artists such as Ellsworth Kelly and John Cage adopted chance techniques and noncompositional strategies in order to obviate or withdraw authorship, I argue that the organic line actuates a realm *alongside* making that compels us to consider the double-sided nature of boundaries such as the limits of a canvas or the temporal demarcations of a score. Rereading Cage's *4'33"* (1952) vis-à-vis the organic line, I suggest that the line's doubly negative character allows us to recover a sonic and social texture to the work in which emptiness is not simply inverted, but a site of lateral movement. Bringing the queer African American composer Julius Eastman's response to Cage into dialogue with the serial and cross-medial aspects of Clark's experiments, I suggest how the organic line allows us to comprehend the subject as neither an autonomous nor a self-evacuated entity, but a fissured surface porous to the world and structured by the pressures that this world exerts on all sides.

The third chapter, "Inhabiting Networks, Subjecting Space," considers how the organic line structures spatial, social, and affective networks. In 1955, Clark made a series of architectural maquettes of multicolored paneled rooms in which the organic line acts as a hinge between doors, cabinets, and walls, but dissolves into a graphic pattern when such elements are not in use. Her interest in the capacities of such "modulated" environments was indebted to period discourses on architecture and the synthesis of the arts. Yet the frictionless standardization and substitutability embraced within this discourse exists in tension with the organic line's inherent contingency and unpredictability. In 1954, Le Corbusier envisioned how the "universal applicability" of his proportional *Modulor* system might revolutionize transnational shipping by permitting "stowage without gaps." The organic line invites us to attend to such zones of facilitation and expediency, but it also signals how channels swell and stick, often as they bind together with observers and users. I explore the ramifications of such networks and their attendant forms of subjectivity in relation to contemporary forms of global capitalism in which the accumulation, depletion, and circulation of life energies follow from previous regimes of coloniality. Considering the contemporary work of artists Mika Rottenberg and Ricardo Basbaum, whose deviant systems of production shuttle between virtual and material objects and space, I suggest how works of art can conform to, but also thwart, protocols for ever smoother globalization today.

The coda, "Of Mutant Coordinates and Living Things" concludes the book by considering the biological metaphor of the organic line and what it means to treat the work of art and its multivalent boundaries as living entities. In 1927, Malevich described Suprematism as a biological infection that would disturb and ultimately overhaul preexisting pictorial systems. This vision coincides with the modernist dream of total political and artistic revolution. By contrast, the organic line encourages us to conceive of the relation between a work of art and its contiguous systems in terms of a paradoxically relational autonomy. Drawing upon theories of autopoiesis — the autoproducing or self-producing capacities of organisms — advanced by the Chilean cognitive biologists Humberto Maturana and Francisco Varela and later by Wynter, among others, I suggest how works of art are coupled with their environments in relations of dynamic interaction and response. While such couplings can stabilize a given system, I argue, following Félix Guattari, that the capacity of art is to "invent mutant coordinates" that "auto-affirm themselves as . . . autopoietic machines." Utilizing the organic line as a conceptual tool thus allows us to trace how such artistic perturbations transform the topology of the systems with which they interact. It follows that a central task of a contemporary history of modernist art is to excavate the organic lines that lie between such configurations and to chart the "mutant coordinates" produced in their wake. Insofar as such coordinates also *specify* the worlds they call into being, this charting is a constructive operation and a political act.

CHAPTER ONE

Circling the Square:

Discovery against Invention

Introduce a real door into the canvas entirely...
—Kazimir Malevich

I am "the before and the after," since in me the future is present.
—Lygia Clark

Black Dada your history of art.
—Adam Pendleton

Pictures tell stories in peculiar ways. They condense, suspend, and short-circuit events; they plant clues with materiality; they are excessive and terse at the same time. But narrative trucks with representation, and so a significant strain of modernist art tried to banish both.[1] The imperative was to show, not tell; to embody, not recount. Even abstraction was suspect, because it might entail a progressive distillation from a natural or figurative state. As one eminent modernist manifesto put it, a painting should have "no other significance than 'itself.'"[2]

What would it mean, then, to paint a picture of discovery? To *discover*, after all, is not quite to *invent*, a term thick with associations of ingenuity, origins, and ex nihilo creation. As the self-proclaimed Invencionistas declared in Buenos Aires in a 1946 manifesto,

"NEITHER FIND NOR ENCOUNTER: INVENT!"[3] For these artists, to invent was to throw off the "representational fiction" of art in favor of an "art of the act." It was to inaugurate a new age by "habituating man to a direct relation to things rather than the fiction of things."[4] To *discover*, by contrast, was precisely to find or encounter what already exists. Its implication lies in disclosure; its temporality is stratified; it requires narration. To paint a picture of modernist discovery therefore entails a certain predicament of ends and means. The painting must rehearse its befores and afters, but it must also manifest the revelation in present tense. It must transform discovery into the beholder's share.

Such are the stakes of Lygia Clark's *Descoberta da linha orgânica* (Discovery of the organic line), a 1954 painting that names and narrates the artist's decisive epiphany of that year and quite possibly of her entire artistic trajectory (fig. 1.1). At first glance, one might be hard-pressed to identify the work's foundational character. The painting features white, black, and red geometric forms arranged on a square, creamy-white canvas, and its titular element — the organic line — manifests as a channel of space that flows between the canvas and its painted white frame. Unlike Clark's associated *Quebra da moldura* (Breaking the frame) series of the same year, the pictorial elements do not extend onto the frame itself, and the organic line appears, at least initially, actively to participate in neither the interior composition nor its pictorial undoing. The organic line is present, in short, but what the painting intends to convey about it or its discovery is not immediately clear.

Writing about Clark in 1958, the Brazilian critic Ferreira Gullar situated *Descoberta da linha orgânica* as the inaugural moment within a series of formal moves that chart the organic line's sundering and suturing of the painterly plane (fig. 1.2) His chronicle begins with the function of the frame: "A middle term, a neutral zone born with the work, where all the conflict between virtual space and real space, between the 'free' work and the practical-bourgeois world, is erased."[5] *Descoberta da linha orgânica* — identified

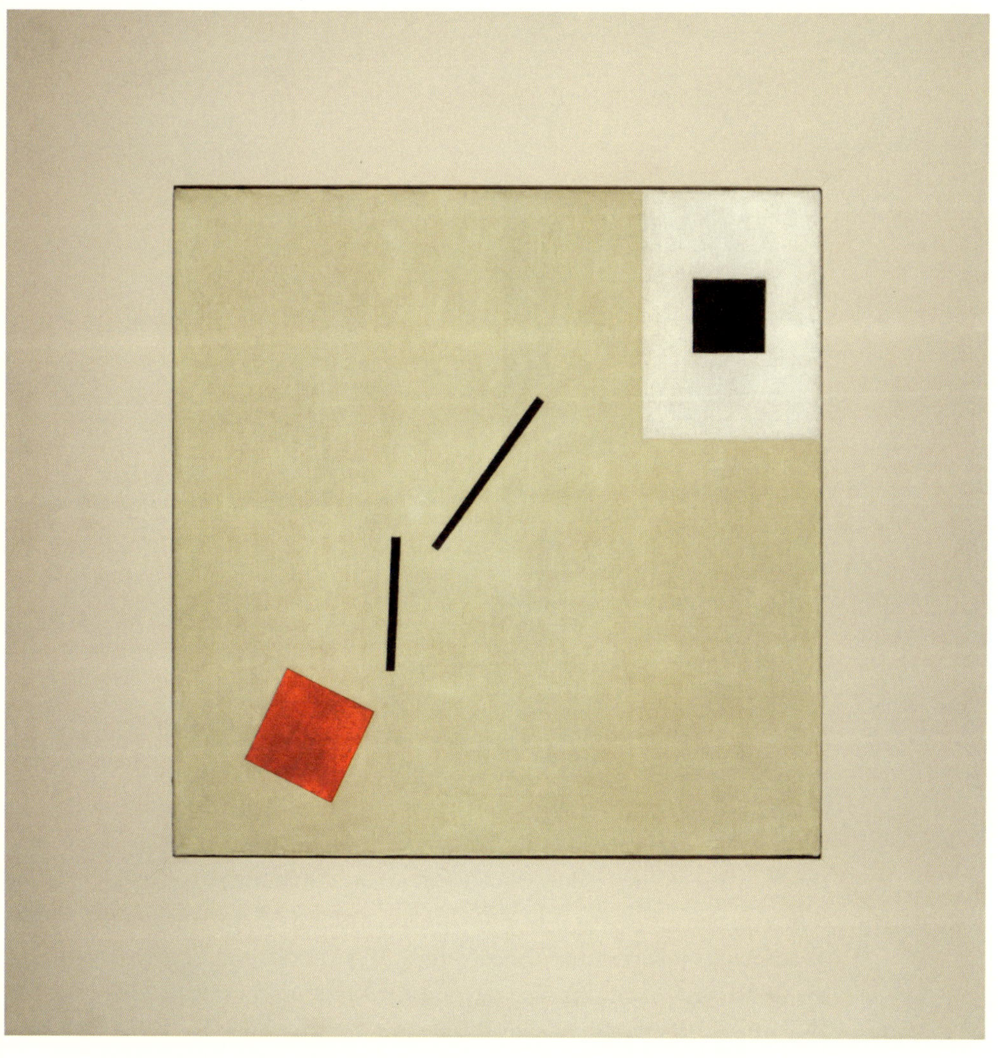

Figure 1.1. Lygia Clark, *Descoberta da linha orgânica* (Discovery of the organic line), 1954. Oil on canvas and wood, 90×90 cm. Photo: Jaime Teixeira Acioli. Courtesy of Associação Cultural "O Mundo de Lygia Clark."

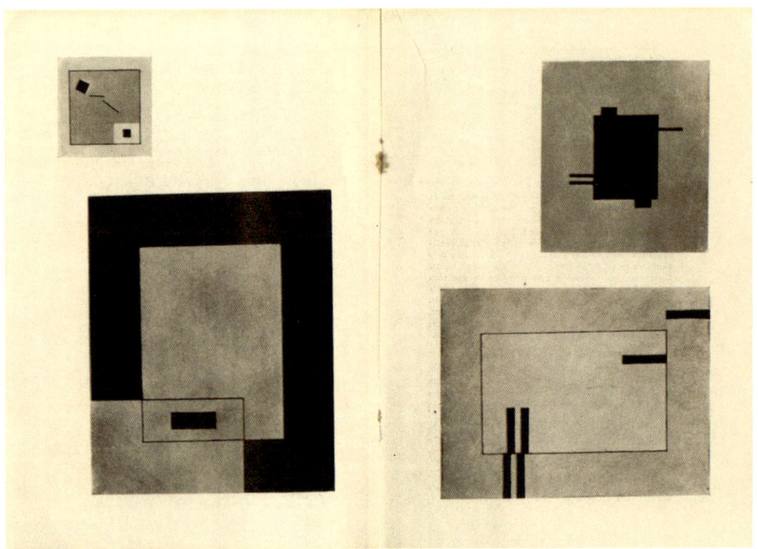

Figure 1.2. Ferreira Gullar, *Lygia Clark: Uma experiência radical, 1954–1958* (Lygia Clark: A radical experience, 1954–1958), exh. cat. (Rio de Janeiro: Departamento de Imprensa Nacional, 1958). Courtesy of Associação Cultural "O Mundo de Lygia Clark."

in Gullar's narrative only as "fig. 1" — commences the colossal inversion of this existing social and aesthetic order. "When I breach the frame, I destroy this impervious space, reestablishing the continuity between the general space of the world and my fragment of surface," Gullar writes, adopting Clark's voice. At first the artist "still relies on the convention of the painting (pictorial space) in order to launch its destruction." Accordingly, this "initial painting" of the series largely maintains the conventional relation between canvas and frame, although the painted frame, "being the same color as the canvas, already starts to invade or be invaded by the 'picture.'" Subsequently, with "fig. 2," Gullar writes, "pictorial space almost entirely disappears," and the painterly surface "extends" over canvas and frame alike. Only a symbolic system of "color/noncolor" signals their difference: the canvas is green (color), while the frame is black (noncolor). Gullar continues: "fig. 3" takes "a new step toward the disarticulation of the painting," as here the "frame" (signaled by the "noncolor" black) moves to the interior of the work while pictorial space (signaled by the "color" blue) is expulsed to the margins, "liberated" from the frame. The final step is achieved when Clark "eliminates" the painting's "center of reference" by propelling its residual pictorial elements to the edges in "fig. 4." *Surface* is finally isolated as the "pure nucleus of painting," Gullar writes, thereby establishing the conditions for a new phase of work.

Despite its formal brilliance, the self-evident logic and economy of this account recedes when details are pressed. Gullar describes a seemingly complete set of four paintings, beginning with the work known as *Descoberta da linha orgânica*, followed by *Quebra da moldura composição no. 5* (Breaking the frame composition no. 5, fig. 2.20), *Quebra da moldura* (Breaking the frame, fig. I.2), and *Quebra da moldura (pxb) versão 1* (Breaking the frame [bxw] version 1, fig. I.24).[6] Yet Clark noted that she completed six paintings in the series and moreover titled the second work in Gullar's narrative *Quebra da moldura composição no. 5*, thus situating it after another painting, *Quebra da moldura composição no. 4* (Breaking the frame composition no. 4), absent from the critic's account (fig. 1.3).[7] Where, further, to place the similarly absent *Quebra da moldura versão 1* (Breaking the frame version 1, fig. 1.4) and how would that painting's concatenation of blue and brown figure in Gullar's argument about the symbolic character of color/noncolor?[8] From there, questions only proliferate. Scale and orientation, for example. Why is "fig. 1" reproduced in miniature in the 1958 publication, when the actual painting approximates or exceeds the others in actual size? Is *Quebra da moldura (pxb) versão 1* meant to lie on the horizontal, as in the 1958 publication, or on the vertical, as it is usually displayed? Did Gullar in fact reproduce the painting, or its associated cardboard maquette? What is the relationship between this maquette and the one described in Clark's own narrative of her discovery, which occurs not upon a painting, but in relation to the black surface of a horizontal collage and its neutral framing mat? If that experiment was the initial point

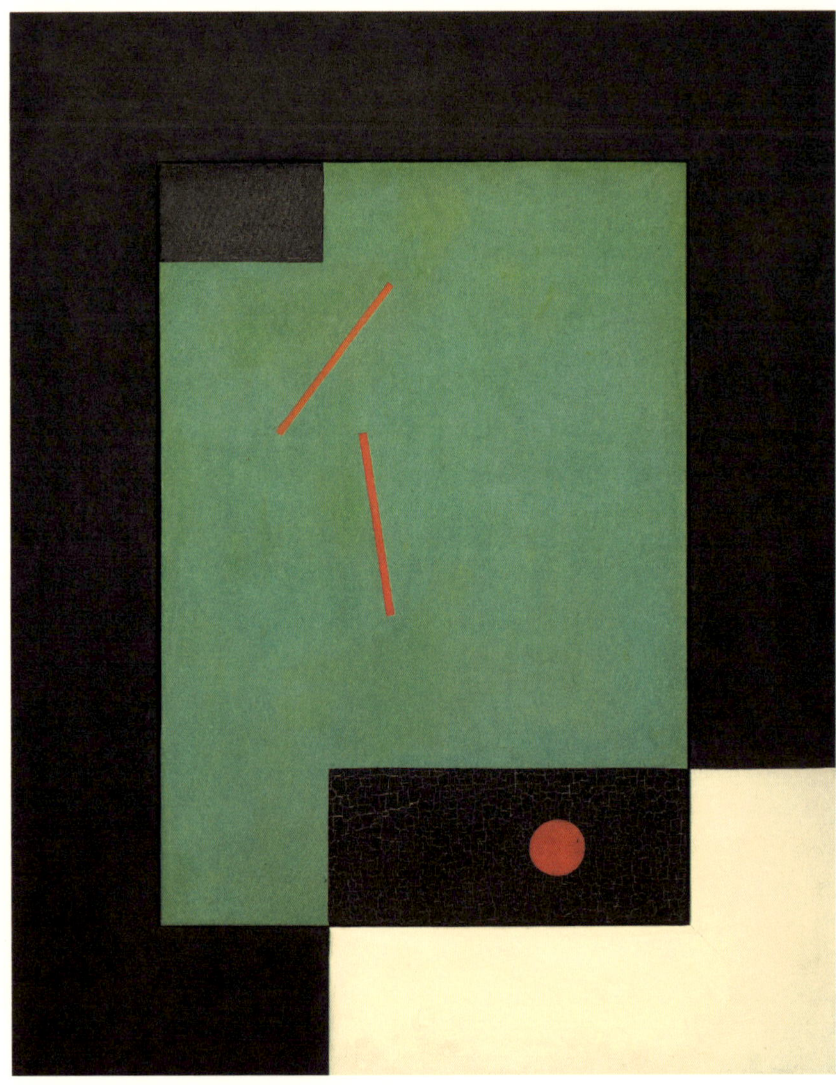

Figure 1.3. Lygia Clark, *Quebra da moldura composição no. 4* (Breaking the frame composition no. 4), 1954. Oil on canvas, 106.5 × 91 × 2 cm. Photo: Sergio Roberto Guerini. Courtesy of Associação Cultural "O Mundo de Lygia Clark."

Figure 1.4. Lygia Clark, *Quebra da moldura versão 1* (Breaking the frame version 1), 1954. Photo: Romulo Fialdini. Courtesy of Associação Cultural "O Mundo de Lygia Clark."

of revelation, is *Descoberta da linha orgânica* the inauguration of an investigative process, or its retrospective recounting?

That Gullar's account dabbles in apocryphal origins is not unusual in the history of modernist art. In fact, it is precisely this affinity for a rhetoric of origins that underscores a pivotal maneuver of *Descoberta da linha orgânica*. For the painting's pictorial grammar is explicitly citational and conjures the Suprematist vocabulary of the Polish-Ukrainian Russian avant-garde artist Kazimir Malevich, specifically, his *Chorny kvadrat* (Black square) of 1915 (fig. 1.5). Gullar's description of the organic line as "irrigating the desert plane" likewise appears to respond to Malevich's evocation of the Suprematist canvas as a "desert" suffused with "sensibility."[9] If Clark's painting concerns the discovery of the organic line, it would also appear to entail a discovery of *Black Square* — and subsequent iterations and responses to its "zero of form" — at a distance of almost half a century.[10] For much of art history, this alone would situate her own work within a well-worn paradigm of delay and derivation endemic to the so-called periphery.[11] What I propose in this chapter, however, is that Clark's painting allows us to recover, *dis-cover*, another paradigm of discovery, one that refutes the one-way temporalities of origin so intimately tied to Malevich's work and the modernist penchant for invention more broadly. Such a paradigm faces in more than one direction and shifts in sequence and time. In what follows, I offer an account of *Descoberta da linha orgânica* that in turn circles around *Black Square*, mobilizing the multitemporal and real-time tenses of the organic line to reimagine the stakes of the modernist inheritance for the present.

———

Let me begin with a few words about the politics of discovery and invention. In Latin, the root word *inventio* carries both the connotations of revelation or disclosure and the fabrication or creation of the new. Classical rhetoricians "invented" by generating novel arguments from existent ideas.[12] In Western discourse, the link between

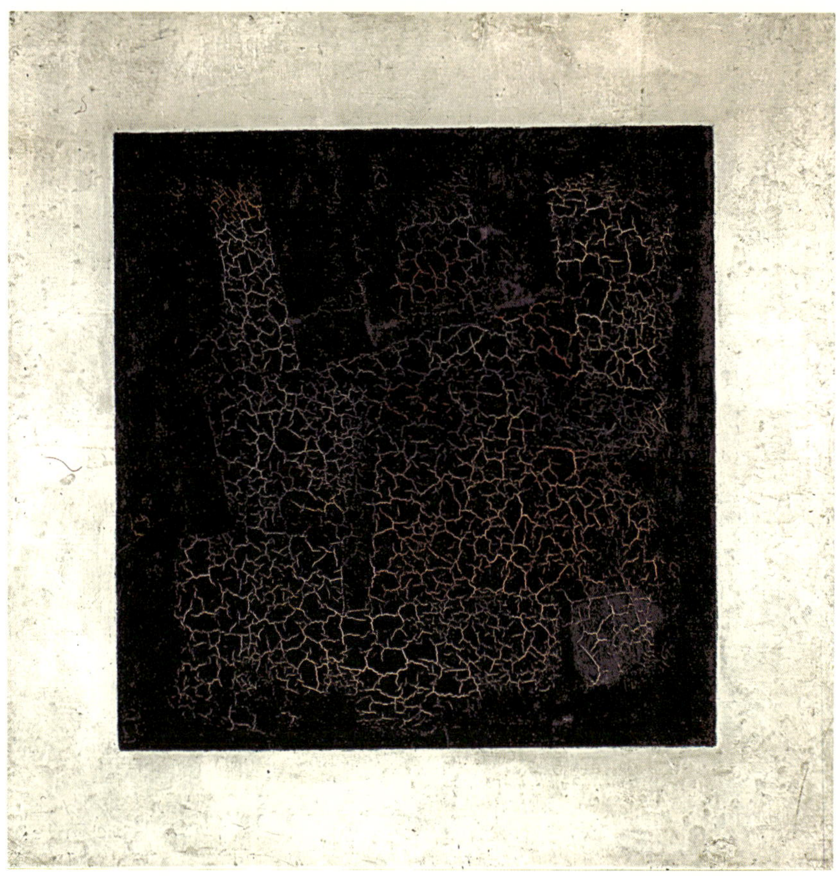

Figure 1.5. Kazimir Malevich, *Chorny kvadrat* (Black square), 1915. Oil on canvas, 79.5 × 79.5 cm. State Tretyakov Museum.

the existent and the novel began to disengage and rearticulate in the early modern period, such that "invention" came to imply a form of origination unique to its author (and the world), while "discovery" was associated with the divulgation and nomination of existing phenomenon.[13] But the concepts continued to be entwined in significant ways.

Lurking within the semantic distinctions between discovery and invention, for example, is the inexorable fact of coloniality and what the sociologist and decolonial theorist Boaventura de Sousa Santos has called the "abyssal line" that emerged in its wake.[14] For de Sousa Santos, the abyssal line organizes the sociopolitics of inclusion and exclusion. In 1493, for example, Pope Alexander VI issued the papal bull *Inter caetera*, which granted Spanish monarchs the right to colonization west of a border drawn from the North to South Poles. The Treaty of Tordesillas further divided the New World between Portugal and Spain the next year. The Doctrine of Discovery that followed validated the conquest and seizure of indigenous territories under European and later US law for several hundred years.[15] Such demarcations are symptoms of what in 1950 the political philosopher Carl Schmitt termed the "nomos of the earth" operative between the fifteenth and nineteenth centuries.[16] Within this spatialized juridical order, the act of land appropriation inaugurated the law that justified it. This, Schmitt argued, is "the reproductive root in the normative order of history."[17]

Like Schmitt, de Sousa Santos comprehends coloniality as both a spatial and conceptual operation, although he applies his analytic toward insurgent, rather than "normative" ends. For de Sousa Santos, the abyssal line is not simply a threshold of colonial power; it structures an epistemological framework that allows the line to operate without becoming visible as such. The abyssal line is what emboldened Christopher Columbus to conceive of his encounter with the populated territories of what the Taínos called Ayiti as the discovery of "virgin" land. It is what spurred the veritable invention of the Americas in the refracted image of the European, as the

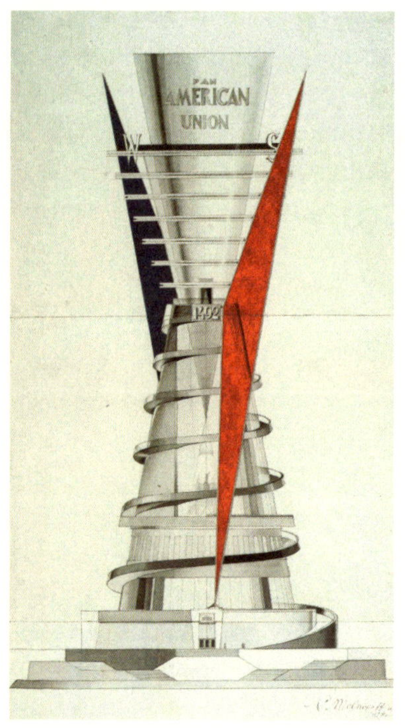

Figure 1.6. Kostantin Mel'nikov, submission to Pan-American Union design competition for a lighthouse dedicated to Christopher Columbus in Santo Domingo, Dominican Republic, 1929. Photo: Album / Alamy Stock Photo.

Mexican historian Edmundo O'Gorman argued in his polemics of 1952 and 1958.[18] And in the discourse of modern art, it is what produces the designations "local" and "universal"—or "derivative" and "original"—as incommensurate and hierarchical terms, wherein the latter are inextricably tethered to the West. *Discovery thus makes way for invention*, but in such a way that conceals its geopolitical tracks.

We need look no further than a 1929 competition entry by the Soviet architect Konstantin Mel'nikov for a monumental lighthouse dedicated to Christopher Columbus in Santo Domingo, Dominican Republic to see how the early modern period, stretching back to the age of exploration, was metabolized by the modernist avant-garde (fig. 1.6). Hosted by the Pan-American Union and guided by US imperial interests, the competition resulted in hundreds of international entries.[19] Mel'nikov's submission utilizes a Suprematist and Constructivist vocabulary to allegorize the relations between Old and New Worlds. The lower cone, which was to house Columbus's physical remains, embodied "European civilization." This volume provided the basis for "the culture of America" above, whose ever-increasing independence was symbolized by massive red and black wings that extended to either side. Propelled by the wind, these wings would slowly rotate the monument on its base, "sending waves over the entire surface of the earth," Mel'nikov wrote, "stirring up humanity day and night to the unceasing performance of great works and exploits like those of Christopher Columbus."[20]

As Mel'nikov's submission suggests, Soviet avant-garde artists aligned themselves with a central myth of Western European self-identity even as they occupied a position geographically peripheral to this West.[21] El Lissitzky, writing around this same time, went so far as to render it a familial relation: "A few centuries ago our ancestors had the luck to make the voyages of great discovery / We, the grandchildren of Columbus, are creating the epoch of the most glorious inventions. / They have made our globe very small but have expanded our space and intensified our time."[22]

Like many modern artists, Lissitzky embraced the conversion of discovery into invention under the sign of universality, specifically, the utopian conviction that communism would unite all the peoples and geographies of the world. Like Mel'nikov, as well, he subscribed to a formal vocabulary that rooted this claim in the radical experimentation of the years around Russia's October Revolution, symbolized, above all, by *Black Square*, the icon of modernist rupture writ large. Indeed, more than anyone other than Malevich himself, Lissitzky was key to propagating and disseminating Suprematism within the immediate context of postrevolutionary Russia and beyond. In 1920, he helped Malevich realize the pamphlet *Suprematism: 34 Drawings*, which narrates the style's formal development, beginning with the square and progressing to circle, cross, multiform, and white-on-white compositions (fig. 1.7). The same year, Lissitzky created *About*

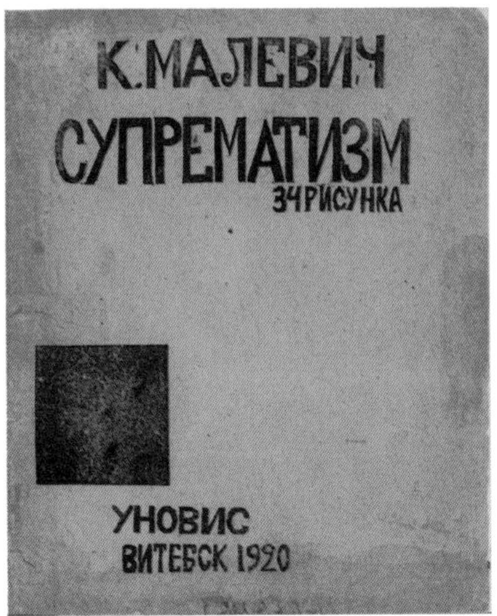

Figure 1.7. Kazimir Malevich, *Suprematizm: 34 risunka* (Suprematism: 34 drawings), 1920. Illustrated book with thirty-five lithographs, page (each) 21.8 × 18 cm. Publisher: UNOVIS, Vitebsk. Printer: probably El Lissitzky, Vitebsk. Edition: approximately 100. Gift of the Judith Rothschild Foundation. Digital images © The Museum of Modern Art / Licensed by SCALA / Art Resource, NY.

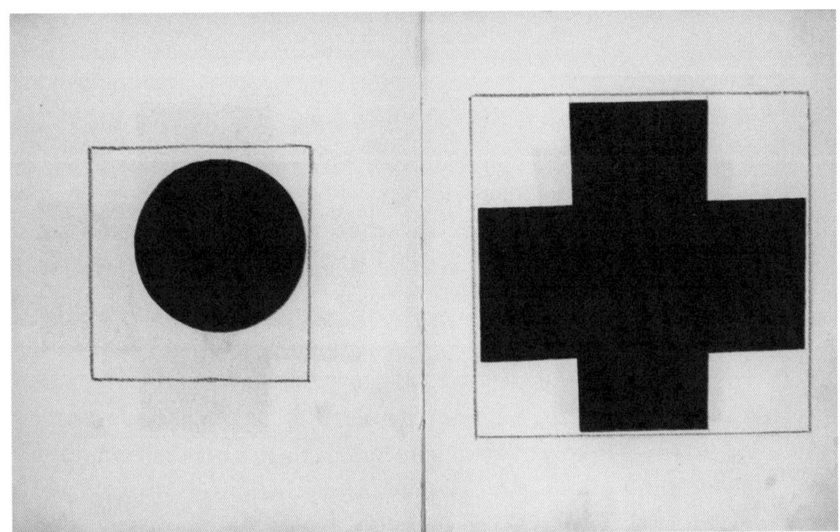

Two Squares: A Suprematist Tale of Two Squares in Six Constructions, which built explicitly from the red and black elements of Malevich's *Painterly Realism of Boy with Knapsack — Color Masses in the Fourth Dimension* (1915) to construct a cosmic drama of revolutionary destruction and renewal (fig. 1.8).[23] And in 1925, he worked with Hans Arp to publish *Die Kunstismen / Les ismes de l'art / The Isms of Art*, a widely circulated booklet that in several cases was the direct link for Latin American artists such as Lygia Clark to encounter Suprematism in turn (fig. 1.9). Tomás Maldonado, leader of the Invencionistas mentioned at the start of this chapter and a key proponent of Concrete art in Argentina and Brazil, recalls the importance of encountering this publication in Buenos Aires in the 1940s.[24] As Maldonado's 1945 *Sin título* (Untitled) painting attests, Malevich's Suprematism provided the foundation to work through formal problems pertaining to figure, ground, and frame in what the Argentine artist called "the battle for an authentically modern art," which was itself "the battle for invention" (see fig. 1.21).[25] For Maldonado, like Lissitzky, this "battle for invention" was aligned — at least initially — with the political aim of a collective communist art in which the banishment of metaphor, anecdote, and representation would free viewers from the mystifying function of ideology.[26]

I will return to Maldonado's and Clark's responses to Malevich and Lissitzky. For now, I want to note that for a historian of modern art, this forward march from one formal innovation — or invention — to another is deeply familiar. Since the 1970s, in particular, various methodologies have nuanced, contextualized, and demythologized this narrative. We now talk of interventions, rather than inventions. We attend to modernism's internal contestations. We attempt to ground experiments in their historical conditions of possibility. Even so, a certain faith in the universality of formal invention has continued to shape the story of modernism, particularly that of the avant-garde. This faith is so deeply entrenched that it easily eclipses the contextual histories that undergird artistic practices themselves. Thus, critics and curators as distinct as Alfred Barr in New York and Gullar in Rio could look to the Russian and

Figure 1.8. Kazimir Malevich, *Painterly Realism of Boy with Knapsack—Color Masses in the Fourth Dimension*, 1915. Oil on canvas 71.1×44.5 cm, 1935. Acquisition confirmed in 1999 by agreement with the Estate of Kazimir Malevich and made possible with funds from the Mrs. John Hay Whitney Bequest (by exchange). Digital image © The Museum of Modern Art/Licensed by SCALA/Art Resource, NY.

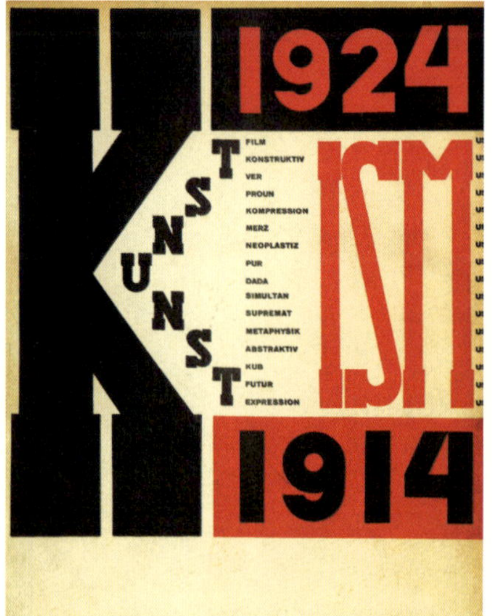

Figure 1.9. El Lissitzky and Hans Arp, *Die Kunstismen / Les isms de l'art / The Isms of Art* (Munich and Leipzig: Eugen Rentsch Verlag, 1925). Photo: Special Collections, Marquand Library of Art and Archaeology, Princeton University. El Lissitzky © 2023 Artists Rights Society (ARS), New York. Hans Arp © 2023 Artists Rights Society (ARS), New York/ VG Bild-Kunst, Bonn.

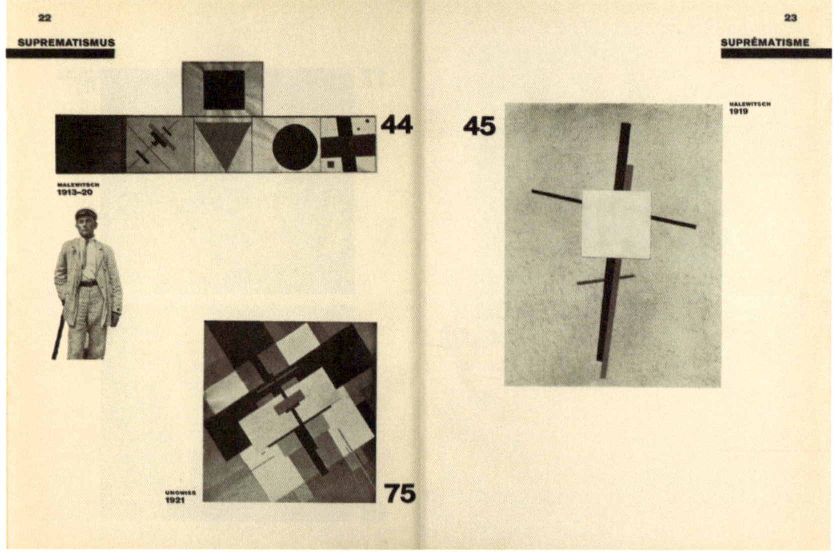

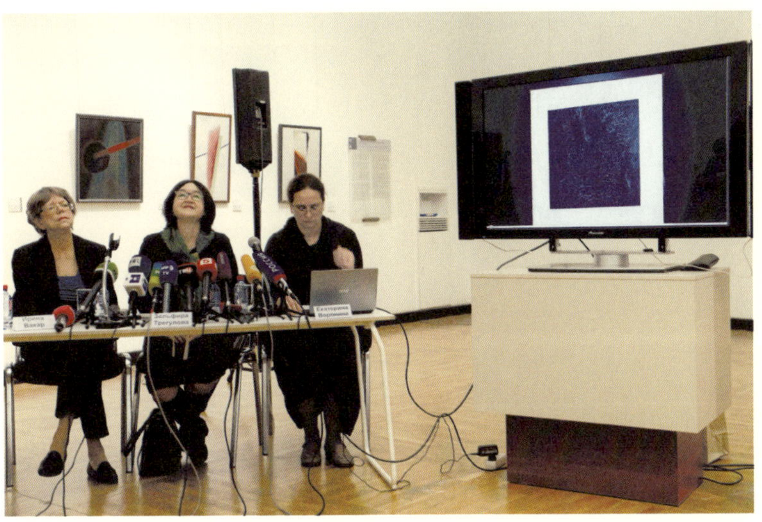

Figure 1.10. Senior research associate at the State Tretyakov Gallery and expert in the Russian avant-garde Irina Vakar, State Tretyakov Gallery director Zelfira Tregulova, and research associate at the Tretyakov Gallery's scientific expertise department Yekaterina Voronina at a press briefing on the research of Kazimir Malevich's painting *Black Square*, November 18, 2015. Photo: Vladimir Vyatkin. Source: Sputnik.

Soviet avant-garde as a storehouse of formal experiments all but stripped of the political investments that motivated them. Conversely, members of that same Russian and Soviet avant-garde were equally confident constructing a formal lineage from earlier movements such as Cubism that culminated in their own work.

What to make, then, of the very different discovery, in 2015, on the occasion of *Black Square*'s centennial, of a pencil inscription that runs along the white perimeter of the painting that reads, "Battle of negroes..." (fig. 1.10)?[27] Written in Russian on already-dried paint, the inscription appears to refer to the series of monochrome "jokes" that the French humorist Alphonse Allais published in 1897 in his pamphlet *Album primo-avrilesque* (April-foolish album) (fig. 1.11). The black iteration of these monochromes, titled *Combat de nègres dans une cave, pendant la nuit* (Battle of negroes in a cave, during the

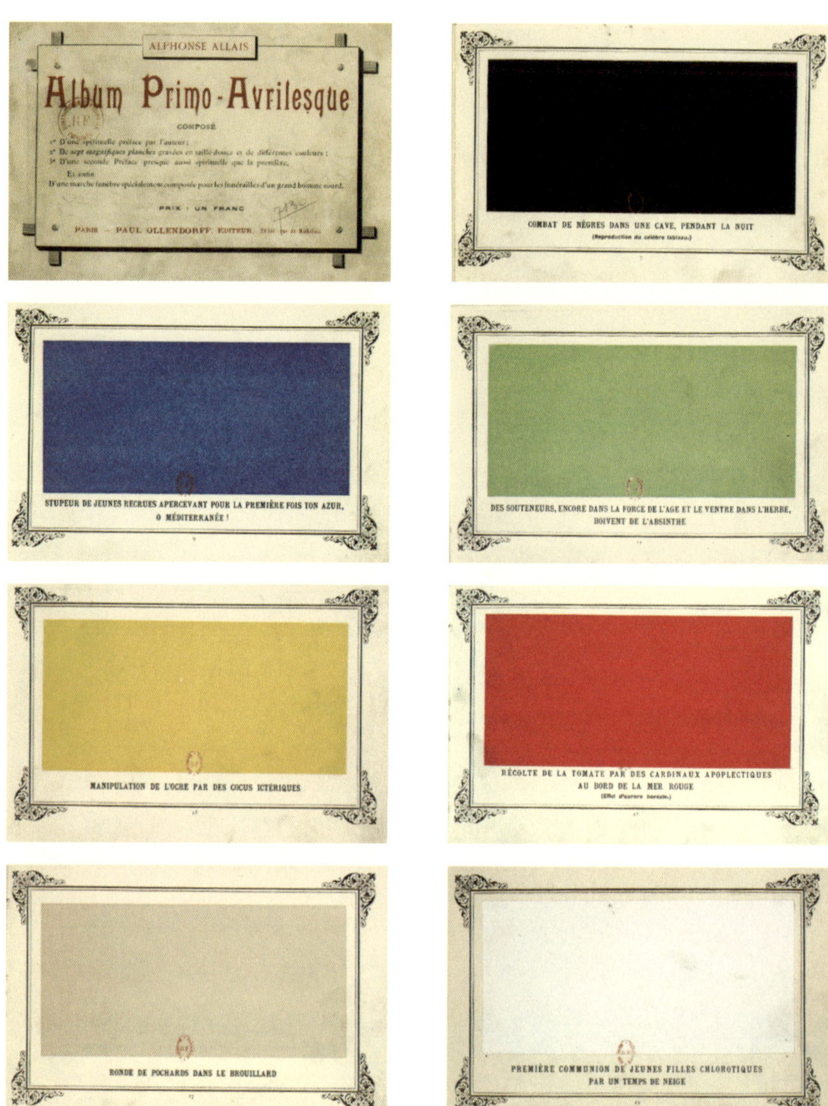

Figure 1.11. Alphonse Allais, *Album primo-avrilesque* (April-foolish album), 1897. *Combat de nègres dans une cave, pendant la nuit* (upper right). Source: gallica.bnf.fr / Bibliothèque nationale de France.

night), is itself a citation of an 1882 painting displayed in a Paris club by Allais's one-time friend Paul Bilhaud.[28] It is hardly overreach to observe that this earlier painting is in turn an abstract sedimentation of countless visual tropes that circulated within the colonial imaginary in the nineteenth century and continued well into the twentieth. Universal expositions across Europe mounted "native villages" populated by indigenous peoples simulating daily tasks and choreographed dances, rituals, and battles. Parisian cabarets abounded with "grands tableaux sauvages de l'Afrique," in which colonial subjects were compelled to perform fantastical spectacles of racialized difference for visitors from near and far (fig. 1.12).[29] Contary to the forward march of invention, such displays participated in an "image loop," as Nanette Jacomijn Snoep has observed, wherein exoticizing and racist tableaus gave rise to further imitations and repetitions.[30]

In 1911, a group of students at the Moscow School of Painting, Sculpture, and Architecture held a gag exhibition that included a "black ink banner with white dots" titled "A Fight of Negroes at Night."[31] It is not known if Malevich was aware of this exhibition or its subsequent mention in a newspaper report. Nor do we know of his exposure to the various cultures of Blackness in Russia at the time.[32] In Moscow, for example, the city's largest entertainment center, the Aquarium, was co-owned by the African American entrepreneur Frederick Bruce Thomas, aka Fyodor Fyodorovich.[33] In 1912, Thomas invited the famed African American fighter Jack Johnson to Russia, fresh off his defeat of the racist white boxer James Jeffries in the so-called "fight of the century" (fig. 1.13).[34] In Moscow, Johnson was to fight another African American, Sam McVey, in a highly publicized event initially set for January 1, 1913.[35] Between 1913 and 1914 — years that were likewise crucial to Malevich's development of Suprematism — several articles in the Russian press recounted the "discovery" of Negro settlements in the Caucasus region.[36] Somewhat later, in 1922, as Malevich began to reorganize the State Institute of Artistic Culture (GINKhUK) in Leningrad, the Fourth Congress of the Communist International declared that "the Negro problem has become

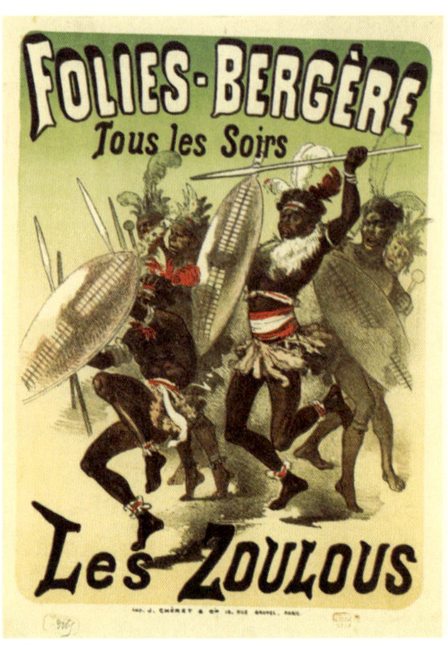

Figure 1.12. Jules Chéret, *Les Zoulous, Tous les Soirs, Folies-Bergère*, Paris, 1878. Source: gallica.bnf.fr / Bibliothèque nationale de France.

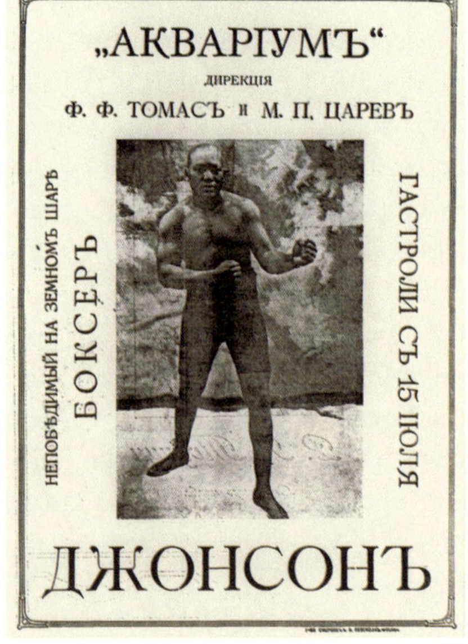

Figure 1.13. Advertisement for Jack Johnson exhibition fights in Moscow: "Aquarium Directors F. F. Tomas and M. P. Tsarev, Appearances Beginning July 15." Photo from *Stseni i arena*, July 15, 1914, as reproduced in Vladimir Alexandrov, *The Black Russian* (New York: Atlantic Monthly Press, 2013).

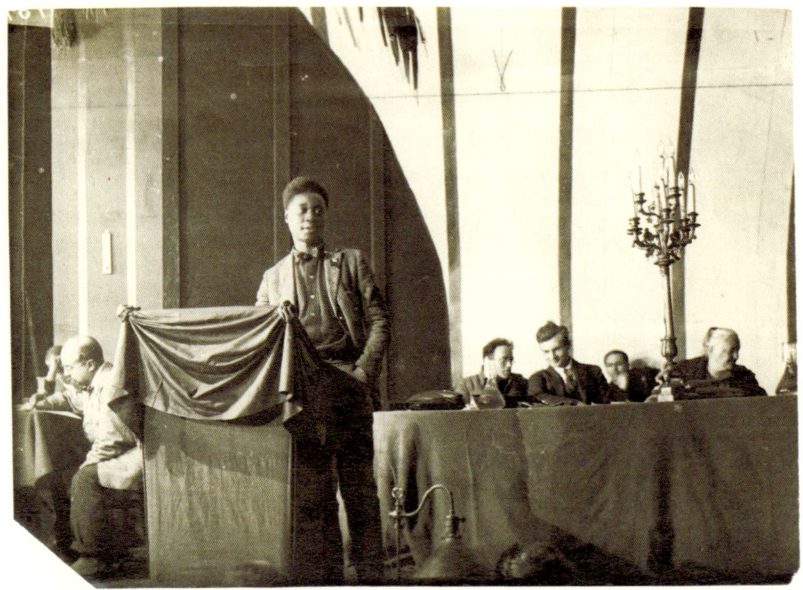

Figure 1.14. Claude McKay speaking in the Throne Room at the Kremlin, Moscow, Fourth Congress of the Communist International, 1922. Claude McKay Collection, Yale Collection of American Literature, Beinecke Rare Book and Manuscript Library.

the urgent and decisive question of world revolution."[37] While attending that congress in Leningrad and Moscow, the Jamaican American poet Claude McKay met with political leaders such as Leon Trotsky, as well as with avant-garde figures such as Vladimir Mayakovsky and Vsevolod Meyerhold (fig. 1.14).[38] In his recollections, McKay noted the Soviets' tendency to subsume political and historical distinctions among African and African diasporic groups while exacerbating differences in skin tone.[39] When presented with a lighter-skinned African American representative to the congress, the revolutionaries, making recourse to the same Russian word for the color "black" used to describe *Black Square*, would ask after the darker-skinned McKay, "But where is the *chorny*?" Where is the Black?[40]

After comparing the inscription on *Black Square* with other known Malevich works, researchers at the State Tretyakov Gallery, including at least one graphologist, have indicated that the writing is likely the artist's.[41] This is hardly a scholarly consensus. The prominent Malevich scholar Aleksandra Shatskikh maintains that the inscription must have been a contemporaneous act of vandalism, insisting "with absolute conviction that Kazimir Malevich had nothing at all to do with it."[42] Irina Vakar, equally respected in Malevich studies, who was part of the Tretyakov research team, is more equivocal, observing that the inscription is of a piece with Malevich's propensity to label works and use linguistic shorthand during his Alogic experiments of 1914–15.[43] Indeed, Shatskikh, too, has argued that by writing words or phrases such as "Village" or "Brawl on the Boulevard" within otherwise blank rectangles, Malevich transformed "figurative ready-made objects . . . into verbal ready-made objects."[44] That Malevich appears to have written "silly" or "stupid" (*glupo*) in the margin of his set design for the 1913 Futurist opera *Victory over the Sun* likewise suggests that such sardonic captions may have acted as dialectical anticipations of a critical or negative response (fig. 1.15).

It will probably be impossible to ascertain definitively if Malevich himself wrote the phrase, and if he did so, if it occurred between 1915 and 1920, when the painting was acquired, or in 1929, when he was asked to restore the work and to paint an exact copy.[45] But none of these scenarios can refute the fact that, contrary to longstanding arguments against pseudomorphology, an aesthetic ontology of blackness operative in *Black Square* cannot be separated from a racial one and that a tense equivocation about their imbrication was at play from the start.[46] After all, even if Malevich was not its author, the inscription was contemporaneous with the work, and the phrase was in active circulation immediately preceding its creation. How, then, can we begin to comprehend, or rather *re-cognize*, the apparent universality of modernist formal invention when it coincides with an articulation of anti-Black racism? And how can we take account of Clark's *Descoberta da linha orgânica*, with its clear citation of *Black Square, now,* which is to say after the 2015 discovery of the inscription, when this knowledge was not available to Clark herself?

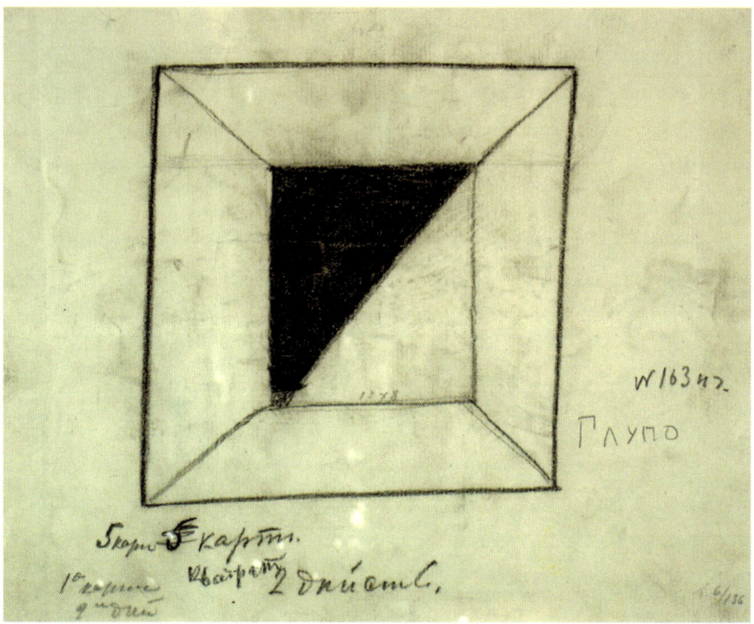

Figure 1.15. Kazimir Malevich, set design for the opera *Victory over the Sun*, by M. Matyushin and A. Kruchenykh, act 2, scene 5, First Futurist Theatre, Petersburg, 1913. Italian pencil on paper, 21.5 × 27.5 cm. The State Museum of Theatre and Music.

In an incisive 1997 essay, Briony Fer argued that *"Black Square* powerfully expresses the fantasy of a place of origin without literally inhabiting it."[47] Here Fer refers to the host of anxious pictorial and discursive supplements by which Malevich retroactively narrated *Black Square* as the "zero of form." These include numerous publications and statements such as *Suprematism: 34 Drawings* and *Die Gegenstandslose Welt* (The Non-Objective World) (1927), as well as drawings Malevich made immediately after completing the painting in 1915 that sought to locate its origins in his designs for *Victory over the Sun.*[48] In light of the discovery of *Black Square*'s inscription, however, we must admit that these supplements follow a far more unruly trajectory, crisscrossing past and present as they oscillate

99

between abstraction and representation. In the following two sections, I track a history of reception and response to Malevich's work for Latin American artists such as Clark and Maldonado, one that ultimately will be interrupted by the present in significant ways. By attending to both these situated and anachronic histories, I want to suggest that Clark's painting and its staging of the organic line return an urgent materiality and metaphoricity to *Black Square* — to its b(B)lackness and to the peculiar status of its white ground — but on the other side of narrative, transmission, and delay.

━━━━━

Black Square's identity as a painterly paradigm has always been highly dependent on discursive and visual supplements. As such, the work has been comprehended through its transmissive apparatus, qualities that in turn came to be ascribed to the painting itself. In 1923, fellow artist Ivan Puni declared that Malevich's work was primarily "proclamational," noting its relative lack of "artistic merits," since "the square was simply made by pouring on paint, coloring it in."[49] At best, "a brochure could be squeezed out of Suprematism," Puni continued, as if the works exuded little more than a slogan.[50] The ease by which the painting's composition could be translated into a schematic illustration — marked form on unmarked support — likewise exacerbated the graphic quality of its figure-ground opposition.[51] Finally, the symbol's portability — from paper and print to fabric squares pinned to lapels and Suprematist signatures on porcelain teacups — facilitated its pictorial citation, bringing to bear a host of philosophical and aesthetic commitments with an extraordinary economy of means. Students associated with Malevich's UNIVOS group in Vitebsk, for example, took to wearing black fabric squares in a gesture of allegiance to the Suprematist ethos (fig. 1.16).[52] For large portions of its public life, in short, *Black Square* was discursive, graphic, and performative, but not necessarily *painterly*.

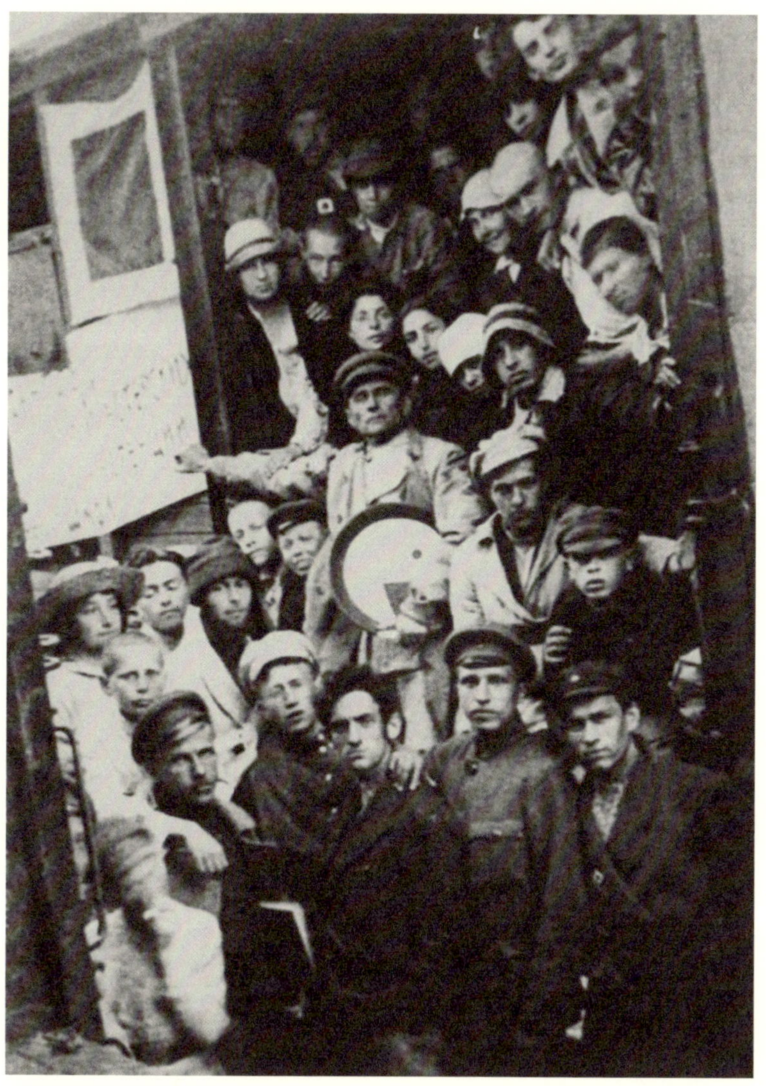

Figure 1.16. Kazimir Malevich and students of the UNIVOS group departing from Vitebsk for the First All Russian Conference of Teachers and Students, Moscow, 1920. Photo: Album/Alamy Stock Photo.

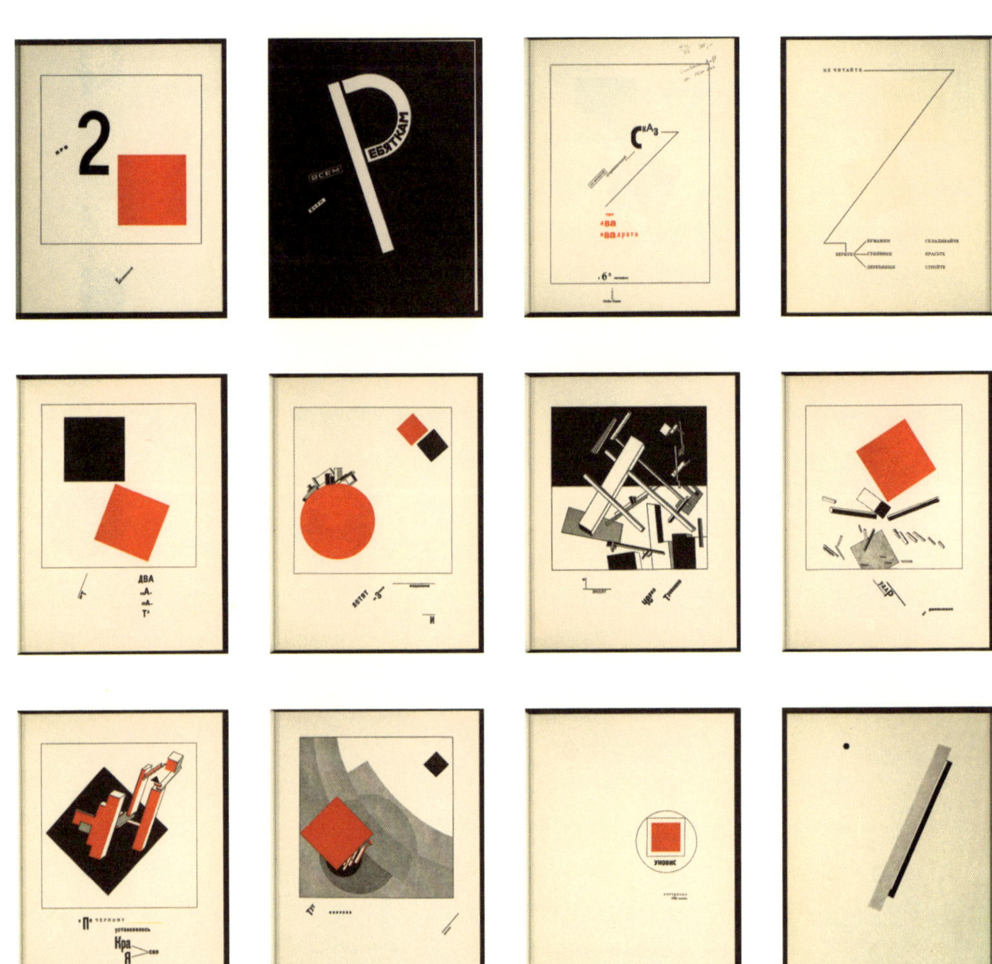

Figure 1.17. El Lissitzky, *Pro dva kvadrata: Suprematicheskiĭ skaz v 6-ti postroĭkakh* (About two squares: A Suprematist tale of two squares in six constructions), 1922. Photo: Special Collections, Cotsen Children's Library, Princeton University.

It is not surprising that subsequent artistic responses to *Black Square* likewise emphasized these mediated qualities. Lissitzky's *About two squares: A Suprematist tale of two squares in six constructions,* "constructed" in 1920, the same year he helped Malevich realize *Suprematism: 34 Drawings,* for instance, is purposefully narratival and anticipates reproductive dissemination (fig. 1.17).[53] Unlike the fantasy of origins that drives Malevich's tract, Lissitzky's Suprematist story for children is deliberately intertextual and referential, building from the sequentiality already enacted in Malevich's Suprematist works. Lissitzky's tale also dilates the rhetorical qualities of Malevich's missives, transforming formal progression into explicit plot, politics, and pedagogy.[54] Most significantly, Lissitzky experimented with the medium of narratival transmission. The book's prologue exhorts the reader not to read, but to "fold, color, build" with "paper, columns, blocks." The final text likewise announces, "It is all over," only to continue, "and then . . . ," suggesting a cyclical, rather than linear reading. By transforming the book's traditional format, typography, and syntax, Lissitzky rendered it "a body moving in space and time," as he wrote, "like a dynamic relief in which every page is a surface carrying shapes, and every turn of a page a new crossing to a new stage of a single structure."[55] Significantly, it was in relation to medial convention that Lissitzky was most critical of Malevich. As he wrote in 1920–21, "For all its revolutionary force, the Suprematist canvas remained in the form of a picture . . . like any canvas in a museum."[56] In response to this conventional pictorial address, Lissitzky's *PROUN*s (Project for the Affirmation of the New), multiplied the possibilities of spatial orientation. In rotating these canvases, he wrote, "we were putting ourselves in space."[57]

The multiple orientations of Lissitzky's *PROUN*s dissolved the canvas's conventional identity and orientation as a picture, but they maintained its traditional *format* as a rectilinear support. And it was against this format's function as a "containing organism," as Maldonado put it in 1946, that a group of Latin American artists associated with the Buenos Aires–based journal *Arturo: Revista de* *artes abstractas* took aim.[58] For these artists, Malevich's Suprematism was already a heavily mediated phenomenon, one that, as Andrea Giunta has incisively observed, was "extracted and generated" from a print culture of art publications that "flattened or eliminated texture and modified color," effectively "diverting the original programs" of the works in question.[59] Significantly, this formal simplification amplified figure-ground distinctions, which became a locus of experimentation and debate among the Argentine group. It was no doubt intentional, for example, that both Maldonado and fellow artist Lidy Prati took on Malevich's *Painterly Realism of Boy with Knapsack — Color Masses in the Fourth Dimension*, already the well-known source material for Lissitzky's *About Two Squares*, in their works of 1945 and 1946, both of which explore the possibilities of the *cuadro* or *marco recortado*, the cut-out canvas or frame.

For Maldonado, the first encounter with irregularly shaped paintings occurred by way of Lissitzky and Arp's publication *Die Kunstismen*, in illustrations of László Péri's work of the midteens.[60] But the impetus for his and Prati's experiments were closer to home, theorized in the Uruguayan artist Rhod Rothfuss's article "El marco: Un problema de plástica actual" (The frame: A problem in contemporary art), published in the single issue of *Arturo* in 1944 (fig. 1.18). Rothfuss's text draws from the Universalismo Constructivo platform of the Uruguayan artist Joaquín Torres-García, who had founded the abstract art group Cercle et Carré with Michel Seuphor in Paris before returning to Montevideo in 1934 to inaugurate his own Latin American–oriented Escuela del Sur.[61] Rothfuss's tract was also indebted to the Creationismo philosophy of the Chilean poet Vicente Huidobro, who argued that the poem or work of art should express its own reality entirely, ceasing to imitate the outer forms of nature and instead producing art "as Nature makes a tree."[62] For Rothfuss, the frame was the crystallization of these concerns. By imposing a regularized format upon the picture (even a fully abstract one), it presumed a pictorial continuity beyond its borders, thereby reducing the work of art to a fragment. In order

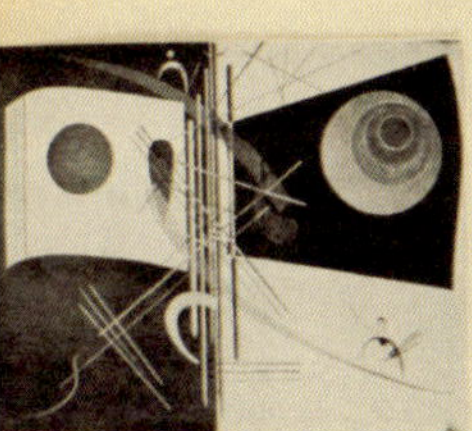

EL MARCO:

UN PROBLEMA DE PLÁSTICA ACTUAL

Motivada por la revolución burguesa del 79 en Francia, una fuerte corriente naturalista invade las artes, especialmente la pintura, a la que por largos años relegará a una condición de máquina fotográfica.

Será necesario que surja un Cézanne, en el panorama plástico, con un concepto tan pictórico que le permitió decir: "He descubierto que el sol es una cosa que no se puede reproducir, pero que se puede representar"; o un Gauguin que escribió: "El arte primitivo procede del espíritu y amplía la naturaleza. El arte que se hace llamar refinado, procede de la sensualidad y sirve a la naturaleza. La naturaleza es la servidora del primero y el amo del segundo. Convirtiéndolo en su servidor, haciéndose adorar por el artista, lo envilece. Así es como hemos caído en el abominable error del naturalismo que comenzó con los griegos de Pericles..." (1), para que, lentamente, la pintura vuelva a sus viejas leyes, por tanto tiempo olvidadas.

Esto se concretará en 1907 (2), con la aparición del cubismo, con el cual cobrarán nuevamente todo su valor en la creación del cuadro, las leyes de proporción, de colorido, la composición, y todo lo relativo a técnica.

El cubismo será definido suscintamente por Guillaume Apollinaire en "Le Temps" del 14 de octubre de 1914, refiriéndose al "Aspecto geométrico de esas pinturas, donde los artistas habían querido restituir, con una gran pureza, la realidad esencial". Y será este deseo de *expresar* la realidad de las cosas, lo que llevará la pintura a una plástica cada vez más abstracta, pasando por el futurismo, hasta culminar en las últimas épocas del cubismo, no objetivismo, neo-plasticismo y también, en su modo abstracto, el constructivismo.

(1) Paul Gauguin. — Notes Éparses.
(2) Dado por Guillermo Janneau en ART CUBISTE.

En este momento, cuando más lejos parece que está el artista de la naturaleza, Vicente Huidobro dirá: "Nunca el hombre ha estado más cerca de la naturaleza, que ahora que no trata de imitarla en sus apariencias, sino haciendo como ella, imitándola en lo profundo de sus leyes constructivas, en la realización de un todo dentro del mecanismo de la producción de formas nuevas."

Pero, mientras se solucionaba el problema de la creación plástica, pura, la misma solución (por un principio dialéctico inquebrantable) creaba otro, que se siente menos en el neoplasticismo y en el constructivismo, por su composición ortogonal, que en el cubismo o en el no-objetivismo, y fué: *el marco.*

El cubismo y el no objetivismo, por sus composiciones basadas, ya en ritmos de líneas oblicuas, ya en figuras triangulares o poligonales, se crearon a sí mismos el problema de que un marco rectangular, cortaba el desarrollo plástico del tema. El cuadro, inevitablemente, quedaba reducido a un fragmento.

Pronto se intuye ésto. Y los cuadros muestran las soluciones buscadas. Por ejemplo MAN RAY, LÉGER, BRAQUE y más cerca nuestro, el cubista de otoño Pettoruti, entre otros, componen algunas de sus obras en círculos, elipses o polígonos, que inscriben en el cuadrilongo del marco. Pero esto no es tampoco una solución. Porque, precisamente es lo regular de esas figuras, el contorno ininterrumpido, simétrico, lo que domina la composición, cortándola.

Es por esto que la generalidad de esos cuadros siguieron en aquel concepto de *ventana* de los cuadros naturalistas, dándonos una parte del tema pero no la totalidad de él. Una pintura con un marco regular hace presentir una continuidad del tema, que sólo desaparece, cuando el marco está rigurosamente estructurado de acuerdo a la composición de la pintura.

Vale decir, cuando se hace jugar al borde de la tela, un papel activo en la creación plástica. Papel que debe tenerlo siempre. Una pintura debe ser algo que empiece y termine en ella misma. Sin solución de continuidad.

RHOD ROTHFUSS

Figure 1.18. Rhod Rothfuss, "El marco: Un problema de plástica actual" *Arturo: Revista de Artes Abstractas*, no. 1 (1944): n.p.

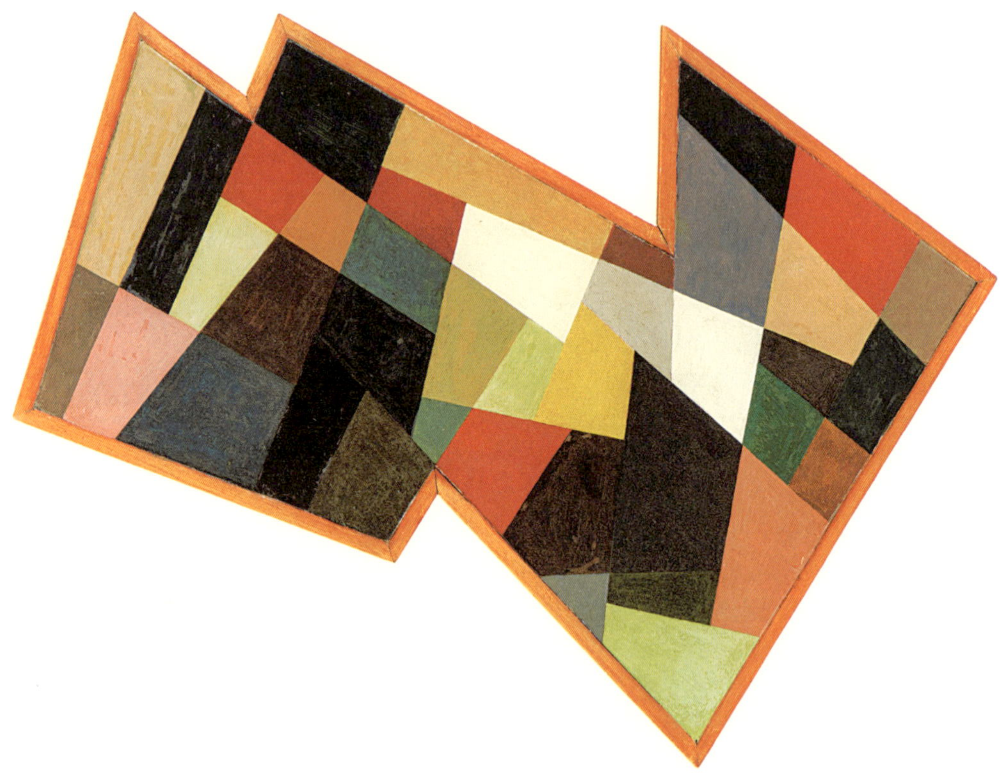

Figure 1.19. Tomás Maldonado, *Pintura*
(Painting), 1944. Oil on chipboard, 38×51 cm.
Private collection, Pasedena, California.

to break with this representational fiction, Rothfuss wrote that "the frame [must be] rigorously structured according to the composition of the painting." He continued, "The edge of the canvas takes an active role in the plastic creation.... A painting should be something that begins and ends with itself."[63]

Rothfuss's statement was followed by a bevy of painterly experiments, political and theoretical debates, and internecine battles, resulting in splinter groups among the artists initially associated with *Arturo*.[64] Key for our purposes is the highly unresolved status of the *marco recortado* and its ability to dispense (or not) with the convention of pictorial illusionism in order to express a work's concrete reality (fig. 1.19).[65] As Maldonado observed in 1946, such irregularly shaped works presented new aesthetic possibilities, but also new complications.[66] A view of the 1948 Argentine contribution to the Salon des Réalités Nouvelles in Paris reveals the sheer variety of experiments that were generated by the *marco recortado*: works penetrated by actual space are joined by articulated and multipanel paintings, moveable sculptures, irregularly shaped works in relief, canvases with both flat and built-up frames, even pieces that are little more than frames themselves (fig. 1.20).

In working through such possibilities, several artists associated with Maldonado's group Asociación Arte Concreto-Invención concluded that neither enclosing external space within a continuous perimeter nor materializing painterly elements in three dimensions were sufficient to destroy pictorial illusion. Instead, artists such as Raúl Lozza, Juan Melé, and Alberto Molenberg began to disintegrate the continuity of the plane by physically separating "the constitutive elements of the picture."[67] For Maldonado, the resulting coplanal structures, in which individual forms radiated outward to create taut constellations fully permeated by space, finally achieved "the conquest of the concrete."[68] Yet as the artist Alfredo Hlito observed in a retrospective analysis, when pictorial elements fully disengaged from a single structure, the wall itself "immediately assumed the optical function previously fulfilled by

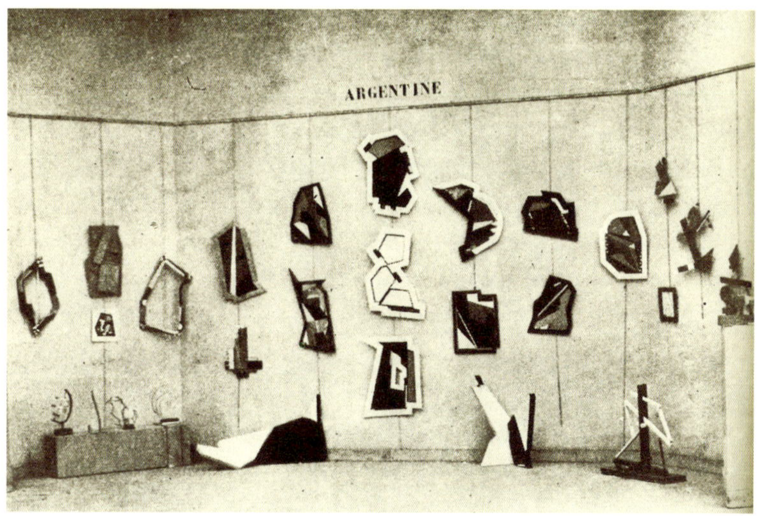

Figure 1.20. Madí works at the Salon des Réalités Nouvelles, Paris, 1948. Published in *Arte Madí Universal*, no. 2 (October 1948).

the canvas," thereby reproducing the problem of figure and ground at a new, environmental level.[69] Faced with the seeming inevitability of the figure-ground opposition, Maldonado and several others found themselves at a theoretical and perceptual impasse, and in 1947, they returned to the orthogonal frame.

Maldonado's and Prati's paintings of 1945 and 1946 must be situated within this theoretical progression. In Maldonado's *Sin título*, the conventional rectilinear border is transformed into an irregular heptagonal support, while Malevich's (and Lissitzky's) black and red squares are stretched, topologically deformed, and rendered as collage elements in relief pasted upon a white enamel ground (fig. 1.21). In texts of 1946 and 1948, Maldonado makes clear the logic for using Malevich's composition as a starting point: although members of the Russian and Soviet avant-garde battled to eliminate the "residues" of the old pictorial space, their efforts were insufficient because the orthogonal plane remained static and disconnected from any consideration of its

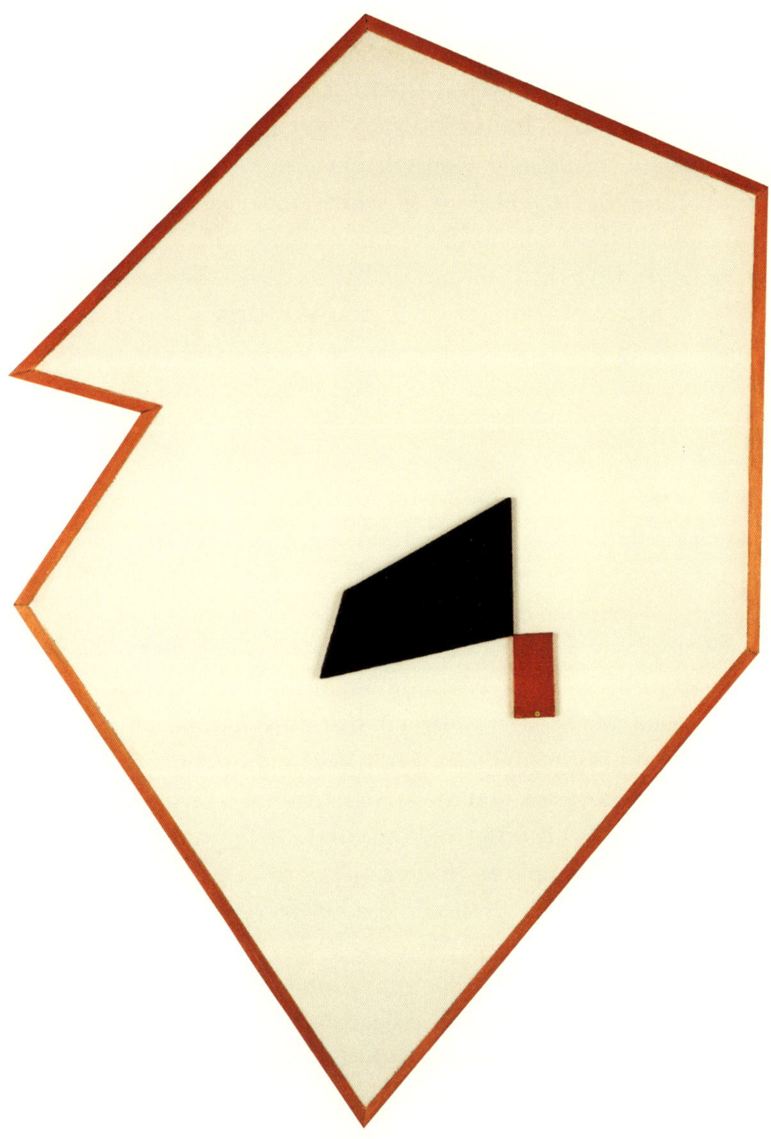

Figure 1.21. Tomás Maldonado, *Sin título*
(Untitled), 1945. Tempura on board attached
to enamel on cardboard, 79×60 cm.
Private collection, Buenos Aires.

constitutive spatial structure. As Maldonado insisted, "SO LONG AS THERE IS FIGURE AGAINST GROUND, ILLUSORILY EXHIBITED, THERE WILL BE REPRESENTATION" (fig. 1.22).[70]

As Sean Nesselrode Moncada has observed, Maldonado's *Sin título* "proposes a genealogy in which Malevich's project culminates in a different hemisphere three decades after its initial creation."[71] And yet the painting's ability to stave off representational illusion by transforming figure-ground relations is equivocal, at best. While the work's irregular perimeter and compositional elements are hardly static, the correlations between them do not resolve into a mappable matrix of reciprocal or responsive relations.[72] Although Maldonado sought to use the three-dimensionality of the collaged red and black forms to break through representational conventions of figure and ground, he soon admitted that this solution was ultimately a "deferral" and that a problem innate to the two-dimensional needed to be solved within that same register.[73] Moreover, as María Amalia García has noted, Maldonado's *Sin título* remains a "self-containing organism" (precisely the quality Maldonado sought to eliminate) in that its frame and white ground isolate and enclose the two centralized pictorial elements.[74] Fellow artists likewise found the work's center too "autonomous" and sought methods for offsetting the contradictory relation between perimeter and compositional forms.[75]

In this sense, Lidy Prati's *Concreto* (Concrete) of 1946 is both an elaboration and corrective (fig. 1.23).[76] Here, the red and black polygons are transformed into vectors of force, the implicit right angle of their moment of contact in Maldonado's earlier work now materialized as a black cross that carves the previously neutral ground into radiating white slabs that stretch across the horizontal. As Gabriel Pérez-Barreiro has observed, Prati's work constitutes a crucial bridge to coplanals such as Lozza's, in which the "entrances and exits" of the work's perimeter are exaggerated to such a degree that exterior space fully "interrupts" the interior of the work, as Maldonado later described it (see fig. 3.18).[77] And yet, much as with these

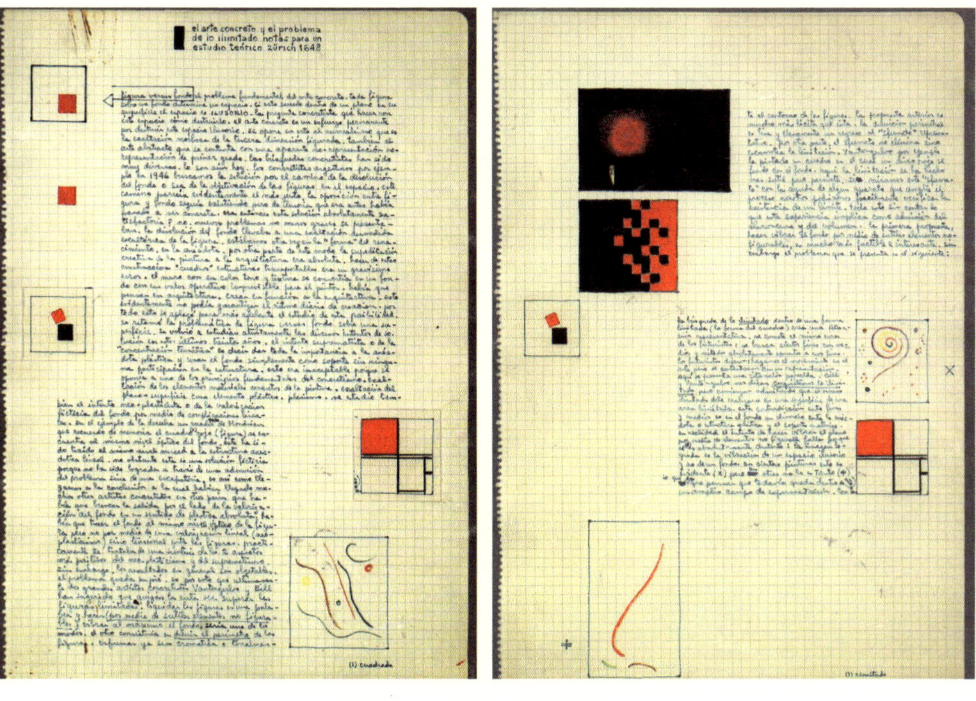

Figure 1.22. Tomás Maldonado, "El arte concreto y el problema de lo ilimitado: Notas para un estudio teórico," ca. 1948. (Buenos Aires: Ramona, 2003).

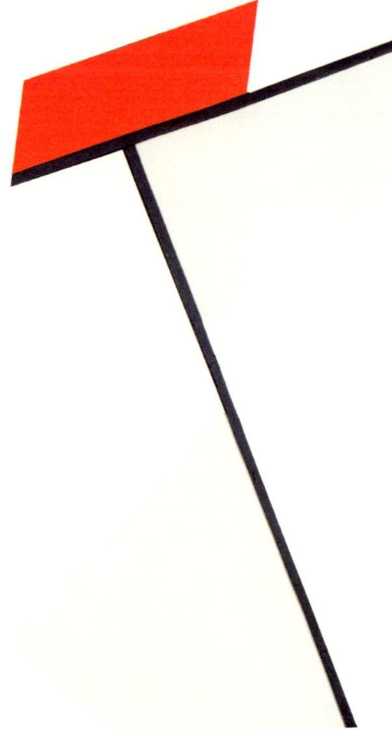

Figure 1.23. Lidy Prati, *Concreto*, (Concrete), 1945. Oil on board, 62 × 48 cm. Private collection, Buenos Aires.

subsequent coplanals, in which colored constellations entirely abolished a single pictorial support, the viewer still cannot but apprehend Prati's work within a pictorial schema of figure and ground in relation to the wall. The impasse that Maldonado, Prati, and their cohort faced circa 1947 thus hinged not on the concrete reality of the work so much as on the inescapable presence of the viewer, who could not be extracted from the aesthetic equation.[78] Faced with the incontestable return of figure and ground, Maldonado ultimately turned his investigations to the theory of Gestalt, the psychology of perception, and the project of a "total design" that would unite viewer and work with the environmental surrounds.

The antirepresentational achievements of the *marco recortado* and the coplanal fall apart when the perceiving body is acknowledged.

Yet the mere fact that such works inscribed themselves so actively within the history of art likewise belied their identity as fully autonomous, concrete works of art. After all, how could a work excise referentiality when it depended upon the *reflexivity* of the history of art, beginning with the convention of the rectangular canvas, itself a signal of the artifice and intertextuality of its own tradition? The self-reflexivity of art and the representational referentiality of figuration are, of course, different beasts. But insofar as the latter is inscribed in the former, they can never be fully disengaged. While Maldonado's and Prati's works dispensed with one form of referentiality by casting off the orthogonal frame, they allowed another to enter when they used Malevich's work as a pictorial conceit. *Black Square* cannot help but function as a decoy in this scenario, cracking open a metaphoric door of art-historical reflexivity that cloaks its historical investments in the apparent self-evidence of the picture plane.[79]

It is difficult to know if Clark's impetus for citing Malevich in *Descoberta da linha orgânica* came by way of Maldonado or Prati or neither. It is likely that Clark encountered some *marco recortado* works in Paris at the Salon des Réalités Nouvelles when she lived there from 1950 to 1952 and that she saw shaped paintings by Lozza, Gyula Kosice, and Martín Blaszko at the São Paulo Bienal of 1953, at which she likewise exhibited.[80] Certainly she saw Maldonado's work and that of other artists previously associated with Asociación Arte Concreto-Invención when they exhibited at the Museu de Arte Moderna do Rio de Janeiro, also in 1953. At this point, however, all of the artists had returned to the orthogonal frame. One of Clark's paintings from that year reveals the fleeting influence of Maldonado's distributed, linear style, now entirely contained within "the expressive field of the canvas," as the Argentine critic Jorge Romero Brest put it.[81]

Maldonado himself traveled to Brazil on several occasions, including in 1951 and 1953, when he met Clark and several members of her circle.[82] At this time, Concrete art was fast becoming the

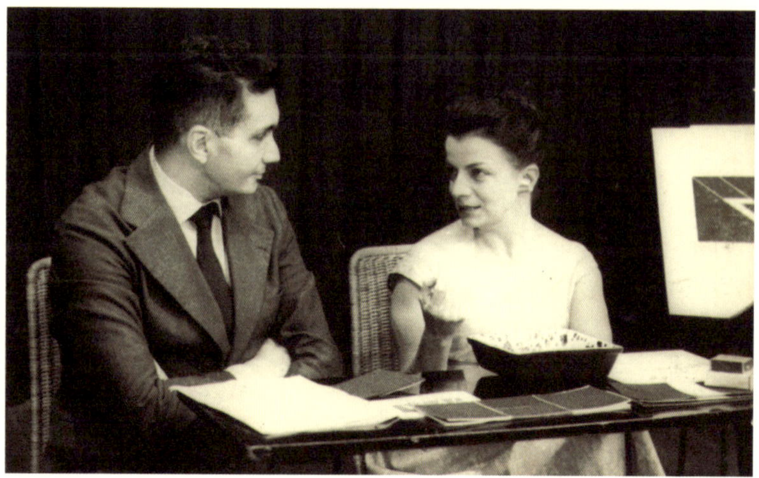

Figure 1.24. "Lygia Clark explicando o concretismo" (Lygia Clark explaining concretism), "Mulheres famosas num programa de TV, roteuri das artes," Caderno feminino, *Correio da Manhã*, June 7, 1959. Arquivo Nacional, Rio de Janeiro.

dominant discourse of Brazilian geometric abstraction and Maldonado a chief disseminator of the work and theories of the Swiss Concretist Max Bill.[83] Although there are important exceptions, as in Argentina, this burgeoning language of Brazilian Concretism was indebted to discourses of invention and creation that often rejected the figurative, representational, regional, and natural. At first glance, the organic line would seem primed for adoption within such idioms. What could be more real, actualized, and universal than space itself? Clark was quickly integrated within the circles of Concrete art that formed in Brazil and her mid-1950s work described accordingly (fig. 1.24).[84] Yet the organic line is a blind spot in many such formulations, not least because the literal space that it constitutes takes part equally in the work and the "natural" world beyond it.[85] Moreover, as we will see, in its peculiar courting of narrative, citation, and referentiality, *Descoberta da linha orgânica* brashly resists several protocols of the self-evident Concrete work of art.

In 1956, Maldonado returned to Rio, now in his capacity as director of the Hochschule für Gestaltung, the institution founded by Bill in Ulm, Germany. In a series of lectures given on the occasion, Maldonado's main concern was calibrating Gestalt phenomena and by extension the optical relations that inhere between the perceiving subject and work of art.[86] We do not know if he discussed experiments with the irregular frame and his own return to the orthogonal format. In much later texts, several Brazilian artists and critics in Clark's circle indicated that the experiment of the shaped canvas was a dead end. In 1960, Waldemar Cordeiro, the main theorist of the Brazilian Concretists in the 1950s, noted that the problem of the frame had already been exhausted by the Argentine group.[87] In a response to Cordeiro, Ferreira Gullar added that those artists had merely "brushed up against [a] problem" more rigorously explored by earlier artists such as Tatlin.[88] A few years later, Hélio Oiticica, Clark's closest artistic interlocutor, diagnosed irregular frame works as "ultraformalist" and unable to "propose the creation of a new color structure that would extend beyond the canvas or the architectonic wall."[89] For her part, Clark's investigation of the relation between external space and the pictorial plane—the action of the organic line—was necessarily tied to the conventionality of the orthogonal frame, for it was there that she could pinpoint the lacunae and inconsistencies of the pictorial apparatus. In this sense, *Descoberta da linha orgânica* does not excise referentiality, citation, narrative, and metaphor, precisely because they are innate to the historicity of painting.

It is not surprising that in the process of advancing a new artistic paradigm—that of the organic line—Clark made recourse to previous one. In Brazil in the 1950s, *Black Square* was largely a myth, as it was for most of the world at the time.[90] In a striking coincidence, the Brazilian critic Mário Pedrosa was studying in Berlin in 1927, the same year Malevich staged a major exhibition and published *The*

Non-Objective World in that city. We do not know if Pedrosa saw or heard of the exhibition.[91] But it was likely that it was through the critic's formidable library—in books such as Alfred Barr's *Painting and Sculpture in the Museum of Modern Art* (1948), Michel Seuphor's *L'art abstrait: Ses origines, ses premiers maîtres* (1949), and Jorge Romero Brest's *La pintura europea contemporánea 1900–1950* (1952)—that members of Clark's circle encountered Malevich's work.[92] None of these volumes illustrated *Black Square*, however, and so despite its extensive citation and description, the painting remained primarily a conceptual proposition.[93]

In 1953, one year before Clark painted her organic line series, the critic Jayme Maurício translated and published excerpts from Malevich's texts in a Rio-based newspaper under the title "'Choix de Malewitsch' o quadrado negro em fundo branco—Suprematismo" ("Malevich's choice": The black square on white ground—Suprematism).[94] Once again, *Black Square* itself is not illustrated, but it is vividly invoked in Malevich's incantatory words: "The midnight of art ringing. Fine art is banished. The artist-idol becomes a prejudice of the past. Suprematism presses the entirety of painting into a black square on a white canvas. I invented nothing, I only felt the night in me, and it was there that I perceived the new thing I nominated Suprematism. It expressed itself by a black surface formed in a square."[95]

Maurício undoubtedly drew this passage from Lissitzky and Arp's *Die Kunstismen*, in which, unlike other texts, Malevich actively distances himself from the notion of invention.[96] *Die Kunstismen* also appears to have been the source for an illustration that accompanied an extract from Malevich's *The Non-Objective World* that Gullar published in a Rio-based newspaper supplement in 1957 (fig. 1.25).[97] There, as in Lissitzky and Arp's layout, *Black Square* appears rather mysteriously upon an elongated rectangular rather than square ground. The puckering toward the center indicates that the image used for the original 1925 publication was of an ink-and-paper illustration of the work, rather than a photograph of the painting itself. Indeed, it is this equivocation about the *ground* of Malevich's icon that indicates

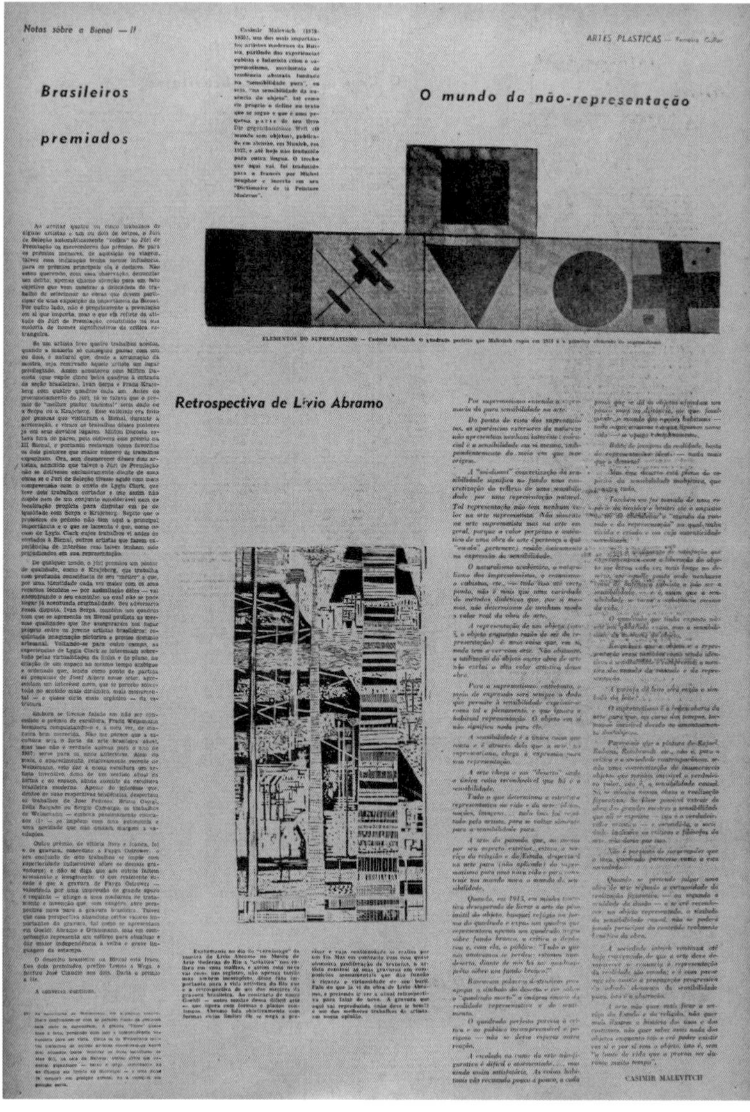

Figure 1.25. "O mundo da não-representação" (The Non-Objective World), *Suplemento Dominical do Jornal do Brasil*, October 13, 1957, p. 3. Centro de Pesquisa e Documentação do Jornal do Brasil.

first, how the promulgation of *Black Square* as a painterly paradigm entailed a loss of its singular materiality, and second, how Clark's *Descoberta da linha orgânica* allows us to reorient the relation between figure and ground by way of the third term of the organic line.

What would happen, for example, if we allowed the ostensible ground of *Black Square* to rise as a material, painterly figure in its own right? For one thing, it would destroy the fiction of the painting's neutral surface, which was the point of departure for Lissitzky's as well as Maldonado's and Prati's critiques.[98] Reconsidering the painting's ground likewise compels us to consider the relation between figure and ground not as a self-evident Gestalt phenomenon, but as a calibration of the aesthetic, discursive, and epistemological means by which these elements become legible — indeed, logical — as a dichotomous relation. Moreover, insomuch as disseminating *Black Square* through mediated reproduction short-circuited the relation between painting and narrative, rethinking the relation between figure and ground initiates a painterly archaeology that transits the other way, from mediation to material specificity in the process of *Descoberta da linha orgânica*'s real-time unfolding.

We can begin with the picture within a picture that is the fulcrum of *Descoberta da linha orgânica*, a clear invocation of Malevich's modernist icon and the first indication that Clark's ostensibly abstract painting is suffused with representation and reference (see fig. 1.1). In Clark's painting, the painterly paradigm of *Black Square* is signaled by a black square that hovers upon a bright white rectangle that, depending on its orientation, is situated horizontally at the interior edge of the bottom right corner of the canvas or vertically at its top right. In the 1958 pamphlet that accompanied an exhibition of Clark's work, Gullar reproduced the painting in the former orientation, possibly following Clark's own indications (see fig. 1.2).[99] If Clark's visual encounter with *Black Square* came by way of Lissitzky and Arp's *Die Kunstismen* (as had Maldonado's and likely Maurício's and Gullar's), this horizontal orientation preserves in material form the reproductive deformations of *Black Square*'s visual transmission. While Maldonado virtualized

Malevich's work as portable concept, in other words, Clark formalized its transmission at the point of reception.

This idiosyncratic rectangular citation, however, deserves further elaboration, for even if Clark encountered Malevich's work in *Die Kunstismen*, ample verbal descriptions of the work noted its square format. Moreover, Clark's own painting has a square format, as do its prominent red and black pictorial elements. The rectangular painting within a painting is therefore even more pronounced, because it disrupts the larger work's symmetries and reciprocities. Luis Pérez-Oramas has compellingly hypothesized that the represented painting's shape and horizontal orientation form a system with the related works *Quebra da moldura composição no. 4* and *Quebra da moldura composição no. 5*, in which a rectangle located on the lower left or right of the canvas locks the painting and frame together, thereby denoting the action of the organic line between them (see figs. 1.3 and 2.20).[100] *Quebra da moldura composição no. 4*, however, contains a similar element at top left, and traces of green beneath the top layer of paint in *Quebra da moldura composição no. 5* indicate that Clark once activated the top right corner of her painting with a similar rectangular tab. Further, a faint arrow and pronounced hanging holes on the back of *Descoberta da linha orgânica* indicate that at some point, it was hung with the painting within a painting oriented vertically, at top right.[101] If the white rectangle is oriented on the lower right, in other words, it is certainly not *only* to be so. Regardless of its placement, Clark's curiously elongated citation of *Black Square* situates that work, first, within a genealogy of transmission, and second, within a much longer painterly tradition in which orientation itself is intimately linked to pictorial illusion. What are horizontal and vertical formats, after all, if not signals of the genre typologies of landscape and portrait? In short, Clark's picture within a picture invokes Malevich's *Black Square* not as a moment of totalizing rupture, but *as a picture* of one.

To this extent, Clark shares with Maldonado and Prati a certain critique of the residual pictorial illusionism of *Black Square*, just as she shares their joint allusions to *Painterly Realism of Boy with Knapsack — Color Masses in the Fourth Dimension* and Lissitzky's *About Two Squares*.[102] Yet whereas Maldonado and Prati sought to expunge any residue of naturalist analogy held over by the "containing organism" of the frame, Clark's critique of the plane was that it was not organic *enough*.[103] As she wrote in 1957, the traditional method of composing "inside" a canvas treated the spatial field as "neutral and therefore dead," deprived of the temporality of "living space."[104] By contrast, "if a surface transforms itself into an organic body . . . the idea [of space] is integrated in relation to the actual support."[105] This, in retrospect, was the ambition of the organic line.

While this "living space" is realized in *Descoberta da linha orgânica*, however, the painting's title intimates that it also tells a story of how this space is unleashed. Here we return to Malevich, for whereas Maldonado and Prati attempted to propel Malevich's pictorial forms out of their residual pictorial illusionism via the spatial tensions of the irregular frame, Clark amplified *Black Square*'s illusionism, seating it within a *mise en abyme* of representational referentiality in which the white ground signifies the unrealized potential of the painterly plane. The question posed by the painting is how it might transform the compaction of this *mise en abyme*, "to burst open the spatial enclosure of the canvas," as Clark put it in 1958, such that space itself "might run beyond the frame."[106]

While Clark's application of geometrical measurement was far from precise, she was fascinated with the philosophy and metaphysics of mathematics and kept manuals such as Vicente Nadal's *Técnica gráfica del dibujo geométrico* (Graphic Technique of Geometric Drawing) in her studio (fig. 1.26).[107] Indeed, *Descoberta da linha orgânica* constitutes an intuitive exercise in transforming the concrete identification of numbers with things into vectors of relationality and function. Lissitzky had advocated an analogous mobilization of relationality in his *PROUN*s. Yet the multiple types of spatial perspective he mobilized in those works — axonometric, axial, oblique — stopped short of engaging literal space in the way

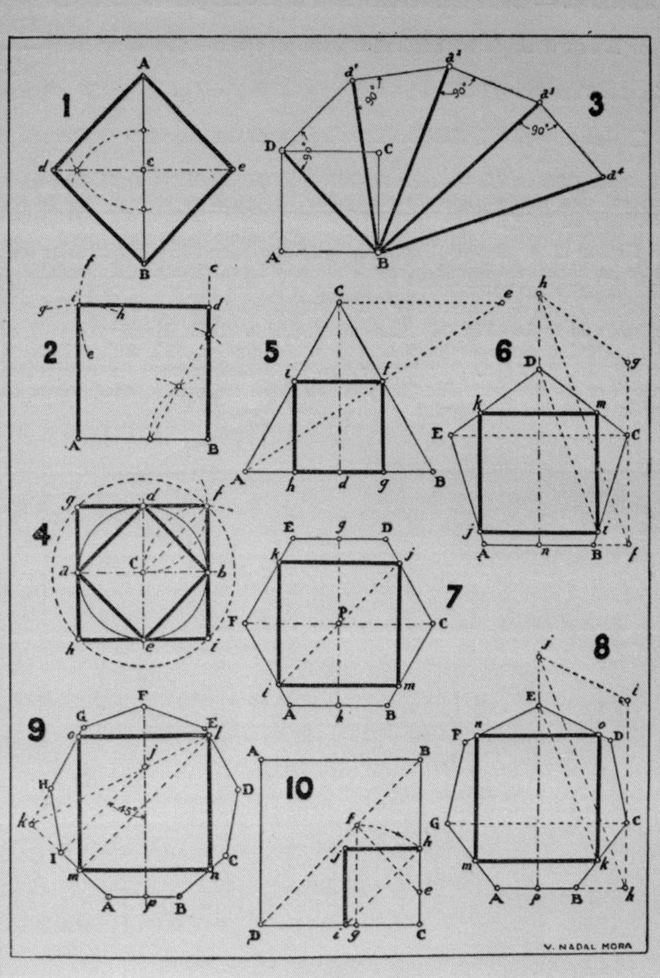

Figure 1.26. Lamina 25, Cuadrado (Square), in Vicente Nadal Mora, *Tecnica grafica del dibujo geometrico, trazados lineales* (Buenos Aires: LA Imprenta Mercantali, 1942), edition in Lygia Clark's library.

that Clark did. As an index of actualized relations within the work of art, Clark's appeal to mathematical measurement anchored its ensuing referential and narratival play in the work's material reality. At the same time, Clark harnessed measurement as both an empirical and rhetorical tool, dilating the tension between metaphor and materiality that is arguably at the core of the modernist rupture with representational art.

Whether oriented horizontally or vertically, the pictorial events of *Descoberta da linha orgânica* proceed from the work's corner, distinguishing it from the centripetal and centrifugal compositions of the *marco recortado* as well as from the self-determining concentricity of *Black Square*. To compose in such a manner, moreover, aligns the painting with certain conceits of narratival, rather than pictorial convention. After all, the picture plane, as Michael Fried famously asserted, is defined by its facingness, and thus its innate condition is to be visually apprehended as a totality: all at once.[108] Contrary to this imperative, *Descoberta da linha orgânica* is patently anecdotal, revealing its story over time. Yet its anecdotes concern purely pictorial and material relations, such that narrative propels, rather than dilutes, painterly reflexivity.

Clark's compositional emphasis on the corner, for example, draws the viewer's attention to the relation between the painting's frame and its citational painting within a painting. This priority of the corner has the effect of foregrounding the diagonal, an element *materially* present in the painted miter of *Descoberta da linha orgânica*'s frame and *rhetorically* present in Clark's citation of *Black Square*. Malevich, we will remember, retroactively sought to locate the genesis of his painting in his drawings for the final set of the opera *Victory over the Sun* (see fig. 1.15). In so doing, he orchestrated a temporal and spatial collapse that effectively reimagined the diagonals denoting the perspectival recession of the theater box as the virtual coordinates of *Black Square*'s white perimeter. In tracts such as *Suprematism: 34 Drawings*, Malevich emphasized the seamless nature of the resulting pictorial space: the relations between form and space "will not be constructed from heterogeneous organisms which together form a whole," he wrote. "The Suprematist apparatus, if one may call it so, will be of one piece with no visible joints."[109] In *Descoberta da linha orgânica*, the haunted perspectival recession of *Victory over the Sun* returns in the form of a critique: a convention of the old representational space and its "visible joints," Clark's work attests, inheres even in the most radical proclamation of modernist abstraction. That the length of the miter (A1) of *Descoberta da linha orgânica* generates the length of its cited painting (A2), seals their connection (fig. 1.27).

But what if we were to comprehend the frame not as a residue of perspectival recession, but, contra Malevich, as an active element of the "heterogeneous organisms" that constitute the work of art as a whole? Clark's ludic mathematical equivalences participate here, too. For over and against the frame's traditional function in securing the pictorial illusion of the plane, here, its width (B1) generates the width of the painting within a painting (B2), clinching a materiality external to the canvas to a representational conceit created within the canvas's bounds. These otherwise incommensurate entities now equalized, this same length propagates a new element in the form of a diagonal rod at the painting's center (B3): a *representation* of this newly activated materiality as an independent pictorial element unleashed on the plane.

This play of equivalencies and analogues amounts to a lesson about the latent materiality and expressivity of those elements — frame and ground — quelled by the traditional aesthetic priority on the pictorial figure. What if we reapply this lesson back to the painting's initial provocation? In *The Non-Objective World*, Malevich offered up the following equation: "The square = feeling, the white field = the void beyond this feeling."[110] By contrast, *Descoberta da linha orgânica* posits that black square and white ground must be comprehended as a material continuity: a single aesthetic "feeling" that stretches from the limits of the square to that of the represented painting (C1). Measuring this continuity is also generative, its length releasing

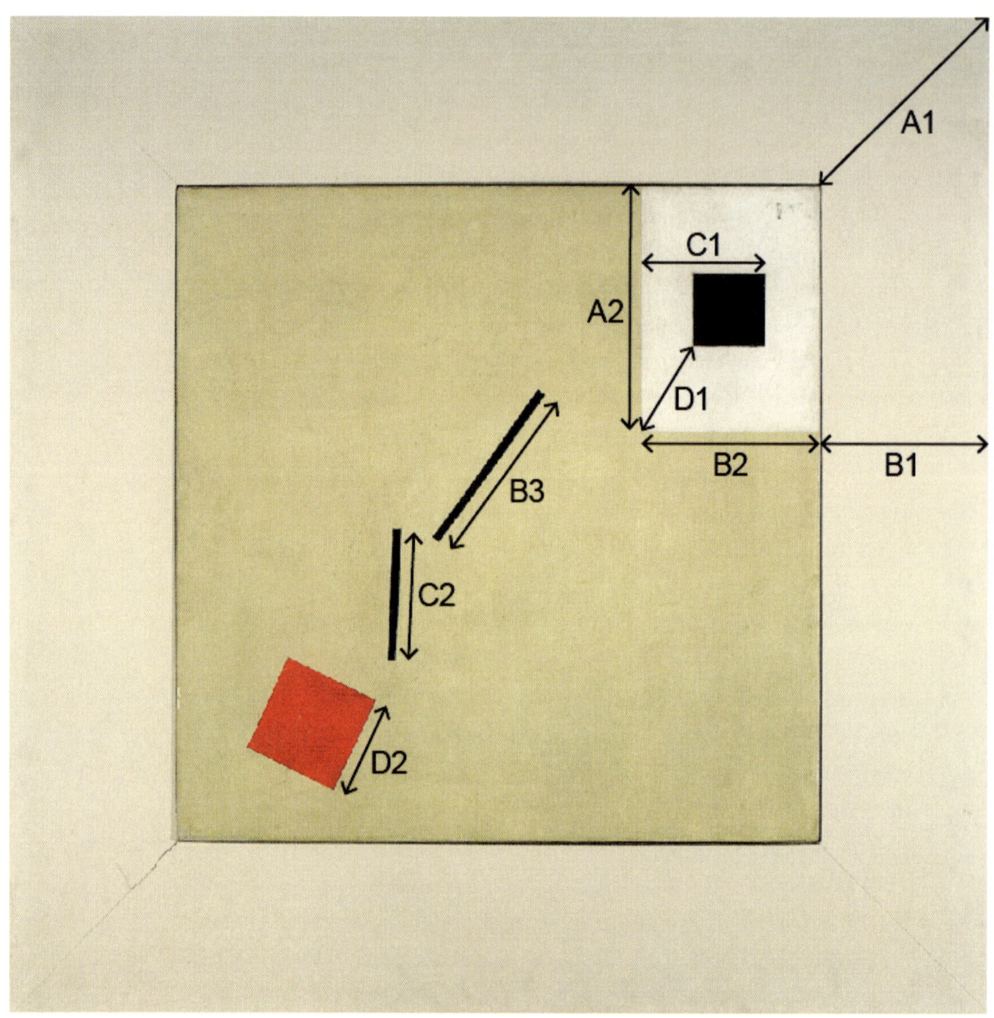

Figure 1.27. Lygia Clark, *Descoberta da linha orgânica* (Discovery of the organic line), 1954. Reference measurements by the author.

a new pictorial element — the second black rod (C2) — into the space of the plane. Finally, we repeat the original operation, now measuring the diagonal of the painting within a painting (D1), but treating it no longer as the residue of representational space, but an index of its newly activated ground. Just as both Malevich and Lissitzky generated their red squares from a black one, Clark, too, applies the results of her experiments, producing a final pictorial element — the red square — each of whose sides (D2) is equivalent to the diagonal of the painting within a painting's ground.

Rotating, tumbling, as if propelled out of the pictorial space of the represented *Black Square* and carried by the cascading motion of the black rods, the red square points us, once again, to the painting's corner, now in the opposite direction from where we began. We can now recognize the chasm of space that triangulates this corner and constitutes the organic line as part and parcel of the work's deliriously heterogeneous materiality, carving up its multiple whites into distinct zones of the painterly apparatus, but ultimately revealing how they partake in a single rhetorical machine. Materiality absorbs and engenders metaphoricity, but also vice versa. Originally the black square — the iconic art-historical representation of the void — appeared to be the work's predominant figure. Due to conventional habit, we ignored both the grounds for this figure and the actual void of empty space that lies between the painting and its frame. Toggling between metaphor and materiality, the work presses this void to the surface as a third element neither figure *nor* ground, but which operates alongside the work's pictorial elements as well as its material architecture. Ultimately, it is the liminality of this spatial cleft that engenders the relation between canvas and frame and facilitates the pictorial progression of compositional elements within and across their bounds.

In *Descoberta da linha orgânica*, narrative — and narratives about abstraction and representation — put the work of art in motion. As we repeatedly return to the work's painting within a painting, accompany the shifting possibilities of its orientation, and recover its spatial chasm, *Descoberta da linha orgânica* becomes comprehensible less as a fixed composition and more as a series of aesthetic events or actions that depend upon the viewer for their linking and relational activation. The narrativity and historicity of Clark's sources are acknowledged as structuring conditions of enactment and reception. But their action is recursively looped with Clark's painting's material and formal specificity. The organic line emerges, in short, as the space of conversion where incommensurate realities meet and are transformed. It is "the hotspot where processes become productive," as Ricardo Basbaum puts it.[111]

In *Descoberta da linha orgânica*, the organic line cleaves aesthetic and literal space apart and together. By harnessing external space as an operative pictorial element, the organic line concedes the representational character of this space as it is incorporated into the painting. External space can be described as a line, after all, only if it is recognized as such by way of a set of pictorial conventions. Once made legible, the organic line thus *represents itself*, abstractly, as a paradigm in the real time of the viewer's observation. This representational operation implicates the perceiving body of the viewer in relation to the material body of the work. As Pérez-Oramas brilliantly writes, recalling the myth of the Corinthian maid who traces an outline of her sleeping lover on a wall, "The organic line is a mnemonic line: suddenly and unexpectedly, it reminds us that painting is and always has been a body—a body, another body, between us and others; a body that harbors other bodies, if only in infra-thin shape."[112]

Binding together the painterly apparatus while making visible its joints, the organic line reveals the corporeal and cognitive investments we bring to painterly surfaces in order that they come to mean in specific historical and aesthetic ways. Yet because the organic line—as a fissure of actual space—also preexists and exceeds the pictorial schema of any given painting, it points to the inability of painting to exist as a self-contained entity. While two-dimensional mathematical relations secure *Descoberta da linha orgânica*'s fabricated compositional elements, the materialized cleavage of the organic line has a spatial plasticity and innate contingency that defies this pictorial dimensionality. It is topological in a way that the canvas and frame are not. The organic line thus also releases itself into the phenomenal space of the world in which it is encountered, which is to say, into the present time of our discovery today.

With these elements of plasticity, conversion, and real-time observation in mind, I want to return to *Black Square*, circling back, as it were, to pose a question from the present time of our own discovery. In this, I want to suggest the analytic potential of the organic line as a third term, neither figure nor ground. The question is, *Onde estão os negros?* — Where are the Blacks? — and it comes from the contemporary Brazilian collective Frente 3 de Fevereiro (F3F), for whom it takes the form of urban interventions: a massive banner unfurled at a soccer game or suspended on the façade of a museum (figs. 1.28a–b). F3F was founded in 2004 in protest of the killing of Flavio Sant'Ana, an Afro-descendent São Paulo resident racially profiled, assassinated, and framed by police. The banner's black text on white ground neatly punctures the country's myth of racial democracy, pointing instead to a dual logic of hypervisibility and invisibility, wherein racialized bodies are submitted to an ongoing regime of state terror while divested of representational agency within other spheres.[113]

Onde estão os negros? Everywhere and nowhere at once.

Onde estão os negros? is a question that reveals the violence of abstraction as operationalized upon bodies and histories made legible and illegible through race. It is also a question that demands to be asked of *Black Square*. The borrowed "joke" of the inscription incites viewers to partake in a representational schema at the level of pictoriality as they inevitably fail to find the "Blacks" within the picture's monochromatic field. In so doing, viewers participate in

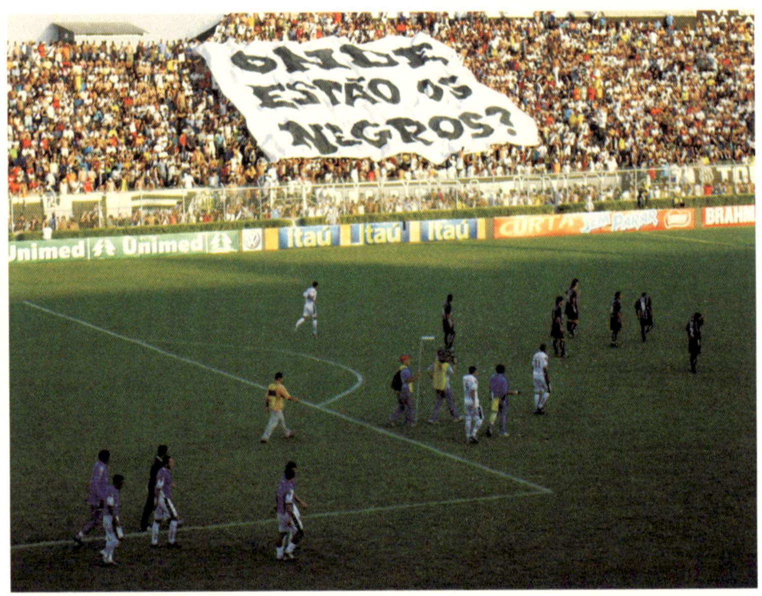

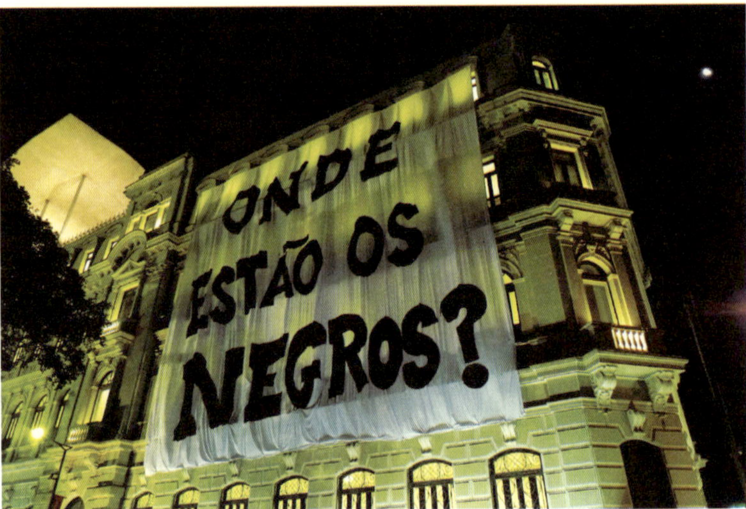

Figure 1.28a. Frente 3 de Fevereiro, *Onde estão os negros?* (Where are the Blacks?), Campinas, Estádio Moisés Lucarelli, August 14, 2005. Photo: Frente 3 de Fevereiro. **b**. Frente 3 de Fevereiro, *Onde estão os negros?* (Where are the Blacks?), MAR, 2015. Photo: Daniel Correia Ferreira Lima.

a "general economy of race," as the cultural theorist Jared Sexton puts it, that "endlessly produces *bodies as images* — not images of bodies, but rather *living images of race*."[114] Such "living images" are materialized targets of police violence, as F3F's contemporary interventions demonstrate. But the Bilhaud-Allais-Malevich inscription maps this conceptual abstraction upon a pictorial one, asking the viewer to summon a representation of racialized bodies where only a blank, black monochrome exists. Annihilating the distinction between figure and ground, the captioned black square deprives the conjured bodies even of their figurability, rendering them, per feminist Hortense Spillers's paradigmatic articulation of racializing violence, as *flesh*: "that zero degree of social conceptualization," as she famously put it in 1987.[115] *Black Square* is thus a plastic totality: all flesh converted into all void, into abstract black form, into all flesh, into all void, and on and on.

In a brilliantly thought-provoking piece written shortly after the 2015 discovery of the inscription on *Black Square*, the critic Hannah Black mused, "If sexual difference is the 'one-plus' of meaning — the extra charge produced by meaning — might race then be the 'one-minus,' that is, meaning's disavowed underneath, its inevitable failure?"[116] Here, Black comprehends the short circuit between race and pictoriality in *Black Square* in terms of nullification: "Negation itself becomes representation," she writes. "What is represented is the nothingness of certain subjects, which indicates a certain nothingness in subjectivity itself."[117] But as the literary theorist Zakiyyah Iman Jackson has argued, perhaps anti-Blackness is not the nullification of Black humanity, but rather its "ontologized plasticity."[118] In other words, Blackness is not what is *excluded* from the liberal notion of the universal human subject; it is what is made "infinitely mutable" in order to subtend that fiction. As Jackson writes, "Blackness is produced as sub/super/human at once, a form where form shall not hold: potentially 'everything and nothing' at the register of ontology."[119]

The violent calibrations of humanity at work in such plasticity find peculiar echoes in Malevich's first theorizations of Suprematism, the text *From Cubism and Futurism to Suprematism: The New Painterly Realism*, which he wrote and revised between 1915 and 1916.[120] While Malevich's title posits a surpassing of Futurism, that earlier movement provided the artist a pivotal programmatic and rhetorical model. As Malevich scholars have noted, the artist copied sections of Italian Futurist manifestos and was closely involved with Filippo Marinetti's 1914 visit to Russia, even as he and fellow Russian Futurists ultimately disavowed his influence.[121] Thus, Malevich almost certainly was familiar with the vertiginous chain of associations in the founding manifesto of Futurism of 1909 in which Marinetti hallucinates his rebirth out of thickly material, maternal blackness: "Oh, maternal ditch, half full of muddy water! A factory gutter! I savored a mouthful of strengthening muck which recalled the black teat of my Sudanese nurse!"[122] Malevich steered clear of Marinetti's explicit racism and fervid colonialism and by all counts was firmly committed to the anti-imperialist struggle. Yet such political investments do not preclude unreconstructed attitudes about race that were rampant at the time.

In the opening section of the 1916 version of his tract, subtitled "The Art of the Savage and Its Principles," for example, Malevich makes recourse to the term *dikar,* or "savage," in contradistinction to the more enveloping term *primitivnyi*, or "primitive," used frequently at that time in Russia in reference to pre-Renaissance European, non-Western, folk, and religious art.[123] Unlike *primitivnyi*, *dikar* encompasses a racializing inflection: an entry for a 1915 Russian dictionary gives its first definition as, "An uncultured colored native of non-European countries: *the dance of the savages.*"[124] In his own text, Malevich aligns "the savage" with the naturalistic and mimetic: "In drawing a dot and five little sticks, [the savage] attempted to transmit his own image."[125] Even art of the Renaissance was merely a bid to "perfect the savage's idea: the reflection of nature on canvas, as in a mirror."[126] For Malevich, Suprematism was the definitive overturning of this representational drive in favor of art in its true sense. Thus, in a perverse machination, to look for "negroes battling in a cave" in *Black Square* is to *look as a savage would.*

Onde estão os negros? On what side of the picture does Blackness reside?

It is significant that Malevich's genealogy of representation, wherein "the realist academists are the savage's last descendants," runs counter to the contemporaneous formulations of his colleague Vladimir Markov.[127] Markov was a key member of the Union of Youth which, among other pursuits, produced *Victory over the Sun* in 1913, the putative origin of Malevich's first drawings of *Black Square*.[128] Earlier that year, Markov had traveled to multiple ethnographic museums in Western Europe to photograph African sculptures, an endeavor he saw as intimately linked to the theorization and regeneration of contemporary art. In his 1914 manuscript *Iskusstvo negrov* (Negro art), Markov argued that it was the antinaturalist tendencies of African artists—their love of "free and independent masses"—that pointed the way toward a new art for the present (fig. 1.29).[129] In short, Markov conceived of African art as a storehouse of nonmimetic aesthetic possibilities, the "conceptual methods" of which, he wrote, "we Europeans can only envy."[130] By contrast, Malevich pegged the history of Western representation to the mimetic impulse of "the savage," reinscribing, while rewiring, a long tradition of anti-Blackness in Western philosophy that posited Africans as ahistorical and governed by "mere nature."[131] Thus, when Malevich developed his own play of "free and independent masses" in Suprematism, he both assimilated and repressed Markov's proposition concerning the aesthetic potential of African art. In this sense, the inscription "Battle of negroes…" can be understood as an injunction against a certain kind of *seeing*, as well as an acknowledgment of formal belatedness, repressed and recalled in equal measure.

Such operations have broader implications, both materially and conceptually. Researchers at the Tretyakov Gallery have revealed that *Black Square* is painted over two prior compositions: a Cubo-Futurist work and a multicolored proto-Suprematist composition.[132] Malevich covered those earlier compositions with the area that

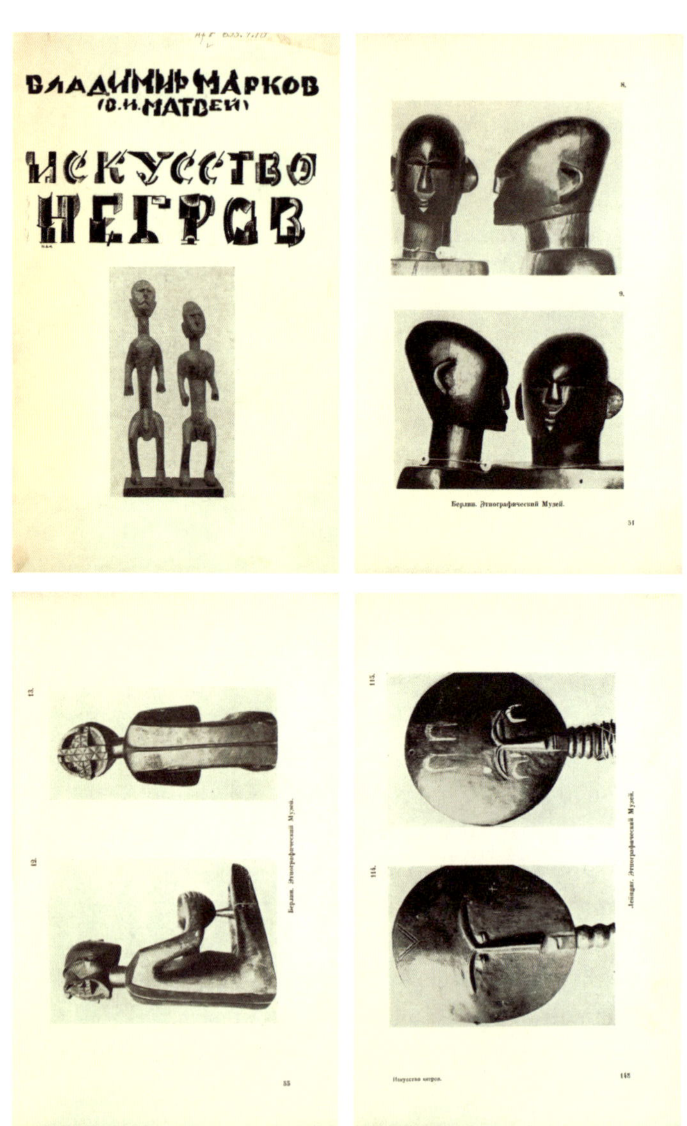

Figure 1.29. Vladimir Markov, pages from *Iskusstvo negrov* (Negro art), 1914 (Petersburg: Izd. Otdela izobrazitel'nykh iskusstv Narodnogo komissariata po prosveshcheniĭu, 1919). Photo: Special Collections, Marquand Library of Art and Archaeology, Princeton University.

is now the black square and subsequently painted the white border around it. Detail images of *Black Square* and the lesser-known *Black Quadrilateral* reveal that the surrounding white border often slightly encroaches on the black, rather than vice versa.[133] Thus, contrary to almost all descriptions of the work, the black square is *not* a black figure painted upon a white ground. Rather, blackness — as iconoclastic, multiple, heterogeneous, and consummately historical — is the means by which whiteness comes to be *perceived* as ground, the neutral condition that allows figuration or meaning to come into view. In the epistemological sense, an abyssal line, to invoke de Sousa Santos, courses between the two.

Neither figure nor ground, the organic line is a site of conversion, a bivalent threshold in which incommensurabilities are held and transformed. Thus, while materially absent from *Black Square*, the organic line is *conceptually* present in the plasticity of its social, aesthetic, and ontological reversals. In 1922, Malevich wrote elliptically, "Introduce a real door into the canvas entirely."[134] *Black Square* can be imagined to introduce such a door only at a metaphoric level by which the black form is pictorialized as a void. But to "introduce a *real* door into the canvas" is to enact an entirely different operation: it is to pry open — *to dis-cover* — the passage of conversion that existed there all along. This, I believe, is what the organic line of *Descoberta da linha orgânica* allows us to do.

⸻

Is it possible for a work of art to be both a beginning and an end, to face in more than one direction, to shift in sequence and time? Over the course of its formal gestation, *Descoberta da linha orgânica*'s pictorial citation of *Black Square* blossoms from a conceptual notation into a material singularity that transforms our comprehension of the painterly apparatus as a whole. Once compacted within the representational space of a painting within a painting, the black square becomes an index of the viewer's temporal comprehension as we return, again and again, to its shifting propositional status, materializing the metaphor of its interior void in the exterior channel of actual space that runs along its border. In the process, the pictorial citation acquires a spectacularly anachronic temporality, embodying both the befores and afters of *Black Square*, but also Clark's organic line paintings in and of themselves. For while the painting's horizontal orientation formalizes a point of reception for *Black Square* as a theoretical phenomenon, transmitted transnationally through pictures, pamphlets, and artistic lore, its vertical orientation simultaneously signals the other works in Clark's own series, the majority of which are rectangular in format and vertical in orientation. It is these paintings, after all, that literally "break the frame," revealing the action of the organic line upon the plane. Disobeying the temporal linearity of discovery, *Descoberta da linha orgânica* performs both the inaugural moment of a painterly investigation that proceeds over the course of the *Quebra da moldura* paintings *and* the retrospective recounting and condensation of the significance of this same process.

Indeed, if we take a cue from the fundamental provocation of the *marco recortado*, the proliferating viewpoints of Lissitzky's *PROUNs*, the cyclical insurgency inscribed in his *About Two Squares*, and finally the topological character of the organic line itself, we can continue to rotate *Descoberta da linha orgânica*, transforming its square shape via a circular action. This spiraling motion recalls the ambiguous orientation of Clark's charcoal studies of stairs from the 1940s, which I discuss in Chapter 3. But it also anticipates Clark's *Ovo linear* (Linear egg) of 1958 (fig. 1.30).[135] In this circular painting, the organic line is recast as a "light line" that traverses the outer ring of the black tondo, breaking at one point such that the painting's interior space spills outward, making contact with the exterior space of the wall. In Paulo Herkenhoff's elegant observation, the plane's "contagion" of the world deforms the regularity of the circle, evoking the ovoid shape of the work's title while retaining the memory of the breaking of the frame. In so doing, he writes,

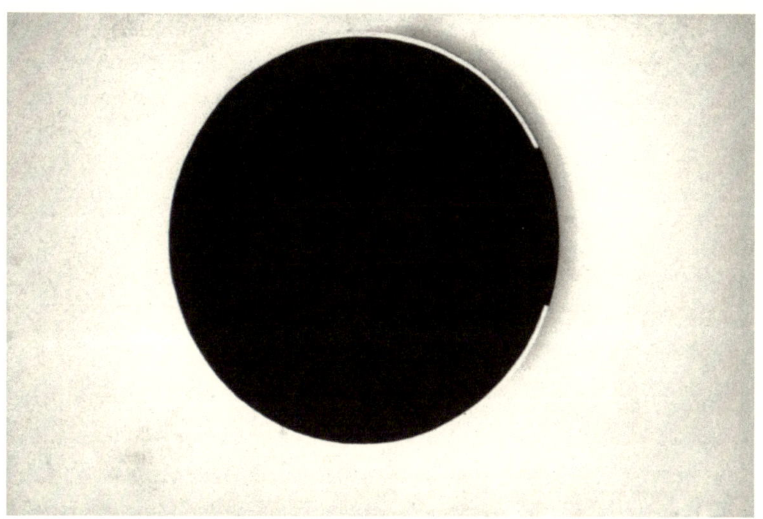

Figure 1.30. Lygia Clark, *Ovo linear* (Linear egg), 1958. Photo: Valentino Fialdino. Courtesy of Associação Cultural "O Mundo de Lygia Clark."

the work enacts "gerundial time: the birth being born."[136] A painting without direction, a surface that is a porous body, an egg that is simultaneously a touching eye, *Ovo linear* marks the definitive overturning of the rectilinear as the abstract instantiation of planarity.

In a 1960 text titled "The Death of the Plane," Clark described a wholesale dissolution of the concepts of orientation, opposition, and rationality by which man attempts to project himself mimetically into the world in the form of God and art alike.[137] Years earlier, Malevich had offered up the square as an affront to such naturalizing tendencies. "The square is a living, regal infant," he wrote. "The first step in pure creation in art. Before it there were naïve distortions and copies of nature."[138] But for Clark, even the "magical meaning" of this square, its "total vision of the universe," was no longer relevant. "The plane is dead," she wrote. And now there is nothing to do but to "swallow the shattered rectangle" that remains in its wake, to "absorb" it in order to become a "living and organic whole."[139] While for Malevich, Suprematist forms "announce that man has attained his equilibrium," Clark imagined a total loss of balance altogether:

> We dive into the totality of the cosmos; we are part of this cosmos, vulnerable on all sides: above and below, right and left, in short, good and evil — all concepts are transformed. Contemporary man escapes the laws of spiritual gravitation. He learns to float in the cosmic reality as in his own inner reality. He feels overcome by dizziness. The crutches which supported him fall far from his arms. He feels like a child who has to learn to steady his balance in order to survive. It is the first experience which is beginning.[140]

In Clark's account, the "swallowing" and "absorption" of the rectangle in pieces releases the viewer into a vertiginous, nonorientable space akin to the child's primordial experience of the world. In this floating, nonbinary atmosphere, the subject becomes a monadic unit of sensation, a vibrating particle of the universe at large. The old epistemologies are no longer sufficient for comprehending such an experience, but they have not fallen away so much as been transformed. "Man" is the primary locus of this transformation, and Clark aligned this entity with the philosophical and painterly tradition of the plane in no uncertain terms. As she wrote in 1960,

> The concept of the plane, of the surface, is an abstract construction created by Man. Woman gives it perpetuity, Man, transcendence. Woman is nature and Man the adventurer who seeks to surpass this very nature. Woman is water, Man the diver who searches in this water for his origin in order to transcend it. Constituted in that passivity of love is the entire unification of two persons into a single being.[141]

The act of sexual intercourse is the means of overcoming binaries, "an equivalent process" of which, Clark continued, "occurs in the work of art."[142]

Heterosexual, cisgender symbiosis is of course a highly clichéd metaphor for artistic making, and it would be a mistake to limit the structuring epistemology of Clark's paradigm to this notion of sexual union. In fact, Clark returned far more often to metaphors of ingestion, ovulation, pregnancy, gestation, parturition, and postpartum transition, commencing with the action of the organic line upon the orthogonal support. As she wrote to a friend in 1961, "It was necessary for the artist to burst the rectangle...to swallow it and feel it not from the outside but inside of it itself" in order "to create the totality of a living thing."[143] The new space that emerges from the "death of the plane" ultimately takes as its organizing metaphor neither sexual union nor the infant born from the ingestion and absorption of the "shattered rectangle," but the process of birth.

Clark felt her way there. In a 1957 interview, she noted that after discovering the organic line in 1954 and realizing a number of paintings with it, she put aside her research, "not knowing how to use this liberated space."[144] A smattering of mentions in the art section of Rio newspapers suggest that she had started to use the term "organic line" as early as March 1955.[145] That same year, she realized a number of little-known gouaches on cardboard titled *Geometria amorosa* (Amorous geometry) in which swaths of pastel-colored shapes are laid down in contiguous and overlapping configurations on schematic renderings of paintings and frames, their division signaled by a graphite line (figs. 1.31 and 1.32). In these studies, as in the *Quebra da moldura* works of the previous year, pictorial elements disobey the conventional boundary of the canvas, flowing across the frame and mobilizing the juncture between them within the composition.

Unlike the earlier series, however, *Geometria amorosa* foregrounds the synergy of curved and rectilinear forms, an interplay narrated in an illustrated text of the same title and year in which the shapes themselves take on explicitly gendered terms (fig. 1.33). In this story of geometric love, a spatial tension triggered by the expansion of the circle brings about the "disaggregation" of the former universe and the "birth of two planes": a circle inscribed within a square and the triangle that had previously contained the two. But the circle—"being a full form without limits"—continues its transformation, stretching beyond the square and generating two separate entities, the feminine principle now identified with the circle and the

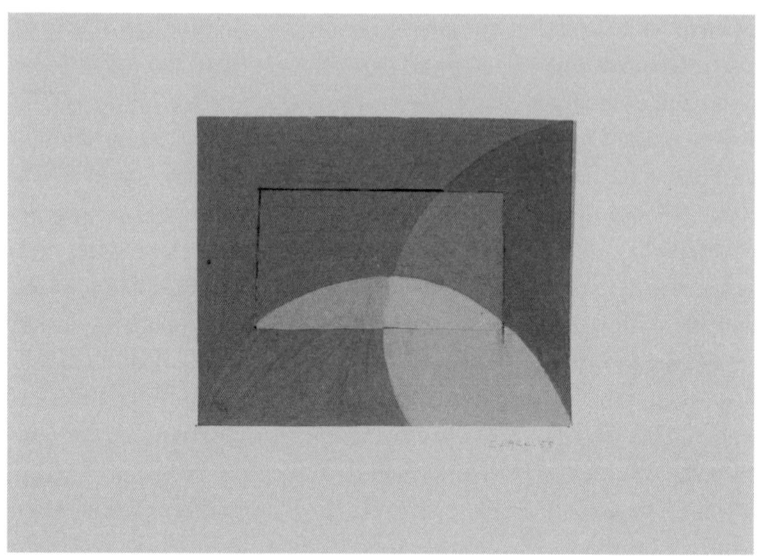

Figure 1.31. Lygia Clark, *Geometria amorosa* (Amorous geometry), 1955. Photo: Marcelo Ribeiro Alvares Corrêa. Courtesy of Associação Cultural "O Mundo de Lygia Clark."

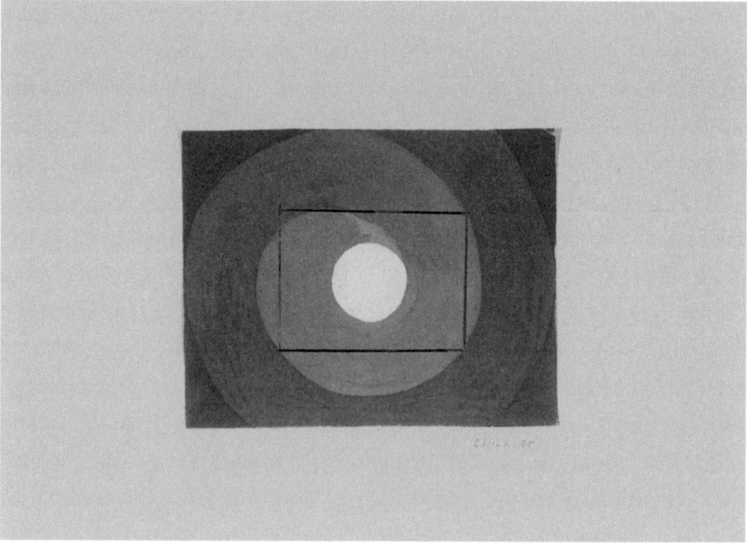

Figure 1.32. Lygia Clark, *Geometria amorosa* (Amorous geometry), 1955. Photo: Marcelo Ribeiro Alvares Corrêa. Courtesy of Associação Cultural "O Mundo de Lygia Clark."

masculine with the square. In the next episode, the shapes are over-laid with the gendered associations of Christian theology (Clark, not surprisingly, was the rebellious and unhappy product of a Catholic upbringing). The triangle is rendered as both *Pae* (father) and *Padre* (father or priest); the circle as mother and son; and the square as son and holy spirit. "Love" entails the "reintegration of the circle within the square" and "Gestation" this circle's "surpassing" of the square as it swells to circumscribe the latter's exterior, rather than interior limits.[146] Birth, finally, is rendered as the "disintegration of the square from within the circle." And the cycle begins again.

In a general sense, the iconography and overarching narrative of Clark's *Geometria amorosa* are structured by the binaries of male and female, circle and square. Clark may well have drawn her symbols from alchemical traditions, wherein the chemical union between male and female forces results in the mythical philosopher's stone.[147] In Clark's version, however, the plot's action is carried by something quite distinct, namely, the capacity of the circle to eclipse fixed geometric schemas by virtue of its fluid contours, dilating to disrupt the universe's original proportional order, waning, stretching, and contracting anew both to absorb and to expel the more static form of the square. Thus, whereas the alchemical narrative hinges on the magical "squaring of the circle," Clark's epistemology is one of parturition and passage: in other words, of *circling the square*.

The circle passes everywhere, but it is also a means of passing through: of transforming, entwining, disengaging, and reconstituting. As I will elaborate in Chapter 2, Clark first described the organic line as occurring in relation to a *passe-partout*, the term for a framing mat that can be placed over any picture (as Jacques Derrida notably observed), but also a master key that opens any door. The organic line, importantly, is not this *passe-partout*, but rather an element of space that appears along its border. In other words, it is neither the frame nor the picture, but the interval between them; not the key or the lock, but the spatial cavity that allows their

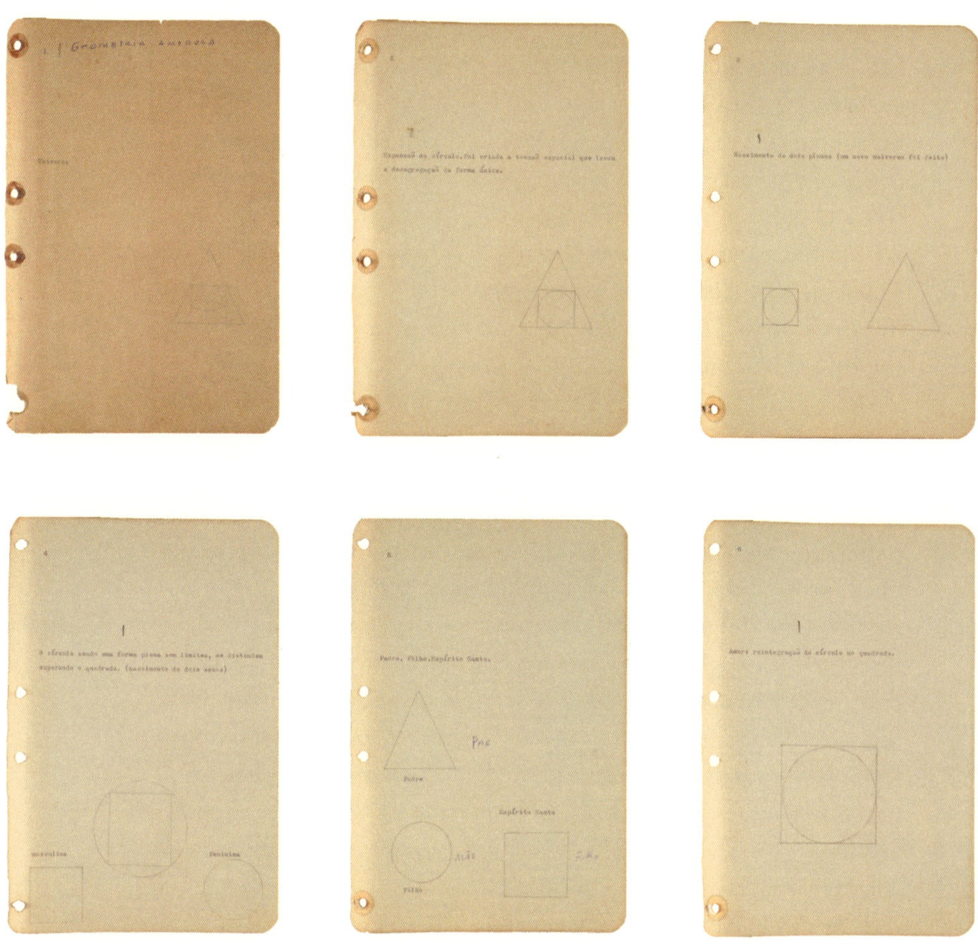

Figure 1.33. Lygia Clark, *Geometria amorosa*
(Amorous geometry), 1955. Courtesy of
Associação Cultural "O Mundo de Lygia Clark."

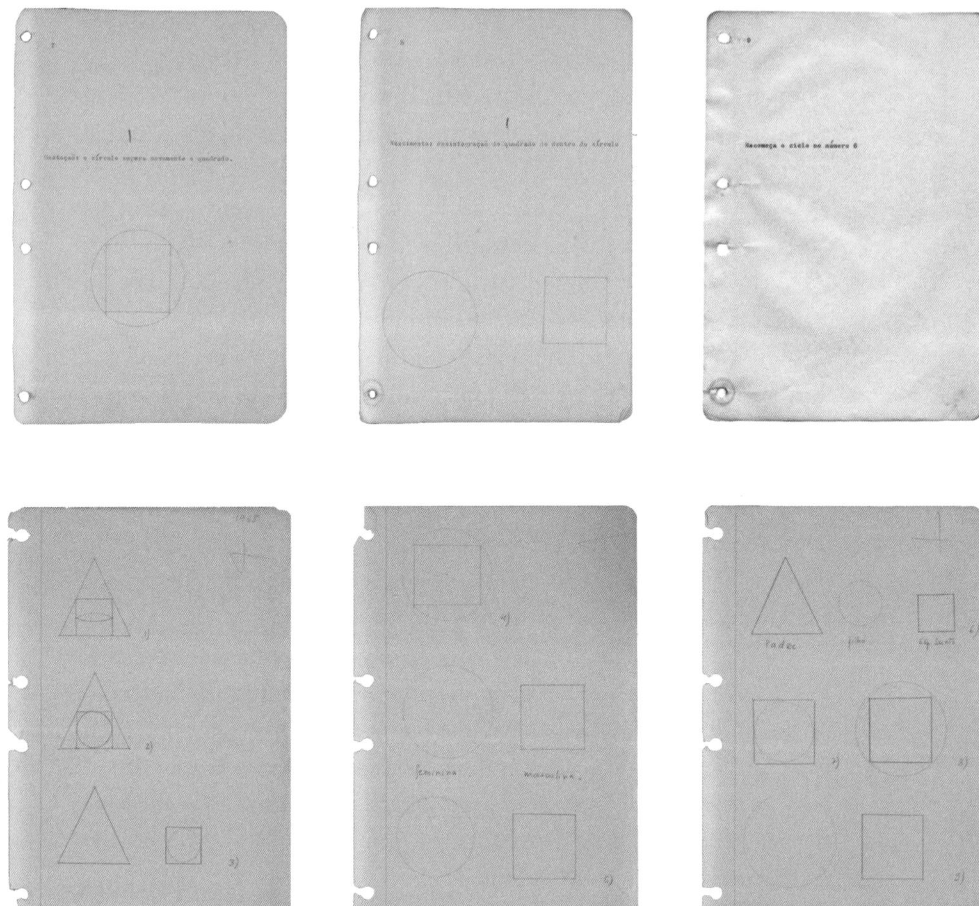
Continação: o círculo supera novamente o quadrado.
Nascimento: reintegração do quadrado de dentro do círculo
Recomeça o ciclo no número 6

machinic combination. A small, but crucial difference, for simply to invert a given hierarchy (woman/man, circle/square) is to leave a binary epistemology in place. Attending to the junctural status of *passage*, by contrast, leaves the notion of a dominant figure — circle or square — aside.

In the *Geometria amorosa* gouache studies, the rectilinear forms of the schematic canvases are pressed into dynamic relationship with their implied frames, their edges forming secants to circles while curved arcs intersect corners and swoop across the borders of the interior planes. The rectangles themselves flicker in and out of focus. But their demarcation is most pronounced when a single color spreads over both zones of the represented canvas and frame. Here, the organic line — rendered as the thickness of the graphic mark — prises apart chromatic continuity, and we can imagine its corresponding action in real space. Variegating the surface of the plane, it signals an irrevocable differencing of the painterly apparatus, even as its pictorial elements remain in place.

Clark, like her paintings, was a deeply porous subject. She suffered her searing aesthetic inquietude in her body and her corporeal intensities in her work. She freely drew analogies between the experience of gravity and her artistic practice. "Every time I begin a new phase of my work I feel all the symptoms of pregnancy," she wrote in 1963. "And as soon as the gestation period begins I suffer from real physical disturbances like dizziness, for example, until the moment when I am able to affirm my new space-time in the world."[148] The vertiginous experience of nonorientable space that Clark described in "The Death of the Plane" was thus ingrained in the cyclical process of making itself. Significantly, Clark noted that her adult artistic practice followed immediately upon the postpartum psychosis she suffered after the birth of her third child.[149] She likewise described the experience in terms of an ecstatic passage of bodies and contours not unlike those diagramed in *Geometria amorosa*. "When the youngest was born, the Mother felt all the magic of an eclipse," she wrote. This eclipse, however, was followed by the trauma of separation and hallucination: "The youngest wailed night and day as madness descended upon the body and soul of the Mother."[150]

The organic line is a juncture that, as Tim Ingold has written of the epistemology of lines, entails both a knotting or looping together and a fissuring or sundering apart.[151] In Clark's narration of her postpartum psychosis, it is located between the eclipse and the subsequent agony of difference. But we can also find it elementally in the passage of birth itself, when mother and baby exist in the most attenuated and liminal state of bodily relation. In a text titled *Breviário sobre o corpo* (Breviary of the body), likely written in 1964 or 1965, Clark describes this passage as both creaturely and cathartic:

> The mouth opens in a spasm, letting out a scream that announces birth, and in the act of devouring a soul, closes voraciously over its swollen counterpart that is the nipple of the breast, giving immediate function to the gill-throat in an act of swallowing that goes from the stomach to the duodenum, from the intestines that undulate like cobras, to the anus that expels digested food but does not have the power to expel the expressive and signifying breath that, inhabiting a body, lends it the identity of a being. The act of swallowing, the spasm of a fish out of its element, sea, placenta, uterus, enveloping cosmic ocean, sleep or death. The bellows that propel air toward the interior of the entrails, the lung that gives meaning to the frenetic rush of life, tingling as it circulates from tiny veins to ever larger ones, veins that return where the oily valve opens, where the folds are invisible, and licks, pushes, flips, nerves that direct the brain in the entire sensation of "being" that is planted in life, in the act of the transplant, the appendage is plucked from the main trunk and life grafted, after having penetrated the great tunnel of the vagina, alive subterraneously, and torn in a rite of joy, relief, and violence. Slime that once clung superimposed in layers is now expelled in the effort to survive, opening the passage for air to penetrate, drying the palate, a swimmer rushing in a race, plunging between tendons into the throat, virgin flagpoles now hoisted to unfurl lungs that give themselves over to be aerated as loosened membranes enveloped by the space of the exterior world.[152]

The metaphor of birth (like that of sexual union) has permeated artistic discourse; here is Malevich: "But a surface lives; it has been born."[153] In Clark's rendering, this singular event becomes a durational condition of spatialized human liminality that inheres not simply in the emergence of a work into the world, but in the ontology of the work's being. Coursing between symbiosis and separation, the organic line becomes legible as a deeply corporeal entity, a void flushed into figurality in relation to a ground utterly transformed as a result.

In the preface to *The Order of Things*, Michel Foucault famously wrote that "man is only a recent invention...a new wrinkle in our knowledge, and that he will disappear again as soon as that knowledge has discovered a new form."[154] But as the theorist Sylvia Wynter has observed, man was not simply invented; a particular genre of man — white, European, heterosexual, cisgender — was *overrepresented*, as if the concept of the human itself.[155] In Leonardo da Vinci's iconic Vitruvian Man, as Walter Mignolo notes, this conception of "Man" joins "the colonization of space and the perfection of geometric forms."[156] Clark's amorous geometries do not replace the male figure within da Vinci's circle. Rather, they potentialize the circle itself as a principle of passage rather than possession or enclosure. As Clark's rapturous incantations in *Breviário sobre o corpo* indicate, the organic line, as the spatial embodiment of this principle of passage, is a metaphor riven with materiality. Through it, the universal and transcendental concepts of "Man" and "the plane" fall into the grasping, sensing thickness of the body as it cleaves in birth. Differentiation in turn emerges as the generative pulse of being.

The organic line is not an invention within modern art. Rather, its discovery, which is also always *our own discovery in real time*, points up a series of lacunae innate to that field. The recurring citation that makes its way onto the white surface of Malevich's

Black Square reveals that anti-Blackness traveled along avant-garde circuits, despite their revolutionary and emancipatory impulses. Transnational, nomadic, and eminently plastic, the anti-Blackness of the avant-garde *births.* We have only to recall Marinetti *rebirthed* in his roadside ditch to see how the corporeality of the maternal Black body is phantasmatically conjured, diffused, and weaponized against itself. But as the organic line suggests, *when disclosed as the very space of conversion*, the plasticity of this racialization can also become a site of generative reversal.

In his excursus on "the case of blackness," the poet and theorist Fred Moten has observed that ontologies have "dangerous supplements" and "fugitivities" that trouble their drive toward essence.[157] Here, Moten contrasts the painter Ad Reinhardt's insistence on the ontology of blackness as pure absence with a Black aesthetic founded on sociality and disruption, an "inhabitation of a break or border" that saturates the jazz-intoned dissonance of Piet Mondrian's *Victory Boogie Woogie.*[158] For Moten, the "case of blackness" is "the gap between fact and lived experience . . . a kind of broken bridge or cut suspension between the two."[159] In formal terms, the organic line gives body to this break, for it converts absence into an incontrovertible presence actualized in the time and space of encounter. Yet the organic line also refuses to remain singly within the register of either abstraction or representation, absence or presence. The blackness of its void, like the Blackness invoked by Moten, is a fluctuating and heterogenous entity that resists ontological fixture.

To this point, it is both curious and philosophically urgent that in Brazilian Portuguese, Malevich's painting is known as *Quadrado negro em fundo branco*, rather than *Quadrado preto em fundo branco* (the latter uses *preto*, the literal term for the color black, not *negro*).[160] But this slippage reveals its own peculiar logic. Although Malevich originally exhibited his painting under the title *Chetyreugol'nik* (meaning quadrilateral, quadrangle, or tetragon), it was immediately described by the artist and others as "the black square" (*chorny kvadrat*), and this title has remained with the work until the present.[161] In light of the invocation of the distinct term "Negro" (*herp, negrov*) on the painting's inscription, however, the appeal to the term *chorny* betrays a semantic equivocation concerning the philosophical work that color might be impelled to do. Malevich wanted his blackness to be an *ontological* phenomenon, not simply a perceptual one. Paradoxically, it follows that there was a use value to converting the metaphoric weight of racial otherness into formal, aesthetic ends. After all, if Malevich drew a direct line from "the savage" to European Renaissance representation, annihilating this mimetic impulse may have required a return to its putative "origins." It will be all but impossible to resolve if this deeply problematic use value aligns with the intentionality and authorship of the inscription on *Black Square*. But this use value is recovered, or better *dis-covered*, in both this inscription and the Brazilian Portuguese translation of the work, *Quadrado negro em fundo branco*.

In 1954, the same year as Clark's discovery of the organic line, the Black Brazilian sociologist Guerreiro Ramos contributed an article to the recently inaugurated art and design magazine *Forma* (which also reported on Clark's work), titled "O negro desde dentro," or "The Black [Negro] from the inside."[162] Here, Ramos reflects on the colors black and white, making explicit the racialized inflection of their metaphoric associations: *black destiny, black list, black soul, black dream*, and so on, all expressions that use the term *negro*, rather than *preto* for "black." Coloniality has produced a "fog of whiteness," Ramos writes, that blinds even people of color to the prejudice ingrained in aesthetic and everyday language alike. To "reveal blackness [*negrura*] in its intrinsic validity," he continued, is therefore "one of the heroic tasks of our age" (fig. 1.34).[163]

For Ramos, blackness was never an essential quality. As he wrote in 1955, Black life "is evasive, protean, multiform … it cannot be defined, for what it is today was not what it was yesterday, and what it will be tomorrow is not what it is today."[164] In this vein, I want to conclude this chapter with Adam Pendleton's *Black Dada*:

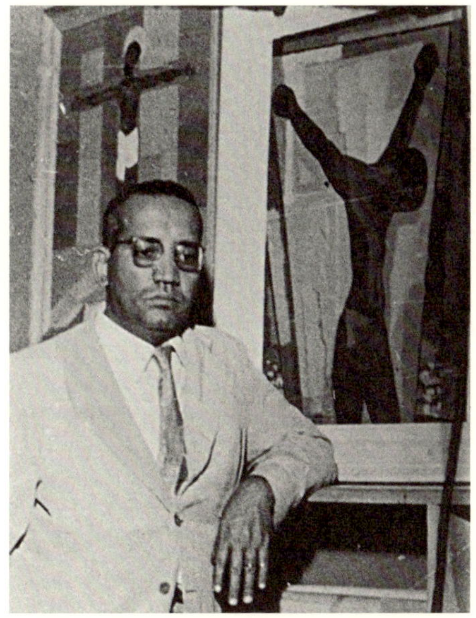

Figure 1.34. Guerreiro Ramos with works from the Concurso Cristo de Cor contest organized by Teatro Experimental do Negro, Rio de Janeiro, 1955. Courtesy of Acervo Abdias Nascimento/IPEAFRO.

a manifesto, series of artworks, reader, and conceptual program that the artist commenced in 2008 (fig. 1.35).[165] *Black Dada* joins the historical avant-garde figure of Hugo Ball with LeRoi Jones's (soon to be Amiri Baraka's) *Black Dada Nihilismus* of 1964, constellating them with a host of thinkers and artists ranging from W. E. B. DuBois and Gilles Deleuze to Adrian Piper, Gertrude Stein, Sun Ra, and Julius Eastman. In so doing, *Black Dada* instantiates a proliferating archive in which the noise produced through citation, dissemination, and circulation becomes a visual and conceptual trope in its own right.

Pendleton's *Black Dada* diptychs, for example, are generated through a process of remediation that begins with photocopied reproductions of Sol LeWitt's *Incomplete Open Cubes*. Begun in 1974, LeWitt's series expresses a permutational logic that signals one of the older artist's key contributions to conceptual art.[166] Scanned, cropped, enlarged, and divided into adjoining panels in Pendleton's works, these source images are overlaid with the letters that make

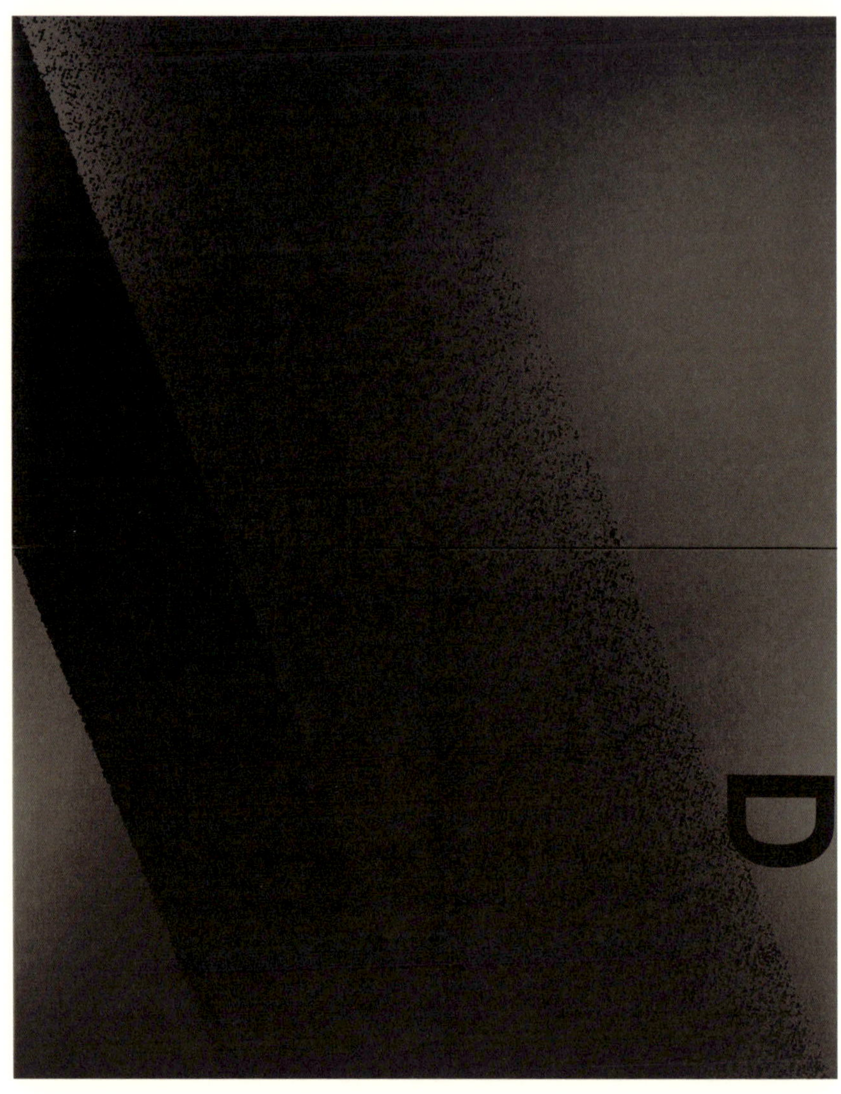

Figure 1.35. Adam Pendleton, *Black Dada (D)*,
2017. Silkscreen ink on canvas, two parts, overall:
96 x 76 in (243.8 x 193 cm) (17-035).

up the words "BLACK DADA." These letters are arranged along the paintings' edges, with one character withdrawn from each iteration within the series. Pendleton's citational method is thus additive and accumulative, while his permutational process is subtractive and extractive. The image's legibility disperses through repetition, while language concretizes as its units go missing. Neither operation answers the question posed in the artist's manifesto: "Did our conceptual artists join hands with our freedom fighters?" (or its unspoken rejoinder, "Why not?").[167] But their simultaneous enactment within Pendleton's diptychs invites the contemporary viewer to inhabit and remobilize this space of historical misalignment.

In Pendleton's wall works, meanwhile, the degradation from the repeated photocopying of the texts that made up the artist's self-published compilation, *Black Dada Reader*, begins to color and mark the whiteness of the texts' ground (fig. 1.36). Mediation is amplified, rather than disavowed, transforming the putatively neutral support of the page or wall into a surface of inscription and transmission. In this sense, *Black Dada* is a web of historical points of reference, but also an artistic practice that dramatizes — in formal terms — the archival urgency to *visibilize* both this network and the gaps that condition its legibility. It renders multiplying iterations of b(B)lackness as both figure and ground while the whole "pulls at the burden of representation," as Pendleton puts it.[168]

In Kobena Mercer's influential articulation, the "burden of representation" is the structural mapping of identity and artwork such that artists of color are trapped within an essentialist logic of "representing" their race.[169] Contrary to this disciplining imperative, *Black Dada* initiates a set of historical relays in which Blackness emerges as a capacious site of proliferating connection.[170] The organic line is a third term — neither figure nor ground — that designates the recursive operation by which representation engenders abstraction and vice versa. While the Bilhaud-Allais-Malevich inscription locks this operation in a loop of anti-Black visuality, the organic line's capacity for encounter and conversion suggests how incommensurability

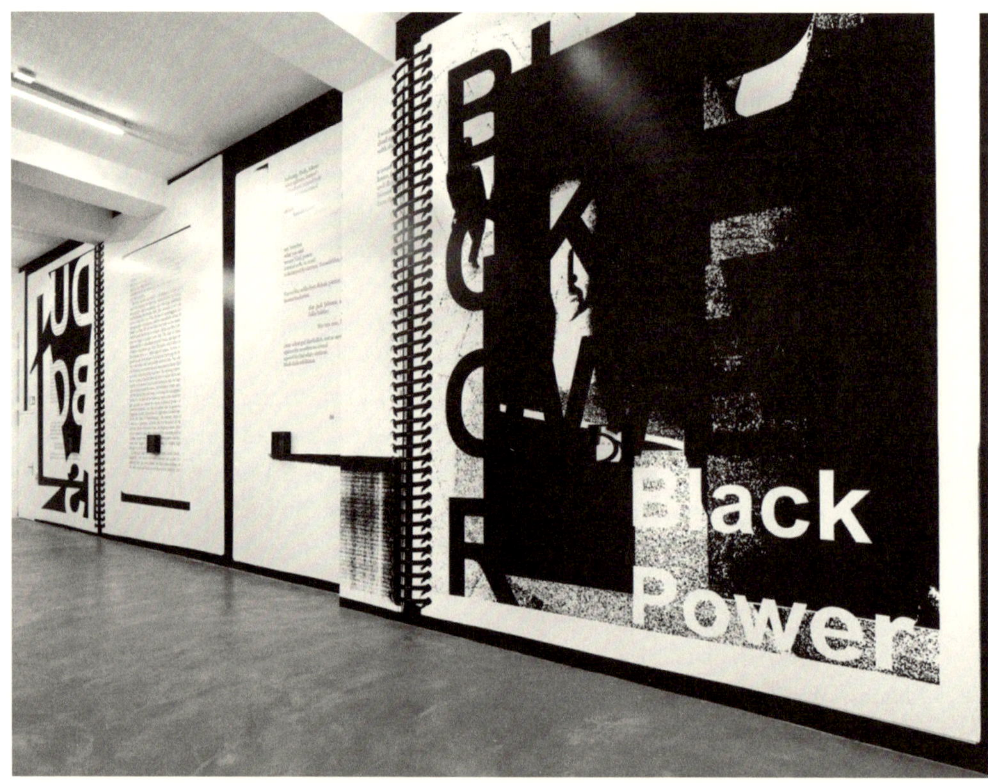

Figure 1.36. Adam Pendleton, *Black Dada Reader (Wall Work #1)*, 2016. Latex ink on adhesive vinyl, dimensions variable (16–092), installation view, *Adam Pendleton: Midnight in America*, Galerie Eva Presenhuber, Löwenbräu Areal, Zurich, November 19, 2016–January 21, 2017.

and ontological distinction can be surfaced and redirected, rather than subsumed. *Black Dada* operates toward similar aims, though by distinct means. Mobilizing both, we can begin to sketch the archival (re)constellations that might follow in turn. Think of Rubem Valentim's incorporation of Afro-Brazilian symbols in his paintings circa 1955, resulting in an abstract geometric syntax infused with cultural content that was largely disavowed by period discourses of the "concrete."[171] Or Francis Newton Souza's *Black Paintings*, begun in 1954, where thickly materialized figures and grounds become the medium of geopolitical reflection and transnational political affiliation.[172] These examples connect to *Descoberta da linha orgânica* only by means of a set of weak links. But this fragility is itself a form of defamiliarization. In Omar Berrada's cogent formulation, "Black Dada names a blind spot of modernist aesthetics, a fissure in the historical fabric of visuality. Black Dada is a seam, ever so elegantly bursting open."[173] It is not insignificant that this description doubles as a working definition of the organic line.

Black Dada is part and parcel of an alter archaeology necessitated by the erasures and willful forgettings of both modernist art and modernist art history. It follows that a *contemporary* art history of modernist art — one that seeks discovery in a decolonial sense — must look to artistic practice for its critical orientations. In the "Afterward" to *Black Dada Reader*, Pendleton writes that "abstraction is a force whenever and wherever the subject is misrecognized as an object." But he submits that abstraction is also a practice that works against this misrecognition. "One day there are masters and tools, and the next, only people," Pendleton writes. "No forces, just relations. Black Dada is the name I borrow for the immanent historical possibility of this transformation: Black for the open-ended signifier projected onto resisting objects, Dada for yes, yes, the double affirmation of their refusal."[174]

Yes, yes, I'd add, as we follow the organic line to circle the square.

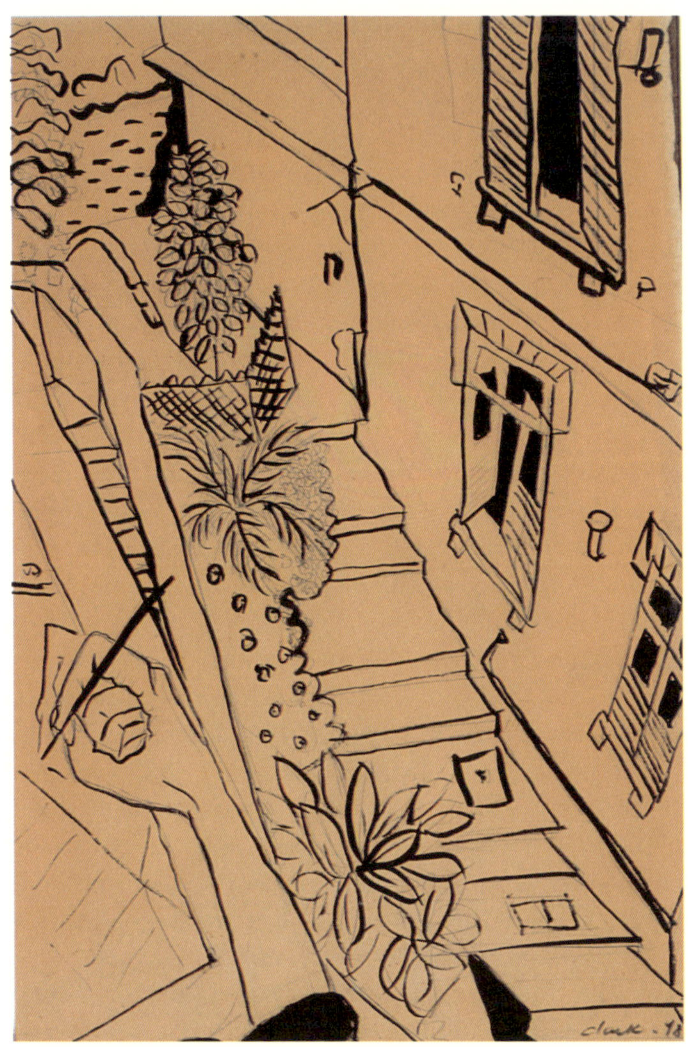

Figure 2.1. Lygia Clark, *Escadas* (Stairs), 1948.
Photo: Marcelo Ribeiro Alvares Corrêa. Courtesy
of Associação Cultural "O Mundo de Lygia Clark.

CHAPTER TWO

Not/Making/Marks:

On the Side of Composition

As soon as man tries to intervene in the natural order to which he is subject,
from the moment he begins to push a pointed instrument or a sharp edge into
some hard material in order to split it and give it form,
his primitive labor contains in itself its whole future development....
Trainer of man, the hand multiplies him in time and space.
—Henri Focillon

Next I would like to show you the hands... the hands, stroke, and...
the fingers.... You see, one never uses the palm, but ...
the tops of the fingers... we stroke, gently. Stroke, gently....
—Julius Eastman

The organic line is not merely a void; it organizes.
—Lula Wanderley

In a rare example of Lygia Clark's early figurative work from 1948,
the artist renders her hand sketching the drawing we currently
view, her elbow perched on the corner of a balcony, knees tucked
behind a tilted paper mount. The border of her drawing doubles as
the width of the balcony's rim as well as the rampart of the stairs
below (fig. 2.1). The bulk of the picture is devoted to the corridor of urban space that abuts the balcony, its shuttered windows,

narrow swath of foliage, and hairpinned stairs set at a steep angle of perspectival recession. Upon the depicted page are preliminary marks toward the representation of these same stairs, the skewing of their incline a register of drawing's embodied nature, seated as it is within both the subjectivity of vision and the placedness of limbs, hands, instruments, and supports in space. A reflexive and nested representation, then, in which both the alignment and ambivalence of space index the event of the work's making.

By her own account, Clark was obsessed with stairs and easels during her years under the tutelage of the Brazilian artist and landscape architect Roberto Burle Marx and the sculptor and painter Zélia Ferreira Salgado in Rio de Janeiro from 1947 to 1950.[1] This interest returned in Paris, where she studied from 1950 to 1952, and in a canvas from 1951, the two themes come together, a scaffolding of stacked paintings, upturned stretcher bars, and a wooden easel concatenated with the slabs of a staircase at right (fig. 2.2). Here, the work of art is revealed as so much hardware: stuff made of independent joints and surfaces, physical matter just like the architecture of a house. Mostly, the ensemble stays in place. But there are small breaches: a sheet askance on its stand; a gully opened along the edge of a canvas's verso; the progressive slant of pictures leaning cheek by jowl against the wall. Much like Clark's treatment of the staircase, these details are about the thickness — even recalcitrance — of matter and space. They also concern the scene of artistic practice. But whereas the 1948 sketch foregrounds making as a matter of the artist's *hand*, the body of the artist is altogether absent in the 1951 oil.

Hands, of course, are a primary signal of human action, linking art and artifacts with the ontology of human distinction. As Henri Focillon put it in his 1934 essay "In Praise of Hands," "The hand touches the world itself, feels it, lays hold of it and transforms it."[2] More recently, David Summers has sketched an entire world art history departing from the notion of facture as the elemental register by which humans acknowledge their molding and shaping of the world.[3] In a section of her *Breviário sobre o corpo* (Breviary of the

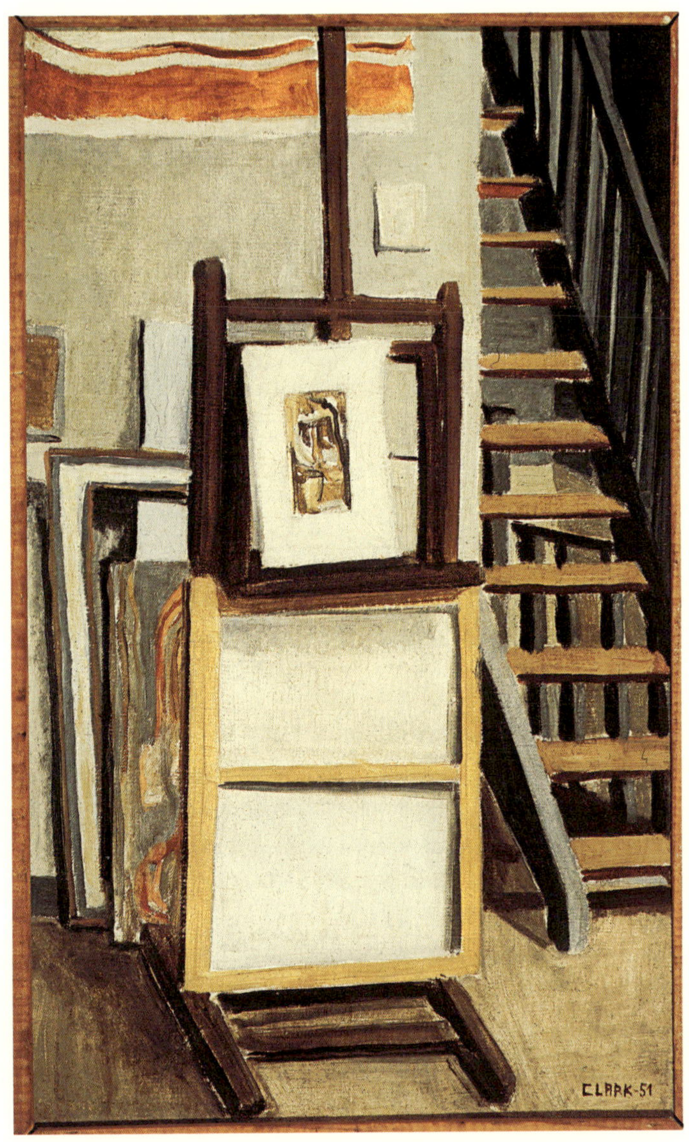

Figure 2.2. Lygia Clark, *Ateliê* (Studio), 1951.
Photo: André de Arruda Pimentel. Courtesy of
Associação Cultural "O Mundo de Lygia Clark."

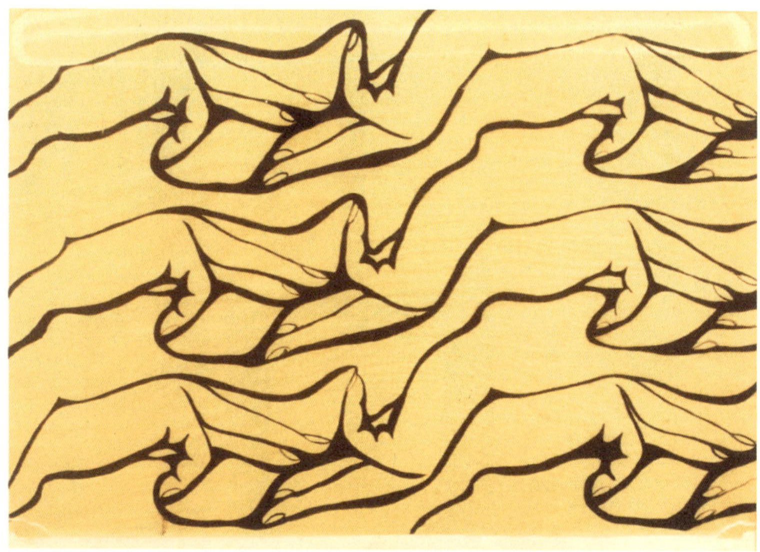

Figure 2.3. Lygia Clark, *Mãos* (Hands), undated (late 1940s–early 1950s). Courtesy of Associação Cultural "O Mundo de Lygia Clark."

body), the same incantatory text that describes the newborn's first gasps of air, Clark likewise offers an homage to hands, describing them as the locus of creation and communication: instruments that "excavate my continuity in the world," "carry stones," "caress," and "commit injustices," but are also "blind eyes" that "rediscover the skin, hair, fat, bluntness of bones."[4] In an undated drawing, Clark's pen performs the recursive touching of hands as the continuity of the graphic line (fig. 2.3). Hands here are decoupled from the body, but they are synonymous with making and marks, fingers stroking fingers unravelling figuration into a sinuous abstract pattern across the page.[5]

In Clark's *Breviário sobre o corpo*, hands also chart fragments of a psychic and artistic autobiography. In Clark's recounting, her own hands "stilled spasms" and the "uncontrollable nerves" of a "great crisis," before they "stretched" greedily toward Picasso and the "knowledge of art books … passed on top of every line, every color, absorbing, swallowing, vomiting the excess." They "sketched the first drawings of stairs," too, before "hands unfold[ed] themselves inside out, [the] glove of form itself in the search of making and destroying." "*Bichos* they are in their form," Clark writes toward the conclusion of her text, describing hands with the same term — *animal*, *critter*, or *beast* — of the series of manipulable works she began in 1960 (see fig. I.12). Interacting with those hinged metal *Bichos*, the hands in question are no longer those of the artist, but of the viewer. This passage into the participatory displaces the primacy of the artist as the maker and shaper of form. But Clark's text intimates that her corresponding conception of the subject was already as creaturely as it was human.[6] At the beginning of the twentieth century, the Belgian artist Henry van de Velde described lines as "transferred gestures" that contain within their expressivity and extension the developmental history of the human race, a sentiment cloaked in racial and cultural hier-archies.[7] Clark's subject is not this heroic molder of this world, but a configuration of being that "feels the world by form, by touch, knowledge that goes far beyond the eyes."[8]

As Focillon, Summers, and van de Velde indicate, art in many of its foundational articulations has been historically coincident with making, a correlation often condensed in the graphic line. It was against precisely this presumed equivalence that some of the most radical gestures of modernist art took aim: the aggressive undo-ing of Robert Rauschenberg's 1953 *Erased de Kooning Drawing*, but also willed strategies of antiproduction or deskilling, as in Marcel Duchamp's readymades, Ellsworth Kelly's noncompositional strate-gies, and the chance techniques of Hans Arp and later John Cage. Clark's organic line bears a resemblance to several of these tech-niques and in some instances shares elements of their procedures. But the organic line is distinct in both a conceptual and material sense. It does not constitute a shift in the register of making in terms of quality, expressiveness, or intent. Rather, it actuates a realm *alongside* making. It is a by-product: a collateral, residual, and even parasitic effect. While the graphic line we observe in Clark's early drawings signals the primordial act of human making, the organic line compels a wholly different set of questions: How can a mark *not* be made? And what kind of author or human subject is assumed as a result? In this chapter, I pursue these questions with an eye toward an assemblage of practices that thematize the implications of making (and nonmaking) for surface, subjectivity, and space. As I will argue, the organic line's emergence *on the side* of composition offers a paradigm of misalignment, rather than cohesion, that defamiliarizes the autonomy and self-evidence of subjects and works of art alike.

———

In the late 1970s, upon returning to Rio de Janeiro after a final sojourn in Paris from 1968 to 1976, Clark stacked her canvases against the wall of her old atelier and transformed the studio into a consulting room for an experimental therapy she would call *Estruturação do Self* (Structuring of the Self, fig. 2.4).[9] Recounting his own experience of this therapy, the singer Caetano Veloso recalled asking Clark how she first began to make art. Her response was that it had its origins in a form of autotherapy. Having passed through an extraordinarily difficult period, she began to cut out paper forms. "I did this to cure myself," she remarked, and only then began to seek out other artists.[10] As noted in Chapter 1, Clark mentioned on several occasions that her artistic practice followed the postpartum psychosis she suffered after the birth of her third child in 1945.[11] Distinct in her recounting to Veloso, however, is that her autocure came in the form of *cutting*, a practice that seems to have emerged (or reappeared) in the process of investigating the organic line as she fit together and shifted independent cardboard elements in low relief. Clark repeatedly described this moment, too, as a period of intense psychic difficulty, her 1954 discovery so startling that she went almost two years before pursuing research of this "liberated space."[12]

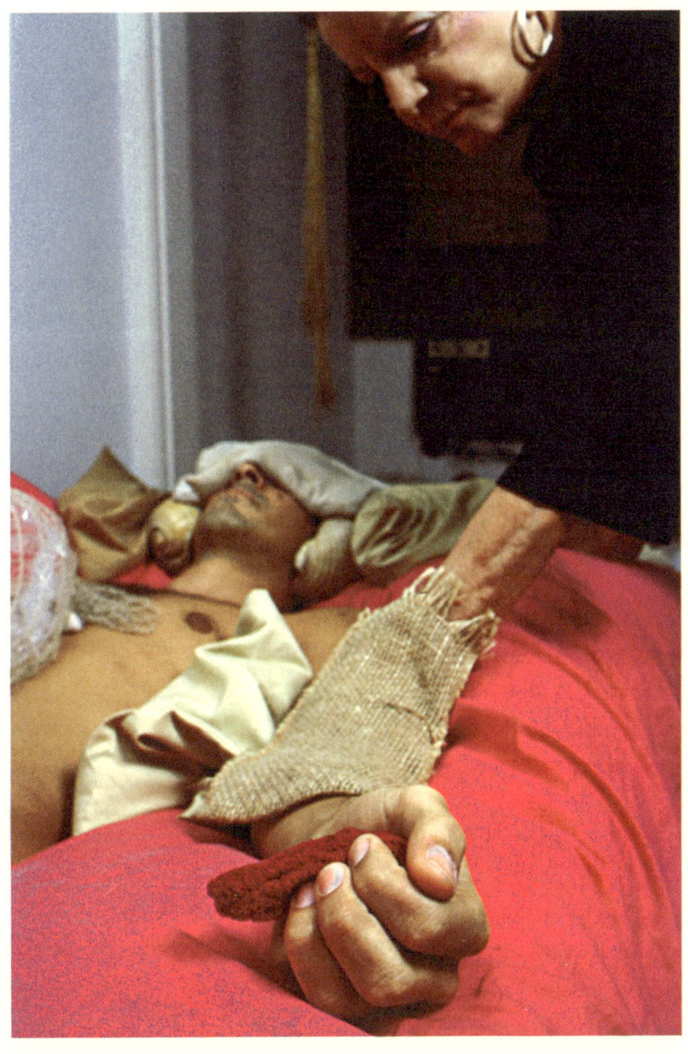

Figure 2.4. Lygia Clark, *Estruturação do Self*
(Structuring of the Self), 1978. Courtesy of
Associação Cultural "O Mundo de Lygia Clark."

Notebook sketches indicate that Clark had begun to draw well before beginning her lessons with Burle Marx and Salgado in 1947, and further, that the years between her discovery of the organic line in 1954 and her self-acknowledged pursuit of the phenomenon in 1956 were not devoid of experiments. As I will detail, Clark included two paintings from what is now known as the *Quebra da moldura* (Breaking the frame) series as part of her contribution to the Brazilian representation at the Venice Biennale in 1954. The organic line of these two works, as in *Descoberta da linha orgânica* (Discovery of the organic line), appears between the canvas and its wooden frame. A year later, at Museu de Arte Moderna do Rio de Janeiro, she exhibited architectural maquettes structured according to the organic line alongside paintings in which the fissures of space from her 1954 works migrated to the paintings' frontal faces. Paintings from this series — titled *Superfícies moduladas* (Modulated surfaces) — were also exhibited at the São Paulo Bienal of 1955. Here, Clark experimented with building up the painterly plane from separate wooden parts, much like a puzzle, carpentering the verso such that the spatial voids of the organic line work in conjunction with chromatic blocks to form a partial map of the work's material construction (fig. 2.5).[13] These paintings entail a model of surface that holds together *as a surface* by means of division and accumulation as much as by continuity.[14]

Around this time, Clark spent two months as an apprentice in a carpentry shop in order to learn the mechanics of cutting, joining, compressing, gluing, and finishing wood.[15] At this point, the painterly apparatus of canvases and frames recorded in her early studio paintings was entirely displaced by panels of industrial plywood that she cut, arranged, and appended to a base with hot glue before applying industrial paint with a spray gun.[16] As she subsequently described this process, "I compose, or better, *materialize* my pictures with pieces of cut and glued wood."[17] In order to create the conditions for the appearance of the organic line in such works, Clark often worked from cardboard studies, a system she extended

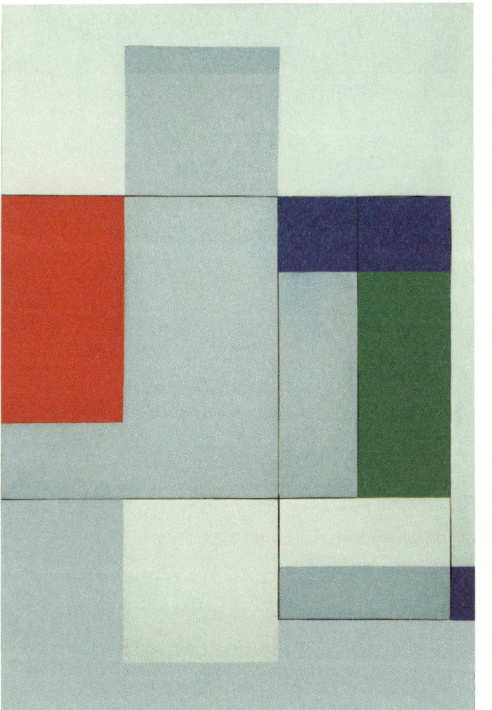 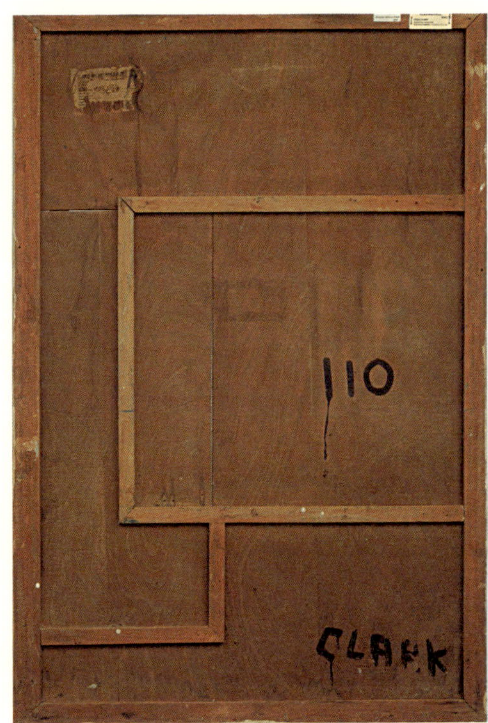

Figure 2.5. Lygia Clark, *Superfície modulada* (Modulated surface), 1955 (recto, verso). Industrial paint on wood, 114 × 77 cm. Photo: André de Arruda Pimentel. Courtesy of Associação Cultural "O Mundo de Lygia Clark."

around 1957, when the practice of cutting and fitting together positive and negative forms—always separated by a slivered void—generated hundreds of cardboard maquettes (fig. 2.6). Some of these maquettes served as models for larger paintings made from condensed plaques of wood, titled *Planos em superfície modulada* (Planes in modulated surface).[18] While at the beginning of her artistic practice, Clark associated cutting with a form of autocure, the lacerating action of the blade proof of an otherwise elusive reality, by the mid-1950s, it was simultaneously linked to a technique of composition in which the line, *unlike the cut*, was catalyzed, *but not made.*

In a 1986 interview, Clark remarked that she freely "absorbed" artistic influences from her mentors and other sources until the discovery of the organic line, after which, all external references fell away.[19] While part and parcel of Clark's self-mythology, it suggests that during the liminal period between 1954 to 1956, in which the organic line was present in her practice, yet still nascent in its conceptualization, Clark was actively working through its capacities as a means of differentiating the modernist painterly plane. As I outlined in Chapter 1, the stakes of this engagement were nothing less than a wholesale reconstitution of the support, a transformation of its abstract, neutral, and a priori quality into a "living space," an "organic body" that expressed a reality in and of itself.[20] If Clark's selective narration of her aesthetic and biographical investments is any indication, it is likewise clear she conceived of this reconstitution in terms not unlike those of psychic reconstruction. Having plunged into the dizzying, nonorientable space unleashed from the breaking of the frame, the painterly support had to be rehabilitated, albeit on radically different terms.

That the painterly plane could be a site of psychic reconstitution was an idea in active circulation when Clark turned definitely to artistic practice in Rio in 1947. In February of that year, paintings created by participants in an occupational therapy workshop run by the psychiatrist Nise da Silveira and the painter Almir Mavignier at the Centro Psiquiátrico Nacional Engenho de Dentro were exhibited

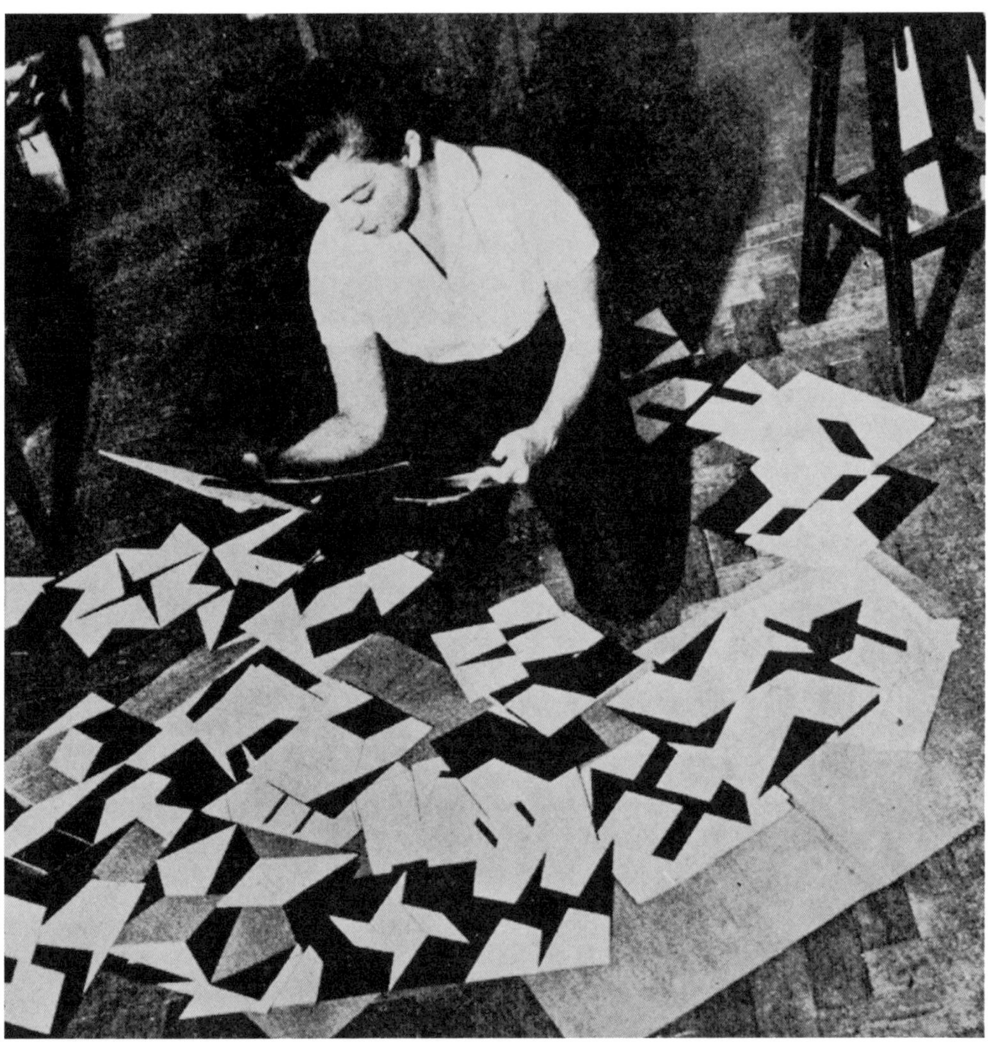

Figure 2.6. Lygia Clark with studies for modulated surfaces, ca. 1957. In Ferreira Gullar, *Lygia Clark: Uma experiência radical, 1954–1958* (Lygia Clark: A radical experience, 1954–1958), exh. cat. (Rio de Janeiro: Departamento de Imprensa Nacional, 1958). Courtesy of Associação Cultural "O Mundo de Lygia Clark."

at the Ministério da Educação e Saude, soon to be provisional head-quarters of the Museu de Arte Moderna.[21] The exhibition's great-est apologist was none other than the critic Mário Pedrosa, who lauded the works' ability to visualize the "psychological origins" of art, the affective impulses of which had long been a central concern of modernism.[22] Directly opposing the rhetoric of "degenerate art" advanced by Nazi propaganda one decade earlier, Pedrosa noted that in the realm of art, the boundaries between "psychological normal-ity and abnormality" are far "fainter" and "cease to have any decisive meaning." "Each individual is a separate psychological system, as well as a potentially malleable and formal organization," he remarked.[23] To this degree, the art of the mentally ill, or "alienated," as they were termed, expressed the "urgent vitality" of art itself.[24]

As Kaira Cabanãs has explored in her important work on Bra-zilian art and the mentally ill, Silveira drew great inspiration from Antonin Artaud and likewise spoke of the "imprecise frontiers of normalcy."[25] Unlike Pedrosa, however, Silveira's therapeutic and theoretical interest in her clients' paintings resided in how the works registered an autocurative force for clients suffering from states of psychic dissociation. For Silveira, the most explicit signal of such psychic reintegration was the spontaneous appearance of the regularized, circular structure of the mandala, about which she corresponded with Carl Jung in 1954.[26] But autocure took other expressive forms, as well. Analyzing a series of paintings created by a schizophrenic client named Fernando Diniz from roughly 1952 to 1955, for example, Silveira observed that the restructuration of the fragmented psyche unfolded vis-à-vis the representation of domestic space (fig. 2.7).[27] Whereas in his earlier paintings, depicted objects careened chaotically within an indeterminate visual field, Diniz isolated individual entities in subsequent paintings, anchor-ing them in a coherent space organized above all by the repetitive lines of floorboards, fit tightly to the wooden molding of the wall (fig. 2.8). For Silveira, the firmness of this depicted ground and its accompanying quotidian space—compiled piece by piece as if "the

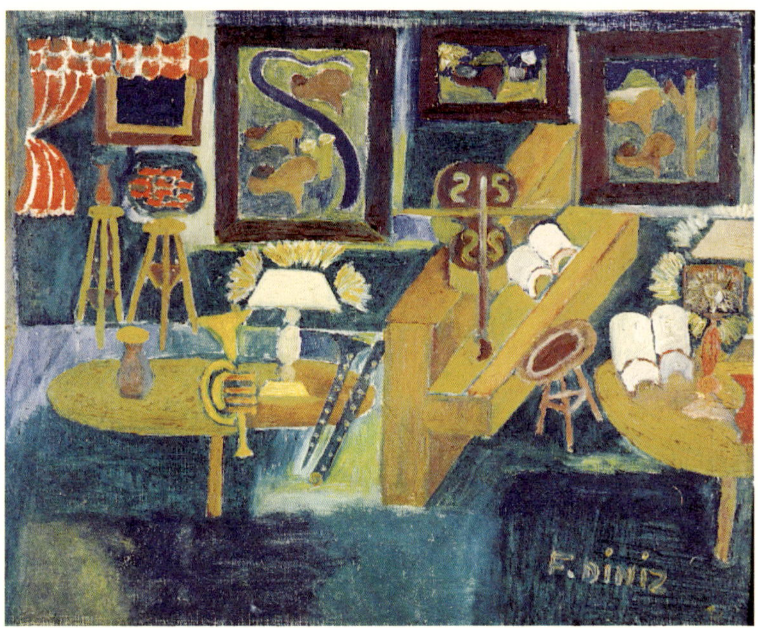

Figure 2.7. Fernando Diniz, *Untitled*, December 1, 1953. Courtesy of Sociedade Amigos do Museu de Imagens do Inconsciente.

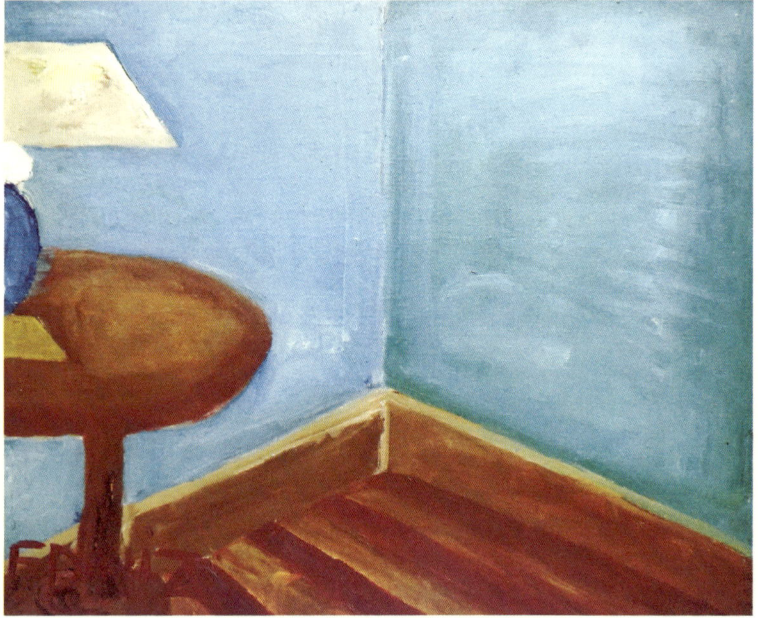

Figure 2.8. Fernando Diniz, *Untitled*, March 4, 1954. Courtesy of Sociedade Amigos do Museu de Imagens do Inconsciente.

letters *a e i o u*," as Diniz described it—corresponded directly to the recuperation of the ego.[28] Silveira found ultimate evidence of this progress in the sudden appearance of an open window in one of Diniz's paintings from 1955: an aperture to the exterior world where previously only a represented painting, securely enclosed in a thick frame, had hung (figs. 2.9 and 2.10).

Although Clark herself did not visit Engenho de Dentro, she certainly knew of the works produced there and the heated debate around art of the mentally ill that ensued in the popular press.[29] Numerous exhibitions of patients from Engenho de Dentro and other psychiatric institutions were organized in Brazil in the late 1940s and early 1950s, and several figures intimate to Clark's circle visited Silveira's and Mavignier's workshop.[30] As Cabañas has noted, works by inmates from Brazilian psychiatric institutions were also included in the much-publicized Exposition international d'art psy-chopathologique (International exhibition of psychopathological art) in Paris in late 1950, where Clark had arrived in February that same year.[31] In a letter to fellow artist Hélio Oiticica in 1970, Clark expressed her preference for the "magisterial expression" of certain inmates over the buttoned-up mediocrity of the Parisian art world, which in her view was in need of "a bit of madness."[32] Not surpris-ingly, however, her own articulation of the painterly plane as a site of therapeutic recuperation deviated markedly from that of Silveira. For while Silveira may have celebrated the "breaking of the frame" in Diniz's painting of the open window, she nevertheless retained a notion of the plane as a *representational* construct, one that might deliver, just like that window, a transparent view onto both interior psychology and the exterior world. By contrast, Clark comprehended the plane as a materially embodied, rather than virtual surface, and thus any process of reconstruction had to occur in those terms.

Clark's attention to the cut is an obvious outgrowth—and per-haps provenance—of this position, because any cut necessarily physicalizes the plane. But as a phenomenon that is observed and even generated, but is not *made*, the organic line is not coincident

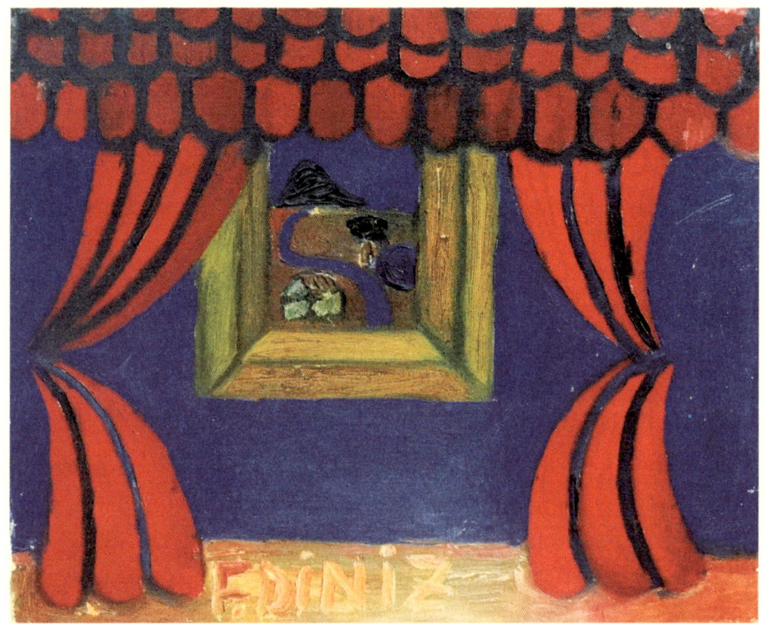

Figure 2.9. Fernando Diniz, *Untitled*, 1955. Courtesy of Sociedade Amigos do Museu de Imagens do Inconsciente.

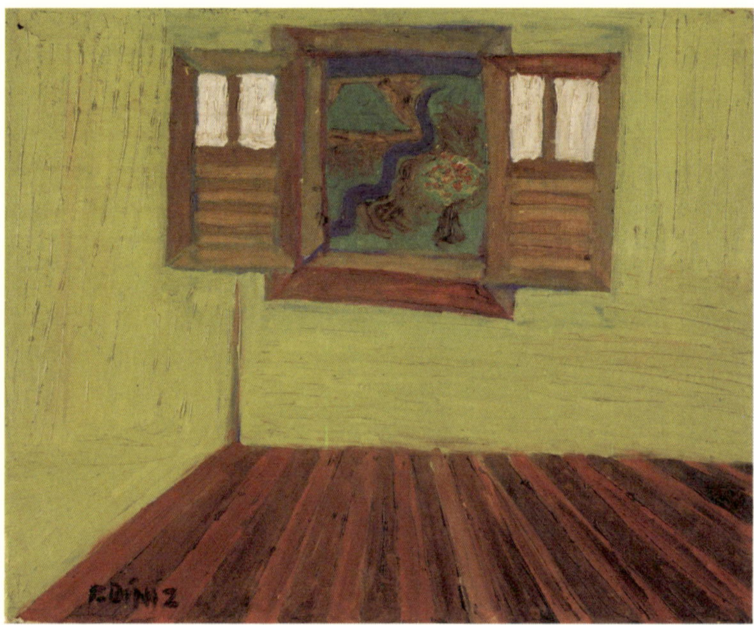

Figure 2.10. Fernando Diniz, *Untitled*, February 2, 1955. Courtesy of Sociedade Amigos do Museu de Imagens do Inconsciente.

with the cut as cure. As a chasm of actual space, the organic line is what refuses any normative notion of the cure as a resuscitation of the plane as a continuous surface. There is a materialist and spatial logic for this, but also a psychic one. If, as I explored in Chapter 1, the organic line finds one analogue in the differentiation of the mother and child in birth, the baby grasping for the "space of the exterior world" as air travels to its lungs for the first time, its counterpart is that same baby's drive for satiety as it nurses. Writing in the 1980s, now from a position deep within her own therapeutic practice, Clark remarked that the "anthropophagous" baby lives "as part of the mother's body." "The baby has no limits" and "lives the 'lack' that pursues him until 'finitude.' He substitutes this void with appropriations, his phantasmatic will be solidly incorporated."[33] For Clark, who herself always seemed on the "edge of an abyss," it would be imperative not simply to fill — and thus satiate — the lack, but to identify the potentiality contained within it.[34] As she commented to one her clients, when emptiness appears, one should not attempt to escape it, but "rest" with it, as the void is also a source of creativity.[35] Returning to the question of the support, the process of its reconstitution thus pivots on how to actuate not the materiality of the cut, but the materiality of the space that occurs *alongside, before, after, and despite it*. As for the subjects who catalyze and observe this liminal space, at stake is how to transform composition and line from conventions cognate with human agency, individual will, and artistic making into a means of lateral activation that unfolds in relation to the world at large. As I hope to demonstrate, the mutual imbrication of the viewer and these liminal spaces enacts a model of porous, serial, and processual subjectivity. "I am afraid of space," Clark once observed, "but I rebuild myself from it."[36]

In February of 1950, Clark, accompanied by her sister Sonia Lins, moved to Paris with her three small children in tow with the aim of pursuing her burgeoning interest in art. We know precious few details about the subsequent two years, the majority gleaned from Clark's occasional mentions of her studies, which occurred in succession with Árpád Szenes, Isaac Dobrinsky, and Fernand Léger.[37] In June 1952, toward the end of her stay, Clark exhibited sixteen paintings at L'Institut Endoplastique, a beauty salon that doubled as a gallery, at the invitation of the Paris-based Iraqi artist Jamil Hamoudi. In the short text that accompanied the invitation, Hamoudi noted that the exhibition demonstrated an intensification of Clark's sensibility and the "essentially living" quality of her compositions. These were traits that one could anticipate Clark developing as she traveled "her avant-garde path."[38] The exhibition garnered a number of positive mentions in the French press that were reproduced in a pamphlet for a solo exhibition organized upon Clark's return to Rio in November 1952.[39] This Rio exhibition resulted in a prize that effectively launched the artist's career. Clark herself was ambivalent about this recognition, however, and recalls that it was an impetus for reevaluating her work (fig. 2.11).[40]

According to Lins, Clark returned to Brazil with suitcases overflowing with art books.[41] In this vein, the Parisian sojourn from 1950 to 1952 appears to have afforded her ample exposure to modern art, but no great epiphanies. Nevertheless, at least one important historiographic detail bears underscoring about the significance of this period for Clark's subsequent conceptualization of the organic line. This is that in all likelihood, Clark's initial point of reference for the idea of a "concrete art" would not have been Max Bill, but rather Hans Arp, who expressed interest in Clark's 1952 Paris exhibition and at some point acquired one or more examples of her work.[42] By the mid-1950s, Bill, with his mathematical approach to art, emerged as the most visible protagonist of Concretism in Brazilian circles, in large part due to the advocacy of Tomás Maldonado.[43] Clark's own work of the mid-1950s was described as "concrete," and she was a key member of the dissenting Neoconcrete movement inaugurated in 1959. Yet Clark missed both Bill's influential 1951 solo exhibition

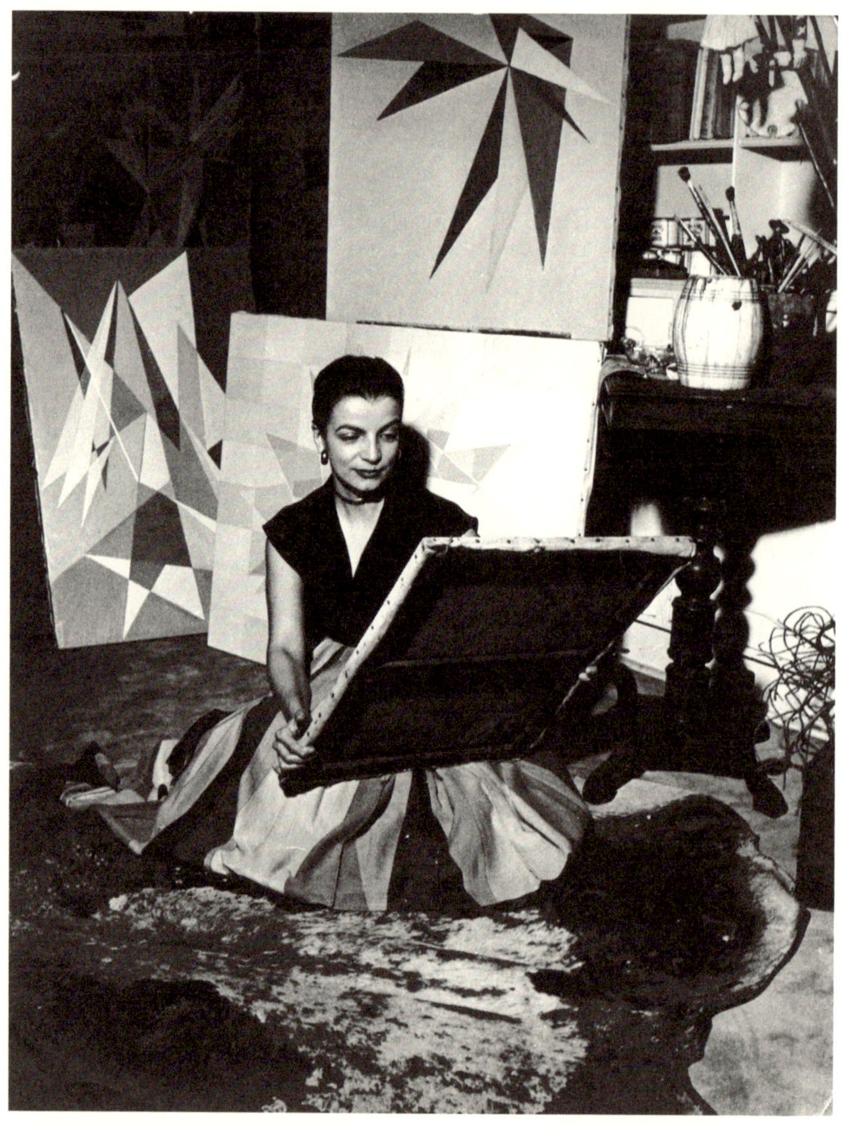

Figure 2.11. Lygia Clark in her studio, Rio
de Janeiro, 1953–54. Courtesy of Associação
Cultural "O Mundo de Lygia Clark."

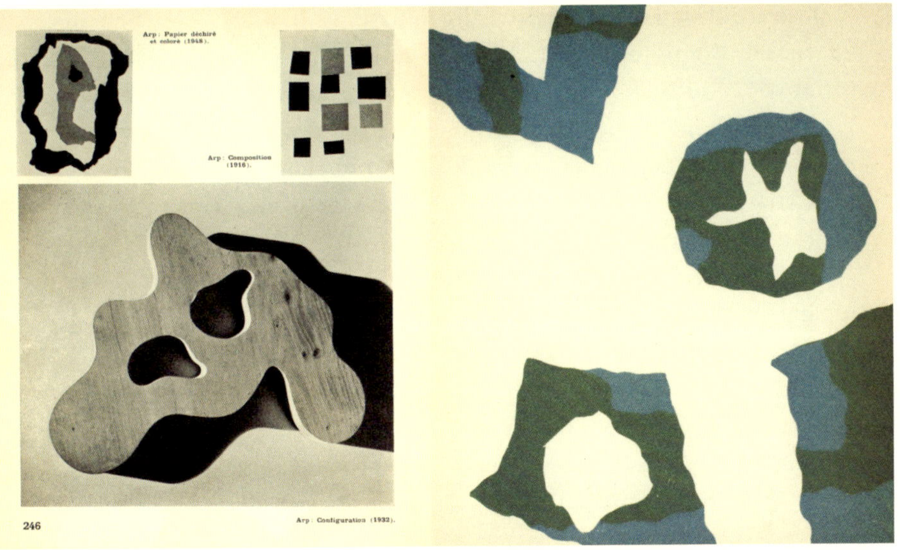

Figure 2.12. Hans Arp's works, illustrated in Michel Seuphor, *L'art abstrait: Ses origins, ses premiers maîtres* (Paris: Maeght, 1950), pp. 246–47. © 2023 Artists Rights Society (ARS), New York / VG Bild-Kunst, Bonn.

at the Museu de Arte de São Paulo and his highly remarked upon prize at the first São Paulo Bienal, also in 1951.[44] By contrast, in Paris, her coordinates for the notion of the "concrete" were more likely to have followed from Michel Seuphor's 1949 catalogue for his renowned two-part historical exhibition, *L'art abstrait: Ses origines, ses premiers maîtres* (fig. 2.12). In this catalogue, which featured Arp's work prominently, Seuphor quotes the artist's distinction between abstract and concrete art. As Arp wrote, "I understand why one would name a Cubist painting abstract, because the parts have been subtracted from the object that serves as the model for the painting. But I find a painting or a sculpture that doesn't take an object for its model as concrete and sensual as a leaf or a stone."[45]

That Arp would seek recourse in the organic and mineralogical in order to explicate the "concrete" already indicates his distinction from Bill's quasi-rationalistic formulations. In a 1953 interview in Brazil, Bill noted that a Concrete artist "always departs from an abstract idea, from a generating and almost always geometric schema," and in 1955, Maldonado rehearsed the Swiss artist's statement that Concrete art is the "pure expression of form and law."[46] Clark herself later noted that the conflation of the "concrete" and the "geometric" was a false affinity, one that could not fully account for her own appeal to the organic as a quality that entails "entering" or "participating" in "that place, that space, of the picture."[47] Already predisposed to the vital quality of the plane as a result of her studies with Burle Marx, Clark would have found ample support in Arp, who wrote, "We want to produce like a plant produces fruit, and not reproduce. We want to produce directly and not by way of an intermediary. Since this art doesn't have the slightest trace of abstraction, we name it: concrete art."[48]

Arp's formulation echoes his friend and one-time collaborator, the Chilean poet Vicente Huidobro, who in 1917 declared that the poet should "make a poem as nature makes a tree."[49] Significantly, as I noted in Chapter 1, it was to Huidobro that Rhod Rothfuss had looked when he formulated the irregular frame, or *marco recortado*, in 1944.[50] Yet as I also noted there, the appeal to natural or biological metaphors and the imperative to establish pictorial autonomy were not always reconciled within the discourse of the *marco recortado*. While Huidobro argued that art should not imitate nature's outer "appearances," but act according to its "constructive laws," Maldonado initially rejected the traditional frame because it functioned as what he called a "containing organism."[51] Yet didn't an organism's "containment" offer the very self-sufficiency artists desired? Huidobro's poem-as-tree provided an apt metaphor for the self-generating, centrifugal action of the irregularly shaped canvas. Theorizing the *edge* was more of a problem, however, since a composition might determine the shape of a frame, but did not proscribe the character of that delimitation. The widely varying approaches the actual *frame* of the irregular frame, as well as the ambivalent status of the field in Maldonado's *Sin título*, discussed in Chapter 1, are all indications of this lack of specification. Arp's work offers fortuitous insight into this problem, for while Rothfuss and Maldonado each objected to the conventionally framed work of art as a fragment of a presumed continuity, Arp looked to the fragment in order to formulate a concept of edge.[52] After all, what were Arp's cut-out wood reliefs, their globular edges carefully calibrated to secure chromatic continuity from one section to the next, if not "containing organisms"? If Arp's corporeal formulation of edge had any purchase for Clark, it likely came in 1954, when both artists exhibited at the Venice Biennale. Never a fully realized dialogue, Arp's idiosyncratic theorization of the concrete forms a characteristically plagiotropic link within Clark's theoretical horizon, as does her possible (or possible lack of) exposure to the Río de la Plata discourse of the *marco recortado*.[53] In light of the oblique relations I seek to chart over the course of this book, however, these and other weak links form a constellation of historical and conceptual possibility through which the organic line emerges into view.

Between her return from Paris and her discovery of the organic line in 1954, Clark's fully realized paintings consist primarily of two types and occasionally their combination. One entailed gridlike compositions in which multicolored squares, rectangles, or bands are punctuated by elongated strips that either project as figures or are absorbed as ground. A second type consists of crystal-like configurations formed from intersecting triangles that slice through one another in space, carving up the painting's ground into a series of flat, neutral fields. In a work from 1953, Clark complicated this ambiguous spatial quality by materializing the surface with differing textures, paint treatments, and most strikingly, by scraping the outline of several shapes upon the canvas (fig. 2.13). While Clark had previously tested the varying autonomy or integration of figure

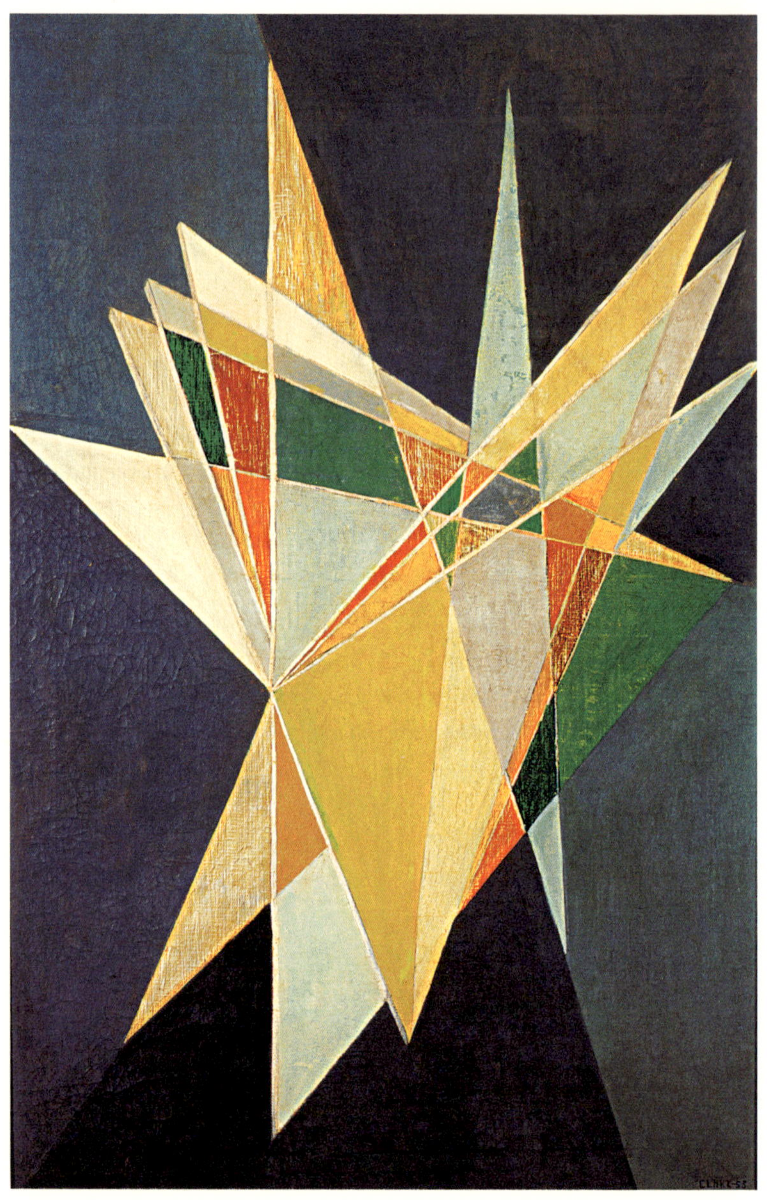

Figure 2.13. Lygia Clark, *Composição*
(Composition), 1953. Photo: Marcelo Ribeiro
Alvares Corrêa. Courtesy of Associação
Cultural "O Mundo de Lygia Clark."

and ground through shape and chromatic interaction, these incised lines abruptly admitted the materiality of the plane as a factor, as well. As I note in the Introduction, however, it was only with her *Quadro objeto* (Painting object), submitted in 1954 to the Salão Preto e Branco, or Black and White Salon, that space itself began to emerge as a material element in its own right.[54]

Because the Salão Preto e Branco opened in Rio in May of 1954 and the Venice Biennale in June that same year, it is all but impossible to know if Clark was at work on pieces for these exhibitions simultaneously or sequentially.[55] We do know that of the five paintings Clark contributed to the Venice Biennale, two belong to the series now known as *Quebra da moldura* and include organic lines between their canvases and frames (fig. 2.14). At Venice, however, the works were displayed under the generic term *Composição* (Composition). Considering that there are only scattered mentions of the organic line in 1955, and that it was not until 1956 that Clark publicly described the phenomenon, it appears that in the liminal period around 1954, the organic line was still an imminent, rather than articulated concept. For this reason, the rich constellation of artistic experiments concerning what a plane might *be* or *do* likewise on display at Venice allows us to comprehend how Clark may have charted the distinctiveness and direction of her own investigations.[56]

Alongside Clark in the Brazilian representation, for example, were a series of collages made by fellow artist Ivan Serpa, an influential art educator who gathered artists at his Rio home to share books and conversation. In June of 1954, the same month the Biennale opened in Venice, Serpa and Clark exhibited along with other members of the newly founded Grupo Frente, which served as a vital locus of experimentation for artists in Rio until 1956.[57] Serpa also worked as a restorer of rare books and manuscripts at the Biblioteca Nacional, and starting in 1953, began using a press at the library to make collages in which layers of thin Japanese paper were bound together with heat-activated cellulose acetate (figs. 2.15 and

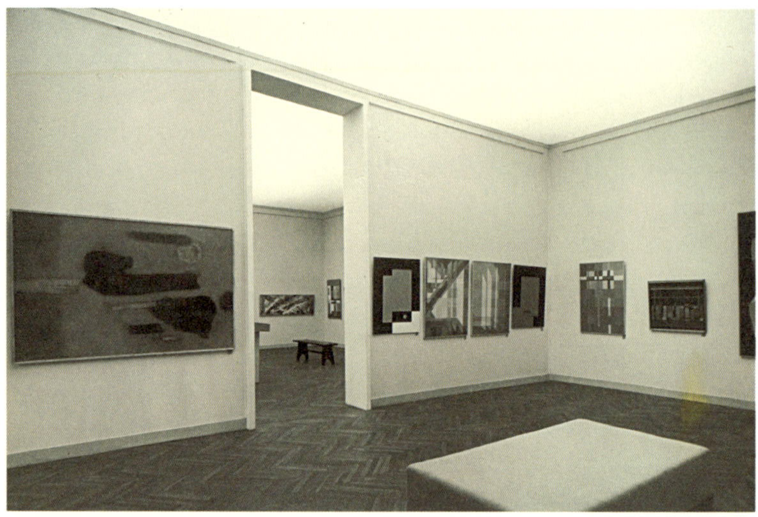

Figure 2.14. Brazilian representation, Venice Biennale, 1954, showing five Lygia Clark works to the right of door. Courtesy of Arquivo Histórico Wanda Svevo/Fundação Bienal de São Paulo and Associação Cultural "O Mundo de Lygia Clark."

2.16).[58] Rather than laminating a document between acetate, Serpa layered the acetate between contiguous layers of paper, titling the works after the process, *Colagens sob calor e pressão* (Collages under heat and pressure). At a material level, the collages eliminated spatial intervals through the bonding action of the melted cellulose, merging separate elements into a single, ultraflat plane. Aesthetically, the resulting compositions of floating, translucent shapes approximate an evanescent veil of colored light. Pedrosa described this effect as "spectral filmic color" unfolding within a "purely imaginary space."[59] This insubstantiality, even idealization, was likewise reflected in Serpa's method, which involved mocking up a composition twice, the second time from memory, in order to distill the essence of a given arrangement. While Serpa's process has origins in a conservation technique for protecting individual documents, his collages convert the interiority of the ostensible document into

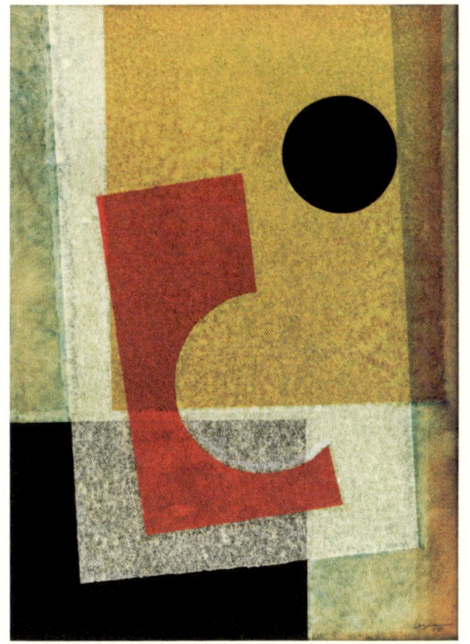

Figure 2.15. Ivan Serpa, *Colagem sob calor e pressão* (Collage under heat and pressure), 1955. Photo: Ding Musa.

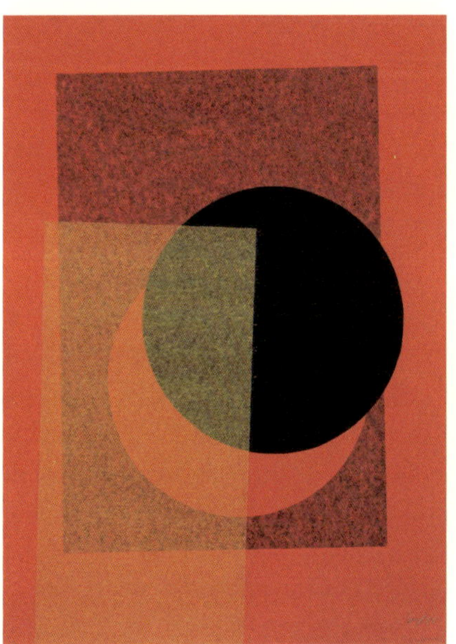

Figure 2.16. Ivan Serpa, *Colagem sob calor e pressão* (Collage under heat and pressure), 1955. Photo: Ding Musa.

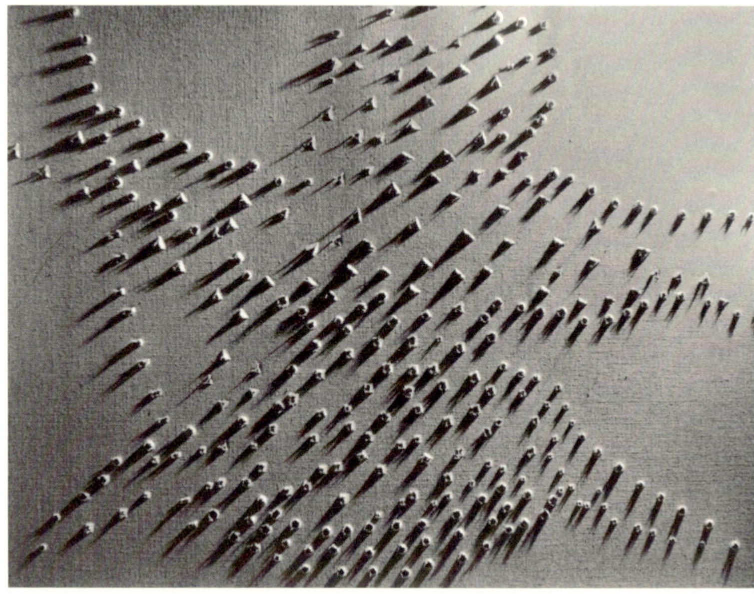

Figure 2.17. Lucio Fontana, *Concetto spaziale* (Spatial concept), 1952. In *La Biennale di Venezia*, exh. cat. (Venice: Lombroso Editore, 1954). Archives of the Venice Biennale. © 2023 Artists Rights Society (ARS), New York/SIAE, Rome.

a combinatory and infinitely connective exterior surface. In short, the collages imagine the seamless integration of informational units through the pure aesthetic values of color, texture, and shape.[60]

Nothing could be further from Lucio Fontana's *Concettos spaziales* (Spatial concepts), exhibited as part of the Italian representation at Venice in 1954. These belonged to the *Buchi* (Holes) series Fontana had begun in 1949, in which the artist punctured a paper or canvas support, resulting in a constellation of lesions that singularize and dimensionalize the otherwise neutral surface of the plane. This effect is particularly pronounced in the raking light photograph included in the Venice catalogue (fig. 2.17). Here, perforations throw long shadows onto the surface of the support, making visible the real, rather than representational action of their sculptural irruptions. These punctures also reveal the canvas "as a membrane . . . a surface permeable from both sides," as Pia Gottschaller has put it.[61] Aesthetic space is no longer solely coincident with the plane, but extends into the actual space behind it. For Fontana, this visual access, minimal with the *Buchi*, but greatly intensified with the slashing cuts of the *Tagli* (Cuts) he began to make in 1958, provided entry to an "infinite dimension" beyond the painting.[62] In short, this space was not literal, but cosmic, metaphoric.

That Fontana's works equivocated about the relations between metaphoric and actual space is particularly fascinating in light of the artist's patchy relation to the irregular frame experiments of the Río de la Plata artists of the 1940s. Born in Argentina and raised in Italy, Fontana returned to Argentina in 1922 and worked between the two countries until 1948, when he established himself permanently in Milan. He was based in Buenos Aires and close friends with Maldonado and other proponents of vanguard abstraction between 1945 and 1947, precisely those years in which the *marco recortado* and its attributes—its concrete character, ability to stave off representation, and radical aesthetic and social potential—were most hotly debated.[63] Recent scholarship has indicated that while Fontana did not join any of the groups associated with the irregular frame, the force of their debates impelled his own turn toward spatial and material experimentation.[64] While Clark was not privy to such details, she was doubtless attentive to, first, how one orchestrates an irruption of actual space within and beyond the plane, and second, how one conceives of the *character* of this space upon its emergence. Fontana remained wholly committed to the authorial mark of puncturing, incising, and lacerating the plane, gestures the critic Giampiero Giani underscored in his essay for the 1954 Biennale catalogue.[65] For Clark, by contrast, the organic line was a *found* phenomenon—a line devoid of mark—and her practice in the years immediately following its revelation entailed exploring the implications of this authorial withdrawal. Whereas Giani described Fontana's void as "the deprivation of form," Clark's fissure is a space deprived not of form, but of *mark*. It therefore disrupts the dualistic register of life/

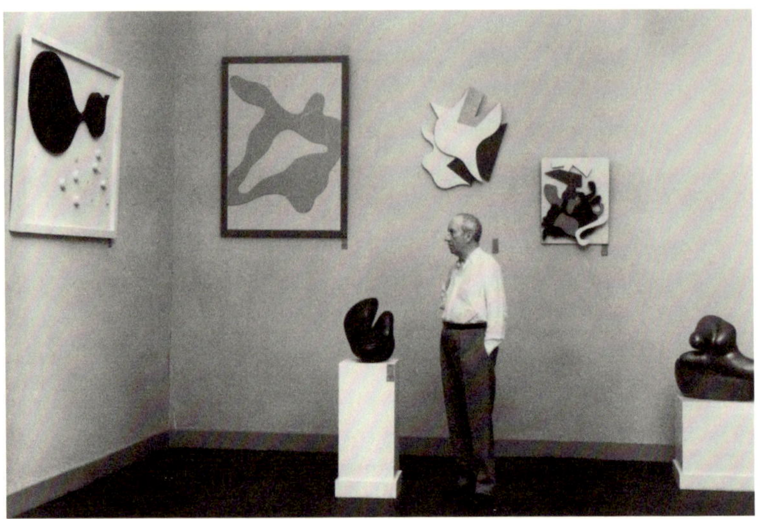

Figure 2.18. Hans Arp exhibition, Venice Biennale, 1954. Photo: Archives of the Venice Biennale. © 2023 Artists Rights Society (ARS), New York / VG Bild-Kunst, Bonn.

death, figure/ground, form/void upon which Giani's interpretation unfolded.[66] Likewise, whereas the varying strands of Concrete art that Fontana and Clark encountered sought to abolish metaphoric space, Fontana remained dedicated to a delirious, if vague register of the infinite.[67] For her part, Clark's developing notion of the organic conformed neither to this abstract spatial topos nor to the relentless factuality espoused by figures such as Maldonado or Bill. Here, Arp emerges again as a fruitful counterpoint (fig. 2.18).

In Venice in 1954, Arp exhibited numerous freestanding sculptures and spatial reliefs, the latter of which included orthogonal as well as irregular, amoebalike works in which compositional elements either rise in thick relief or were stamped in the negative, throwing shadows onto the wall. *Horloge* (Clock), 1924, which was illustrated in the exhibition catalogue and won the prize for sculpture, combines both strategies (fig. 2.19).[68] Here the circular form of the work's titular reference is delicately misshapen, its surface studded with

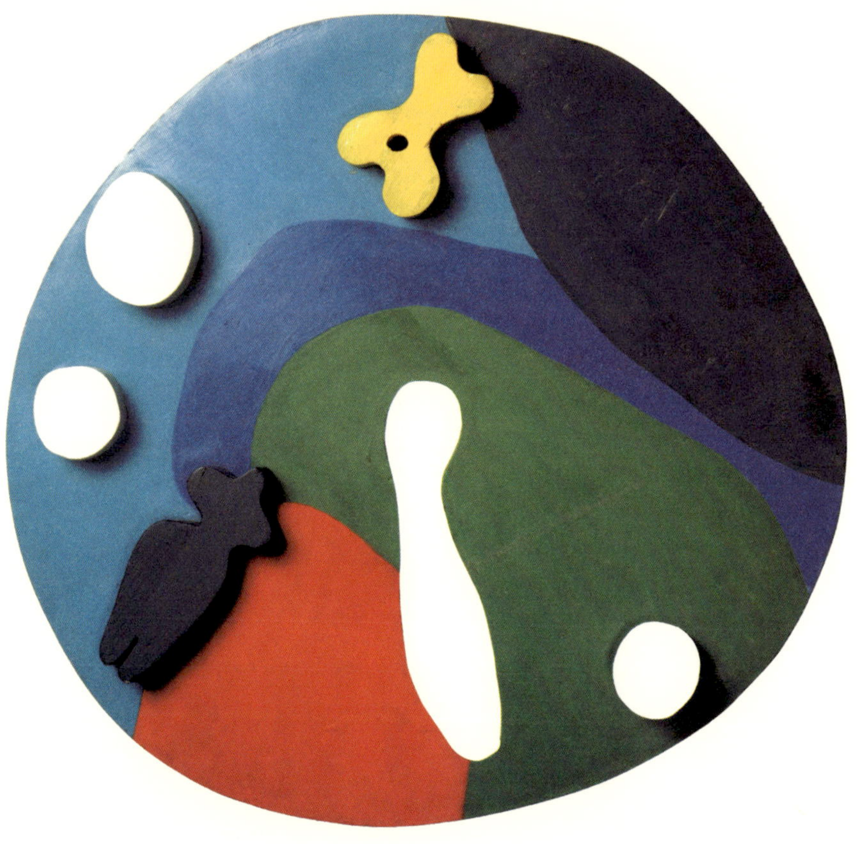

Figure 2.19. Hans Arp, *Horloge* (Clock), 1924. Painted wood relief, 53.5 × 53 × 6 cm (76.8 × 79.8 × 11.8 cm). Image courtesy Kunstmuseum Basel. © 2023 Artists Rights Society (ARS), New York/VG Bild-Kunst, Bonn.

painted wooden nodules. Placed at the edges of the tondo, these nodules appear propelled by veils of flat color, in turn driven by a tubular void that opens to the wall. This void functions as the memory of a clock's hand, rooting the relief's action and directing it transversely, from the relief's interior edge to its projected shadows.[69] Thus, unlike the empty, infinite space of Fontana's punctures and slashes, the space admitted into Arp's relief is metaphoric not in its quality *as space*, but in its pictorial action within the structure of the artwork as a whole. The relief's tubular void appears to motivate this system of relations, suggesting that this action, while metaphoric, has real effects. Indeed, the cohesiveness of this pictorial economy is perhaps the reason that Arp wrote of the frame and pedestal as "useless crutches."[70] His reliefs had no need to be insulated from external space. Not only did they incorporate space within them, the resulting configurations generated an autonomy akin to "a new body among us" that would "suffice unto itself," as Arp wrote.[71] The "perfection of an organic form," as Seuphor put it, thus does not refer to the undulating character of a relief's contours so much as to the work's ability to maintain its integrity as something like a "body," despite its permeability to space.[72]

Arp's thick sedimentation of vertical slabs enacts an opposing model of surface to Serpa's orchestration of a superflat horizontal plane. But both practices remained deeply invested in the integrative capacity of the work of art. For Arp, the cut and its resulting edge brought the plane into an actualized dimensionality, allowing it to join other such surfaces in order to articulate a body that might "suffice unto itself." Serpa's achievement in flattening out the space interleaved between his sheets of paper, meanwhile, was a material plane so paradoxically *de*materialized that its colored elements, as Pedrosa put it, were "freed of their immemorial association with objects."[73] In contrast to an autonomy of material form, in Arp's case, and formal content, in Serpa's, Fontana's lacerations of the plane breach the self-sufficiency of the work of art as a material and aesthetic construct. And while Fontana's formulation of space was inadequately theorized — on the one hand, actualized and material, on the other, metaphoric and ultimately pictorial — this space nevertheless troubled the conceit of an art object as an internally cohesive entity.

A work of art's frame is the conventional signal of this cohesion. But in securing the work's vulnerabilities, the frame also reveals the contradictory character of this putative autonomy. Thus, it is not surprising that Clark found it imperative to commence her articulation of the organic line there, or more accurately, at the frame's internal margins, where a liminal space that is not infinite, pictorial, or self-evident was propelled into action and view. Of the five works Clark sent to Venice and designated as numbered compositions *(Composição 1–5)*, three correspond to the quasi-gridded compositions I described earlier and were enclosed in a typical manner by thin wooden frames.[74] The two other works, now known as *Quebra da moldura composição no. 4* and *Quebra da moldura composição no. 5*, feature thick wooden frames painted in conjunction with their canvas interiors (see figs. 1.3 and 2.20). What we now recognize as the organic line appears between these structural elements at the juncture between the malleability of the canvas and the rigid surface of the wooden frame.[75] Like the tubular void in Arp's *Horloge*, the organic line participates in the larger compositional economy of these works, extending graphic elements with nothing more than a spatial abyss. Yet whereas Arp's void is fully integrated in the pictorial logic of the work, the organic line's inextricability from the frame renders it by turns active and latent, surfacing as an operative element of the composition in selected areas, but also retreating into an unrecognized and unseen fixture in others. A literal shifter, the organic line refuses to signal rupture consistently, like Fontana, or integration, like Arp or Serpa. While for Arp the cut was a means to draw the plane into a dimensional, quasi-corporeal materiality, Clark's imperative, by contrast, was to render thick the ostensible emptiness of *space*. Whereas Serpa sought to fuse discrete elements into a single field, the organic line in Clark's Venice works decouples the heterogeneous units of an ostensibly singular plane.

In so doing, the works expose the multiplicities of surface as well as structure, such that plane can no longer be isolated from either its supporting or presenting apparatus. The infrathin space pressed out of Serpa's collages and elided by the chromatic continuity between Arp's vertical wooden layers thus thickens along the edges of Clark's planes, dilating and contracting according to the material variability of canvas and frame along each point of their mutual articulation. The organic line is a real-time effect of contiguous material elements, not unlike the shadows thrown by Fontana's punctures or Arp's reliefs. Unlike these instances, however, Clark's works prioritize this collateral effect — parasitic, dependent, *neither mark nor made* — as the primary site of conceptual and aesthetic investigation.

Quebra da moldura composição no. 5 is the best known of the 1954 organic line series, due in no small part to its canonization in Clark's artist's book, *Livro-obra* (1964, 1983, see fig. I.35). Here, the work is schematized as a cardboard frame that, when lifted from its mount, reveals the graphic interaction of composition and space. Yet the painting itself is infinitely more complex (fig. 2.20). There, the binary oppositions of the cardboard version are rendered in gray, green, black, and rust. The painted black line strikes a vertical and horizontal just shy of the frame's corresponding L, orchestrating the slightest compaction toward the painting's interior. Finally, a ghost of green haunts the sides of the frame at its top right corner, where technical analysis reveals that a similar L shape lingers beneath the final coat of paint.[76] Such details suggest that Clark worked out compositional elements as she painted, rather than merely transferring a finished composition from a study or maquette. Moreover, while this painting is frequently harnessed to illustrate the action of the organic line, in Venice in 1954, the concept remained unnamed, unannounced, and in all likelihood was still in development.

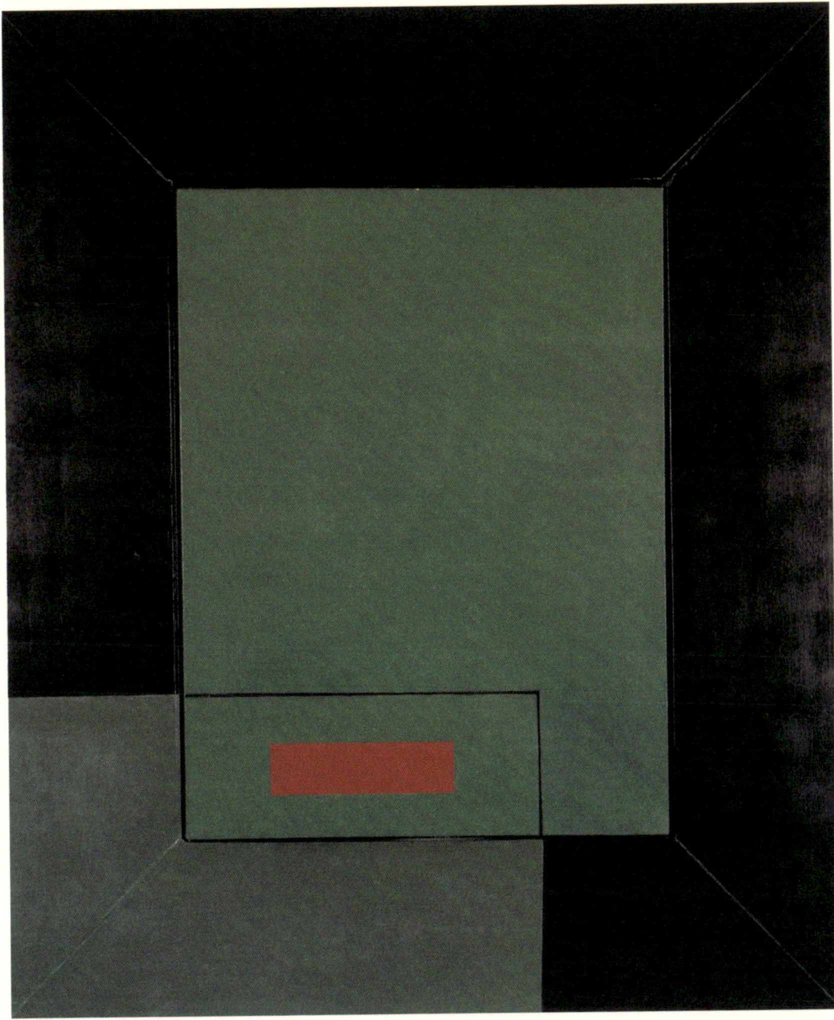

Figure 2.20. Lygia Clark, *Quebra da moldura composição no. 5* (Breaking the frame composition no. 5), 1954. Oil and oleoresin on canvas and wood, 106.5 × 91 × 2 cm. The Museum of Modern Art, New York. Gift of Patricia Phelps de Cisneros through the Latin American and Caribbean Fund. Courtesy of Associação Cultural "O Mundo de Lygia Clark."

In shifting the title of the Venice Biennale works from *Composição* (Composition) to *Quebra da moldura* (Breaking the frame), Clark intentionally recalibrated emphasis from the paintings' pictorial configuration—formal arrangements traditionally designated by the generic term "composition"—to the works' material and spatial architecture. The retention of *composição* in the two subtitles of the *Quebra da moldura* works is telling, however, for even if a result of habit or oversight, the double titles indicate the way composition as an artistic and philosophical problem remains innate—if purposely residual—in the concept of the organic line. In a general sense, composition entails the combination, placement, and arrangement of independent elements. A musician scores a composition; a schoolchild formulates essays in a composition book; a painter composes a picture through line, shape, and color. The author is typically the subject who resolves these parts into a discrete entity, thus transforming a compositional *process* into the composition as an individual *work*. (It was precisely against the expressive associations of such authorship that Soviet avant-garde artists prioritized construction *over* composition.) Etymologically, the Latin and French roots of the word join the sense or being *with* or *together* (*com-*) with *placing, pausing,* and *position* (*-poser/pausare/ponere*). Thus, while the thrust of composition lies in unification or synthesis, the term implies passage through a state of material and temporal disconnection and instability.

Although Clark's earliest resolved manifestations of the organic line were painterly, she repeatedly described her discovery of the phenomenon apropos of working on a cardboard collage. In these accounts, the organic line first appeared as a spatial interstice between a collage element and a *passe-partout*, the framing cardboard mat intended, apropos of its title, to "go everywhere" around a work (see fig. I.1). As Clark put it in one interview, "I observed that the moment in which there was a contrast in color between the collage [piece] and the *passe-partout*, the line was integrated, absorbed, and disappeared, while with another piece with which there was no contrast, the line not only continued to appear but, as I came to later ascertain, became a 'line of space.'"[77]

In his influential excursus on the frame, Jacques Derrida describes the *passe-partout* as the "frame within a frame" that "works the frame, makes it work, lets it work, gives it work to do."[78] Lying between inside and outside, the *passe-partout* unsettles binaries, thereby revealing how the frame (*parergon)* produces the fiction of the unity and self-sufficiency of the work (*ergon*) by means of epistemological presumptions beholden to the *parergon* itself. The putative truth or self-evidence of a given entity such as painting is thus demonstrated to be a dependent and even parasitic effect. To this end, the *passe-partout* operates as an analytic instrument through which to pry open relations between interior and exterior. In the Derridean articulation, the *passe-partout* is thus an emblem of the *parergal* condition: the frame (a frame) is always at stake.

For Derrida, the *passe-partout* implies a particular spatial stratum, the representational and epistemological assumptions of which follow in turn. In his description, the *passe-partout* is placed *over* the work, which appears in its empty center. But another work can just as easily be slotted into its place. "To that extent," he writes, "the *passe-partout* remains a structure with a moveable base."[79] The work consigned to existing beneath or behind it can also be substituted without changing the fundamental structure and disciplinary force of its accompanying interpretive apparatus. The nearly imperceptible plane of horizontal space that exists between the *passe-partout* and the work upon which it is placed thus contains the contradictions that render work and frame at once incommensurable (at an ontological level) and mutually dependent (at an epistemological one).

The implications that proceed from Clark's experiments with the *passe-partout* are distinct in kind. Three interlinked observations emerge from her description, in which the organic line appears when a collage element—a materialized and temporarily mobile pictorial entity—is placed next to a *passe-partout* of the same color, but disappears when the colors diverge. First, the work is no longer a dematerialized representational entity that presumes its self-sufficiency. Rather, it is an element that shares in the same physicality and dimensionality as the *passe-partout* itself. Second, the recognition of this materiality displaces the horizontal thickness that exists *beneath* the *passe-partout* onto the vertical corridor of space that lies *next* to it. While this contradictory space is a veritable locus of the work-frame relation — at once facilitating the distinction between the two and masking their interdependence — it now also emerges as a functioning element within the work's larger aesthetic and material ecology. Third, while always a by-product of the *parergal* apparatus, this spatial interstice entails distinct and contingent behaviors. When it appears, it interrupts the chromatic continuity between work and *passe-partout*, but when it disappears, it "integrates" itself to the work, thereby suppressing its disruptive capacity.[80] In short, the organic line materializes the philosophical problem of the *ergon-parergon* relation, but it does not remain a symptom of this relation, gesturing, as in Derrida's *mise en abyme*, to a framing device that always gives rise to another frame. Instead, it actively *deforms and reforms* the work through its dual behaviors of irruption and fugitivity.

We will remember that the term "composition" evokes placing, pausing, and position, wherein any arrangement of parts belies their prior or future discontinuity. In Clark's description of her discovery, the organic line emerges as a result of the physical shifting of collage elements within a material field, which is to say during precisely this period of compositional malleability. The *Quebra da moldura* paintings that followed from this collage experiment are thus complex articulations. They attempt, much like *Descoberta da linha orgânica*, both to record an experimental process and to enact its resulting discoveries.[81] In 1958 and 1959 newspaper articles recounting the development of her artistic research, Clark illustrated her experiment with a diagram in which a white, tablike collage element placed upon a black ground abuts the white border of the *passe-partout*, catalyzing the appearance of the organic line between them (fig. 2.21).[82] In this concise demonstration, the organic

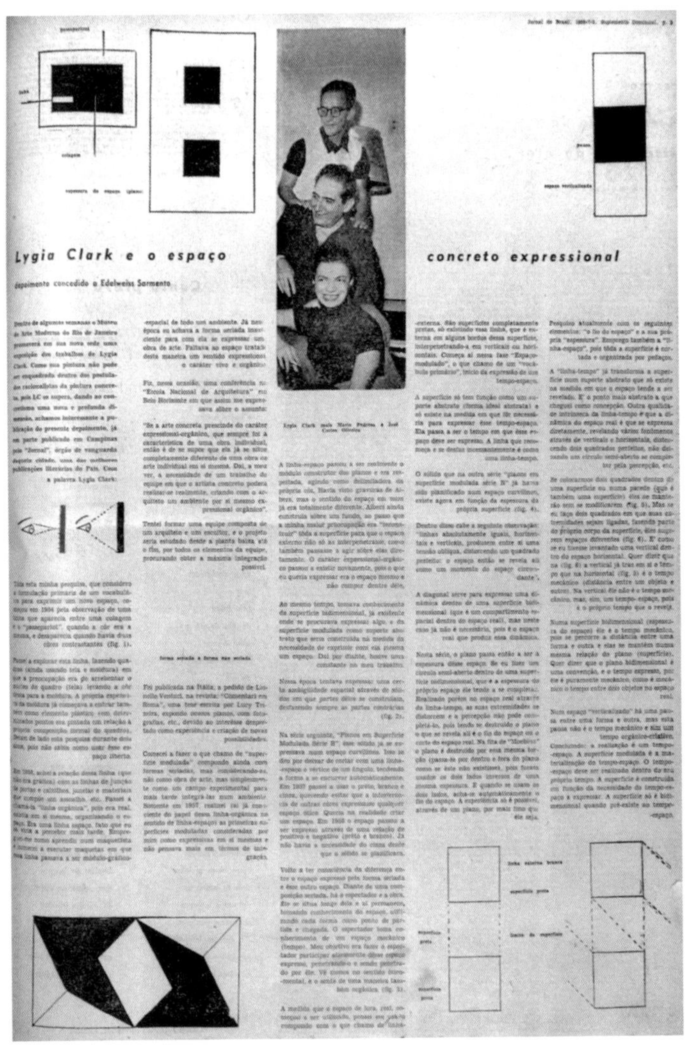

Figure 2.21. "Lygia Clark e o espaço concreto expressional: Depoimento concedido a Edelweiss Sarmento," *Suplemento Dominical do Jornal do Brasil*, July 11, 1959, p. 3. Courtesy of Associação Cultural "O Mundo de Lygia Clark." Centro de Pesquisa e Documentação do Jornal do Brasil.

line arises from the interaction between the tab, a metonym of compositional processes writ large, and those processes' organizing constraint, the *passe-partout*. The designation *p(reto)* x *b(ranco)* — b(lack) x w(hite) — of the painting *Quebra da moldura (p x b) versão 1* recalls the binary schema of this illustration, even as the painting itself is rendered in black, white, and green (see fig. I.24). In the painting, black tabs recall Clark's original collage element and retain in their doubling and misalignment a memory of the physical movement by which the organic line was revealed. Now, in a signal of the torquing of the work-frame relation, however, these black strips cluster not only at the interior edge of the canvas, but along the interior and exterior edges of the surrounding wooden frame. As Ricardo Nascimento Fabbrini observes, the painting's lack of central axis means that our vision slides to its lateral edges, beyond the frame, and to the wall itself.[83] Moreover, the frame is insistently present and impossible to separate from "the work." It does not merely partake of the work's epistemological infrastructure, per Derrida's analysis, but actively participates in its pictorial and material content. To wit, the black strips are nothing less than pictorial transfers of the measure of the frame itself. Thus, while these tabs initially function as metonyms for composition in general, they now simultaneously register the material constraint by which this *particular* composition interpolates its frame.

Within this pictorial and material economy, the action of the organic line is somewhat opaque, for unlike Clark's diagram of her collage experiment, the tabs do not generate the optical appearance of a line as an interruption of a chromatic field. Rather, they direct our attention to the void that lies between the canvas and frame. Here, in this caesura, the materiality of both elements comes into view as the black tabs and the base color of white or green turn the corner of the planar surfaces, revealing the dimensionality of their corresponding edges (see fig. I.25). But while edge is continuous with surface, it also links recto to verso, the facingness of painting with its hidden back. The strangely autonomous bodies formed by

Arp's stacked reliefs are consistent with this conceit: the aperture of *Horloge* functions like a bodily orifice insofar as it also secures the continuity of its enveloping corpus. But in Clark's *Quebra da moldura (pxb) versão 1*, something distinct occurs. For while we can imagine the black tabs wrapping around the canvas from front to back, much like string around a package, this circularity does not account for the migration of the tabs to the frame, where they similarly wrap from front to back, only to reappear, dislocated, on the painting's face. Spaces shuffle as pictorial elements are displaced. The resulting model of surface is thus not the looped enclosure of the membrane of skin, as in Arp's work, but a recursively generated topology that radically transforms along the void of the organic line.

Indeed, while the organic line provides a topological hinge between work and frame, it does not simply bridge their difference. In each painting of the *Quebra da moldura* series, the natural dilation, contraction, and swelling of wood and canvas result in clefts of space that are widely variable, squeezed to a sliver in some places, widened to a yawning gap in others. The doubling, displacement, and topological extension of the black tabs of *Quebra da moldura (pxb) versão 1* signal that the thickness and plasticity of the organic line is a causal agent, as well, pressing elements out of alignment, holding open fissures, appearing and disappearing from view. In this sense, while integrated in the work's aesthetic operations, the organic line also disrupts the putative coherence of these operations. As Ricardo Basbaum observes, it is an "in-between space…where productive events are generated, created, and triggered" by the very fact of disjunction.[84] In short, the organic line is a device for registering the constitutive *misregistration* of content and form.

———

Clark's experiments that give rise to the organic line unfold within a cross-medial space in which compositional processes are distributed across divergent material and medial conventions. But as a fissure of empty space, the organic line is always anterior to — and in excess of — composition as such. Significantly, this approach to composition diverges from that of several artists working in Europe and the United States in the wake of World War II for whom composition became a particularly fraught enterprise. For such artists, whose experiments form a major thread of the historiography of modernist art, the notion of composition was exhausted and overdetermined by the faith and subsequent disillusionment in scientific progress, rational decision making, and the coherent human subject upon which both were premised. While artists working in gestural abstraction reanimated earlier avant-garde investments in the irrational and the subjective, others turned to anticompositional strategies that sought to absent both the rational and expressive self. As Yve-Alain Bois writes, the "simultaneous and independent use of chance" in the 1950s by the US composer John Cage and the French artist Françoise Morellet "was above all a means for avoiding constant decision making, for avoiding the traditional authorial model of 'invention' (and thus for deflating the status of the author)."[85] For Bois, the US artist Ellsworth Kelly, who lived in Paris from 1948 through 1954, is a central protagonist within these articulations of authorial withdrawal, for while Kelly made use of chance, he developed a further arsenal of techniques for obviating composition that had a particular purchase on painting.

Although it does not appear that Kelly and Clark met while they lived in Paris in the early 1950s, their artistic circles and sensibilities overlapped in significant — though significantly weak — ways. Kelly exhibited at key venues for abstract art such as the Salon des Réalités Nouvelles alongside Latin American artists associated with the *marco recortado* experiments.[86] He also participated in *Abstractions*, a 1952 group show organized by none other than Almir Mavignier, who had worked in Nise de Silveira's art therapy workshops at Engenho de Dentro and had relocated to Europe from Brazil the year before. Kelly also sought out Arp, whom he visited on three occasions between 1950 and 1951. As Bois has noted in his extensive

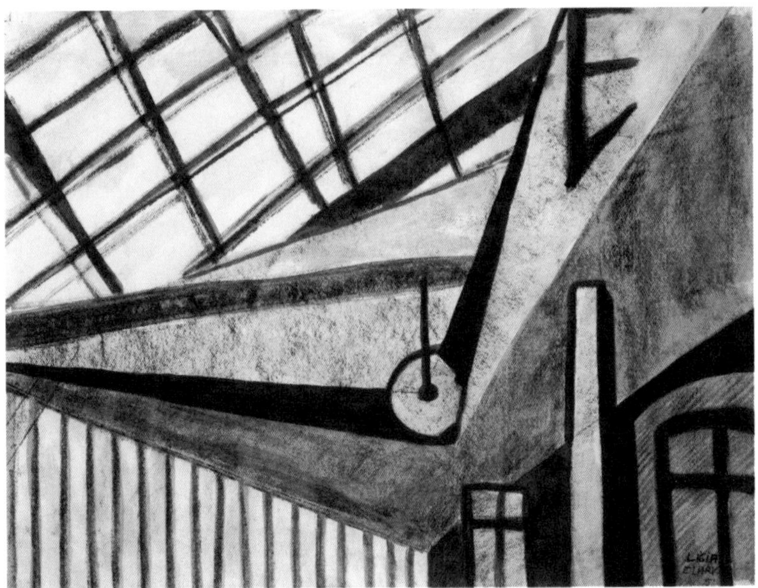

Figure 2.22. Lygia Clark, *Untitled* (Studio), 1951. Photo: Mario da Costa Grisolli. Courtesy of Associação Cultural "O Mundo de Lygia Clark."

work on Kelly, the collages Arp made on his own and in collaboration with Sophie Taeuber-Arp were likely a spur to Kelly's burgeoning interest in chance and anticompositional operations.[87] Such operations were key to Kelly's technique of the transfer, which Bois defines as "the mere recording, without any indication of a point of view or a recession in depth, of a flat pattern observed in the world onto a flat support, paper or canvas."[88] Kelly elaborated this technique over the course of numerous experiments beginning in 1949 involving motifs such as windows, building facades, stairs, and pavement stones, as well as patterns created by shadows.

In a little-known group of works made in Paris and apparently sold at her 1952 Rio exhibition, Clark likewise appears to have experimented with automatically recording shapes generated by shadows (fig. 2.22). As she and her sister recalled in separate accounts, after observing geometric patterns cast upon the wall by hooks or objects "suspended by chance" on the mirror of a hat rack, Clark traced — or "captured," as Lins put it — the forms on paper. Clark described the process this way: "I copied [them] literally. I put a paper down and drew the contours in black, white, and gray."[89] In the 1986 interview in which she recounts this experience, Clark accords it little importance. Likewise, had she seen works Kelly made by similar indexical transfers, she would not have recognized the technique, since he did not reveal his sources until 1967.[90] Nevertheless, that Clark would have engaged in such experiments at all indicates a shared interest in chance and the registration of found or already made compositions, concerns that once again link her to Arp and even possibly to Marcel Duchamp, who had photographed the shadows of his own readymades — including a hat rack — in his studio years before.[91] Yet as her subsequent practice attests, Clark had distinct investments in the reimagination of compositional processes that emerge in sharper relief when compared with Kelly's experiments of this time.

In 1951, Kelly had a solo exhibition in Paris that included a number of works now recognized as noncompositional in nature (fig. 2.23). These include *La combe II*, 1951, the patterns of which were generated by the shadows of a stair railing, and *Window, Museum of Modern Art*, 1949, exhibited under the generic title *Construction-relief en blanc, gris, et noir* (Construction-relief in white, gray, and black). The former consisted of a nine-panel folding screen connected by hinges, recalling, however obliquely, Kelly's muted source of stairs. The latter was a stacked diptych, the lower portion consisting of a canvas turned backward so that its stretcher bars faced out. If Clark saw the exhibition, she almost certainly would have noted the works' material aspect, which echoed the paintings of easel backs she first made in Rio and had taken up again in Paris (see fig. 2.2). The distinction, of course, is that in Kelly's works, the material support was made present as such: the spaces between hinges, joints, and frames are actual, rather than pictorial. The existence of this actual space was further mobilized in Kelly's *Cité* and *Colors for a Large Wall*, polyptych

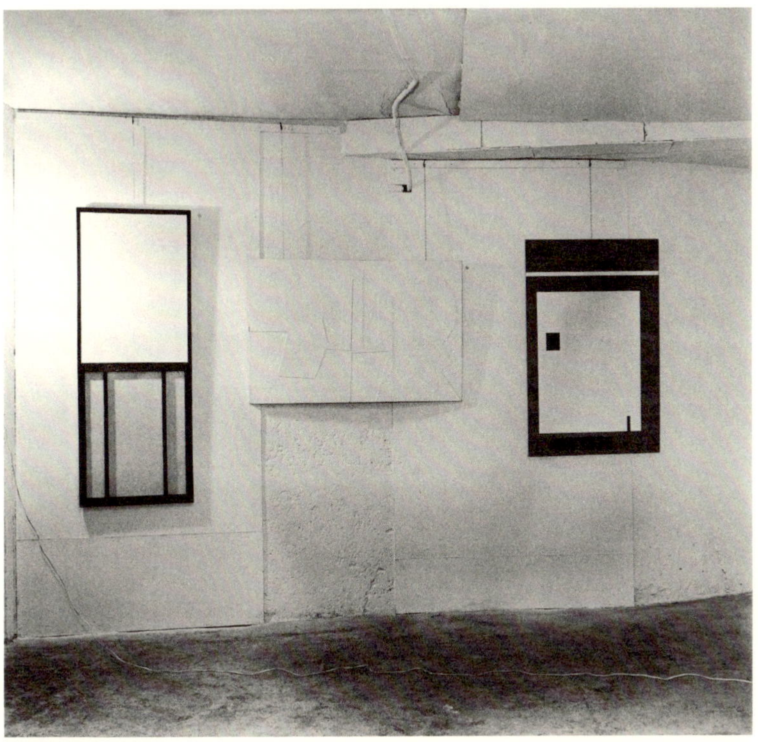

Figure 2.23. Ellswsorth Kelly, *Kelly peintures et reliefs*, Galerie Arnaud, Paris, 1951. Photo: Emeril Bronson. Courtesy Ellsworth Kelly Studio.

works exhibited in Paris in 1951 and 1952, respectively, in which a grid is established by physical adjoinment, rather than by pictorial lines (fig. 2.24).[92] As Bois observes, the grid as a series of "marks applied *onto* a support" is thereby replaced with an assemblage of canvases "whose edges would constitute the sole marks of the work."[93] Kelly himself later described the process as "throwing things out—like marks, lines, and the painted edge" in a drive for an autonomous, impersonal practice liberated from the legacy of pictorial composition and its associated trappings of the authorial subjectivity.[94] One can easily see how Kelly would have been attracted to the thread of

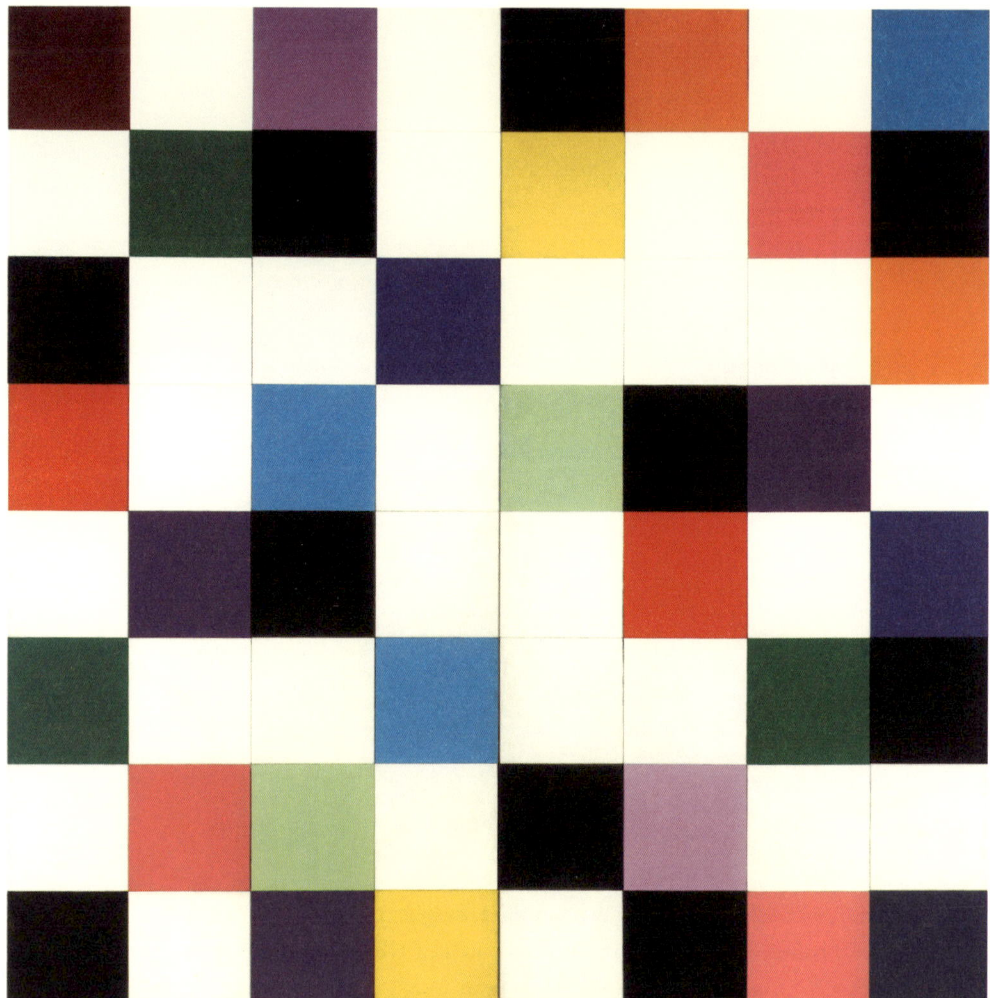

Figure 2.24. Ellsworth Kelly, *Colors for a Large Wall*, 1951. Oil on linen, sixty-four joined panels, 240×240 cm. The Museum of Modern Art, New York. Gift of the artist, 1969. Image courtesy Ellsworth Kelly Studio. © Ellsworth Kelly Foundation.

"depersonalization" in Arp's work, in which, as Seuphor put it in 1953, "nothing is made, but everything found."[95]

This quality of *not being made* likewise became fundamental to Clark when she arrived at the organic line in Rio in 1954. But the implications that follow from Kelly's and Clark's strategies of not making significantly diverge. For Kelly, the enemy was composition, and the various techniques he elaborated to avoid it were materialist insomuch as the physical existence of a canvas edge or backing could short-circuit—and thus dissemble—representation and its implications within a compositional process. The flatness of a source motif was a priority because the painterly plane was flat. That a relief might cast actual shadows attested to its presentational, rather than representational character. And in a work such as *Colors for a Large Wall*, Kelly's intervention pivots on the fact that by obviating the lines of the grid, he sought to deliver the absolute self-referentiality of canvas and edge.[96]

By contrast, Clark had no dispute with composition and in fact harnessed it toward the appearance of the organic line. Like Kelly, she was invested in the actuality of the plane. But her interest was not in the way in which the lines of an implicit grid could be eliminated ("thrown out," as Kelly put it), but in the way in which such lines—while no longer marks—*persisted as such*.[97] Moreover, insomuch as a channel of real space could act in conjunction with the flat marks of a represented line, as occurs in *Quebra da moldura composição no.5*, Clark disallowed the fiction of either the plane's self-evidence or the possibility of entirely casting off representation (fig. 2.25). After all, the organic line can be recognized as a line only once we draw it into pictorial visibility, in essence transforming a literal interval of space into a representation of line as such. Moreover, because the organic line describes not edge, but the space that occurs *alongside* it, the organic line delimits that edge's exterior, rather than interior limit. In so doing, the organic line dissolves the possibility of rendering an edge "self-referential." Rather, an edge must be comprehended in terms of a mutual dependence upon entities understood as positivities (such as the plane), but also negativities (the void of

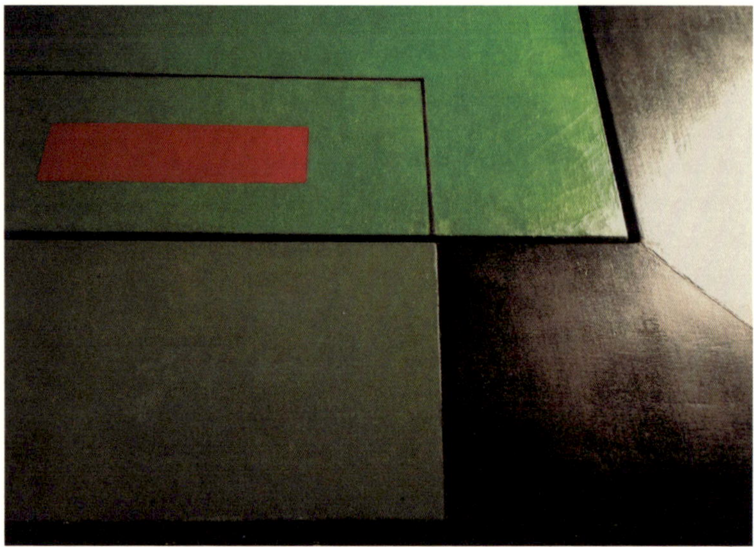

Figure 2.25. Lygia Clark, *Quebra da moldura composição no. 5* (Breaking the frame composition no. 5) (detail). Photo: Irene V. Small. Courtesy of Associação Cultural "O Mundo de Lygia Clark."

space beside it). The organic line is thus both adjunctive and disjunctive in its action. Most importantly, the organic line situates the very appearance of the line — and thus of the mark and of representation more broadly — within the purview of the viewer. It is the viewer, after all, who in recognizing the spatial cavity *as a line*, pulls it into the constellation of art, or more neutrally, meaning-laden visual things. Perhaps this is why Clark, unlike Kelly, was not concerned with the problem of artistic choice. The subject she was most interested in was not the artist, but the viewer.

In his notebooks on art and painting, Leonardo da Vinci posited a surface as the limit or boundary interposed between two contiguous bodies: an "invisible thickness" with no body of its own. "The limits of bodies are not part of these same bodies," he wrote.[98] Over the course of several decades, Duchamp elaborated what we might call a sibling concept of the *inframince*, or infrathin, through a series of examples that inhabit the limits of cognitive distinction: the separative difference between two mass-produced objects cast from the same mold; the melding of vapors; the divergence between an object and that same object a second later.[99] The infrathin is sensorially fugitive. As Thierry de Duve has noted, an "infra-thin separation is working at its maximum when it distinguishes same from same, when it is an indifferent difference, or a differential identity."[100]

Clark's organic line shares with Duchamp's concept of the infrathin a heightened attention to perceptual experience and cognitive distinction: the observer must draw each phenomenon into conceptual legibility against its tendency to disappear from recognition or analysis. Yet the organic line is paradoxically agential in a way the infrathin is not. It is not an "indifferent difference," as de Duve puts it, but a difference that *makes a difference* in both a material and conceptual sense.[101] In this, we might say that the organic line is *extrathick*, rather than infrathin. It dilates space within the terms of material relation, and in so doing compels both mental and phenomenal recognition. Clark's line is therefore akin to Leonardo's conception of surface in its negative and relational ontology. But it transforms his purely abstract notion of an interface into an organic and material paradigm: a thickness that is not only visible, but that exerts pressures on the bodies along which it coincides. The "modulated surfaces" that result from the organic line are thus no longer constituted by the pure positivity of physical matter, but by the spatial thickness of the interval itself. Such surfaces do not resuscitate the old homogeneity of the plane. Rather, as I will elaborate, they mobilize the plane's newly riven, porous character as a network that stretches beyond the work in space, through time, and includes the viewer as a constitutive element of its recursive structure.

In order to investigate this interstitial quality further, I want to suggest how the paradigmatic character of the organic line offers a distinct point of entry into an urform of modernist emptiness and authorial withdrawal: John Cage's *4'33"* of 1952.[102] While Cage's work can be seen to mobilize a certain Duchampian logic of nomination — the difference between unattended silence and silence that is noticed and named — *4'33"* is also structured by intervals that exceed this difference and that trouble the autonomy by which "sounds in themselves," as Cage famously put it, are brought to the fore.[103] Like Kelly, Cage had investments in absenting the self from typical compositional processes. Yet in such absenting, "sounds in themselves" also came to analogize a certain autonomy and freedom of the subject. Pressing on the abstractness of this presumption, I want to argue that the thickness of the organic line allows us to recover a distinct social as well as sonic texture to Cage's work and its critical legacy.

As is well known, Cage's composition, which consists of four minutes and thirty-three seconds of silence, was inspired by Robert Rauschenberg's *White Paintings* of 1951. Those paintings comprise five iterations of stretched canvases in distinct configurations of one, two, three, four, and seven panels (fig. 2.26). Rauschenberg understood the paintings to be statements of gestural and authorial withdrawal.[104] He famously painted the panels with a house painter's roller and authorized friends and assistants to repaint and even remake them in order to maintain their pristine, unblemished appearance.[105] Writing in 1951, he remarked, "It is totally irrelevant that I am making them — Today is their creat[o]r."[106] Cage, who saw the paintings at Black Mountain College and incorporated at least one of them into his *Theater Piece # 1* of 1952, comprehended the works in terms of a negative ethos. In his statement for Rauschenberg's 1953 exhibition, Cage contributed a litany of negatives: "No subject / No image / No taste / No object / No beauty / No message / No talent / No technique (no why) / No idea / No intention / No art / No object / No feeling / No black / No white (no *and*)."[107] In his 1961 book *Silence,* Cage further described the paintings as "airports for lights, shadows, and particles," an interpretation that remains the works' predominant art-historical explanation today.[108]

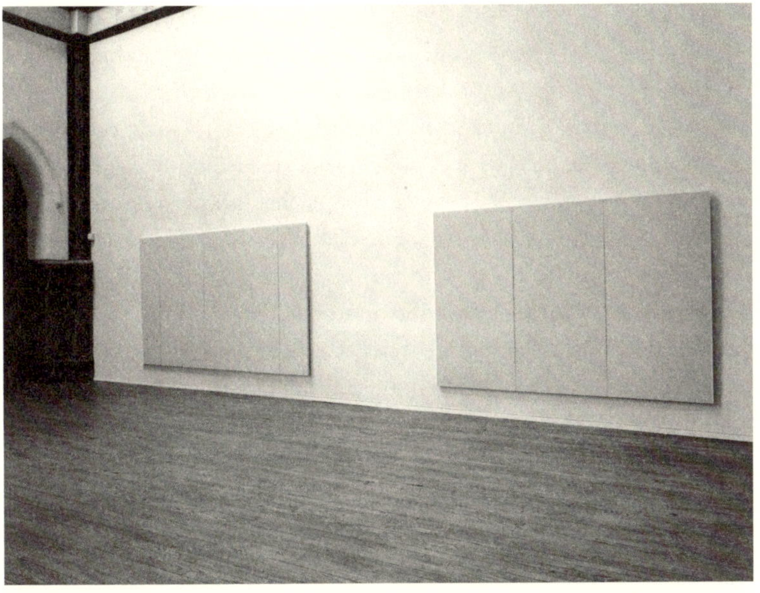

Figure 2.26. Robert Rauschenberg, installation view of *White Painting (Three Panel)* and *White Painting (Seven Panel)*, 1951, in the artist's Lafayette Street Studio, New York. Photo: © Dorothy Zeidman, 1991. Robert Rauschenberg Foundation (VAGA/ARS).

In Cage's reading, the primary zone of pictorial incident occurs across the surface of the Rauschenberg's paintings. These surfaces act as screens or receptacles for otherwise invisible incidents of environmental activity that unfold within the envelope of space that lies between the work and the viewer. Put another way, the shifting contents of the empty room "fill" the negative space of the canvas.[109] In so doing, as Brandon Joseph has argued, "Rauschenberg's pure white monochrome canvases" brought the US critic Clement Greenberg's theory of medium specificity to its logical conclusion while "reprising the historical role played by the monochrome as a degree zero of painting."[110] Joseph and other scholars have traced how Cage's courses on experimental composition at the New School in the late 1950s elaborated the score as an empty field within which to materialize content. As Liz Kotz has observed, the resulting "event score" became an expansive and flexible compositional device for artists associated with Fluxus and Happenings: a textually notated "temporal container" for sound, but also gesture, action, behavior, even the mere act of noticing.[111] Kotz notes that artists were attracted to the "conceptual simplicity" of *4′33″* in part due to the conventional, typewritten nature of its notation, which allowed it to act as a structural device capable of encapsulating an infinite variety of content.[112] In this vein, we might trace a modernist genealogy from the object as material container to the textual and temporal container of the score, the two impulses held together in the blank template of the monochrome.

Yet Cage realized at least three scores for *4′33″* and also divided the piece into three movements, details that trouble the self-evidence of what such a container or template might be.[113] As Kyle Gann has elaborated, Cage's original score was written in conventional musical notation, complete with treble and bass clefs, staff lines, and a time signature of 4/4 (fig. 2.27). A second score in "proportional" notation followed, in which the movements of silence (or tacets, the technical term for a period in which an instrument is not played) were demarcated by vertical lines (fig. 2.28). The durations of these tacets, further, were metrically calibrated to the space of the score's otherwise empty pages. Finally, in a third typewritten score, the three movements were notated by roman numerals and the word "TACET," followed by a verbal description that indicated that although initially composed of three set durations, the piece could be performed for "any length of time" (fig. 2.29).[114]

While several scholars have noted that the lines of Cage's second, most "visual" score mimic the panel edges of Rauschenberg's paintings, they have largely maintained the basic premise of Cage's description. In Joseph's gloss: "The score acts just as one of Rauschenberg's *White Paintings*; the lights, shadows and particles falling on it become analogues of the environmental sounds occurring within the piece when 'performed.'"[115] Yet if we attend to the organic lines *between* the panels of Rauschenberg's paintings, we

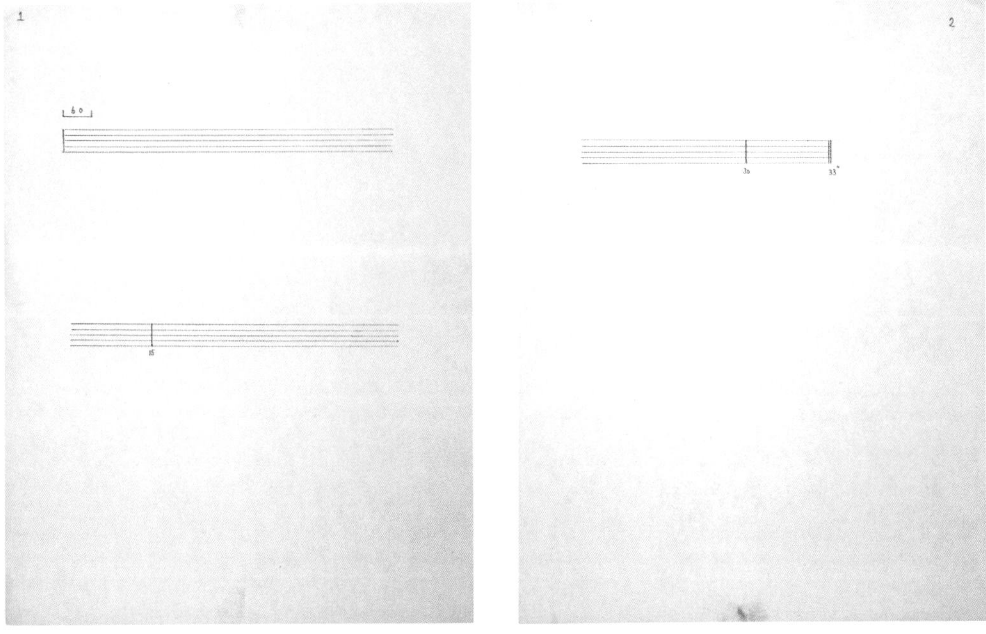

Figure 2.27. David Tudor, John Cage, *4'33"*,
1952. Pencil on paper, 27.9×21.6 cm.
© J. Paul Getty Trust, Getty Research Institute,
Los Angeles (980039).

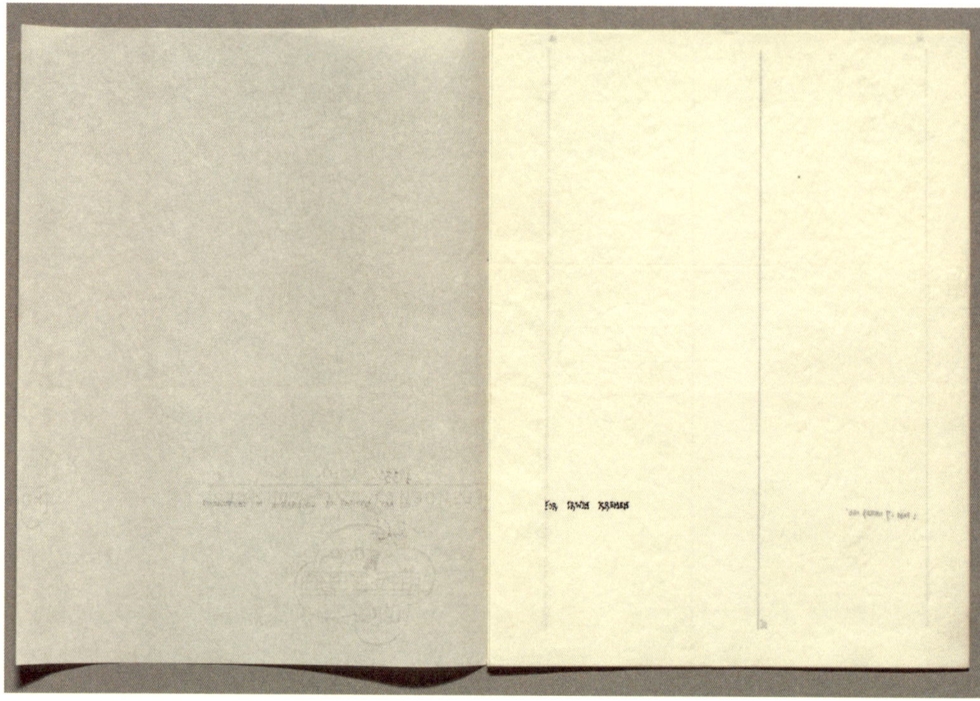

Figure 2.28. John Cage, *4'33"* (in proportional notation), 1952/1953. Ink on paper, page (each): 27.9 × 21.6 cm; sheet (each, unfolded): 27.9 × 43.1 cm. Acquired through the generosity of Henry Kravis in honor of Marie-Josée Kravis. Digital image © The Museum of Modern Art / Licensed by SCALA / Art Resource, NY. John Cage © 1960 by Henmar Press Inc. Permission of C. F. Peters Corporation. All rights reserved.

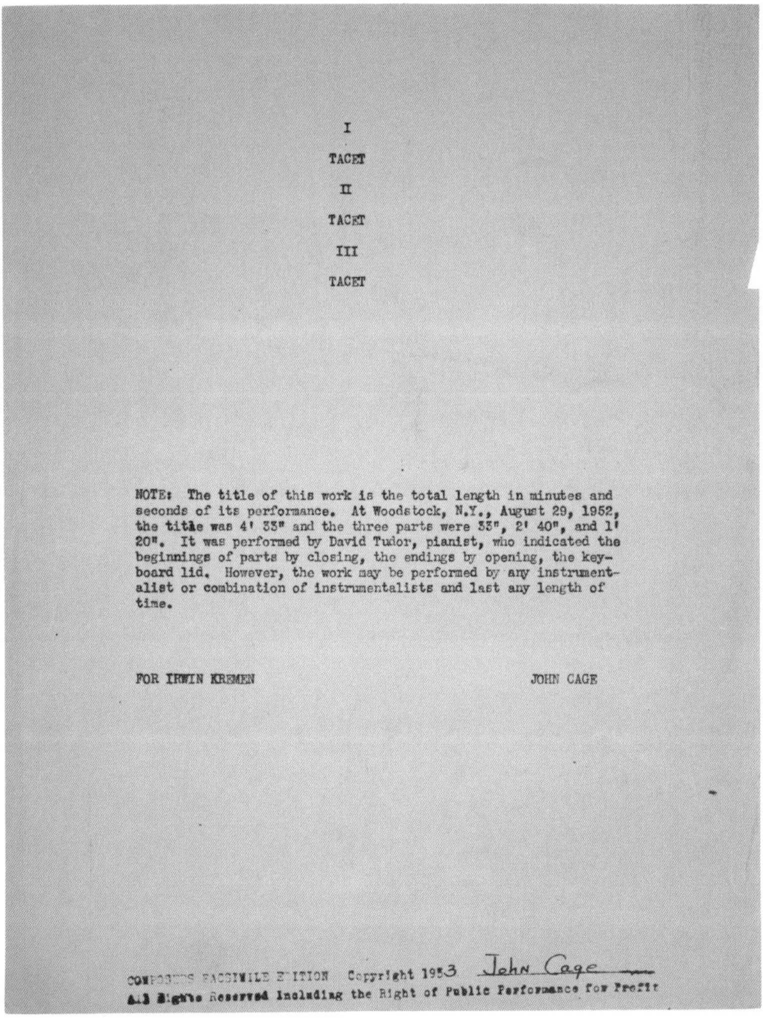

I

TACET

II

TACET

III

TACET

NOTE: The title of this work is the total length in minutes and
seconds of its performance. At Woodstock, N.Y., August 29, 1952,
the title was 4' 33" and the three parts were 33", 2' 40", and 1'
20". It was performed by David Tudor, pianist, who indicated the
beginnings of parts by closing, the endings by opening, the key-
board lid. However, the work may be performed by any instrument-
alist or combination of instrumentalists and last any length of
time.

FOR IRWIN KREMEN   JOHN CAGE

Figure 2.29. John Cage, *4'33"* (For Irwin Kremen).
Pencil on paper, 27.9 × 21.6 cm. Image: J. Paul
Getty Trust, Getty Research Institute, Los Angeles
(980039).

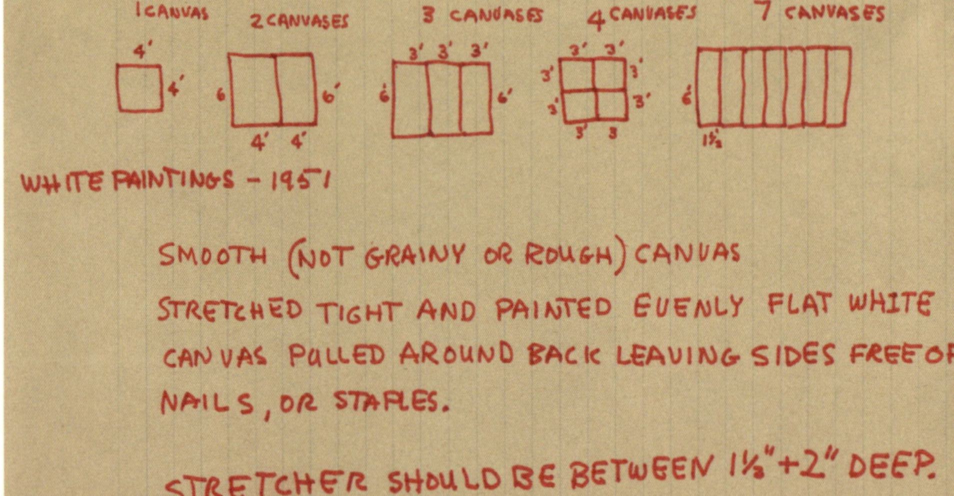

Figure 2.30. Robert Rauschenberg and Billy Klüver, instructions for fabrication of *White Paintings* (1951), 1965. Felt-tip pen on lined paper stapled and glued to board 20.6 × 37.1 cm. Gift of the Gilbert B. and Lisa Silverman Instruction Drawing Collection, Detroit. Robert Rausuchenberg Foundation. © 2023 Robert Rauschenberg Foundation / Licensed by VAGA at Artists Rights Society (ARS), NY.

are faced with a cavity or void that resists recuperation into such content: a negative space that *remains* negative, but structures the possibility of allowing the other negative space — that of the paintings — to be comprehended as full. Instead of a principle of inversion, in other words, we are faced with a triadic relation in which content and form never fully coincide.

Attending to these unacknowledged organic lines likewise calls our attention to the dual character of edge. Viewed from the *internal* limits of their edges, Rauschenberg's paintings may indeed represent a terminal case in the logic of medium specificity. But viewed from their *external* limits — those margins that link panels together within a given work and across the series as a whole — the paintings reveal a sequential, modular structure, a one-unit panel of 48 by 48 inches giving rise to a diptych of 72 by 48 inches, then a triptych of 72 by 36 inches, a four-panel piece of 72 by 72 inches (each square 36 by 36 inches), and finally a seven-panel piece of 72 by 18 inches (fig. 2.30).[116] In short, far from embodying the pure white degree zero of a single monochrome, the series constitutes a performance of motif and variation, wherein the motif is a measurement or span that gives rise to myriad configurations of what *configuring* whiteness, or blankness, or emptiness, might be.

What might 4′33″ look — *or sound* — like from the perspective of these unacknowledged organic lines? Initially, Cage used chance methods to peg the work's three movements at 30″, 2′23″, and 1′40″.[117] He subsequently shifted the proportions of the movements to 33″, 2′40″ and 1′20″, maintaining the total time at 4′33″. Performing the work entails signaling these movements in some fashion, for example, by closing the lid of the piano to begin a movement of silence and opening it to indicate that movement's end. This is how David Tudor performed the work at its first appearance in 1952, and subsequent performances have often emulated this precedent.

Two logical consequences follow that to my knowledge have strangely escaped commentary. First, the performative acknowledgment of the commencement and conclusion of each movement means that the piece's total performance time is, in fact, not coincident with its title. Rather, the piece exceeds itself by a temporal factor coincident with the span of this internal acknowledgment, a variability clocked to the work's real-time embodiment. Content and form are thus fundamentally *misregistered*, rather than aligned. Second, the piece's auditory soundscape does not emerge simply from the ambient noise flushed to cognition by the work's durational frame: "sounds in themselves," as it were, analogous to the environmental incidents rendered visible on Rauschenberg's white surfaces. Rather, this soundscape is also inflected by the performative designation of each movement, the assertion of which constitutes a distinct auditory and visual figuration in and of itself. (Imagine the eventlike nature of opening and closing a piano.) Thus, the noise of silence exists in a ratio with the *noise of notation*, and the work's temporal realization is always in excess of that same work as it is realized *in its actual time* (fig. 2.31).

These dual excesses correspond to a sonic-structural form of the unacknowledged organic lines that punctuate Cage's work. But here, we can likewise locate the sonic-structural and ultimately social forms that the work intentionally forgets, if not outright suppresses. I refer here to commercial music and the improvisatory ethos of jazz, both of which Cage vigorously disavowed. As scholars have noted, *4'33"* was anticipated by a 1948 proposal by Cage for a three- or four-and-a-half-minute piece of silence he planned to sell to the Muzak company, timed to its conventions for mass-produced sonic commodities.[118] As Douglas Kahn puts it, the proposed *Silent Prayer* would be a kind of intermission or silencing of this "canned" music, which was designed to grease the wheels of consumption and labor through pleasant background noise.[119] The image conjured by such "canned" music — of a sealed and standardized container — helps elucidate all that *4'33"* is not. While strikingly close in duration to its canned cousin, *4'33"* entails the stubborn temporal snag of an extra three seconds, derailing any attempt to slot the piece within commercial protocols of substitution and equivalence.

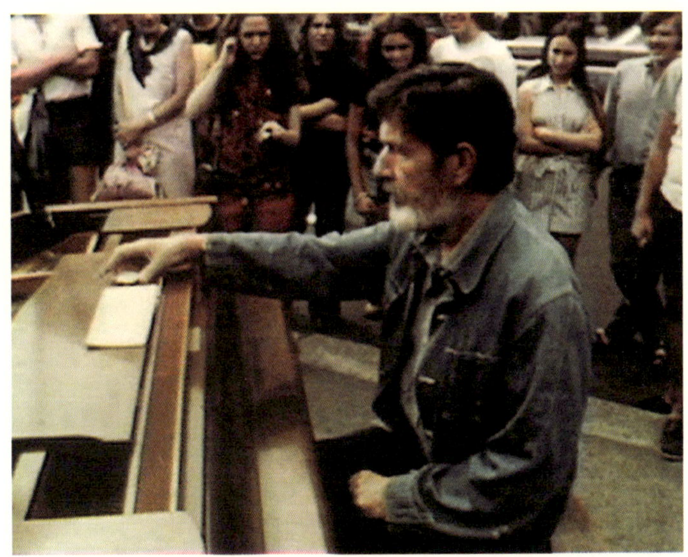

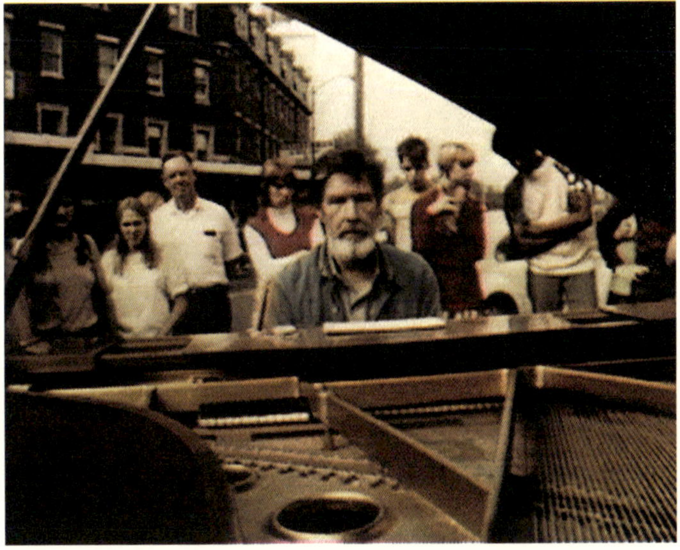

Figure 2.31. John Cage performing *4'33"* (1952), from *Tribute to John Cage* by Nam June Paik, 1973. Courtesy of the Estate of Nam June Paik and Electronic Arts Intermix (EAI), New York.

Cage's use of indeterminacy to establish the piece's three internal movements, as well as his decision to stage the work within the conventions of the concert hall involving a stage, performer, and audience, likewise align *4′33″* with the specific legacy of classical music in the West.[120] In this sense, orchestrated chance, intentional composition structure, and embodied reception are all fundamental to the work's sonic landscape of unintended sound.

Paradoxically, these same three qualities also coincide with the core characteristics of jazz, which Cage repeatedly dismissed as derivative of "serious music."[121] As the trombonist and music theorist George Lewis has observed, jazz, and specifically the radical bebop styles that emerged in the 1940s (of which Cage was certainly aware), remain a willful blind spot in both contemporaneous narratives and the historiography of American experimental music.[122] Cage, for example, differentiated his own use of indeterminacy from improvisation: "Improvisation is generally playing what you know," he opined, "it doesn't lead you into a new experience."[123] Contra Cage, one can define the practice of improvisation as the mobilization of preexisting elements — such as a bebop "head" drawn from popular music — for the purposes of "new experience" (fig. 2.32).[124]

Moreover, *4′33″* internalizes an improvisatory structure at the elemental level of temporal demarcation. We will remember that Rauschenberg's *White Paintings* enact a play of motif and variation wherein an opening "phrase" of 48 inches gives rise to a series of planar iterations, each of which repeats a prior unit of measurement while generating another in length or width. Cage surely recognized the analogy between spatial and temporal phrasing, and his decision to peg the movements of *4′33″* to aleatory durations was perhaps a way of "correcting" Rauschenberg's use of repetition and variation from a framework of improvisation to one of indeterminacy. Nevertheless, by translating the visual effect of the *White Paintings*' side-by-side panel structure into compositional lines in his second score, Cage laid bare the fact that the formal structuring of the piece's unintentional sound depends upon the

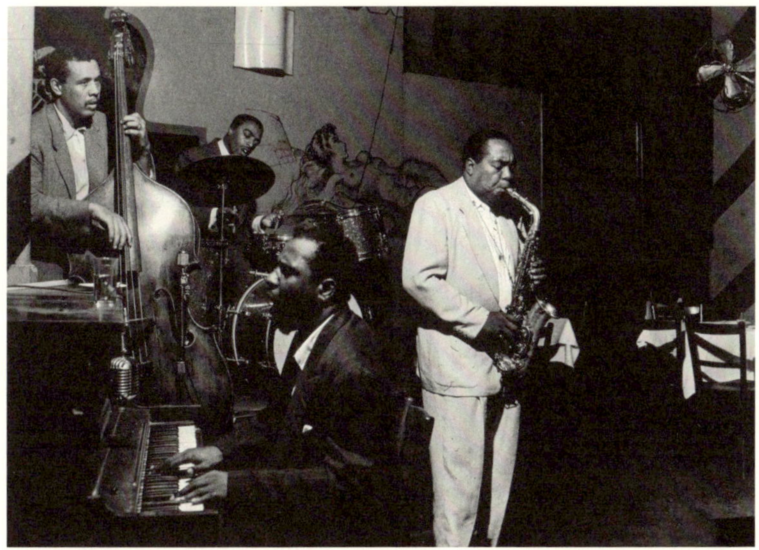

Figure 2.32. Bassist Charles Mingus (1922–1979), drummer Roy Haynes (1925–), pianist Thelonious Monk (1917–1982), and saxophonist Charlie Parker (1920–1955) perform at the Open Door, New York, New York, September 13, 1953. Photo: Bob Parent/Getty Images. Hulton Archive.

compositional convention of the musical movement and its repetition. Cage's drawn lines signal the written and graphic notation of this convention. And at a temporal level, they correspond to each movement's internal demarcations. But within their *external* temporal demarcations — the piece's sonic organic line — the performer *improvises notation as such* through a series of embodied, real-time actions: opening and closing a piano lid, preparing the conductor's baton, lifting up an instrument, setting a timer, turning a page of the score, and so on. Improvisation as a practice of repetition and variation thus emerges as an unwitting by-product of the score.

As Lewis and other scholars remind us, written notation is one of the key ways in which practitioners of the "Eurological" musical tradition such as Cage dismissed musical forms embedded in distinct sociocultural histories. The discounting of bebop is an attenuated instance of this lacuna, because its harmonic and rhythmic innovations demonstrate an acute reflexivity to popular and experimental jazz forms alike.[125] Moreover, bebop emerged during the same period from 1942 to 1944 in which the American Federation of Musicians (AFM) instituted a ban on recordings in an effort to protect musicians' income as live performers.[126] Thus, for a precise interval, it was a form of highly sophisticated, embodied improvisation that elided both notation *and* recording. Moreover, it was a form premised on the transformation of commercial musical fragments into something entirely defamiliarized, or to (re)use Cage's term, "new." Improvisation was thus also a means of resisting commodity capture.[127] In his argument that Cage's ethos of silence was also *silencing*, Kahn notes that the composer's 1948 *Silent Prayer* can be understood as an aesthetic riposte to a second AFM ban from 1947 to 1948. As Cage mused, "I allowed myself to indulge in the fantasy of how normalizing the effect might have been had [James C. Petrillo, the president of the AFM] had the power, and exerted it, to ban not only recordings, but radio, television, the newspapers, and Hollywood."[128] Kahn argues that Cage imagined that this "normalizing effect " would result in greater attention to the living, present-time qualities of sound. Yet as his dismissal of jazz indicates, Cage admitted only certain forms of liveness into his spectrum of interest.

On several occasions, Cage aligned his embrace of chance strategies and indeterminacy with anarchist inclinations.[129] Yet his circumvention of the political as a sphere of action as well as a factor in his own compositional affinities amounts to a "normalization" of another order. As the dancer and choreographer Yvonne Rainer observed of Cagean aesthetics, chance strategies do not simply signal an abstract concept of freedom; they are also used "to equalize and suppress hierarchical differentiations of meaning."[130] To this end, excavating the organic line of *4′33″* reveals how its temporal and auditory excesses map onto the suppressed historical form of another experimental music (bebop), but also the "hierarchical differentiations" (condensed in the symbolic form of the score) that facilitated this suppression at one and the same time.

After all, both the Cagean circuit and that of bebop jazz were racially coded forms of experimental music, but only the former has been consistently described as "experimental," while only the latter has been marked as racially specific. The fundamental asymmetry that structures this distinction compels the recognition that abstract freedom is the purview only of abstract subjects. By contrast, embodied subjects — which is to say, all of us — inhabit the world in highly divergent ways. These manners of inhabitation correspond to social inscriptions that mutually reinforce and mediate against the legibility of such terms as agency, intentionality, and experimentation. When Clark returned from Paris to Rio in 1952, for instance, she was described in the press as "pretty and intelligent, with far too elegant a manner for a painter."[131] Presumptively, for this critic, "painter" and "woman" were still incommensurate terms. As this anecdote indicates, to withdraw authorship assuming the self-evidence and autonomy of the author is thus willfully to remain within a purely theoretical realm.

The fallout from the tension between abstract and embodied conceptions of authorship was amply evident in 1975, when African American composer and self-proclaimed "gay guerilla" Julius Eastman radically queered his performance of Cage's *Song Books* (1970), much to the older composer's outrage.[132] The *Song Books* consisted of ninety solos "relevant or irrelevant to the subject: We connect [Erik] Satie with [Henry] Thoreau," to be "used" by any number of performers in any order.[133] As one of four musicians from the S.E.M. ensemble realizing the concert, Eastman chose to perform *Solo for Voice 8*, designated as "irrelevant" to the theme, "theatrical" in character, and whose main instruction was to "perform a disciplined action" (fig. 2.33).[134] Eastman's interpretation involved bringing two

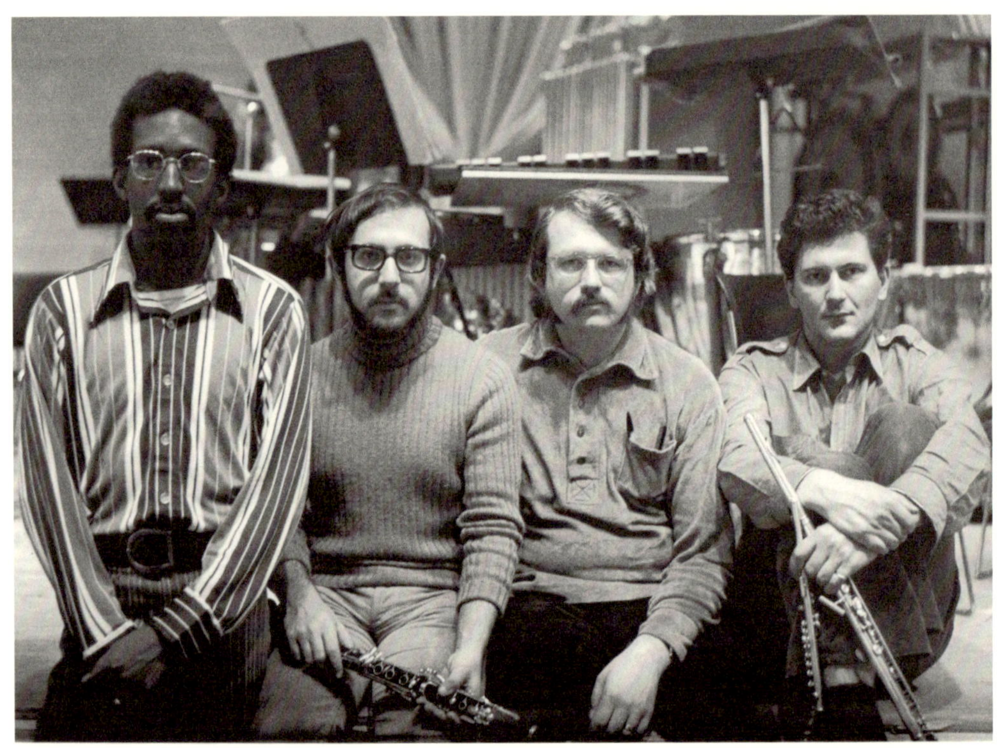

Figure 2.33. S.E.M. Ensemble: Julius Eastman, Roberto Laneri, Jan Williams, and Petr Kotik, seated at edge of stage, 1971–72. Photo: Jim Tuttle. © Jim Tuttle. All rights reserved 2023/Bridgeman Images.

assistants to the stage—a white man (Eastman's boyfriend) and a Black woman (erroneously described in some accounts as his sister). Eastman then proceeded to deliver a burlesque lecture in the guise of an imaginary Professor Padu that advocated replacing the existing and normative "system of love" (the "In-and-Out-System") with a new "Sideways-and-Sensitive System." In the guise of Professor Padu, Eastman demonstrated his new method by leisurely undressing his two racially distinct "specimens," as he called them, rapturously drawing attention to their body parts and capacities to stroke, kiss, elongate, rise, embrace, encompass, as well as be receptors of the same.[135]

In a much-reported lecture the following day, Cage accused Eastman of numerous faults and misrepresentations of his work: of using three performers in a solo; of being "constricted" in his ego against the desired "flow" of Zen; of being "closed in on the subject of homosexuality"; of not understanding "discipline."[136] Cage began his lecture with an anecdote previously relayed in a 1966 lecture, "How to Improve the World: You Will Only Make Matters Worse." The "touching story," as Cage termed it, concerned his visit to an aging anarchist who had recently adopted "two Negro children." After devoting his life to anarchy, Cage recounted, the man was forced to make a rule: "No jumping up and down on the beds."[137] Without commenting on the strident paternalism, racism, and philosophical contradiction of the story and its retelling, Cage extracted the following lesson: "Now, the misinterpretation of [Eastman's performance] consists in, 'If anything goes, I can do anything I want!' And that's precisely the wrong interpretation."[138]

According to one of Eastman's friends, the younger composer was shaken by Cage's negative reaction and insisted that the question of sex had to be addressed: "I had to bring him out!" he recalls Eastman exclaiming.[139] Another friend noted that a year later, Eastman deadpanned, "Well, it says 'perform a disciplined act,' so I gave this lecture on how to make love. What could be more disciplined?"[140] This pithy comment compels us to probe the antagonisms and willed misinterpretations that permeated compositional discourses of demarcation, interpretation, and freedom in these years. Significantly, the piece Eastman performed, *Solo for Voice 8*, is also known as *0'00" (4'33" No. 2)*, in reference to the 1962 piece Cage dedicated to the Japanese composer Toshi Ichiyanagi and his then wife, the artist Yoko Ono. As Ono recounted, while she greatly respected Cage, the two had several disagreements about composition when they toured Japan with Ichiyanagi in 1962. Ono recalled asking why *4'33"* had to have a specific time, to which Cage replied that Western music required a frame. (This deflection is puzzling, since Cage frequently invoked Asian philosophies and texts such as the *I Ching* and Zen.)[141] Ono recounts that Cage created *0'00" (4'33" No. 2)* in recognition of their exchange.[142]

Cage's homage to Ono's dispute in *0'00" (4'33" No. 2)* is fascinating. One could argue that by asking the performer to "perform a disciplined action" within an undefined duration, the score removes the piece's *temporal* frame in order to internalize *framing as content*, wherein the performer's actions delineate a protocol or convention that becomes visible over time. Significantly, Cage first performed the piece by simply notating his score for the work with microphones attached to instruments such as his pen. Here, the noise of notation that arises from within the unacknowledged organic lines of *4'33"* becomes the sonic event of "discipline" itself. Cage opined in his 1975 response to Eastman that the value of discipline is to "dissolve the boundaries of the ego" so as to liberate it from its "likes and dislikes."[143] By making queer desire and racial difference explicit and performative, Eastman clearly transgressed this concept of "discipline" while refusing its purported aim of authorial withdrawal. Instead, Eastman proposed that "discipline" involves the theatrical mobilization of an expository convention — the lecture — toward what spectacularly conforms to as well as exceeds convention: the intersubjective erotics of making love. Thus, in his interpretation of *Solo for Voice 8 (0'00" [4'33" No. 2])*, he, too, internalized framing as content, but a content that pivots on its comic *inability* to contain yet another content: the proliferating, "sideways-and-sensitive" possibilities of human desire.

To extend this lateral impulse in a plagiotropic vein, we might observe that while Duchamp has long been linked to Cage through an "aesthetics of indifference" that foregrounded nomination and authorial withdrawal, the older artist continued to make works long past his supposed retirement from art.[144] Many of these works were explicitly erotic, as in the four cast bronzes Duchamp made in the early 1950s in which the irregular cleavages and orifices of the female body are extruded as abstract forms. While the infrathin designates an "indifferent difference" all but imperceptible to human sensation, these objects materialize the thick voids and convergences of bodily encounter: "difference" run amuck in organicity, corporeality, desire.[145]

In 1980, when Eastman was invited to present a program of his own compositions at Northwestern University, he chose to perform several works from his *Nigger Series* (1978–79), despite complaints from students regarding the offensiveness of the works' titles (fig. 2.34). In his introduction to the concert, Eastman explained that his use of the term was to refer to "that thing which is fundamental, that person or thing that attains to a basicness, a fundamentalness, and eschews that thing which is superficial." He further linked the foundation of American capitalism with the labor of the "first and great nigger, the field niggers."[146] Eastman's "basicness," here, emerges in stark contradistinction to Cage's dissolution of the ego's boundaries. Against the latter's abstraction and disembodiment, Eastman offers the inescapable fact of US economic and political history as it is sedimented upon the racialized body. In titling pieces such as *Crazy Nigger*, *Evil Nigger*, and *Nigger Faggot*, moreover, Eastman gave names to the far more slippery opprobrium directed his way due to his open embrace of his racial and sexual identity. The titles also act as injunctions: unlike the unmarked authorship presumed (but socially inhabited) by Cagean

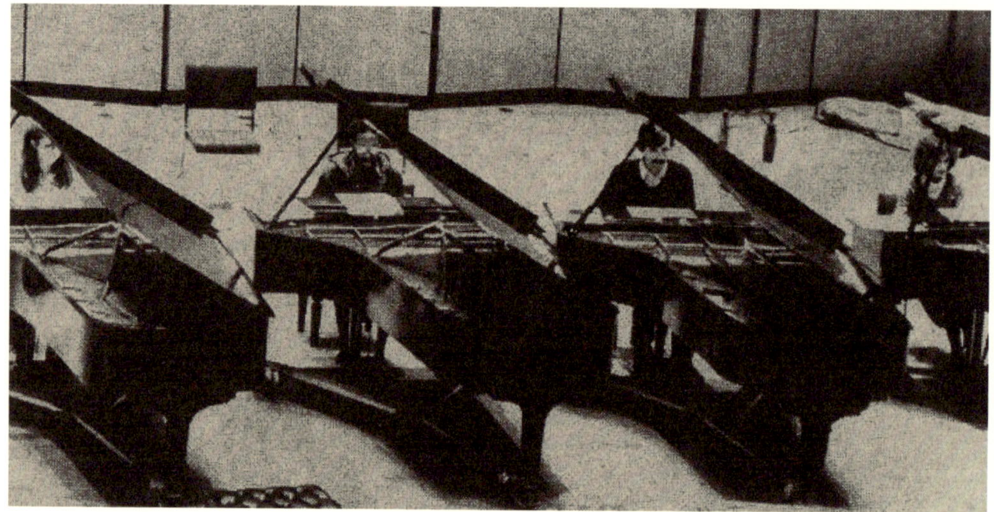

Figure 2.34. Julius Eastman with Patricia Martin, Frank Ferko, and Janet Kattas in performance at Northwestern University, 1980. From Julius Eastman *Nigger Series*, 1978–79. Photo: Lee Urban.

notation, enunciating Eastman's titles compels an acknowledgment of a given speaker's social positionality vis-à-vis the history of race, sexuality, and the multiple circuits of experimental music.

But in his introduction to his 1980 concert, Eastman did not speak only about the provocative character of his titles. He also described these compositions as an attempt to create "organic form." As he explained, "the third part of any part has to contain all the information of the first two parts, and then go from there.... There's an attempt to make every section contain all the information of the previous sections, or else, taking out information at a gradual and logical rate."[147] In this sense, "organic form" refers to the iterative absorption, growth (or reduction), and continuity between parts sustained across the composition as a whole. Within the tradition of classical Western music, we can locate this organic impulse in Romantic philosophies that found expression in such techniques as compositional variations, tonal progressions, and melodic-rhythmic motifs developed, differentiated, and recalled over the course of a given piece. Eastman's use of the term "information" acknowledges the outer edges of this tradition in contemporary musical movements that rejected Romantic emotionalism and narrativity by valuing all tones equally (as in serialism) or by limiting their range in order to explore their intensity through repetition (as in minimalism).[148]

But the Black tradition of music also has a relation to organicism that manifests through what Amiri Baraka influentially called "the changing same," a understanding of sociality and cultural expression in which disruption is a means of continuity.[149] Such vitalism is expressed from micro to macro in formal qualities such as polyrhythm and syncopation, performative techniques such as call and response and improvisation, and broader processes of adaptation, survivance, and innovation (Baraka gives the example of Afro-Christian hybridity). In this sense, Eastman's "organic form" also describes how dyadic structures are transmuted into overlapping triadic relations through iteration. In so doing, a principle of repetition, as James Snead has written of Black culture, becomes the vehicle of transformation.[150]

Considering these multiple lineages of organicism, it is notable that Eastman used clock time for his organic compositions, an intentional citation of Cagean music and its outgrowths. *Evil Nigger*, for instance, is set to 21 minutes and 5 seconds and internally divided by time markers, though, importantly, not with movement breaks (fig. 2.35).[151] Thus, unlike either *4'33"* (which exceeds its own time) or *0'00" (4'33" No. 2)* (which circumvents any specific time), *Evil Nigger* proposes sequential sections of exact clock time, even as the score invites elements of improvisation and variation within (and sometimes across) their temporal bounds. Performers might play a given note at different octaves, for instance, or vary the intensity and repetition of a musical pattern within a given duration. Moreover, Eastman doubled, quadrupled, and deliriously

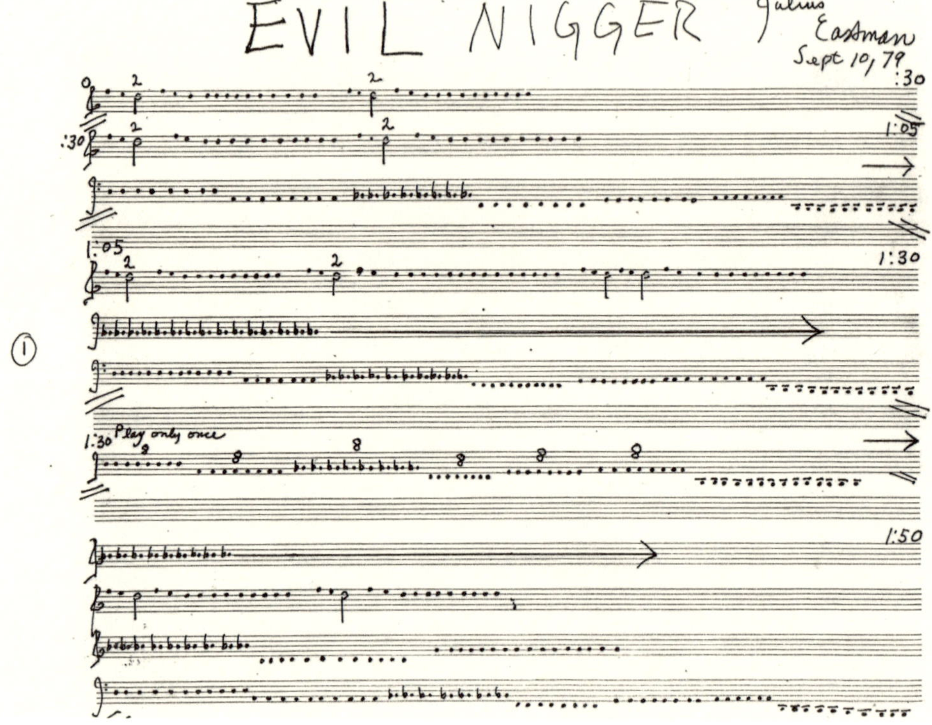

Figure 2.35. Julius Eastman, page 1 of score for *Evil Nigger*, 1979. © 2018 by Music Sales Corporation and Eastman Music Publishing Company. All rights administered by Music Sales Corporation. International Copyright secured. All rights reserved. Used by permission.

multiplied identical instruments in his organic compositions. *Evil Nigger* is typically staged for four pianos, but other compositions call for seven trumpets, eight metronomes, ten cellos, and so on. As Malik Gaines has observed, there is "something very homosexual about using 'multiple instruments of the same kind,'" because their proliferation acts as a surrogate for the similitude of bodies.[152] This multiplication catalyzes a specific aural quality, as well, since every situated instrument has a unique timbre and frequency, while identical notes, even if played in unison, are always slightly discrepant in time. As Gaines notes, Eastman's compositions result in sonic landscapes in which "visual cues and subtle spatial arrangements separate layers of sound, setting off differences within a thick field of sameness."[153]

Eastman differentiated clock time and sonic, social texture in other ways, as well. At four temporally designated points in his 1980 rendition of *Evil Nigger*, he cued all performers to play a single phrase in unison by calling out "1 2 3 4," an audible enunciation of coordinated gathering wholly antithetical to the conventions of Western musical notation. Significantly (or not, we cannot know), the first of these callouts occurs at 2'40", which is also the duration of the middle and longest movement of Cage's *4'33"*. This is to say, Eastman articulated what I have called the noise of notation, now in a manner specifically coded to Black music, at precisely a time stamp that registers Cage's reinscription of the European classical tradition as a structuring constraint. If, as I have argued, we should understand *4'33"* not as three movements that tally up to the work's eponymous time, but three movements punctuated by unacknowledged sonic organic lines that together *exceed* this putative temporal container, we can comprehend Eastman's time-stamped callouts as materializing and socially marking this relation of liminality. Thus, even as Eastman asserted temporal demarcation as an external frame, he opened up lateral interstices *within* his composition, wherein repetition, variation, and socially coded performative conventions recursively generate difference from the same. Rather than a withdrawal of authorship, such "sideways-and-sensitive" sonic relations emerge *on the side of* composition as a function of real-time realization and reception. In the process, they explode the notion of "sounds in themselves" and the fiction of the autonomous subject they analogize.

———

The word *cleave* has two seemingly opposed significations: to *cleave to* something, meaning to cling or adhere; and to *cleave from* something, meaning to split or separate. Several bodily descriptions retain both connotations: we speak of a cleft palate, the cleavage of breasts, or a cloven hoof, in each case designating a liminal space held together and apart through division. In a series of charcoal drawings made between 1948 and 1951, Clark returned again and again to depict her two young sons, Eduardo and Álvaro, as if amid such a cleaving (figs. 2.36–42).[154] Heads touching, they share or intermingle ears, the shirt collar of one doubling as his brother's shoulder. Twinned in profile, their left arms drape over a single rectangular plane; seen from behind, they draw close in a whisper. Paired sets of eyes tilt up or down as if the paper had been pressed together and unfolded, one side imprinting itself on the other. Yet even as the boys conjoin within the compressed space of the page, the drawings are studies in difference. One boy's mouth gapes open; another turns away ever so slightly, compelling a rearticulation around the ear. Their eyes shift in focus, suggesting a dispersal rather than fusion of attention. Rather than replication, they model iterative difference rendered visible through similarity.

In her work on siblings, the psychoanalyst Juliet Mitchell contrasts the traditional privileging of vertical relations in the Oedipus complex and its corresponding "law of the father" with the lateral relations established by what she calls the "law of the mother." The "law of the mother," she writes, "introduces seriality—one, two, three, four siblings, playmates, school friends…tinker, tailor,

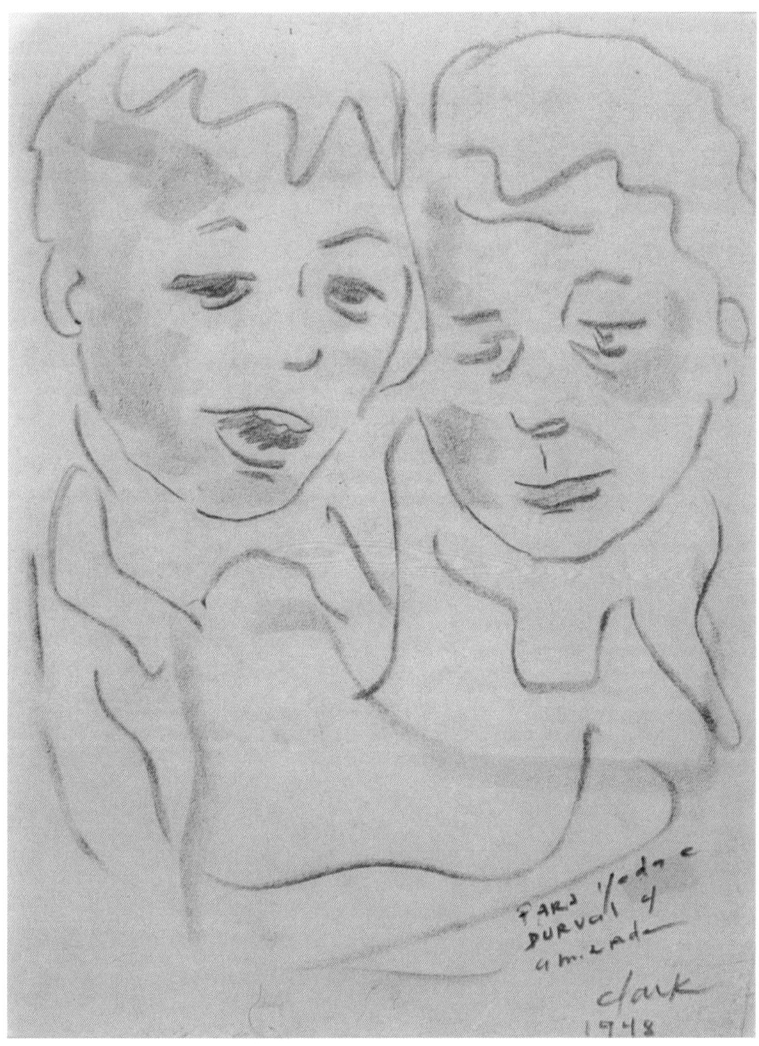

Figure 2.36. Lygia Clark, *Família* (Family), 1948.
Photo: Marcelo Ribeiro Alvares Corrêa. Courtesy
of Associação Cultural "O Mundo de Lygia Clark."

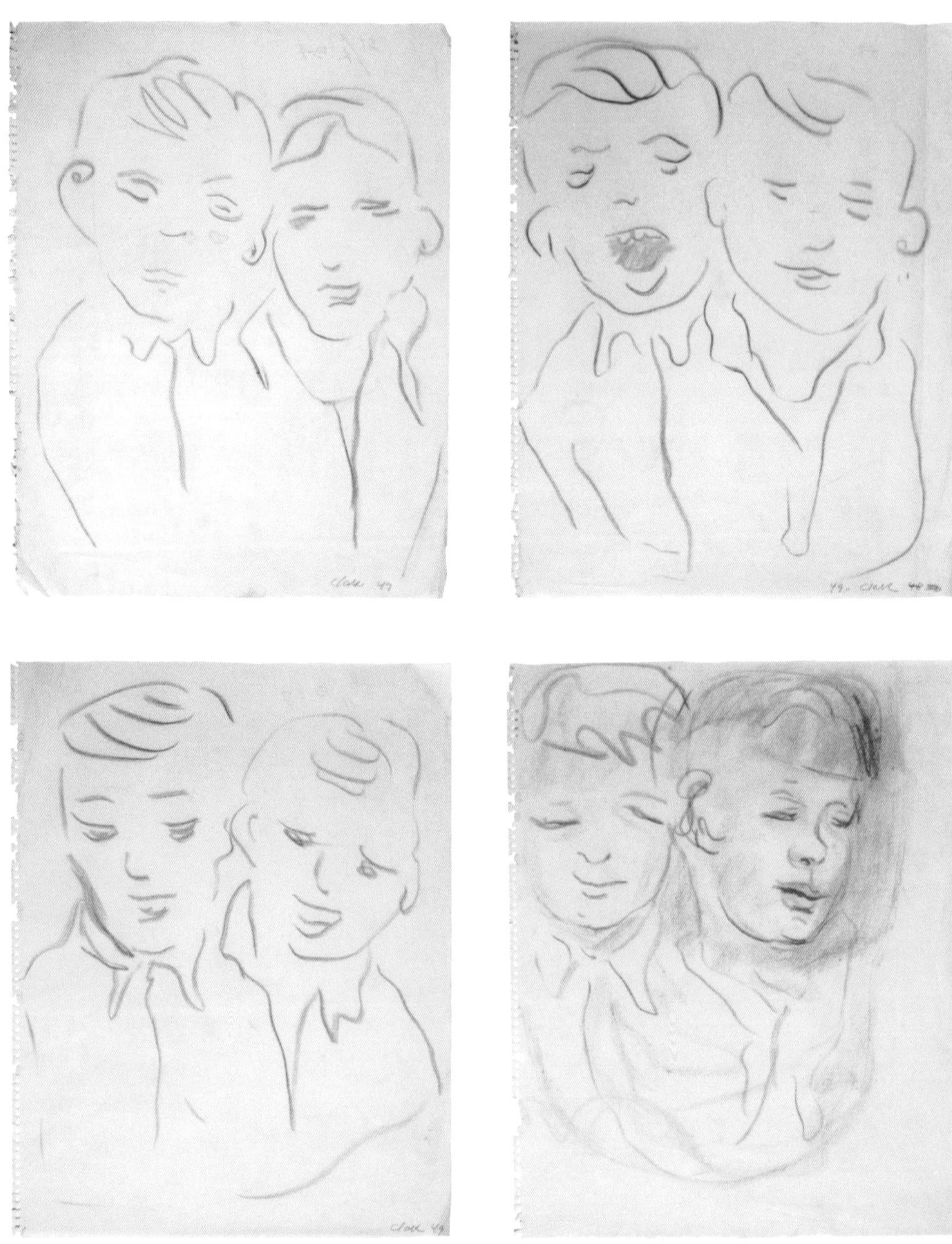

Figures 2.37–40. Lygia Clark, *Família* (Family), 1949. Photos: Marcelo Ribeiro Alvares Corrêa. Courtesy of Associação Cultural "O Mundo de Lygia Clark."

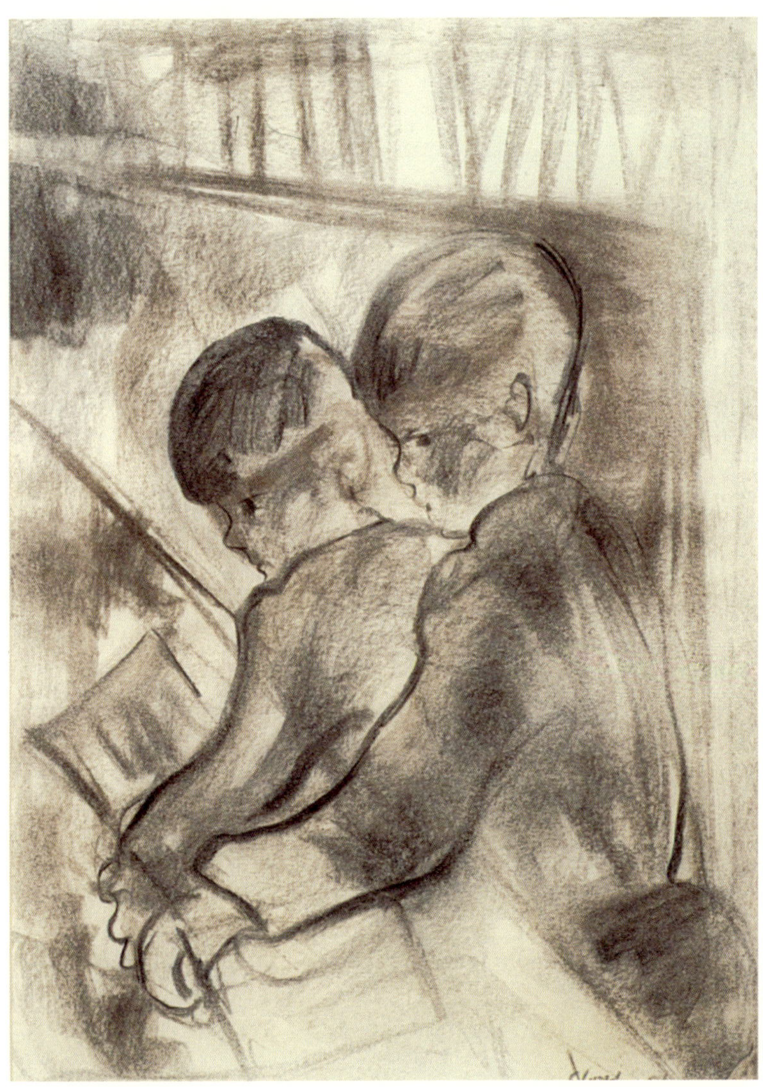

Figure 2.41. Lygia Clark, *Família* (Family), 1951. Photo: Marcelo Ribeiro Alvares Corrêa. Courtesy of Associação Cultural "O Mundo de Lygia Clark."

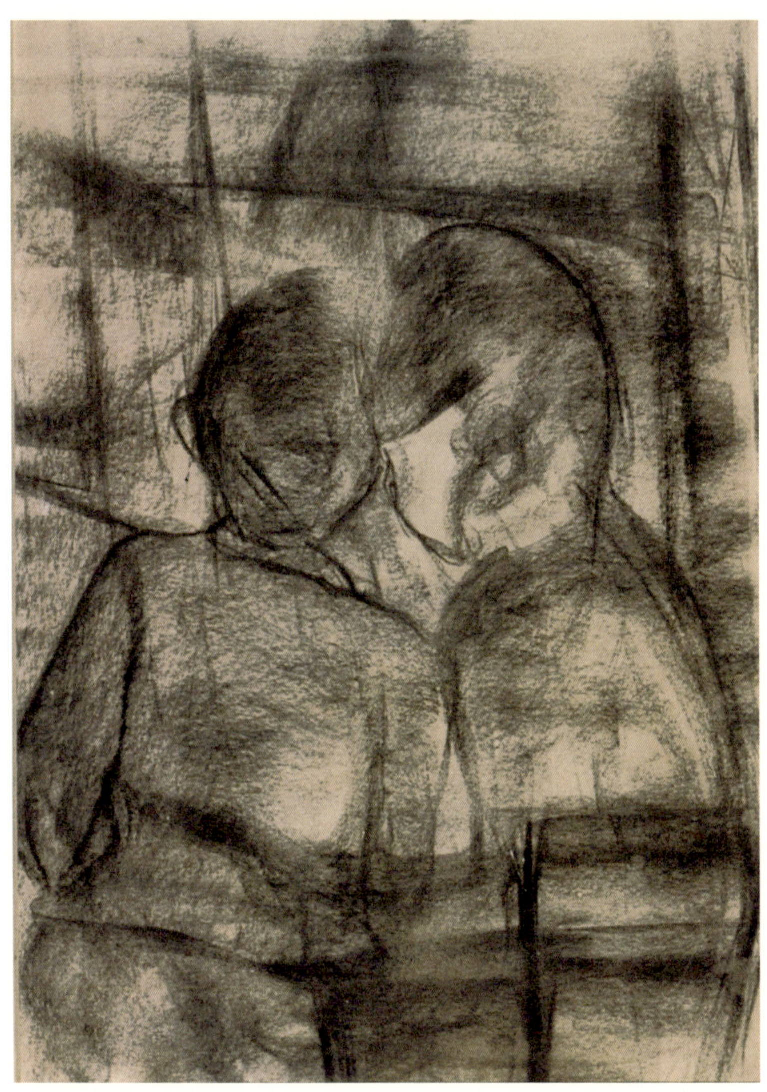

Figure 2.42. Lygia Clark, *Família* (Family), 1951. Photo: Marcelo Ribeiro Alvares Corrêa. Courtesy of Associação Cultural "O Mundo de Lygia Clark."

soldier, sailor."[155] Through such differentiation, the child is forced to contend with a primal displacement: the singular position it once occupied is taken by a "self-same other," whom it must not kill, but love as if itself.[156] This "threat of sameness" can produce a phobic assertion of difference, as in the dominating impulse of racism or sexism.[157] Yet because siblings and sibling types are lateral and serial, rather than vertical and dichotomous, their psychic relations are not formed within a paradigm of sexual difference (that is, having or not having a phallus or a womb). Rather, as Mitchell argues, their relations *engender* gender as a spectrum in which one finds "likeness in unlikeness, unlikeness in likeness."[158] Professor Padu himself might have observed that Eastman's Blackness and queerness linked him equally, though differently, to both "specimens" that he brought on stage in his rendition of Cage's *0'00" (4'33" No. 2)*. In short, the sibling is a "boundary object," as literary theorist Stefani Engelstein puts it, that "reveals the openness of the subject to its own variants."[159] Cage clearly interpreted Eastman's provocation as an Oedipal aggression, and this is not surprising, considering that a vertical relationship of generational inheritance and antagonism has long conditioned the history of art. But Mitchell's psychoanalytic model allows us to comprehend Eastman's relation to the unacknowledged multiplicity of experimental music as one of lateral slide. (It bears noting that Eastman's own brother, Gerry, is an accomplished jazz musician and composer in his own right.) Eastman's intervention was not to kill the father, in other words. It was to differentiate and pluralize Cage's noise of notation from within.

A photograph published in a Rio newspaper from 1957 appears to picture Clark with her sons in the midst of making cardboard studies with scissors, ruler, stylus, and pen, their dark locks of hair and crisp white shirts rhyming with the geometric shapes dispersed across the table (fig. 2.43). Here, the law of the mother is transformed into a process of making, wherein the boundary object of the sibling becomes a compositional method writ large. Scoring the

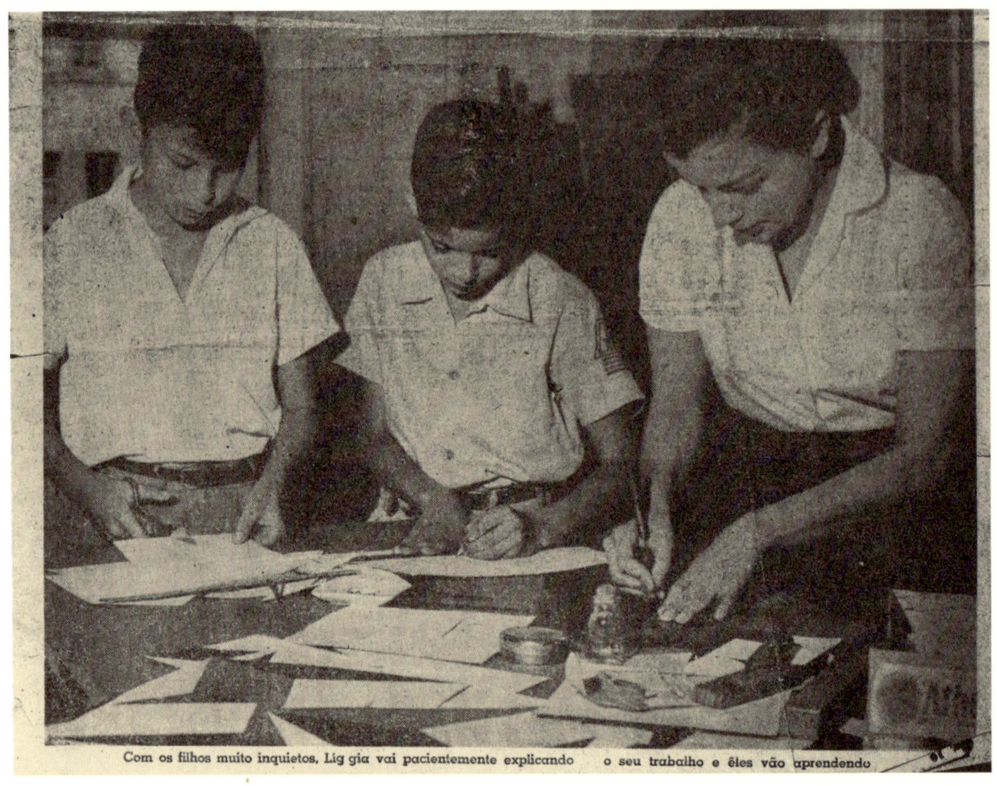

Figure 2.43. "Com os filhos muito inquietos, Líggia vai pacientemente explicando o seu trabalho e êles vão aprendendo." "Lígia Clark—Prêmio 'Diário de Notícias' na IV Bienal," *Diário de Notícias: A Revista Feminina*, October 13, 1957. Courtesy of Associação Cultural "O Mundo de Lygia Clark."

plane, Clark and the boys differentiate its unity and abstract extension; cutting, they sunder its singularity; assembling and reassembling the parts via the void of the organic line, they generate a new, amalgamate entity whose integrative form is dependent upon prior division and rupture. While the authorial gesture of the mark goes missing with the organic line, here, the hand returns as a means of participatory construction.[160]

Interestingly, while the captioned photograph describes the boys as Clark's sons, the article itself notes that only one of the two, Eduardo, currently lived with her. "As the boy was very lonely, I adopted a companion for him," Clark recounted to the journalist, who observed that the "adopted son" was the same size as Eduardo and similarly skilled with scissors.[161] Condensed within this anecdote about process is a mutual mapping of formal composition and intersubjective relations: seriality as an engine of similitude and linkage across rupture.

While Clark realized several *Planos em superfície modulada* in wood on the basis of these cardboard maquettes, the sheer number of studies vastly outnumber realized paintings, and she described the studies as "an experimental field" in and of itself.[162] The above anecdote indicates this field's aesthetic and psychic character at the level of compositional process, but I want to suggest that these works have implications *after and alongside* composition, in the position that we as viewers take in relation to surface and space.

In 1957, the same year as the newspaper article cited above, Clark noted the importance of Josef Albers's work for her thinking. She seems to have been particularly drawn to the "pluridimensional" space of Albers's *Structural Constellations*, begun in 1950, which mobilize graphic lines to create the illusion of geometric solids and voids protruding and recessing in space.[163] As early as 1952, Clark had used variations in color and orientation to produce ambiguous geometric spaces in gouache studies that suggest a dialogue with these *Structural Constellations*, as well as possibly with Albers's *Homage to the Square*, also begun in 1950. Clark titled this small group of

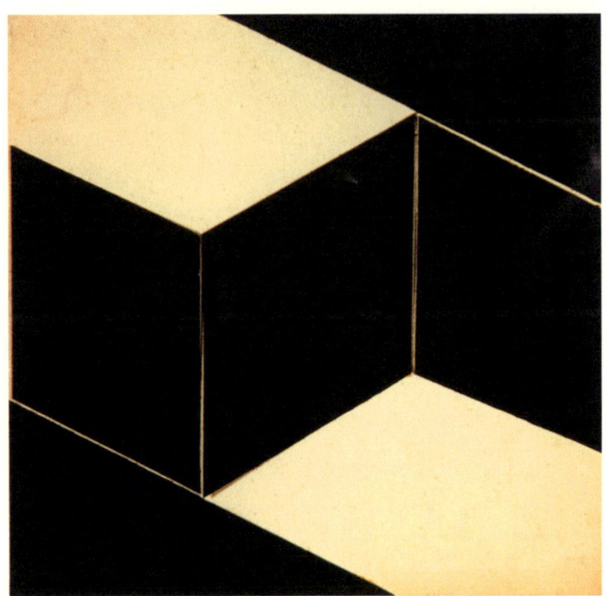

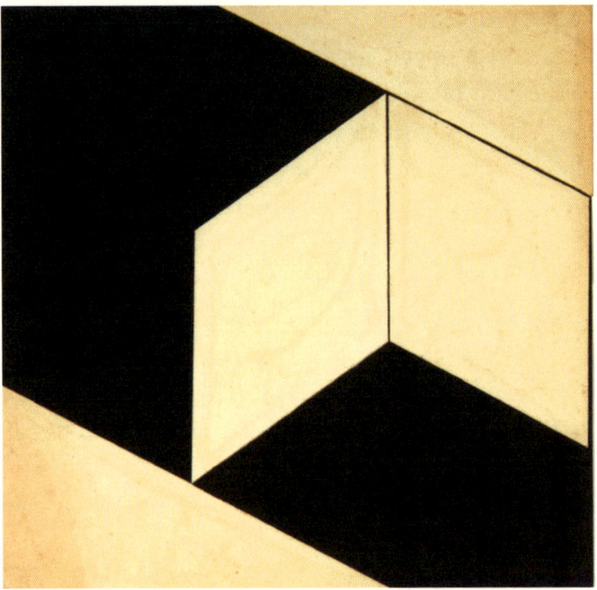

Figure 2.44. Lygia Clark, Studies for *Planos em superfície modulado* (Planes in modulated surface), 1957–58. Photo: Marcelo Ribeiro Alvares Corrêa. Courtesy of Associação Cultural "O Mundo de Lygia Clark."

studies *Planos em superfície modulada* (Planes in modulated surface), likely retroactively, when she returned to their modulated forms around 1957. The majority of Clark's cardboard studies from this later period, too, are similarly constructed according to interlocking Gestalt patterns. Yet unlike in Albers's work or Clark's earlier explorations, the shapes in these studies are no longer delineated by graphic lines, but by the edges of physical matter as one or more cut-out forms are placed upon supports of contrasting colors. The spatiality of the resulting configurations thus occurs in actual, rather than illusionistic space. As Clark put it, "What I seek is to *compose a space* and not compose in it."[164]

Moreover, this spatiality pivots on the organic line's dilatory action, which holds apart the geometric shapes through minute distinctions in measurement and alignment (fig. 2.44). Encountering these formal arrangements, a viewer might imagine the shapes contracting or shifting, as if to join together to create a continuous field. Yet such resolution is continuously thwarted, since fitting one shape into the crevice of a contiguous section would result in a gap elsewhere upon the support. If viewers initially search for matching forms *within* a given work, they are quickly compelled to seek such joins beyond that work in the series' proliferating combinations of positive and negative forms. I noted earlier that in *Quebra da moldura (p×b) versão 1*, a phenomenon revealed in the process of making a collage was translated into the misalignment of painterly tabs that cluster along the surface and sides of the work's canvas and frame, wrapping from front to back in a paradoxically disjunct continuity. In Clark's experimental field of cardboard collages, this recursively generated topology is redirected toward the temporalized modality of the series.

As Fabbrini has observed, the recurrence of forms in Clark's series is always irregular and erratic, producing a "latency" that "invalidates" the expectation of the series' consistency.[165] Indeed, Clark took issue with contemporaneous models of seriality that utilized iterative compositions to establish a closed field of formal development and resolution. Clark objected to this part-by-part approach, arguing that it falsely treated space as a set of determinate points upon a surface, rather than as an encompassing and immersive medium.[166] Clark's surfaces, of course, do not lack delimitation. But she mobilized edges not to enclose a composition within an autonomous space, but to activate an interface with the environment at large.[167]

This practice of composing with external space is the essence of what Clark called the "modulated surface." As I explore in Chapter 3, a period discourse of art and architecture frequently invoked the module as a standardized geometric unit that, through repetition and addition, forms a larger assembly or structure. The related term "modulation" entails a principle of variation or adjustment that implies a continuity between differences as much as the recurrence of a fixed entity.[168] For Clark, modulation was first and foremost a means to compose a surface by weaving together segments of matter and space.[169] The void of the organic line thus comes to signal the paradoxical materiality of these spaces, but also the way they bind elements together through disjunction. Modulation generates seriality from the moment that two like entities almost, but do not quite align. Far from facilitating compositional resolution, the series thus becomes a vehicle for manifesting the constitutive *lack* that inhabits any single work and the series at large.

In the stacked positive and negative forms of Clark's cardboard studies, there is always a seam that remains open to space, not only frontally, in the space perpendicular to the support, but laterally, where a prior cut gives rise to the organic line. By cleaving units of matter together and apart across potentially infinite permutations, the interval of the organic line opens the work into the environment. The spectator inhabits this space of separation and suture. And so the consequences of not making marks and its serial, sibling logic are spatialized at the site of observation. This occurs, however, only when the viewer *re-cognizes* the spatial voids within and between works as "lines." The modulated surfaces thus relocate representation to the side of the viewer while materially withholding *what is represented* from the work of art itself.[170]

In his path-breaking 1975 analysis of Neoconcretism, the Brazilian art historian Ronaldo Brito observed that the Neoconcrete work's "mode of insertion into real space entails a certain *negativity*, something that surpasses the limits of function."[171] Absorbing the frame's qualities of liminality, contingency, and mediation and transposing them from matter onto space, the organic line embodies and thus anticipates this "certain negativity."[172] Extrapolating the line's analytic value beyond Neoconcretism, we can recognize its operation in the excesses and lacks that riddle the putative self-sufficiency of works of art and the interpretive frames by which we comprehend them. Figuring forth this "certain negativity" does not entail a simple inversion, however. After all, even as Cage rendered empty as full and silence as sound in *4′33″*, he subscribed to a structure of containment that undergirds the old notion of autonomy for the subject and the work of art alike.[173] Excavating the organic lines implicit to a work's structure thus entails searching out misregistrations of form and content. It occasions looking to what occurs *on the side* of composition: what is liminal to a work's self-understanding, but emerges as a node of relations in the world writ large.

———

I observed at the beginning of this chapter that Clark once suggested that the process of cutting and compiling forms had a quasi-therapeutic function. But I also noted that the organic line inheres not in the cut as cure, but in what occurs *alongside* the cut: the hollow that resists satiety; the emptiness that endures. One should "rest" within this void, Clark counseled the clients who took part in her *Estruturação do Self*. For it was there, rather than in plenitude, that one cultivates creative force.

Although Clark's self-described abandonment of art for therapy in the late 1970s invites the retrospective projection of her later therapeutic interests onto her earlier work, one must be circumspect about drawing too tidy a picture of their relations. Clark's deeply corporeal notion of the psyche arose not only from the decades-long trajectory of her artistic practice, but from her teaching experiences at the Sorbonne in the mid-1970s and a host of intellectual and therapeutic influences that she freely absorbed, blended, and transformed. As Suely Rolnik, Christine Macel, and Kaira Cabañas have noted, these include her early acquaintance with the ideas of Silveira, but also her sessions in the 1970s with the psychoanalyst Pierre Fédida, various practitioners of relaxation techniques, as well as her exposure to the work of such theorists as Didier Anzieu (the "skin-ego"), Donald Winnicott (transitional objects, the "good enough mother"), Melanie Klein (object relations theory), and experimental educators and psychiatrists associated with the La Borde clinic, among others.[174] An accounting of Clark's engagement with this constellation of references is beyond the scope of this chapter. Nevertheless, if we understand Clark's therapeutic practice as one of many outgrowths of the revelation of the organic line, I want to bring this chapter to conclusion by limning some of the line's implications for conceiving of subjectivity and the psyche, even if in embryonic form.

In 1955, the same year that Clark began to modulate surfaces by way of the organic line's spatial voids, Nise da Silveira founded a Jungian study group at Engenho de Dentro that continued well after her death. One of the themes that held Silveira's attention was the question of opposites: their "conflicts, withdrawals, approximations, union."[175] Jung believed that the structure of the psyche is formed by the dynamic tension between polar principles, the most "formidable" among them that of masculine and feminine. As we saw in Chapter 1, Clark's *Geometria amorosa* (Amorous Geometry) shares in this elemental (and often clichéd) conceit. But as I argued there, the organic line reveals how Clark transformed this epistemology of opposites into one of *passage*, the line's cavity of space demarcating the juncture of the two principles, as well as spatializing their transmutation. The serial structure of Clark's "modulated surfaces" similarly trouble a binary epistemology, for although this seriality depends on the repetition of contrasting forms, its recursive model of rupture as seam continuously produces a generative lack that derails any notion of equilibrium. For Silveira, the series was a diagnostic tool through which to evaluate the psychic reintegration of patients such as Fernando Diniz, discussed at the beginning of this chapter.[176] Clark's organic line, by contrast, offers a model of subjectivity as *itself* serial and permeable to the outside.

To this end, I want to highlight a key insight articulated by the artist and psychotherapist Lula Wanderley, who, together with Gina Ferreira, are the only individuals whom Clark trained in her therapeutic methods. Wanderley adapted and extended Clark's practice of *Estruturação do Self* for years in an experimental nucleus he called "O Espaço Aberto ao Tempo" — The Space Open to Time — located in the same Engenho de Dentro complex where Silveira began working in the 1940s.[177] Wanderley's insight is simple, namely, that "the organic line is not merely a void; it *organizes*."[178] At a purely formal level, his observation helps articulate how the organic line, while a negative entity — an absence, a cavity — is simultaneously a means of structuration. But his insight indicates how organization can be an experimental practice, as well.

Describing the mobilization of what she called *Relational Objects* in her therapeutic practice of *Estruturação do Self*, Clark noted that these objects, which ranged from seashells and textured sacks to pillows and plastic bags filled with water or air, gained a phantasmatic dimension for her clients (fig. 2.45). They thus could be used as a site of both "acting out" and reconstitution. Clark described locating "holes" or "fissures" in the client's body during her sessions, wherein "the body" is a corporeal and psychic entity that

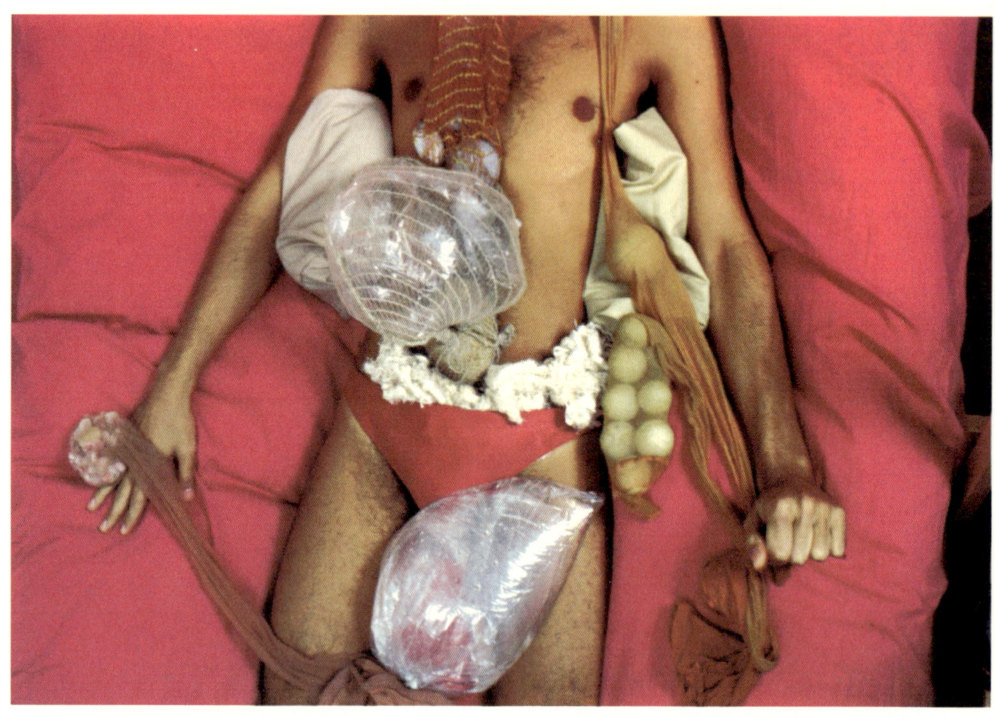

Figure 2.45. Lygia Clark, *Estruturação do Self*
(Structuring of the Self), 1978. Courtesy of
Associação Cultural "O Mundo de Lygia Clark."

exceeds literal anatomy.[179] The *Relational Objects*, together with Clark's touch, variously "stitch," "unstitch," and "join" these voids.[180] Here the hand returns as a gesture of care, rather than authorial making. While for some clients the resulting sensation was of "'gluing' or 'soldering' pieces of the body," for others it was one of "'closing' the 'holes' of the body or 'moving them' to other areas."[181] Such descriptions resonate with the topological character of the organic line and the serial logic of Clark's cardboard maquettes, where edges and their corresponding fissures are both propulsive and integrative in character. As psychically fluid supplements and focalizations (rather than illustrative substitutes), the *Relational Objects* form elastic seams with a client's existing corporeal schema (or "phantasmatic of the body," as Clark called it), shifting as this schema is molded and reshaped. As Luiza Martelotte has observed, "the body" reconstituted by means of such objects is never a fixed unity, but a flexible and reconfigurable mesh.[182] That the organic line *organizes* thus signals its capacity to reconfigure spatial and psychic formations alike.

In *Estruturação do Self*, Clark was concerned primarily with the subject comprehended within a "preverbal space" in which the ego is formed and potentially reshaped.[183] In this sense, as Cabañas writes, her use of the *Relational Objects* was a means to "trigger new patterns of subjective self-organization (or 'self-structuring,' to retain Clark's vocabulary)" at the elemental level of "subjective emergence."[184] Yet the organic line's capacity to knit the viewer together with the work of art within a spatial network, as we see in her "modulated surfaces," suggests that it has implications as a social insertion, as well. In their various recountings of *Estruturação do Self*, Clark, Wanderley, and Ferreira each point at different moments to the social inscription of their clients. In her own research on Clark's therapeutic practice, Rolnik has likewise underscored the psychic terror unleashed by the Brazilian dictatorship for many of Clark's clients, who had lived through the most repressive phase of that regime from 1968 to 1974.[185]

In relation to this chapter, we need look no further than the discordance between Eastman and Cage to recover the social implications of this model of porous subjectivity. For while Cage described his model of authorial withdrawal in terms of dissolving the ego's boundaries, his subsequent reassertion of authorship demonstrates that subjectivity is articulated and rearticulated within a complexly striated, rather than borderless space. Eastman's caustic appeal to "that which is fundamental" in the titles of his own compositions gives names to some of these striations. But in acknowledging their structuring capacity, Eastman's compositions — like the organic line — also imagine ways in which their organization might be remade. "What the relational object appears to do is to entangle lines," Martelotte writes. "To create knots or nodes that compose us and compose the world in a sinuous cartography."[186] To this end, we might say that the sheer multiplicity of Eastman's evocation of "that thing which is fundamental" ("there are 52 niggers," he observed at his Northwestern concert) suggests how striations of power are entwined with organic lines of refusal as well as active lines of flight.[187]

David Summers has written that "the idea of a *real plane* is inherently paradoxical because any actual format in a social space has some definite shape and size."[188] We might say the same of a subject, since actual subjectivities are not abstract constructions, but sedimentations of psychic, historical, and sociobiological experiences and the conditions of which they manifest. At the beginning of this chapter, I suggested that the organic line disturbs the apparent coincidence between making and human action signaled by the graphic line. If the plane — the real plane — finds its analogue in a subject, the organic line's paradigm of liminality allows us to reconceive of this subject not as a unitary, dissolvable, or self-evident entity, but as a modulated and fissured surface, not only porous to the world, but structured by the pressures that this world exerts on all sides. Looking to what occurs *alongside* the work of art, where content and form do not match, we recover a radical, constitutive negativity that cleaves the subject into the social and material realm. Approached from this perspective, the human itself is no longer an a priori entity, but one recursively produced by acts of making and not making, the latter given form by the negative and relational ontology of the organic line.

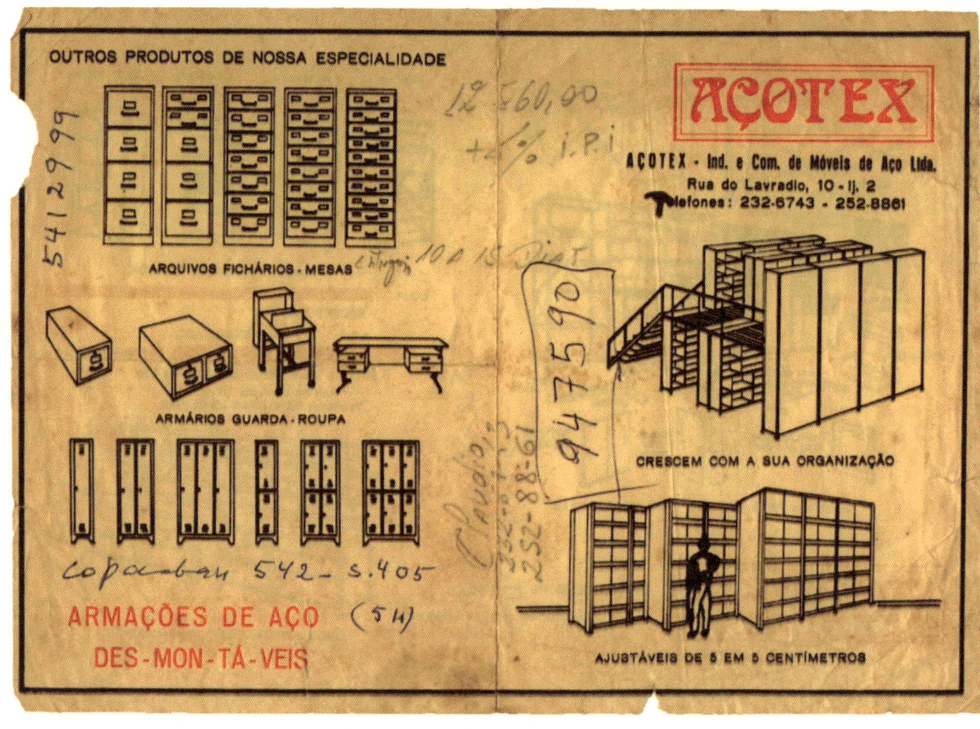

Figure 3.1. Açotex advertisement.
Publication source unknown.

CHAPTER THREE

Inhabiting Networks,

Subjecting Space

There exists yet another container: a container of men: scaffoldings.
—Le Corbusier

The needles chuckled and conversed with the fabrics—
"Don't be afraid, making two into one multiplies the laughs."
—Lygia Clark

You're the weave of the cloth and I put all you are in the cloth,
I roll it up and take it away. . . .
—Josephine Baker, as recalled by Le Corbusier

Retained in the archive of Lygia Clark's personal papers is an unusual, if innocuous, document: an advertisement for a set of expandable storage systems for home or office manufactured by the Brazilian company Açotex (fig. 3.1). Clark notated various phone numbers on the page, and it was likely preserved for this reason. But in retrospect, it is the advertisement itself that compels interest, for in its guileless technical illustrations of stacked filing cabinets, subdivided armoires, and neatly compartmentalized shelving units—products that are "adjustable," "grow with your organization," and "DIS-MOUN-TA-BLE" (the hyphenated syllables performing the furniture's segmentation and connectivity)—

is a dream of another kind of "modulated surface." Unlike the recursive and ever-incomplete serial structure of Clark's *Superfícies moduladas* (Modulated surfaces), discussed in the previous chapter, this is a surface that is wholly standardized and rational. It is a surface whose graphic divisions transparently signal corresponding partitions of volume and whose extensibility suggests an infinite capacity for the capture of information, objects, and subjects alike. Serialized and regularized, the storage system's modular sectioning of space analogizes its epistemic ordering. And so, contained within this illustration of containment is an entire *dispositif* of space and its segmentation, one that stretches from the gridded towns of colonial cartography to the developmentalist mandates of midcentury Latin America, where standardization promised the means to a modernized and wholly integrated world.[1] As the Brazilian architect Henrique Mindlin wrote in 1956, the year of Clark's first public exposition of the organic line, "an enormous body of specifications and standards" newly instituted in the country was "paving the way for the use of modular coordination."[2]

The *dispositif* embedded in the Açotex storage system corresponds in part to what media theorist Bernhard Siegert describes as the "cultural technique" of the grid, that is, a "materiality of communication" with constitutive properties and capacities that condition its application in discourse, representation, and practice.[3] According to Siegert, the grid not only diagrams actual space from a specific point of view, thus imposing representational control upon it. It also "presupposes the ability to write absence."[4] In other words, it treats empty space as a placeholder, rather than a void. The storage system makes this abundantly clear: its unoccupied compartments do not lack demarcation; rather, they are demarcated as compartments for future data or things. Thus, the grid's expansion into space and regulation *of* space is exerted whether or not its portals are empty or full. For Siegert, the globalizing logic of this matrix is epitomized by the "dwelling machines" Le Corbusier imagined building by the kilometer across the metropolises of Montevideo and São Paulo in 1929 (fig. 3.2). The Swiss-French architect pegged the size of these prefabricated modular units to the dimensions of the ship quarters he occupied during his voyage from Paris to Buenos Aires that year. Thus, the ideal unit of habitation was not only scalable, but transportable: a module in movement; a node in a network of gridded enclosures.

And yet, perhaps the grid is not as totalizing as it appears. Siegert demonstrates how the grid's digital logic of empty/full marshals even unoccupied space into utility, but his argument elides the fact that the graphic demarcations that generate the grid occupy space in and of themselves. The blacked-out zones constituted by these lines are neither empty nor full, according to a logic of content. But the grid's capacity to *organize* content depends upon the irreducible thickness of the line. Figured as positive mark in graphic representations such as the Açotex advertisement, the line materializes as negative space when realized in physical form. And here, in the hollow regions where part meets part and units join structure, we arrive again at the organic line.

The graphic or spatial lines that denote a grid in a representational or material construction exceed that grid's spatialization of content. Yet it is important to underscore that there is nothing essentially fugitive or insurgent about line, and even the organic line. Although line is rhetorically linked to expressivity and emancipatory flight, it has always been submitted to techniques of regulation and standardization. In 1936, the German architect Ernst Neufert released the first edition of his influential handbook of architectural norms, which promised a fully formatted world of divisible components, from paper sizes and filing cabinets to windows, doors, buildings, and beyond.[5] A Latin American edition appeared in 1948, and the handbook continues to be an international point of reference today (fig. 3.3).[6] As Anna-Maria Meister has argued, Neufert designed a system of dimensioned norms, as well as the representation of that system.[7] The drawn outline of an object prescribed a thickness that managed the material variability

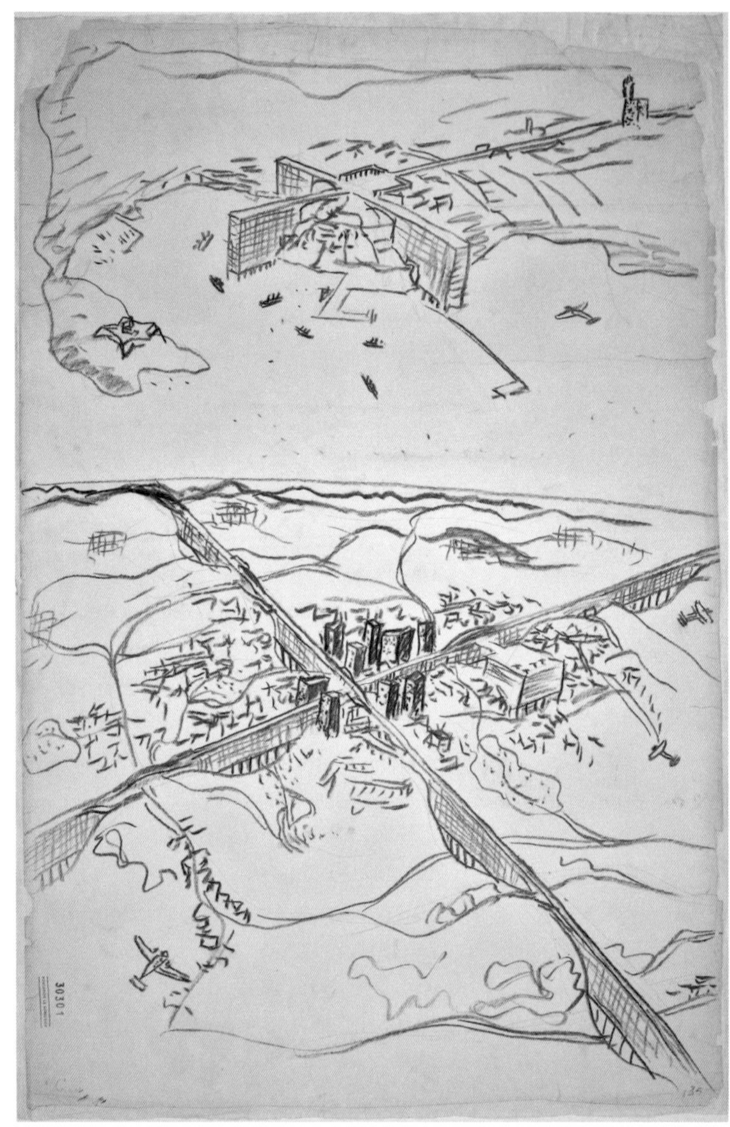

Figure 3.2. Le Corbusier (Charles-Édouard Jeanneret), urban projects for Montevideo and São Paulo, aerial perspectives, 1929. Ink on paper, (27 × 16.5 cm. Digital image © The Museum of Modern Art / Licensed by SCALA / Art Resource, NY. © F.L.C. / ADAGP, Paris / Artists Rights Society (ARS), New York, 2023.

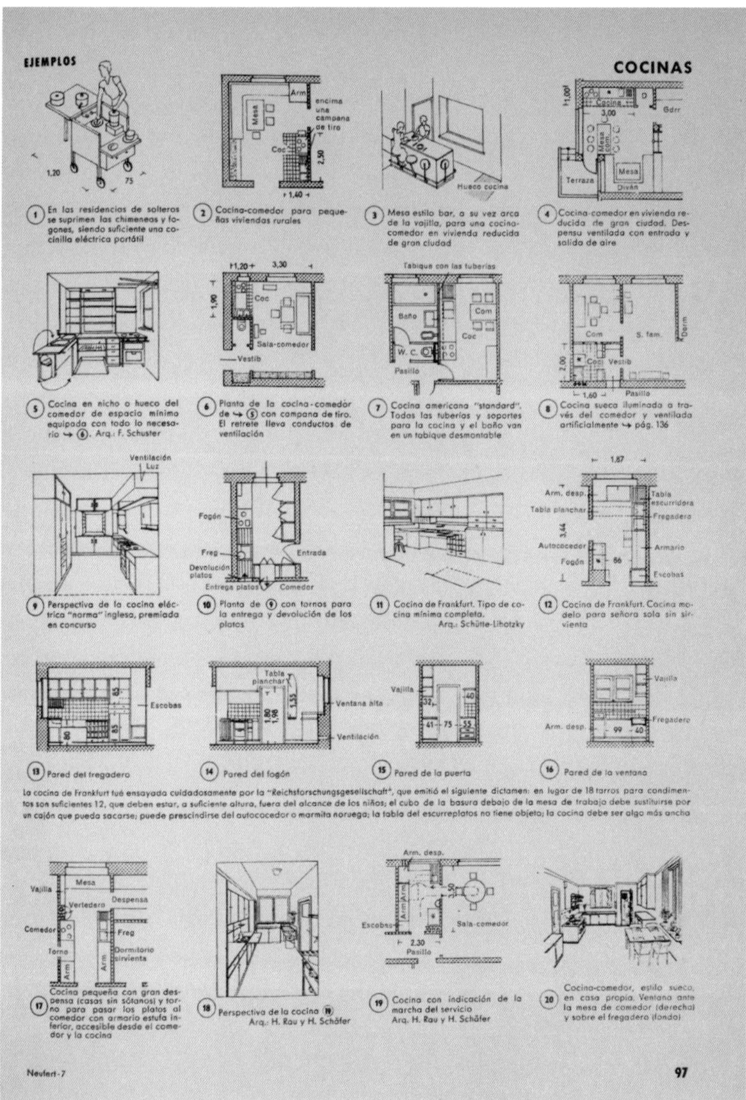

Figure 3.3. Ernst Neufert, "Cocinas" (Kitchens),
from *Arte de proyectar en arquitectura:
Fundamentos, normas y prescripciones sobre
construccion* (Buenos Aires: Cili, 1948).
© Bauentwurfslehre, 13th ed. by Neufert Ernst,
1937, Springer Nature.

of the represented object in real space. The potential deviation that results when abstract geometry takes material form was thus controlled by the drawn line's exterior edge, with variation and error absorbed toward its interior. Such technical specifications resulted in an "alphabet of lines" that made for a "universal graphical language of the industrial world," as one 1953 engineering manual put it.[8] Technical meanings internal to the pictorial codes of illustration thus regulated the transit of forms between representation and embodiment.

Such conventions were particularly vital for the management of material and spatial tolerances: allowable variations in dimension or angle that permitted two or more components to operate in combination. Tolerances pertain to junctures and seams, as in so-called "mating" surfaces (the match of a nut and bolt) or positional relations (the alignment of a door and its frame). While an "alphabet of lines" managed the material tolerance of a form's delimiting contours, spatial tolerances expressed such limits vis-à-vis intervals within an actualized system of relations. Yet as Francesca Hughes has written, architecture has been remarkably *intolerant* of material error, and one way of telling the story of modern architecture is as a series of intensifying techniques (the stripping away of ornament, standardization, industrial materials, formatting, digital rendering, and so on) for combatting the inherent variability of matter in space.[9] Moreover, as Hughes observes, this drive for precision is always also political, for it entails the coding as well as the disciplining of heterogeneity, variation, and error.

Consider another advertisement, likewise with scribbled notations, that Le Corbusier reproduced in his famous *The Modulor: A Harmonious Measure to the Human Scale Universally Applicable to Architecture and Mechanics* (1950/1954) (fig. 3.4).[10] This advertisement publicizes rectangular shipping cartons manufactured by the French national railway association and proclaims that such containers—ideal for "your fruit and vegetable exportations from North Africa"—are already "in use in the metropole and abroad."[11]

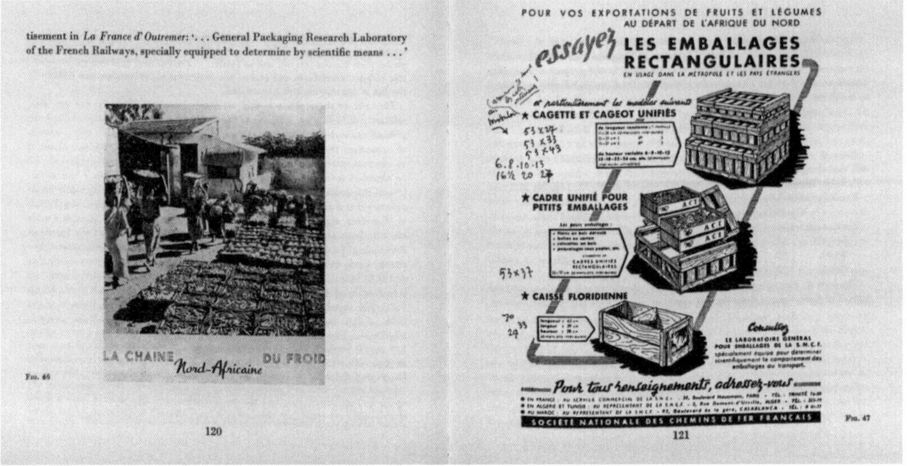

Figure 3.4. Le Corbusier, illustration from *The Modulor: A Harmonious Measure to the Human Scale Universally Applicable to Architecture and Mechanics* (Cambridge, MA: Harvard University Press, 1954), pp. 120 and 121. © F.L.C./ADAGP, Paris/Artists Rights Society (ARS), New York, 2023.

Le Corbusier devised his Modulor system as a uniquely modern instrument of aesthetic proportions that would translate between imperial and metric systems of measurement. Such conversion was pivotal in order to aid "the *flow* of the world's products," wrote the architect.[12] Such networks were far from neutral, of course, and it is not incidental that both Le Corbusier and the French railway association highlighted the transit of products from the colony to the metropole even as Algerians agitated for independence in these same years.[13]

In an attempt at scientific standardization, the French railway association proposed regularized sizes for shipping crates based on their interior dimensions. In attending solely to content — the commodity capacity of the crates — the railroad treated each unit as an abstract volume joined in a hypothetical grid of cargo. But the crates themselves added an additional thickness, which would logically result in problems of fit and unprofitable spatial remainders. Le Corbusier thus recognized that it was the containers' *exterior* dimensions that affected the efficiency of long-distance transport, and used the Modulor to calculate the ideal sizes of shipping containers to facilitate "isotropic stowage," or "stowage without gaps."[14] In the architect's vision, the abstract operations of the grid as a mechanism of infinite capture and scalability would then be reconciled with the materiality of physical things.

How does Clark's organic line figure in such a networked world, where, as Le Corbusier enthused, "everything is exchanged, linked and interlinked"?[15] Much like the lines of a grid, the organic line demarcates a liminality that resists a binary paradigm of empty or full. Yet unlike the graphic construct of the grid or the contour lines of a technical illustration, the organic line is not a positive mark. Instead, like an expression of spatial tolerance, it concerns a void between forms. As I argued in Chapter 2, it is a negative *that remains negative*. Thus, although Le Corbusier drew upon an interstitial logic in order to correct the French railway association's dimensioning, the organic line does not correspond to the material thickness of his hypothetical containers, but rather to the thickness of space that occurs *alongside* them. This space, too, is instrumental. After all, a spatial interval, however narrow, is necessary for material units to be assembled and disengaged. Neufert attended to just this issue when he reduced the length and width of his dimensioned brick by one centimeter in order to account for the mediating function of mortar.[16] To this extent, both Neufert's system of norms and Clark's organic line demonstrate that Le Corbusier's "stowage without gaps" remains in a metaphoric spatial register: an idealization of the mechanics of global connectivity, rather than a view from its seams.

As I have begun to suggest, the organic line is a zone of integration and expediency, allowing for the juncture of parts while easing the mechanics of their organization and mobility. But while Neufert's fully formatted and divisible world approached the gaps between materials and objects as opportunities for control, the organic line is a capricious (no)thing. Contingent, relational, and temporal, it can shrink to barely a sliver or dilate to a chasm, according to external conditions. Thus, while the organic line facilitates flows along channels of space, communication, and even subjectivity, it also causes such channels to swell, stick, or leak, thwarting their purported efficiency. The organic line is therefore in service of the "linked and interlinked" world Le Corbusier presaged in *The Modulor*, but it also sabotages its smooth functioning from within.

The role of the viewer in such circuits is complex. As a perceptual phenomenon, the organic line is a function of observation and cognition: it requires a viewer to draw literal space into legibility and aesthetic signification. To this degree, the organic line entails a virtuality characteristic of the image, even as we comprehend its actuality in space. As I noted in Chapter 1, *the organic line represents itself, abstractly, in the real time of the viewer's observation.* Insomuch as the line is a spatial phenomenon formed in relation to material entities, however, it preexists the viewer's recognition and persists beyond it. Just as a tension between real and metaphoric space exists in the cultural technique of the grid, a related one occurs here, in the distinction between visual perception and material structure.

What happens when this relentless abstraction confronts the specificities of subjects, surfaces, and gaps — when walls become permeable, compositional lines become seams, and fissures become apertures and thresholds of passage? Here we come to Clark's architectural experiments of 1955, which construe the organic line as a graphic ornament, as well as a literal aperture between interior and exterior space (fig. 3.5). These maquettes cast the viewer/user within a spatial network that shuttles between real and representational space by means of the threshold. Such experiments participate — for the most part positivistically — in a broader period discourse concerning modularity and the integration of the arts. Yet even as Clark sought to assimilate the organic line into this architectural rhetoric, the line itself flushes to the surface, as it

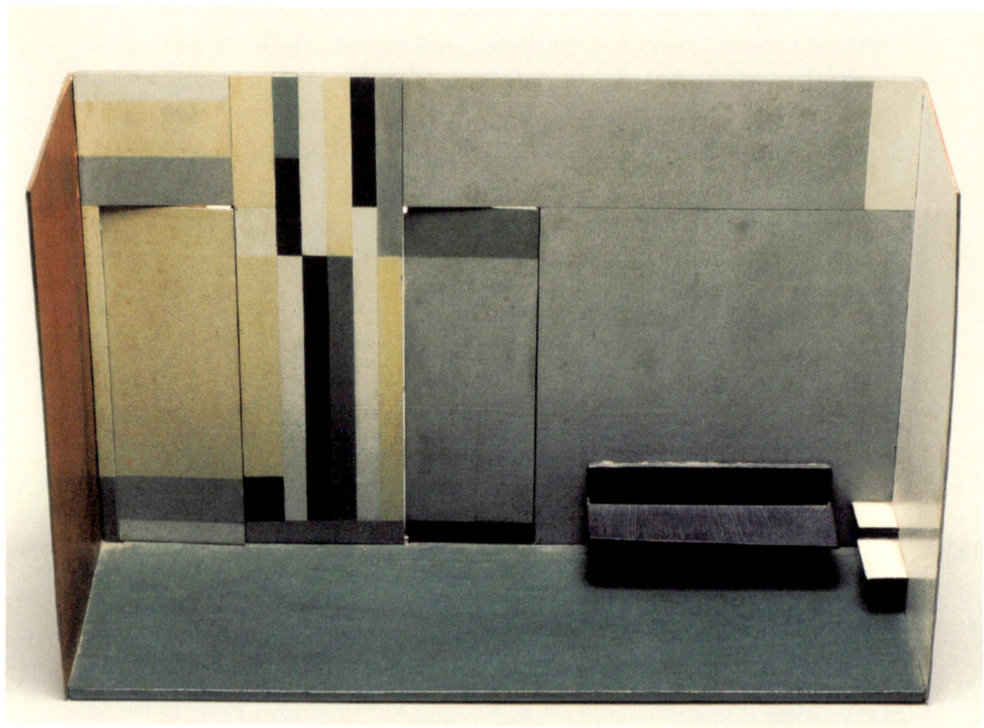

Figure 3.5. Lygia Clark, *Maquette para interior*
(Maquette for interior), 1955. Photo: Marcelo
Ribeiro Alvares Corrêa. Courtesy of Associação
Cultural "O Mundo de Lygia Clark."

were, much that this architecture sought to sideline and repress. The dream of modularity revealed in period advertisements hinges on the notion of "universal applicability," as well as a proportional reciprocity between "Man" and the environment.[17] By contrast, the contingency of the organic line intensifies spatial, bodily, intersubjective, and environmental relations. In other words, human and module are not configured toward ever-smoother integration and rationality, but by means of a mutually decentering reciprocity and variability. The organic line thus throws into relief energies and affects that normative forms of period architecture sought to harness and control.

Clark was enthusiastic about the formal and metaphoric capacities of architecture, and several later projects demonstrate that her engagement with the discipline was a sustained, rather than passing interest. Among others, these experiments include a patent registration for a house that inhabitants could modify themselves, matchbox structures in which the organic line becomes a mechanism for spatial transformation, as well as participatory "biological architectures."[18] Over the years, too, Clark's relationship to architecture became both more participatory and explicitly disruptive. As Fernando Cocchiarale and Anna Bella Geiger have observed, Clark's 1968 *A casa é o corpo: Penetração, ovulação, germinação, expulsão* (The house is a body: Penetration, ovulation, germination, expulsion) pointedly inverted Le Corbusier's dictum that "a house is a machine for living" by constructing a "living architecture" that spatialized the interior of the maternal body (figs. 3.6 and 3.7).[19] Entering the structure's dark chambers of fabric scrims and plastic sheeting, interacting with balloons, pausing within a translucent membrane, and finally squeezing through a tunnel-like passageway outfitted with colored balls, thread, and distorting mirrors before emerging into light, the participant allegorically and haptically experiences the processes of reproduction, gestation, and birth detailed in the work's subtitle.[20] The corporeality is unequivocal, and there is no need to ask after the "organicity" of the architecture.

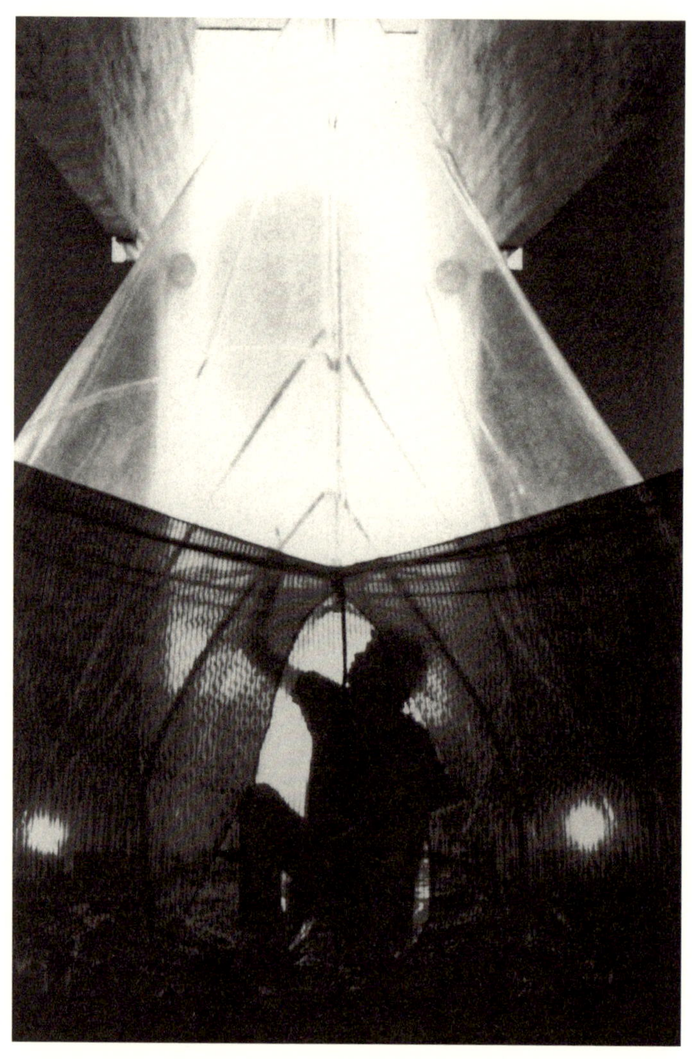

Figure 3.6. Lygia Clark, *A casa é o corpo* (The house is a body), 1968, showing "germination." Courtesy of Associação Cultural "O Mundo de Lygia Clark."

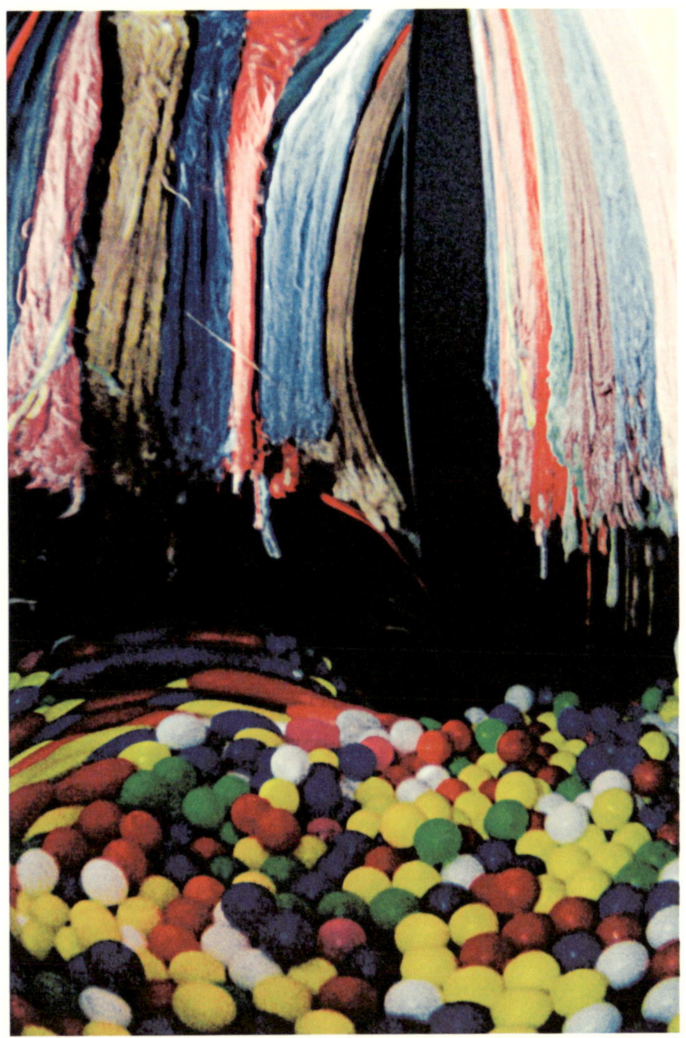

Figure 3.7. Lygia Clark, *A casa é o corpo* (The house is a body), 1968, showing "expulsion." Courtesy of Associação Cultural "O Mundo de Lygia Clark."

In 1975, while in Paris undergoing psychoanalysis, Clark wrote a kind of fairytale she published as *Meu doce rio* (My sweet river) in 1984 after her return to Brazil. The story's conceit is a myth from a far-away time of fairies and genies in which the world was a giant, multisexed, and self-copulating creature. This creature eventually gives rise to "the virgin," whose plastic and malleable body is a veritable geography of desire. As Sérgio Bessa has argued, the text is a complex processing not only of Clark's childhood traumas and psychic formation, but of key elements of her work. There are references to specific projects, such as her "relational objects" and *Cabeça coletivo* (Collective head, 1969), as well as allusions to more generalized themes of cannibalism and copulation.[21] Notable for our purposes is Clark's description of the virgin's body as "elaborated in stages," stitched together from fabrics in an image that recalls her early descriptions of the organic line as seam.[22] Clark also described the virgin's mutating body/landscape, which harbors teeming plant and animal life, as a house without privileged orientation, a "topological" and "future model of an architecture as yet to be elaborated," comprising elastic walls, a tunnel, and an interior cavern containing millions of eggs, each one fantastically different from the next.[23]

Across Clark's notes and final version of her fable, objects, body parts, and concepts talk to one another about their ligation, combination, and mutual dependence, often with humorous sexual innuendo. "The virgin's breasts . . . tapped on the shirt — knock, knock, can we come out yet?" Or, "Said the head to the belly — I know that you exist. Said the belly to the head: I feel your knowledge." And, "Said one mouth to another — The shape can be different, but the opening always fits."[24] Spatial intervals and categorical difference, here, are not mathematically managed tolerances, but occasions for unruly desire, touch, and affective connection. Stylistically, Clark's early maquettes exhibit none of this bodiliness and carnality. But as I seek to demonstrate in this chapter, what appears like formal restraint and assimilation into modernist architectural modularity was in fact a mutation of its protocols. In a certain way, Clark's later corporeal articulations of reciprocal and relational identity-in-difference were already immanent in the organic line.

On January 27, 1957, a headline in the regional newspaper *Diário de Minas* announced: "Minas Gerais Painter (Lygia Clark) Discovers New Organic Lines in the Plastic Arts." The text was a transcription of a lecture Clark had given at the architecture school of the federal university in Belo Horizonte the previous September, and the article's lede framed the discovery in specifically architectural terms: "Necessity of integration for artists and architects encountering new solutions — Dynamic panels in prefabricated houses."[25] Three illustrations of Clark's works accompanied the text, likely drawn from an exhibition the architecture students organized to accompany her lecture. They include a *Superfície modulada* (Modulated surface) painting (fig. 3.8), another painting designated *Solução para painel* (Solution for a panel), and *Maquette do interior para armário embutido* (Maquette of the interior for a built-in closet).[26] As if to cement the resonance with period design, an advertisement for furniture, including units with modular elements similar to those in the Açotex advertisement, appeared on the opposite page.

While Clark's first revelation of the organic line occurred in relation to the pictorial support and its frame, the article underscores that her second revelation was undoubtedly architectural in nature. In accounts of her trajectory, Clark noted that she went for an extended period between her initial discovery and her subsequent pursuit of the line's perceptual and structural implications. According to Clark, the interim period was one of considerable disorientation and uncertainty. As she recounted in 1958, "I went practically one and a half to two years without knowing how to move forward with this research, until one day I came across the direct relation between this so-called 'organic' line and the line

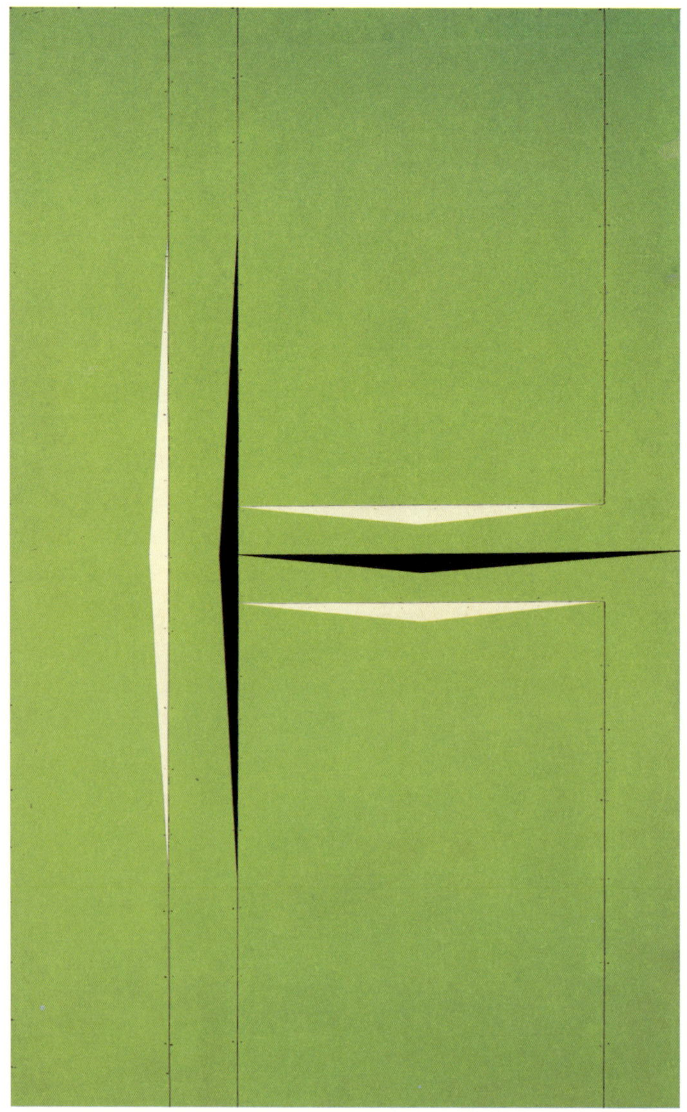

Figure 3.8. Lygia Clark, *Superfície modulada no. 5* (Modulated surface no. 5), 1955. Lacquer on wood, 116×72 cm. Photo: Jaime Teixeira Acioli. Courtesy of Associação Cultural "O Mundo de Lygia Clark."

that separates a door and its casement, [and] then this same line as the seam between various materials such as the tiles of parquet flooring. I thought as well of the seams between fabrics and other lines that create the junction between two surface planes."[27] As noted in Chapter 1, Clark did in fact use the term "organic line" at some point in early 1955 and that same year explored its character in terms of the *Superfícies moduladas* paintings created using single or stacked wooden supports. Faced with the limits of her own technical skills and spurred by her new interest in the line's architectural import, Clark decided to apprentice at a carpentry shop in order to learn the mechanics of woodworking.[28]

As a result of this training, she executed at least three maquettes of architectural interiors composed with the organic line in mind. These maquettes each consist of a single-room enclosure composed of three walls and a floor and perforated by one or two doors or hinged apertures that open and close (fig. 3.9). In keeping with Clark's paintings of the time, the maquettes' walls display abstract geometric patterns made up of ribbons of rectangular panels or elongated triangles in muted shades of forest green, burgundy, blue, lavender, and yellow, as well as gray, white, and black. They likewise incorporate scoring and actual slits to convey the presence of the organic line. The maquettes were exhibited at the second Grupo Frente exhibition at the Museu de Arte Moderna do Rio de Janeiro in July of 1955, along with three works from Clark's *Superfícies moduladas* series.[29] It was not until the following year, however, that Clark explicitly named the organic line and publicly elaborated its discovery and use. Clark's architectural revelation was thus fundamental in consolidating the phenomenon as an aesthetic concept and instrument.

Clark's interest in both the structural solidity and spatial ambiguity of the built environment was already visible in the drawings of stairs she made while studying with Roberto Burle Marx and Zélia Ferreira Salgado between 1947 and 1950, as discussed in Chapter 2. Her time in Paris between 1950 and 1952 likewise coincided

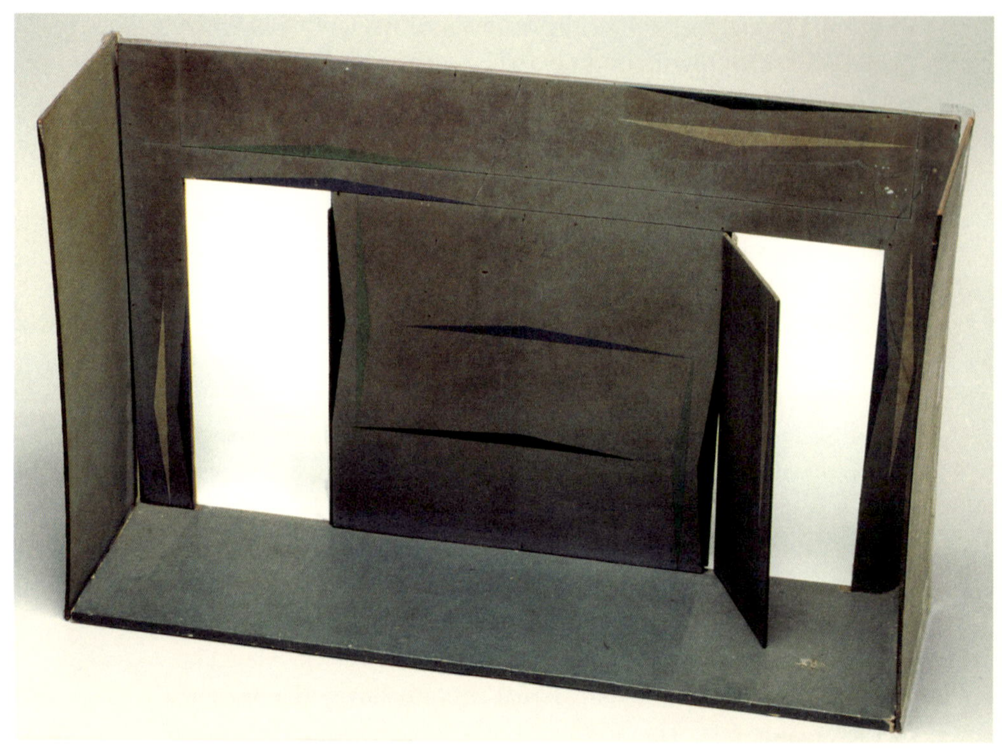

Figure 3.9. Lygia Clark, *Maquette para interior*
(Maquette for interior), 1955, 30×48×15 cm.
Photo: Marcelo Ribeiro Alvares Corrêa. Courtesy
of Associação Cultural "O Mundo de Lygia Clark."

with the prominent discourse on the synthesis of the arts in which an approximation between painting, sculpture, and architecture was imagined to model a broader social and technological cohesion. In the early twentieth century, many artists and architects explored notions of integrative design: members of De Stijl such as Piet Mondrian theorized architectural polychromy; Sonia Delaunay designed fabrics and environments so that compositional patterns anticipated function; Le Corbusier expounded the unifying force of architecture; and Fernand Léger declared that an "agreement among the wall—the architect—the painter" was an aesthetic and humanist imperative.[30]

In the wake of the Second World War, as Romy Golan has written, the humanist inflection of such concerns became ever more urgent, even as practitioners sought to dispense with the more problematic associations of the total work of art.[31] In 1952, while Clark was one of his students, Léger noted that the mural amounted to a new "collective" art form, one in which painting would "lose its frame" and, together with the "elastic rectangles" of polychrome architecture, revitalize the "dead surface" of the wall.[32] While in the United States, the critic Clement Greenberg argued that the solution to the "crisis of the easel picture" was a fully autonomous art in which painting approximated the scalar ambition of the mural, European practitioners proposed the mural, the polychrome wall, and the tapestry as antidotes to the individualism and commodification of canvas painting and the potential anonymity of modern architecture.[33]

The discourse of the synthesis of the arts was likewise prominent in Brazil in the early 1950s, where it joined first-hand encounters with the early work of artists such as Delaunay, Mondrian, and Sophie Taeuber-Arp, all of whom had experimented with integrating painting with the environment (fig. 3.10).[34] In Latin America, there was much enthusiasm for the Venezuelan architect Carlos Raúl Villanueva's ambitious Ciudad Universitária in Caracas, considered a prime example of the synthesis of the arts, to say nothing

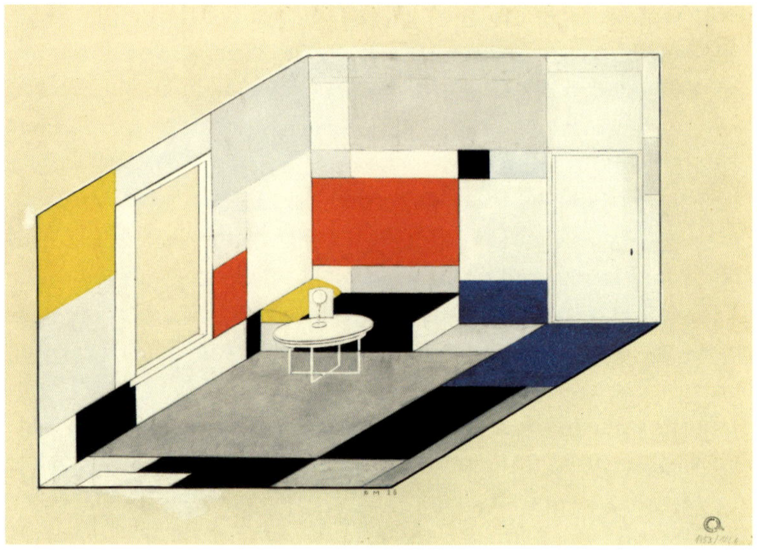

Figure 3.10. Piet Mondrian, *Design for the Salon of Ida Bienert* (*Axonometrie II*), 1926. Courtesy of Kupferstich-Kabinett, Staatliche Kunstsammlungen Dresden. Photo: Herbert Boswank.

of the excitement around the planned capital city of Brasília, begun in 1956. Clark participated in an exhibition that accompanied an inter-American conference hosted at Ciudad Universitária the year of its inauguration, in 1954. In March 1955, the Museu de Arte Moderna do Rio de Janeiro held an exhibition of Groupe Espace, a French collective dedicated to a synthesis of art and architecture under the sign of the "constructive" and "nonfigurative."[35] In July that year, when the museum hosted the second Grupo Frente exhibition, newspaper accounts described it as similar to Groupe Espace and other European "nuclei."[36] It was at this exhibition that Clark first displayed her architectural maquettes featuring the organic line. The catalogue noted that she was dedicated to research on murals and polychrome architecture.[37] These terms suggest that at least for the moment, Clark subscribed to the period rhetoric with some degree of enthusiasm, as did her critics, who lauded her "incessant search...to resolve the problem of painting in relation to the wall."[38]

In early 1956, Clark solicited statements from a number of Brazilian architects about the significance of her research, among them Mindlin (author of the 1956 volume on modern Brazilian architecture), Affonso Eduardo Reidy (whose design for the Museu de Arte Moderna in Rio was then in construction), and Oscar Niemeyer (who had recently realized the Bienal buildings in Parque Ibirapuera, founded the architectural journal *Módulo*, and would soon design the buildings of Brasília).[39] None of the letters name the organic line as such, but it is clear that it was the core of Clark's investigations. Jorge Machado Moreira noted that her maquettes "integrate the openings" of architectural components, thereby "aggregating the entire wall."[40] And Niemeyer wrote that in her proposals, doors, windows, and other such elements "no longer constitute obstacles or interruptions to the composition," but are instead "modules and rhythms that enrich and discipline it."[41] In a feature on Clark's work published in the Rio-based newspaper *Correio da Manhã* in April of 1956, snippets from these statements recount Clark's discovery of the organic line — now explicitly designated for the first time — as well as indications of her ambition to apply it to the totality of a building project, from interior and exterior walls to ceilings, floors, and even curtains. The article mentions that Niemeyer had included her in a project in Belo Horizonte and that the critic Mário Pedrosa had likewise invited her to contribute to the renovation of his house.[42] These projects do not seem to have materialized, but it may have been the publicity from this article that led to Clark's invitation to lecture and exhibit at the school of architecture in Belo Horizonte in September of 1956.

In this 1956 lecture, Clark framed her discussion in terms of the importance of collaboration among architects and artists in order to create "harmonious atmosphere[s] in which to live and work," sentiments that hewed closely to period discourse in Europe and Latin America.[43] However, while in Europe, the synthesis of the arts encompassed a desire for social and civic reconstruction through a renewed form of public monumentality, in Brazil, it was associated with the construction of a new, modern society through the democratizing potential of design.[44] Faced with a spate of construction that accompanied Brazil's rapid industrialization in the early 1950s, architects such as Niemeyer, Lúcio Costa, and Rino Levi urged artists and architects to work together so that buildings would not act as mere backdrops for isolated paintings or sculptures.[45] Collaboration offered the possibility of integrating aesthetic decisions with industrialized design processes such as prefabrication. Artists associated with the burgeoning Concrete movement embraced the idea of creating prototypes for mass production, even as their work often exhibited a fascinating hybrid of artisanal and industrial techniques.[46] In her 1956 lecture, Clark noted that the geometric simplification of Concrete art made it particularly suited for integration with architecture.[47] "The artist may also research the function of lines I will call 'organic' — functional lines of doors, seams of fabrics, etc. — in order to modulate an entire surface," she wrote. As in the *Correio da Manhã* article, she noted the cross-medial applicability of the line, from textile designs to prefabricated houses. "In my view, this is the most revolutionary thing that will present itself as new techniques and malleable materials become available for the artist and the architect to plan together the future habitat of man."[48]

The Brazilian discourse concerning the relations between art and architecture tended to foreground integration, rather than synthesis. As Costa observed in 1953, "synthesis implies the idea of fusion," but fusion was only one path, and not necessarily the most desirable one for considering the relations between painting and contemporary architecture.[49] For Clark, the organic line was a unique contribution to these debates, for in suturing discrete planar elements into a composition or pattern, the organic line acts as a literal bridge between the heterogeneous surfaces of the built environment.[50] Writing about Clark's engagement with architecture in

1957, Pedrosa noted that unlike the mural (an "unjustifiable survival" not terribly distinct from the "anachronistic privilege" of easel painting), the organic line allowed for "planimetric modulation" that interpolated multiple architectonic features.[51] The planar surfaces of painting and architecture were not treated in isolation, in other words, but mutually articulate one another by way of the module. The organic line was the instrument of this integrative articulation. Left unstated, however, was what exactly it meant for a line of space to be *organic*.

In the early 1950s, the term "organic" was used to describe multiple and sometimes conflicting qualities and phenomena relating to architecture and design. In a 1951 book on mural painting deeply invested in the synthesis of the arts, Groupe Espace member Antoine Fasani described painting in explicitly biological terms as the "organ of a superior organism" and the means by which to "pigment the skin of architecture."[52] (In a tantalizing aside, Fasani notes that "the question of joints remains open" and imagines the possibility of a large-scale mural assembled from a series of panels.)[53] Since the early twentieth century, Frank Lloyd Wright sought explicitly to align architecture with nature, as late as 1953 defining the organic in terms of an intrinsic integrity and integration — "Part-to-Whole-as-Whole-to-Part" — that should characterize architecture and society alike.[54] Many critics and practitioners used the organic in a functionalist sense to convey the harmonious interrelation of parts, much like "the segments of a finger and the finger as a whole, the finger to the arm and so on," as Mies van der Rohe put it.[55] Already in the Renaissance, Leon Battista Alberti had written of the parts of a building relating to one another through lineaments and structure much like an animal's members.[56] In the context of twentieth-century modernism, this emphasis on structure and proportion allowed the organic to implicate the machinic and the mechanical, as well. As Amédée Ozenfant wrote in 1952, "NATURAL forms are mechanistic, for they are the product of universal forces."[57] Le Corbusier's calls for "universal applicability" vis-à-vis

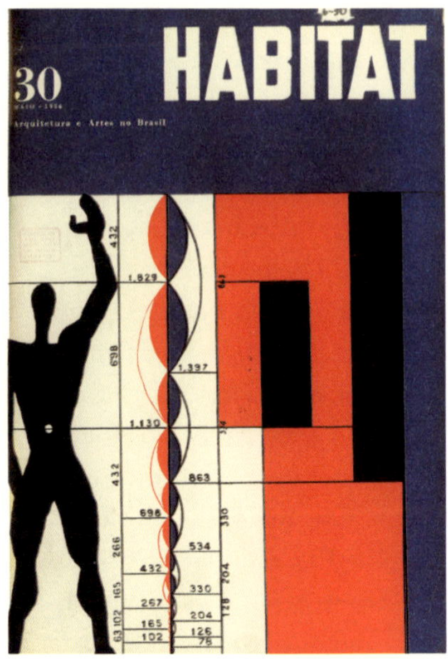

Figure 3.11. *Habitat: Arquitetura e Artes no Brasil*, no. 30 (May 1956). Le Corbusier, The Modulor. © F.L.C./ADAGP, Paris/Artists Rights Society (ARS), New York, 2023.

the proportional system of the Modulor likewise appealed to this sense of the organic.[58] The Modulor received wide exposure in Latin America, and in a 1963 diary entry, Clark herself suggested that the "organicity" and "living totality" of Le Corbusier's approach was the most important expression of modern architecture (fig. 3.11).[59]

Yet a rich tradition of thought going back to ancient philosophy also sought to differentiate the mechanical from the organic. For Aristotle, Baruch Spinoza, Johann Wolfgang von Goethe, Samuel Taylor Coleridge, Henri Bergson, and many others, the organic was not simply a functional arrangement of parts, but an inner purpose and innate life force that separated animate from inanimate entities.[60] The organic implied a self-organizing capacity that endowed a given entity with autonomy and innate behaviors. These vitalist associations of organicism could disrupt other, more functionalist senses of the term. A 1941 exhibition on organic furniture design at the Museum of Modern Art, New York, highlighted the possibilities of standardization such that units might be "completely interchangeable," for instance.[61] Yet the curator noted that modular parts ran into problems with the variability of organic materials such as wood. Factors such as heat and humidity (particularly at issue in the tropical climate of Brazil) meant that drawers "were often too loose or too tight when interchanged."[62] In this case, the living, breathing, "organic" quality of matter was also what sabotaged the standardization of "organic" design.

Many modern architects and critics sought to split the difference by emphasizing process or cohesion among elements. Sigfried Giedion wrote that "to mechanize things is to give them a mechanical life, a dead life, but to mechanize *the process* by which they are made is to win life."[63] Meanwhile, in Brazil, Mindlin asserted that "the house should be considered as an organic conjunction of elements . . . that integrate . . . to form an indissolvable totality," while Costa wrote of an "organic-functional concept" of construction in which "architectonic expression" develops as if it were a "live organism."[64] Clark, too, seemed to be working between these double inflections of the organic in her early articulations of the line. On the one hand, she clearly understood the organic line as a means of functional connection between elements of an architectural environment and that a modulated surface was the result of this ligation. As she observed in 1956, "All of my work departs from the architectonic module, which will always be the disciplinary element, moderating, if you like. In the same way that mathematics is the discipliner of the so-called 'concrete' [artists], the architectonic module will be my discipline."[65] In keeping with the utopian rhetoric of the period, Clark likewise understood the functional relationality enacted by the organic line and its corresponding modular units as performing the ideal collaborative relations between artists, architects, sculptors, and psychologists.[66]

Yet Clark also understood this connective operation as occurring in relation to the viewer in terms that moved beyond the functional and that explicitly counterposed the mechanical and the bodily or biological. In contrast to serial works that presumed a fixed distance between the viewer and the work of art, Clark wrote that in her modulated surfaces, the spectator "participates actively within this expressive space, penetrating it and being penetrated by it." It was this sensation, moreover, that was "organic."[67] Clark likewise argued that the "expressional organic character" previously accorded to the subject and the autonomous work of art must be transmuted to the environment at large.[68] As Pedrosa wrote about the architectural potential of the organic line, "Everything in a building taken as a living body becomes part of the same creative thought."[69] To this degree, even in Clark's (and her supporters') early articulations, the organic line had a contingency, vitality, and expressivity that resisted full inscription within the mechanical.[70] Thus, while architects looked to standardize Brazil's "undeveloped … buildings materials industry" in order to *overcome* variability, Clark's invocation of the organic opened up an entirely divergent possibility: that the organic would *enliven* modularity through a shifting ecology of spatial forces and bodily affects.[71]

In her orientation toward the organic, Clark clearly built from her studies with Burle Marx in the late 1940s. By this time, Burle Marx was already well known for his landscape designs and botanical cultivation. Although Clark's studies revolved around painting, she was certainly aware of his approach to the plane as an organic topography and would have been intimately familiar with his terrace garden for Rio's most iconic modernist building, the Ministério da Educação e Saúde of 1938, also the temporary headquarters of the Museu de Arte Moderna do Rio de Janeiro.[72] As Paulo Herkenhoff has eloquently observed, the sinuous, amoebic curves of Burle Marx's designs for gardens are echoed in the snail-like spiraling of Clark's drawings of stairs from this period, while the landscape architect's treatment of compositional segments as the variable surfaces of a "latent living plane" ultimately found its way into her conception of the plane as "the potential place of life."[73] Burle Marx was extraordinarily active with projects and exhibitions throughout the mid-1950s period in which Clark discovered and nominated the organic line, and the artist herself noted his formative influence.[74] Yet comprehending Clark's organic line vis-à-vis Burle Marx's practice demands complicating assumptions about what an organic or natural form might entail.

As a stylistic description, the organic is typically associated with the undulating, serpentine lines of biomorphic abstraction: works that foregrounded "the silhouette of the amoeba," rather than "the shape of a square," as Alfred Barr memorably put it in 1936.[75] Such curvilinear contours were a trademark not only of Burle Marx's designs, but of Brazilian architects such as Niemeyer, whose "capricious and gratuitous curves" Max Bill famously criticized in 1953.[76] Barr distinguished the quasi-representational character of the biomorphic from a purer geometric abstraction entirely divorced from nature. Yet Clark's organic line is straight, even as it swells. In this sense, it is closer to what theorists have more recently described as a "biocentric," rather than "biomorphic" conception of the organic, which prioritizes neither style nor naturalistic association, but the enactment of vitalist energies and integrative life.[77] Moreover, as a contingent, actualized, and present-time phenomenon, the organic line is the antithesis of the transferrable compositional lines that migrate from drawings and plans to buildings or garden contours in Burle Marx's work (fig. 3.12). Indeed, pressing on the question of *contour* reveals where Clark's biocentric and Burle Marx's biomorphic conceptions of line diverge.

A garden is an eminently artificial endeavor in which the raw and inconstant matter of plant life is corralled into a fabricated configuration. To this degree, the garden is a prime example of human action upon the environment, and in classic French garden design, elements such as sight lines and rigidly controlled geometries assert this ontology of making. Burle Marx's modernist designs, by contrast, do not impose the rectilinear outlines of an abstract geometric order on nature, but rather the transfigured forms of nature itself.[78] In his garden for the estate of Odette Monteiro, begun in 1947, the

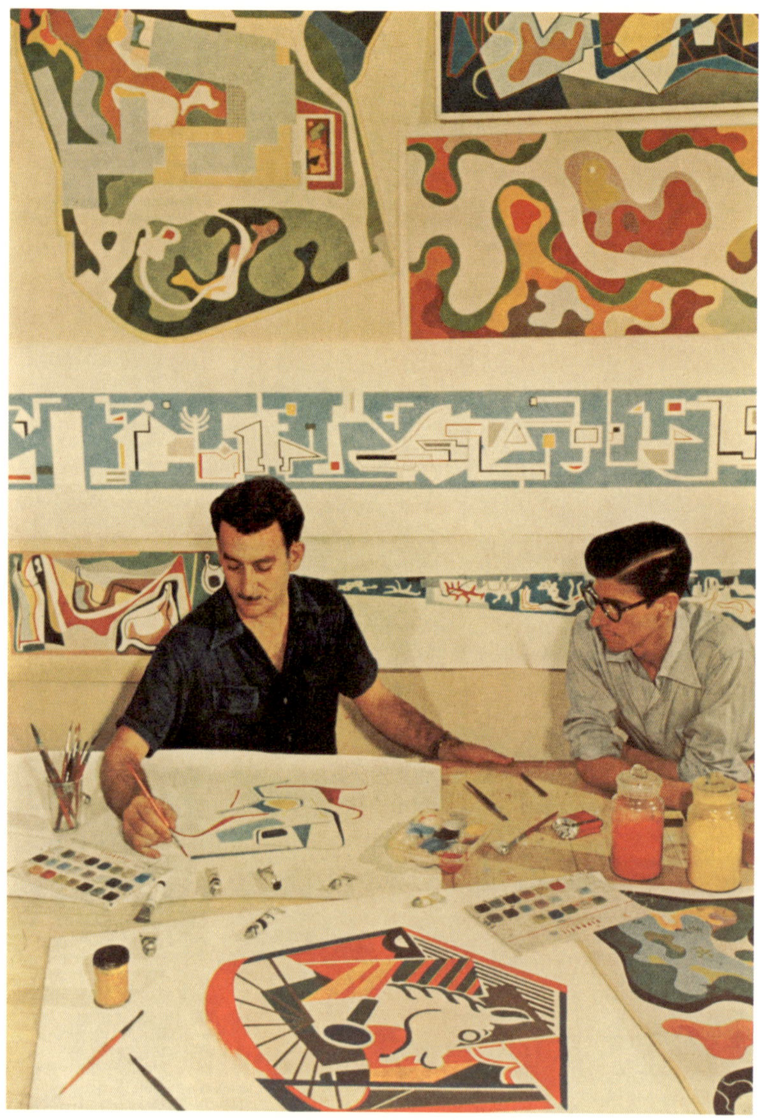

Figure 3.12. Roberto Burle Marx, 1955.
National Geographic, March 1955. Photo:
Charles Allmon, National Geographic Staff.

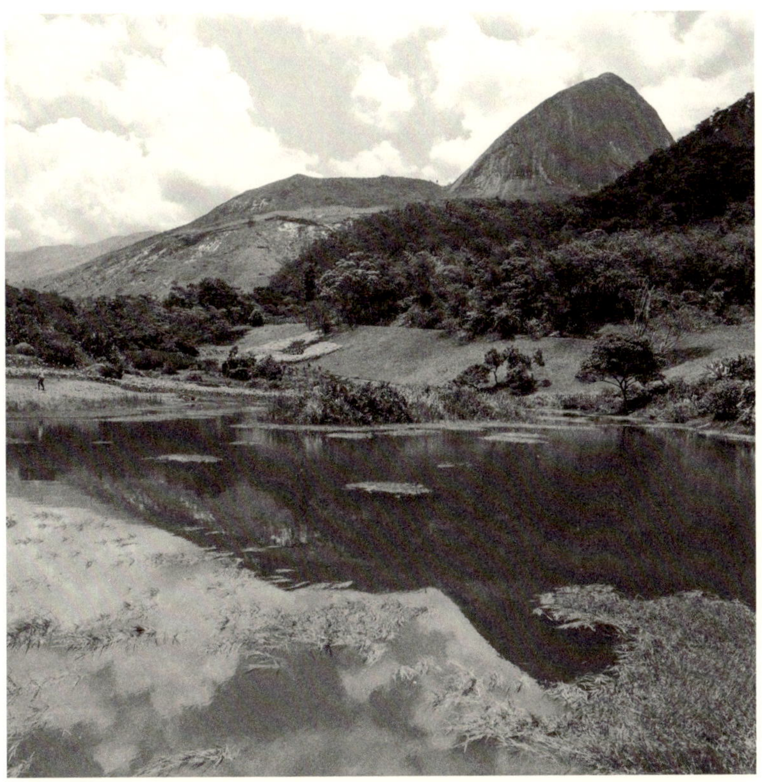

Figure 3.13. Marcel Gautherot, residence of Odette Monteiro, by Roberto Burle Marx and Wladimar Alves de Souza, ca. 1960. Courtesy of Instituto Morreira Salles.

same year Clark commenced her studies, the arching contours of nested plant beds, stones, and an artificial lake pictorially register the surrounding topography by "foreshortening and analogy," as Mindlin put it (fig. 3.13).[79] Mapping three-dimensional natural phenomena onto a two-dimensional composition, Burle Marx used the garden to transform his original source into a landscape, a picture.

Such dimensional transfers were crucial to Burle Marx's aesthetic. Elevated vistas frequently recreated the two-dimensional plane of a garden's original pictorial composition, as in the Ministério da

Educação e Saude building in Rio. Moreover, Burle Marx established the legibility of his compositions through the precise delineation of edges, often underscored by juxtapositions of color and scale.[80] At a practical level of upkeep, these contour lines were preserved by uprooting new growth so that a conduit of bare earth remained between any two plantings. Beneath this channel, a *divisor de canteiro* (plant-bed divider) made of concrete or aluminum was often buried in the ground, thereby preventing the intermingling of roots.[81] In this case, the drawn line of the original composition was transformed into a subterranean wall. Gardens were thus designed so that plant growth would dilate a vertical topography. Lateral swelling, however, was by and large disallowed. For this reason, although the empty spaces between elements in Burle Marx's gardens afford a superficial affinity to Clark's organic line, they are evidence of a diametrically opposed strategy: the elimination of organic growth as a means to *secure* compositional line.

Clark's only experiment with mosaics offers a useful comparison. In her mural for a building in Copacabana finished only after she left for France in 1950, Clark, like Burle Marx, harnessed tesserae toward sinuous, biomorphic curves (fig. 3.14). Because each colored mosaic establishes its own contour, such compositional lines coincide with the interior edges of the mosaic units. By contrast, the organic line inheres in the space *between* units. In so doing, it migrates line as such to these units' *exterior* edge. Tim Ingold has observed that we tend to think of constructions such as a brick wall as composed of solid forms, but we might instead conceive of such structures in terms of the connective network of mortar or plaster that holds these solids in place.[82] It is this tensile web that establishes the wall's durability, because it absorbs shifts and changes in the planarity of the individual units and allows for the breathing, swelling, and contracting of material over time. The organic line catalyzes just such a network, but in terms of empty space. In so doing, it also enacts a dimensional and ontological transfer of the organic, transposing the temporalized dilation and variability of

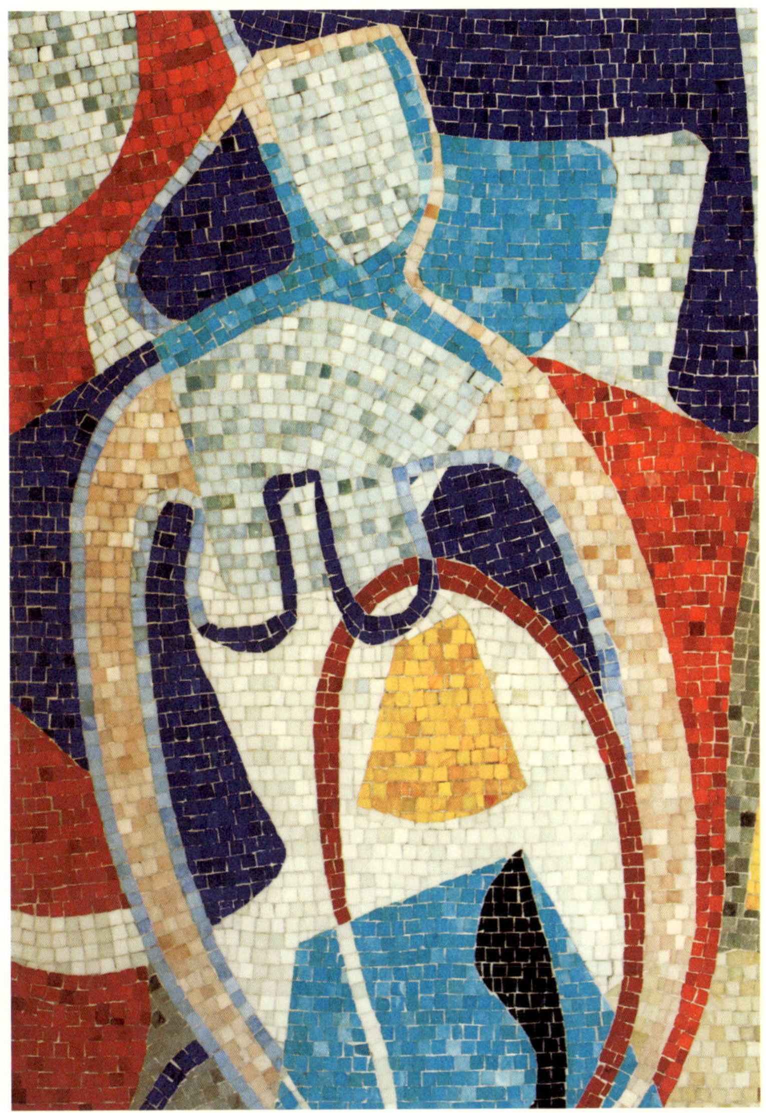

Figure 3.14. Lygia Clark, mosaic mural at Prédio
Mira Mar, Avenida Atlântica, 3992, Copacabana,
Rio de Janeiro, 1948–51. Photo: Pat Kilgore.
Courtesy of Associação Cultural "O Mundo de
Lygia Clark."

the organic plane Burle Marx established in his gardens in a *vertical* register onto the *lateral* edge of seemingly inert matter. This matter is now comprehended as constituting the responsive and contiguous limits of an "organic" line, drawing each element — limit and line — into a reciprocal, inflective ecology.

For critics such as Pedrosa, Clark's emphasis on the vitality of architectonic surfaces modulated by way of the organic line was an invigorating departure from the contemporaneous incorporation of murals within architecture. Although Clark and others participated in a robust dialogue about abstraction in early 1950s, the dominant idiom of Brazilian contemporary art remained representational. This representational art was often mobilized toward nationalist and ideological ends, resulting in the frequent commission of artists such as Candido Portinari to complete murals for the boom of new buildings in cities such as Rio and São Paulo. In 1948, Barr described Portinari in glowing terms as "the leading mural painter of South America."[83] But for Pedrosa, works by Portinari, Emiliano Di Cavalcanti, and others constituted a "muralist invasion" that "monopolized" the cities' available walls.[84] While Pedrosa's comments express a specific stylistic sensibility, they also throw into relief the problematic status of the wall for several Latin American practitioners at this time. While Pedrosa and others objected to representational murals as little more than images artificially affixed to walls, geometric abstraction appeared to offer a more cogent solution to integrating painting and architecture. Yet the pictorial status of the resulting surface was often unresolved.

Walls, of course, have long occupied an ambivalent position in relation to art and its display. As photographs of the inaugural exhibition staged by the Museu de Arte Moderna in Rio demonstrate, it was common practice well into the 1950s to cloak the walls of an exhibition space with curtains (figs. 3.15–3.16).[85] Such

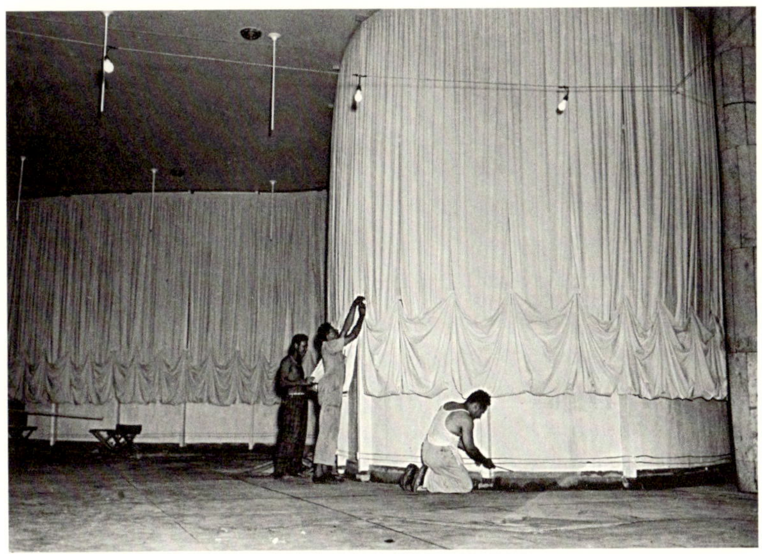

Figure 3.15. Museu de Arte Moderna do Rio de Janeiro, preparing for first exhibition, 1952. Courtesy of the Museu de Arte Moderna do Rio de Janeiro.

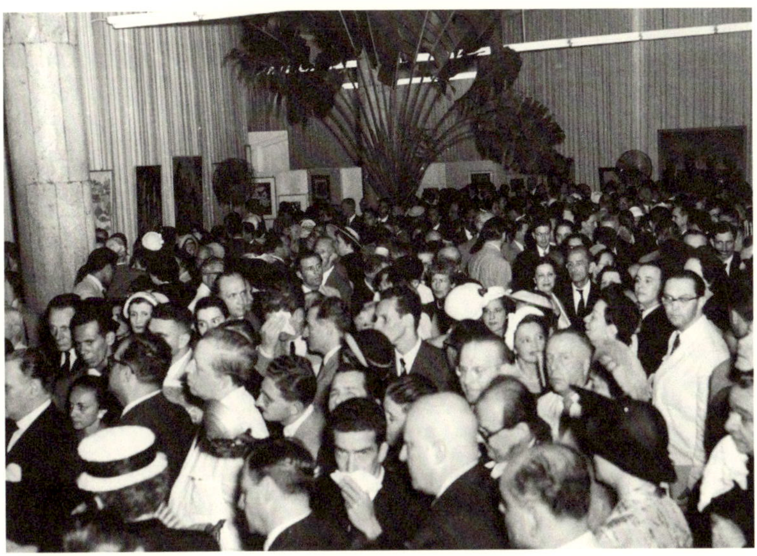

Figure 3.16. Museu de Arte Moderna do Rio de Janeiro, visitors at first exhibition, 1952. Courtesy of the Museu de Arte Moderna do Rio de Janeiro.

veiling shielded both viewers and works of art from the literal functionality of architecture and was often used — as in the 1955 Grupo Frente exhibition where Clark first showed her architectural maquettes — even when works were displayed on moveable panels. Conventional frames intensified this mediation, securely enclosing works of art from their environments. It was exactly in this sense that Ferreira Gullar described the frame in his 1958 text on Clark as "a middle term, a neutral zone born with the work, where all the conflict between virtual space and real space, between the 'free' work and the practical-bourgeois world, is erased."[86]

As discussed in previous chapters, the problem of the frame was the primary locus of experimentation for artists from Argentina and Uruguay working in Buenos Aires in the mid- to late 1940s who sought to abolish all residues of illusionistic pictorial space. This dynamic was often encapsulated in the problem of figure against ground, which, as Tomás Maldonado wrote, always "determines [an illusory] space."[87] As noted in Chapter 1, between 1944 and 1948, Maldonado and others affiliated with Asociación Arte Concrete-Invención and Arte Madí experimented with various methods of neutralizing the figure-ground relation, first through irregular or broken frames and subsequently through "coplanal" works in which constellations of colored shapes raised in relief were attached directly to a wall (fig. 3.17). While this approach eliminated the problem of the frame, the ground proved a more recalcitrant issue, since at a perceptual level, the wall itself inevitably took on this role.

After arriving at the coplanal format in 1946, artists such as Alberto Molenberg, Raúl Lozza, Alfredo Hlito, and Juan Melé began to investigate how shapes could retain their compositional unity even while spatially disengaged.[88] How far could individual units move apart while maintaining formal tension? How would color affect this equation? Should the orientation of elements be fixed or free? Believing that an "integral art" that combined art and architecture was all but impossible, Melé put forward the notion of the "delimited ground" in order to manage such variables.[89] As

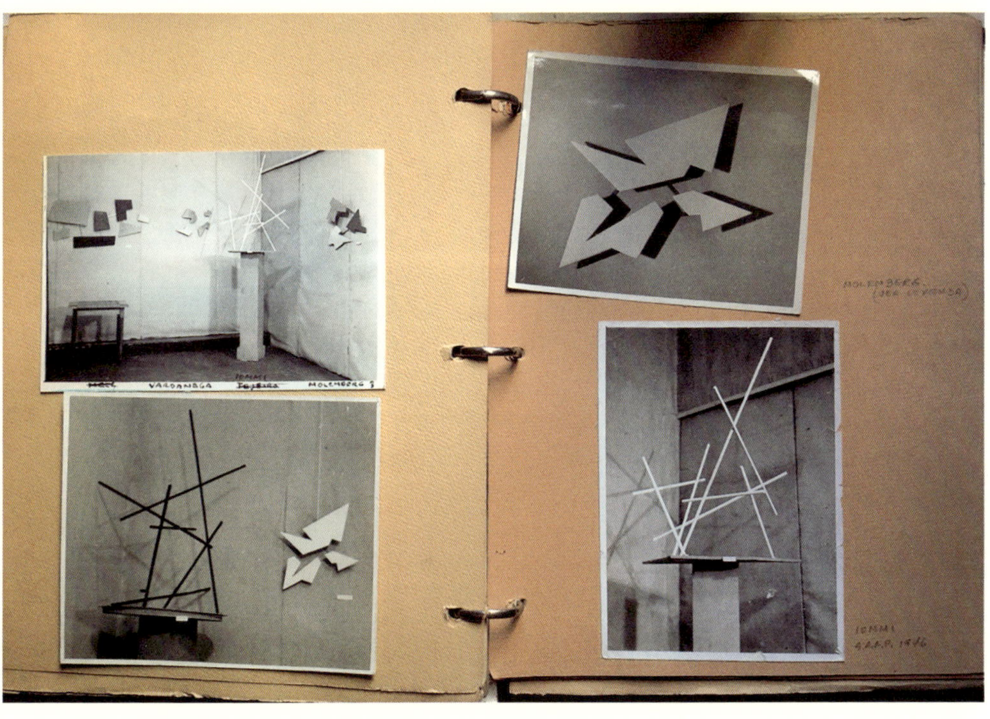

Figure 3.17. Juan N. Melé, page from portfolio
Grupo Concreto 1948, Sociedad Argentina
de Artistas Plásticos, October 1946, with works
by Melé, Maldonado, Vardánega, Iommi, and
Molenberg. Courtesy of Carlos H. Brasero.

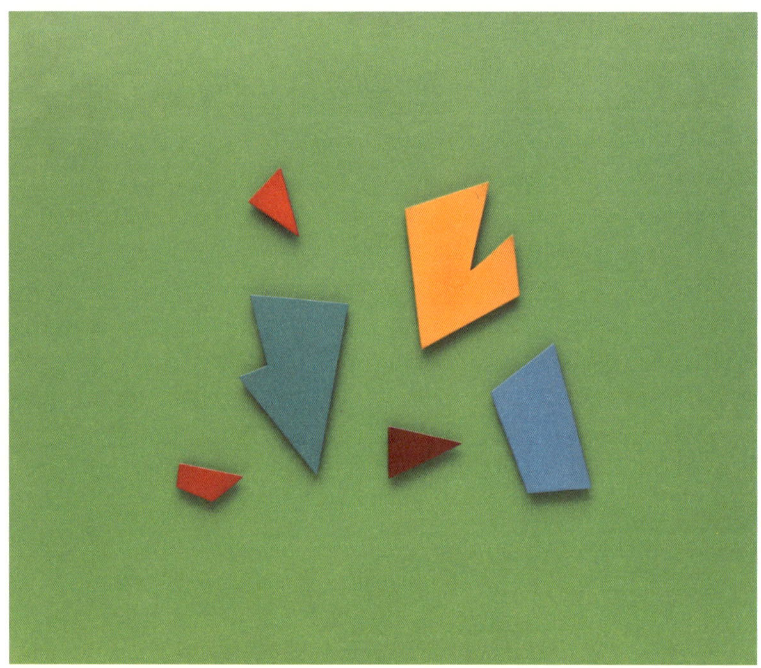

Figure 3.18. Raúl Lozza, *Pintura no. 171* (Painting no. 171), 1948. Oil and enamel on plywood, 99.5 × 119 cm. Photo: Museo de Arte Moderna de Buenos Aires.

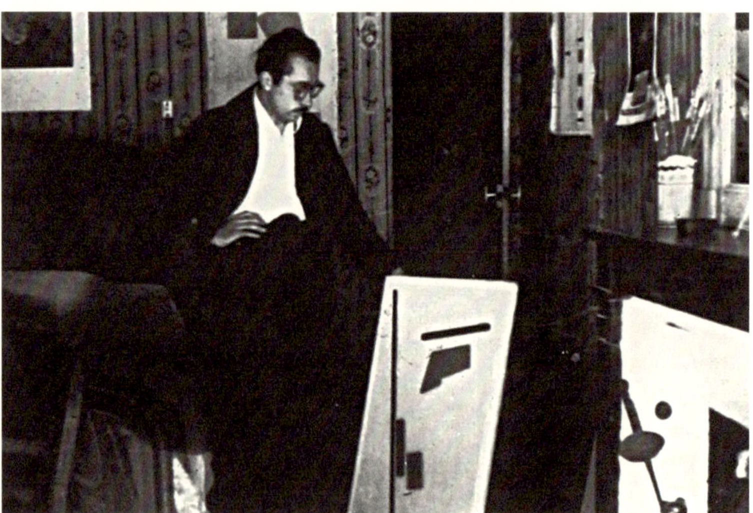

Figure 3.19. Juan N. Melé looking at his works in his atelier at 16 rue du Bac, Paris, 1949. Courtesy of Carlos H. Brasero.

demonstrated by such works as Lozza's *Pintura no. 171* (Painting no. 171, 1948), this convention allowed the artist to continue to exert aesthetic control over a composition by disengaging the coplanal from the wall and locating it on its own colored support (fig. 3.18). This solution of the *muro portátil*, or portable wall, as it came to be known, had the advantage of both control and mobility, and when Melé traveled to Europe in 1948, he brought at least one of these works with him (fig. 3.19).

In 1948, several artists intimate to these debates felt that they had reached an impasse and returned to the orthogonal frame. Others, such as Maldonado, concluded that an engagement with architecture was inevitable and embraced the notion of total design.[90] By contrast, Lozza, together with his brother Rembrandt and the theorist Abraham Haber, inaugurated a new movement called Perceptismo that continued the pursuit of nonrepresentational art in space. The core of Perceptismo was the development of a mathematical method for calibrating the relations between size, shape, composition, and color that Lozza called *cualimetría*, a neologism combining the terms "quality" and "geometry."[91] A housepainter and interior decorator by profession and a Marxist by political persuasion, Lozza sought to activate *cualimetría* not in relation to a ground, but by way of the concept of a *field* given by physics, wherein each point within a region is affected by a set of forces.[92] As Gabriel Pérez-Barreiro has observed, because Lozza's compositions were centrifugal, he considered the spatial limits of a given field accidental, rather than determinate, and thus entirely unlike the delimitation of either traditional or irregular frames.[93] For Lozza, a field was sufficient as long as it was large enough to preserve a composition's chromatic relations, and period photographs show that he not only displayed his works on portable supports, but differentiated compositions installed on a gallery wall with wooden dividers (fig. 3.20). Ideally, however, the chromatic ground would coincide with the wall, and in the first issue of the movement's self-published journal, *Perceptismo: Teorico y Polemico*, in 1950, Lozza

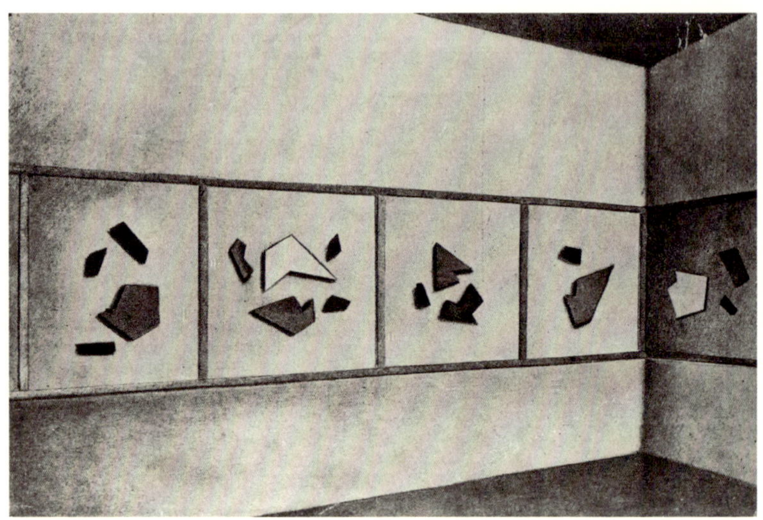

Figure 3.20. Raúl Lozza, works exhibited at first Perceptismo exhibition, Galería Van Riel, October 1949. *Perceptismo: Teorico y Polemico*, no. 1 (October 1950).

created a photocollage that positioned one of his compositions within a domestic environment (fig. 3.21). Although the image is black and white, the walls appear as if painted, establishing a chromatic field for the artist's formal constellation.

Yet the status of the wall vis-à-vis this field is ambiguous. In a 1951 article, Haber wrote, "For Perceptismo, architecture does not offer its forms to painting, but provides the plane upon which pictorial forms stand out." He continued, "The synthesis between architecture and painting" is thus achieved by comprehending "the flat wall as a determinate limit of the architectonic space, which neither disappears nor is incompatible with the pictorial plane, but serves as its background."[94] As the redoubling and contradictory language of this passage suggests, Perceptismo approached the wall as both a literal, material boundary and a protopictorial plane. This plane, however, does not assert its pictorial status so much as act as a "background" for what can only be understood as *yet another*

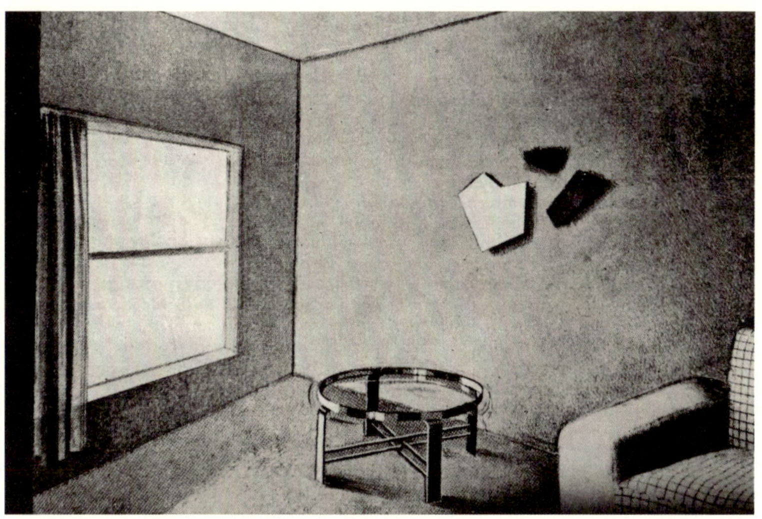

Figure 3.21. Illustration of work by Raúl Lozza in Abraham Haber, "Pintura y Perception," *Perceptismo: Teorico y Polemico*, no. 1 (October 1950).

pictorial plane. It was *this* plane that Perceptismo understood as a field, even as it materially coincided with the wall.[95]

In Lozza's photomontage, the conceptual distinction between the plane as a pictorial or architectural support is signaled at the junctures of the walls, ceiling, and floor, which the artist accentuated with a dark, ruled line. It is unclear if this line is meant to indicate a flat painted element or the three-dimensional architectural feature of a *zócalo* — a baseboard molding in its convex iteration, a negative cut-out in concave form.[96] When Lozza's environments were restaged for his 1997 retrospective at the Museo de Arte Moderno de Buenos Aires, this edging element was retained, indicating its intentional, rather than incidental use for differentiating the plane.[97] As a demarcation, however, it both sublimates and represses Perceptismo's equivocations regarding the pictorial status of the wall.

Lozza's edges enact both the theoretical originality and the contradiction of Perceptismo. Indeed, as Isabel Plante has compellingly

argued, the heavily retouched photographs Lozza and other associated artists used in their publications signal the "as if" tense of their
ambition to materially project a future world into being.[98] But the
architectural feature of the *zócalo* also signals a far wider condition in modern architecture by which walls came to signify their
complex and shifting historical relation to function. In classical and
Beaux-Arts traditions, convex moldings concealed joints between
architectural elements as well as the potential errors that inhered
in these junctions. In this role, they developed an ornamental value
of their own. Modern artists and architects seeking to elementa-
rize construction stripped away such decorative additions in order
to highlight structure and planarity, as well as the ever-increasing
value of precision.[99] Because modern construction meant that walls
functioned primarily as spatial dividers, rather than as load-bearing
devices, architects were eager to emphasize their lightness and flex-
ibility. Such walls, in turn, had formal affinities with the floating
partitions of modern exhibition design (fig 3.22).[100] A highly reflexive,
if little-noticed feature, a *zócalo* or recessed molding is one way of
visually disengaging the modern wall from its traditional function as
a structural support. Paradoxically, the result is an aesthetic reitera-
tion of the planar surface of the wall not unlike that proposed by Perceptismo, although for radically divergent ends. While Perceptismo
sought to derealize the wall in order to differentiate between literal
architecture and a chromatic field, modern architecture did so in
order to *approximate* literal architecture to the pictorial.

Now widespread in museum and exhibition architecture, a version of the *zócalo* or recessed molding appears to have been used in
Brazil as early as 1953 at the São Paulo Bienal, where we can identify it, aptly enough, in installation images of Lozza's works in the
Argentine pavilion (fig. 3.23).[101] Here, distinct genealogies of the
plane clash and overlap with practical constraints and genre conventions like mismatched Russian nesting dolls. For while Lozza's
works appear alongside irregularly shaped canvases by fellow artist
Martín Blaszko, cueing the historical dialogue of *marco recortado*, the

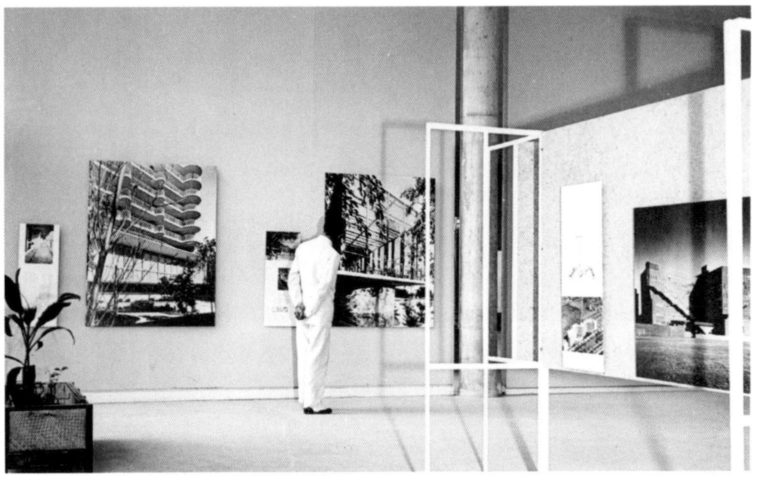

Figure 3.22. Exposição Internacional de Arquitectura, Second São Paulo Bienal, 1953. Courtesy of Fundação Bienal de São Paulo/Arquivo Histórico Wanda Svevo.

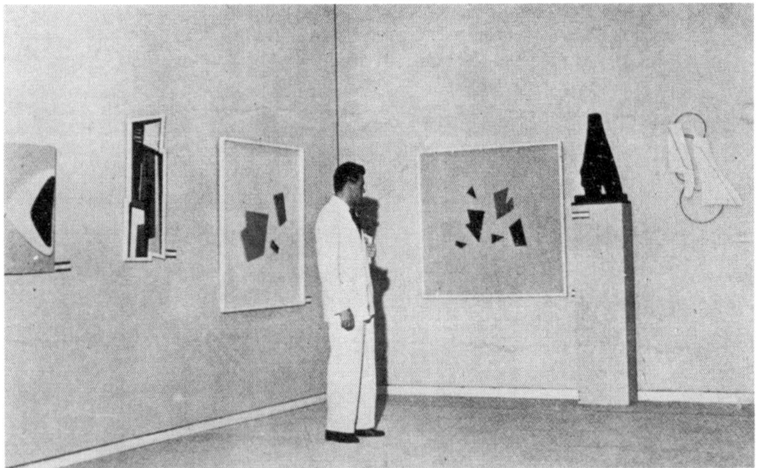

Figure 3.23. Argentine representation at the Second São Paulo Bienal, 1953, including works by Raúl Lozza and Martín Blaszko. *Arte Madí Universal*, nos. 7–8 (1954), p. 31.

installation reveals that the delimited ground or portable wall was not so different from the traditional orthogonal frame. Either Lozza himself or the biennial's exhibition designer appeared to reinstate the frame as a matter of protective security for his works' compositional fields. Meanwhile, the architecture's recessed molding — itself a novel design development of the two new buildings constructed since the biennial's first iteration in 1951 — declares the wall a pictorial plane freed from structure. This move gestures to the possibilities of an integrated art and architecture. But these possibilities, at least from a certain perspective, were ones that Lozza's unhappily constrained constellations had already foreclosed under the pressure of display.

The sociologist Georg Simmel famously declared that the door "speaks" while the wall is "mute."[102] As the prior discussion submits, however, walls are far from dumb. Clark's maquettes of 1955, moreover, draw the wall into a new loquaciousness by way of the organic line. In her work, the equivocation of the *zócalo* regarding the pictoriality of the wall becomes an integrating, structuring, and expressive architectonic element. In the context of De Stijl, Theo Van Doesburg declared, "nowhere there appears simply a hole or void," while Mondrian understood the "corporeality" of architecture as its curse.[103] Imploding these modernist preoccupations with planar flatness in architecture, Clark's maquettes treat surfaces as bodied entities riven by spatial intervals.[104] And while such surfaces do not lend themselves easily to construction or inhabitation, this virtuality enacts a pointed commentary on the transitivity of subjects and space.

When Clark exhibited her architectural maquettes in 1955 and 1956, she showed them alongside paintings from her *Superfície modulada* series constructed from glued, segmented, and scored panels of wood. As Herkenhoff has argued, the material support of these paintings retains the vestige of the frame — and its rupture — from her *Quebra da moldura* (Breaking the frame) series of 1954.[105] Illustrations that accompany a 1957 article by Lucy Teixeira for the Italian design journal *Commentari* signal the shared pictoriality of Clark's paintings and maquettes.[106] The illustrations commence with two *Superfícies moduladas*, followed by images of three maquettes with their doors in open and closed positions. One of the paintings, now known as *Superfície modulada no. 5*, 1955, is identified as *Bozzetto per la pareti dipinte* (Study for a painted wall) and reappeared in a 1957 article as *Solução para painel* (Solution for [a] panel) (see fig. 3.8). Both early titles indicate that Clark directed her compositions toward the built environment. In the photographs of the associated maquette, these compositional elements begin to signify in an architectural sense, the white triangles pointing to the aperture of a door or to the room's corner (fig. 3.24a). When these doors are set in motion, the triangles likewise seem to suggest the directionality of their opening. *Opening itself* becomes a pictorial event as the narrow fissure of the organic line swells into a shape, the resulting void of black space in turn absorbing its contiguous black triangle. As the comparative photographs demonstrate, the modules of empty space unleashed by these apertures are as integral — and integrated — into the composition as the thin lines of space that exist when the doors are closed.

This compositional mobilization of the organic line as void is even more pronounced in the photographs of the second two maquettes (figs. 3.24b–c). Formally, these works relate to *Superfície modulada no 2.* (1955), illustrated in the Teixeira article and constructed from rectangular bands of color that weave a surface by way of chromatic contrast and channels of literal space.[107] But the maquettes depart strikingly from that painting's tightly centered and self-enclosing square configuration. Instead, they display a dynamic asymmetry that steps down from left to right in Teixeira's figures 5 and 6, and is concatenated and fully dispersed in figures 7 and 8. Clark clearly positioned the opened doors of the maquettes at a precise angle when she photographed them, because in each case, the perceived width of the resulting black

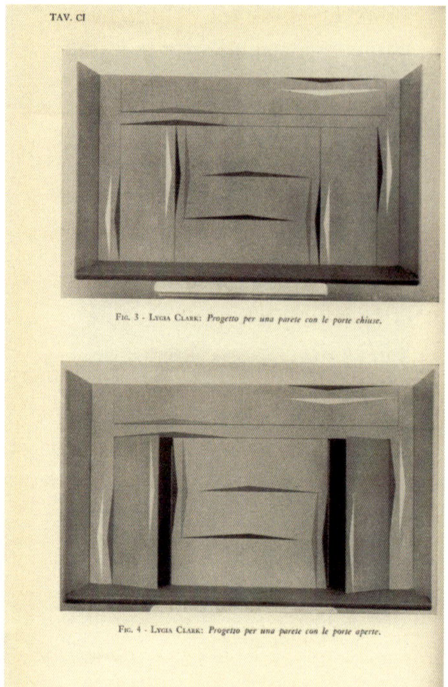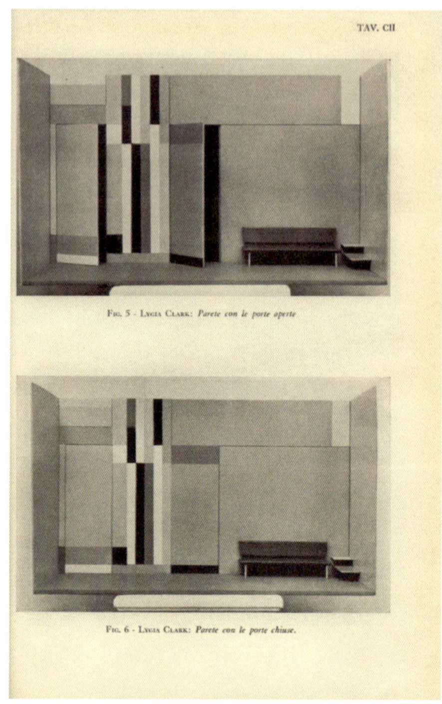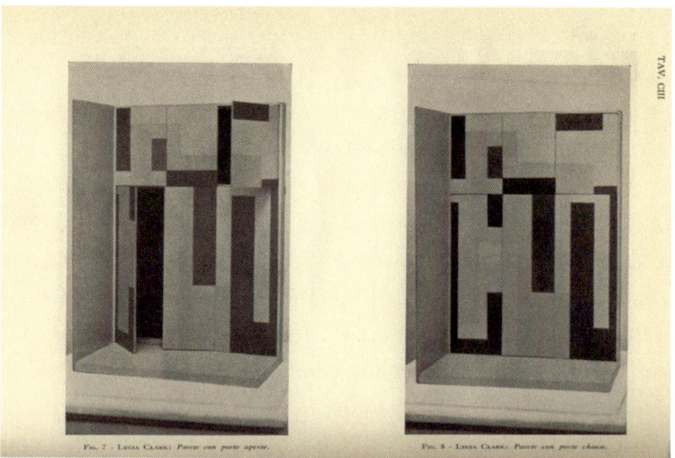

Figures 3.24a–c. Lucy Teixeira, "Una esperienza brasiliana," *Commentari* (October–December 1957), figures 3–4, 5–6, and 7–8.

void is equivalent to a matching painted element. But whereas in the first maquette, compositional elements act subtly to call attention to function, in the second and third maquettes, the formal doubling of black voids and panels triggers a dizzying set of possibilities of openness and closure that defy function or navigability. In this blended environment, painted and actual space are equally pictorialized: the room is always an image of itself, even when its planar surfaces are ruptured. One can only imagine that a viewer interacting with such an environment would experience this virtuality *phenomenologically*. To this degree, Clark's maquettes do not use architectural apertures to turn an exterior environment into a picture; they render architecture itself as a spatially immersive pictoriality.[108]

In 1959, discussing her early paintings of stairs, which often confuse spatial orientation, Clark spoke of the problem of "entering the space of the picture."[109] Later, she described this quality as *organic*: "When I said to enter the picture it was exactly this organic thing that I wanted. Not for the picture to be contemplated from afar [but that] one could enter the place, the space of the picture."[110] In this sense, the organic line was not simply a means of integrating painting with architecture or surface with space, but of embedding the viewer within their mutually constitutive networks. Mark Wigley has remarked that the concept of total design can be divided into implosive and explosive impulses, the former "subjecting every detail, every surface, to an overarching vision," resulting in "a space with no gaps, no cracks, no openings onto . . . other worlds," the latter attempting to expand in order "to touch every possible point in the world."[111] In contrast to both of these tendencies, Clark's maquettes imagine a fully modulated interior architecture that depends precisely on its *porosity* to the exterior world.

Clark's maquettes propose an architectural environment in which the bounding surface of the wall that typically divides interior from exterior is perforated and rearticulable, rather than fixed. In this sense, her maquettes imagine a situation in which the wall is always potentialized as a threshold. Writing about the door as cultural technique, Bernhard Siegert notes that for figures such as Simmel or Gottfried Semper, the door enacts "the primordial difference of architecture — that between inside and outside."[112] It is for this reason that Simmel wrote that the door *speaks*: it is the image of a boundary that also establishes the possibility of "permanent interchange."[113] But Siegert recognizes that the door's symbolic character does not lie simply in the difference between outside and inside, but in the way the door instantiates the paradox of a symbolic order. "The door and the gatekeeper implement the differential law of the signifier itself," he writes. The result is "the logic of a door that is closed while it is open."[114] Here we might think of the exclusionary capacity of the state, the authority of religion, or inscriptions of gender, class, and race. The door — and in Clark's case, the entirety of the architectural membrane — is therefore a site that produces asymmetries of power, but also the possibility of their narrativization.

Sergio Delgado Moya has argued that Clark's *Relational Objects*, mentioned in Chapter 2, deliberately reconfigure the quotidian objects and everyday gestures of domestic space against the backdrop of Latin America's burgeoning consumer culture.[115] In light of the symbolic character of the threshold, however, we might locate the incipient politics of this defamiliarization in Clark's earliest foray into architecture, not in relation to objects so much as to the notion of the architectural enclosure as a presumptively social space. In her 1956 lecture at the school of architecture in Belo Horizonte, Clark closed her discussion of the collaborative potential of art and architecture with a parable: "Do not call upon the artist at the end of a project, thereby having the 'patriarchal' attitude of a *mineiro* from the hinterland who, in offering a good spread of food to his friend, leaves his wife behind the kitchen door, listening to the praise which the friend gives regarding the food that she herself has prepared."[116] In this anecdote, Clark analogizes the artist to the wife who listens behind the kitchen door — seething, we can imagine — as her husband (and by extension, the architect) takes credit for her labor. That Clark's ex-husband and father were both *mineiros* (inhabitants from the region of Minas Gerais) — and traditional ones, at that — is highly significant.[117] As Adele Nelson has argued, Clark's decision to include this anecdote in her lecture, as well as her broader self-presentation in these years, constitutes a "politics and performance of gender" that intervenes in period discourses of femininity, decorum, and taste.[118]

Yet Clark's parable does not simply stage a complaint. It thematizes the wall as an apparatus for the circulation of information, energies, and affects, a circulation that occurs within — indeed *produces* — uneven conditions.[119] The sustaining food the wife makes transits from kitchen to dining room by means of an opened door; the husband's comments filter back to the wife through the wall, despite this door's closure; the wall's materiality cordons sociality into distinctly gendered zones; its visual absenting of the wife thematizes the invisibility and force of her anger. We can only imagine that Clark had a vested interest in recalibrating these relations in her own experiments with architecture. Indeed, when approached comparatively through contemporaneous articulations of domesticity and integrated, efficient living, Clark's maquettes offer a mutant model of the ways in which sociality congeals within surface and space.

———

At a purely formal level of abstract design, Clark's maquettes are not so different from the architectural configuration featured in a 1951 article, "Un armario multiple," published in the Buenos Aires-based journal *Nuestra Arquitectura* (figs. 3.25 and 3.26).[120] The article includes drawings and photographs of a modular armoire wall unit, paying particular attention to the transitional moments when flat elements extend into three-dimensional space. The accompanying text notes that the unit fuses a bedroom, wardrobe, and ironing room within a highly reduced space of twelve square meters. Features include a closet, a retractable table that doubles as a nightstand, a full-sized bed, a large table, an ironing board, shelves, and

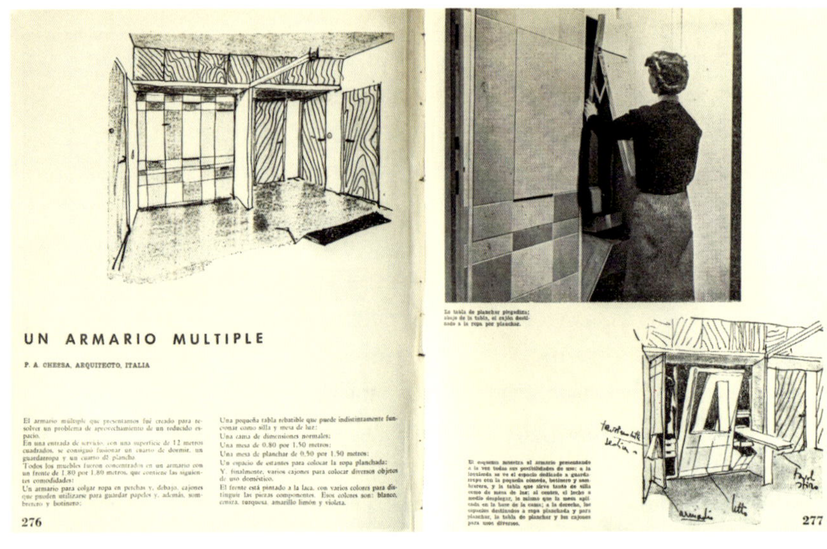

UN ARMARIO MULTIPLE

P. A. CHESSA, ARQUITECTO, ITALIA

El armario múltiple que presentamos fué creado para resolver un problema de aprovechamiento de un reducido espacio.

En una entrada de servicio, con una superficie de 12 metros cuadrados, se consiguó fusionar un cuarto de dormir, un guardarropa y un cuarto de plancha.

Todos los muebles fueron concentrados en un armario con un frente de 1,80 por 1,80 metros, que contiene las siguientes comodidades:

Un armario para colgar ropa en perchas y, debajo, cajones que pueden utilizarse para guardar papeles y, además, sombrerero y botinero;

Una pequeña tabla rebatible que puede indistintamente funcionar como silla y mesa de luz;

Una cama de dimensiones normales;

Una mesa de 0.80 por 1.50 metros;

Una mesa de planchar de 0.50 por 1.50 metros;

Un espacio de estantes para colocar la ropa planchada;

Y, finalmente, varios cajones para colocar diversos objetos de uso doméstico.

El frente está pintado a la laca, con varios colores para distinguir las piezas componentes. Esos colores son: blanco, ceniza, turquesa, amarillo limón y violeta.

276

La tabla de planchar plegadiza; abajo de la tabla, el cajón destinado a la ropa por planchar.

El esquema muestra el armario presentando a la vez todas sus posibilidades de uso: a la izquierda se ve el espacio dedicado a guardarropa con la pequeña cómoda, botinero y sombrerera, y la tabla que sirve tanto de silla como de mesa de luz; al centro, el lecho a medio desplegar, lo mismo que la mesa aplicada en la base de la cama; a la derecha, los espacios destinados a ropa planchada y para planchar, la tabla de planchar y los cajones para usos diversos.

277

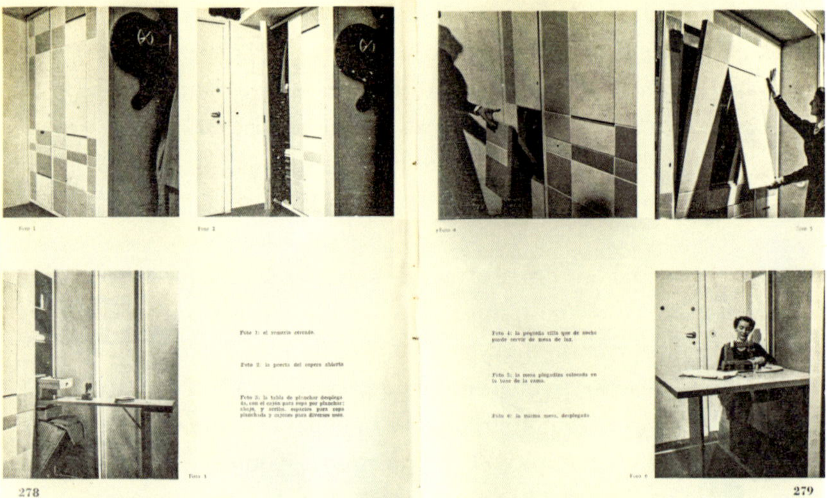

278

279

Figures 3.25 and 3.26. P. A. Chessa, "Un armario multiple," *Nuestra Arquitectura* (Buenos Aires) 22.264 (July 1951), pp. 276–79. Photo: Milena Pazos.

a set of drawers. The text underscores functions that revolve primarily around apparel and its maintenance: the closet is for hanging clothes; the ironing board for pressing; the shelves for storing already ironed items, and so on. The article explicitly codes the space as feminine: photographs picture a woman opening and closing the hinged modular units as well as operating a sewing machine; another image features the all-important ironing station, waiting to be activated. We are led to imagine a solitary woman, perhaps with an office job, endlessly reproducing her sartorial respectability for a world that exists on the other side of the wall.

Yet the dormitory space itself is hermetic, and there are no visual apertures to this outside. When the armoire's panels extend, they reveal only shallow storage, and the illustration's three doors remain emphatically closed. What is more, the armoire's capacity for articulation is oriented entirely toward the room's interior. To this extent, the architecture aids and mimics the woman's cyclical domestic labor, extending and retracting its surfaces into neat rectangles, just as she presses, folds, and stores her clothing within their modular compartments. Insofar as no mention is made of a kitchen or bathroom, *un armario multiple* is not technically a *machine-à-habiter*, or machine for living, as in Le Corbusier's influential appellation.[121] Rather, it is a mechanism for the self-reproduction of the petit-bourgeois female subject as worker. In short, a certain kind of labor occurs inside so that another kind of labor can occur outside.

How different this vision is from Le Corbusier's own articulations of labor and space. As I noted at the beginning of this chapter, the architect elaborated his 1921 formulation of a "machine for living" during his voyage from France to Buenos Aires in 1929 aboard a luxury ocean liner. On the return trip, he compiled his recollections of his South American lectures, publishing them in the 1930 volume *Precisions on the Present State of Architecture and City Planning: With an American Prologue, a Brazilian Corollary, Followed by "The Temperature of Paris" and "The Atmosphere of Moscow."* In these lectures, Le Corbusier makes much of the visual perspective offered by the airplane, by which he comprehended the vastness of the South American landscape and envisioned ribbons of mass-produced housing unfurling across its surface (see fig. 3.2). But it was the ocean liner itself that inspired his reflections on the character of these dwellings.

In his fourth lecture, Le Corbusier notes that one of the controversies provoked by his concept of a "machine for living" was that "among the different social classes, we do not agree on an intellectual point of great important: *the reason for living.*"[122] Rather than elaborating these differences, Le Corbusier launches into a description of his quotidian life on the ship, where for fifteen days, "I am cut off from the rest of the world, from my barber, my laundress, from my baker, my greengrocer, and my butcher. I opened my trunks, I settled in my house, I'm in the skin of a gentleman who has rented a small house" (fig. 3.27).[123] The architect makes an inventory of his sparse, but efficiently equipped cabin, noting that the whole area is only 15.75 square meters. But within this, he writes, "A man is happy, carries on all the functions of domestic life, sleeps, washes himself, writes, reads, invites his friends."[124] Le Corbusier then imagines a skeptical interlocutor: "Well, and eating? The kitchen and the cook, the valet de chambre, and the femme de chambre?" His reply is euphoric, and proceeds from the question of food ("I'm not concerned by it. It is the job of the dining room, using refrigerators, kitchens, cookers, washing machines, etc., etc."), to personal assistance ("At seven in the morning my valet de chambre, who is extraordinarily polite and helpful, wakes me.... He has prepared my dinner jacket discreetly at 7 p.m., and when at night the bed is ready, the night-light lit. God, how easy my life is"), to cleaning ("My valet has done the room, the toilet, and the bath"), and washing ("John, here is my laundry, have it washed for me the day after tomorrow, but have my trousers ironed while I am at the barber's"), and so on. The brilliant solution of the ocean liner — a discovery Le Corbusier likens to the apocryphal story Christopher Columbus's egg — is the *quantification* of service, by which a single worker's labor is distributed across multiple passengers.[125]

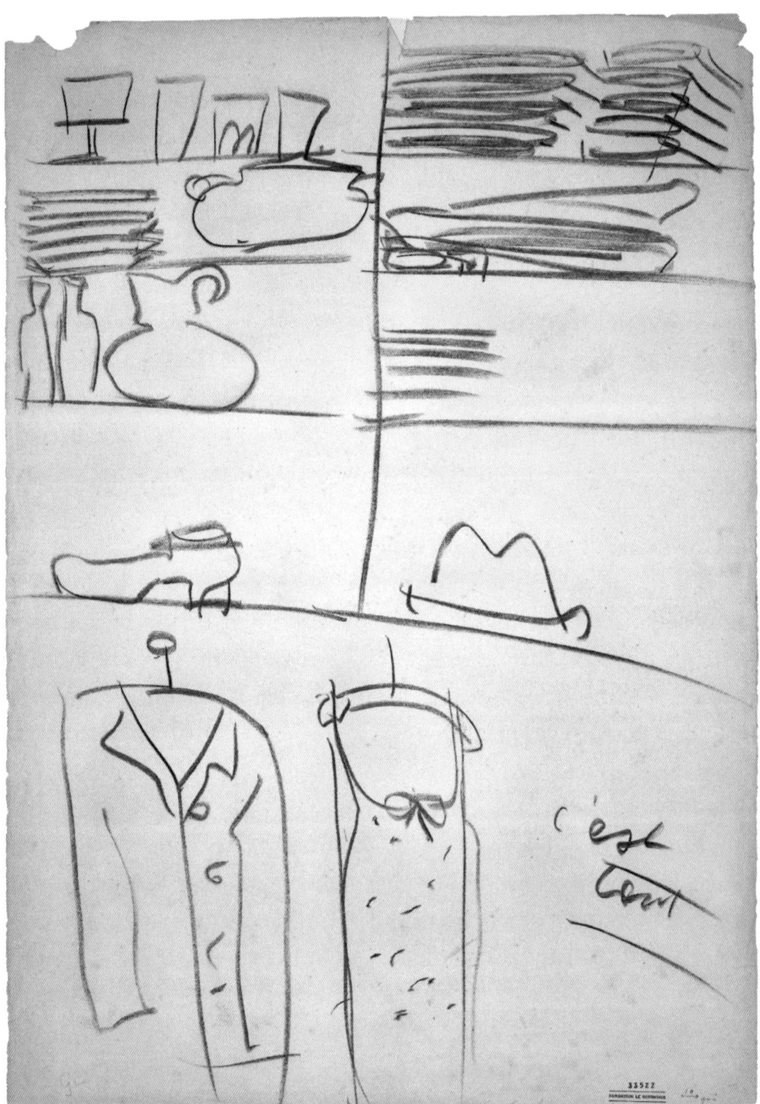

Figure 3.27. Le Corbusier, from *Precisions on the Present State of Architecture and City Planning: With an American Prologue, a Brazilian Corollary, Followed by "The Temperature of Paris" and "The Atmosphere of Moscow,"* 1930. © F.L.C./ ADAGP, Paris/Artists Rights Society (ARS), New York, 2023.

"Ladies and gentlemen, I employ a fortieth of a cook," he enthuses. "I have … at my service one-twentieth of a valet de chambre. How the cost of living goes down!"[126] But Le Corbusier's excitement is not driven solely by the ability to fragment, quantify, and agglomerate labor, but in the interchangeability and anonymity of the servants themselves. "I don't have to know whether John smokes cigarettes and reads novels, or wants to go the movies," he writes. "At two in the morning, I call John on the telephone: 'John is in bed, I'll send you someone.' Here is Paul. 'Paul, be so good as … .'"[127] In a stunning turn of phrase, Le Corbusier notes that by releasing oneself from the "false surfaces" of the traditional home, individual servants, "and the frightful cares they cause," "*liberty appears*, to us who are slaves."[128]

The division, multiplication, and financialization of labor that facilitates Le Corbusier's "liberated" existence on the ocean liner depends upon both the security and permeability of architectural barriers. Within the "false surfaces" of a traditional home, master and servant overlap within domestic space, such that the needs and affects of the latter are impossible to be ignored by the former. The ship, by contrast, provides a strict containerization of social relations, resulting in *true* surfaces, Le Corbusier might say. The master now controls his 15.75-square-meter cabin and solicits services by means of the telephone. Information and affects move across the boundary of the wall, but now primarily in one direction. John (or Paul) may be "extraordinarily polite and helpful," but the master no longer knows if he smokes, reads, watches films, or falls sick. Provisions and services, meanwhile, transit in the other direction, transmitted from exterior to interior such that labor itself is largely invisible from view. In *un armario multiple*, architecture's enclosure and quasi-anthropomorphic extension aids (impels!) the female inhabitant in the labor of her own social and self-reproduction. By contrast, Le Corbusier's cabin mobilizes the architectural apparatus of the wall to outsource the reproductive labor of biological maintenance while sealing off the socioaffective repercussions of this labor from within.

But what of the wall itself? Unlike the impermeable outer surfaces of *un armario multiple*, Le Corbusier's machine for living depends on the wall as a mechanism of circulation and exchange. For the most part, these operations are carefully managed and in this are akin to several of the architect's other articulations of bounding surfaces. In his second South American lecture, Le Corbusier imagines the wall as a mechanical, pneumatic structure, constructed of two membranes separated by a few centimeters of empty space (fig. 3.28). This "neutralizing wall" would allow for the heating and cooling of air so as to prevent undue "influence" from the outside by means of its "exact breathing."[129] Le Corbusier's attentiveness to the thickness of boundaries, likewise, was what allowed him to reimagine "the *flow* of the world's products" in *The Modulor* vis-à-vis the shipping crates and colonial networks of the French railway line. But while both of these cases suggest how a material border is scrutinized and adjusted to facilitate movement, the management of affects is a far stickier affair. Although Le Corbusier imagined his ship cabin as a container sealed from the "frightful cares" of John (or Paul), his voyages to and from South America were also occasions in which the threshold operated as a site of discomfort and desire.

It was on the ocean liner from Bordeaux to Buenos Aires, after all, that Le Corbusier met and had an affair with the legendary dancer and singer Josephine Baker, who, as Anne Anlin Cheng has persuasively argued, embodied "the dream of a second skin—of remaking one's self in the skin of the other."[130] In her pathbreaking work on eugenics and modern architecture, Fabiola López-Durán has demonstrated that Le Corbusier was complicit with some of the most heinous articulations of "perfecting" and "whitening" the human race.[131] Although he publicly subscribed to these ideologies only on his second trip to South America in 1936, already by 1930, Le Corbusier spoke of a desire to join architecture with "breeding, the constitution of a healthy race."[132] That the architect had an affair with Baker, an African American woman known for her

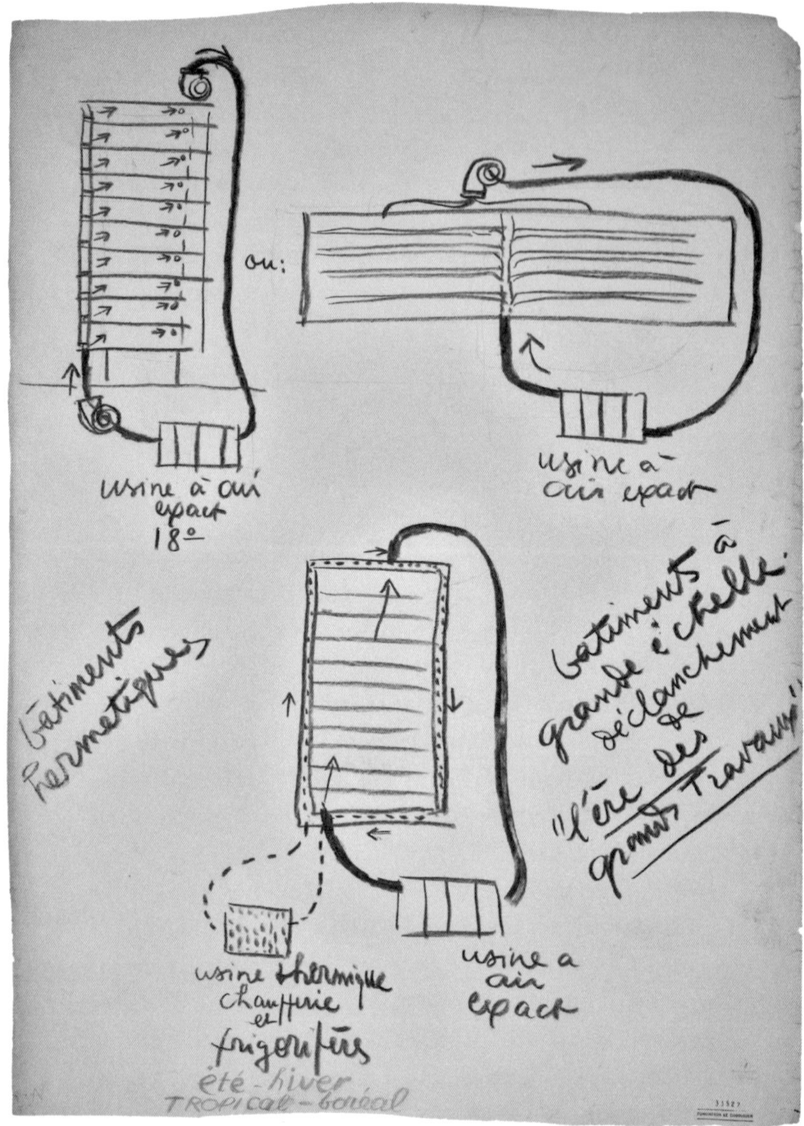

Figure 3.28. Le Corbusier, from *Precisions on the Present State of Architecture and City Planning: With an American Prologue, a Brazilian Corollary, Followed by "The Temperature of Paris" and "The Atmosphere of Moscow,"* 1930. © F.L.C./ADAGP, Paris/Artists Rights Society (ARS), New York, 2023.

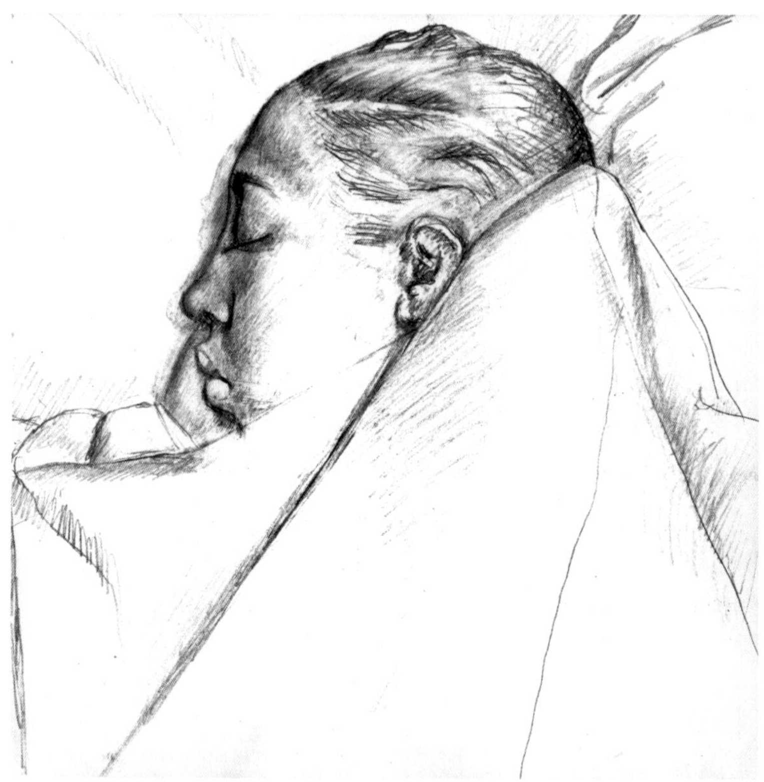

Figure 3.29. Le Corbusier, *The Sleeping Josephine Baker*, 1929. © F.L.C./ADAGP, Paris/ Artists Rights Society (ARS), New York, 2023.

primitivizing performances, is not surprising, however, since racial fetishization is of a piece with suprematist phantasies. It is not diffi-cult to imagine that when Baker "came to his cabin and he sketched her, nude," Le Corbusier conceived of his sexual access as one more iteration of his blithe existence on the ship, "liberated" from the "false surfaces" of the traditional home (fig. 3.29).[133]

But as Cheng argues, surface itself was very much at stake with Baker, and the affective charge of her relationship with Le Cor-busier was not solely one of freedom and release. As Le Corbusier recounted in his prologue to *Precisions*, he visited Baker's steamship

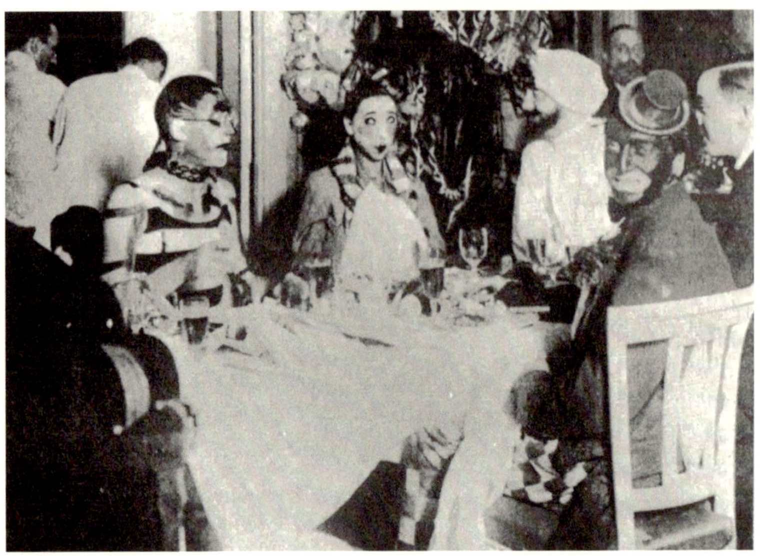

Figure 3.30. Le Corbusier, Josephine Baker, and others at a costume party abord the *Lutétia*, bound for Paris from Buenos Aires, 1929. Photographer unknown.

cabin, as well, and when she crooned to him of being "the weave of the cloth" that she might "roll up and take away," or sang "Baby" in a São Paulo nightclub, it moved him to tears, allowing him to "break out of his own skin," as Cheng puts it.[134] Already Le Corbusier associated settling into his ship cabin with an erotic charge of epidermal displacement: "I'm in the skin of a gentleman who has rented a small house."[135] His relationship with Baker only intensified this obsession with surface as a means of cloaking, revealing, and transforming the subject. While labor and service could be quantified and managed, desire occupied the threshold itself. To wit, for a costume ball on their return voyage from South America aboard the *Lutétia*, Le Corbusier appeared to dress up *as* Baker, in blackface, with his hair dyed black and slicked down in her characteristic "Bakerfix" (fig. 3.30). For his clothing, the architect donned a black-and-white striped singlet, painting black bands across his bare arms to extend the pattern to his (white) skin. The year before, the architect Adolf Loos had designed a house for Baker prominently featuring a black-and-white striped façade in which the mechanical and the animalistic "speak through one another," as Cheng puts it.[136] How apt that Le Corbusier, railing against "false" architectural surfaces while engaging in a cross-racial, cross-gender masquerade, dressed as "Josephine Baker" conjured *as a wall* through another architect's eyes!

One wonders how Le Corbusier would have described the "reason for living" of the Johns and Pauls who served him in his steamship cabin, such that they, too, might enjoy a "machine for living" in the modern world. One can speculate that it was some version of *un armario multiple*, in which the worker ceaselessly reproduces his or her own readiness for labor outside of the home. Although Le Corbusier would have disapproved of the thick enclosure of the dormitory's walls at the level of architectural style, in terms of social class, he might have appreciated their insulating and isolating properties. After all, not everyone was accorded the privilege of freely crossing architectural boundaries, let alone the transgressive thrill of inhabiting the membrane itself. Put another way, while in *un armario multiple*, architecture aids the social reproduction of its inhabitant at a mechanical level — extending, storing, supporting, folding up — Le Corbusier's cabin walls facilitate the transit and accumulation of vital energies at a biological and psychic level, but by means of externalized labor. While the first corresponds to the organic in its machinic inflection, the second evokes the organic in terms of a network of energies generated and sustained by multiple bodies in space. In *The Modulor*, Le Corbusier strategized how to transport containers of commodities from colony to metropole. In *Precisions*, the ocean liner indicated how human service might likewise be quantified, packaged, and deployed within a global network "without gaps."

Triangulating Clark's maquettes with these distinct architectural formulations, we can begin to see how her maquettes catalyze the dual inflections of the organic as a property of the wall itself. As Clark would have learned during her apprenticeship in a carpentry shop circa 1956, all material planes have a thickness and temporal elasticity that repudiates the idealization of absolute geometry.[137] As noted earlier, tolerances are thus built into designs in order to account for the swelling, shrinking, and mutability of constructed elements. But in Clark's maquettes, this spatial and temporal variation and deviation becomes a structuring and aesthetic element in and of itself. In other words, Clark's maquettes *introvert the organic as the defining quality of the architectural seam.* Returning to our comparison, what was directed toward the interior of domestic space in *un armario multiple* and transited across the walls of Le Corbusier's cabin is now held in tension by a grid of spatial fissures dispersed across the architectural surface itself. I explored in Chapter 2 how the organic line amounts to a thickening of the painterly plane. With regard to the architectural plane, it results in a corresponding *thinning*, such that the technological, material, and affective elements normally contained within or managed by the wall are pushed to its edges and intervals. Rather than carving out a channel of space within the architectural membrane to "neutralize" external conditions, as Le Corbusier imagined, the spatial conduits of Clark's maquettes *absorb* these conditions, such that it is the wall itself that breathes and reacts, in concert with the participatory touch of the user. Energies and affects are not transparently exchanged across or forestalled by the wall. Rather, they are distributed across the architectural membrane by means of the organic line. Wall and user thus exist in a mutually constitutive network in which the organic implicates subjectivity, materiality, and space in equal measure.

Notably, this "mutual shaping" of energies and affects underscores architecture as a specifically social construction.[138] As discussed above, Clark concluded her 1956 lecture by invoking domestic space and the gendering of labor. In a certain lineage of architectural discourse, the origins of architecture were to be located not in monumental forms such as the temple, but in domestic space and elemental activities such as meal preparation, craftwork, and socialization that take place in and around it.[139] Le Corbusier's ship cabin sits at the opposite end of this conceptualization, for while the cabin becomes a prototype of domestic space, it does so only by outsourcing labor to an external realm. In stark contrast to the interiorization of *un armario multiple*, it demands an infrastructure that moves between public and private spheres. As Beatriz Colomina has argued, Loos's interiors, by contrast, posit an unresolved tension between domestic and public space (each ostensibly gendered in their own way), such that the wall itself performs — and produces — the splitness of the subject.[140]

Considering this fraught genealogy of the domestic, it is significant that Clark's maquettes are largely denuded of any indications of function. Designated primarily as "maquettes for an interior," they conjure the indeterminate space of a living room, office, or waiting room: spaces that themselves express a liminal relationship to public and private.[141] Moreover, they do not offer a pragmatic or buildable architecture: witness the lack of handles or doorknobs, the confusion of spatial orientation, the absence of institutional specificity, and the impracticality of architectonic surfaces perforated by channels of space. Suspended between genres and functions, the maquettes are abstractions of architecture significant for their deformation of period architecture's normative aims. Simmel recognized that architectural thresholds enact the paradox of human activity: as humans, he writes, "we are at any moment those who separate the connected or connect the separate."[142] In Clark's maquettes, this theoretical relationality and permeability of the threshold is rendered in material form. The corresponding model of the subject is not split between public and private, but the site of their suture.

———

The performative character of Clark's 1955 maquettes likely had some roots in her brief experiences with scenography and interior design.[143]

The maquettes likewise suggest Clark may have been familiar with Mondrian's set designs, published in Michel Seuphor's 1949 volume *L'art abstrait*.[144] Those illustrations feature a small cardboard figure positioned against a shifting pattern of abstract geometric elements within a recessed stage. In Clark's photographs of her maquettes, even the semblance of such a figure disappears. Instead, their visual drama lies in the articulation and disarticulation of the architectural surface as doors and panels open and close and modules of surface and void advance and retreat. That architecture might act as a spatial protagonist is not novel in and of itself. The illustration for *un armario multiple* suggests an absurdist, even threatening activation of architectural function, wherein the wardrobe seems to deploy its full repertoire of modular fixtures on its own accord. Moreover, as Spyros Papapetros has persuasively argued, the animation of inorganic objects is part and parcel of a fundamental, though deeply ambivalent impulse within modernist thought.[145] While Clark's maquettes participate in this longer history, I want to suggest that their significance lies more precisely in how they perform the mutable boundaries of global capitalism that we navigate and inhabit today. Le Corbusier's shipping containers and steamship cabins anticipate the corporate, multinational dream of this capitalism, wherein material objects and laboring subjects are seamlessly integrated within global networks. The organic lines of Clark's maquettes offer a view distinct from these networks' "liberated" and omniscient masters, one that allows us to dilate the complexity, asymmetry, and vitality of the seam itself.

As political theorists Sandro Mezzadra and Brett Neilson have argued, the conditions of contemporary capitalism and the demand for ever-cheaper and more mobile labor have not resulted in the elimination of borders, but their proliferation. Following Étienne Balibar, who writes of the polysemy and heterogeneity of borders, Mezzadra and Neilson observe that the border is a "productive" device for "sorting and filtering flows, commodities, labor, and information."[146] In this sense, borders do not simply separate or exclude, as Simmel and Semper wrote of the wall; they integrate through "differential inclusion."[147] To recall Siegert and the paradox of the symbolic order, a door may be open to guest workers and closed to citizenship, or open to material and immaterial commodities, but closed to the bodies of the laborers who produce them.

In the contemporary world, the bordering functions of regulating and channeling movement are increasingly mobilized through administrative logics and biopolitical techniques that are spatially dispersed within a given territory, rather than located solely at its physical limits.[148] Even as such borders multiply, however, those who view them from below — the migrant, the fugitive, the marginal — are skilled at discerning "their thickness and heterogeneity," as Mezzadra and Neilson put it.[149] Unwanted flows of objects, subjects, affects, and ideas are therefore never truly stemmed, but simply diverted. It is for this reason that the material forms of traditional borders have gained new symbolic force. As Wendy Brown argues, with the fundamental theatricality of politics and the dissolution of the nation-state under the pressures of globalization, physical walls have become screens for fantasies about the sovereignty of the state and the preservation of national culture. "Viewed as a form of national psychic defense," she writes, "walls can be seen as an ideological disavowal of a set of unmanageable appetites, needs, and powers."[150] In other words, walls project visual power, but embody exposure and contestation, a dynamic Brown understands as explicitly gendered in its implications. "The heterosexual coupling of the feminized nation and masculinized sovereign state is no minor matter here," she observes. "Absent the protection of the sovereign state, the nation stands vulnerable, violable, and desperate. Walling restores an *imago* of the sovereign and his protective capacities."[151]

But walls, borders, and networks are gendered — and gendering — not simply in a metaphoric sense. As the anthropologist Kalindi Vora has argued, the outsourcing of labor that characterizes contemporary global capitalism has its precursor in the kind of colonial networks Le Corbusier extolled in *The Modulor*.[152] In these earlier stages of capitalism, such networks accumulated value through the extraction of labor power and natural resources. These were embodied jointly in slavery and indentured servanthood, on the one hand, and the material commodity, on the other, each of which were physically displaced from one location in order to be mobilized in another. Contemporary capitalism, by contrast, increasingly operates according to a global distribution of vital *energies* that Vora terms "life support." These energies are produced by embodied subjects in some parts of the globe for the biological and affective consumption of embodied subjects in other parts of the globe. They are thus racialized and gendered in every sense, but they no longer necessarily entail the physical movement of the protagonists themselves.

In the classical Marxian formulation, reproductive labor replenishes the body of the worker, who then commodifies his or her labor outside of the home. Because this reproductive labor is frequently performed by women within the domestic sphere, however, it is often invisible or classified as unskilled. (Think here of the female inhabitant of *un armario multiple*, pressing and folding her clothes at the end of each day, only to return to her office in the morning.) Within the contemporary networks of capitalism, Vora argues, the "draining of vital energy in service of the rehumanization of the worker" is now enacted across geopolitical and racial lines, wherein "those aspects of the subject or parts of the body useful for reproducing life elsewhere travel easily without the whole."[153] Vital energy is transmitted across boundaries in transnational markets ranging from gestational surrogacy (where women's productive and reproductive labor redoubles upon itself) to call centers (where workers are compelled affectively to embody fictive identities, thereby absenting their own subjectivity). The depletion, extraction, and accumulation of this "life support" constitutes a "membrane" as Vora writes, "through which unequal social relations occur and across which new socialities are formed and imagined."[154] While Le Corbusier envisioned containing and transferring commodities "without gaps," Vora's insights—together with Clark's organic line—teach us that spatial

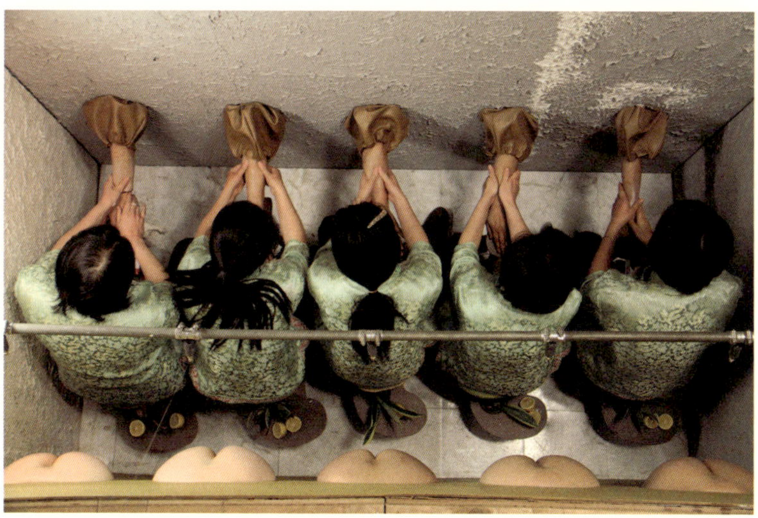

Figure 3.31. Mika Rottenberg, *Squeeze* (still), 2010. Single-channel video installation with sound and digital C-print, 20 min., dimensions variable. © Mika Rottenberg. Photo: Courtesy of the artist and Hauser & Wirth.

fissures are equally constitutive of networks and that the resulting membranes are agential in their own right.

The organic vitality of the membrane analyzed by Vora and materially prefigured by Clark is a symptom of the asymmetrical conditions of global capitalism and its devaluation of certain forms of life. But it also gestures toward the creation of aberrant and resistant possibilities that redirect the smooth transfer of energies for the purposes of accumulation, interrupting its networks and harnessing flows toward the production of new life practices, forms, and events. Contemporary art gives us a picture of such possibilities, and here, the work of the New York–based, Buenos Aires–born Israeli artist Mika Rottenberg is particularly apt, for in Rottenberg's work, the fantastical implications of inhabiting geopolitical thresholds (recall Le Corbusier dressed as Josephine Baker *as a wall*) become the raw materials of aesthetic composition (fig. 3.31).

The diegetic worlds of Rottenberg's video installations often revolve around the creation of mutant commodities: maraschino cherries rolled from fingernail clippings; lemon-scented towelettes moistened with sweat; allergen-catalyzed noodles; sculptural cubes made from compressed lettuce and cosmetics. The videos track the material and affective connectivity of the laboring bodies that produce these bizarre objects, attending to the corporeal and spatial idiosyncrasies of the workers and their material environments. Rottenberg frequently collaborates with actors who advertise their bodily distinctiveness as a form of niche commodity value: individuals who squeeze, squash, or wrestle, or who are unusually tall, large, flexible, or strong. She often builds her physical sets around these unique qualities and capacities, as well, such that the biological-corporeal informs the spatioarchitectural and vice versa. In *Meu doce rio*, Clark conjured a libidinal world in which the malleable body acts as a support, protagonist, and event. Rottenberg's works insist that we must inject capital and its myriad transmutations into the geopolitics of this corporal equation, as well.

In Marx's analysis of the conditions of industrial production, abstract labor power extracted from the worker congeals in the material form of the commodity. In Vora's contemporary update, this commodity is vital energy itself. Rottenberg's videos refer to aspects of both of these historical phases of capitalism: assembly lines coexist with corporeal modification, while rudimentary mechanisms such as pulleys and rotating discs deliver affects and objects across impossible geographic divides.[155] Likewise, while the actors featured in Rottenberg's videos possess their own means of distinctive corporeal production, the artist's eccentric systems harness their vital energies in absurdist, literal form: the growth capacity of hair or fingernails; the plasticity of the body; secretions such as sweat or tears. However, while late-capitalist networks tend to *invisibilize* the transfer of vital energies, Rottenberg's video installations emphatically rematerialize the relationality of bodies, objects, information, and systems as they interact to produce (or negate) value. (One would like to imagine John and Paul chain-smoking and watching movies, gaily ignoring Le Corbusier's calls from his cabin.)

In Rottenberg's videos, cinematic cuts blend documentary elements with fictive constructions to create improbable scenarios on the edge of possibility. In *NoNoseKnows* (2015), footage from a pearl-harvesting factory in Zhuji gives way to smoke-filled bubbles mysteriously floating in a polychromed office. In *Cosmic Generator* (2017), an early twentieth-century network of tunnels dug by Chinese railway workers beneath the US/Mexico border facilitates the movement of a miniaturized businessman between a generic restaurant on *la frontera* and a wholesale market for kitsch plastics in Yuwi (figs. 3.32a–b). As Rottenberg notes, the structuralist logic of the cinematic cut means that diegetic and formal differences between one visual segment and another generate new meanings. This cut corresponds to the organic line in its mechanical inflections, wherein the correlation of independent units creates a new, functionally interrelated entity. But Rottenberg also uses an affective logic of relation that moves *across* the cut by means of temporal looping and sensory continuity.[156] Deploying sound and image in the synesthetic vein of ASMR (autonomous sensory meridian response) triggers, Rottenberg's videos catalyze physical responses in the viewer that are akin to the organic line in its second, biological and affective sense. To this end, Rottenberg's works invite the viewer to "penetrate and be penetrated" by their "expressive space," to use Clark's memorable turn of phrase.[157]

I noted earlier that Clark's maquettes posit a virtuality experienced phenomenologically. Rottenberg's works amplify this immersive pictoriality by embedding videos in sculptural environments that share key material and spatial elements of their diegetic content. Thus, in *Cosmic Generator*, one has to crouch in a crudely constructed tunnel haphazardly indicated by plastic decorations before entering the space of projection. In *Mary's Cherries* (2004), the gloopy, meringuelike plaster that coats the surfaces of the makeshift

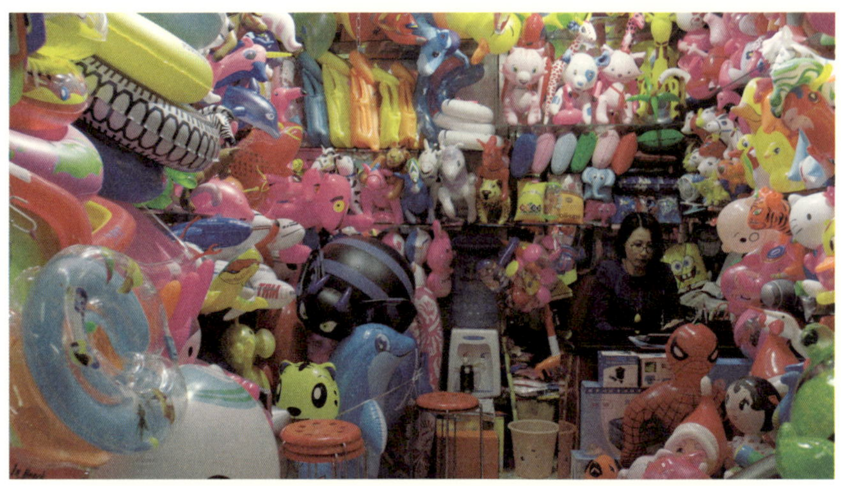

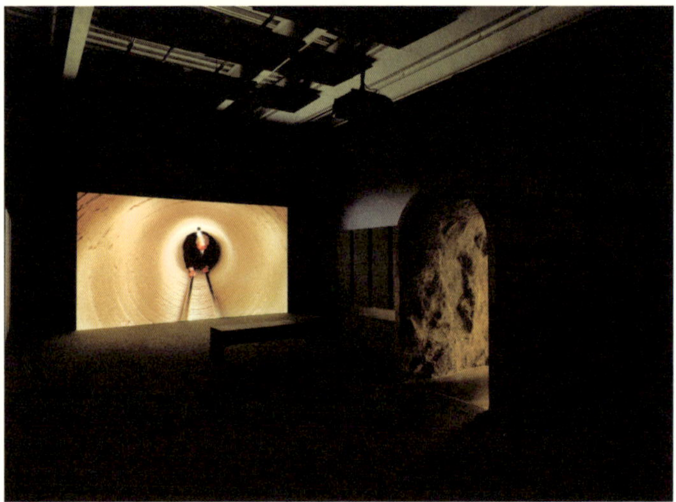

Figure 3.32a–b. Mika Rottenberg, *Cosmic Generator*, 2017. Single-channel video installation, sound, color, 26:36 min. Dimensions variable. © Mika Rottenberg. Courtesy of the artist and Hauser & Wirth. Commissioned by Skulptur Projekte Münster. Produced with generous support from the Louisiana Museum of Modern Art, Humlebæk, Denmark; Outset Contemporary Art Fund, London; and Polyeco Contemporary Art Initiative, Piraeus, Greece. Video still (tunnel variant). Installation view of *Mika Rottenberg: Easypieces*, 2019, New Museum, New York. Photo: Dario Lasagni.

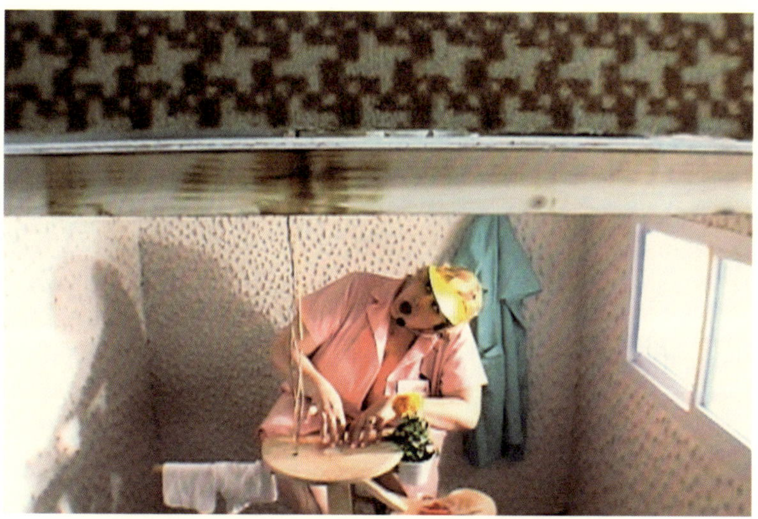

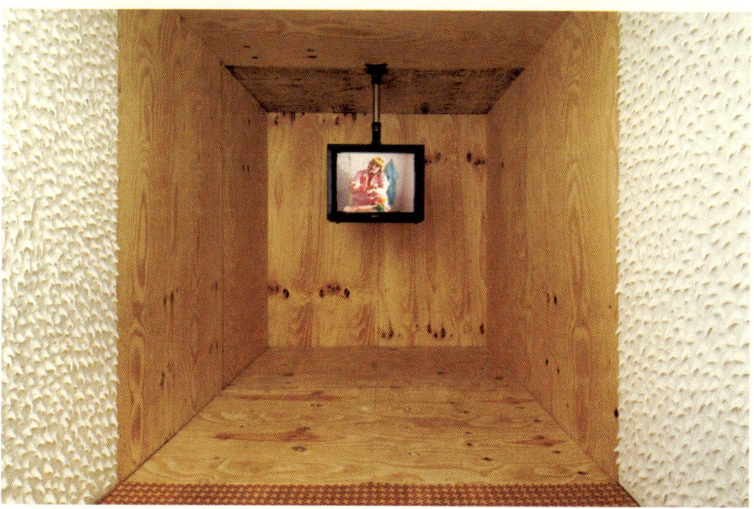

Figure 3.33a–b. Mika Rottenberg, *Mary's Cherries*, 2004. Single-channel video installation, 5:50 min. Dimensions variable. Lower image: Installation view from *The Irresistible Force* at the Tate Modern, London, 2007. © Mika Rottenberg. Courtesy of the artist and Hauser & Wirth.

factory where Mary, Barbara, and Rose work likewise covers the plywood walls of the video viewing room (figs. 3.33a–b). This wall texture, too, is of a piece with the puttylike substance Barbara uses to reconstitute Mary's red nails into malleable cherries.

These pliable, quasi-corporeal materials reappear across Rottenberg's videos and installations, perhaps most literally in the revolving door for *Bowls Balls Souls Holes (Bingo)* (2014) (fig. 3.34). Here, hundreds of wads of chewed and discarded gum spackle a door along with their metallic wrappers, marking and remarking the spatial aperture of the installation with the indexically registered refuse of a multitude of now-absent mouths. Having passed from the interior to the exterior of these bodies, these masticated, exhausted bits of matter demarcate a new threshold at a social and collective scale. On one side of the wall, viewers undertake another form of sensory consumption that, if successful, triggers bodily sensations such as pleasure, boredom, and disgust. Such sensations knit viewers into a temporary network of material, affective, and diegetic relationalities that stretch across screens and space. When it is most successful, the work inaugurates new formations of vital energies by means of this network and its ligations. Unlike the networks to which global capitalism aspires, these formations are inevitably lumpy and leaky, rather than transparent and smooth. When the video is least successful, the work is simply consumed and forgotten, but this possibility is already prefigured by the wads of gum deposited on the revolving door. Matter energized and depleted by organic contact, but bearing the unmistakable trace of this encounter, the gum is a token of the errant possibilities of inhabiting networks and subjecting space.

═══

The etymology of the word "symbol" lies in the Greek *symbolon*, which refers to a token or tally — "that which is thrown or cast together" — in order to convey a meaning beyond the thing itself.[158]

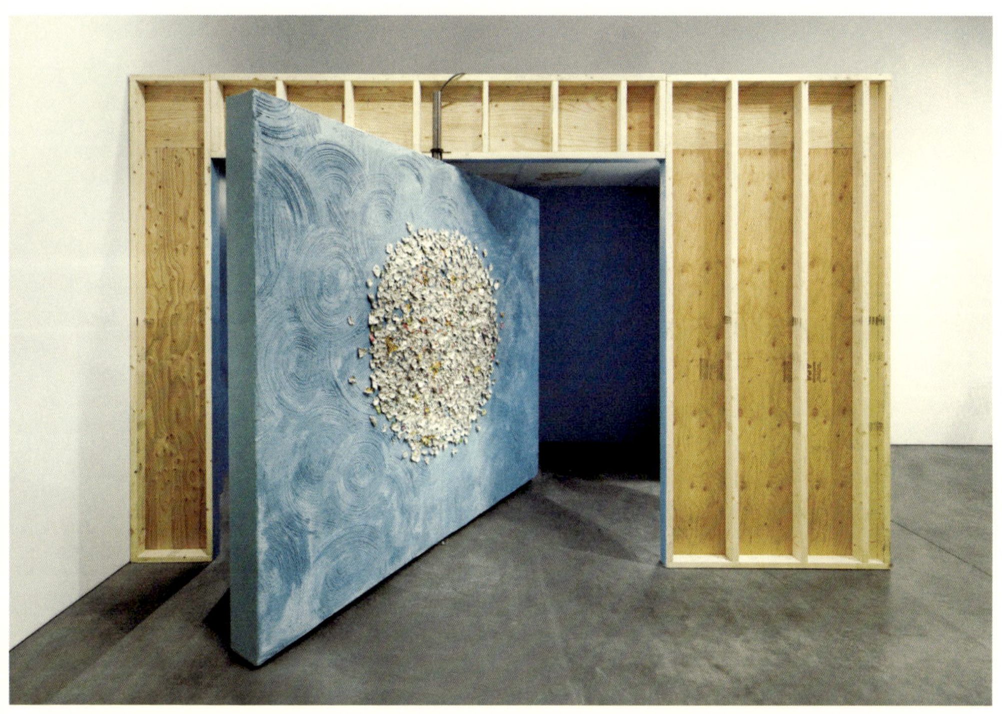

Figure 3.34. Mika Rottenberg, *Bowls Balls Souls Holes (Bingo)*, 2014. Video and sculpture installation, 27:54 min. Dimensions variable. © Mika Rottenberg. Courtesy of the artist and Hauser & Wirth. Installation view, 2014, Andrea Rosen Gallery, New York. Photo: Lance Brewer.

Already in the ancient world, the term was used in an immaterial sense. In *De interpretatione*, Aristotle notes that in contradistinction to inarticulate sound, nouns and names take on the character of a *symbolon*, thereby suggesting a linguistic agreement formed through convention.[159] But in its original and literal meaning, the term referred to a genre of material object, perhaps most primally instantiated in the *astragalos*, the knucklebone of a sheep or goat broken between friends to commemorate a promise or encounter. The fragment retained by each party was evidence of the authenticity of this relationship; together, they formed a guarantee as well as an anticipation of future reunification and hospitality.[160] As in the double inflection of cleaving, splitting and linkage are combined.

As Anne Carson and David Graeber have noted in their respective writings on the social relationality of debt, the *symbolon*, as a form of mutual obligation akin to the gift, stands in contradistinction to the quantification and alienation brought about through the exchange of money.[161] As Carson writes, "A gift is not a piece broken off from the interior life of the giver and lost into the exchange, but rather an extension of the interior of the giver, both in space and in time, into the interior of the receiver. Money denies such extension, ruptures continuity and stalls objects at the borders of themselves."[162] Considering this metaphoric thematization of boundaries and bordering, it is significant that the *symbolon* first took the form of a bone that was simultaneously a hinge, an anatomical element that, as Peta Carlin writes, facilitates "the movement of the hand, its gestures of pointing, of opening and closing, of beckoning and dismissing, releasing and grasping."[163]

In 1900, Louis Sullivan described the organic as a "ten-fingered grasp on reality," a formulation popularized midcentury by Frank Lloyd Wright as well as architectural critics and historians such as Sigfried Giedion and Bruno Zevi to refer to the symbiosis between the human subject and built environment (fig. 3.35).[164] Paradoxically, Clark's maquettes seem to offer little in terms of such phenomenological anchoring or scalar proportion. Despite

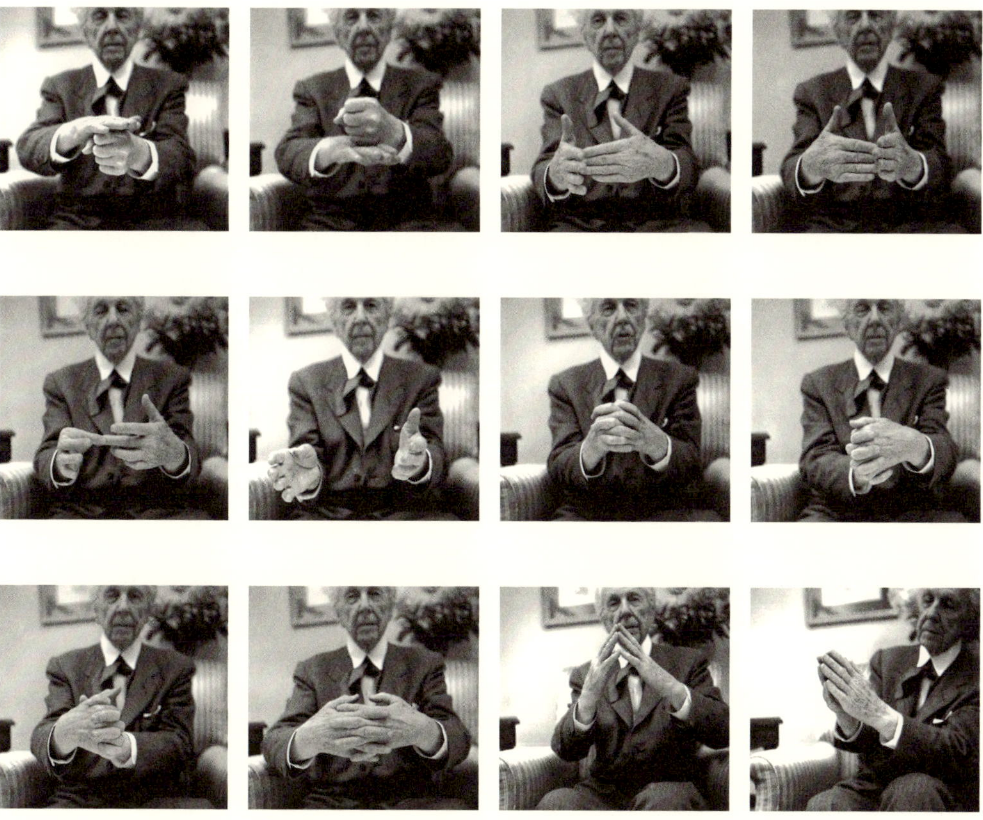

Figure 3.35. Pedro Guerrero, *Wright's Hands*, 1953. © The Estate of Pedro E. Guerrero.

the spatial permeability activated by the organic line, most period photographs of Clark's maquettes do not show an exterior world on the other side of the works' doors and panels, and only one maquette gives any indication of inhabitation in the form of an austere table and bench. Taken at face value, one might observe that this abstraction is of a piece with modernism's projective impulse, wherein a maquette — modeling futurity — skips over the contingencies of the present. Yet unlike so many of modernism's heroic architectures, the structuring principle of Clark's maquettes — the organic line — depends precisely on what resists standardization and exceeds projection. In Clark's formulations, it is the real-time variability of matter, space, and encounter that lends the resulting environments vitality and expressivity. It therefore behooves us to understand the maquettes' abstraction as a theorization of architecture wherein the mutability of human life force is not excised, but *internalized* as the organic quality of architectural surface itself.

There is one photograph of Clark's maquettes, however, that stands apart from the others by explicitly evoking human touch. The image in question shows Clark and the critic Ferreira Gullar at the Second Grupo Frente Exhibition in 1955 standing next to a work that now appears lost (fig. 3.36). One of the maquette's doors is ajar, and Clark's and Gullar's fingers entwine across its threshold, the artist's and critic's bodies playfully out of proportion as if giants peering into a doll's house. Linked at the knuckle, Clark and Gullar perform the mutual reciprocity of the *symbolon*, their touch registering a friendship and occasion that anticipates future reactivation. But the gesture is also performed in relation to the spatial porosity of the maquette, lending it the character of a *symbolon*, as well. Here, the maquette facilitates recognition and reciprocity, in contradistinction to the closed kitchen door of Clark's 1956 Belo Horizonte lecture, which regulates and enforces gendered divisions of space. The touch from the interior draws in the touch from the exterior, in keeping with the integrative capacity of the organic line. Vitalizing edges, the maquette foregrounds the connective

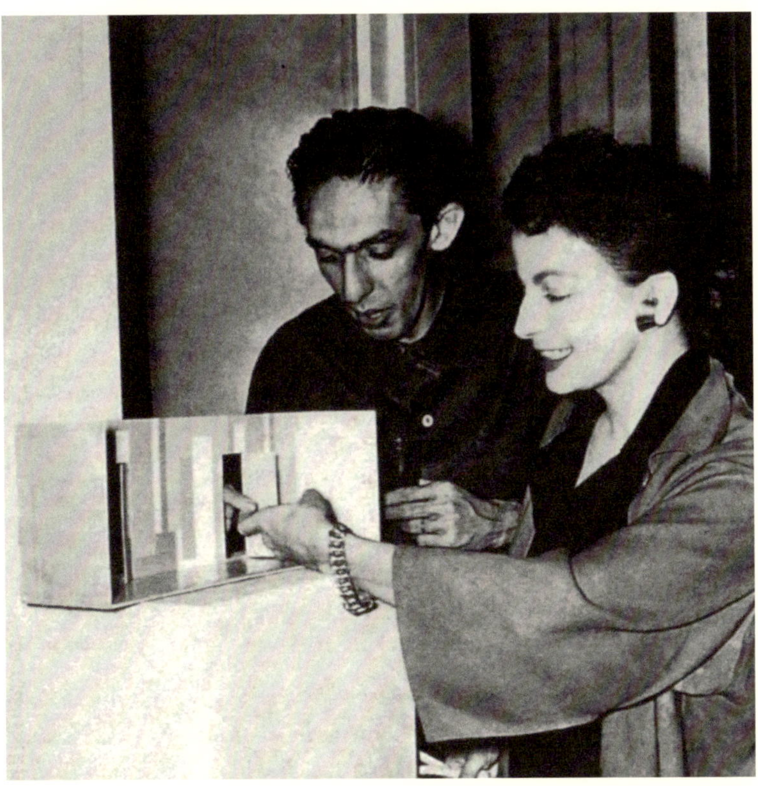

Figure 3.36. Lygia Clark and Ferreira Gullar with Clark's *Maquette para Interior* at the Second Grupo Frente Exhibition, Museu de Arte Moderna do Rio de Janeiro, 1955. Courtesy of Associação Cultural "O Mundo de Lygia Clark.

function of apertures and intervals for subjects and space alike.

But there is another way in which the maquette functions as a *symbolon*, namely, by performing its contingency and fragility as a material object *in order to* stand for something else. To this degree, Clark's maquettes are not realizable architectures in miniature so much as materialized conceptualizations of an agreement between surface and space and the subjects implicated therein. Writing about the inflections of the term "culture" in "cultural techniques," Siegert notes that for the philosopher Theodor Adorno, techniques

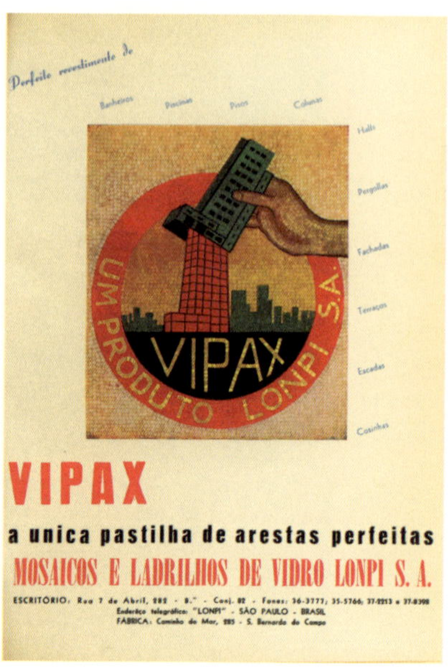

Figure 3.37. Advertisement, *Habitat: Arquitetura e Artes no Brasil*, no. 14 (January–February 1954).

were a means of anthropomorphizing the world around us, as in the way a door handle answers human gesture. But for Siegert, even "human touch" is "constituted by and dependent on cultural techniques."[165] "In this sense," he writes, "cultural techniques allow actors involved to be both human and nonhuman; they reveal the extent to which the human actor has always already been decentered *by* the technical object."[166]

A 1954 advertisement for Vipax mosaics and glass bricks that appeared in the magazine *Habitat: Arquitetura e Artes no Brasil* allegorizes this paradox (fig. 3.37). Promoting the ability of its prefabricated units to deliver "perfect edges," the advertisement pictures a disembodied female hand lifting off the gridded façade of a highrise building, only to reveal yet another surface, likewise gridded, but hermetically sealed. Here, the illustration imagines a superhuman power over an environment organized entirely for the subject's control. And yet, as *un armario multiple* and Le Corbusier's shipping crates alike reveal, it is *the grid* that coordinates human action, rather than the other way around. Ironically, the term that the Vipax advertisement uses for the mosaic and glass bricks is *pastilha*, which refers to a modular unit, but also a padded or elastic element placed *between* units, as in the brake pads of a car or a stick of chewing gum. As I noted at the beginning of this chapter, one of the blind spots of modernist formulations of standardization was the failure to recognize the thickness of the grid's demarcation and, as a corollary, the space between modules themselves. Vipax mosaics and glass bricks can create "perfect edges" only by means of the adhesive mortar that binds them together. Thus, while the advertisement's graphic demarcations are meant to connote total enclosure through the perfect matching of edges, they also indicate those liminal zones where units of matter fall apart.

The conceptual intervention of Clark's maquettes is not only to prioritize these liminal zones, but to comprehend them as spatial, rather than simply material intervals, which is to say, as a means of *fissuring* a surface, rather than sealing it up. To this end, it is not surprising that the maquettes exhibit a fragility that has only been exacerbated over the years. After all, the spatial ligations that allow the organic line to integrate a surface also contain the equal and opposite possibility of that surface's fragmentation. To wit, while two of Clark's three surviving maquettes have largely held together, various photographs of one of the maquettes reveal panels that have gone missing or were entirely disengaged over the years (fig. 3.38). But perhaps this is the most apt indication of the maquette's character as *symbolon*. In reassembling their disengaged pieces, the maquettes invite us to learn how their material and spatial agreements posit historical cultural techniques, but also signal divergent ones. Approximating ourselves to these material *symbolons*, we might discover novel ways to reorient ourselves to each other and the world in turn.

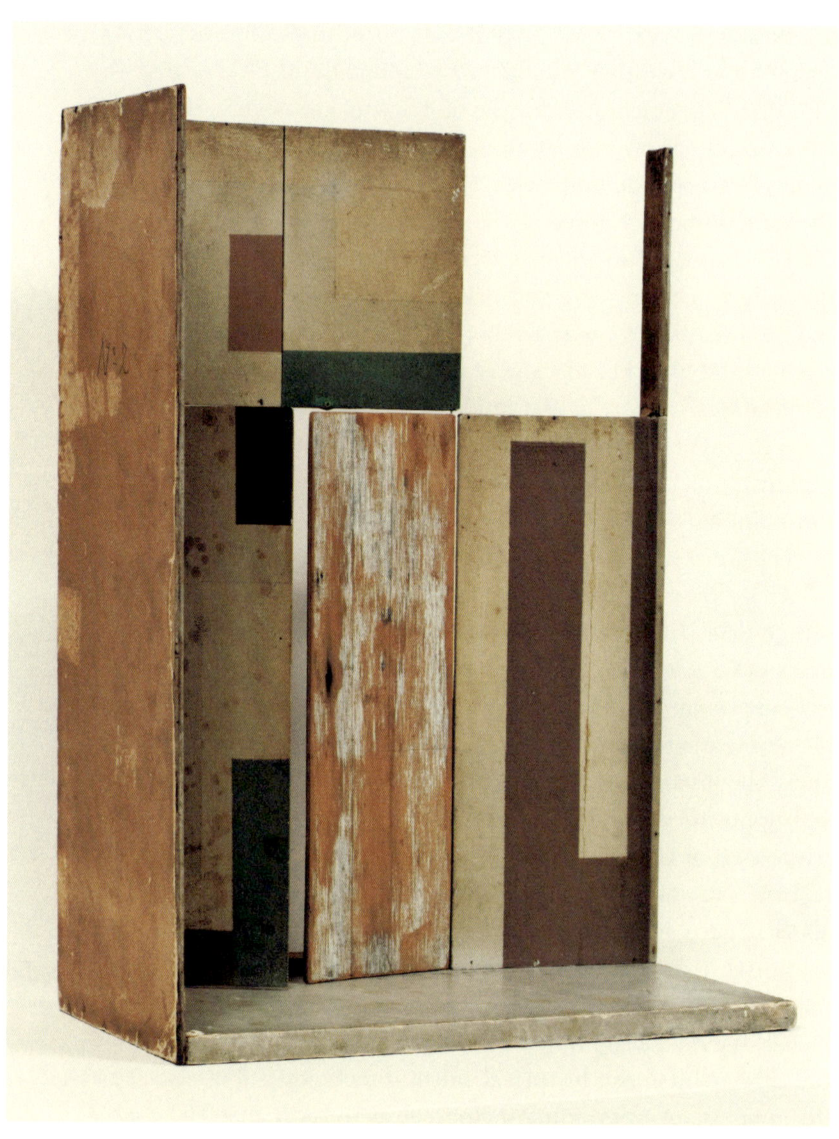

Figure 3.38. Lygia Clark, *Maquette para Interior*
(Maquette for interior), 1955. Courtesy of
Associação Cultural "O Mundo de Lygia Clark."

In 1994, the artist Ricardo Basbaum introduced a peculiar object into circulation under the aegis of an ongoing project titled *Would you like to participate in an artistic experience?* As a Brazilian artist who came of age in the 1980s, Basbaum was deeply informed by the 1960s and 1970s propositional works of Clark and Hélio Oiticica, among others, and similarly conceived of his object as an open-ended catalyst for participation (fig. 3.39). For his project, Basbaum invited individuals and groups to experiment with the object any way they liked, documenting their experiences before sending it on to other parties in their own or Basbaum's network. To bring this chapter to conclusion, I want to suggest how his object acts as a symbolic riposte — in the sense of the *symbolon* given above — to the organic line, materializing the virtual qualities of its architectural inscription while intensifying its affective cues.

Made of metal, painted white with minimal blue edging, and large enough to require at least two people to move or transport it comfortably, Basbaum's object is based on a shape called NBP, an acronym for Nova Bases para Personalidade, or New Bases for Personality. The NBP shape first emerged in the artist's work around 1990 and subsequently served as the matrix for all of his future practice. The immediate precedent was a drawing of an eye Basbaum affixed to surfaces in various public spaces between the mid- to late 1980s in the years immediately following Brazil's redemocraticization. Whereas the eye functioned as a visual logo, invoking surveillance and perceptual reciprocity in equal measure, the NBP form dispensed with recognizable iconography while retaining an iconic charge. The shape recalls elements of the eye, but refuses to stabilize them, instead catalyzing a host of visual associations — ear, monitor, stamp, electrical outlet, orifice, computer chip, and so on — while escaping strict identification with any of them. As NBP drawings from Basbaum's early 1990s notebooks indicate, the artist was particularly invested in the shape's mnemonic power, specifically, its ability to implant itself cognitively in the viewer's body in a manner analogous to a virus.[167] Basbaum studied biology before

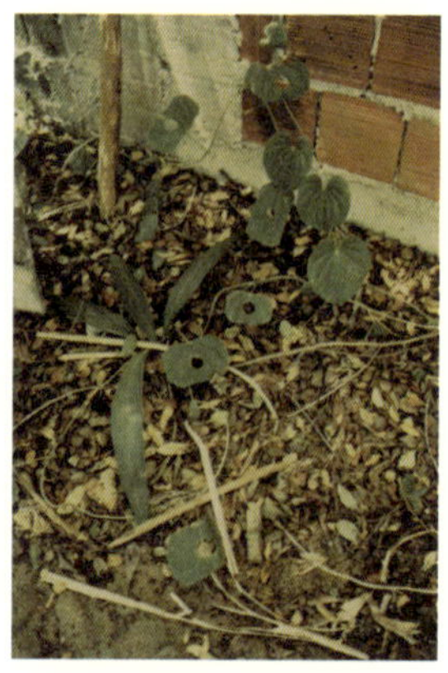

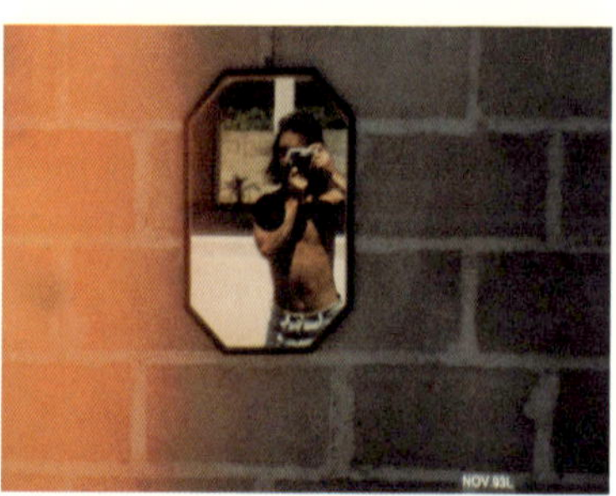

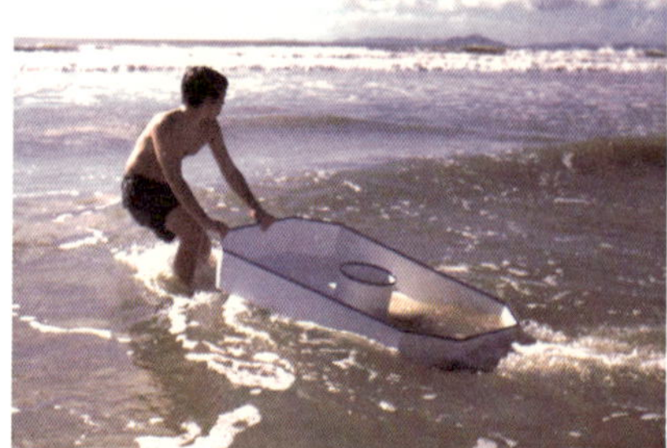

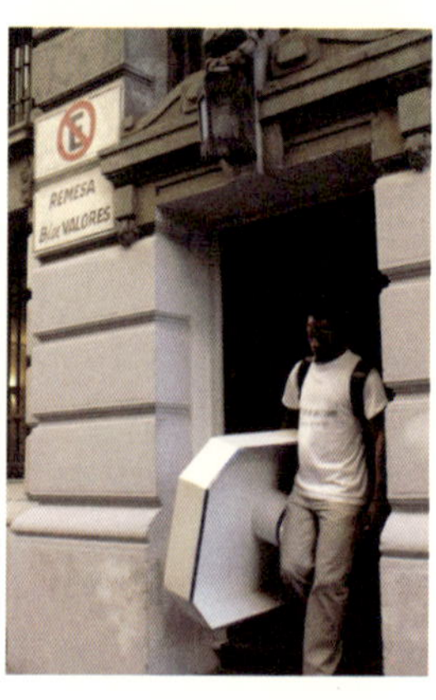

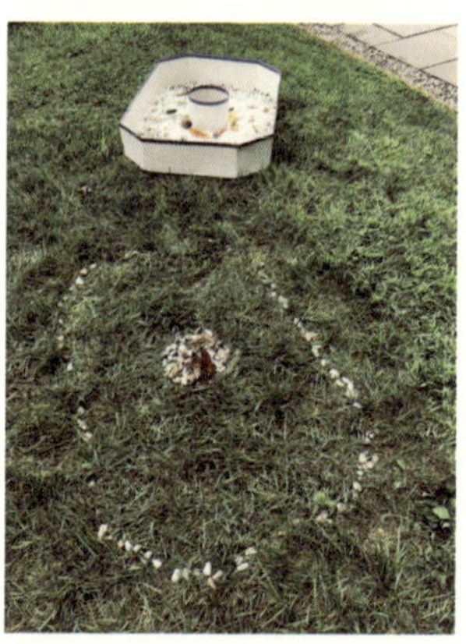

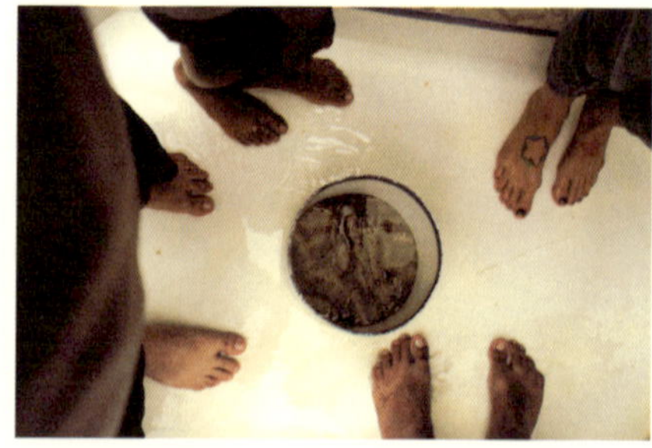

Figure 3.39. Ricardo Basbaum, *Você gostaria de participar de uma experiência artística? (trabalho em progresso desde 1994)* (Would you like to participate in an artistic experience? [work in progress since 1994]). Painted steel object, experience, 125×80×18 cm (object). Participation SIM ou ZERO, Enseada das Garças, Brasil, 1994. Participation Brígida Baltar Verão, Vermelho, Brazil, 1997. Participation Jaes Caicedo, Valparaiso, Chile, 2007. Participation Asia Komarova, Rio de Janeiro, Brazil, 2017. Participation Lulu Baring, Sofie Baring, and Kha-ai Mosaka, Princeton, New Jersey, 2020. Photos courtesy of participants, Ricardo Basbaum, and the project *Você gostaria de participar de uma experiência artística?*

turning to art, and this ability to "contaminate" the viewing subject, as he put it, was an explicit alternative to the circulation of art objects within the market. In contrast to such material commodities, the NBP shape was immaterial, yet instantly recognizable. It could be transmitted between people, like a rumor, as well as materialize in an infinite variety of ways without losing its conceptual integrity as a form.

In this latter sense, the NBP shape is diagrammatic par excellence, and not surprisingly, the diagram was key to Basbaum's thinking of this time. Among other sources, Basbaum recalls encountering illustrations created by Kurt Lewin, a key figure of social psychology who had studied alongside the psychologists Max Wertheimer and Wolfgang Köhler, who in turn were fundamental references for Pedrosa's influential 1940s writings on Gestalt form.[168] In 1936, Lewin published *Principles of Topological Psychology*, with a preface by Köhler, in which Lewin sought to describe and account for "psychological life space," that is, the way in which individual behaviors are determined within a given psychological environment. Lewin explained that such behaviors result from relationships and events that establish regions delimited by boundaries of greater or lesser permeability.[169] Every point of a life space is a boundary point that can be influenced by internal and external relations, and because these spatialized psychological regions are topological, they are capable of transformation — stretching, bending, twisting, and so on — without tearing. Lewin frequently illustrated his texts with diagrams that describe a psychological field at a given time. Such diagrams are abstract theorizations of social relations, yet they inevitably evoke corresponding spatial dynamics. Viewing Lewin's diagrams of the shifting life spaces of a husband and wife from his 1951 study *Field Theory in Social Science*, for instance, we immediately recall Clark's description of a wife who serves dinner to her husband and his friends and then is compelled to listen behind the kitchen wall as he takes credit for her meal (fig. 3.40).[170]

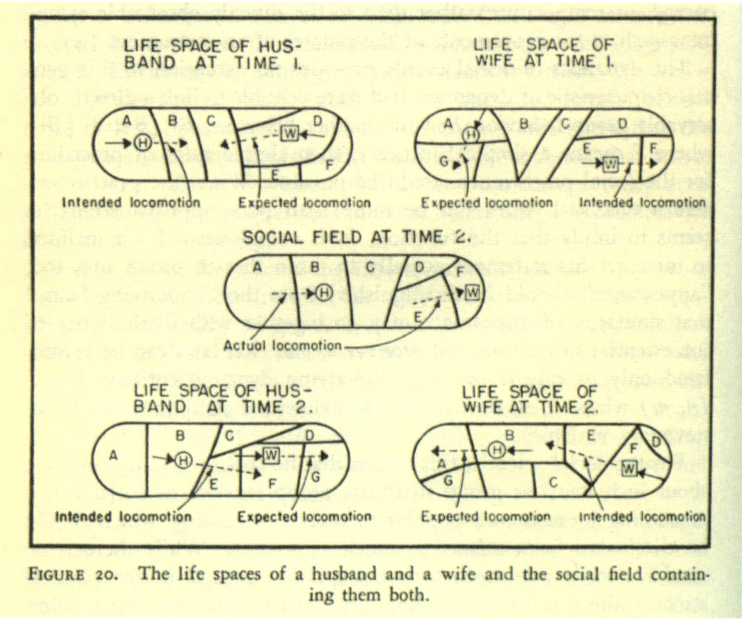

Figure 3.40. Kurt Lewin, "The life spaces of a husband and a wife and the social field containing them both," *Field Theory in Social Science: Selected Theoretical Papers* (New York: Harper and Row, 1951), p. 196.

For Basbaum, Lewin's illustrations resonated with long-standing interests in the diagrammatic as a means of connective modeling. In 1994, the same year he introduced the NBP object, the artist created his first public diagram, *love songs*, which concerned the shifting dynamics of a romantic relationship (fig. 3.41). As I explore in this book's Coda, thinkers such as Humberto Maturana and Félix Guattari have described love as an affective domain in which the "structural plasticity" of the individual dissolves by way of mutually shared vulnerability.[171] Basbaum's diagram underscores that "love" is also a domain for the renegotiation of "me" and "you" as dynamic, responsive, and conflictual behavioral entities that do not simply meld, but continually reform in relation to one another. For Basbaum, the diagram was a graphic instrument for visualizing such

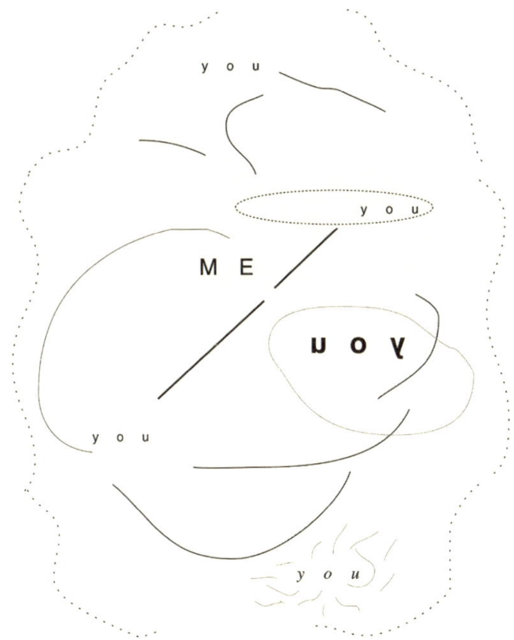

Figure 3.41. Ricardo Basbaum, *diagram (love songs series)*, 1994. Variable dimensions. Digital vectorial drawing. Courtesy of Ricardo Basbaum.

forces of intersubjective attraction, repulsion, and recombination. But it was also a conceptual tool that exceeded the registers of representation or inscription, allowing for both abstract virtuality (the diagram can map noncontiguous phenomena and transit between media, materialization, and scale) and real-time encounter (the diagram invites cognitive activation, adaptation, and projection).

Basbaum's NBP object likewise partakes of this dual character. Its singularity lies in the formal specificity of its shape: an irregular polyhedron formed by a rectangle whose four corners have been modified as diagonals and that features a cylindrical aperture at its center. But the object itself is not unique and has been replaced and multiplied since the initiation of *Would you like to participate in an artistic experience?* in 1994. Moreover, several participants have replicated and propagated its shape in their quotidian environments: on the leaves of a growing plant; as a contour of stones on grass; inscribed as a tattoo; as a photograph in which the object is subject matter and mirrored lens, and so on (see fig. 3.39). These reproductions transmit NBP as an "epidemiology of culture," in Basbaum's words, and are retained in the memory of participants and passersby, despite the ephemerality of the actual iterations.[172]

The NBP object joins abstract virtuality and real-time enactment in its character as interface, as well. In an installation created while Basbaum was still working to specify the NBP shape, the artist painted colored rectangles directly on a wall, leaving a sliver of space to delineate a smaller rectangle within each monochrome (fig. 3.42). We can imagine the three-dimensional NBP object arising from this even more reductive form, edges folding up along the installation's unpainted organic lines to create the prototypical form of a box. Here, the organic line — itself a residual contour that belongs strictly to the materiality of the wall — becomes an agent of topological transformation. Intensifying the line's liminal and topological qualities, the NBP object is a container perforated by its own form: its outer contours delineate an interior and an exterior, yet its circular aperture is itself an interior form that holes out to exterior space. Containment is thus always bordering, wherein the border itself catalyzes inversions and oscillations of spatial relations.

Such oscillations return us to Basbaum's acronym, NBP, for in *Would you like to participate in an artistic experience?* the object is a prompt for experimentation among a shifting cast of *yous* and *mes*. Such activities and behaviors are never programmatic: Basbaum's titular invitation is intentionally neutral: the object's obdurate quality evades normative use, and the "new bases for personality" are deliberately cryptic and vague. The collaborative work of "participating in an artistic experience" in large part is figuring out *what to do.* In the resulting propositions, experiments, modifications, and redescriptions, participants negotiate and collectively produce idiosyncratic bodily techniques and "life spaces" prompted by the

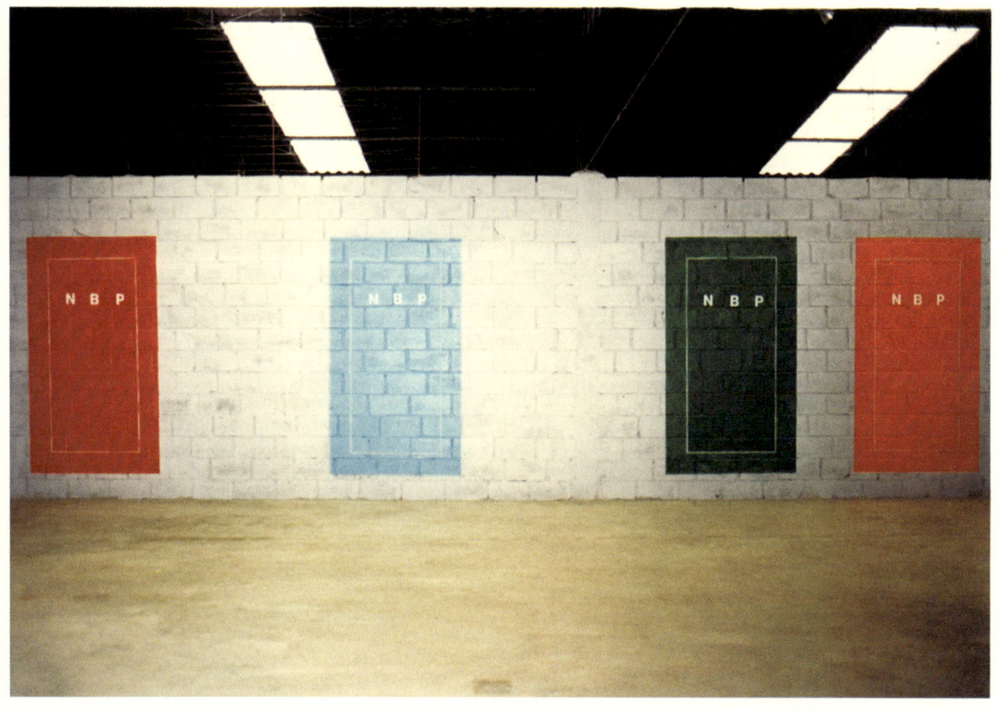

Figure 3.42. Ricardo Basbaum, *NBP—
New Bases for Personality*, 1990. Acrylic-
polyurethane paint, latex, jasmine essential oil,
228×129 cm (each panel). Installation view
at the "4-44" group show, Ateliê Livre de
Petrópolis, Petrópolis, Rio de Janeiro. Photo:
Márcio R. M. Courtesy of Ricardo Basbaum.

object. They share and carry forward the strangeness and novelty of these experiences, even as the object reenters circulation. As the object has multiplied and moved across regions and continents in subsequent years, it has catalyzed a slow-moving and fragmentary network: "linked and interlinked," as Le Corbusier wrote of a future globalized world, but, in this case, deliberately riddled with gaps.

Unlike for the great majority of artists discussed in this book, Basbaum's relationship to Clark's organic line is one of direct influence. However, Basbaum's metabolization of this influence in *Would you like to participate in an artistic experience?* is notably plagiotropic in character. The project constellates Lewin and Vito Acconci with Pedrosa's Brazilian legacy of Gestalt form; obdurate metal alongside pliant topology; viral transmission by way of sensory participation; flux punctuated by periods of dormancy. Each collaboration with the NBP object involves a conceptual and geographically distanced accord with Basbaum. Each likewise institutes set of situated intersubjective, sensorial, and material connections where and when a given NBP experiment takes place. Like the *symbolon*, *Would you like to participate in an artistic experience?* depends on reciprocity, connection, and encounter, even as it refuses strict contractual obligation. Tellingly, the online and mnemonic archive collectively formed by these experiences is discontinuous, erratic, and always incomplete. Internalizing the organic line as a social experiment, Basbaum's "new bases for personality" is a testament to an ongoing community of weak links.

Of Mutant Coordinates
and Living Things

Patently, art does not have a monopoly on creation,
but it takes its capacity to invent mutant coordinates to extremes:
it engenders unprecedented, unforeseen and unthinkable qualities of being.
The decisive threshold constituting this new aesthetic paradigm
lies in the aptitude of these processes of creation to auto-affirm themselves as
existential nuclei, autopoietic machines.
—Félix Guattari

The knowledge of knowledge compels.
—Humberto Maturana and Francisco Varela

"Life wishes not to live but to rest," wrote Kazimir Malevich in *The Non-Objective World*; "it strives not for activity but passivity."[1] In this 1927 text, Malevich analogized the persistence of artistic conventions to homeostatic equilibrium. New creative forms such as Suprematism disturb this tendency toward stability. The effect of such "additional elements" was not unlike that of "bacteria on the human organism," Malevich offered.[2] Through their "activated and activating particles," old pictorial systems would be disrupted, dynamically bringing about a new order. As Malevich's commentary and teaching didactics attest, the artist's comparison between bacterial elements and aesthetic innovation was inspired by the late nineteenth-century isolation of the tuberculosis bacillus and experiments with inoculation contemporaneous to his own time (fig. C.1). The metaphor was not incidental: Malevich wore a white lab coat, "infected" his students with stylistic elements, and dubbed his department at the State Institute of Artistic Culture the Bacteriology Art.[3] In this delirious vision of artistic change as biological infection and cure, Suprematism represented the ultimate overhaul of existing pictorial norms.

In a 1957 text, Lygia Clark recounted that she came to call the line of space she had discovered "the organic line" because it was "real, existing in itself."[4] We can better grasp this claim to self-existence by contrasting it with Malevich's paradoxical statement that "life wishes not to live but to rest." Clark's remark associates the organic with a kind of actualized, but provisional autonomy. The line's "reality" is generated from materially dependent conditions of adjacency, cleavage, and chasm, but it also "exists in itself" in that it automatically forms and persists as a spatial entity. Like liquid in a container, it is self-organizing and expansive in relation to its material limits. In other words, the interstitiality and contingency of the organic line is also the occasion for its self-production. It "lives" because it "rests" within the passivity of the boundary. But as we have seen across this book, the interval of the organic line is also a zone of intense activity. In *Descoberta da linha orgânica*, it is a site for the encounter and conversion of incommensurate pictorial and ontological operations. In *Quebra da moldura (p×b) versão 1*, it transforms metric spaces into topological envelopes and generates recursive difference. In *Planos em superfície modulada*, it actuates edges and distributes this material, phenomenological, and psychic difference across the lateral, sibling logic of the series. And in *Maquette para interior*, it absorbs and distributes affects along the architectural seam. In short, the liminality and quiescent self-formation of the organic line cannot be disengaged from its dynamic, transformational qualities.

In 1971, the Chilean cognitive biologists Humberto Maturana and Francisco Varela defined living beings as *autopoietic*, that is,

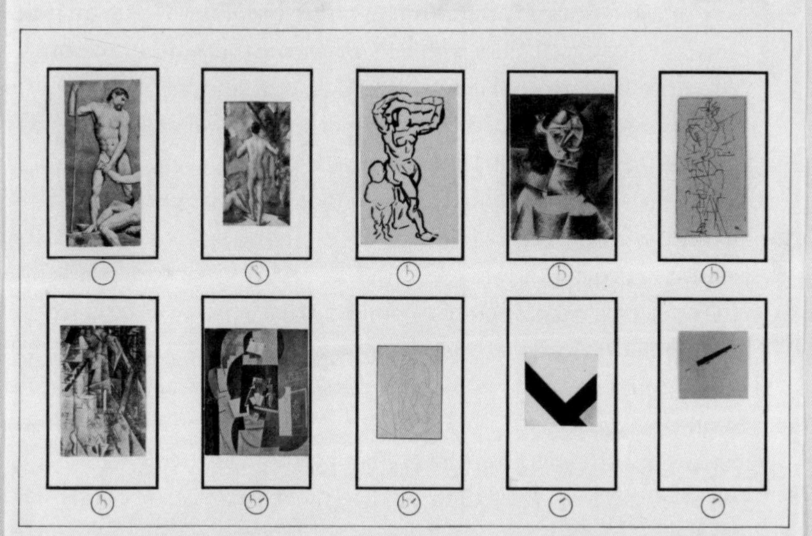

Figure C.1. Kazimir Malevich, *Analytical Chart* (ca. 1925). Cut-and-pasted printed and painted papers, gelatin silver prints, ink and crayon on paper mounted on paper, with ink and pencil inscriptions, 72.39 × 98.43 cm. A 1935 acquisition confirmed in 1999 by agreement with the Estate of Kazimir Malevich and made possible with funds from the Mrs. John Hay Whitney Bequest (by exchange). Digital image © The Museum of Modern Art / Licensed by SCALA / Art Resource, NY.

autoproducing or self-producing entities with neither vitalist teleology nor evolutionary aim.[5] Against the dominant representational epistemology that comprehends organisms as simply reacting to stimuli within the outside world, Maturana and Varela argued that perception entails not "the grasping of an external reality, but rather the *specification* of one."[6] Moreover, they insisted that this quality of self-referential autonomy is not ancillary, but the central feature of living systems. As autopoietic unities, living systems sustain their identity through internal feedback. Their autonomy depends upon the continual generation of a boundary that separates the entity — or "autopoietic machine," as Maturana and Varela put it — from its environment and allows for its recursive production (fig. C.2). Since such boundaries are porous and have internal and external limits, however, autopoietic unities are not hermetically sealed, but "structurally coupled" with their environments in relations of dynamic interaction and response. External events may produce perturbations that require adjustment to an entity's internal functioning. Such couplings may also result in wholesale deformations of the living system and environment involved, as when an animal shifts its metabolic rate in response to climate change or a plant develops a plagiotropic growth pattern to take advantage of soil and light. To recall René Thom's language, as noted in this book's Introduction, such changes amount to "catastrophes": radical shifts in a system's disposition. If the entity is able to maintain its autopoietic organization plastically after such structural changes, it continues to live. Conversely, the disintegration of autopoiesis entails the loss of identity and life. Yet living systems can also experience a loss of identity through repeated interactions that result in a novel unity. In this case, interrelations generate a new organization of life.

Can we appeal to the theory of autopoiesis to account for works of art and the multivalent ecologies in which they interact? In the following section, I want to suggest that the organic line's *living* and *liminal* character illuminates this possibility. Maturana and Varela's topological conception of biology allows us to conceive of works

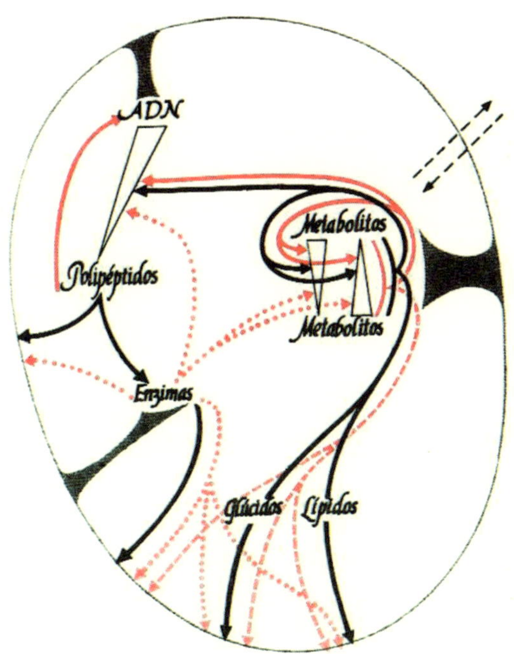

Figure C.2. Diagram from Humberto Maturana and Francisco Varela, *De máquinas y seres vivos, autopoiesis: La organization de lo vivo* (1973; Santiago de Chile: Editorial Universitaria, 1994).

of art in terms of a paradoxically relational autonomy. The organic line provides a model for this autonomy, but also the architecture for describing the space and behavior of its relationality. As a membrane between entities, it embodies the operation of "structural coupling." In so doing, it also allows us to comprehend how works of art — conceived as living systems — enact the possibility of change. This paradigm leaves aside the dream of totalizing revolution that animated Malevich's and so much modernist thought. But it retains an investment in Malevich's idiosyncratic metaphor of biological agency, wherein aesthetic entities carry unique potential for disruption and reorientation. Such entities plot "mutant coordinates" within existing configurations of the world, to borrow the philosopher Félix Guattari's phrase, and in so doing chart possibilities for its respecification. The organic line teaches us how to describe and activate such coordinates as they "auto-affirm themselves as existential nuclei, autopoietic machines."[7]

═══

Works of art are situated within interactive ecologies, some of which involve other works of art, but many of which do not. In order to comprehend how art might perturb or deform such ecologies, I want to chart—at a formal level—how works can exist as autopoietic machines that actuate membranes such as the organic line. Consider installations by three contemporary artists whose practice involves insertions into—or diversions of—political, economic, and aesthetic systems. For *Maria Eichhorn Public Limited Company*, commissioned for Documentaii in 2002, the artist Maria Eichhorn established a public limited company with a single shareholder, the artist herself (fig. C.3). Eichhorn stipulated that the company's assets—the required initial investment of €50,000—must never appreciate in value. She then transferred all her shares to the company, thereby eliminating her role as a shareholder. Stripped of the possibility of profit, the company forfeited its raison d'être, but also could not fold. The €50,000 investment, meanwhile, lost its representational and mobile character as capital and became mere matter, static and dead. Yet the conceptual form inaugurated by Eichhorn's work is recursive and autopoietic and remains, in essence, alive. A legal entity continually divesting itself of its own financial potentiality, it is a glittering kernel of autonomy within a market system premised on the capital of art. Documentation regarding the company's establishment can be and has been purchased, thus participating in an external appreciation of value that the holding company's internal rules disallow. Yet the company *itself* is owned by itself. Impervious to market fluctuation, it simultaneously evacuates and gives form to capital, each operation a figure to the other's ground.

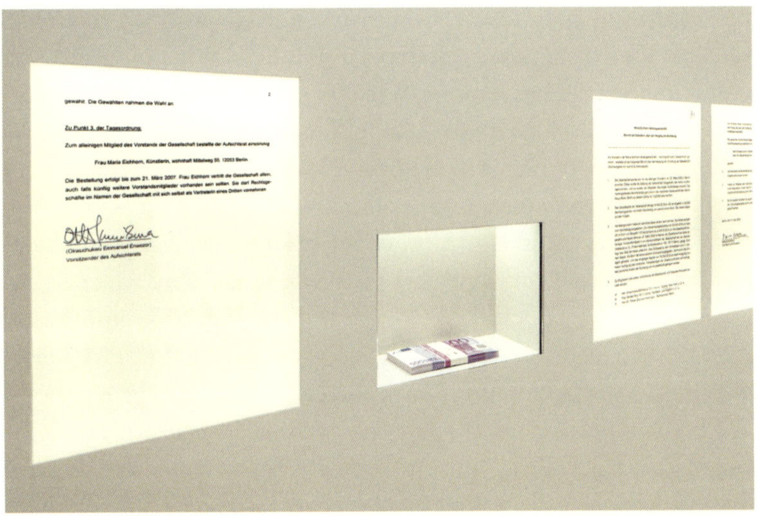

Figure C.3. Maria Eichhorn, *Maria Eichhorn Aktiengesellschaft, 2002*, exhibition view, *Maria Eichhorn*, Kunsthaus Bregenz, 2014. © Maria Eichhorn/VG Bild-Kunst, Bonn. Photo: Markus Tretter. Collection Van Abbenmuseum, Eindhoven.

The mediums for *Maria Eichhorn Public Limited Company* are the legalistic discourse of financial institutions, the profit motive of capitalism, the aesthetic valuations of the art world, and the means by which such valuations translate into financial worth. Eichhorn did not reinvent these mediums. Rather, she charted a mutant form *within* them capable of endless self-production. But this form is also a constant irritation within the mediums from which it is plied. While capital produces "generalized equivalence," as Guattari observes, Eichhorn's autopoietic machine refuses this operation at the interstice where aesthetic objects are converted into financial value.[8] While typically immaterial and invisible, Eichhorn dilates this interval to reveal how her work is structurally coupled with legal and financial protocols. In so doing, the work galvanizes an organic line where incommensurate entities meet, but in this case do not equalize and combine.

While similarly invested in art's interface with institutions, Michael Riedel's practice catalyzes a strikingly different politics of recursion. Riedel has expressed particular interest in the German sociologist Niklas Luhmann, who in the 1980s and 1990s elaborated a systems theory drawn initially from Maturana and Varela's concept of autopoiesis to explicate the communicative structures of sociology, science, art, and law. A totalizing theory of social production, Luhmann's framework privileges the mechanisms by which social systems achieve operational closure and homeostatic equilibrium, even as they incorporate difference within their bounds. As Riedel puts it, glossing Luhmann, "Each system needs a good container."[9] For his 2011 installation *The quick brown fox jumps over the lazy dog* at David Zwirner Gallery in New York, Riedel activated the physical enclosure of the gallery, first by plastering its interior surfaces with wallpaper printed with text cut and pasted from the gallery's website. Reidel then affixed a series of silkscreened "poster paintings" on top of this wallpaper. The content of these paintings followed from a "Select All" operation, which similarly copied and pasted text of other sites that mention Riedel's work, together with the digital junk of HTML code and computational commands. This text was visually punctuated with circular forms that refer to the color wheel: a ubiquitous icon that captures the "density" and informational capacity of the internet, but also its "digital drag," as one critic aptly put it.[10] Certain of the gallery's walls, finally, were replicated and extruded as sculptures, as if to rematerialize the container itself (fig. C.4).

Paradoxically, while these sculptures duplicated and fragmented the gallery at an architectural level, they underscored the security of its institutional closure. For Riedel, unlike for Eichhorn in *Maria Eichhorn Public Limited Company*, recursion involves the algorithmic production of ever more artworks that can be converted into exhibitionary (and financial) value. Thus, a PowerPoint presentation of images of his work becomes the digital source for a new set of silkscreened paintings made from screenshots of the transition between slides. Posters are collected in artist's books, which

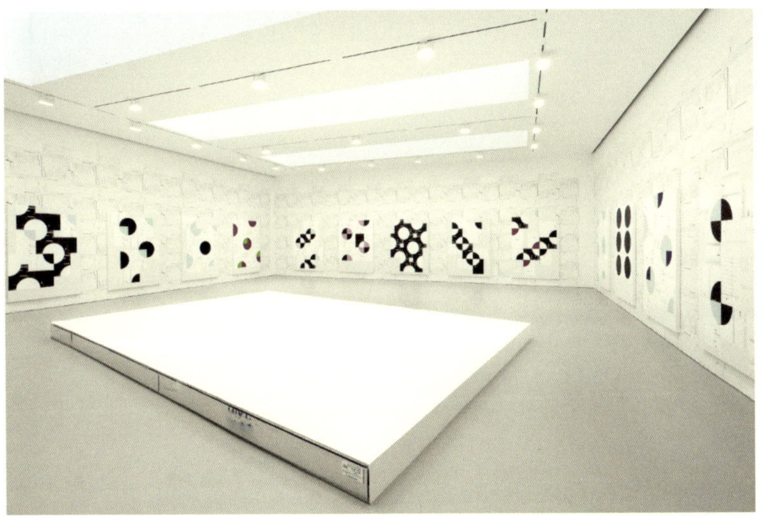

Figure C.4. Michael Riedel, *The quick brown fox jumps over the lazy dog*, 2011. © Michael Riedel. Courtesy the artist and Michel Rein, Paris/Brussels.

trigger exhibitions, catalogues, and more documentation, which in turn can be reinserted back into the system. In short, the digital hiatus of the color wheel—an indication of computational processing—becomes an engine of infinite production. Riedel has likened these transitions to "voids" of unoccupied territory that can be harnessed toward further aesthetic processes.[11] Thus, while his work ingeniously identifies and engages fissures and intervals akin to the organic line, he directs his autopoietic machine toward capturing and exploiting their liminality in a manner not unlike the colonial gesture of appropriation Carl Schmitt traced in *The Nomos of the Earth*.[12] There is no exit from the autopoietic machine's operational closure, moreover. As Riedel remarks, "I am overwriting myself. In other words, I'm not just the artist making art but also the artist watching himself making art and perceiving this process of art."[13]

What would it look like to trouble such closure, to open autonomy to an alterity that might shift an autopoietic machine's

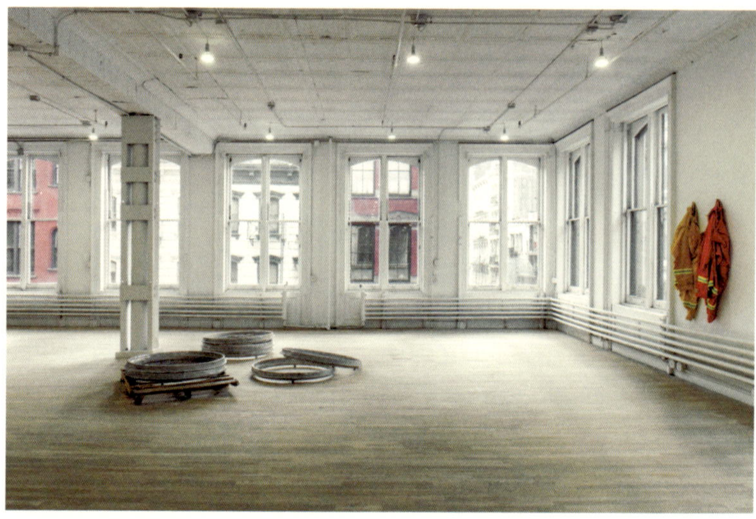

Figure C.5. Cameron Rowland, *91020000*, Artists Space, New York, 2016. Installation view.

organization and structural coupling with its environments?[14] Here I turn to the work of Cameron Rowland, who has long been interested in the financial and juridical legacies of slavery in the United States. For his renowned 2016 exhibition *91020000* at Artists Space in New York, Rowland displayed a number of ordinary objects—courtroom benches, office desks, manhole rings, fire safety jackets—all of which were produced by prison labor in California and New York and remunerated at the nominal rate of between \$0.10 and \$1.14 an hour (fig. C.5). These objects were procured from quasi-commercial entities such as Corcraft, which is affiliated with the Division of Industries of the New York State Department of Correctional Services and Community Supervision. Corcraft sells such goods to governmental, educational, and nonprofit entities, which must be registered with a customer number. The Thirteenth Amendment, which abolished slavery, is notoriously riddled with the exception that involuntary servitude is allowable "as a punishment for a crime." Given this exception, the history of leasing convict labor to private and public industries, the staggering racial disproportion of incarceration rates, and the development of the prison industry since the 1970s, the prison labor system continues the historical institution of slavery by another name.

Rowland's choice of objects underscores the recursive logic of this structural and systemic racism. Manhole rings constructed by inmates at the Elmira Correctional Facility recall the use of chain gangs to pave public roads for the expansion of state infrastructure. Benches made by prisoners at the Green Haven Correctional Facility in New York are sold to that same state's court system, where defendants receive sentencing under the terms of a vastly unequal criminal justice system. As Rowland writes, "The court reproduces itself materially through the labor of those it sentences" (fig. C.6).[15] Rowland's installation, in short, identifies and makes visible the autopoietic machine of state carcerality. But his work also structurally couples this system with *aesthetic* systems, and the discomfort of this coupling likewise drives the conceptual and political power of his work. Encountering the installation, viewers must reconceive of the sculptural entities as sedimentations of state violence, the former as immobile and inert as the latter is active and ongoing. But viewers must also contend with various levels of complicity and inscription within this equation. In order for the objects to appear in the gallery to render this violence visible, Artists Space had to become a nonprofit customer of Corcraft, in essence participating in an institutional agreement with the carceral system itself. The first work in the exhibition, *Partnership* (2016), is little more than the documentation of Corcraft's customer registration for Artists Space and its identificatory number, 91020000. The work thus materializes the structural coupling of the two institutions, and in so doing, the disquieting thickness of their shared organic line. The logic of possession and accumulation that drives racial capitalism, of course, also subtends museum collecting. Since Rowland does not sell these works to museums, but requires institutions to lease them at cost, this institutional interface circumvents the museum's

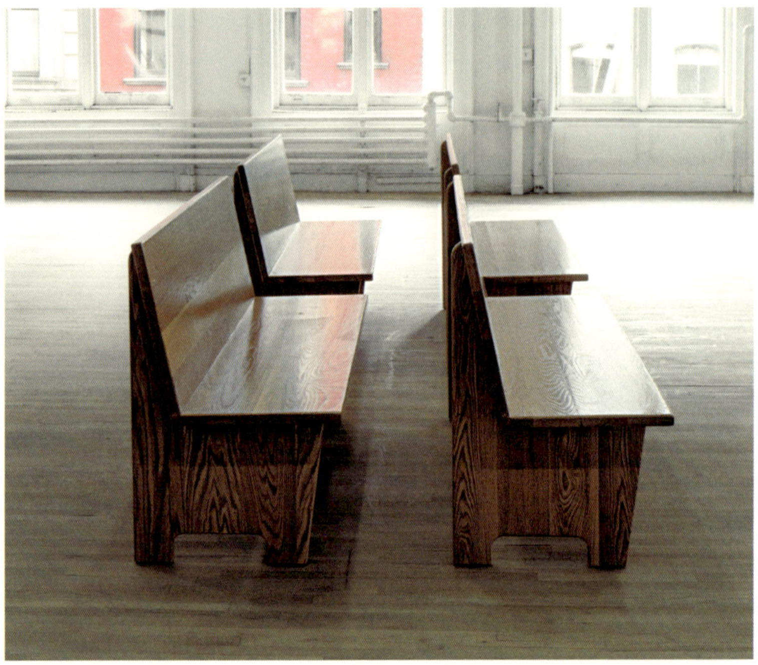

Figure C.6. Cameron Rowland, *New York State Unified Court System*, 2016. Oak wood, distributed by Corcraft, 419.10 × 146.05 × 91.44 cm, rental at cost. Courtrooms throughout New York State use benches built by prisoners in Green Haven Correctional Facility. The court reproduces itself materially through the labor of those it sentences. Rental at cost: Artworks indicated as "rental at cost" are not sold. Each of thee artworks may be rented for 5 years for the total cost of the Corcraft products that constitute it.

drive toward acquisition and the accrual of financial value. Thus, while the work's organic line reveals the art institution's structural coupling with the carceral system, it also compels a shift in any given museum's protocols.

As these examples demonstrate, the organic line can be mobilized as a conceptual tool that exceeds its historical inscription by Clark's work. But I want to underscore the urgency of attending to the *historicity* of appearance and description, as well. Although autopoiesis was always conceived as a philosophy of life, for example, its epistemological extension was never a foregone conclusion.

When Maturana and Varela first published their study in 1973, they remained split regarding the theory's applicability to social and ethical, rather than simply biological phenomena. On September 11 of that year, Chile's experiment with democratic socialism was violently crushed, inaugurating a brutal military dictatorship that sent Varela and countless others—including Mário Pedrosa, as mentioned in this book's Introduction—into exile. Both Maturana and Varela have since noted that their conception of autopoiesis was indebted to the cultural and political ferment of 1968 and the "collective creativity" that unfolded in Chile during the ensuing Salvador Allende years.[16] In his introduction to the first English edition of their study, in 1980, Maturana likened this period to learning to speak anew. "Language was a trap," he wrote, but the process of trying to say something different "was a wonderful school in which one could discover how mute, deaf, and blind one was." He continued, "One began to listen and one's language began to change; and then, but only then, new things could be said."[17]

Both Maturana and Varela have remarked that a society, comprehended autopoietically, drifts toward stabilization and even totalitarianism when a given specification of reality affords no other points of view.[18] For Varela, this kind of "boundary maintenance" has historically devolved into fascism and authoritarianism.[19] For him, autopoiesis was thus a dangerous analytic beyond its strictly biological inscription. Maturana's 1980 introduction, by contrast, identified two phenomena that productively disturb such conservative tendencies and more broadly position the social as the logical outgrowth of biological cognition. The first is "love," because it transforms the "structural plasticity" of the individual.[20] As Fred Moten might say, it creates "blur" apropos of the axiom, "consent not to be a single being."[21] (Recall here the elasticity of the circle in Clark's amorous geometries, as well as her dilation of the temporal passage of birth.) The second phenomenon is "social creativity," insofar as it mediates against a system's homeostasis by generating novel "modes of conduct."[22] Here, Maturana's description echoes elements of Malevich's aesthetic bacteriology. Yet for Maturana, such creativity is a cognitive, rather than merely a stylistic phenomenon and thus lies in the domain of the observer, rather than the maker per se. It is observers who, in recursively reacting to their own descriptions and representations, propel autopoiesis into time and diachronic change.[23]

It is the possibility — indeed the *necessity* — of redescription that inspired Sylvia Wynter to turn to autopoiesis as a rubric for exposing the racial underpinnings of the Western conception of the human. As noted in Chapter 1, Wynter argues that since the onset of Renaissance secularism and the subsequent development of the biological and economic sciences, Western thought has produced a self-description of the human as a purely biological being, even as it actively curtails this conception to a highly specific *genre* of performative human enactment. This privileged genre — which Wynter terms "Man(2)" — is autopoietically produced through the descriptive statements of a Western world-societal order premised on racial hierarchy. Yet these descriptive statements occlude their character *as descriptions*.[24] The result is a myth of naturalized biocentrism that enacts ontological violence at a planetary scale. Exiting this order of consciousness, Wynter suggests, requires that we recognize our agency as observers and redescribe ourselves as "hybridly human." Put another way, we must newly "auto-institute" ourselves as beings constructed through biology and mythology alike.[25]

Art, I wager, acts as a pivotal engine of such autoinstituting, not only because it plots "mutant coordinates" within existing systems, but because it demands description and redescription in practice and analysis alike. Because such actions and observations have an epistemological character, they also plot political effects. That Clark's *Descoberta da linha orgânica* and Adam Pendleton's *Black Dada* allow us to recover and *redirect* the racial ontologies that subtend the inscription on Malevich's *Black Square* is a crucial way of moving us "toward the Human, after Man."[26] That the near elision of Julius Eastman's historical legacy has sparked a host of contemporary artworks that riff and reflect on the problem of artistic genealogy (among them, Jace Clayton, *The Julius Eastman Memorial Dinner*, 2013; The Otolith Group, *The Third Part of the Third Measure*, 2017; and Pendleton, *That Which Is Fundamental*, 2018) is a reminder that the weakness of the organic line also binds.

———

As an interval between entities, the organic line can be harnessed toward the recursion or dissolution of its bounding systems and even come to act as an autopoietic entity in and of itself. This is because the *living* and *liminal* quality of the organic line is inherently plastic, even as it is generated by means of constraints. Recall Clark's inaugural description of her discovery apropos of making a collage. The organic line emerges when a spatial fissure persists between the collage's cardboard elements and its encompassing *passe-partout*. Such a line can be absorbed within the collage's pictorial system, but it catalyzes a fundamental reorganization of its material and medial ecologies. Suddenly, space — what previously existed as a neutral, encompassing, and unspecified entity — becomes a material element of the work. The work's medium ceases to be cardboard collage, but cardboard collage *and space*. This activated space likewise propels the collage's compositional elements and the *passe-partout* into a new, sculptural dimensionality and dissolves the categorical distinction between work and frame.[27] But space is also a medium in the technical and nondisciplinary sense of a facilitating substance or channel. When the organic line emerges as a legible linear form, it creates a tight configuration of space that differentiates itself from the loose configuration of space in which the collage sits. In short, the organic line introduces alterity into the preexisting medium of collage. In so doing, it remobilizes the collage's *specific* medial condition within a more expansive and *aspecific* medial ecology that exceeds any strictly historical delimitations in art.[28] Within this ecology, neither medium nor form are stable entities, but capable of constituting and reconstituting each other over time.

It is for precisely this reason that we can trace protean emanations, or *re-formations*, of the organic line across Clark's subsequent work. In her *Ovo linear* (Linear egg), *Unidades* (Units), and *Espaços modulados* (Modulated spaces) of 1958, the organic line is recast as a materially recessed "light line" that optically deforms its accompanying planes, opening them into virtual and phenomenological space (see figs. I.32 and 1.30). In her manipulable *Bichos* (Critters), begun in 1960, the organic line, as a seam of affective possibility and transition, is transformed into a hinge that vitalizes metal panels with "quasi-corporeal" movement (see fig. I.12). In the *Obras moles* (Soft works) (1964), the organic line's topological character is materialized in coils of clinging rubber (fig. C.7). In *Caminhando* (Walking, 1963), the line's sundering quality is reconceived as an active cut that extends indexical presence into theoretically infinite duration (see fig. I.28). In *Pedra e ar* (Stone and air, 1966), breath (the organic line that flows through the lungs) is externalized in the thin membrane of a plastic bag, where it dialogues with the condensed materiality of a stone as an empty spatial form (fig. C.8). In *Baba antropofágica* (Anthropophagic slobber, 1973), this capacity to traverse corporeal boundaries is reimagined as a line of thread unspooled from the mouth, which together with other such threads forms a collective epidermis for a supine subject (fig. C.9).[29] And finally, in *Estruturação do Self* (Structuring of the Self), begun in the late 1970s, the organic line emerges as a psychic and corporeal void that can be molded, repositioned, and transformed (see figs. 2.4 and 2.45).

In this book, I have chosen to concentrate on Clark's earliest instantiations of the organic line — its revelation as a fissure of found, interstitial, and empty space — in order to expound its paradigmatic character. In this elemental iteration, the organic line is a fugitive entity that must be sought within the particular conditions of each work. Vestigial and contingent, it disrupts the continuity the plane and the entire epistemology of self-evidence embedded

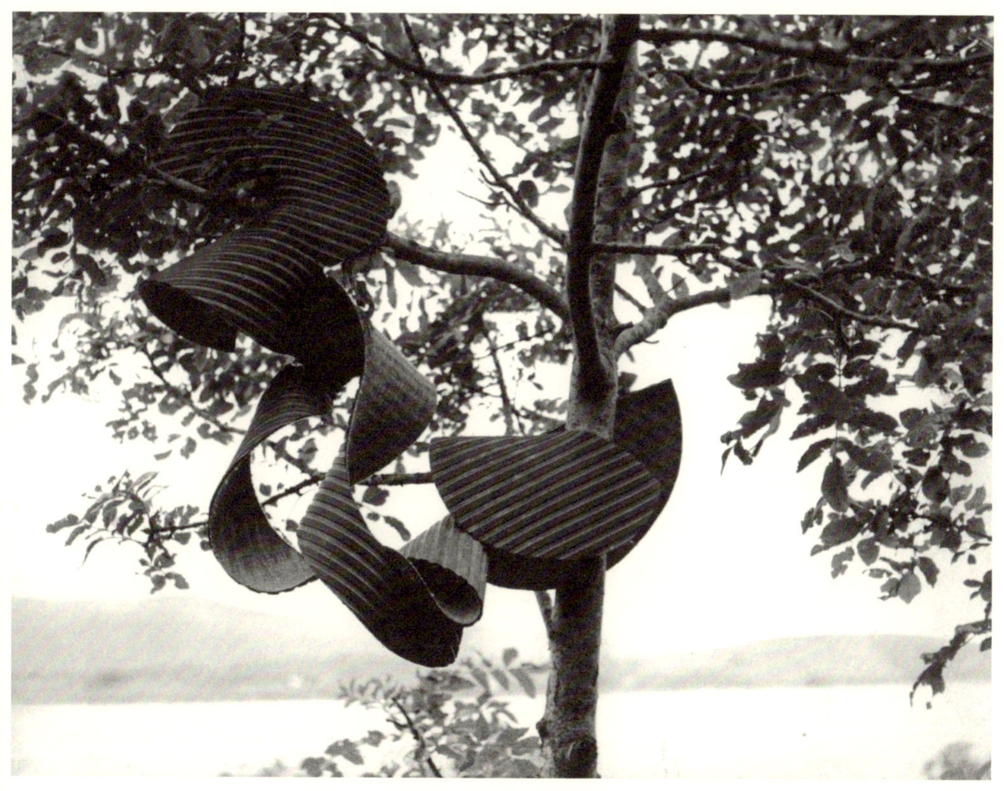

Figure C.7. Lygia Clark, *Obra mole no. 1* (Soft
work no. 1), 1964. Courtesy of Associação
Cultural "O Mundo de Lygia Clark."

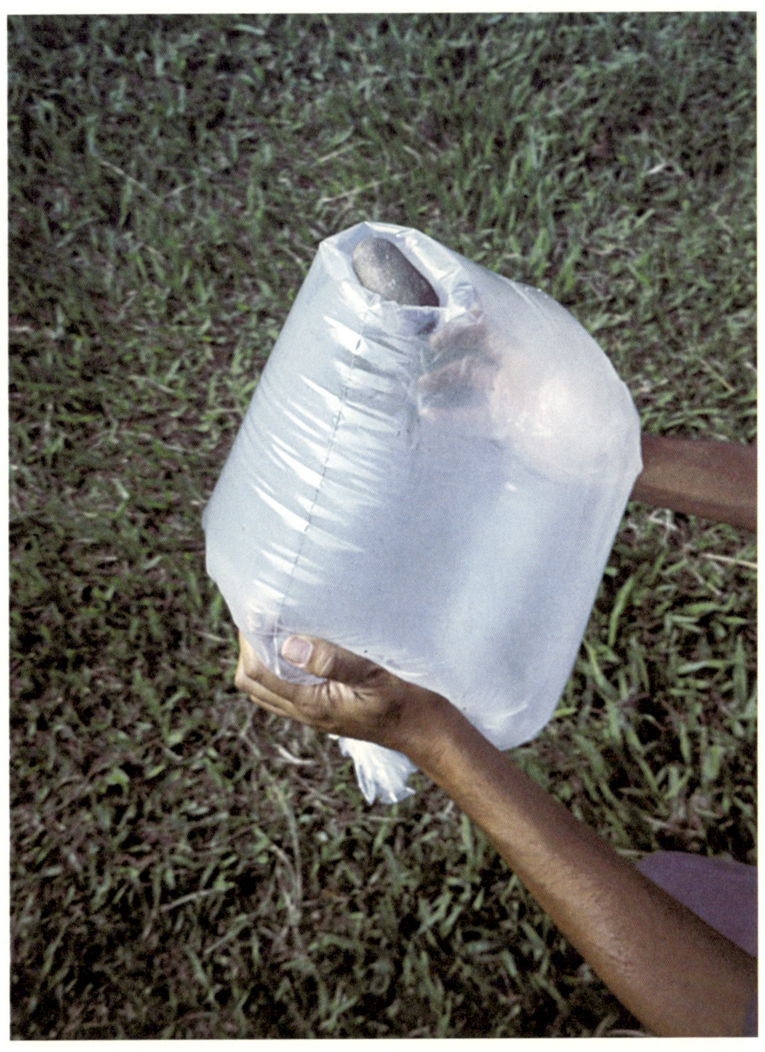

Figure C.8. Lygia Clark, *Pedra e ar* (Stone and air), 1966. Courtesy of Associação Cultural "O Mundo de Lygia Clark."

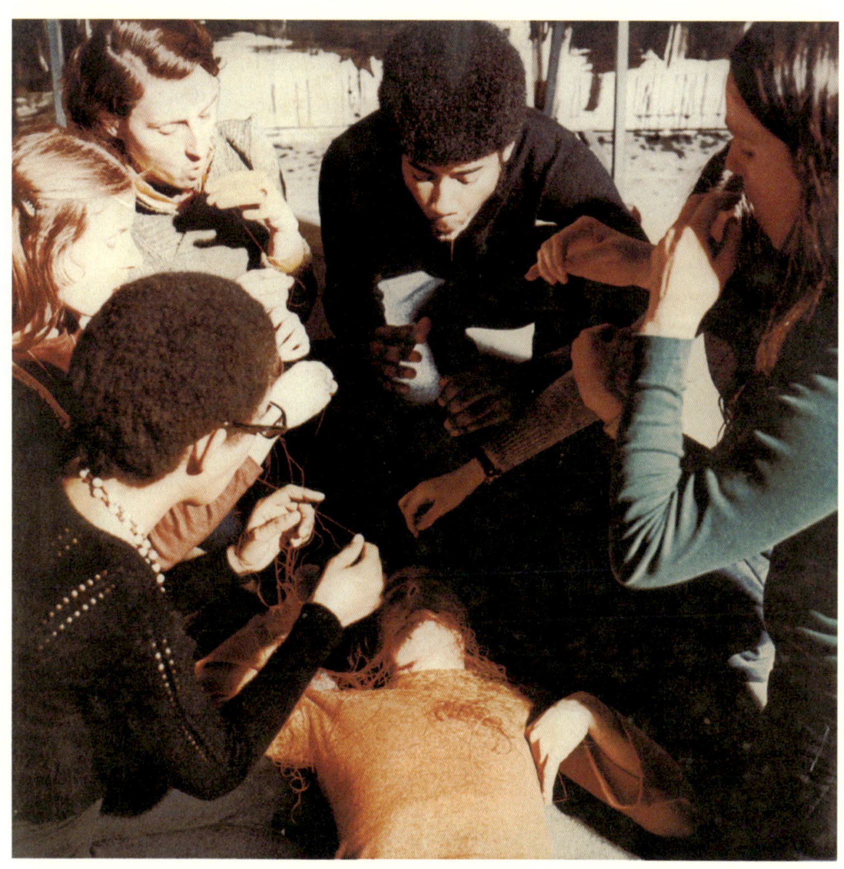

Figure C.9. Lygia Clark, *Baba antropofágica* (Anthropophagic slobber), 1973. Courtesy of Associação Cultural "O Mundo de Lygia Clark."

in it.[30] The organic line inheres in this doubly negative status: a line that is not a line, whose very emergence entails an unraveling of the a priori existence of the plane as a continuous, homogenous surface.[31] Yet as the philosopher Avrum Stroll has observed, what we consider a surface *to be* is often conditioned by "the operations we perform or intend to perform" upon it.[32] A surface that we can materially disengage from its support (such as the peel of an orange) is divergent from the uppermost limit of a materially uniform entity (such as a wooden tabletop). A plane constructed by knitting together matter and void is ontologically distinct from a preexisting support carved by spatial incisions. An edge conceived as the terminal limit of a form differs from that same edge comprehended as a porous membrane. In her early explorations of the organic line, Clark investigated a range of such possibilities in order to consider the minimal and maximal conditions under which a cavity of space might behave as a chasm, shape, contour, or seam. The organic line is historically significant in part because it allows us to produce and hold these distinctions in a way that can be named.

But the organic line was never a static phenomenon in Clark's own work. Between 1956 to 1958, for instance, she experimented with catalyzing the organic line by assembling independent panels, as well as by incising lines upon a panel with a scalpel. Although the resulting channels of the latter process have largely the same optical and spatial effect, the subtractive process of cutting reestablished both the a priori status of the plane and the coincidence of mark and line that Clark's earliest investigations had so vigorously decoupled. But Clark's priorities were also shifting, and as she became increasingly interested in the phenomenological instigation of the viewer, she subsumed artistic process to the beholder's share. To this extent, she herself treated the organic line as a resource for rediscovery, and her singular trajectory—only a few instances of which I mention above—is testament to this capacious experimentation.

This book has set out to identify the organic line in its paradigmatic form in order to demonstrate its extraordinary analytic potential beyond Clark's own practice. In treating the organic line as a conceptual instrument that can be activated in the present, however, I want to hold on to the line's spatial and historiographic particularity as a *weak link*. For such weak links, latency, discontinuity, and disjunction carry their own efficacy for the reconfiguration and the perturbation of existing systems, to recall Malevich's biological analogy. In a late interview, contrasting her work with that of fellow artist Hélio Oiticica, Clark commented, "I, as a woman — which must have been my weakness and my force — went more toward things that were no longer so visible, so touchable."[33] An art history under the sign of the organic line attends to this conjunction of "weakness and force." It recognizes that artistic practices may demand nonlinear temporalities or evade tracking within recognized vocabularies or interpretive frames. It does not seek to produce genealogies of influence, but to multiply constellations of possibility that allow us to topologically reorient *the shape* of modernism in the present.

With such latent constellations in mind, I want to invoke one of Maturana and Varela's key axioms: "Everything said is said by an observer."[34] Here, Maturana and Varela underscore that the designation of an autopoietic system cannot be separated from the activity of description.[35] When Clark observed a fissure of space and drew it into legibility as an organic line, she made a distinction between the living quality of the line and its bounding systems. She occupied a historical position from which to describe this distinction, as well as a blind spot from which she could not see. When we attend to the organic lines that Clark's works help us see, those lines become indexical structures through which the contemporaneity of our own observation enters and differentiates the work, as well. Describing and redescribing these multiple levels of distinction encourages us to excavate and activate organic lines at play within other artistic phenomena and the plural ecologies with which they interact. This plotting of coordinates and their liminal relations is qualitatively distinct from the utopian predilection for triumphant

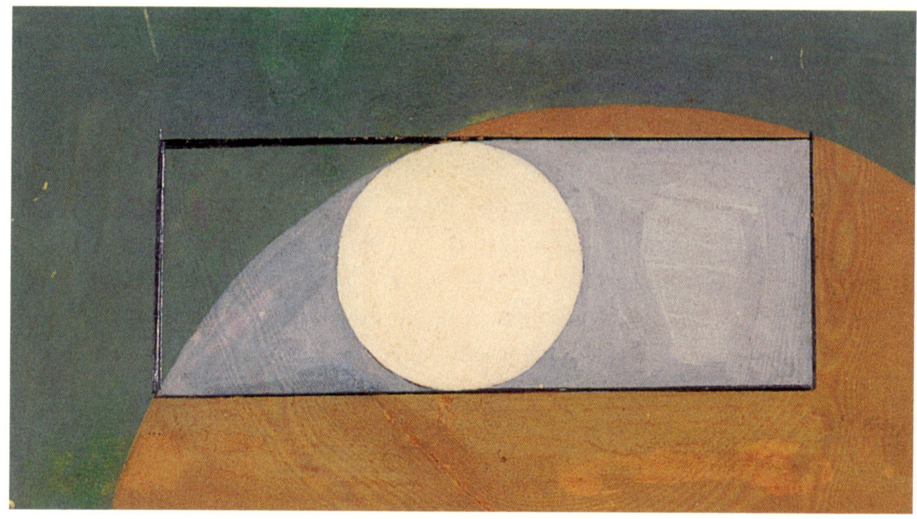

Figure C.10. Lygia Clark, *Geometria amorosa* (Amorous geometry), 1955. Graphite and gouache on cardboard, 24.5×34 cm. Photo: Marcelo Ribeiro Alvares Corrêa. Courtesy of Associação Cultural "O Mundo de Lygia Clark."

progress and sweeping overhaul that animated so much modernist rhetoric. Tracing plagiotropic relations and weak links may seem a pale version of those galvanizing pronouncements. But as Wynter argues with reference to Maturana and Varela, being human in a decolonial sense is a praxis, not an achievement, one that requires the continuous dismantling of colonial epistemologies through an adaptive "realization of the living."[36] As catastrophe theory reminds us, an aggregate of small pressures can catalyze structural change, as well. Viewing modernism from the present — which it to say, specifying modernism *by means of* our present — we can recognize and reanimate pressures that were there all along.

In 1969, as Maturana and Varela began to formulate the theory of autopoiesis, the mathematician George Spencer-Brown published *Laws of Form*, a text that would become key for the cognitive biologists' subsequent elaborations of self-referentiality.[37]

Spencer-Brown's work departed from an emphasis on Gestalt figure/ground relations in order to focus on the operation of differentiation. As he began his excursus: "A universe comes into being when a space is severed or taken apart. The skin of a living organism cuts off an outside from an inside. So does the circumference of a circle in a plane."[38] The foundational act of distinction, Spencer-Brown argued, creates a marked and an unmarked space—an inside and residual leftover—the separation of which is ultimately undermined by the reentry of difference within the space of demarcation. It was this quality of topological recursion that was attractive to Maturana and Varela, as well as to later systems theorists. Yet for Spencer-Brown, distinctions were synonymous with marks, just as line has been for much of the history of art. They are thus positivities that cut, delineate, and sunder and ultimately are returned to the system itself.

The organic line, by contrast, teaches us to apprehend the negativity and interstitiality of a distinction: to open self-referentiality to heterogeneity, misalignment, and lateral slide. In Clark's amorous geometries, a universe is not inaugurated with a cut. Rather, an existing configuration of a universe is disaggregated and reformed through the circle's capacity for plasticity, passage, and ontological recombination (fig. C.10). Spencer-Brown's injunction was: "Draw a distinction."[39] The organic line offers the following rejoinder:

> Find a distinction! *Dilate its liminality*
> and attend to what occurs along its sides.

Acknowledgments

I have been thinking about both the fragility and potent elasticity of linkage for some time. When I was researching my first book, I was often in Brazil and periodically trying to find my way to South Africa to reconnect with my partner and, in time, our daughter. Flight paths didn't follow affective ties though, and for a long time passing through Europe or other complicated paths was the only way of making the connection. My friend, the artist Thiago Rocha Pitta, was obsessed with Pangea, and finding himself on the western coast of South Africa, made a work in which he dripped honey from the cliffs that once nestled South America's littoral contours, the viscosity of the liquid a material metaphor for sculpting the earth in deep time. What irony that it was so hard to bridge the same geographies in the temporality of embodied experience.

The challenges of networking from the South are ever present for those who live and work there. For an art historian, it can manifest in everything from the inaccessibility and fragmentation of archives and collections, to the precarity of institutions and funding, from the sluggishness of bureaucracy to the mercurial hostilities of power and anemic possibilities for publishing. Navigating within such networks never erases their gaps or asymmetries, nor one's place within them. But to be situated in a network is also to be oriented to its multiplicity and light. I am honored and humbled to be in community with thinkers, scholars, and curators whose brilliant work in and from

Latin America continues to inspire from points near and far. For the gift of their intellectual exchange and friendship over the years, my thanks to Frederico Coelho, Ricardo Basbaum, Heloisa Espada, María Amalia García, Isabel Plante, Silvia Dolinko, Cristina Freire, Fernanda Pitta, Zanna Gilbert, Daniel Quiles, Sérgio Martins, Kaira Cabañas, Inés Katzenstein, Sofía Hernández Chong Cuy, Tatiana Ferraz, and Maria Iñigo Clavo. I am grateful as well for continued dialogues with Ondine Chavoya, Mónica Amor, Gabriel Pérez-Barreiro, Thiago de Paulo Souza, Felipe Scovino, Gabriela Rangel, Lilia Schwarcz, Hélio Menezes, Mari Carmen Ramírez, Andrea Giunta, Amy Buono, Cecilia Fajardo-Hill, Roberto Conduru, Aleca Le Blanc, Luiz Camillo Osorio, Alex Alberro, Edward Sullivan, Sérgio Bessa, Elena Shtromberg, Sebastian Vidal, Ana María Reyes, Vivian Crockett, Dorota Biczel, Adele Nelson, Megan Sullivan, Jennifer Josten, Miguel López, Marina Reyes Franco, Max Jorge Hinderer Cruz, Joaquín Barriendos, Sean Nesselrode Moncada, Harper Montgomery, Michael Asbury, Mariola Alvarez, Dária Gorete Jaremtchuk, Leonard Folgarait, and Thomas Cummins. During key periods of research, many a Sunday *almoço* were spent with Lais Myrrha, Thiago Rocha Pitta, Marilá Dardot, Hector Zamora, Sara Ramo, Carol Nogueira, Fábio Tremonte, André Komatsu, Cinthia Marcelle, Daniel Steegman Mangrané, Ana Linnemann, and Rosângela Renno, as well as a roving band of kids. It is impossible to imagine this book without the laughter and acute intelligence of these artists and friends. I owe a special thanks to camofe-in-arms Matheus Rocha Pitta, who spent a late night indulging my giddy mathematical speculations regarding *Descoberta da linha orgânica*, and whose own work and magnetic thinking have inspired me for years.

I am indebted to many individuals who facilitated my research in institutions, collections, and archives. My first thanks are to the Associação Cultural "O Mundo de Lygia Clark" and the kind facilitation of Julio Werneck, Fabiane Moraes, Álvaro Clark, and Sonia Menezes. Profound thanks as well to Agustín Díez-Fischer, Sofía Frigeiro, Clarissa Diniz, Luiz Guilherme Vergara, Angélica

Pimenta, Maria Tsantsanoglou, Maria Mazzillo Costa, Beatriz Olivetti, Joaquín Medina Warmburg, Aline Siqueira, Karen Bucky, Marisa Daley, Jessica Hoppe Dagci, Rachael Nutt, Nicola Shilliam, Brianna Cregle, Holly Hatheway, Rebecca Friedman, John Blazejewski, Julia Gearhart, Michele Mazeris, and Yichin Chen, who offered crucial institutional support. I am most grateful to the Fadel family (Sérgio, Hecilda, and Marta), Marisa Monte, Luiz Paulo Montenegro, Reynaldo Abucham, and Jones Bergamin, who kindly allowed me to study key works of art in their collections in person. For deeply meaningful conversations regarding their own areas of expertise, I thank Pino Monkes, Geeta Kapur, Maria Kokkori, Mónica de la Torre, Francesco Perrotta-Bosch, Carla Machiavello, Cynthia Albertsen, Juliet Koss, Gordon Hughes, Jason Treuting, Adam Sliwinski, Maya Kronfeld, Sumanth Gopinath, and Ittai Weinryb. I am especially grateful to Juan Carlos Letelier and Jorge Mpodozis for stimulating discussions in Santiago de Chile and facilitating my meeting with Humberto Maturana.

A huge thank you to Kerry Gaertner Gerbracht for the herculean task of tracking down image rights and acquisitions. For their help with particular images, I am indebted to Lynn Gamwell, Víctor Ortiz-Palau, Thomas Keenan, Yasmil Raymond, Alex Alberro, Rafael Cesar, Eve Reifert and Claudia Bank, María del Carmen Carríon, Inés Katzenstein, Mathilde Sauquet, and Kristine Genevive Khouri. For research assistance at various points, my heartfelt thanks to Julian Rose, Alice Heeren, Sasha Whittaker, Curt Gambetta, Luiza Repsold Franca, and Isabela Muci Barradas. I am most grateful to Maureen Killeen, as well as the late Susan Lehre, whose administrative genius and great heart will never be forgotten.

The first inklings of this book lie in a short essay, "Medium Aspecificity/Autopoietic Form," commissioned for the volume *Contemporary Art, 1989–Present* (London: Wiley Blackwell, 2013). Although my points of reference have shifted since then, it was in the process of writing that piece that I began to comprehend the astonishing conceptual value of the organic line, and I am indebted to Alexander Dumbadze and Suzanne Hudson for their warm invitation to contribute to that book. I am likewise grateful to have published an initial articulation of the weak link and elements of my second chapter in the essay "Cut, Fuse, Fissure: Planarity circa 1954" in Zanna Gilbert, Andrew Perchuk, Pia Gottschaller, Tom Learner, and Andrew Perchuk, eds., *Purity Is a Myth: The Materiality of Concrete Art from Argentina, Brazil, and Uruguay* (Los Angeles: Getty Research Institute, 2021). I appreciate permission to republish elements of those texts in this book. Zanna and Pia deserve special thanks for welcoming me at the Getty Research Institute during research for the exhibition *Making Art Concrete: Works from Argentina and Brazil in the Colección Patricia Phelps de Cisneros.* Our ongoing dialogues, and the opportunity to inspect several pivotal works in close proximity, were vital to this project.

Over the several years of this book's gestation, my research was supported by a Clark-Oakley Fellowship from the Sterling and Francine Clark Art Institute and Williams College, as well as a Harold Willis Dodds Presidential Preceptorship and a Barr Ferree Foundation Publication Grant from Princeton University. A number of smaller grants were indispensable to my research, and I am thankful to the Graham Foundation for Advanced Studies in the Fine Arts, the Dedalus Foundation, the Stanley J. Seeger Center for Hellenic Studies, and the Program in Latin American Studies at Princeton. I am particularly grateful to my marvelous hosts in Williamstown, Caroline Fowler, Gage McWeeny, Krista Birch, and Caitlin Woolsey, as well as the cohorts of Clark fellows during my fellowship year, especially Cecilia Fajardo-Hill, Roberto Conduru, Sarah Hamill, Lisa Paravisini-Gebert, Anne Lafont, and Lisa Lee, who provided helpful feedback on work in progress. Alena Williams, Emmelyn Butterfield-Rosen, Ohan Breiding, Mari Rodriguez Binnie, Shoghig Halajian, William Binnie, Susan Cross, Wendy McWeeny, Sara Rara, Luke Fischbeck, and Aruna D'Souza provided ongoing intellectual community and many fabulous nights of eating, drinking, and animated discussion.

It has been a great privilege to discuss Lygia Clark's work with several individuals, formidable in their own right, who knew the artist personally. For sharing conversations and recollections with me, my deep gratitude to Luciano Figueiredo, Yve-Alain Bois, and Lula Wanderley. I am immensely grateful to Luis Pérez-Oramas, who generously engaged in multiple discussions about Clark, and whose exquisite writing on her oeuvre motivates my own. Although I did not speak with them about this specific project, the pioneering work of Suely Rolnik, Paulo Herkenhoff, and Guy Brett remain glittering points of reference. This book has benefitted from the feedback of several talks, workshops, and lectures. For their warm invitations, sincere thanks to George Flaherty and Robin Greeley at the Clark; Sabeth Buchmann at the Academy of Fine Arts, Vienna; Christa Noel Robbins and Amanda Phillips at the University of Virginia; Megan Sullivan and Ricardo Basbaum at the University of Chicago; Markus Klammer at Eikones, Zentrum für die Theorie und Geschichte des Bildes; Tim Barringer, Joanna Fiduccia and Jordan Troeller at Yale University; Taisa Palhares at the Universidade Estadual de Campinas; Ioannis Mylonopoulos, Eleonora Pistis, and Janet Kraynak at Columbia University; Michael Asbury at TrAIN; Pia Gottschaller at the Courtauld; Sofia Hernandez Chong Cuy at the Kunstinstituut Melly; and Geaninne Gutiérrez-Guimarães, Vivien Greene, and Naomi Beckwith at the Guggenheim.

Thank you to my kith and kin and oddkin: Leslie and Loan-Anh Small, Ivan Small, Na-Rae Kim, Ana Kim Small; my family in South Africa, especially Ofentse and Nonhle Mosaka; my sistren Sarah Hsia; and my Brooklyn family, especially Shayla Harris, Jess Atwood-Gibson, Sam Greenleaf Miller, Max Greenleaf Miller, and our ever-expanding tribes, who have sustained and energized me across several cities and life phases. Heartfelt thanks to friends, fellow travelers, and colleagues Philipp Ekardt, Jennifer Greenhill, Michelle Kuo, Sharifa Rhodes-Pitts, Jennifer Allora, Guillermo Calzadilla, Megan Luke, Yasmil Raymond, Beatriz Balanta, Adrienne Edwards, Gabi Ngcobo, Thomas (T.) Jean Lax, Katrina Dodson,

Fia Backstrom, Molly Nesbit, Kellie Jones, and David Joselit, whose thoughts and conversations about this and other projects have invigorated me more than they know. I am most grateful for the camaraderie of my colleagues at Princeton, particularly Hal Foster, Rachel Price, Bridget Alsdorf, Rachael DeLue, Spyros Papapetros, Chika Okeke-Agulu, Carolyn Yerkes, Gabriela Nouzeilles, Anna Arabindan-Kesson, Beatriz Colomina, Tina Campt, Javier Guerrero, Beatrice Kitzinger, and Devin Fore. A reading group convened by Monica Huerta and Russ Leo threw me a lifeline during the dark days of the lockdown. For the practice of writing in community, I especially thank Christina León and fellow scrawlers Paul Nadal and V. Mitch McEwen.

Three dear friends read my manuscript at a crucial early stage — Jess Atwood-Gibson, Zanna Gilbert, Daniel Quiles — and I am endlessly grateful for their ongoing interlocution and critical perspectives, generative and generous in equal parts. As readers, Felipe Scovino and Matthew Jesse Jackson approached the project with expertise and expansiveness, and the book has been immeasurably improved by their astute observations. Spyros Papapetros, Rachel Price, Natalia Brizuela, Laura Harris, Amy Sara Carroll, Sergio Delgado Moya, and Bridget Alsdorf all read drafts of individual chapters; their feedback and encouragement came at vital points and spurred me to keep going. Thank you to the tremendous team at Zone, who have been a joy to work with — Meighan Gale, Julie Fry, Bud Bynack, Kyra Simone — and especially Jonathan Crary for his enthusiasm in taking on the organic line.

My final and most profound thanks are to Tumelo Mosaka, who has lived, breathed, and nurtured this project by my side in Brooklyn, Princeton, Rio de Janeiro, Capetown, São Paulo, San Juan, Williamstown, and parts beyond, and to Kha-ai, who, since the earliest glimmerings of this endeavor, has been quick to recognize organic lines in the world around her, including the all-important ones that lie between the pages of a book.

Notes

Note on the text: Documents pertaining to Lygia Clark's archive at Associação Cultural "O Mundo de Lygia Clark" are cited with document ID number where available and preceding folder designation if not. I use existing English translations of Clark's texts when published versions are available, although I modify translations in several instances and also resort to originals, particularly when a text exists in multiple versions. Unless noted, all other translations are mine. Variant spellings of Clark's name are retained in archival citations, but otherwise regularized as "Lygia."

INTRODUCTION: ON WEAK LINKS AND PLAGIOTROPIC RELATIONS

1. Lygia Clark, "1956," in *Livro-obra*, artist's book, self-published (1964, 1983). Archives of the Associação Cultural "O Mundo de Lygia Clark," ID 7355.

2. Luis Pérez-Oramas, "Lygia Clark: If You Hold a Stone," in Cornelia Butler and Luis Pérez-Oramas, eds., *Lygia Clark: The Abandonment of Art, 1948–1988*, exh. cat. (New York: Museum of Modern Art, 2014), p. 38.

3. Ricardo Basbaum, "Within the Organic Line and After," in Alexander Alberro and Sabeth Buchmann, eds., *Art After Conceptual Art* (Cambridge, MA: MIT Press; Vienna: Generali Foundation, 2006), pp. 87–99. See also Basbaum, "Antropofagia and the Strategies of Permanent Hybridization," in Elke aus dem Moore and Giorgio Ronna, eds., *Entre Pindorama*, exh. cat. (Stuttgart: Künstlerhaus Stuttgart, 2004), pp. 65–69; and Basbaum, "The Sensorial + Conceptual Mix," in *Conceptual Paradise*, symposium at Kunstraum of Leuphana University, Lüneburg, January 28, 2010, https://kunstraum.web.leuphana.de/de/events/the-sensorial-the-conceptual-mix.

4. See Suely Rolnik, "La mémoire du corps," PhD diss., UER de Sciences Humaines Cliniques, Sorbonne, Université de Paris, 1978; *Cartografia sentimental: Transformações contemporâneas do desejo* (São Paulo: Estação Liberdade, 1989); and "Uma terapêutica para tempos desprovidos de poesia," in Suely Rolnik and Corine Diserens, eds., *Lygia Clark: Da obra ao acontecimento, somos o molde, a Você cabe o sopro*, exh. cat. (São Paulo: Pinacoteca do Estado, 2006), pp. 13–26.

5. Basbaum, "Within the Organic Line and After," p. 98.

6. See, for example, Rosalind Krauss, "Grids," *October* 9 (Summer 1979), p. 52. We can think of such articulations in terms of Michel Foucault's elaboration of the utterance as the constitutive unit of discourse in *The Archaeology of Knowledge and The Discourse on Language*, trans. A. M. Sheridan Smith (1969; New York: Pantheon, 1972). When such utterances compose apparatuses, or *dispositifs*, they exert a distinct form of power. See Gilles Deleuze, "What is a Dispositif?" in *Michel Foucault, Philosopher: Essays Translated from the French and German*, trans. Timothy Armstrong (New York: Routledge, 1992), pp. 159–68, and Giorgio Agamben, *What Is an Apparatus? and Other Essays*, trans. David Kishak and Stefan Pedatella (Stanford: Stanford University Press, 2009).

7. Mikhail Bakhtin, "Discourse in the Novel," in *The Dialogic Imagination: Four Essays*, ed. Michael Holquist, trans. Caryl Emerson and Michael Holquist (Austin: University of Texas Press, 1981), pp. 259–422.

8. See, for example, Bernhard Siegert, *Cultural Techniques: Grids, Filters, Doors, and Other Articulations of the Real*, trans. Geoffrey Winthrop-Young (New York: Fordham University Press, 2015).

9. Shklovsky first articulated the notion of the artistic device in his essay "Art as Technique," also translated in English as "Art as Device" (1917, 1919), in Alexandra Berlina, ed., and trans., *Viktor Shklovsky: A Reader* (New York: Bloomsbury Academic, 2017), pp. 73–96. He elaborated the concept of "baring the device" in subsequent writings gathered as *On the Theory of Prose*, trans. Shushan Avagyan (1925; Dallas: Dalkey Press, 2021), particularly the essay "The Parody Novel: Sterne's Tristam Shandy" (see pp. 214–51).

10. Gottfried Semper, "The Structural Significance of the Seam," in Semper, *Style in the Technical and Tectonic Arts; or, Practical Aesthetics* (1860–1862), trans. Harry Francis Mallgrave and Michael Robinson (Los Angeles: Getty Research Institute, 2004), p. 154.

11. Ibid., p. 155.

12. Mário Pedrosa, "Da natureza afetiva da forma na obra da arte" (1949), in *Mário Pedrosa, Textos escolhidos II: Forma e percepção estética*, ed. Otília Arantes (São Paulo:

EdUSP, 1996), pp. 124–25. Pedrosa here quotes in part from Laurence Binyon, *The Spirit of Man in Asian Art* (Cambridge, MA: Harvard University Press, 1936). Although neither engages the organic line as a specific site of articulation, Pedro Erber, in *Breaching the Frame: The Rise of Contemporary Art in Brazil and Japan* (Berkeley: University of California Press, 2014), and Mariola Alvarez, in "Calligraphic Abstraction and Postwar Brazilian Informalist Painting," in Mariola Alvarez and Ana M. Franco, eds., *New Geographies of Abstract Art in Postwar Latin America* (New York: Routledge, 2019), pp. 25–40, have touched on resonances between Brazilian and Japanese art that occurred by way of transnational and diasporic figures such as Pedrosa, Manabu Mabe, Tomie Ohtake, and Flavio Shiró. Although certain elements of these and other artists' works (Franz Weissman's *Amassados* series from the 1960s, created after his trip to Japan, or Clark's 1960 architectural proposition, *Construa você mesmo o seu espaço para viver* (Build your own living space, 1964), in which moveable walls recall Japanese sliding screens, were likely influenced in part by Asian art, Clark's archive has not as yet revealed references to specific philosophical or aesthetic concepts such as *sunyata* (emptiness) and *qi* (vital energy).

13. Wendy Ikemoto, *Antebellum American Pendant Paintings: New Ways of Looking* (New York: Routledge, 2018). See also Siegert, "Door Logic, or, The Materiality of the Symbolic," in *Cultural Techniques*, pp. 192–205.

14. Ikemoto, *Antebellum American Pendant Paintings*, p. 3.

15. Catherine de Zegher, "A Century Under the Sign of Line: Drawing and Its Extension (1910–2010)," in Cornelia H. Butler and Catherine de Zegher, eds., *On Line: Drawing Through the Twentieth Century*, exh. cat. (New York: Museum of Modern Art, 2010), p. 24.

16. Aleksandr Rodchenko, "The Line," (1921), in Alexander Lavrentiev, ed., *Aleksandr Rodchenko: Experiments for the Future. Diaries, Essays, Letters and Other Writings*, trans. Jamey Gambrell (New York: Museum of Modern Art, 2004), p. 113.

17. Eric de Bruyn, "Beyond the Line or a Political Geometry of Contemporary Art," *Grey Room* 57 (Fall 2014), pp. 24–49. De Bruyn appeals to Gilles Deleuze and Félix Guattari's reading of Paul Klee's pedagogical sketchbooks in *A Thousand Plateaus: Capitalism and Schizophrenia*, trans. Brian Massumi (Minneapolis: University of Minnesota Press, 1987).

18. See George Jackson, *Les frères de Soledad*, trans. Catherine Roux (1970; Paris: Gallimard, 1971); Michelle Koerner, "Line of Escape: Gilles Deleuze's Encounter with George Jackson," *Genre* 44.2 (Summer 2011), pp. 157–80, and Fernand Deligny, *The Arachnean and Other Texts*, trans. Drew Burk and Catherine Porter (Minneapolis: Univocal, 2015).

19. Deleuze and Guattari, *A Thousand Plateaus*, pp. 204–205.

20. Paul Klee, *Pedagogical Sketchbook* (1925), trans. Sibyl Moholy-Nagy (New York: Frederick Praeger, 1953), pp. 16–21. Klee's work featured in the São Paulo Bienal of 1953 in a special exhibition of sixty-five works. Pedrosa also had a 1925 edition of Klee's book in his library and referred to sections pertaining to the line in his essay "Problemática da arte contemporânea" (1954/1959–1960), in *Mário Pedrosa, Textos escolhidos II*, pp. 267–300.

21. Here my analysis departs from Megan Sullivan's argument in *Radical Form: Modernist Abstraction in South America* (New Haven: Yale University Press, 2022) that the organic line establishes pure presence with the viewer and is anti-indexical because it does not point back to an action or inscription. While the latter is undoubtedly true, as I explore in Chapter 2, I would insist that the organic line is *always and only* indexical to its contiguous material borders. Because this structural relation precedes and lasts beyond the viewer's encounter, the organic line also exceeds any self-evident notion of presence.

22. Despite such differences, Paulo Herkenhoff has elaborated fascinating points of contact between the two artists in *Lucio Fontana / Brasil: A ótica do invisível*, exh. cat. (Milan: Charta, 2001), pp. 15–55.

23. On Orozco's sculpture, see Natasha Adamou, "Impossible Objects: Gabriel Orozco's Empty Shoe Box and Yielding Stone," in Sophie Halart and Mara Polgovsky Ezcurra, eds., *Sabotage Art: Politics and Iconoclasm in Contemporary Latin America* (London: I. B. Tauris, 2016), pp. 130–50.

24. Among other interviews, Orozco mentions his interest in Clark in Benjamin Buchloh, Carrie Lambert-Beatty, and Megan Sullivan, "To Make an Inner Time: A Conversation with Gabriel Orozco," *October* 130 (Fall 2009), p. 180.

25. See notebook entry "Memoria del espacio," in *Gabriel Orozco*, exh. cat. (New York: Museum of Modern Art, 2009). See also Benjamin Buchloh, "Gabriel Orozco: La escultura como recolección," in *Gabriel Orozco*, exh. cat. (London and Mexico City: Museo del Palacio de Bellas Artes, 2006), pp. 154–207.

26. Gordon Hughes, *Resisting Abstraction: Robert Delaunay and Vision in the Face of Modernism* (Chicago: University of Chicago Press, 2014), p. 51.

27. Jorge Romero Brest, *La pintura europea contemporánea 1900–1950* (Mexico City: Fondo de Cultura Económica, 1952), p. 154. The painting is also reproduced in *Dictionnaire de la peinture moderne* (Paris: F. Hazan, 1954), which Pedrosa had in his library.

28. *Quadro* translates both as "painting" and "picture." An article described it this way: "A moldura, o chassis, e a assinatura de Lígia Clark anunciam a falta de telas no

mercado" (the frame, the stretcher, and the signature of Lygia Clark announce the lack of canvases in the market). Clemente de Magalhães Bastos, "160 pinturas em discussão, no Salão Preto e Branco," *Diário de Notícias*, June 20, 1954, p. 5.

29. On the artists' protest, see Paulo Herkenhoff and Gloria Ferreira, eds., *A arte e seus materiais. Salão Preto e Branco: III Salão Nacional de Arte Moderna, 1954* (Rio de Janeiro: FUNARTE, 1985), as well as Aleca Le Blanc, "The Agency of Artists at the Salão Preto e Branco," in Luis Antônio Cruz Souza, Maria Amélia Bilhões, Marília Andrés Ribeiro, and Yacy-Ara Froner, eds., *Arte concreta e vertentes construtivas; Teoria, crítica e história da arte técnica*, Jornada ABCA (Belo Horizonte: Editora ABCA, 2018), pp. 18–33.

30. Irene V. Small, "Ready Constructible Color," in *Hélio Oiticica: Folding the Frame* (Chicago: University of Chicago Press, 2016), pp. 131–80. The debate about artistic materials lasted well past the salon and rose to international discussion. "Os artistas marcham para a unidade," *Forma* 3 (October 1954), n.p., notes that a Brazilian delegate participated in an international artists' advocacy conference in Venice in September that year.

31. See Sylvia Wynter, "Beyond the Categories of the Master Conception: The Counterdoctrine of Jamesian Poiesis," in Paget Henry and Paul Buhle, eds., *C. L. R. James's Caribbean* (Durham: Duke University Press, 1992), pp. 63–91, and "Unsettling the Coloniality of Being/Power/Truth/Freedom: Towards the Human, After Man, Its Overrepresentation—An Argument," *CR: The New Centennial Review* 3.3 (Fall 2003), pp. 257–337, as well as Aníbal Quijano, "Coloniality of Power, Eurocentrism, and Latin America," *Nepantla: Views from the South* 1.3 (2000), pp. 533–80, and "Coloniality and Modernity/Rationality," *Cultural Studies* 21.2–3 (March–May 2007), pp. 168–78. See also Cedric Robinson's pioneering analysis of racial capitalism in *Black Marxism: The Making of the Black Radical Tradition* (1987; Chapel Hill: University of North Carolina Press, 2000).

32. Hal Foster, "Who's Afraid of the Neo-Avant-Garde," in Foster, *Return of the Real: The Avant-Garde at the End of the Century* (Cambridge, MA: MIT Press, 1996), pp. 1–32. On the subsumption of Latin American modernist articulations within universalizing versions of modernism, see Rafael Cardoso, *Modernity in Black and White: Art and Image, Race and Identity in Brazil, 1890–1945* (Cambridge: Cambridge University Press, 2021).

33. The literature on multiple, alternative, and comparative modernities emerged as a useful corrective to totalizing narratives of globalization at the turn of the twenty-first century. See, for example, "Multiple Modernities," *Daedalus* 129.1 (Winter 2000); Timothy Mitchell, ed., *Questions of Modernity* (Minneapolis: University of Minnesota Press, 2000); Dilip Parameshwar Gaonkar, ed., *Alternative Modernities* (Durham: Duke University

Press, 2001); and Dipesh Chakrabarty, *Provincializing Europe: Postcolonial Thought and Historical Difference* (Princeton: Princeton University Press, 2007). With specific relation to art and art history, see also Kobena Mercer, ed., *Cosmopolitan Modernisms* (Cambridge, MA: MIT Press, 2005); Nicolas Bourriaud, *Altermodern*, exh. cat. (London: Tate, 2009); "African Modernism," special issue, *South Atlantic Quarterly* 109.3 (Summer 2010); and Terry Smith, *What Is Contemporary Art?* (Chicago: University of Chicago Press, 2009). Subsequent inflective nominations — for example "refugee modernisms" or "diasporic modernisms" — have usefully foregrounded many transnational practices, but have often left the presumption of modernism as a shared aesthetic language intact. The more recent term "intersectional modernisms" is one way of thinking with and beyond the limits of the "multiple modernisms" discourse.

34. Giorgio Agamben, *The Signature of All Things: On Method*, trans. Luca di Santo and Kevin Attell (New York: Zone Books, 2009), p. 17. Agamben's examples include paradigms of power such as Foucault's Panopticon, as well as those of aesthetics such as Aby Warburg's *Pathosformel*.

35. Ibid., pp. 31 and 20.

36. Michel Foucault, "Nietzsche, Genealogy, History," in Donald F. Bouchard, ed., *Language, Counter-Memory, Practice: Selected Essays and Interviews*, trans. Donald F. Bouchard and Sherry Simon (Ithaca: Cornell University Press, 1977), pp. 139–64. As Ricardo Nascimento Fabbrini observes, the organic line "instantiates difference at the origin of meaning." *O espaço de Lygia Clark* (São Paulo: Editora Atlas, 1994), p. 41.

37. In Rio de Janeiro, Clark circulated among artists and critics such as Pedrosa and Ivan Serpa, who shared books and catalogues with friends at weekly gatherings. Beginning in 1956, the *Suplemento Dominical do Jornal do Brasil* also published extensive art criticism covering major movements and texts of European modern art.

38. See David Medalla, ed., special issue on Lygia Clark in *Signals* 1.7 (April–May 1965); Jean Clay, "Dossier Lygia Clark," *Robho* 4 (1968), pp. 12–19, and "Unite de champ perceptif," *Robho*, nos. 5–6 (1971), pp. 8–13. Guy Brett was closely involved in Clark's exhibition at Signals Gallery, London, in 1965. To this list we must add the art historian Yve-Alain Bois, who notes that Clark, along with Mathias Goeritz, exerted her own "anxiety of influence" on him when they met in Paris in the early 1960s and Bois was yet a teenager. Yve-Alain Bois, "Some Latin Americans in Paris," in *Geometric Abstraction: Latin American Art from the Patricia Phelps de Cisneros Collection*, exh. cat. (Cambridge, MA: Harvard University Art Museums, 2001), p. 81. Particularly significant is Bois's recollection of

how Clark disrupted his initial, Neoplatonic understanding of Mondrian, resonances we might see in the art historian's later "The Iconoclast," in *Piet Mondrian, 1872–1944*, exh. cat. (New York: Little, Brown, 1995), pp. 313–72. Bois recalls that he wrote his first piece of art criticism on Clark's work, as the short text "Lygia, l'art hors des enceints" *Réforme*, March 8, 1969, p.14. Although he discussed coauthoring a book about Clark with Brett, and discussed her work in letters exchanged with the German artist Franz Erhard Walther, he did not write about her work again or his formative encounter until his introduction to Clark's texts in "Nostalgia for the Body," *October* 69 (Summer 1994), pp. 85–88, surely due to the "paralyzing 'lack of distance'" regarding her work he notes in "Angels with Guns," *October* 179 (Winter 2022), pp. 11–77. Bois's recollections are reprinted in Yve-Alain Bois, *An Oblique Autobiography*, ed. Jordan Kantor (Cambridge, MA: MIT Press, 2022), pp. 17–77 and 187–203.

39. Brandon Joseph, *Beyond the Dream Syndicate: Tony Conrad and the Arts after Cage (A "Minor" History)* (New York: Zone Books, 2008), p. 48. See Gilles Deleuze and Félix Guattari, *Kafka: Toward a Minor Literature*, trans. Dana Polan (Minneapolis: University of Minnesota Press, 1986).

40. On Clark's departure from art as institution, see Kaira Marie Cabanãs, "Art's Histories without Art History," *ARTMargins* 11.3 (2022). pp. 126–33.

41. Donald Judd, "In the Galleries," *Arts Magazine* (April 1963), reprinted in *Donald Judd: Complete Writings 1959–1975* (Halifax: Nova Scotia College of Art and Design, 1975), p. 85. A brief article published in Brazil notes that Louise Nevelson and Dore Ashton attended Clark's opening in New York, among other critics. "Intercâmbio entre galeries de arte," *Jornal O Estado de São Paulo*, March 10, 1963. The Louis Alexander Gallery archives at the Smithsonian Archives of American Art do not document this exhibition.

42. On the Neoconcrete non-object, see Ferreira Gullar, "Theory of the Non-Object" (1959), trans. Michael Asbury, in Kobena Mercer, ed., *Cosmopolitan Modernisms*; Ronaldo Brito, "Neo-concretism, Apex and Rupture of the Constructive Project," trans. Gabriel Pérez-Barreiro with Irene V. Small, *October* 161 (Summer 2017), pp. 89–42; and Mónica Amor, *Theories of the Nonobject: Argentina, Brazil, Venezuela, 1944–1969* (Oakland: University of California Press, 2016). See also Michael Asbury, "Neoconcretism and Minimalism: Cosmopolitanism at the Local Level and a Canonical Provincialism," in Mercer, ed., *Cosmopolitan Modernisms*, pp. 174–89 and Donald Judd, "Specific Objects" (Arts Yearbook 8 [1965]), reprinted in *Donald Judd: Complete Writings*, pp. 181–89.

43. Paulo Herkenhoff, "Divergent Parallels: Toward a Comparative Study of

Neoconcretism and Minimalism," in *Geometric Abstraction: Latin American Art from the Patricia Phelps de Cisneros Collection*, p. 106. See also Michael Asbury, "Abstract Impulses," in *Impulse, Reason, Sense, Conflict: Abstract Art from the Ella Fontanals-Cisneros Collection*, exh. cat. (Miami: Cisneros Fontanals Art Foundation, 2015), pp. 16–31.

44. Blake Gopnik, "Lygia Pape and Frank Stella: Separated at Birth?," *Artnet* (April 19 2017), https://news.artnet.com/opinion/lygia-pape-met-929204. Though not cited directly, Gopnik's reference is to Yve-Alain Bois, "The Uses and Abuses of Lookalikes," *October* 154 (Fall 2015), pp. 127–49.

45. Erber, *Breaching the Frame*, p. 4.

46. Ibid., pp. 10 and 11. See Piotr Piotrowski, "Toward a Horizontal History of Art," expanded as "Toward a Horizontal History of the European Avant-Garde," in Sascha Bru and Peter Nicholls, eds., *European Avant-Garde and Modernism Studies* (Berlin: De Gruyter, 2009), pp. 49–58. See also Kobena Mercer, ed., *Discrepant Abstraction* (Cambridge, MA: MIT Press, 2006).

47. Lygia Clark, "Letter to Mondrian (May 1959)," trans. in *Lygia Clark*, exh. cat. (Barcelona: Fundacío Antoni Tàpies, 1997), pp. 114 and 115.

48. On revisibilizing as a more primal operation of "radical pictoriality," see Whitney Davis, "The Archaeology of Radical Pictoriality," in Richard Heinrich, Elisabeth Nemeth, Wolfram Pichler, and David Wagner, eds., *Image and Imaging in Philosophy, Science and the Arts: Proceedings of the 33rd International Ludwig Wittgenstein-Symposium in Kirchberg, 2010, Volume 1* (New Brunswick: Ontos, 2011), pp. 191–218.

49. Pape comments on her own and Clark's work in Frederico Morais, "Entrevista com Lygia Pape," *O Globo*, July 22, 1975, p. 3.

50. See William Rubin, *Frank Stella*, exh. cat. (New York: Museum of Modern Art, New York, 1970), p. 16.

51. See Clement Greenberg, "The Crisis of the Easel Picture (1948), in John O'Brian, ed., *Clement Greenberg: The Collected Essays and Criticism, Vol 2: Arrogant Purpose* (Chicago: University of Chicago Press, 1988), pp. 221–25, and Michael Fried, "Shape as Form: Frank Stella's Irregular Polygons" (1967), in *Art and Objecthood: Essays and Reviews* (Chicago: University of Chicago Press, 1998), pp. 77–99.

52. Carl Andre, "Cuts," quoted in Maria Gough, "Frank Stella Is a Constructivist," *October* 119 (Winter 2007), p. 100. However, as Gough notes, it was vital that Stella understood the untouched side of Andre's works as "sculpture too."

53. Fried, "Shape as Form," p. 23.

54. In his 1970 essay, Rubin points to Fried's equivocation in the concept of the deductive structure, calling attention to the fact that "the edge of the canvas—which is 'negative' in the sense that it demarcates one border of the outer bands—is thereby equated with the 'negative' space that indicates their inside borders." *Frank Stella*, p. 47. Rubin notes that Fried himself admitted the limitations of the term, substituting the term "acknowledgment" for "deductive structure" in a footnote in his essay for *Jules Olitski: Paintings 1963–1967*, exh. cat. (Washington, DC: The Corcoran Gallery, 1967), pp. 59–60. Neither discussion, however, concentrates on the problem of the spatial interval itself.

55. For a related, but divergent reading of Stella's paintings articulated by the German critic Max Imdahl, see Megan Luke's excellent essay, "A Picture Is a Shaped Thing," *October* 168 (Spring 2019), pp. 148–65.

56. On mediums as a function of socially networked objects, see also Craig Dworkin, *No Medium* (Cambridge, MA: MIT Press, 2013).

57. Hélio Oiticica, "February 16 1961," and "August 13 1961," in Susanne Gaensheimer, ed., *Hélio Oiticica: The Great Labyrinth*, trans. Steve Berg (Ostfildern: Hatje Cantz, 2013), pp. 76 and 83.

58. Hélio Oiticica, "June 1960," in Gaensheimer, ed., *Hélio Oiticica*, p. 67 ("um marco que faltava").

59. I want to underscore that the organic line has long been influential within Brazilian art, however. Its formal and conceptual prominence within the exhibition *Artevida*, curated by Adriano Pedrosa and Rodrigo Moura (Rio de Janeiro: Secretaria de Estado de Cultura do Rio de Janeiro, 2015), for example, suggests how the line is a means to comprehend trajectories of contemporary art more broadly. Frederico Coelho's beautiful text "Uma Linha," in Myria Sepúlveda, ed., *Entre utopias e memórias: Arte, museus, patrimônia* (Rio de Janeiro: Mórula, 2021), pp. 138–45, likewise suggests how the organic line might philosophically dialogue with a host of other artistic lines, from those of Giacometti to Tunga.

60. Alfred Barr, *Cubism and Abstract Art*, exh. cat. (New York: Museum of Modern Art, 1936). On the diagram, see Astrit Schmidt Burkhardt, "Shaping Modernism: Alfred Barr's Genealogy of Art," *Word & Image* 16.4 (2000), pp. 387–400. The 2012 diagram was created for Leah Dickerman, ed., *Inventing Abstraction, 1910–1925*, exh. cat. (New York: Museum of Modern Art, 2012). Pedrosa criticized Barr for characterizing Latin American Concretism as mere "Bauhaus exercises" in "Pintura brasileira e gosto internacional"

(1957) in Glória Ferreira and Paulo Herkenhoff, eds., *Mário Pedrosa: Primary Documents*, trans. Steve Berg (New York: Museum of Modern Art, 2016), pp. 192–93.

61. Real points of connection and resonance do certainly exist, as María Amalia García has explored in *Abstract Crossings: Cultural Exchange between Argentina and Brazil*, trans. Jane Brodie (2011; Berkeley: University of California Press, 2019). See also Aracy Amaral, "Abstração geométrica no América do Sul: A Argentina como precursora," and "Artes visuais: Contatos com a Argentina," in Amaral, *Textos do Trópico de Capricórnio, Volume 2: Artigos e ensaios (1980–2005): Circuitos de arte na América Latina e no Brasil* (São Paulo: Editora 34, 2006), pp. 102–11 and 170–72, as well as Elizabeth Catoia Varela, "Arte concreta além da Europa: Diálogos entre Brasil e Argentina através do MAM RJ," PhD diss., Universidade Federal do Rio de Janeiro, 2016.

62. Mark Granovetter, "The Strength of Weak Ties," *American Journal of Sociology* 78.6 (May 1973), pp. 1360–80.

63. Ibid., p. 1360.

64. Ibid., p. 1374.

65. Ibid., p. 1360.

66. See Claudia Zaldívar, ed., *40 Años Museo de la Solidaridad por Chile: Fraternidad, Arte y Política 1971–1973* (Chile: Museo de la Solidaridad Salvador Allende, 2012) as well as Andrea Giunta, "Joan Miró y la solidaridad con Chile: Las obras que el artista donó al pueblo de Chile como um manifiesto contra la dictadura," in Giunta, *Contra el canon: El arte contemporáneo en un mundo sin centro* (Buenos Aires: Editores, Siglo Veintiuno, 2020), pp. 109–27.

67. On Hamoudi, see Nada M. Shabout, *Modern Arab Art: Formation of Arab Aesthetics* (Gainesville: University Press of Florida, 2007), and Wijdan Ali, *Modern Islamic Art: Development and Continuity* (Gainesville: University Press of Florida, 1997). Before moving to Paris in 1947, Hamoudi had already founded the review *Al Fikr Al Hadith* (Modern thought). In 1958, he founded the journal *Ishtar of the East and West* and in the 1960s and 1970s held curatorial posts at the Iraq Museum and the Ministry of Culture. On the debated chronology of *Hurufiyya*, see also Charbel Dagher, *Arabic Hurufiyya: Art and Identity*, trans. Samir Mahmoud (Milan: Skira, 2016), particularly pp. 22–24.

68. On transnational synergies in Paris at this time, see Dana Miller, ed., *Carmen Herrera: Lines of Sight*, exh. cat. (New York: Whitney Museum of Art, 2016), particularly Edward Sullivan's essay "Carmen Herrera: South to North," pp. 69–81, which draws from Mary Louise Pratt's notion of "contact zones" of cultural convergence to suggest the existence of resonances without explicit connections. A crucial case in point is

that while Herrera began to construct works using multiple panels in Paris in the early to mid-1950s, she never appeared to theorize or comment upon the resulting spatial interstices, and neither she nor Clark nor Ellsworth Kelly seem to have engaged their contemporaneous practices.

69. Abdias Nascimento notes his rejection of the "gheto" and "linha de côr" in his inaugural editorial for *Quilombo*, "Nós" 1.1 (December 1948), pp. 1 and 6. See also Rachel Queiroz's, "Linha de côr" in the same issue, which argues against the dominant view that there is no color prejudice (and hence no color line) in Brazil (p. 2). On the Museu de Arte Negra and for a partial list of artist supporters, see Abdias Nascimento, "Cultura e estética no Museu de Arte Negra," *GAM: Galeria de Arte Moderna* 14 (1968), pp. 21–22, and "Abdias Nascimento fala do Museu Negra," in *O Quilombismo* (Brasília/Rio: Fundação Cultural Palmares/OR Editor, 2002), pp. 146–49. My thanks to Roberto Conduru for bringing Clark's donation to my attention. Ramos was key to the Cristo de Cor (Christ of color) competition realized in 1955 (see fig. 1.33).

70. In Brazil, related initiatives focusing on regional networks include the First Bienal Latino Americano in 1978 and the Mercosul Bienal, founded in 1996.

71. See Mulk Raj Anand, "Second Triennale India — 1971," in Anand, *Second Triennale India 1971* (New Delhi: Lalit Kala Akademi, 1971), n.p., as well as John Berger, untitled statement, London, January 10, 1968, *First Triennale India 1968* (New Delhi: Lalit Kala Akademi, 1968), n.p. Certain protagonists continued to perpetuate center-periphery presumptions, such as Barr, who described the presence of Euro-American artists in India as a "friendly invasion." Alfred H. Barr, Jr., untitled statement, January 26, 1968, *First Triennale India 1968* (New Delhi: Lalit Kala Akademi, 1968), n.p.

72. Nancy Adajania, "Globalism before Globalization: The Ambivalent Fate of the Triennale India," in Shanay Jhaveri, ed., *Western Artists and India: Creative Inspirations in Art and Design* (London: Thames and Hudson, 2013), pp. 168–85.

73. This controversy was largely due to the entrenched institutionality and bureaucracy of the exhibition's host, the Lalit Kala Akademi. Several artists boycotted the 1971 version, and critics such as Geeta Kapur were notoriously critical of the effort. See "Triennaletters," special issue, *Vrishchik* 2.1 (November 1970). Kapur has revised her criticism of the Triennale in "When Was Modernism in Indian Art?," in Kapur, *When Was Modernism: Essays on Contemporary Cultural Practice in India* (New Delhi: Tulika Books, 2000), pp. 295–324.

74. See Kristine Khouri and Rasha Salti, eds., *Past Disquiet: Artists, International Solidarity and Museums in Exile* (Warsaw: Muzeum Sztuki Nowoczesnej, 2018).

75. For period discussions, see "Topology," in A. D. Aleksandrov, A. N. Kolmogorov, and M. A. Lavrent'ev, *Mathematics: Its Content, Methods, and Meaning*, trans. S. H. Gould and T. Bartha, 3 vols. (1953; Cambridge, MA: MIT Press, 1963), vol. 3, pp. 193–225, and Waclaw Sierpinski, *General Topology* (Toronto: University of Toronto Press, 1952), the latter of which was in Pedrosa's library.

76. Lygia Clark, "The Death of the Plane," trans. in *Lygia Clark: The Abandonment of Art*, p. 158.

77. Joan Kee offers a resonant articulation in *The Geometries of Afro Asia: Art Beyond Solidarity* (Oakland: University of California Press, 2023).

78. René Thom, "Structural Stability, Catastrophe Theory, and Applied Mathematics," *SIAM Review* 19.2 (April 1977), pp. 189–201.

79. Ibid., pp. 189 and 193.

80. See Paul K. Saint-Amour's edited issue and introduction, "Weak Theory, Weak Modernism," *Modernism/Modernity* 25.3 (2018), pp. 437–59. Several decades earlier, theorists of architecture put forward a notion of "weak architecture" against both classical and modernist monumentality, informed in part by Gianni Vattimo's 1985 *La fine della modernità*, later explored in volumes such as Gianni Vattimo and Pier Aldo Rovatti, eds., *Weak Thought* (Albany: State University of New York, 2012). See Ignasi de Sola-Morales, "Arquitectura dedil," *Quaderns d'Arquitectura I Urbanisme* 175 (October–December 1987), p. 175.

81. See Wai Chee Dimock, "Weak Theory: Henry James, Colm Tóibín, and W. B. Yeats," *Critical Inquiry* 39.4 (2013), pp. 732–53, and "Weak Network: Faulkner's Transpacific Reparations," *Modernism/Modernity* 25.3 (September 2018), pp. 587–602.

82. Eve Sedgwick, "Paranoid Reading and Reparative Reading, or, You're So Paranoid, You Probably Think This Essay Is About You," in Sedgwick, *Touching Feeling: Affect, Pedagogy, Performativity* (Duke University Press, 2003), pp. 123–51.

83. Here I would also note a distinction from Hans Ulrich Gumbrecht's approach to meaning that "seems to lie 'under' a surface" in *After 1945: Latency as Origin of the Present* (Stanford: Stanford University Press, 2013), p. 23.

84. Bois appeals to Bloom's "anxiety of influence" and Guillaume Apollinaire's concept of "foreignness" in order to comprehend the relationship to "the symbolic authority of a center" of Latin American artists such as Clark, Jesús Rafael Soto, Carlos Cruz-Diez, and others who lived in Paris for various periods during the 1960s. Bois, "Some Latin Americans in Paris," p. 70.

85. See "A quebra da moldura: Entrevista de Lygia Clark a Luciano Figueiredo e

Matinas Suzuki Jr.," *Folhetim de Folha de São Paulo*, March 2, 1986, pp. 2–7. This Bloomian misreading features in the "1955a" entry of the textbook Hal Foster et al., *Art Since 1900: Modernism, Antimodernism, Postmodernism, Vol. 2: 1945 to the Present* (London: Thames and Hudson, 2005), which discusses Japanese Gutai and Brazilian Neoconcretism as "similarly born out of the reinterpretation, from a peripheral outpost, of a canonical trend of Western modernism" (pp. 375–76). In "La invención concreta," Gabriel Pérez-Barreiro suggests that the delinking of works of art (or published illustrations of works of art) from artistic intentionality (as in the case of the reception of Mondrian among the Río de la Plata artists in the 1940s) suggests that a model of active "interpretation" might be usefully substituted for existing models of passive "influence." Pérez-Barreiro, *La invención: Colección Patricia Phelps de Cisneros, Reflexiones en torno a la abstracción geométrica latinoamericana y sus legados*, exh. cat. (Madrid: Museu Nacional Centro de Arte Reina Sofia, 2013), pp. 17–27.

86. "Entrevista Lygia Clark," in Fernando Cocchiarale and Anna Bella Geiger, eds., *Abstracionismo geométrico e informal: A vanguarda brasileira nos anos cinqüenta* (Rio de Janeiro: FUNARTE, 1987), p. 148.

87. Following from this interest, Simone Oshtoff has appealed to topology as a way to comprehend the fluid boundaries between artworks, artists' writings, and archives among Brazilian artists including Clark, Hélio Oiticica, Paulo Bruscky, and Eduardo Kac, as well as the nomadic philosopher Vilém Flusser, in *Performing the Archive: The Transformation of the Archive in Contemporary Art from Repository of Documents to Art Medium* (New York: Atropos Press, 2009).

88. Tania Rivera, "Ensaio sobre o espaço e o sujeito: Lygia Clark e a psicanálise," *Agora* 11.2 (July–December 2008), p. 222.

89. Mário Pedrosa, "Problemática da arte contemporânea," quoted in Adrian Anagnost, *Spatial Orders, Social Forms: Art and the City in Modern Brazil* (New Haven: Yale University Press, 2022), p. 146. As Pedrosa states in this essay, "Topology would be the geometry of contemporary sensibility" (p. 287).

90. Explorations of the anachronic as method include Georges Didi-Huberman, "Before the Image, Before Time: The Sovereignty of Anachronism," in Claire Farago and Robert Zwijnenberg, eds., *Compelling Visuality: The Work of Art In and Out of History* (Minneapolis: University of Minnesota Press, 2003), and Alexander Nagel and Christopher Wood, *Anachronic Renaissance* (New York: Zone Books, 2020).

91. Haroldo de Campos, "A escritura mefistofélica," in de Campos, *Deus e o diabo no Fausto de Goethe* (São Paulo: Perspectiva, 1981), pp. 75 and 76 n. 5. See also "Post scriptum:

Transluciferação mefistofaústica," in the same volume, pp. 179–209. De Campos notes that he first used the term "plagiotropic" in a spring 1978 course given at Yale University on the evolution of forms in Brazilian poetry. Significantly, Harold Bloom was a faculty member in the department of English at this time.

92. De Campos, "Post scriptum," pp. 181 and 208.

93. Deleuze and Guattari, *A Thousand Plateaus*, p. 7.

94. Daniel Barthélémy and Yves Caraglio, "Plant Architecture: A Dynamic, Multi-level and Comprehensive Approach to Plant Form, Structure and Ontogeny," *Annals of Botany* 99.3 (March 2007), p. 376.

95. Clark also participated in this biennial with three paintings titled *Composição* (Composition). Having missed the inaugurating biennial of 1951, she would have certainly traveled to São Paulo on the occasion. The Mondrian exhibition was particularly catalyzing for artists and critics later associated with Neoconcretism. Ferreira Gullar, for example, staked the group's difference from Brazilian Concrete art in part on the distinction between Mondrian's theoretical positions and the "alive and fecund" nature of his actual paintings. Ferreira Gullar, "Manifesto neoconcreto," *Suplemento Dominical do Jornal do Brasil*, March 22, 1959, pp. 4–5.

96. Lygia Clark, "Carta ao Luiz Almeida Cunha, 1959," diário 2, Archives of the Associação Cultural "O Mundo de Lygia Clark," ID 61676.

97. Ibid.

98. Rocco Sinisgall, ed. and trans., *Leon Battista Alberti: On Painting: A New Translation and Critical Edition* (Cambridge: Cambridge University Press, 2013), p. 23. Alberti's description here differs from Euclid's description of a surface as one of infinite extension "which has length and breadth only." T. L. Heath, ed., *The Thirteen Books of Euclid's Elements*, 3 vols. (Cambridge: The University Press, 1908), vol. 1, book 1, p. 153.

99. "Tapeçaria, arte mural," *Forma* 2 (August 1954), n.p.

100. Clark noted, "In cloths, the artists could base themselves on the width of the material, and using the very line of the finishing not only to modulate, but also for a series of rhythms, if they study the possibilities of reversing several strips of cloth." "Lecture at the Escola Nacional de Arquitetura, Belo Horizonte, Fall 1956," trans. in *Lygia Clark: The Abandonment of Art*, p. 55. In Almeida Cunha, "Ligia Clark busca na pintura a expressão do próprio espaço," *Folha da Noite*, September 22, 1958, Clark likewise noted, "I thought, moreover, of the lines of seams between cloths." Archives of the Associação Cultural "O Mundo de Lygia Clark," ID 4567.

101. On the autoreferentiality and alloreferentiality of the grid, see Siegert, "Introduction: Cultural Techniques, or, The End of the Intellectual Postwar in German Media Theory," in *Cultural Techniques*, p. 13.

102. Partha Mitter, "Decentering Modernism: Art History and Avant-Garde Art from the Periphery," *Art Bulletin* 90.4 (December 2008), pp. 531–48.

103. Griselda Pollock, *Differencing the Canon: Feminism and the Writing of Art's Histories* (London: Routledge, 1999). More recently, Mónica Amor has drawn from Chakrabarty's injunction to "provincialize Europe," Niklas Luhmann's systems theory formulation of modernity, and Achille Mbembe's notion of the threshold in order to suggest how otherness is recursively produced in "Edge," in Amor, *Gego: Weaving the Space in Between* (New Haven: Yale University Press, 2023), pp. 1–13.

104. Lygia Clark, "Letter to Mário Pedrosa, May 22, 1969," trans. in *Lygia Clark: The Abandonment of Art*, p. 233. Clark had already identified herself as "Escorpião Clark" in a prior text, "O homem como suporte vivo," diário 2, Archives of the Associação Cultural "O Mundo de Lygia Clark," ID 65300.

105. Clark, "Letter to Mário Pedrosa, May 22, 1969," translation emended.

106. Ibid. Clark was not alone in her appeal to eggs and processes of birth, and such images and metaphors appear in the work of fellow Brazilian artists such as Lygia Pape and Anna Maria Maiolino. But Clark not infrequently commented on her feelings of isolation, sensations exacerbated in the early 1980s, when she was detached from the worlds of both contemporary art and psychoanalysis. See Lula Wanderley, "Through the Broad Windows of MAM," in *Lygia Clark (1920–1988): 100 anos*, exh. cat. (Rio de Janeiro: Edições Pinakotheke, 2021), pp. 295–306.

107. Examples of this dynamic within art, mythology, and literature are legion, from Zeus spawning Athena from his head, to the Pygmalion myth, to Mary Shelley's *Frankenstein* and beyond. On the Aristotelian figuration of female passivity within procreation, see Luce Irigaray, "How to Conceive (of) a Girl," in Irigaray, *Speculum of the Other Woman*, trans. Gillian Gill (1974; Ithaca: Cornell University Press, 1985), pp. 160–67. On the gendered dynamics of generation and creation in art history, see, for example, Linda Nochlin's classic essay, "Why Have There Been No Great Women Artists?" (1971), in Nochlin, *Women, Art, and Power and Other Essays* (New York: Routledge, 2018), pp. 145–78, as well as Anne Wagner, *Mother Stone: The Vitality of Modern British Sculpture* (New Haven: Yale University Press, 2005).

108. Clark, "Letter to Mário Pedrosa, May 22, 1969."

109. Clark, *Livro-obra*, n.p.

110. Clark, "A quebra da moldura," p. 3. Guy Brett has subsequently observed, "It seems to me that the evolution of her work is so coherent that it can be seen forwards or backwards so to speak (it was the artist Tunga who first suggested this perspective to me)." "Lygia Clark: Six Cells," in *Lygia Clark* (1997), p. 33.

111. A significant body of Clark's writings were published in Brazil in Mário Pedrosa and Ferreira Gullar, eds., *Lygia Clark* (Rio de Janeiro: FUNARTE, 1980). Suely Rolnik, who collaborated with Clark to write "Objeto relacional" for that publication, has been key to the study of the artist in Brazil, organizing several projects related to her work and therapeutic practice and orienting numerous students researching Clark, including Maria Alice Milliet, whose dissertation was published as *Lygia Clark, obra-trajeto* (São Paulo: EdUSP, 1992), and Beatriz Helena Scigliano Carneiro, *Relâmpagos com claror: A construção da vida como obra de arte em Lygia Clark e Hélio Oiticica* (São Paulo: FAPESP, 2004). See also Paulo Herkenhoff, "A aventura planar de Lygia Clark — de caracóis, escadas e caminhando," in *Lygia Clark*, exh. cat. (São Paulo: Museu de Arte Moderna de São Paulo, 1999), pp. 6–65, which is an expanded version of his essay "Lygia Clark," in *Lygia Clark* (1997), pp. 36–53. The earliest monograph to be published outside of Brazil is Sylvie Coellier, *Lygia Clark (l'enveloppe): La fin de la modernité et le désir du contact* (Paris: Hartmattan, 2003).

112. See for example relevant chapters in Susan Best, *Visualizing Feeling: Affect and the Feminine Avant-Garde* (New York: I. B. Tauris, 2011); Amor, *Theories of the Nonobject*; Alexander Alberro, *Abstraction in Reverse: The Reconfigured Spectator in Mid-Twentieth-Century Latin American Art* (Chicago: University of Chicago Press, 2017); Adele Nelson, *Forming Abstraction: Art and Institutions in Postwar Brazil* (Oakland: University of California Press, 2022); Sullivan, *Radical Form: Modernist Abstraction in South America*; and Mariola Alvarez, *The Affinity of Neoconcretism: Interdisciplinary Collaborations in Brazilian Modernism, 1954–1965* (Oakland: University of California Press, 2023).

113. Interestingly, Clark herself remarked, "The work is always more intelligent than the artist; it is what gives direction, and the theoretical concept of thing." "Encontro de Lygia Clark com psicotêrapeutas, clínica 'Canto da Gávea,'" in *Lygia Clark: Da obra ao acontecimento*, p. 59.

114. George Kubler, *The Shape of Time: Remarks on the History of Things* (New Haven: Yale University Press, 1965). Significantly, Kubler describes "actuality" as a "gap," "interval," and "void between events" (p. 17).

115. On what Elizabeth Freeman calls the "chrononormativity" of such generational

relations, see *Time Binds: Queer Temporalities, Queer Histories* (Durham: Duke University Press, 2010); Sarah Ahmed, *Queer Phenomenology: Orientations, Objects, Others* (Durham: Duke University Press, 2006); and Ismail Muhammad, "The Misunderstood Ghost of James Baldwin," *Slate*, February 15, 2017, in which a "queered definition of reproduction" allows exit from Oedipal repetition of "literary patricide."

116. Lygia Clark (1963), diário 2, Archives of the Associação Cultural "O Mundo de Lygia Clark," ID 62059. A female fetus develops and sheds about five to six million eggs during the period of gestation, such that only one to two million remain at the time of birth.

117. Clark, "A quebra da moldura," p. 4. When Gullar recalled the impetus for his 1959 term, he described it in relation to a constructed relief by Clark made of double bars such that interior and exterior "frames" interpenetrate in the work's pictorial space and physical structure. Since the relief in question was not an art object such as a painting or sculpture but also not a quotidian object such as a table or chair, Gullar contended that it was a "non-object." See Ariel Jiménez and Ferreira Gullar, *Ferreira Gullar in Conversation with Ariel Jiménez* (New York: Fundación Cisneros, 2012), pp. 52–53, and Small, *Hélio Oiticica: Folding the Frame*, p. 53.

118. On the fraught nature of such dynamics, see Roberto Conduru, "*Roda* and *Terreiro*: The Historiography of Brazil's Visual Arts at the Crossroads of Globalization," *Arts* 12.103 (2023), as well as Aruna de Souza and Jill Casid, eds., *Art History in the Wake of the Global Turn* (Williamstown: Sterling and Francine Clark Art Institute, 2014); Sérgio Martins, letter to the editor regarding Professor Caroline A. Jones's article "Anthropophagy in São Paulo's Cold War," *ARTMargins*, February 20, 2014, https://artmargins.com/letter-to-the-editor; and "A Questionnaire on Global Methods," *October* 180 (Spring 2022), pp. 3–80.

119. Here my approach is distinct from Boris Groys's invocation of topology as a rubric to understand a relationship between art and nonart as a condition of the contemporary in "The Topology of Contemporary Art," in Terry Smith, Okwui Enwezor, and Nancy Condee, eds., *Antinomies of Art and Culture: Modernity, Postmodernity, Contemporaneity* (Durham: Duke University Press, 2008), pp. 71–80. I do not observe a strict delineation between the modern and contemporary, but rather seek to use the contemporary to defamiliarize and excavate elements of the modern.

120. Clark, "Lecture at the Escola Nacional de Arquitetura, Belo Horizonte, Fall 1956," p. 54, translation emended.

121. Ibid.

122. Lygia Clark, "1957—Entrevista para o jornal de Campinas," diário 4, Archives of the Associação Cultural "O Mundo de Lygia Clark," ID 61701. Although it does not appear that this text was published in *Jornal de Campinas*, it provided the basis for the article "Lygia Clark e o espaço concreto expressional," edited by Edelweiss Sarmento, published in the *Suplemento Dominical do Jornal do Brasil*, July 2, 1959, p. 3. "Lygia Clark and the Concrete Expressional Space," in *Lygia Clark* (1997), p. 83, translation emended.

123. See for example Cunha, "Ligia Clark busca na pintura a expressão do próprio espaço," and Clark, "A quebra da moldura."

124. Herkenhoff, "A aventura planar de Lygia Clark," pp. 18 and 26.

125. Pedrosa, "Da natureza afetiva da forma na obra da arte."

126. Gullar, "Manifesto neoconcreto."

127. Jayme Maurício, "As novas dimensões de Lygia Clark," *Correio da Manhã*, June 19, 1965. Archives of the Associação Cultural "O Mundo de Lygia Clark," ID 8840.

128. "Lygia Clark: A coragem e a magia de ser contemporânea," *Correio da Manhã*, November 10, 1971, supplement, 1.

129. Sylvia Wynter and Katherine McKittrick, "Unparalleled Catastrophe for Our Species?," in McKittrick, ed., *Sylvia Wynter: On Being Human as Praxis* (Durham: Duke University Press, 2015), pp. 9–89.

130. See Bois, "Angels with Guns." André Lepecki has suggested that Clark's antipathy to "performance art" in fact allows a generative rethinking of the concept of performance itself in "Affective Geometry, Immanent Acts: Lygia Clark and Performance," in *Lygia Clark: The Abandonment of Art*, pp. 278–89.

131. Rolnik, "Uma terapêutica para tempos desprovidos de poesia," p. 22. It is telling that describing her own role in *Estruturação do Self*, Clark drew from Donald Winnicott's concept of the "good enough mother," whose psychoanalytic function in relation to a child's developing subjectivity is to build autonomy through her own gradual withdrawal. See Lygia Clark, "Relational Object" (1980), in *Lygia Clark* (1997), pp. 319–27. Best has likewise noted that the subject that emerges across Clark's trajectory is "a precarious subject: a subject whose enigmatic body is at once its own and yet inhabited by wild imaginings; a subject who grasps but is also grasped by the world, thus active, open and vulnerable at one and the same time." *Visualizing Feeling*, p. 66.

132. See Laura Harris's excellent article, "At the Egg's Edge: Lygia Clark's Indiscretions," *Women and Performance: A Journal of Feminist Theory* 24.2–3 (2014), pp. 167–85.

133. See Eve Sedgwick, *The Epistemology of the Closet* (1990; Berkeley: University of California Press, 2008), Beatriz [Paul] Preciado, "Queer Cartographies: The Perverse Flâneur, the Topophobic Lesbian and the Cartographical Whore*, or How to Construct a 'Foxy' Cartography with Annie Sprinkle," in José Miguel Cortés, ed., *Dissident Cartographies* (Seacex, 2008), n.p.; and Freeman, *Time Binds*.

134. Eve Sedgwick, *Tendencies* (Durham: Duke University Press, 1993), p. 8.

135. Irigaray, "How to Conceive (of) a Girl," p. 166.

136. As this book goes to press, it joins a resonant, though distinct formulation of "an amonograph or counter-monograph, a feminist queering of the monograph form" in Julia Bryan-Wilson's *Louise Nevelson's Sculpture: Drag, Color, Join, Face* (New Haven: Yale University Press, 2023), p. 3.

137. On the commons and undercommons, see Michael Hardt and Antonio Negri, *Commonwealth* (Cambridge, MA: Harvard University Press, 2009), and Stefano Harney and Fred Moten, *The Undercommons: Fugitive Planning and Black Study* (New York: Autonomedia, 2013), who write of the "undercommons" as a way of thinking "where the commons give refuge, where the refuge gives commons" (p. 26). Conduru has suggested that such a space might be analogized to Afrobrazilian religious spaces of encounter in "*Roda* and *Terreiro*."

CHAPTER ONE: CIRCLING THE SQUARE

The epigraphs are from Malevich's response to a question posed by artist, Vitebsk student, and collaborator Lev Iudin in 1922: "Why is there a limit still in Cubism that no one crosses (in the sense of the format of canvases)?" See Iudin, "Diaries, 1921–1937," in Irina A. Vakar and Tatiana N. Mikhienko, eds., *Kazimir Malevich: Letters, Documents, Memoirs, Criticism, Volume 2: Memoirs and Criticism*, trans. Antonina W. Bouis (London: Tate, 2015), p. 230; Lygia Clark, 1963, diário 2, Archives of the Associação Cultural "O Mundo de Lygia Clark," ID 62059. See also Lygia Clark, "On the Act," *Livro-obra* (1964, 1983), in *Lygia Clark*, exh. cat. (Barcelona: Fundacío Antoni Tàpies, 1997), pp. 164–65. Clark named one of her *Bichos* "O antes é o depois," "The before and the after," as well; Adam Pendleton, "Black Dada" (2008), in *Black Dada Reader* (London: Koenig Books, 2017), p. 345.

1. Clement Greenberg's 1940 essay "Towards a Newer Laocoön" is perhaps the most influential articulation of this impulse. In John O'Brien, ed., *Clement Greenberg: The Collected Essays and Criticism*, 4 vols. (Chicago: University of Chicago Press), vol. 1, pp. 23–38.

See also Norman Bryson's plotting of the tension between discursive meaning and aesthetic figurality in *Word and Image: French Painting of the Ancien Régime* (Cambridge: Cambridge University Press, 1982).

2. Theo Van Doesburg, et al., "Manifest de l'Art Concret," *Art Concret* 1 (1930), p. 1.

3. "Manifiesto invencionista," *Arte Concreto Invención* (Buenos Aires) 1 (August 1946), p. 8. This manifesto was reprinted in the Brazilian journal *Joaquim* 9 (March 1947), p. 12, however, we do not have evidence that Clark encountered it then or later. On the relations between the Brazilian and Río de la Plata artists of Argentina and Uruguay, see María Amalia García, "Vanguardia en doble página: Intervenciones del invencionismo argentino en la revista *Joaquim*," *Revista do Instituto de Estudos Brasileiros* 61 (August 2015), pp. 159–82, and *Abstract Crossings: Cultural Exchange between Argentina and Brazil*, trans. Jane Brodie (2011; Oakland: University of California Press, 2019).

4. "Manifiesto invencionista," p. 8. The limits and inflections of the concepts of discovery and invention were far from stable. In 1944, Tomás Maldonado and artists associated with *Arturo: Revista de artes abstractas* equated invention with creation, but also *descubrir* (to discover) and *hallar* (to find) in a signal of the influence of the older Uruguayan artist Joaquín Torres-García, who in 1918 wrote, "To invent is not to create. The etymology of this great word tells us that it is to find. To create is another thing. Finding and creating are generally achieved by the work of the true artist's spirit." Torres-García, "Naturaleza y Arte" (1918), in Jorge Schwartz, ed., *Las vanguardias latinoamericanos: Textos programáticos y críticos* (Mexico City: Fondo de Cultura Economica, 2002), pp. 427–28. While initially drawn to Torres-García's program to blend constructivist and figurative idioms from ancient American indigenous culture, the recalibrated language of "Manifiesto invencionista" disavowed this prior influence. Maldonado's new position was that Torres-García's "eclectic pastiche" had no place in the march toward an "absolute, CONCRETE," and nonrepresentational art. "Torres-García contra el Arte Moderno," *Boletín de la Asociación de Arte Concreto Invención* 2 (December 1946), n.p. See also Gabriel Pérez-Barreiro, "The Argentine Avant-Garde, 1944–1950," PhD diss., University of Essex, 1996, and Alexander Alberro, "To Find, To Create, To Reveal: Torres-García and the Models of Invention in Mid-1940s Río de la Plata," in Luis Pérez-Oramas, ed., *Joaquín Torres-García: The Arcadia Modern*, exh. cat. (New York: Museum of Modern Art, 2015), pp. 106–21.

5. Ferreira Gullar, *Lygia Clark: Uma experiência radical, 1954–1958*, exh. cat. (Rio de Janeiro: Departamento de Imprensa Nacional, 1958), n.p. All subsequent quotes from Gullar are from this publication.

6. In an early scholarly monograph, Ricardo Nascimento Fabbrini follows Gullar in reiterating the analytic progression and orientation of this sequence of four paintings. *O espaço de Lygia Clark* (São Paulo: Editora Atlas, 1994), pp. 29–34.

7. Almeida Cunha, "Ligia Clark busca na pintura a expressão do próprio espaço," *Folha da Noite*, September 22, 1958, Archives of the Associação Cultural "O Mundo de Lygia Clark," ID 4567. These six works do not include two small paintings known as *Descoberta da linha orgânica* that may have been studies for the larger work, which do not in fact contain actual organic lines.

8. Gullar's binary system seems to respond as much to the polarization of black-and-white reproductions as to the paintings' heterogeneous character, which includes multiple kinds and applications of paint, as well as shades of a single color such as white or blue.

9. Gullar, *Lygia Clark: Uma experiência radical*, n.p. Malevich's 1927 description of arriving at *Black Square* in *Die Gegenstandslose Welt* is reproduced in Michel Seuphor's *L'art abstrait: Ses origines, ses premiers maîtres* (Paris: Galeria Maeght, 1949), which Clark likely encountered in Paris between 1950 and 1952. This passage is translated in the 1959 English version of Malevich's book as: "When, in the year 1913, in my desperate attempt to free art from the ballast of objectivity, I took refuge in the square form and exhibited a picture which consisted of nothing more than a black square on a white field, the critics and, along with them, the public sighed, 'Everything which we loved is lost. We are in a desert.... Before us is nothing but a black square on a white background!'... No more 'likenesses of reality', no idealistic images — nothing but a desert! But this desert is filled with the spirit of non-objective sensation which pervades everything." Kasimir Malevich, *The Non-Objective World*, trans. German Howard Dearstyne (1927; Chicago: Paul Theobald and Company, 1959), p. 68.

10. Malevich appeals to this language of the "zero of form" in "From Cubism and Futurism to Suprematism: The New Painterly Realism, 1915," in John Bowlt, ed. and trans., *Russian Art of the Avant-Garde: Theory and Criticism, 1902–1934* (London: Thames and Hudson, 2017), pp. 116–36, among many other texts.

11. Contrary to this presumption, Andrea Giunta has proposed that Latin American artists looked to the historical vanguards to generate "simultaneous vanguards and neo-vanguards." See "Adiós a la perferia: Vanguardias y neovanguardias en el arte de América Latina," *Blanco sobre Blanco* 5.8 (2013), pp. 9–20, and *Contra el canon: El arte contemporáneo en un mundo sin centro* (Buenos Aires: Editores, Siglo Veintiuno, 2020).

12. As Cicero put it, "Invention is the discovery of valid or seemingly valid arguments to render one's cause possible." *De inventione*, trans. H. M. Hubbell (Cambridge. MA: Loeb Classical Library, 1993), p. 19.

13. See James Dougal Fleming, ed., *The Invention of Discovery, 1500–1700* (Burlington: Ashgate, 2011).

14. Boaventura de Sousa Santos, *Epistemologies of the South: Justice against Epistemicide* (London: Routledge, 2014).

15. See Ken MacMillan, *Sovereignty and Possession in the English New World: The Legal Foundations of Empire, 1576–1640* (Cambridge: Cambridge University Press, 2009), and Robert Miller, Jacinta Ruru, Larissa Behrendt, eds., *Discovering Indigenous Lands: The Doctrine of Discovery in the English Colonies* (Oxford: Oxford University Press, 2010).

16. Carl Schmitt, *The Nomos of the Earth in the International Law of the Jus Publicum Europeaum* (1950; Candor: Telos Press, 2006). For a compelling reading of Schmitt's "global linear thinking," see Eric de Bruyn, "Beyond the Line, or a Political Geometry of Contemporary Art," *Grey Room* 57 (Fall 2014), pp. 24–49.

17. Schmitt, *The Nomos of the Earth*, p. 48. As Walter Mignolo observes, Schmitt's "global linear thinking traced lines in land and sea [as well as] racial lines." "Sylvia Wynter: What Does It Mean to be Human?," in Katherine McKittrick, ed., *Sylvia Wynter: On Being Human as Praxis* (Durham: Duke University Press, 2015), p. 111.

18. See Edmundo O'Gorman's essays "La idea del descubrimiento de América" (1952) and "La invención de América" (1958), expanded in *The Invention of America: An Inquiry into the Historical Nature of the New World and the Meaning of Its History* (Bloomington: Indiana University Press, 1961). See also Walter Mignolo, *The Idea of Latin America* (Malden: Blackwell, 2005).

19. See Albert Kelsey, *Program and Rules of the Competition for the Selection of an Architect for the Monumental Lighthouse Which the Nations of the World Will Erect in the Dominican Republic to the Memory of Christopher Columbus* (New York: Stillson Press, Pan American Union, 1928), and Robert Alexander González, *Designing Pan-America: U.S. Architectural Visons for the Western Hemisphere* (Austin: University of Texas Press, 2011).

20. K. S. Mel'nikov, "The Project for a Memorial to Christopher Columbus in a Global Competition, 1929," in *Mastera sovetskoj arkhitektury ob arkhitekture* (Moscow: Isskustvo, 1975), pp. 166–67, quoted in Mario Fosso, Otakar Macel, and Maurizio Meriggi, eds., *Konstantin S. Mel'nikov and the Construction of Moscow* (New York: Skira, 2000), p. 250, English in the original. See also S. Frederick Starr, *Melnikov: Solo Architect in a Mass*

Society (Princeton: Princeton University Press, 1978), and Rishat Mullagildin, ed., *Architecture of Konstantin Melnikov: 1920s–1930s* (Tokyo: Toto Shuppan, 2002), pp. 70–73.

21. On the Soviet government's interest in the competition as a form of international diplomacy, see Igor Kazus, "How Soviet Architects Designed the Monument to Christopher Columbus in Santo-Domingo," *Otechestvennaia istoriia* 5 (2013), pp. 59–76.

22. El Lissitzky, "The Film of El's Life" (1928), in Sophie Lissitzky-Küppers, ed., *El Lissitzky: Life, Letters, Texts* (Greenwich: New York Graphic Society, 1967), p. 325. El Lissitzky's father visited the United States in the 1890s and considered emigrating with the entire family. See also Vladimir Mayakovsky, *My Discovery of America*, trans., Neil Cornwell (1926; London: Hesperus Press, 2005).

23. El Lissitszky, *Pro dva kvadrata: Suprematicheskiĭ skaz v 6-ti postroĭkakh* (Berlin: Skify, 1922).

24. Giancinto di Pietrantonio, "Interview to Tomás Maldonado," in *Arte abstracto argentino: Arte Concreto-Invención, Madi, Perceptismo* (Buenos Aires: Fundacion Proa, 2003), p. 25.

25. See Maldonado, "Torres-García contra el Arte Moderno," and Edgar Bayley, "La batalla por la invención: Manifiesto," *Invención* 2 (1945), n.p.

26. On the political investments of artists aligned with Maldonado, see statements in *Arte Concreto-Invención* 1 (August 1946), including "Manifiesto invencionista" and "Nuestra militancia"; Alfredo Hlito, "Notas para una estética materialista"; Edgar Bayley, "La batalla por la invención," *Invención* 2 (1945), n.p.; and "Sobre arte concreto," *Orientación: Órgano central del Partido Comunista* (February 20, 1946) in Rafael Cippolini, ed., *Manifiestos argentinos: Politicas de lo visual 1900–2000* (Buenos Aires: Adriano Hidaldo, 2003), pp. 195–98.

27. See Irina Vakar, *Kazimir Malevich: The Black Square* (Moscow: The State Tretyakov Gallery, 2015), and "New Information Concerning *The Black Square*," in Christina Lodder, ed., *Celebrating Suprematism: New Approaches to the Art of Kazimir Malevich* (Boston: Brill, 2019), pp. 11–28. The words "Battle of negroes" (Битва негров—Bytva negrov) is legible; the rest of the phrase, while visible, is illegible.

28. See James Smalls, "Visualizing Racial Antics in Late Nineteenth-Century France," in Adrienne L. Childs and Susan H. Libby, eds., *Blacks and Blackness in European Art of the Long Nineteenth Century* (London: Routledge, 2014), pp. 145–74, and Phillip Dennis Cate, "The Spirit of Montmartre," in Cate and Mary Shaw, eds., *The Spirit of Montmartre: Cabarets, Humor, and the Avantgarde, 1875–1905* (New Brunswick: Rutgers University Press, 1996), pp. 29–31. On Allais's publication, see also Denys Riout, *La peinture monochrome:*

Histoire et archéologie d'un genre (Nîmes: Editions Jacqueline Chambon, 2003), particularly "Des monochromes pour rire," pp. 169–86. *Cave* translates as both "cave" and "cellar."

29. On such phenomena, see Sylvie Chalaye, "Théâtre et cabarets: Le 'nègre' spectacle," in Pascal Blanchard, Nicolas Bancel, Gilles Boëtsch, Éruc Deroo, and Sandrine Lemaire, eds., *Zoos humains et exhibitions colonials* (Paris: La Découverte, 2004), pp. 396–406, as well as Pascal Blanchard, Gilles Boëtsch, and Nanette Jacomijn Snoep, eds., *Human Zoos: The Invention of the Savage* (Paris: Musée du Quai Branly, 2012). Chalaye recounts, among other examples, an 1878 presentation of "les terribles Zoulous" at Les Folies Bergère, as well as staged battles of warriors from Dahomey and elsewhere at the Casino de Paris and the Theater Châtlet following the victory of the French army in Abomey the year before. Exhibitions of non-Western individuals multiplied after 1870, often in the form of "human zoos" and universal expositions. The 1889 Exposition Universelle, seen by over 28 million visitors, included a Village Nègre, which displayed over four hundred indigenous people.

30. Nanette Jacomijn Snoep, "Savage Imagery," in Blanchard et al., eds, *Human Zoos*, p. 105.

31. This incident is reported in "Khudozhestvennye parodii," *Russkoe slovo* 290 (December 17, 1911), p. 7, quoted in Vakar, "New Information Concerning *The Black Square*," p. 23.

32. On the Black presence in Russia, see period texts such as Albert Parry, "Negroes in Russia," *Opportunity* 3 (October 1925), pp. 306–307, and "Black Folk in Russia," *Abbott's Monthly* (April 1931), pp. 11–16 and 56–57, as well as Allison Blakely, *Russia and the Negro: Blacks in Russian History and Thought* (Washington, DC: Howard University Press, 1986), and Maxim Matusevich, ed., *Africa in Russia, Russia in Africa* (Trenton: Africa World Press, 2007).

33. On Thomas's fascinating trajectory from a sharecropping family to an entertainment entrepreneur, see Vladimir Alexandrov, *The Black Russian* (New York: Atlantic Monthly Press, 2013).

34. The race riots that followed the Johnson-Jeffries fight were widely covered in the international press. In Russia, see, for example, *Niva* 41.33 (1910), p. 458.

35. Alexandrov notes that Johnson didn't end up arriving in Russia until July of 1914.

36. See, for example, F. Elius, "Chernokozhie rossiiane," (Black-skinned Russians), *Argus* 10 (1913); Pavel Ivanovich Kovalevskii, *Kavkaz* (The Caucasus) (St. Peterburg: Tip. M.I. Akinfieva, 1914–1915); and Viacheslav Panteleimonovich Vradii, *Negry Batumskoi*

oblaski I Kutaisskoi gubernii (Negroes of Batumi Province and Kutais Governorate) (Batumi: G. S. Tavartkiladze, 1914).

37. "Theses of the Fourth Congress on the Negro question" (1922), quoted in Kate Baldwin, "The Russian Routes of Claude McKay's Internationalism," in Matusevich, ed., *Africa in Russia, Russia in Africa*, p. 92. On depictions of Blackness and anti-racism in the 1920s and early 1930s see Christina Kiaer, "Inventing an Aesthetics of Anti-Racism: African Americans in Early Soviet Visual Culture," in Denise Milstein and Matvei Yankelevich, eds., *The Wayland Rudd Collection: Exploring Racial Imaginaries in Soviet Visual Culture* (Brooklyn: Ugly Duckling Press, 2021), pp. 94–113.

38. On the relations between artists and poets of color such as McKay and the Soviet avant-garde, see Steven S. Lee, *The Ethnic Avant-Garde: Minority Cultures and World Revolution* (New York: Columbia University Press, 2015), as well as Otto Huiswoud and Claude MacKay [*sic*], "Speeches to the 4th World Congress of the Comintern on the Negro Question [22nd Session–November 25 1922]," http://www.marxisthistory.org/history/international/comintern/1922/1125-huiswoudmckay-cispeeches.pdf.

39. Claude McKay, *A Long Way From Home* (New York: Lee Furman, 1937). See also McKay's *Negroes in America* (Port Washington: Kennikat Press, 1979), originally commissioned and published in Russian by the State Publishing House, Moscow, as *Negry v Amerike* in 1923.

40. McKay, *A Long Way From Home*, p. 177.

41. See Ekaterina Voronina and Irina Rustamova, "Annex: The Results of the Technical Analysis of K. S. Malevich's Black Suprematist Square," in Vakar, *Kazimir Malevich: The Black Square*, pp. 56–63.

42. Aleksandra Shatskikh, "Inscribed Vandalism: The Black Square at One Hundred," *e-flux Journal* 85 (October 2017), http://www.e-flux.com/journal/85/155475/inscribed-vandalism-the-black-square-at-one-hundred, and "Revelations and Sensations in the Centenary Year of Kazimir Malevich's Black Square," *Art Studies Magazine* 3 (2016), pp. 10–25. On the controversy, see also Khadija von Zinnenburg Carroll and Dina Gusejnova, "Malevich's *Black Square* under X-Ray: A Dialogue on Race, Revolution and Art History," *Third Text Online Forum*, September 9, 2019, http://www.thirdtext.org/malevich-blacksquare. Matthew Jesse Jackson has suggested that if Malevich wrote the inscription, it is conceivable only as an attempt to sidestep art bureaucrats in the subsequent Stalinist regime who might have claimed that the painting was ideologically hostile. Communication with the author, December 14, 2022.

43. See Vakar, *Kazimir Malevich: The Black Square*, and "New Information Concerning *The Black Square*."

44. Alexandra Shatskikh, *Black Square: Malevich and the Origin of Suprematism*, trans. Marian Schwartz (New Haven: Yale University Press, 2012), p. 12. See Andréi Nakov, ed., *Malevich: Painting the Absolute*, catalogue raisonné, 4 vols. (London: Lund Humphries, 2010), vol. 1, F477 and F478.

45. See Vakar, *Kazimir Malevich: The Black Square*; E. A. Voronina and I. T. Salakhov, "On the History of Studying the Painting *Black Suprematist Square* (1915) by K. Malevich from the Collection of the Tretyakov Gallery," in L. I. Iovleva and T. B. Yudenkova, eds., *Tretyakov Readings, 2016: Proceedings of the Scholarly Reports Conference* (Moscow: Tretyakov Gallery, 2017), pp. 264–73, and Irina Vakar, "K. S. Malevich's 1929 Exhibition at the Tretyakov Gallery," in I. N. Karasik and J. Kiblitsky, eds., *The Russian Avant-Garde: Problems of Representation and Interpretation* (Saint Petersburg: Palace Editions, 2001), pp. 121–38.

46. On pseudomophology and the monochrome, see Yve-Alain Bois, "On the Uses and Abuses of Look-alikes," *October* 154 (Fall 2015), pp. 127–49.

47. Briony Fer, "Imagining a Point of Origin: Malevich and Suprematism," in Fer, *On Abstract Art* (New Haven: Yale University Press, 1997), p. 10. See also Fer, "Abstraction at War with Itself," in Iwona Blazwick, ed., *Adventures of the Black Square: Abstract Art and Society 1915–2015*, exh. cat. (London: Whitechapel Gallery, 2015), pp. 225–31.

48. See Malevich, Letters to Mikhail Matiushin, May 27, 1915, Kuntsevo (no. 35); Letter to Mikhail Matiushin, beginning of June (?) 1915, Kuntsevo (no. 37); and Letter to Mikhail Matiushin, beginning of June 1915, Kuntsevo (no. 38), in Irina A. Vakar and Tatiana N. Mikhienko, eds. *Kazimir Malevich: Letters, Documents, Memoirs, Criticism, Volume 1, Letters and Documents*, trans. Antonina W. Bouis (London: Tate, 2015), pp. 65–66, which entreat Matiushin to include a drawing of the black square as a backdrop in a second-edition publication devoted to *Victory over the Sun* in 1915.

49. Ivan Puni, "Contemporary Painting" (Berlin, 1923), in Vakar and Mikhienko, eds., *Kazimir Malevich: Letters, Documents, Memoirs, Criticism, Volume 2*, p. 167.

50. Ibid., p. 169. Ironically, an unexpected visit by Puni to Malevich's studio caused him to consider "[putting] out a booklet on my work no matter what and christen it, thereby giving notice of my copyright." Kazimir Malevich, Letter to Matiushin, September 24, 1915, quoted in Shatskikh, *Black Square: Malevich and the Origin of Suprematism*, p. 55.

51. The presumed equation between conceptual and pictorial reduction is reflected in Stedelijk Museum curator Willem Sandberg's 1958 statement that the ground of Malevich's paintings was of little importance to the artist: "The white surface serves only as the place where the movement of forms unfolds." Ferreira Gullar published and translated extracts of Sandberg's article from a *L'Architecture d'Ajourd'hui* special on Malevich in the *Suplemento Dominical do Jornal do Brasil*, "Malevith," (*sic*), April 27, 1958, p. 3.

52. As the students proclaimed in their first UNIVOS leaflet of November 20, 1920, "Let the overthrow of the old world of arts be marked out on the palms of your hands. Wear the black square as a mark of the world economy. Draw the red square in your workshops as a mark of the revolution in the arts. Clear the areas of the wide world of the whole chaos that prevails in it." Quoted in Patricia Railing, *More about Two Squares* (Cambridge, MA: MIT Press, 1991), p. 7. On various painterly and graphic versions of the square, see Nakov, *Malevich: Painting the Absolute.*

53. *About Two Squares* was printed two years later in Berlin in 1922.

54. T. J. Clark has argued that Lissitzky transformed the "signifying collapse" of *Black Square* into an instrumentalized language of politics in "God Is Not Cast Down," in Clark, *Farewell to an Idea: Episodes from a History of Modernism* (New Haven: Yale University Press, 1999), pp. 225–97. However, if we admit that plot, narrative, and proselytism were innate to *Black Square* from the outset, this move is less a volte-face than an intensification of the earlier work's rhetorical character.

55. El Lissitzky quoted in Railing, *More about Two Squares*, p. 37. Yve-Alain Bois has argued that the work's revolutionary provocation lies in its medial innovation, rather than its semblance of ideological content. "El Lissitzky: Reading Lessons," *October* 11 (Winter 1979), pp. 113–28.

56. Lissitzky wrote that the Suprematist picture "possessed one specific perpendicular axis (vis-à-vis the horizon), and when it was hung any other way it looked as if were sideways or upside down." El Lissitzky, "Prouns: Towards the Defeat of Art" (1920–21), in *El Lissitzky, Austellung vom 9 April bis Ende Juni 1976*, exh. cat. (Zürich: Galerie Gmurzynska, 1976), p. 65. Malevich himself clearly felt otherwise and displayed paintings such as *Painterly Realism of a Football Player — Color Masses in the Fourth Dimension* in inverted positions.

57. Ibid., p. 65. On the PROUNs' principle of rotation, see Yve-Alain Bois, "El Lissitzky: Radical Reversibility," *Art in America* 76.4 (1988), pp. 160–81. The movement into space can be traced to Malevich's articulations in *The Non-Objective World*, p. 100.

Lissitzky's PROUNs were illustrated in several period catalogues to which Clark would have had access, including Michel Seuphor's *L'art abstrait.*

58. Tomás Maldonado, "Lo abstracto y lo concreto en el arte moderno," *Arte Concreto Invención* 1 (August 1946), pp. 5–7. As he wrote, "Because neither Peri nor the Neoplasticists dared to relativize the painting itself: to question its traditional function as a 'containing organism,' a surface in which an event, necessarily, must take place" (p. 6).

59. Andrea Giunta, "Simultaneous Abstractions and Postwar Latin American Art," in Okwui Enwezor, Katy Siegel, and Ulrich Wilmes, eds., *Postwar: Art Between the Pacific and the Atlantic, 1945–1965,* exh. cat. (Munich: Haus der Kunst, 2016), p. 485. On the performativity of print materials for these artists, see Isabel Plante, "Printing Invention: Artwork, Project, or Device," in Zanna Gilbert, Pia Gottschaller, Tom Learner, and Andrew Perchuk, eds., *Purity Is a Myth: The Materiality of Concrete Art from Argentina, Brazil, and Uruguay* (Los Angeles: Getty Research Institute and Getty Conservation Institute, 2021), pp. 181–99. In his interview with di Pietrantonio, Maldonado notes the importance of Lissitzky and Arp's *Die Kunstismen*; he also recalls his access to Alfred Barr's 1936 *Cubism and Abstract Art* catalogue from the Museum of Modern Art, New York, which contains a black-and-white illustration of Malevich's *Painterly Realism of Boy with Knapsack—Color Masses in the Fourth Dimension.* In Barr's catalogue, Malevich's painting is in inverted form, an orientation Maldonado retained in his illustration of the work in *El arte concreto y el problema de lo ilimitado: Notas para un estudio teórico, Zürich 1948* (Buenos Aires: Ramona, 2003), n.p. As Pérez-Barreiro notes in "The Argentine Avant-Garde, 1944–1950," the German émigré Grete Stern brought many modernist publications with her when she relocated to Buenos Aires in 1936, including examples of the famous Bauhausbücher, which included Malevich's *Die Gegenstandslose Welt.* Juan Melé likewise noted that he knew European vanguard works primarily from reproductions in lectures and publications. Juan Melé, *La vanguardia del 40: Memorias de un artista concreto* (Buenos Aires: Ediciones Cinco, 1999).

60. Di Pietrantonio, "Interview to Tomás Maldonado." As Maldonado recounts, "In January (or February) of 1943, I traveled to Montevideo to visit the Uruguayan artist Torres-García, who in 1930 had shown his works at the exhibition 'Cercle et carré' in Paris. On that occasion, Torres-García gave me some books, booklets, and manifestos that referred to what he called 'Universalismo Constructivo" [Constructive Universalism]. In the months that followed, my inclination toward nonfiguration became stronger and more definite.... In August (maybe September) 1932 [1942], I met Arden Quin, who

explained Rothfuss's theory of the 'cut out frame' for me. At first sight, I found it quite stimulating, even when it was not entirely new to me. In fact, I knew a series of works in that style, painted in the 1920s and 30s. I'm concretely referring to the paintings by Popola [*sic*] in 1916 and Peri in 1913 — as they appeared in 'Die Kunstismen.' Anyhow, I decided I would follow that path. So that's how I made my first paintings with an irregular frame" (pp. 23–25).

61. On Rothfuss's regional references, see María Amalia García, "Rhod Rothfuss and the *marco recortado*: A Synthesis of Cultural Traditions in the Río de la Plata Region," in Gilbert et al., eds., *Purity Is a Myth*, pp. 27–45.

62. Vicente Huidobro, "Prologue to *Horizon Carré*" (1917), in *Square Horizon*, trans. Tony Frazer (Bristol: Shearman Books, 2019), pp. 14–15. See also "La creación pura," and "El creacionismo," in Huidobro, *Obras completas de Vicente Huidobro* (Santiago: Editorial Andres Bello, 1976), pp. 718–22 and 731–40.

63. Rhod Rothfuss, "El marco: Un problema de plástica actual," *Arturo: Revista de artes abstractas* 1 (Summer 1944), n.p. As Sean Nesselrode summarizes the gambit, the purely pictorial autonomy advocated by Theo Van Doesburg in his 1930 manifesto of Concrete art was thereby converted into the material autonomy of the physically self-contained work of art. Nesselrode, "Art for Partisan Life: Nonobjectivity Translated to Buenos Aires, 1944–48," *ICAA Documents Project Working Papers* 3 (November 2013), pp. 3–13. In 1950, Rothfuss differentiated between the distinct strategies of the *marco recortado* (cut-out or broken frame), the jagged frame of which resulted from an operation of cutting, and the *marco estructurado* (structured frame), in which the centrifugal radiation of compositional forms determines the delimitations of the bounding perimeter or frame, and the composition expands from the inside outward, thereby determining the work's bounding perimeter. See Mario H. Gradowczyk and Nelly Perazzo, eds., *Abstract Art from the Río de la Plata: Buenos Aires and Montevideo 1933–1953*, exh. cat. (New York: The Americas Society, 2001), p. 55.

64. Formidable studies of these practices and debates include Pérez-Barreiro, "The Argentine Avant-Garde, 1944–1950"; García, *Abstract Crossings*; Alejandro Crispiani, *Objectos para transformar o mundo: Trayectorias del arte concreto-invención, Argentina y Chile, 1940–1970: La Escuela de Arquitectura de Valparaíso y las teorías del diseño para la periferia* (Bernal: Universidad Nacional de Quilmes, 2011); Mónica Amor, *Theories of the Nonobject: Argentina, Brazil, Venezuela, 1944–1969* (Oakland: University of California Press, 2016); Alexander Alberro, *Abstraction in Reverse: The Reconfigured Spectator in Mid-Twentieth-Century Latin American Art* (Chicago: University of Chicago Press, 2017); and Pino Monkes, "Argentine Concrete Art,

the First Decade: Between Material and Formal Innovation," in Gilbert, et. al., eds., *Purity Is a Myth*, pp. 236–51. This scholarship follows seminal catalogues by Nelly Perazzo, *El arte concreto en la Argentina en la decada del 40* (Buenos Aires: Ediciones de Arte Gaglianone, 1983), and Gradowczyk and Perazzo, *Abstract Art from the Río de la Plata*. Although initially exhibiting together, artists associated with *Arturo* and its Invencionista platform split sometime the following year, eventually forming the rival groups Asociación Arte Concreto-Invención (AACI) and Arte Madí. Although the *marco recortado* was a point of departure for both groups, they staked out different aesthetic and political approaches, with Maldonado and Bayley of AACI, for example, seeking to align formal experimentation more tightly with a Marxist critique of ideology and with Madí artists experimenting in a more ludic and performative vein, even as they saw their works, too, as deeply political.

65. See also Tomás Maldonado, "Los artists Concretos, el 'realismo' y la realidad," *Arte Concreto Invención* 1 (August 1946), p. 10.

66. Maldonado, "Lo abstracto y lo concreto en el arte moderno," and Rhod Rothfuss, "Super estructuras," *Arte Madí Universal* 2 (October 1948), p. 2.

67. Maldonado, "Lo abstracto y lo concreto en el arte moderno," p. 7. See also Alfredo Hlito, "El tema del espacio en la pintura actual," *Nueva Visión* 8 (1955), pp. 10–13, and Melé, *La vanguardia del 40*, particularly chapter 3.

68. Maldonado, "Lo abstracto y lo concreto en el arte moderno," p. 7

69. Hlito, "El tema del espacio en la pintura actual," p. 11.

70. Maldonado, "Lo abstracto y lo concreto en el arte moderno," p. 5. See also Maldonado, *El arte concreto y el problema de lo ilimitado*.

71. Nesselrode, "Art for Partisan Life," p. 3.

72. These elements generate what Nelly Perazzo describes as a "stress field" in which the picture is "relativized," as Maldonado characterized the ambition in 1946. Although Maldonado likewise stated that the relations between forms and perimeter are linked by "a complex connective network," attempts to disclose this network are almost entirely frustrated. Perazzo, *Abstract Art from the Río de la Plata*, pp. 29 and 32, and Maldonado, "Lo abstracto y lo concreto en el arte moderno," p. 6.

73. Maldonado, "Lo abstracto y lo concreto en el arte moderno," p. 6.

74. *Tomás Maldonado in Conversation with María Amalia García*, trans. Jen Hofer and Kristina Cordero (New York: Fundación Cisneros, 2010), p. 29. In this interview, Maldonado concurs with this assessment, although he notes the work's importance within debates of the time.

75. Subsequent works by Lozza and Manuel Espinosa that actualize the structuring grid of the painting's bounding perimeter offer one thread of response because here, the mechanism of generating the plane is simultaneously the means of disrupting the pictorial illusion of figure and ground.

76. Prati's work was published in *Arte Concreto Invención* alongside Maldonado's *Sin título* and works by Lozza and Espinosa in the 1946 "Manifiesto Invencionista."

77. Pérez-Barreiro, "The Argentine Avant-Garde, 1944–1950," and *Tomás Maldonado in Conversation with María Amalia García*, pp. 34–36.

78. On the implications of spectatorship in relation to these experiments, see Alberro, *Abstraction in Reverse*.

79. On this historical dynamic, see Rosalind Krauss's description of the lurking perspectivism of Frank Stella's stripe paintings in "A View of Modernism," *Artforum* (September 1972), pp. 48–51.

80. Carmelo Arden Quin, who relocated to Paris with the intention of launching Madí as an international movement, participated in several iterations of the Salon des Réalités Nouvelles in Paris between 1949 and 1954 and exhibited at Galerie Colette Allendy in 1951. In his 1950 volume *L'art abstrait*, Michel Seuphor dismissively described Quin's irregular frames and articulated works as having "the air of a joke, as in general everything that is new does" (p. 91). The Argentine representation for the 1953 São Paulo Bienal included Alfredo Hlito, *Anedota sobre vermelho*, 1953; Gyula Kosice, *Planos e côr liberados (pintura Madí)*, 1953; Raúl Lozza, *Estrutura em amarelo*, 1953, and *Mural perceptista*, 1953; and Tomás Maldonado, *Construção com elementos eguais*, 1953, and *15 elementos, 11 espaços*, 1953.

81. Jorge Romero Brest, *Grupo de artistas modernos argentinos*, exh. cat. (Rio de Janeiro: Museu de Arte Moderna do Rio de Janeiro, 1953), p. 8. Brest likewise organized a conference in Rio on the occasion of the exhibition.

82. In an interview given for the *Museu de Arte Moderna do Rio de Janeiro: Boletim de Setembro* 11 (September 1953), p. 1, Maldonado mentions Clark among four young Brazilian artists with whose works he had become acquainted.

83. See Tomás Maldonado, ed., *Max Bill* (Buenos Aires: Editora Nueva Visión, 1955). Importantly, as Bill's presence became increasingly visible in Brazil in the mid-1950s, Rio-based artists associated with Grupo Frente, including Clark, sought to assert their independence from his positions and work. See Adele Nelson, "Artist as Model Citizen: Grupo Frente and Rio Institutions," in Nelson, *Forming Abstraction: Art and Institutions*

in Postwar Brazil (Oakland: University of California Press, 2022), pp. 209–52. Likewise, although several Grupo Frente members came to be associated with Concrete art, the group included representational painters such as Elisa Martins da Silva.

84. Prior to the term "Concrete" taking hold among artists from Rio, Clark already received recognition in such exhibitions as the I Exposição Nacional de Arte Abstrata, held at the Hotel Quitandinha in Petrópolis, where she was awarded the Augusto Federico Schmidt prize. Clark likewise participated in the important I Exposição Nacional de Arte Concreto in 1956, held at the Museu de Arte Moderna de São Paulo and subsequently at the temporary headquarters of the Museu de Arte Moderna do Rio de Janeiro.

85. Theo Van Doesburg differentiated actually existent forms of nature ("a woman, a tree, and a cow") from pictorial entities such as planes or lines in "Manifeste de l'art concret."

86. Maldonado's 1956 course at the Museu de Arte Moderna do Rio de Janeiro was titled "Iniciação Visual." According to newspaper reports, he discussed the importance of topology, the history of Gestalt psychology, and theories of symmetry, among other things. See articles in *Correio da Manhã*, July 5 and 7, 1956. "Curso relâmpago Maldonado," *Última Hora*, July 20, 1956, notes that a study group had already formed to pursue questions Maldonado had presented in his lectures.

87. Waldemar Cordeiro, "Néo-Retórico," *Correio da Manhã*, literary supplement, section 1, August 6, 1960, p. 8, and section 2, p. 2.

88. Ferreira Gullar, "Resposta a Cordeiro," *Suplemento Dominical do Jornal do Brasil*, August 13, 1960, p. 7. It is likewise conceivable Gullar had the Argentine groups in mind when he distinguished Clark's series from efforts to "break out of the frame," arguing instead that she "assimilated" the frame into the painting in "Lygia Clark," *Suplemento Dominical do Jornal do Brasil*, March 15, 1959, p. 5.

89. Hélio Oiticica, "Nota," August 10, 1964, Arquivo Hélio Oiticica / Projeto Hélio Oiticica, ID 2089.64. Oiticica's charge of "ultraformalism" is interesting, considering that artists associated with the *marco recortado* experiments in Buenos Aires understood the battle against representation to be an explicitly Marxist political imperative, in line with their Soviet avant-garde predecessors. Corresponding experiments with format by their Brazilian counterparts, as well as the reception of Suprematism and Constructivism, by contrast, were formal, phenomenological, and at least at first, largely apolitical. See García, *Abstract Crossings*. As Ronaldo Brito persuasively argued in his groundbreaking 1975 essay, this reception paradoxically laid the groundwork for the far more radical and

politicized Brazilian experiments of the mid- to late 1960s. See "Neo-concretism, Apex and Rupture of the Constructive Project," trans. Gabriel Pérez-Barreiro with Irene V. Small, *October* 161 (Summer 2017), pp. 89–142.

90. On the postwar reception (or reputation) of *Black Square*, see Tom McDonough, "The Mercurial Monochrome, or the Nihilation of Geometric Abstraction," in Blazwick, ed., *Adventures of the Black Square*, pp. 243–51. In an unpublished section of her 1986 interview with Luciano Figueiredo and Matinas Suzuki, Jr., Clark remarked that "I saw very little of those Russians, they were trapped in the basement of the Moscow Museum of Modern Art. So, I know, for example, the reproduction of the *Black Square*, Kazemir [*sic*] Malevich, which I think is beautiful. . . . But if you don't see it, it's completely different, seeing only the reproduction is not the same thing." "Late Afternoon in Copacabana," in *Lygia Clark (1920–1988): 100 anos*, exh. cat. (Rio de Janeiro: Edições Pinakotheke, 2021), p. 285. It is possible that Clark saw examples of Malevich's work from the Museum of Modern Art, New York, in the exhibition *Artwork of the 20th Century*, organized by Alfred Barr and held at the Musée National d'Art Moderne in 1952 while she was living in Paris.

91. Vera Pedrosa, the critic's daughter, does not believe her father encountered Malevich himself in Berlin. Interview with author, October 23, 2017, Rio de Janeiro.

92. Other volumes include Michel Seuphor, *Dictionnaire de la peinture moderne* (Paris: Hazan: 1954), and Christian Zervos, *Historie de l'art contemporain* (Paris: Éditions Cahiers d'Art, 1938).

93. *Die Gegenstandslose Welt* illustrates *Black Square* as a drawing, rather than as a photograph of the painting.

94. Jayme Maurício, "'Choix de Malewitsch' o quadrado negro em fundo branco—Suprematismo," *Correio da Manhã*, September 5, 1953, section 1, p. 11. Maurício opens his article noting: "One more ism for the long lists of isms with which the painters of the twentieth century reacted against the pictorial conformism is being resuscitated: Suprematism." He may also have been referring to Juan Eduardo Cirlot's Spanish-language *Diccionario de los ismos* (Buenos Aires: Argos, 1949).

95. I have modified the English translation of Malevich's text in *Die Kunstismen* to hew closer to Maurício's Portuguese translation from that same text.

96. See, by contrast, Malevich's "From Cubism and Futurism to Suprematism."

97. In Gullar's introduction to "O mundo da não-representação," *Suplemento Dominical do Jornal do Brasil*, October 13, 1957, p. 3, he notes the accompanying text was drawn from Michel Seuphor's *Dictionnaire de la peinture moderne*. Gullar translates Malevich's

title into Portuguese as *The World of Non-Representation* rather than *The Non-Objective World*, as it is known in English.

98. On the expressive character of Malevich's Suprematist surfaces, see Nakov, "Devices, Style and Realisation: Professionalism in Malewicz's Painting Technique," in *Malevich: Painting the Absolute*, vol. 4, pp. 133–90. Nakov observes that even the white border of *Black Square* exhibits fingerprints and evidence of brushstrokes and further notes that misguided restoration of the work has flattened much of this texture, in addition to regularizing the deliberate geometric idiosyncrasies of Malevich's stretchers. Malevich himself observed, "Usually the public says, 'But the canvas is empty?' What do you mean it's empty, when you can see that the canvas is painted with white paint?" Quoted in Shatskikh, *Black Square: Malevich and the Origin of Suprematism*, p. 269.

99. The publication *Lygia Clark* (Rio de Janeiro: FUNARTE, 1980), produced in consultation with the artist, prints *Descoberta da linha orgânica* with the rectangle in horizontal orientation. However, the catalogue also publishes two *Quebra da moldura* works using photographs of cardboard maquettes, rather than the paintings themselves. The maquette for *Quebra da moldura (p x b) versão 1* is likewise printed in horizontal orientation, even though the painting is otherwise exhibited vertically. Luciano Figueiredo, who collaborated with Clark on several projects during this period, has noted that the artist was not always attentive to such details, and it is possible that the orientation of the 1958 and 1980 catalogues reflected design and printing constraints as much as anything else. Interview with author, October 24, 2017, Rio de Janeiro.

100. Luis Pérez-Oramas, conversations with author, June 16 and 21, 2016, Museum of Modern Art, New York.

101. I am extremely grateful to the collectors Sérgio and Hecilda Fadel, who allowed me to study this work closely for several hours during my research in Rio. Problems of orientation have followed *Descoberta da linha orgânica* in its public life, as well. During Clark's retrospective exhibition at the Museum of Modern Art, New York, in 2014, the painting was hung in two different orientations, the first conforming to significant indications on the work's back, the second "corrected" to Gullar's orientation in his 1958 pamphlet. It was published in the catalogue in error in a third orientation. Pérez-Oramas, conversations with author, June 16 and 21, 2016. Ultimately, however, these vacillations are productively symptomatic and also follow issues of orientation that accompany other works in Clark's *Quebra da moldura* series.

102. Clark may have encountered illustrations of Lissitzky's *About Two Squares* in

publications circulating in either Rio or Paris, such as Seuphor's *Dictionnaire de la peinture moderne*, which was also in Pedrosa's library.

103. See, for example, Maldonado, "Lo abstracto y lo concreto en el arte moderno"; Hlito, "El tema del espacio en la pintura actual"; and Gyula Kosice, "Naturaleza y estructura," *Arte Madí Universal* 3 (October 1949), n.p.

104. Lygia Clark, "1957 sobre o espaço," diário 4, Archives of the Associação Cultural "O Mundo de Lygia Clark," ID 61717.

105. Ibid.

106. Cunha, "Ligia Clark busca na pintura a expressão do próprio espaço."

107. See "Lígia Clark—Prêmio 'Diário de Notícias' na IV Bienal," *Jornal Diário de Notícias: A Revista Feminina*, October 13, 1957, which notes that she also had a copy of Edward Kasner and James Newman's book *Matemática é imaginação*. Archives of the Associação Cultural "O Mundo de Lygia Clark," ID 4590.

108. See Michael Fried's memorable treatment of this quality in *Manet's Modernism, or, The Face of Painting in the 1860s* (Chicago: University of Chicago Press, 1998).

109. *Malevitch: Suprematism, 34 Drawings* (1920; New York: Artists Books Distribution, 1974), n.p.

110. Malevich, *The Non-Objective World*, p. 76.

111. Ricardo Basbaum, "Within the Organic Line and After," in Alexander Alberro and Sabeth Buchmann, eds., *Art after Conceptual Art* (Cambridge, MA: MIT Press; Vienna: Generali Foundation, 2006), p. 96.

112. Luis Pérez-Oramas, "Lygia Clark: If You Hold a Stone," in Connie Butler and Luis Pérez-Oramas, eds., *Lygia Clark: The Abandonment of Art, 1948–1988*, exh. cat. (New York: Museum of Modern Art, 2014), p. 46. Pérez-Oramas connects this quality to Marcel Duchamp's notion of the infrathin.

113. On F3F, see Rodrigo Martí, "Frente 3 de Fevereiro," in Bill Kelly, Jr., and Grant Kester, eds., *Collective Situations: Readings in Contemporary Latin American Art, 1995–2010* (Durham: Duke University Press, 2017), pp. 165–85, and Fabiano Lopes, "Black Performance in Brazil: Hidden Stories and the Rough Vibrancy of Now," *Nka: Journal of Contemporary African Art* 44 (May 2019), pp. 64–76.

114. Jared Sexton, *Amalgamation Schemes: Antiblackness and the Critique of Multiracialism* (Minneapolis: University of Minnesota Press, 2008), p. 29, quoted in Hannah Black, "Fractal Freedoms," *Afterall: A Journal of Art, Context, and Enquiry* 41 (March 2016), pp. 4–9. Sexton also draws from Kara Keeling's work on Gilles Deleuze and cinema; see

The Witch's Flight: The Cinematic, the Black Femme, and the Image of Common Sense (Durham: Duke University Press, 2007). It is worth nothing that Malevich repeatedly described his paintings not as representations of reality, but "living forms." See "From Cubism and Futurism to Suprematism."

115. As Spillers writes, "I would make a distinction in this case between 'body' and 'flesh' and impose that distinction as the central one between captive and liberated subject-positions. In that sense, before the 'body' there is 'flesh,' that zero degree of social conceptualization that does not escape concealment under the brush of discourse, or the reflexes of iconography." Hortense Spillers, "Mama's Baby, Papa's Maybe: An American Grammar Book," *Diacritics* 17.2 (Summer 1987), p. 67.

116. Black, "Fractal Freedoms," p. 5. On the inscription on Malevich's painting as symptomatic of the lacunae of modernist art historical epistemologies, see also Leah Dickerman, Mignon Nixon, and David Joselit, "Afrotropes: A Conversation with Huey Copeland and Krista Thompson," *October* 162 (Fall 2017), pp. 3–18.

117. Ibid., p. 6.

118. Zakiyyah Iman Jackson, *Becoming Human: Matter and Meaning in an Antiblack World* (New York: New York University Press, 2020).

119. Ibid., p. 3

120. Malevich released the first version of this text on the occasion of *The Last Futurist Exhibition 0.10* in December 1915, publishing it in January 1916. An expanded third version, which includes the section "The Art of the Savage and Its Principles," was published in November 1916 (but dated to 1915) and is usually considered the definitive form of the text.

121. See Charlotte Douglas, "Defining Suprematism: The Year of Discovery," in Lodder, ed., *Celebrating Suprematism: New Approaches to the Art of Kazimir Malevich*, pp. 29–43, and "The New Russian Art and Italian Futurism" *Art Journal* 34.3 (Spring 1975), pp. 229–39, as well as Irina Vakar, "Afterward: Kazimir Malevich and His Contemporaries: A Biography in Personalities," in Vakar and Mikhienko, eds., *Kazimir Malevich: Letters, Documents, Memoirs, Criticism, Volume 2: Memoirs and Criticism*, in which she notes that he copied the manifestos by hand (p. 579).

122. F. T. Marinetti, "The Manifesto of Futurism" (1909) in James Joll, *Three Intellectuals in Politics* (New York: Harper & Row, 1960), p. 180. Marinetti's 1909 manifesto appeared in a St. Petersburg newspaper soon after its initial publication. This was followed by the publication of Futurist manifestos in several newspapers and journals

(including the journal of the Union of Youth in 1912) and the release of three translated collections of Italian manifestos in 1914. See, for example, Filippo Tommaso Marinetti, ed., *Manifesty italiyanskogo futurizma*, trans. Vadim Shershenevich (Moscow: Russkago Tovarishchestva, 1914). Marinetti's racist and colonialist predilections were well known. In 1909, he published the violent and pornographic *Mafarka le futuriste: Roman africain*, concerning an Arab warrior who fights armies of Black Africans to become Master of Africa. Marinetti was also involved with Italy's colonial campaign in Libya from 1911 to 1912. During his 1926 trip to Rio de Janeiro, Marinetti requested to tour the predominantly Afro-Brazilian region of the Morro da Favela, because he wanted to see "the places where the racial presence was at its strongest." See Romulo Costa Mattos, "Heavenly Heights, or Reign of the Dangerous Classes? F. T. Marinetti's Visit to the Morro da Favela (1926)," in *International Yearbook of Futurism Studies* 7 (2017), pp. 288–305 and see 289n5.

123. See Jeremy Howard, *The Union of Youth: A Society of Artists in St. Petersburg, 1910–1914* (New York: St. Martin's Press, 1992).

124. Petr Evstaf'evich Stoain, *Malyĭ tolkovyĭ slovar' russkago ī azyka: s 1300 risunkami* (Pechatn ī a K. P. Shrader, 1915). "Некультурный цветнокожий ('tsvetnokozhyi') туземец неевропейских стран. *Пляска дикарей*." The term "tsvetnokozhyi" refers to nonwhite people, literally, "people with colored skin." Translation by Sasha Whittaker.

125. Malevich, "From Cubism and Futurism to Suprematism," p. 119.

126. Ibid., p. 120.

127. Ibid., p. 124.

128. See Howard, *The Union of Youth*, and Jeremy Howard, Irena Buzinska, and Z. S. Strother, eds., *Vladimir Markov and Russian Primitivism: A Charter for the Avant-Garde* (London: Ashgate, 2015).

129. Vladimir Markov, "Iskusstvo negrov" (1914; published 1919), in Howard et al., eds., *Vladimir Markov and Russian Primitivism*, p. 242.

130. Ibid., p. 244. Notably, while Markov's enthusiasm for such aesthetic possibilities led him to purchase African sculptures for institutions back in Russia during his 1913 trip, Claude McKay began his chapter on art in his 1923 volume *Negry v Amerike* with the looting of the Benin bronzes and the travesty of their display at the British Museum.

131. See Jackson, *Becoming Human*. As G. W. F. Hegel notoriously wrote, "At this point we leave Africa, not to mention it again. For it is no historical part of the World; it has no movement or development to exhibit. . . . What we properly understand by Africa, is the

Unhistorical, Undeveloped Spirit, still involved in the conditions of mere nature, and which had to be presented here only as on the threshold of the World's History." *Lectures on the Philosophy of World History*, trans. J. Sibree (1837; New York: Dover, 1956), p. 99.

132. See Vakar, "New Information Concerning *The Black Square*"; Vakar, *Kazimir Malevich: The Black Square*; and M. P. Vikturina, "Secrets of *The Black Square*," *Nauka v Rossii* 3 (1997), pp. 72–79

133. It is worth noting that upon the work's first appearance at *The Last Futurist Exhibition 0.10*, the conservative artist and critic Alexandre Benois described the painting not as a black figure upon a white ground, but as a "black square framed by white" and as having a "white cover." Such descriptions convey a perceived pictorial recession in keeping with Malevich's drawings of the recessed theatrical space of *Victory over the Sun*. Alexandre Benois, "The Last Futurist Exhibition," *Rech'*, January 9, 1916, trans. in Vakar and Mikhienko, eds., *Kazimir Malevich: Letters, Documents, Memoirs, Criticism, Volume 2: Memoirs and Criticism*, p. 517. Malevich also frequently laid down lines in pencil that guided his paint application, often retaining the sliver of a seam between geometric forms. Even when such seams are not visible, it is clear that the paint layers are materially contiguous, rather than the black layered on top of the white. On these points, I am particularly grateful to conversations with Maria Kokkori, who examined *Black Quadrilateral* as part of her conservational analysis of the G. Costakis Collection, Thessaloniki. See also Petra Mandt, "The Paintings of Kazimir Malevich in the Ludwig Collection from the Art-Technological Point of View," *InCoRM Journal* 3 (Spring–Autumn 2012), pp. 49–58.

134. Iudin, *Diaries*, p. 230.

135. Clark noted how *Ovo linear*'s spiraling action catalyzes a topological, rather than simply two-dimensional space in "Entrevista Lygia Clark," in Fernando Cocchiarale and Anna Bella Geiger, eds., *Abstracionismo geométrico e informal: A vanguarda brasileira nos anos cinqüenta* (Rio de Janeiro: FUNARTE, 1987), p. 149.

136. Paulo Herkenhoff, "A aventura planar de Lygia Clark—de caracóis, escadas e caminhando," in *Lygia Clark*, exh. cat. (São Paulo: Museu de Arte Moderna de São Paulo, 1999), pp. 23–24.

137. Lygia Clark, "The Death of the Plane" (1960), trans. in Butler and Pérez-Oramas, eds., *Lygia Clark: The Abandonment of Art*, p. 158. In 1953, when the exhibition of Argentine modern art showcasing Maldonado and other Concrete artists traveled from Rio to the Stedelijk Museum in Amsterdam, the German artist Friedrich Vordemberge-Gildwart noted the necessity of establishing an orthogonal plane due to the vertical stance of the

human body and its corresponding horizontal tension. "Discurso inaugural," *nueva visión: revista de cultura visual: artes arquitectura, diseño industrial, tipografía 5* (1954), pp. 38–40. While Maldonado had once looked to the irregular frame to break the work of art's similitude to natural form, here, the return to the orthogonal was universalist, norma-tive, even disciplinary in character.

138. Malevich, "From Cubism and Futurism to Suprematism," p. 134.

139. Clark, "The Death of the Plane," p. 158. Clark's language of "living forms" echoes Malevich's, who wrote, "Now it is essential to shape the body and lend it a living form in real life. And this will happen when forms emerge from painterly masses, that is, they will arise just as utilitarian forms arose. Such forms will not be repetitions of living things in life, but will themselves be a living thing. A painted surface is a real, living form." "From Cubism and Futurism to Suprematism," p. 130.

140. Clark, "The Death of the Plane," p. 158.

141. Lygia Clark, "Dizem que a parte criadora do artista é a sua parte feminine, 1960," diário 2, Archives of the Associação Cultural "O Mundo de Lygia Clark," ID 61905.

142. Ibid.

143. Lygia Clark, "Minha querida Lucy, 23 de Maio de 1961," diário 2, Archives of the Associação Cultural "O Mundo de Lygia Clark," ID 61933.

144. "1957—Entrevista para jornal de Campinas," diário 4, Archives of the Associa-ção Cultural "O Mundo de Lygia Clark," ID 61701.

145. In the "Artes Plásticas 'Flashes'" section of *Correio de Manhã*, Jayme Maurício noted, "The interview Lygia Clark gave to an evening newspaper is still reverberat-ing in vanguard circles. Everyone is obsessed with the 'organic line' that the interview announced as Lygia's discovery. For her part, the painter is annoyed with the reporter, and called her 'novice.'" Section 1, March 31, 1955, p. 14.

146. Lygia Clark, "Geometria amorosa" (1955), diário 2, Archives of the Associação Cultural "O Mundo de Lygia Clark," ID 61830. Clark's diagram notably recasts the UNI-VOS logo of "construction" under the sign of the pregnant female body.

147. The alchemical iconography of the philosopher's stone (also described as a rivalry, sexual intercourse, and marriage), appears on the second page of Clark's illustrated text. See, for example, Michael Maier's engraving in *Atalanta fugiens*, 1618, emblema XXI, the Latin inscription of which translates as: "Make from the male and female a circle, then a square, afterwards a triangle, from which make a circle, and thou shalt have the Philoso-pher's Stone." My thanks to Cecilia Fajardo-Hill for calling my attention to this alchemical

symbology. Clark may have accessed alchemical ideas through Carl Jung's work, which was widely known within intellectual circles in Rio, particularly those engaged with the psychiatrist Nise de Silveira's experiments with art therapy at Engenho de Dentro. References to the black sun or *sol niger* also appear within alchemical iconography, anticipating Malevich's preoccupation with darkness and light in *Victory over the Sun*.

148. Lygia Clark, "Caminhando" (1965), trans. in Butler and Pérez-Oramas, eds., *Lygia Clark: The Abandonment of Art*, 160.

149. See Lygia Clark, "Carta de Lygia em 6 pontos, 1980" Archives of the Associação Cultural "O Mundo de Lygia Clark," ID 6840.

150. Lygia Clark, "A Mãe," diário 1, Archives of the Associação Cultural "O Mundo de Lygia Clark," ID 65586. Clark wrote, "My postpartum psychosis happened during a lunar eclipse. I experienced it like a prehistoric woman." "Writings, mid-1980s," trans. in Butler and Pérez-Oramas, eds., *Lygia Clark: The Abandonment of Art*, p. 242.

151. Tim Ingold, *The Life of Lines* (London: Routledge, 2015), p. 20.

152. Lygia Clark, "Breviário sobre o corpo — 3," diário 2, Archives of the Associação Cultural "O Mundo de Lygia Clark," ID 65157, published posthumously in *Lygia Clark* (1997), pp. 190–204, and in Brazil in *Arte e Ensaios* 16 (2008), pp. 114–23. This is a new translation from the original texts. In "Breviário sobre o corpo — 4," diário 2, ID 65156, Clark mentions "Last year in 64...."

153. Malevich, "From Cubism and Futurism to Suprematism," p. 134.

154. Michel Foucault, *The Order of Things: An Archaeology of the Human Sciences* (New York: Vintage, 1994), p. xxiii.

155. Sylvia Wynter, "Unsettling the Coloniality of Being/Power/Truth/Freedom: Towards the Human, After Man, Its Overrepresentation — An Argument," *CR: The New Centennial Review* 3.3 (Fall 2003), pp. 257–337. On the relationship between Foucault's and Wynter's thought, see Denise Ferreira da Silva, "Before Man: Sylvia Wynter's Rewriting of the Modern Episteme," in McKittrick, ed., *Sylvia Wynter: On Being Human as Praxis*, pp. 90–105.

156. Mignolo, "Sylvia Wynter: What Does It Mean to Be Human?," pp. 108–109.

157. Fred Moten, "The Case of Blackness," *Criticism* 50.2 (Spring 2008), p. 187.

158. Ibid., p. 189. Significantly, Reinhardt, like Allais, participated in satirical social commentary; unlike his French counterpart, however, Reinhardt strictly differentiated his representational caricatures from his abstract painterly work.

159. Ibid., p. 180.

160. Importantly, in Brazilian Portuguese, art-historical terms such as "black-and-white" are almost always rendered as *preto-e-branco*.

161. See, for example, Benois's review, "The Last Futurist Exhibition," p. 517. In his letters to Matiushan, Malevich also described his retroactively dated set drawings for *Victory over the Sun* in these terms: "The curtain depicts a black square . . . the germ of all possibilities," Shatskikh, *Black Square: Malevich and the Origins of Suprematism*, p. 50.

162. Guerreiro Ramos, "O negro desde dentro," *Forma* 3 (October 1954), n.p.

163. Ibid.

164. Alberto Guerreiro Ramos, "Patologia social do branco brasileiro" (1955), in Ramos, *Introdução crítica à sociologia brasileira* (Rio de Janeiro: Editora UFRJ, 1957), 171.

165. For an excellent overview of the artist's work, see Adrienne Edwards, "Adam Pendleton: Here Is Your Language," in Adrienne Edwards, Alec Mapes-Frances, and Andréa Picard, eds., *Adam Pendleton* (London: Phaidon, 2020), pp. 35–71.

166. I use "remediation" here in the sense given by such scholars as Jay David Bolter and Richard Grusin in *Remediation: Understanding New Media* (Cambridge, MA: MIT Press, 2000).

167. Pendleton, "Black Dada," p. 342.

168. Adam Pendleton, quoted in Adrienne Edwards, *Blackness in Abstraction*, exh. cat. (New York: Pace Gallery, 2016), p. 125. As part of this same exhibition, Edwards commissioned a group of four new works by the artist Ellen Gallagher titled *Negroes Battling in a Cave*, in reference to the inscription on Malevich's painting.

169. Kobena Mercer, "Black Art and the Burden of Representation," *Third Text* 4.10 (1990), pp. 61–78.

170. Pendleton, "Black Dada." As Pendleton has remarked, "We think we know what Black is but we don't. Black is a capacious space, it's about multiplicity, it's about moving in many different directions at once." Artist's talk with Jenny Schlenzka, "Black Dada: How Does It Feel to Be a Problem?," https://www.youtube.com/watch?v=lBOmwns3mXE.

171. See Rubem Valentim, "Statement to Bené Fonteles" (1989–1990), in *Rubem Valentim: Afro-Atlantic Constructions*, exh. cat. (São Paulo: MASP, 2018), pp. 141–49.

172. See Atreyee Gupta, "Francis Newton Souza's Black Paintings: Postwar Transactions in Color," *Art Bulletin* 103.4 (December 2021), pp. 111–37. See also Julia Bryan-Wilson's rethinking of the color black in *Louise Nevelson's Sculpture: Drag, Color, Join, Face* (New Haven: Yale University Press, 2023).

173. Omar Berrada, "Paratactical Haunting: Adam Pendleton's Diasporic Images," in *Adam Pendleton: Who We Are*, exh. cat. (Berlin: Galerie Max Hetzler, 2019), pp. 169–77.

174. Pendleton, "Afterward," in *Black Dada Reader*, p. 348.

CHAPTER TWO: NOT/MAKING/MARKS

The epigraphs are from Henri Focillon, "In Praise of Hands," in Focillon, *The Life of Forms in Art* (1934; New York: Zone Books, 1992), pp. 164–65 and 184; the transcript of Julius Eastman's interpretation of *Solo for Voice 8 (0'00" [4'33" No. 2])*, 1975, from John Cage, *Song Books* (1970), transcribed by Adam Overton in collaboration with G. Douglas Barrett from a recording archived at Music Library, SUNY Buffalo (Concert 2, JB 5), http://library.buffalo.edu.gate.lib.buffalo.edu/libraries/units/music/spcoll/june.html; and Lula Wanderley, interview with author, October 20, 2017, O Espaço Aberto ao Tempo, Engenho de Dentro, and October 21 2017, Botafogo, Rio de Janeiro.

1. Claude, "A mulher na arte moderna," *Querida* 117 (April 1959), p. 46. See also Lygia Clark, "Carta de Lygia em 6 pontos, 1980," Archives of the Associação Cultural "O Mundo de Lygia Clark," ID 6840.

2. Focillon, "In Praise of Hands," p. 168.

3. David Summers, *Real Spaces: World Art History and the Rise of Western Modernism* (London: Phaidon, 2003), p. 74.

4. Clark's text "Mãos" (Hands) exists in several versions. I translate here primarily from that included in "Breviário sobre o corpo—1," diário 2, Archives of the Associação Cultural "O Mundo de Lygia Clark," ID 65154. See also "Mãos 2" and "Mãos 2 (versão II)," Archives of the Associação Cultural "O Mundo de Lygia Clark," ID 6823 and ID 6827.

5. As Clark wrote in "Mãos," "Dar-se as mãos a si mesma." ("To hold hands with yourself.") According to her son Álvaro Clark, this drawing was created as a commission for a textile company (and thus anticipates the displacement of the hand by the machine). The textile itself, however, was never made. Correspondence with Felipe Scovino, July 13, 2022.

6. Clark later developed this "creaturely" orientation in her *Obras moles* (Soft works), 1964, whose horizontal orientation and ability to cling and climb lend them the character of "animais rastejantes" (crawling animals) as Luiz Camillo Osorio writes in "Sem título ou da antiarte à não arte: Interrogações a partir de Lygia Clark" (2003), in Osorio, *Olhar à margem: Caminhos da arte brasileira* (São Paulo: SESI-SP Editora, 2016), p. 140.

7. Henry van de Velde, "The Line" (1908), in Katherine Kuenzli, ed., *Henry van de*

Velde: Selected Essays, trans. Elizabeth Tucker (Los Angeles: Getty Research Institute, 2022), p. 282.

8. Clark, "Mãos." An attentiveness to tactile knowledge resonates strongly with Clark's experience teaching art to deaf and mute children at the Instituto Nacional de Educação de Surdos between 1960 and 1962. See Beatriz Scigliano Carneiro, *Relâmpagos com claror: Lygia Clark e Hélio Oiticica: Vida como arte* (São Paulo: FAPESP, 2004), and Graça Maria Dias da Silva, *Lygia Clark no Instituto Nacional de Educação e Surdos: Arte de histórias de cumplicidades* (Saarbrücken: Novas Edições Acadêmicas, 2015). Marcio Doctors extends the notion of working with blind or deaf subjects in "Catharsis and Lygia Clark: The Healing Power of Art," in *Lygia Clark (1920–1988): 100 anos*, exh. cat. (Rio de Janeiro: Edições Pinakotheke, 2021), pp. 269–74.

9. Luciano Figueiredo, who was one of Clark's clients at this time and also curated her retrospective exhibition at Paço Imperial in 1986, recalls the stacked paintings visible in the consulting room, the same location as her old studio. Interview with author, October 24, 2017, Rio de Janeiro. *Estruturação do Self* is sometimes dated to 1978, even as elements of the practice are continuous with Clark's earlier *Objetos relacionais* and *Nostalgia do corpo*. Suely Rolnik and Felipe Scovino date the practice to 1976.

10. Caetano Veloso, interviewed by Suely Rolnik in Rolnik, ed., *Lygia Clark — Archive pour une oeuvre-evenement* (Paris: Carta Blanca Editions, 2010), DVD 1.

11. Clark, "Carta de Lygia em 6 pontos, 1980."

12. See "Pintora mineira (Ligia Clark) descobre linhas orgânicas nas artes plásticas," *Diário de Minas*, January 27, 1957; Almeida Cunha, "Ligia Clark busca na pintura a expressão do próprio espaço," *Folha da Noite*, September 22 1958; "A quebra da moldura: Entrevista de Lygia Clark a Luciano Figueiredo e Matinas Suzuki Jr.," *Folhetim de Folha de São Paulo*, March 2, 1986, p. 3. See also "1957 — Entrevista para o jornal de Campinas," diário 4, Archives of the Associação Cultural "O Mundo de Lygia Clark," ID 61701, subsequently used for "Lygia Clark e o espaço concreto expressional," ed. Edelweiss Sarmento, *Suplemento Dominical do Jornal do Brasil,* July 2, 1959, p. 3.

13. Clark experimented with different methods of catalyzing the organic line in these years. A pair of *Superfícies moduladas* from 1955 (one included in the São Paulo Bienal) repeats a basic composition with two color treatments. In one, Clark compiled and glued individually cut pieces to construct the painting's frontal layer, while in the other, she merely incised lines upon this top layer, stopping short of a total breach.

14. As Adele Nelson writes, "Clark articulated a conceptual innovation — the

creation of a surface via the multiplication of surfaces. Surface made of multiple surfaces, surface doubled by adhering surfaces on the same plane to support a surface, and surface made thick by building up uniformly sprayed layers of paint." Nelson, "On Gender and Surface in Lygia Clark's Early Abstraction," in *Lygia Clark: Painting as an Experimental Field, 1948–1958*, exh. cat. (Bilbao: Guggenheim Bilbao, 2020), p. 75.

15. "Lígia Clark — Prêmio 'Diário de Notícias' na IV Bienal," *Jornal Diário de Notícias: A Revista Feminina*, October 13, 1957, Archives of the Associação Cultural "O Mundo de Lygia Clark," ID 4590.

16. See Claude, "A mulher na arte moderna"; "Ligia Clark busca na pintura a expressão do próprio espaço"; and "Ligia Clark — Prêmio 'Diário de Notícias' na IV Bienal." For a conservational analysis of Clark's works, see Giulia Villela Giovani, "A análise de técnicas e materias aplicada à conservação de arte contemporânea: O uso da tinta industrial sobre madeira na produção pictórica de Lygia Clark," masters thesis, Universidade Federal de Minas Gerais, 2014.

17. Claude, "A mulher na arte moderna," my emphasis.

18. This process of assembling such surfaces from independent panels was technically demanding, and at a certain point, Clark began to contract out their construction.

19. "A quebra da moldura," p. 3.

20. Lygia Clark, "1957 — Sobre o espaço," diário 4, Archives of the Associação Cultural "O Mundo de Lygia Clark," ID 61717.

21. The exhibition "Exposição de Pintura dos Alienados do Centro Psiquiátrico Nacional" opened on December 22, 1946, at the Centro Psiquiátrico Nacional Engenho de Dentro and was transferred to the temporary headquarters of the Museu de Arte Moderna do Rio de Janeiro on February 4, 1947. The exhibition was subsequently shown at the Associação Brasileira de Imprensa. Already in 1933, artworks created by patients interned at the Hospital do Juquery were exhibited by Dr. Osório Cesar and the artist Flávio de Carvalho in São Paulo. See Raquel Carneiro Amin, "O 'Mês das Crianças e dos Loucos': Um olhar sobre a exposição paulista de 1933," *ARS: Arte, Tecnologia e Novas Mídias* 11.22 (2013), pp. 123–42.

22. Mário Pedrosa, "Arte, necessidade vital" (1947), in Gloria Ferreira and Paulo Herkenhoff, eds., *Mário Pedrosa: Primary Documents*, trans. Steve Berg (New York: Museum of Modern Art, 2016), p. 104. This text was given as a lecture at the exhibition's opening.

23. Ibid., p. 110.

24. Ibid., p. 111.

25. Nise da Silveira, catalogue for *Nove artistas de Engenho de Dentro*, exh. cat. (São Paulo: Museu de Arte Moderna de São Paulo, 1949), quoted in Flávio de Aquino, "Nove artistas de Engenho de Centro," *Diário de Notícias*, December 18, 1949, reprinted in *Raphael e Emygdio: Dois modernos no Engenho de Centro*, exh. cat. (Rio de Janeiro: Instituto Morreira Salles, 2012), p. 182. See Kaira Cabañas, *Learning from Madness: Brazilian Modernism and Global Contemporary Art* (Chicago: University of Chicago Press, 2018).

26. See Nise da Silveira, *Imagens do inconsciente* (Petrópolis: Editora Vozes, 2015). This correspondence led to the exhibition of several works by inmates of Engenho de Dentro (including Fernando Diniz) at the Second World Congress of Psychiatry in Zurich in 1957, in which Silveira participated.

27. Diniz was hospitalized in 1939 and began participating in the workshop in 1947 at the referral of another psychiatrist. See Silveira, *Imagens do inconsciente*. Diniz is also the subject of Leon Hirszman's 1986 film, *Em busca do espaço cotidiano*.

28. Silveira, *Imagens do inconsciente*, p. 51.

29. Pedrosa and the critic Quirino Campofiorito faced off in a number of articles in *Correio da Manhã* following *Nove artistas de Engenho de Dentro*, which debuted at the Museu de Arte Moderna de São Paulo in 1949 and came to Rio at the end of the year.

30. Among them were Lygia Pape, Ivan Serpa, Abraham Palatnik, Ferreira Gullar, and, of course, Pedrosa. See Lucia Reily, José Otávio Pompeu e Silva, and collaborators, eds., *Marcas e memórias: Almir Mavignier e o ateliê de pintura de Engenho de Dentro* (Campinas: Komedi, 2012), and *Raphael e Emygdio: Dois modernos no Engenho de Centro*. Mavignier worked at Engenho de Dentro from September 1946 through November 1951.

31. Kaira Cabañas, "The Artist as Therapist: Isidore Isou and Lygia Clark," in *Lost, Loose and Loved: Foreign Artists in Paris, 1944–1968*, exh. cat. (Madrid: Museo Reina Sofía, 2018), pp. 232–42. Cabañas notes that the exhibition, which was on display from September 21 to October 14, 1950, attracted over ten thousand visitors.

32. Lygia Clark, "Carta a Hélio Oiticica," October 22, 1970, in Luciano Figueiredo, ed., *Cartas 1964–74: Lygia Clark / Hélio Oiticica* (Rio de Janeiro: Editora UFRJ, 1996), pp. 181–82. Landscapes by Emygdio de Barros of Engenho de Dentro were also included in the 1953 São Paulo Bienal, in which Clark also exhibited.

33. Lygia Clark, "Writings, mid-1980s," in Connie Butler and Luis Pérez-Oramas, eds., *Lygia Clark: The Abandonment of Art, 1948–1988*, exh. cat. (New York: Museum of Modern Art, 2014), p. 238.

34. Jards Macalé, interview with Suely Rolnik, recounting Hélio Oiticica's observation. *Lygia Clark—Archive pour une oeuvre-evenement*, DVD 1.

35. Ibid.

36. Clark, "On the Act," *Livro-obra* (1964, 1983), in *Lygia Clark*, exh. cat. (Barcelona: Fundació Antoni Tàpies, 1997), p. 165. Clark noted that she had various dreams and nightmares about space, including one in which she realized that she was seeking an "interior" space represented by the "exterior" beyond her window; the "horror" of this realization was abated when she realized that "space was also my constructive element." Lygia Clark, "Tive o seguinte sonho," (1963) diário 2, Archives of the Associacão Cultural "O Mundo de Lygia Clark," ID 62057.

37. The Hungarian-French painter Szenes fled to Rio during the war and returned to Paris in 1947, holding an exhibition with his students (including Almir Mavignier) at the Instituto dos Arquitetos do Brasil just before he left. Dobrinsky was a former teacher of Zélia Salgado, who recommended him to Clark when the latter went to Paris. Clark recalled that Dobrinsky was the best of her teachers because he emphasized the direct encounter with the work of art. Clark likewise recalled that during her studies with the French painter and muralist Léger, he observed that fundamentally everything she painted was stairs. See Clark, "Meu contato com Burle Marx," in "Carta de Lygia em 6 pontos, 1980," and also "A quebra da moldura," p. 3. Although Clark may well have absorbed certain ideas about architecture and the synthesis of arts from Léger, her training does not appear to have been marked by the same intensity she experienced with Burle Marx. In Clark's sister Sonia Lins's recounting of this period, Léger "would jump off his motorbike" once a week to glance at the work of the young artists in his atelier, remarking, "Ça bouge!"—"It's coming along!"—before moving on to the next student. Sonia Lins, *Artes* (Ghent: Snoeck Ducaju and Zoon Belgica, 1996), p. 103.

38. Jamil Hamoudi, *L. Clark-Ribeiro, artiste brésilienne*, exh. cat. (Paris: L'Institut Endoplastique, 1952), n.p. See also Jayme Maurício, "Artes plásticas: Uma nova e talentosa pintura," *Correio da Manhã*, 1952, Archives of the Associação Cultural "O Mundo de Lygia Clark," ID 4487.

39. *L'Art d'Aujourd'hui* noted the "mural scale" to which Clark's compositions aspired, while *L'actualité Artistique Internationale* described her abstraction as "well built, solidly and broadly conceived." Mário Pedrosa added a brief text of his own to this pamphlet, noting the recurring motif of the stairs, as well as the "structural" character of Clark's

paintings and the "rhythmic force" of her graphic lines. *Lygia Clark: 1950–1952*, exh. cat. (Rio de Janeiro: Salão do Ministério da Educação, 1952), n.p.

40. In the 1980–1981 interviews recorded for Fernando Cocchiarale and Anna Bella Geiger, eds., *Abstracionismo geométrico e informal: A vanguarda brasileira nos anos cinqüenta* (Rio de Janeiro: FUNARTE, 1987), Clark notes that the exhibition was lauded by critics whom she admired such as Pedrosa, as well as conventional critics for whom she had little respect. "Entrevista com Lygia Clark," p. 146.

41. Lins, *Arte*, p. 103.

42. Lygia Clark, "Biografia curriculo portugûes," V Documentos A, Archives of the Associação Cultural "O Mundo de Lygia Clark." This document notes that Clark's 1952 exhibition in Paris attracted "the interest of a number of reputable artists, among them: Jean Arp, Yaacov Agam, and Michel Seuphor. All of them have works by Lígia Clark." On Clark's relationship to Arp, see Heloisa Espada, "'Cher Maître'": Lygia Clark and Hans Arp's Concept of Concrete Art," in Jana Teuscher and Loretta Würtenberger, eds., *The Art of Hans Arp After 1945* (Berlin: Stiftung Arp e. V. Papers, 2017), pp. 80–87. As Espada notes, Clark encountered (or reencountered) Arp in 1964 while in Paris on a fellowship and wrote to him after her return to Brazil, sending him a catalogue of her 1963 exhibition at the Museu de Arte Moderna do Rio de Janeiro and noting that a friend would deliver one of her *Bichos* to him as a gift.

43. Bill's approach to Concretism was not uncontested in Brazil. As early as 1954, Jayme Maurício noted that Brazilian artists would do well to consider Arp's warning about an overly rationalist approach at a moment when "concretism is singled out as the only truth, the only path." Maurício, "Perigo de morte na pintura Concreta: Advertência de Jean Arp," *Correio da Manhã*, June 11, 1954, p. 11. Maurício's text quotes heavily from Arp's own text "Danger de mort," *XXe Siècle* 4 (January 1954).

44. Bill's exhibition was scheduled for 1950, but a series of delays resulted in its opening only on March 1, 1951. See María Amalia García, *Abstract Crossings: Cultural Exchange between Argentina and Brazil*, trans. Jane Brodie (2011; Berkeley: University of California Press, 2019), p. 130.

45. Hans Arp, quoted in Michel Seuphor, *L'art abstrait: Ses origines, ses premiers maîtres* (Paris: Galeria Maeght, 1949), p. 13. Seuphor also reproduced a section from Theo Van Doesburg's formulation of *art concret* in "Commentaire sur la base de la peinture concrete," *Art Concret* 1 (1930), pp. 2–4. Here, the Dutch artist noted that both the attempt to abstract art from nature and the idea of distinct "artistic" and "natural" forms were

obsolete. Now, he wrote, was "the period of the concretization of the creative spirit. Concrete and not abstract painting, because nothing is more concrete than a line, a color, a surface." Seuphor noted that Arp likewise defended this idea, but differently distinguished between the abstract and concrete.

46. Max Bill, "O inteligente iconoclasta: Entrevista de Flavio d'Aquino em Manchete," *Habitat: Arquitetura e Artes no Brasil* 12 (September–October 1953), p. 35, and Tomás Maldonado, "Arte de 'n' dimensões," *Suplemento Dominical do Jornal do Brasil*, May 19, 1957, p. 9. Maldonado's article reproduces a section from his edited monograph *Max Bill* (Buenos Aires: Nueva Vision, 1955). See also Bill's text "The Mathematical Approach in Contemporary Art" in this monograph, pp. 36–38.

47. Clark, "A quebra da moldura," p. 4. She likewise insisted in "Entrevista com Lygia Clark" that "concreta mesmo eu não era" ("I was never truly concrete"). Cocchiarale and Geiger, eds., *Abstracionismo geométrico e informal*, p. 145.

48. Alexandre Partens [Hans Arp], "Concrete Art" (1944), in *Arp on Arp: Poems, Essays, Memories*, ed. Marcel Jean, trans. Joachim Neugroschel (New York: Viking, 1972), p. 139. See also Arp, "I Became More and More Removed from Aesthetics" (1948), ibid., pp. 237–38.

49. Vicente Huidobro, "Prologue to *Horizon Carré*" (1917), in *Square Horizon*, trans. Tony Frazer (Bristol: Shearman Books, 2019), pp. 14–15. Huidobro and Arp collaborated on *Tres inmensas novelas* (Santiago de Chile: Editorial Zig-Zag, 1935).

50. On the relationship between Huidobro and the Río de la Plata group, see Alejandro Crispiani, *Objectos para transformar o mundo: Trayectorias del arte concreto-invención, Argentina y Chile, 1940–1970: La Escuela de Arquitectura de Valparaíso y las teorías del diseño para la periferia* (Bernal: Universidad Nacional de Quilmes, 2011).

51. Huidobro, quoted in Rhod Rothfuss, "El marco: Un problema de plástica actual," *Arturo: Revista de artes abstractas* 1 (Summer 1944), n.p.

52. In her excellent study "Definite Means: Arp's Cut-Outs, 1911–1930," PhD diss., Princeton University, 2015, Tessa Paneth-Pollak argues that Arp's conjunction of the organic and the autonomous was indebted to the German Romantic discourse of the fragment, in which, as Friedrich Schlegel put it in 1798, "A fragment should be like a little work of art, complete and perfect in itself, and separate from the rest of the universe." "Athenäeums-Fragmente" no. 206. On the resonance between this dual action of separation and closure and Arp's repeated motif of the navel, see also Briony Fer, "The Laws of Chance," in Fer, *On Abstract Art* (New Haven: Yale University Press, 1997), p. 76.

53. Such weak connections are all the more pronounced when one considers that in 1948, several artists associated with Asociación Arte Concreto-Invención and Arte Madí traveled to Europe to meet "the masters of Non-figurative art and in particular, Concrete art." Juan Melé, *La vanguardia del '40: Memorias de un artista concreto* (Buenos Aires: Ediciones Cinco, 1999), p. 14. Gyula Kosice met and interviewed many of these "masters" (including Arp), publishing these encounters in *Geocultura de la Europa de hoy / Géoculture de l'Europe d'aujourd'hui: Arp, Aragon, Bill, Bloc, Cassou, S. Delaunay, Domela, Fontana, Gilioli, Guéguen, Herbin, Le Corbusier, Mortensen, Munari, Pasmore, Pevsner, D. René, Schoffer, Seghers, Seuphor, Tzara, Vantongerloo, Varèse, Vasarely* (Buenos Aires: Ediciones Losange, 1959). Maldonado's trip was likewise revelatory, prompting him to revert to the orthogonal frame and increasingly embrace Bill's vision of the concrete, which he advanced in subsequent trips to Brazil in 1951, 1953, and 1956. Carmelo Arden Quin relocated to Paris entirely and sought to relaunch Madí as an international movement. There, he participated in several editions of the Salon des Réalités Nouvelles, a locus of abstract art from 1946 through 1953. On Quin's Parisian period, see the special issue on Arte Madí in *Robho* 3 (Spring 1968). See also Gerardo Mosquera, "Paris est un fête," in *Carmen Herrara*, exh. cat. (New York: Whitney Museum of American Art, 2017), pp. 43–53. Melé remained in the French capital until 1950, where he met figures such as Sonia Delaunay, Georges Vantongerloo, Denise René, and Michel Seuphor, showing them a photographic portfolio of the irregular frame experiments he and his colleagues had exhibited in Argentina in the mid- to late 1940s. As a result of such contacts, Seuphor mentioned the "curious articulated pictures and irregular frames of the Argentine Carmelo Arden Quin" in his 1949 *L'art abstrait* (p. 21), and in his 1954 *Dictionnaire de la peinture moderne*, he observed that *art concret* was becoming "a certain vogue" among avant-garde circles in Switzerland and Argentina (p. 10). Pedrosa had a copy of Seuphor's *Dictionnaire* in his library. Despite these overlapping episodes in Paris and Brazil, Clark never mentioned these earlier South American iterations of Concrete art.

54. A tantalizing and emblematically weak link here is the Dutch artist Cesar Domela's *tableaux-objets*, described as *quadro objetos* in the Brazilian newspaper *Jornal do Commercio*, October 10, 1954, and thus after Clark's own use of the term in the Salão Preto e Branco earlier that year. The article, "Cesar Domela e seus quadro-objetos," notes that the artist would exhibit his works alongside Sophie Taueber-Arp and Jean Arp in an exhibition that opened the following week. Another article, "Domela e os quadros-objetos," illustrated with one of his reliefs, appeared in *Forma* 3 (October 1954), n.p. Clark

appeared to have met with Domela around this time, and Jayme Maurício reported that it was the support and intimacy between the artists that catalyzed Clark's ongoing investigations of the organic line. Maurício, "Itinerário das artes plásticas: Lygia Clark três anos depois: Valorização da linha e cromatismos no plano arquitetônico," *Correio da Manhã*, April 7, 1956, section 1, p. 10.

55. Aleca Le Blanc has proposed that the work now known as *Quebra da moldura composição no. 5* is in fact the work Clark sent to the Salão Preto e Branco, prior to a shift in the frame's color scheme and without its interior frame. See Le Blanc, "The Agency of Artists at the Salão Preto e Branco," in Luis Antônio Cruz Souza, Maria Amélia Bilhões, Marília Andrés Ribeiro, and Yacy-Ara Froner, eds., *Arte concreta e vertentes construtivas: Teoria, crítica e história da arte técnica*, Jornada ABCA (Belo Horizonte: Editora ABCA, 2018), pp. 18–33. Because the Salão Preto e Branco ran from May 16 to June 30, 1954, and the Venice Biennale from June 19 to October 17, 1954, however, this appears to be all but impossible.

56. There is no record of Clark traveling to Venice, but she would have certainly seen the catalogue.

57. On Grupo Frente, see Mário Pedrosa, "Grupo Frente" (1955), in Ferreira and Herkenhoff, eds., *Mário Pedrosa: Primary Documents*, pp. 269–72; *Grupo Frente* (Rio de Janeiro: Instituto Brasil-Estados Unidos, 1994); and Adele Nelson, "Artist as Model Citizen: Grupo Frente and Rio Institutions," in Nelson, *Forming Abstraction: Art and Institutions in Postwar Brazil* (Berkeley: University of California Press, 2022), pp. 209–52.

58. Cellulose acetate was widely used in the mid-1950s by library conservationists to laminate documents for protection. On Serpa's work at the Biblioteca Nacional, see Hélio Márcio Dias Ferreira, ed., *Ivan Serpa* (Rio de Janeiro: FUNARTE, 2004), and Mário Pedrosa, *Ivan Serpa: Collage and Painting, August 17 to September 16 1954*, exh. cat. (Washington, DC: Pan American Union, 1954), n.p. Works from this series were exhibited at the Grupo Frente exhibition in 1955 in which Clark also participated.

59. Mário Pedrosa, "Ivan Serpa expõe em Washington, E.U.A," *Forma: Revista de Arquitetura, Artes Plásticas, Teatro* 3 (October 1954), pp. 10–11. See also Pedrosa, "Serpa, mostra-despedida" (1958), in Otilia Arantes, ed., *Mário Pedrosa: Texto escolhidos, Vol 3, Academicos e Modernos* (São Paulo: EdUSP, 1998).

60. Interestingly, these aesthetic values mapped onto economic investments in the frictionless transfer of commodities and information, as I explore in Chapter 3. Serpa's exhibition of these collages at the Pan-American Union in Washington, DC, in 1954 was supported by a shipping company specializing in the US-Brazil line. As Claire Fox has

noted, José Gómez Sicre, director of the Visual Arts Section of the Pan-American Union, explicitly "based his transnational curatorial projects on the principle of commodity exchange and circulation." Fox, *Making Art Panamerican: Cultural Policy and the Cold War* (Minneapolis: University of Minnesota Press, 2013), p. 5.

61. Pia Gottschaller, *Lucio Fontana: The Artist's Materials* (Los Angeles: The Getty Conservation Institute, 2012), p. 28.

62. As Fontana wrote in an undated text, "The discovery of the cosmos is a new dimension, it is infinity, so I made a hole in canvas, which was the basis of all the arts and I created an infinite dimension." Quoted in Enrico Crispolti, *Lucio Fontana: Catalogo generale* (Milan: Edizioni Electa, 1986), p. 19. Gottschaller, in *Lucio Fontana*, notes that while Fontana allowed the slashes of his earliest *Tagli* to open to the wall behind them, he subsequently spanned black gauze across the canvas stretcher so that the viewer would look through to a pure, dimensionless black. Perhaps this is why Ferreira Gullar, after seeing the *Tagli* at the São Paulo Bienal of 1959, wrote that they were "curious, bizarre, and extravagant objects," amounting to a bold, though ultimately "naïve" and "retardaire attempt to destroy the fictitious character of pictorial space through the introduction within it of a real cut." Gullar, "Theory of the Non-Object" (1959). trans. Michael Asbury, in Kobena Mercer, ed., *Cosmopolitan Modernisms* (Cambridge, MA: MIT Press, 2005), p. 172, translation emended.

63. Giancinto di Pietrantonio, "Interview to Tomas Maldonado," in *Arte abstracto argentino: Arte concreto-invencion, Madi, perceptismo* (Buenos Aires: Fundacion Proa, 2003), pp. 23–24.

64. See Iria Candela, "Fontana's Odyssey," and Andrea Giunta, "The War Years: Fontana in Argentina," in *Lucio Fontana: On the Threshold*, exh. cat. (New York: Metropolitan Museum of Art, 2019), pp. 15–27 and 41–49. Madí artists held their second exhibition in October 1946 at the Escuela Altamira, the short-lived school Fontana founded earlier that year. In 1953, writing to Madí artist Gyula Kosice from Italy, Fontana commented that the Madí movement "is for me the best in the world." It "is the most advanced in everything." Lucio Fontana, Letter to Gyula Kosice, February 3, 1953, quoted in Paulo Herkenhoff, *Lucio Fontana: A ótica do invisível*, exh. cat. (Milan: Charta, 2001), p. 145. Several commentators have suggested that the Manifiesto Blanco, which Fontana and his students from Altamira launched the month after the Madí exhibition in 1946, responded rhetorically to the environment of vanguardism established by such artists and may even refer to specific elements of their programs. See di Pietrantonio, "Interview to Tomas

Maldonado," p. 24, as well as Alexander Alberro, *Abstraction in Reverse: The Reconfigured Spectator in Mid-Twentieth-Century Latin American Art* (Chicago: University of Chicago Press, 2017). This manifesto appears to have catalyzed Fontana's subsequent Spatialist manifestos, as well as the appearance of the *Buchi* in 1949. See Fontana's *Primo manifesto dello Spazialismo*, released in 1947 and *Secondo manifesto dello Spazialismo* of 1948 in *Lucio Fontana: Catalogo generale*, pp. 33–36. See also Fontana's *Proposta per un regolamento* of 1951 in Enrico Crispolti, ed., *Lucio Fontana*, exh. cat. (Milan: Electa, 1998), p. 172.

65. Giampiero Giani, "Lucio Fontana," in *La Biennale di Venezia*, exh. cat. (Venezia: Lombroso Editore, 1954), 115. "The canvas is incised, pierced, all of a sudden."

66. Ibid.

67. As Giani wrote, "It is the magical rhythm of astral spaces, the mystery of the void, which is the mystery of the universe." Ibid.

68. Arp's prize was reported in Brazilian newspapers of the time.

69. There are fascinating resonances between Arp's *Horloge* and Clark's circular *Ovo linear*, discussed in Chapter 1, in the way each pictorially evokes, but also produces a relationship to time and durational intervals. In an undated poem titled "Branco" (White), Clark wrote of a desire to "be like the hand of a clock," which "forgets the other passages of marked time" in each "living moment" when "the hand stops." "The point of the real . . . is the white of the support" that "whitewashes" the other passages of time. "Branco," Archives of the Associação Cultural "O Mundo de Lygia Clark," ID 6377. My thanks to Felipe Scovino for this insight.

70. Arp, "I Became More and More Removed from Aesthetics," p. 237. Both Clark in her 1960 text "A morte do plano," and Pedrosa in 1963 described her work in language that recalls Arp's description of the frame and pedestal as "useless crutches," Pedrosa going so far as to suggest the removal of the frame was akin to a mother who takes away the stroller to which a toddler clings so that it might walk. Mário Pedrosa, "A obra de Lygia Clark" (1963), in Arantes, ed., *Mário Pedrosa, acadêmicos e modernos*, pp. 347–54. This triumphant and developmental language is in keeping with a broader narrative concerning the emancipatory transformation of painting as a representational surface into an actualized body in space.

71. Arp, "I Became More and More Removed from Aesthetics," p. 237.

72. Michel Seuphor, "Jean Arp," in *La Biennale di Venezia*, p. 228. Key here is the concept of a membrane, which defines the limits of a body, but allows for both the passage and exertion of pressures from within to without and vice versa. See Fer, "The Laws of

Chance," and Paneth-Pollak, "Definite Means," particularly Chapter 2, "Integumentary Abstraction."

73. Pedrosa, *Ivan Serpa: Collage and Painting*, n.p.

74. These paintings are currently known as *Composição 1* (1954), *Composição 2* (1954), and *Sem Título* (1952). It is likely that the designations *4* and *5* associated with the *Quebra da moldura* works are residues of this grouping, rather than pertaining to the organic line series as such.

75. Paulo Herkenhoff notes this material juxtaposition in "A aventura planar de Lygia Clark—de caracóis, escadas e caminhando," in *Lygia Clark*, exh. cat. (São Paulo: Museu de Arte Moderna de São Paulo, 1999), p. 16.

76. Pia Gottschaller, "Examination Record, Lygia Clark, Composição no. *5* (from "Quebra da moldura" series)", unpublished document. I am grateful to Gottschaller and Zanna Gilbert for their generous conversations and discussions with me as we studied this and other paintings in 2016 and 2017 as part of research for *Pacific Standard Time: LA/LA* at the Getty Conservation Institute. See also Gottschaller, "Making Concrete Art," in Zanna Gilbert, Pia Gottschaller, Aleca Le Blanc, Tom Learner, and Andrew Perchuk, eds., *Making Art Concrete: Brazilian and Argentine Art from the Colección Patricia Phelps de Cisneros*, exh. cat. (Los Angeles: Getty Research Institute, 2017), pp. 25–59.

77. Cunha, "Ligia Clark busca na pintura a expressão do próprio espaço."

78. Jacques Derrida, *The Truth in Painting*, trans. Geoffrey Bennington and Ian McLeod (Chicago: University of Chicago Press, 1987), p. 12. Mónica Amor appeals to Derrida's discussion of the outside/inside distinction in *Of Grammatology* (1976) to think through a broader disruption of subject/object distinctions in Clark's and Hélio Oiticica's trajectories in "From Work to Frame, In Between, and Beyond: Lygia Clark and Hélio Oiticica, 1959–1964," *Grey Room* 38 (Winter 2010), pp. 20–37.

79. Derrida, *The Truth in Painting*, p. 12.

80. Clark described this dynamic in terms of the "valorization" and "devalorization" of the organic line. "Lecture at the Escola Nacional de Arquitetura, Belo Horizonte, Fall 1956," in Butler and Pérez-Oramas, eds., *Lygia Clark: The Abandonment of Art*, p. 54.

81. While the paintings are usually translated as *Breaking the Frame* to emphasize their insurgent, transformational quality, the original Portuguese is more equivocal, conveying, as well, the more straightforward description, *Break of the Frame*.

82. "Contato: Lygia Clark," *Jornal do Centro de Ciências, Letras e Artes* 2 (October 1958): n.p., and "Lygia Clark e o espaço concreto expressional," p. 3.

83. Ricardo Nascimento Fabbrini, *O espaço de Lygia Clark* (São Paulo: Editora Atlas, 1994), p. 32.

84. Ricardo Basbaum, "Within the Organic Line and After," in Alexander Alberro and Sabeth Buchmann, eds., *Art After Conceptual Art* (Cambridge, MA: MIT Press; Vienna: Generali Foundation, 2006), p. 96.

85. Yve-Alain Bois, "Chance Encounters: Kelly, Morellet, Cage," in Julia Robinson, ed., *The Anarchy of Silence: John Cage and Experimental Art*, exh. cat. (Barcelona: Museu d'Art Contemporani de Barcelona, 2010), pp. 192–93. On noncompositional techniques as a broader modernist phenomenon, see Bois's lecture "The Difficult Task of Erasing One-self: Non-Composition in Twentieth-Century Art," The Institute of Advanced Study, March 7, 2007, https://www.youtube.com/watch?v=dQWssOdMwQ4.

86. Kelly exhibited at the Salons des Réalités Nouvelles of 1950 and 1951, the *Tendance* exhibition at Galerie Maeght in 1952, and the Premier Salon des Jeunes Peintures at the Galerie des Beaux-Arts in 1950. Yve-Alain Bois has noted that despite efforts to link Kelly and the Madí artists, the chronology of Kelly's movements suggests that it was unlikely he ever saw the exhibitions in question. See Bois, "Window V, February 1950," in Eric Banks and Yve-Alain Bois, eds., *Ellsworth Kelly: Catalogue Raisonné of Paintings, Reliefs, and Sculpture, Volume 1 1940–1953* (Paris: Cahiers d'art, 2015), pp 166–69. Although Bois was close with Clark in the 1960s and 1970s, when she returned to Paris, she does not seem to have conveyed to him significant recollections of her earlier 1950s sojourn or artists she may have met at that time, beyond her studies with Fernand Léger. See Bois, "Some Latin Americans in Paris," in *Geometric Abstraction: Latin American Art from the Patricia Phelps de Cisneros Collection*, exh. cat. (Cambridge, MA: Harvard University Art Museums, 2001), pp. 77–103. In a conversation with Estrellita Brodsky, Kelly suggested that he was not aware of other Latin American artists living in Paris. Quoted in Dana Miller, "Carmen Herrera: Sometimes I Win," in Miller et al., *Carmen Herrera: Lines of Sight* (New York: Whitney Museum of Art, 2016), p. 39 n. 31. Much later, Clark may well have encountered Kelly's works as part of the US contingent at the São Paulo Bienal of 1961.

87. See Bois, *Ellsworth Kelly*, in particular pp. 12, 140, 151, 193, 224, 270–71.

88. Ibid., p. 134. Interestingly, Clark experimented with "capturing" indexical forms via airbrushed photograms in at least three untitled works made between 1952 and 1956. See *Sem título (Abstrato informal)*, 1952 (ID 55609); *Sem título (Abstrato informal)*, 1956 (ID 55514); and *Sem título (Abstrato informal)*, 1956 (ID 55515), Archives of the Associação Cultural "O Mundo de Lygia Clark." In these works, which are outliers in her oeuvre, she

may well have been informed by Geraldo de Barros's contemporaneous photographic experiments, which included cameraless photograms and indexical processes alongside more traditional photographic works. De Barros was in turn one of the few artists associated with Concretism in São Paulo to frequent Pedrosa's home alongside artists from Rio. See Heloisa Espada, *Geraldo de Barros e a fotografia* (São Paulo: SESC São Paulo, 2015). My thanks to Daniel R. Quiles for bringing my attention to the resonance with de Barros.

89. Lins's account offers considerably more details about these works and differs slightly from Clark's recollections. As Lins writes, "Once in Paris, at Avenue Kléber, as she went down the hall where the sun came in to see herself in the hat rack's mirror, whose hooks were used to hang frames, Lygia encountered shadows that formed geometric figures traced on the walls. She went in search of material and, manipulating a rectangle of paper, recorded structured forms that rose and descended in white, gray, and black. She discovered new projections of abstract drawings by changing the positions of the frames tied to the hangers with thread. Captured by Lygia, [these drawings were] sold when shown at her first individual exhibition in Brazil (Ministry of Education, Rio de Janeiro, 1952)." Lins, *Artes*, p. 54 and 98, translation emended. Clark describes the experiment in an interview within the context of her lack of interest in color. She recalls, "In a series of very little importance I suspended a thing by chance on a hanger and projected the reflection on the wall. I copied it literally. I put down a piece of paper underneath and drew those outlines in black, white, and gray. Since then I've never again added color to a picture." "A quebra da moldura," p. 3.

90. According to Bois's catalogue raisonné, *La combe I*, *II*, and *III* were shown at the 1951 exhibition, while *La combe IV* was shown at the 1951 Salon des Réalités Nouvelles under the title *La combe I: En collaboration avec une jeune fille de douze ans*. *La combe I* was also reproduced in the June 1951 issue of *L'Art d'Aujourd'hui*.

91. In her 1986 interview, "A quebra da moldura," Clark notes that she didn't think too much of Picasso, but that Duchamp and Mondrian were the "great ones of the era for me," Duchamp for "bringing art to life" and Mondrian for "ending with the space of ground and figure" (p. 5).

92. Bois notes that *Cité* was exhibited at the *Tendance* group show at Galerie Maeght in October 1951 under the title *La rêve, ou Projet mural* and *Colors for a Large Wall* at the same group show in 1952.

93. Bois, *Ellsworth Kelly*, p. 272.

94. Kelly, quoted in ibid., p. 268. In his Institute of Advanced Study lecture, Bois notes that "noncomposition" appears to be "unsustainable" and that artists who experimented with noncompositional modes eventually turned back to subjectivity, composition, and choice.

95. See Gabrielle Buffet-Picabia, *Jean Arp* (Paris: Les Presses Littéraires de France, 1952), n.p., and Michel Seuphor, *Mission spirituelle de l'art a propos de l'oeuvre de Sophie Taeuber-Arp et de Jean Arp* (Paris: Berggruen, 1953), p. 14.

96. Bois, *Ellsworth Kelly*, p. 12.

97. It is interesting to note the visual resonance between the black strips and off-center tabs in Kelly's *Colors on Wood*, shown at his 1951 Paris exhibition, and corresponding elements in Clark's *Quebra da moldura* series. In Bois's assessment, *Colors on Wood* is atypical of Kelly in that it is explicitly compositional and thus belongs to a tradition of geometric abstraction the artist otherwise sidestepped. See Bois, entry 111, *Colors on Wood*, in *Ellsworth Kelly*, p. 232. While for Kelly such formal features signal the kind of compositional decision-making, relationality, and balance he otherwise sought to forgo, for Clark, they track a shift in priority from *composition* to *cognition* wherein the organic line emerges within the viewer's space as a by-product of making. Kelly's work comes closest to the organic line in *Saint Louis II* (1950), which was not shown until the 1970s. Here, stacked and painted cardboard strips mounted on a wooden panel result in linear fissures of space that registered the recessed grooves of a building façade the artist encountered in Paris. Unlike Kelly's first version of this motif, which renders the source grooves in lines of black paint, *Saint Louis II* makes lines in the same way that its model does: through shadows cast in actual space. In retrospect, we can recognize what Kelly "transferred" was nothing less than an untheorized and unrecognized organic line.

98. I translate here from a Brazilian Portuguese version of the writings in Eduardo Carreira, ed. and trans., *Os escritos de Leonardo da Vinci sobre a arte da pintura* (Brasília: Editora Universidade de Brasília, 2000), p. 28 (Br. M. 132a). The philosopher Avrum Stroll contrasts Leonardo's notion of a surface as an immaterial entity with a second, commonly held understanding of surface — the Somorjai conception — wherein a surface remains part of the physical entity to which it is attached. Stroll, *Surfaces* (Minneapolis: University of Minnesota Press, 1988).

99. Paul Matisse, ed. and trans., *Marcel Duchamp Notes* (Paris: Centre National d'Art et de Culture Georges Pompidou, 1983). See notes numbers 1–46.

100. Thierry de Duve, *Pictorial Nominalism: On Marcel Duchamp's Passage from Painting to the Readymade* (Minneapolis: University of Minnesota Press, 1991), p. 160.

101. This formulation echoes Gregory Bateson's definition of information in *Steps to an Ecology of the Mind: Collected Essays in Anthropology, Psychiatry, Evolution, and Epistemology* (1972; Chicago: University of Chicago Press, 2000).

102. The literature on 4'33" is vast. Key recent publications include Kyle Gann, *No Such Thing as Silence: John Cage's 4'33"* (New Haven: Yale University Press, 2010); Robinson, ed., *The Anarchy of Silence*; and Dieter Daniels and Inke Arns, eds., *Sounds Like Silence: John Cage — 4'33" — Silence Today — 1912, 1952, 2012* (Leipzig: Spector Books, 2012). In "Within the Organic Line and After," Basbaum briefly notes the affinity between Clark's organic line and Cage's 4'33" in terms of "opening spaces between existing things" (p. 92). See also Camillo Osorio, "Sem título ou da antiarte à não arte: Interrogações a partir de Lygia Clark," which notes Clark and Cage's distinct desires to deindividualize and reinvent the role of the artist in relation to the public and the institutional category of art.

103. John Cage, "Experimental Music" (1955), in *Silence: Lectures and Writings* (Middletown: Wesleyan University Press, 1961), p. 10. The two artists were linked repeatedly, with Duchamp frequently cast as a father figure to Cage and a slightly younger generation of artists including Rauschenberg, among others. See Moira Roth, *Difference/Indifference: Musings on Postmodernism, Marcel Duchamp and John Cage* (London: Routledge, 1999).

104. On Rauschenberg's work of this period, see Hal Foster, "'Made Out of the Real World': Lessons from the Fulton Street Studio," in Leah Dickerman, ed., *Robert Rauschenberg*, exh. cat. (New York: Museum of Modern Art, 2016), pp. 89–97.

105. See Sarah Roberts, "White Painting [three panel]," Rauschenberg Research Project, July 2013. San Francisco Museum of Modern Art, http://www.sfmoma.org/explore/collection/artwork/25855/essay/white_painting. See also Brandon Joseph, *Robert Rauschenberg and the Neo-Avant-Garde* (Cambridge, MA: MIT Press, 2007), and his earlier iteration of the first chapter, "White on White," *Critical Inquiry* 27.1 (Autumn 2000), pp. 90–121. Rauschenberg asked his assistant, the artist Brice Marden, to recreate the series for a 1968 exhibition of the *White Paintings* and also used some of the original panels from the series for later combine works.

106. Robert Rauschenberg, "Letter to Betty Parsons," October 18, 1951, in Dickerman, ed., *Robert Rauschenberg*, p. 230.

107. Emily Genauer, "Art and Artists: Musings on Miscellany," *New York Herald Tribune*, December 27, 1953, quoted in Roberts, "White Painting [three panel]."

108. John Cage, "On Robert Rauschenberg, Artist, and His Work," in Cage, *Silence*, pp. 102–103. This interpretation was cemented by Rauschenberg's own description of the works as "open compositions responding to the activity within their reach" in his 1968 lithograph *Autobiography*.

109. As Rauschenberg noted, "A canvas is never empty." *Sixteen Americans*, exh. cat. (New York: Museum of Modern Art, 1959), p. 58, repeated in Cage, *Silence*, p. 103. See also Charles Stuckey, "Rauschenberg's Everything, Everywhere Era," in Walter Hopps and Susan Davidson. eds., *Robert Rauschenberg: A Retrospective* (New York: Guggenheim Museum, 1998), p. 31.

110. Joseph, "White on White," p. 92. Joseph locates the art-historical precedent for Cage's comment in Man Ray's photograph of dust "breeding" on the surface of Marcel Duchamp's *Large Glass* and László Moholy-Nagy's description of Malevich's *White on White* paintings as "projection screens" (pp. 97–98).

111. Liz Kotz, "Post-Cagean Aesthetics and the 'Event' Score," *October* 95 (Winter 2001), pp. 54–89. Julia Robinson likewise describes the piece in terms of a sealed container that recalls the composer's famed experience in the anechoic chamber in "John Cage and Investiture: Unmanning the System," in Julia Robinson, ed., *John Cage* (Cambridge, MA: October Files, MIT Press, 2011), p. 193.

112. Kotz, "Post-Cagean Aesthetics and the 'Event' Score," p. 70.

113. Cage likewise composed according to time brackets in his *Theater Piece # 1*. See John Cage, Michael Kirby, and Richard Schechner, "An Interview with John Cage," *Tulane Drama Review* 10.2 (Winter 1965), p. 52.

114. See Gann, "The Piece and Its Notations," in *No Such Thing as Silence*, 167–87.

115. Joseph, "White on White," pp. 107–108.

116. Although not predominant in descriptions of the work, critics have observed this phenomenon. In "The Early Work of Robert Rauschenberg: The White Paintings, the Black Paintings, and the Elemental Sculptures," *Arts Magazine* 61 (September 1987), pp. 28–37, Roni Feinstein suggests that the lines produced by the edges refer to Barnett Newman's zips, an argument repeated in Stuckey's 1998 essay in which he suggests that the modular format also facilitated movement and storage.

117. These are the durations noted in the score used at the piece's first performance in 1952, now lost. In 1990, Cage noted that he used tarot cards to build up the piece, a

practice related to his interest in the *I Ching*. See Gann, *No Such Thing as Silence*, p. 175.

118. As James Pritchett notes, it was through such durational structures that Cage understood the equivalence of silence and sound. See "What Silence Taught John Cage: The Story of *4'33"*, in Robinson, ed., *The Anarchy of Silence*, p. 171. See also Cage, "A Composer's Confessions," Lecture at Vassar College (1948), in *Musicworks* 52 (Spring 1992), p. 15.

119. Douglas Kahn, "John Cage: Silence and Silencing," *Musical Quarterly* 81.4 (Winter 1997), pp. 556–98.

120. Robinson describes Cage's inhabitation of these institutional frameworks and codes as form of "symbolic investiture": a "radical dispersal of subjectivity on the unidirectional control of composing." "John Cage and Investiture," pp. 196–97.

121. As Cage remarked in "History of Experimental Music in America," "Jazz per se derives from serious music. And when serious music derives from it, the situation becomes rather silly." *Silence*, p. 72.

122. George Lewis, "Improvised Music after 1950: Afrological and Eurological Perspectives" (1996), *Black Music Research Journal* 22, supplement, Best of BMRJ (2002), pp. 215–46. Lewis likewise quotes musician Anthony Braxton, who noted, "Both aleatory and indeterminism are words which have been coined . . . to bypass the word improvisation and as such the influence of non-white sensibility" (p. 223).

123. Richard Kostelanetz, "His Own Music: Ur-Conversation with John Cage," *Perspectives of New Music* 25.1–2 (Winter–Summer 1987), pp. 88–106. See also Michael Zwerin, "A Lethal Measurement" (1966), in *John Cage: An Anthology*, ed. Richard Kostelanetz (New York: Da Capo, 1991), pp. 162–42.

124. See Rob Wallace, "Writing Improvisation into Modernism," in Rebecca Caines and Ajay Heble, eds., *Improvisation Studies Reader: Spontaneous Acts* (New York: Routledge, 2015), and Lewis, "Improvised Music after 1950." Per my discussion in Chapter 1, this procedure recalls the classical notion of *inventio*, in which discovery and invention remained entwined.

125. As Fred Moten remarks, "The idea of a black avant-garde exists, as it were, oxymoronically — as if black, on the one hand, and avant-garde, on the other hand, each depends for its coherence upon the exclusion of the other." Moten, *In the Break: The Aesthetics of the Black Radical Tradition* (Minneapolis: University of Minnesota Press, 2003), p. 32.

126. Scott DeVaux, "Bebop and the Recording Industry: The 1942 AFM Recording Ban Reconsidered," *Journal of the American Musicological Society* 41.1 (Spring 1988), pp. 126–65.

127. DeVaux notes that publishers of popular music of the swing era objected to improvisation because it "distorted" and "detracted" from the melody. He cites a publisher who complained, "Who can count on them for just one straight melody chorus to plant the refrain with those who might want to buy the song, if they could only tell what the tune was like—what with their way of going haywire after the first eight bars?" Ibid., p. 135.

128. Cage, "A Composer's Confessions," quoted in Kahn, "John Cage: Silence and Silencing," p. 568.

129. See Eva Díaz, "John Cage's Chance Protocols," in Díaz, *The Experimenters: Chance and Design at Black Mountain College* (Chicago: University of Chicago Press, 2015), pp. 53–100.

130. Yvonne Rainer, "Looking Myself in the Mouth," *October* 17 (Summer 1981), p. 73. As Alan Durant likewise observes, "To isolate 'sounds' themselves as intrinsic, spontaneous or autonomous—imagining them outside some determinate relation of hearing—is an idealization which has its counterpart in the would-be invisible social relations of Cage's politics." *Conditions of Music* (Albany: State University of New York Press, 1984), p. 56. Vaughn Anderson has suggested that both Augusto de Campos and Hélio Oiticica arrived at a related criticism of Cage's refusal to consider power relations within silence, even as the poet and artist enthusiastically engaged his work. See Anderson, "'Revision of the Golden Rule': John Cage, Latin America, and the Poetics of Non-Interventionism," *Journal of Modern Literature* 41.1 (Fall 2017), pp. 58–80. On Oiticica's engagement with Cage via Malevich in his 1973 work with Neville D'Almeida, *CC4 Nogacions—Block Experiments in Cosmococa*, see Sérgio B. Martins, "White on White," in Martins, *Constructing an Avant-Garde: Art in Brazil, 1949–1979* (Cambridge, MA: MIT Press, 2013), pp. 161–80. Vivian Crockett has also discussed Oiticica's white monochromes in relation to the inscription on Malevich's *Black Square* in "War Heroes: Toward a Poethics of Blackness in Hélio Oiticica" in Adriano Pedrosa and Tomás Toledo, eds., *Hélio Oiticica: Dance in My Experience*, exh. cat. (São Paulo: Museu de Arte de São Paulo, 2020), pp. 133–245.

131. Maurício, "Artes plásticas: Uma nova e talentosa pintura." Maurício's reportage revolves around his difficulty resolving his gendered expectations of Clark as a young, beautiful mother, "made up as if a cinema star," with the clear force of her work.

132. This contradiction is all the more acute because Cage himself was gay. On a potential "politics of negation" immanent to Cage's (and Duchamp's) "aesthetics of indifference," see Jonathan Katz, "Identification," in Roth, *Difference/Indifference*, pp. 49–68. Eastman composed the piece *Gay Guerrilla* in 1979, but he had always been overt about his

sexuality. As he put it in a 1976 interview, "What I am trying to achieve is to be what I am to the fullest: Black to the fullest, a musician to the fullest, a homosexual to the fullest." Quoted in Renée Levine Packer and Mary Jane Leach, eds., *Gay Guerrilla: Julius Eastman and His Music* (Rochester: University of Rochester Press, 2015), p. 47. On the historical erasure and recent "recovery" of Eastman's work, see Federica Bueti, Antonia Alampi, and Boaventure Soh Bejeng Ndikung, eds., *We Have Delivered Ourselves From The Tonal: Of, Towards, On, For Julius Eastman* (Berlin: Savvy Contemporary, 2018).

133. John Cage, *Song Books: Volume 1* (New York: C. F. Peters, 1970), p. 1.

134. The entire instruction was: "In a situation with maximum amplification (no feedback), perform a disciplined action. With any interruptions. Fulfilling in whole or part an obligation to others. No attention to be given to the situation (electronic, musical, theatrical)." Ibid., p. 31.

135. Transcript of Julius Eastman's interpretation of *Solo for Voice 8 (0'00" [4'33" No. 2])*.

136. "Lecture by John Cage June 5, 1975," *June in Buffalo*, box 3, reel 3, CD 81, tracks 1 and 2, held at the Music Library, SUNY Buffalo. On the relationship between Cage and Eastman apropos of this incident, see Ryan Dohoney, "John Cage, Julius Eastman, and the Homosexual Ego," in Benjamin Piekut, ed., *Tomorrow Is the Question: New Directions in Experimental Music Studies* (Ann Arbor: University of Michigan Press, 2014), pp. 39–62. See also Steve Schlegel, "John Cage at June in Buffalo, 1975," masters thesis, SUNY Buffalo, 2008. On the relations between queerness, closeting, and Zen in Cage's work, see Jonathan Katz, "John Cage's Queer Silence; or, How to Avoid Making Matters Worse," in David W. Bernstein and Christopher Hatch, eds., *Writings through John Cage's Music, Poetry, and Art* (Chicago: University of Chicago Press, 2001), pp. 41–61.

137. See Cage's June 5, 1975, lecture, as well as "Diary: How to Improve the World (You Will Only Make Matters Worse) Continued 1966," in John Cage, *A Year from Monday: New Lectures and Writings* (Middletown: Wesleyan University Press, 1967), p. 59.

138. Lecture by John Cage, June 5, 1975.

139. See Rocco di Pietro, "Message from Julius Eastman and Memoir," in Bueti et al., eds, *We Have Delivered Ourselves From The Tonal*, pp. 118–34.

140. Recounted by Ned Sublette in Renée Levine Packer, "Julius Eastman: A Biography," in Packer and Leach, eds., *Gay Guerrilla*, p. 46. Cage relays in his June 5 lecture that he confronted Eastman immediately after the performance and asked him why he had changed his interpretation from previous realizations of *Song Books*, to which Eastman indicated that he had been "bored" and didn't intend to perform the piece again.

141. In an intriguing weak link, in his 1935 Harvard lectures, Laurence Binyon (whom Pedrosa quoted in his 1947 thesis) noted a painting *Listening to Silence*, attributed to Chou Fang (780–810 CE), as structured around empty spaces that are "even more significant than the figures. The intervals seem brimmed with a listening silence." Binyon, *The Spirit of Man in Asian Art* (Cambridge, MA: Harvard University Press, 1936), p. 77.

142. See Madeleine Bocaro, "Yoko and John . . . Cage," in Bocaro *In Your Mind: The Infinite Universe of Yoko Ono* (Conceptual Books: 2021), https://madelinex.com/2018/09/05/yoko-and-john-cage, and David F. Hoenigman, "Yoko Ono: Forever a Force for Peace," *Japan Times*, November 7, 2009, p. 10. For a close analysis of Cage's time in Japan, see Serena Yang, "'John Cage Shock' and Its Aftermath in Japan," PhD diss., University of Southern California, 2020, and Miki Kaneda, "The 'John Cage Shock' Is a Fiction! Interview with Tone Yasunao, 1," *Post: Notes on Art in a Global Context*, Museum of Modern Art, New York, March 8, 2013, https://post.moma.org/the-john-cage-shock-is-a-fiction-interview-with-tone-yasunao-1. The premiere of *0'00" (4'33" No. 2)* was at the Sogetsu Art Center on October 24, 1962.

143. Lecture by John Cage, June 5, 1975; here Cage refers to Daisetsu Suzuki's teachings on Zen.

144. Moira Roth, "Aesthetics of Indifference" (1977), in *Difference/Indifference*, pp. 33–47.

145. Here we might locate affinities between the indexical character of the organic line and Duchamp's molds in terms of Georges Didi-Huberman's notion of the imprint. See *La resemblance par contact: Archéologie, anachronism et modernité de l'empreinte* (Paris Éditions de Minuit, 2008).

146. Julius Eastman, "Introduction to the Northwestern University Concert," January 16, 1980, disc 3, *Julius Eastman: Unjust Malaise* (New World Records, 2005), also reproduced in Kyle Gann's liner notes for *Unjust Malaise*, "'Damned Outrageous': The Music of Julius Eastman," p. 13. On Eastman's use of the term and its connection to Malcom X's discourse of resistance, see George Lewis, "The Idea of Eastman: Reflections on the Otolith Group's *The Third Part of the Third Measure*," and "Texts for Elegy V3, March 22nd 2018," in Bueti et al., eds. *We Have Delivered Ourselves From The Tonal*, pp. 36–44 and 168–73.

147. Eastman, "Introduction to the Northwestern University Concert." Ellie Hisama analyzes Eastman's *Crazy Nigger* according to this notion of organic music in "'Diving into the Earth': The Musical Worlds of Julius Eastman," in Olivia Bloechl, Melanie Lowe, and Jeffrey Kallberg, eds., *Rethinking Difference in Musical Scholarship* (Cambridge: Cambridge University Press, 2015), pp. 260–86.

148. On Eastman's agonistic relationship to minimalist music, see Sumanth Gopinath, "'Black Forces': Julius Eastman against Minimalism," in Bueti et. al, eds., *We Have Delivered Ourselves From The Tonal*, pp. 174–93.

149. LeRoi Jones [Amiri Baraka], "The Changing Same (R&B and New Black Music)" (1966), in *Black Music* (New York: Da Capo Press, 1998), pp. 180–211.

150. James Snead, "On Repetition in Black Culture," *Black American Literature Forum* 15.4 (Winter 1981), pp. 146–54. The Otolith Group responds to this triadic structure in their 2017 filmic installation about Eastman, *The Third Part of the Third Measure*. On the misinterpretation of such qualities as repetition and syncopation, see Maya Kronfeld, "The Philosopher's Bass Drum: Adorno's Jazz and the Politics of Rhythm," *Radical Philosophy* 2.5 (Autumn 2019),pp. 34–47.

151. Both 21'30" and 22' have also been given as times for *Evil Nigger*. I use 21'05" here to reflect Eastman's notation on his score, but this lack of agreement itself gestures to the piece's larger troubling of clock time's hegemony over the score.

152. Malik Gaines, "Same Difference: Malik Gaines on Julius Eastman," *Artforum* 56.8 (April 2018), pp. 53–54.

153. Ibid.

154. On the possible relationship between these drawings and Clark's teacher Szenes, see Geaninne Gutiérrez-Guimarães, "Lygia Clark: The Early Years, 1948–1952," in *Lygia Clark: Painting as an Experimental Field, 1948–1958*, p. 25.

155. Juliet Mitchell, *Siblings: Sex and Violence* (Cambridge: Polity Press, 2003), p. 44. On Mitchell's applicability to artistic seriality, I am indebted to Mignon Nixon's brilliant article "O + X," *October* 119 (Winter 2007), pp. 6–20, and her interview with Tamar Garb, "A Conversation with Juliet Mitchell," *October* 113 (Summer 2005), pp. 9–26. On the series as a mode of contending with and differentiating modernism, see Briony Fer's crucial study, *The Infinite Line: Re-Making Art After Modernism* (New Haven: Yale University Press, 2004).

156. Mitchell, *Siblings, Sex and Violence*, p. 35.

157. Ibid., p. 223.

158. Ibid., p. 125.

159. Stefani Engelstein, *Sibling Action: The Genealogical Structure of Modernity* (New York: Columbia University Press, 2020), pp. 2 and 27. In a 1976 performance, for example, Eastman sang, "Why don't you make me feel like a natural woman?" Quoted in Packer, "Julius Eastman: A Biography," p. 49. On this note, we might also consider Eastman's

1984 composition *Buddha*, notated in the shape of an egg, as an unwitting rejoinder to the contamination and fertilization of space staged by Clark's *Ovo linear* of 1958. My thanks to Zanna Gilbert for bringing this composition to my attention.

160. As Felipe Scovino has observed, a part-by-part impulse can be identified across Clark's production, from the articulated *Bichos* to the *Corpo coletivo* to *Estruturação do Self*, in which the parts of the body and the subject's memory are (re)stitched. Conversation with the author, July 2022.

161. "Lígia Clark — Prêmio 'Diário de Notícias' na IV Bienal."

162. See "Entrevista para o jornal de Campinas" and Claude, "A mulher na arte moderna."

163. Lygia Clark, "1957 influencias de Albers," diário 4, Archives of the Associação Cultural "O Mundo de Lygia Clark," ID 5881. In 1956, the exhibition *Escola Superior de Desenho de Ulm* at the Museu de Arte Moderna in Rio included panels with photographs and texts of artists associated with the Bauhaus and Ulm, including Albers.

164. Clark, "Ideas about Diverse Points," in Butler and Pérez-Oramas, eds., *Lygia Clark: The Abandonment of Art*, p. 57.

165. Fabbrini, *O espaço de Lygia Clark*, p. 39.

166. See Clark, "Ideas about Diverse Points," 57.

167. Ibid.

168. Several Brazilian artists of the time appealed to both inflections, particularly to describe the way color interacts with recurring geometric elements upon a painterly plane. See, for example, Willys de Castro's *Estudo para Composição VI, distribuição sobre um sistema modulado* (1953) and Samson Flexor's *Modulacão com dominante vermelo* (1954) and *Modulação com círculos (Cromático)* (1956). Flexor exhibited alongside Clark in Venice in 1954.

169. Traces of a longer historiography of modulation and materiality are embedded in Clark's *Grega No. 4* (1955) from the *Superfícies modulados* series: its geometric patterning and concatenation of spatially, graphically, and chromatically delineated lines remember not only the elongated horizontal panels of antique bas-relief, but the tension between literal and depicted space that animated Cubism. See Clement Greenberg, "Collage" (1959), in Greenberg, *Art and Culture: Critical Essays* (Beacon Press, 1961), p. 80. Significantly, Pedrosa described spatiality in terms of modulation in a 1950 article on Cézanne: "We ought not to say to model…but to modulate," noting that the latter entailed producing "the effects of three-dimensionality" by virtue of planar relations, rather than

color. "Modulations between Sensation and Idea" (1950), in Ferreira and Herkenhoff, eds., *Mário Pedrosa: Primary Documents*, pp. 264–67 and 264.

170. This dynamic dissolves dichotomies that inform a certain line of modern art historiography in which artistic intentionality aligns with art's containment, such that individual and pictorial autonomy are cognate processes of mediating one's relation to the world. The affective response of the viewer has little or no role within this lineage, save as a misguided desire for immediacy and presence. See Walter Benn Michaels, *The Shape of the Signifier: 1967 to the End of History* (Princeton: Princeton University Press, 2004), and Todd Cronan, *Against Affective Formalism: Matisse, Bergson, Modernism* (Minneapolis: University of Minnesota Press, 2013).

171. Ronaldo Brito, "Neo-concretism, Apex and Rupture of the Constructive Project," trans. Gabriel Pérez-Barreiro with Irene V. Small, *October* 161 (Summer 2017), p. 140. Sérgio B. Martins has observed a related quality in Amilcar de Castro's sculptures, positing that this "sheer negativity" suggests failure "as a structural, constitutive character" of the work itself. Martins, *Constructing an Avant-Garde*, p. 46.

172. As Pérez-Oramas puts it, "The organic line is a caesura, a break, a fold — a fissure, an absence, a line in absentia. As a negative presence, a nonline, a minus-line or line-minus, it works as an incision between materials." Luis Pérez-Oramas, "If You Hold a Stone," in Butler and Pérez-Oramas, eds., *Lygia Clark: The Abandonment of Art*, p. 40.

173. At times, Clark described the process of recognizing the line in terms of inversion, rendering "full" what had previously been "empty." See, for example, Jean Clay's gloss of her description in "Lygia Clark: Fusion generalisé," *Robho* 4 (1968), pp. 12–14. This notion of *vazio-pleno*, as she put it in 1960 ("The Full-Emptiness," in *Lygia Clark* [1997], pp. 111–13), resonates in certain ways with Martin Heidegger's discussion of an empty jug in his 1950 essay "Das Ding," translated in Fiona Candlin and Raiford Guins, eds., *The Object Reader* (New York: Routledge, 2009), pp. 113–23. Yet the organic line's action in relation to its contiguous entities is more complex than simple inversion. In *Pedra e ar* (1966), for example, an empty plastic bag filled with air embodies the dichotomy empty/full, yet the membrane of the bag itself is a *materialized* organic line insofar as it separates the contained empty/full air from the uncontained air that circulates in the environmental space itself.

174. See Christine Macel, "Lygia Clark: At the Border of Art," in Butler and Pérez-Oramas, eds., *Lygia Clark: The Abandonment of Art*, pp. 252–61, and Kaira Cabañas, "Art without Art," in Cabañas, *Immanent Vitalities: Meaning and Materiality in Modern and*

Contemporary Art (Berkeley: University of California Press, 2021), pp. 89–109, as well as Clark's own discussion of her therapeutic experiences (as patient and therapist) in "Relational Object" (1980), in *Lygia Clark* (1997), pp. 319–27. Following her encounter with the artist in Paris in the 1970s, Suely Rolnik has engaged Clark's practice and its psychoanalytic and political implications in many texts over the years. See, for example, *Cartografia sentimental: Transformações contemporâneas do desejo* (São Paulo: Estação Liberdade, 1989); "Molding a Contemporary Soul: The Empty-Full of Lygia Clark," in Rina Carvajal and Alma Ruiz, eds., *The Experimental Exercise of Liberty*, exh. cat. (Los Angeles: The Museum of Contemporary Art, Los Angeles, 2000), pp. 59–108; Rolnik and Corinne Diserens, eds., *Lygia Clark: Da obra ao acontecimento, somos o molde, a você cabe o sopro* (São Paulo: Pinacoteca do Estado de São Paulo, 2006); and "Suely Rolnik on Lygia Clark: Interview with Lars Bang Larsen," *Afterall* 15 (May 2009), pp. 24–34. See also Tania Rivera, "Ensaio sobre o espaço e o sujeito: Lygia Clark e a psicanálise," *Agora* 11.2 (July–December 2008), pp. 219–33.

175. Silveira, *Imagens do inconsciente*, p. 272.

176. See Hirszman, *Em busca do espaço cotidiano*.

177. See Lula Wanderley, *O dragão pousou no espaço: Arte contemporânea, sofrimento psíquico e o objeto relacional de Lygia Clark* (Rio de Janeiro: Rocco, 2002), and Kaira Cabañas, ed., *No silêncio que as palavras guardam: O sofrimento psíquico, o objeto relacional de Lygia Clark e as paixões do corpo* (São Paulo: N-1 Edições, 2021). As Wanderley recounts, he first encountered Nise de Silveira at a reading group conducted at her house, after which she invited him to intern with her at the Casa das Palmeiras, an outpatient clinic she had founded in 1956. Wanderley met Clark through his wife, Gina Ferreira, in the early 1980s. Toward the conclusion of his own therapy with Clark as part *Estruturação do Self*, Clark asked Wanderley to continue her methods, providing him with a set of the objects and materials she herself used in the process. See also Cabañas's introduction to an English version of Wanderley's text, "Art's Histories without Art History," and Gina Ferreira's "Lend Me Your Eyes," *ARTMargins* 11.3 (October 2022), pp. 126–33 and 134–38, respectively.

178. Wanderley, interview with author, October 20 and 21, 2017.

179. On the implications of this body, see José Gil, "Abrir o corpo," in Rolnik and Diserens, eds., *Lygia Clark: Da obra ao acontecimento*, pp. 63–66.

180. Lygia Clark, "Relational Object," pp. 320–21. Clark also describes these objects in Mário Carneiro's 1984 film *Memória do corpo*.

181. Clark, "Relational Object," p. 321.

182. Luiza Martelotte Simões de Carvalho Martins, "Linhas e erotismo, encostar na

ponta de agulha: Lygia Clark e a Estruturação do Self," masters thesis, Universidade Federal Fluminense, 2021, pp. 56–57. Martelotte, who underwent sessions of *Estruturação do Self* administered by Gina Ferreira, further suggests that the process can be analogized to a sewing machine that "unmakes" or "unsews," rather than makes.

183. Clark, "Relational Object," p. 322.

184. Cabañas, "Art without Art," p. 107.

185. See Rolnik, "Uma terapêutica para tempos desprovidos de poesia," in Rolnik and Diserens, eds., *Lygia Clark: Da obra ao acontecimento*, pp. 13–26.

186. Martelotte, "Linhas e erotismo, encostar na ponta de agulha," p. 13. As Gil writes, "To open the body is to create a zone in which the body, seen from the exterior to the interior, enters in contagion with the world." "Abrir o corpo," p. 66.

187. Eastman, "Introduction to the Northwestern University Concert," p. 13.

188. Summers, *Real Spaces*, p. 350.

CHAPTER THREE: INHABITING NETWORKS, SUBJECTING SPACE

The epigraphs are from Le Corbusier, *The Modulor: A Harmonious Measure to the Human Scale Universally Applicable to Architecture and Mechanics* (1950; Cambridge, MA: Harvard University Press, 1954), p. 124; Lygia Clark, *Meu doce rio* (1975; Rio de Janeiro: Galeria Paulo Klabin, 1984), p. 15; and Le Corbusier, *Precisions on the Present State of Architecture and City Planning: With an American Prologue, a Brazilian Corollary, Followed by "The Temperature of Paris" and "The Atmosphere of Moscow,"* trans. Edith Schreiber Aujame (1930; Cambridge, MA: MIT Press, 1991), p. 12.

1. On the *dispositif* (apparatus) as an ensemble of relations, see Michel Foucault, "Confessions of the Flesh" (1977), in Foucault, *Power/Knowledge: Selected Interviews and Other Writings, 1972–1977*, ed. Colin Gordon, trans. Colin Gordon, Leo Marshall, John Mepham, and Kate Soper (Brighton: Harvester, 1980), p. 194. On the spatial logic of colonial cartography, see Walter Mignolo, *The Darker Side of the Renaissance: Literacy, Territoriality, and Colonization* (Ann Arbor: University of Michigan Press, 1995); James Ackerman, ed., *Decolonizing the Map: Cartography from Colony to Nation* (Chicago: University of Chicago Press, 2017); and primary documents in Jordana Dym and Karl Offen, eds. *Mapping Latin America: A Cartographic Reader* (Chicago: University of Chicago Press, 2011).

2. Henrique Mindlin, *Modern Architecture in Brazil* (New York: Reinhold, 1956), pp. 9–10.

3. Bernhard Siegert, "Introduction: Cultural Techniques, or, The End of the Intellectual Postwar in German Media Theory," and "(Not) in Place: The Grid, or, Cultural Techniques of Ruling Spaces," in Siegert, *Cultural Techniques: Grids, Filters, Doors, and Other Articulations of the Real*, trans. Geoffrey Winthrop-Young (New York: Fordham University Press, 2015), pp. 1–18 and 97–120. See also Hans Ulrich Gumbrecht and K. Ludwig Pfeiffer, eds., *Materialities of Communication* (Stanford: Stanford University Press, 1994).

4. Siegert, "(Not) in Place," p. 97.

5. Ernst Neufert, *Bauentwurfslehre Grundlagen, Normen und Vorschriften über Anlage, Bau, Gestaltung, Raumbedarf, Raumbeziehungen; Maße für Gebäude, Räume, Einrichtungen und Geräte mit dem Menschen als Maß* (Berlin: Bauwelt, 1936), published in English as *Architects' Data*, ed. and rev. Rudolf Herz, trans. G. H. Berger et al. (London: Lockwood, 1970).

6. Ernst Neufert, *Arte de proyectar en arquitectura: Fundamentos, normas y prescripciones sobre construccion* (Buenos Aires: Cili, 1948). Significantly, Walter Gropius, with whom Neufert studied and worked, won the top prize for architecture at the Second São Paulo Bienal in 1953.

7. Ana-Maria Meister, "From Form to Norm: Systems and Values in German Design circa 1922, 1936, 1954." PhD diss., Princeton University, 2018.

8. Thomas French and Charles Vierck, *A Manual of Engineering Drawing for Students and Draftsmen* (New York: McGraw Hill, 1953), p. vi. See also Molly Nesbit's groundbreaking account of Marcel Duchamp's engagement with the technical drawing as gendered cultural artifact in Nesbit, *Their Common Sense* (New York: Black Dog, 2000).

9. Francesca Hughes, *The Architecture of Error: Matter, Measure, and the Misadventures of Precision* (Cambridge, MA: MIT Press, 2014). Contemporaneous to Clark's discovery, for example, Earle Buckingham expressed an anxiety about the lack of a "common and consistent practice for the expression of tolerances and their application or translation into definite measuring and manufacturing plants." Buckingham, *Dimensions and Tolerances for Mass Production* (New York: The Industrial Press, 1954), p. 4.

10. Le Corbusier, *The Modulor*, pp. 120–21. The first edition was published in French by Editions de l'Architecture d'Aujourd'hui; a second edition and second volume were released in 1954.

11. Le Corbusier, *The Modulor*, p. 121.

12. Ibid., p. 107, emphasis in the original.

13. Although independence movements began much earlier, the Franco-Algerian War commenced in 1954, the same year as the prominent second edition of *The Modulor*.

14. Le Corbusier, *The Modulor*, p. 122.

15. Ibid., p. 125.

16. As Meister notes of this adjustment, "What Neufert designed was the grid, not the object." "From Form to Norm," p. 166.

17. On the humanist implications of proportion, see Rudolf Wittkower, *Architectural Principles in the Age of Humanism* (1949; New York: W. W. Norton, 1998), a 1952 edition of which Mário Pedrosa had in his library. The first issue of *Habitat* features reporting on the Modulor, including Nelson Rockefeller's critique that "human scale" is in fact "variable, adatable, and flexible" and thus potentially dangerous if fixed in a universal canon. "Novo mundo do espaço de Le Corbusier," *Habitat: Arquitetura e Artes no Brasil* 1 (October–December 1950), n.p.

18. See *Construa você mesmo seu espaço para viver* (1960), *Estuturas de caixas de fósforos* (1964), and *Arquiteturas biológicas* (1969), among many others. Clark applied for a patent for the concept of *Construa você mesmo seu espaço para viver* in 1963. On Clark's engagement with architecture, see, for example, Zeuler R. M. de A. Lima, "Ceci n'est pas un mur: The Architecture of Organic Lines," in Cornelia Butler and Luis Pérez-Oramas, eds., *Lygia Clark: The Abandonment of Art, 1948–1988*, exh. cat. (New York: Museum of Modern Art, 2014), pp. 72–75; Megan Sullivan, "Lygia Clark: Interior Spaces," in Sullivan, *Radical Form: Modernist Abstraction in South America* (New Haven: Yale University Press, 2022), pp. 163–205; and Adrian Anagnost, "Scattered Wall: Waldemar Cordeiro and Lygia Clark," in Anagnost, *Spatial Orders, Social Forms: Art and the City in Modern Brazil* (New Haven: Yale University Press, 2022), pp. 130–61.

19. Fernando Cocchiarale and Anna Bella Geiger, "Entrevista Lygia Clark," in Cocchiarale and Geiger, eds., *Abstracionismo geométrico e informal: A vanguarda brasileira nos anos cinqüenta* (Rio de Janeiro: FUNARTE, 1987), p. 150.

20. In a text of the following year, Clark inverted the concepts, writing "now the body is the house." Clark, "O homem, estrutura viva de uma arquitetura biológica e cellular," trans. in *Lygia Clark* exh. cat. (Barcelona: Fundació Antoni Tàpies, 1997), pp. 247–48. On the relation between these propositions, see André Lepecki, "Affective Geometry, Immanent Acts: Lygia Clark and Performance," in Butler and Pérez-Oramas, eds., *Lygia Clark: The Abandonment of Art*, pp, 278–89.

21. Sérgio Antonio Bessa, "Word-Drool: The Constructive Secretions of Lygia Clark," in Butler and Pérez-Oramas, eds., *Lygia Clark: The Abandonment of Art*, pp. 301–305.

22. Clark, *Meu doce rio*, p. 15.

23. Ibid., pp. 16–17.

24. Ibid., p. 41. Clark's typescript "Piadas," appears to have been a source document, because several of its jokes appear in the final version. Archives of the Associação Cultural "O Mundo de Lygia Clark," ID 6459.

25. The lecture appears to have taken place on September 3 or 4, 1956, and was followed by a conference organized by Pedrosa on the synthesis of the arts. See "Itinerário das artes plásticas," *Correio da Manhã*, August 30, 1956, section 1, p. 12. The text of the lecture was first published in *Jornal do Brasil*, October 7, 1956, section 2, p. 5, and as "Uma experiência de integração," in *Brasil-Arquitetura Contemporânea* 8 (1956), p. 45. The following year, it was also published as "Pintora mineira (Ligia Clark) descobre linhas orgânicas nas artes plásticas," *Diário de Minas*, January 27, 1957, n.p., trans. as "Lecture at the Escola Nacional de Arquitetura, Belo Horizonte, Fall 1956," in Butler and Pérez-Oramas, eds., *Lygia Clark: The Abandonment of Art*, pp. 54–55.

26. These latter two works are now known as *Superfície modulada no. 5* (1955) and *Maquette para Interior no. 2* (1955).

27. Almeida Cunha, "Ligia Clark busca na pintura a expressão do próprio espaço," *Folha da Noite*, September 22, 1958. See also Jayme Maurício, "Itinerário das artes plásticas: Lygia Clark três anos depois: Valorização de linha a cromatismos no plano arquitetônico," *Correio da Manhã*, April 7, 1956, section 1, p. 10, and Lygia Clark, "1957—Entrevista para o jornal de Campinas," diário 4, Archives of the Associação Cultural "O Mundo de Lygia Clark," ID 61701.

28. "Lígia Clark—Prêmio 'Diário de Notícias' na IV Bienal," *Jornal Diário de Notícias: A Revista Feminina*, October 13, 1957, Archives of the Associação Cultural "O Mundo de Lygia Clark," ID 4590.

29. The catalogue lists the works as *Superfície modulada no. 4*, *Superfície modulada no. 5*, and *Superfície modulada no. 6* and *Maquette de interior no. 1*, *Maquette de interior no. 2*, and *Maquette de interior no. 3*, all from 1955. The maquette pictured in the photograph of Clark and Gullar at this exhibition does not appear to be one of the three extant maquettes, which suggests Clark may have lost and remade at least one of them.

30. Fernand Léger, "The Wall, The Architect, The Painter" (1933), in Léger, *Functions of Painting* (Thames and Hudson, 1994), p. 95, and Christopher Green, *Léger and the Avant-Garde* (New Haven: Yale University Press, 1974). See also Sonia Delaunay, "The Influence of Painting on Fashion Design" (1926), in Arthur A. Cohen, ed., *The New Art of Color: The Writings of Robert and Sonia Delaunay*, trans. David Shapiro and Arthur A.

Cohen (New York: Viking, 1978), pp. 203–207, and Amédée Ozenfant "La peinture murale: Divorce de l'architecture de la peinture," *Encyclopédie française*, vol. 16 (Paris: Comité de l'Encylopédie Française, 1935), pp. 70–76.

31. Romy Golan, *Muralnomad: The Paradox of Wall Painting, Europe 1927–1957* (New Haven: Yale University Press, 2009), p. 5.

32. See Fernand Léger, "La peinture mural" (March 1952), in *Derriere le miroir* (Paris: Maeght, 1958), p. 6, as well as "The Wall, The Architect, The Painter," p. 95. Paulo Herkenhoff notes Clark's possible debt to Léger in terms of the wall as a living surface in "Lygia Clark," in *Lygia Clark* (1997), p. 37.

33. See Clement Greenberg, "The Situation at the Moment" (1948), and "The Crisis of the Easel Picture" (1948), in John O'Brian, ed., *Clement Greenberg: The Collected Essays and Criticism, Volume 2: Arrogant Purpose, 1945–1949* (Chicago: University of Chicago Press, 1986), pp. 192–96 and 221–25.

34. Sonia Delaunay's work was also exhibited in Brazil in exhibitions such as Leon Degand's *Do figurativismo ao abstracionismo* at the Museu de Arte de São Paulo in 1949. Mondrian was given a special exhibition in the São Paulo Bienal of 1953; the 1955 São Paulo Bienal included a special exhibition of Sophie Taeuber-Arp within the Swiss presentation that included over forty works, including numerous studies for Café Aubette.

35. See the group's inaugural manifesto, "Manifeste du Groupe Espace," *L'Architecture d'Aujourd'hui* 37 (October 1951), p. 9. The collective was founded by André Bloc, who published *L'Architecture d'Aujourd'hui* and *Art d'Aujourd'hui*, both of which were mouthpieces for the synthesis of the arts during the early 1950s. On the period discourse, see Joan Ockman, "A Plastic Epic: The Synthesis of the Arts Discourse in France in the Mid-Twentieth Century," in Eeva-Liisa Pelkonen and Esa Laaksonen, eds., *Architecture + Art: New Visions, New Strategies* (Helsinki: Alvar Aalto Academy, 2007), pp. 30–61.

36. See "A 1a exposição do Grupo Frente," *O Globo*, July 7, 1954, and "Em poucas linhas," *Correio da Manhã*, August 2, 1955. The latter notes that the renowned architect Lúcio Costa accompanied Clark to the exhibition, where she showed him her maquettes.

37. *Grupo Frente: Segunda mostra coletiva, Julho 1955*, exh. cat. (Rio de Janeiro: Museu de Arte Moderna do Rio de Janeiro, 1955), n.p. The article "Tapeçaria, arte mural," *Forma* 2 (August 1954), n.p., regarding the exhibition of French tapestry artist Jean Lurçat at the Museu de Arte Moderna do Rio de Janeiro, which Clark retained in her archives, likewise echoes key elements of the discourse around the synthesis of the arts.

38. A. L. Quadros, "Grupo Frente," *Forma* 2 (August 1954), n.p.

39. See "De Henrique E. Mindlin para Lygia Clark, 8 Março 1956," ID 10844; "De Jorge Machado Moreira para Lygia Clark, 23 Março 1956," ID 10840; "De Oscar Niemeyer para Lygia Clark, 8 Março 1956," ID 10830; "De Affonso Eduardo Reidy para Lygia Clark, 2 Março 1956," ID 10848; "De Carmen Portinho para Lygia Clark, 3 Março 1956," ID 10835, Archives of the Associação Cultural "O Mundo de Lygia Clark." See also Mindlin, *Modern Architecture in Brazil.*

40. "De Jorge Machado Moreira para Lygia Clark."

41. "De Oscar Niemeyer para Lygia Clark."

42. Maurício, "Itinerário das artes plásticas: Lygia Clark três anos depois." Extracts from statements by Mindlin and Pedrosa were also included in an article "Abandono de la decoracion para integrar arquitectura," in the Spanish-language newspaper *El País*, January 7, 1957. As Adele Nelson notes, apropos of Lucy Teixeira's article "Una esperienza brasiliana," *Commentari* (October–December 1957), pp. 287–91, the project for Niemeyer was intended for the Conjunto Kubitschek, now known as Edifício JK, and that another collaboration was planned with the architect Leopoldo Teixeira Leite for a school in the city of Itatiaia. Nelson, "On Gender and Surface in Lygia Clark's Early Abstraction," in *Lygia Clark: Painting as an Experimental Field, 1948–1958*, exh. cat. (Bilbao: Guggenheim Bilbao, 2020), p. 63 n. 4. Lula Wanderley further notes that the architect Sergio Bernardes possessed a document in which he and Clark requested permission to present a project for public housing to the mayor of Rio. "Through the Broad Windows of MAM," in *Lygia Clark (1920–1988): 100 anos*, exh. cat. (Rio de Janeiro: Edições Pinakotheke, 2021), p. 299 n. 2.

43. Clark, "Lecture at the Escola Nacional de Arquitetura, Belo Horizonte, Fall 1956," pp. 54–55.

44. Clark discussed the importance of diffusing art to the general population, as well as her experiments with design and architecture in "A mulher na arte moderna," *Querida* 117 (April 1959), p. 46, and "Lygia Clark (pintora concretista): 'A arte me disciplina e me educa,'" *Jornal do Brasil*, August 8, 1957, Archives of the Associação Cultural "O Mundo de Lygia Clark," ID 5567. In his text for Clark's 1952 exhibition, Jamil Hamoudi describes her work in terms of the "monumental" style, suggesting affinities to Léger's and others' language regarding the synthesis of the arts. Le Corbusier's own rhetoric shifted from "synthesis" to "union" over the years.

45. See, for example, Mário Barata, "A arquitetura como plástica e a importância atual da síntese das arts," *Brasil—Arquitetura Contemporânea* 7 (1956), pp. 11–12; Rino

Levi, "Síntese das artes plásticas," *Revista Acrópolis* 16.192 (September 1954), p. 45; and Mário Pedrosa, "A cidade nova—Síntese das artes," *Habitat: Arquitetura e Artes no Brasil* 57 (November–December 1959), pp. 11–13. See also Fernanda Fernandes, "A síntese das artes e a moderna arquitetura brasileira dos anos 1950," *Cadernos de Pós-Graduação da UNICAMP* 8 (2006), pp. 71–78.

46. On techniques of production and their implications in this period, see Zanna Gilbert, Pia Gottschaller, Tom Learner, and Andrew Perchuk, eds., *Purity Is a Myth: The Materiality of Concrete Art from Argentina, Brazil, and Uruguay* (Los Angeles: Getty Research Institute and Getty Conservation Institute, 2021).

47. António Bento echoes these sentiments in "Lígia Clark," *Módulo* 2.5 (September 1956), pp. 38–39.

48. Clark, "Lecture at the Escola Nacional de Arquitetura, Belo Horizonte, Fall 1956," pp. 54–55, translation emended.

49. Lúcio Costa, "A crise da arte contemporânea," *Brasil—Arquitetura Contemporânea* 1 (August–September 1953), p. 3.

50. Interestingly, a short newspaper item published after Clark's Belo Horizonte lecture suggested the disciplinary instability of the organic line, noting that the audience "ended up thinking 'that' was neither painting, nor art, nor nothing." "Figuras," *Jornal do Brasil*, October 14, 1956, section 2, p. 5. Another critic characterized Clark's work and Concrete art more broadly as mere decoration: any work could be "a bathroom wall, the floor of a living room or terrace, any such thing." "Artes plásticas: Lygia Clark e o concreto," *O Estado de São Paulo*, September 30, 1958. Archives of the Associação Cultural "O Mundo de Lygia Clark," ID 4466.

51. Mário Pedrosa, "Lygia Clark, or the Fascination of Space" (1957), in Glória Ferreira and Paulo Herkenhoff, eds., *Mário Pedrosa: Primary Documents*, trans. Steve Berg (New York: Museum of Modern Art, 2016), p. 286.

52. Antoine Fasani, *Eléments de la peinture murale: Pour une technique rationelle de la peinture. Contribution à l'art monumental modern* (Paris: Bordas, 1951), pp. 8–9 and 238. Le Corbusier wrote the preface for Fasani's book, noting, "The wall has its laws, its rules, its potential, its vitality" (p. 1).

53. Ibid., pp. 25–26.

54. Frank Lloyd Wright, *The Language of Organic Architecture* (Scottsdale: Taliesin West, 1953), p. 3. See also Wright, *The Future of Architecture* (New York: Plume, 1953); Wright, *An Organic Architecture: The Architecture of Democracy* (Cambridge, MA: MIT

Press, 1939); Enrico Tedeschi, *Frank Lloyd Wright* (Buenos Aires: Editorial Nueva Visión, 1955); and Bruno Zevi, *Towards an Organic Architecture* (London: Faber and Faber, 1950).

55. See Detlef Martins, "Living in a Jungle: Mies, Organic Architecture, and the Art of City Building," in Phyllis Lambert, ed., *Mies in America* (New York: Harry Abrams Press, 2001), p. 597.

56. Leon Battista Alberti, *On the Art of Building in Ten Books*, trans. Joseph Rykwert, Neal Leach, and Roger Tavernor (Cambridge, MA: MIT Press, 1988), pp. 23–25.

57. Amédée Ozenfant, *Foundations of Modern Art*, trans. John Rodker (London: Vision Press, 1952), p. 151.

58. The relation between modularity and natural, symbolic proportion is likewise articulated in such texts as Gyorgy Kepes, "Symmetry, Proportion, Module," in Kepes, *The New Landscape in Art & Science* (Chicago: Theobald, 1956), in which he notes that modularity, while an inherent product of industrialized societies, expresses "an absolute measure of interdependence between God and nature" (p. 333).

59. Lygia Clark, "Caramujo da praia rasa," diário 2, Archives of the Associação Cultural "O Mundo de Lygia Clark," ID 61939, published in Butler and Pérez-Oramas, eds., *Lygia Clark: The Abandonment of Art*, p. 162, translation emended.

60. See G. S. Rousseau, ed., *Organic Form: The Life of an Idea* (Boston: Routledge and Kegan Paul, 1972); Caroline van Eck, *Organicism in Nineteenth-Century Architecture: An Inquiry into Its Theoretical and Philosophical Background* (Amsterdam: Architectura and Natura Press, 1994); Peter Collins, "The Biological Analogy," in Collins, *Changing Ideals in Modern Architecture, 1750–1950* (Montreal: McGill-Queens University Press, 1965); and Raymond Williams, s.v. "Organic," in Williams, *Keywords: A Vocabulary of Culture and Society* (Oxford: Oxford University Press, 1985).

61. Eliot Noyes, *Organic Design in Home Furnishings*, exh. cat. (New York: Museum of Modern Art, 1941), p. 28.

62. Ibid.

63. Sigfried Giedion, *Space, Time, and Architecture: The Growth of a New Tradition* (1941; Cambridge, MA: Harvard University Press, 1967), p. 105, my emphasis. Reinhold Martin tracks the subsequent inscription of the organic within corporate systems in *The Organizational Complex: Architecture, Media, and Corporate Space* (Cambridge, MA: MIT Press, 2003).

64. Henrique Mindlin, "Analyse racional do projeto (metodo Klein)," *Acropole* 1.3 (July 1938), p. 39; Lúcio Costa, *Considerações sôbre arte contemporânea* (Rio de Janeiro: Ministério da Educação e Saúde, 1952), pp. 6–7.

65. Clark, quoted in Maurício, "Itinerário das artes plásticas," p. 10.

66. Clark already noted the importance of working in a team in her 1956 Belo Horizonte lecture. See also "1957 — Entrevista para o jornal de Campinas," in which she mentions an architect, sculptor, and psychologist who would work specifically on the question of color.

67. Ibid.

68. Clark, "Lecture at the Escola Nacional de Arquitetura, Belo Horizonte, Fall 1956," p. 54.

69. Mário Pedrosa, "Integration of the Arts," *Brazilian-American Survey* 3 (1955–1956), p. 61.

70. The opposition between the mechanical and the organic became stronger in Clark's later articulations, inflected in part by the context of Neoconcretism. By 1960, she wrote, "A 'living thing' is always in direct contact with space, externally, having at the same time its interior 'expressivity.' Space itself (mimics) movement. A machine only has expression intimately linked to its function and this is exactly why [a living thing] doesn't become a mechanical object, which has nothing transcendent about it ([or] interior time, for that matter)." IV Documentos A Diários, diário 2, 1960, p. 3, Archives of the Associação Cultural "O Mundo de Lygia Clark."

71. See Peter Cramer, "Report on Brazil," *Architectural Review* 116.694 (October 1954), pp. 235–36.

72. On Clark's early work, see Geaninne Gutiérrez-Guimarães, "Lygia Clark: The Early Years, 1948–1952," in *Lygia Clark: Painting as an Experimental Field, 1948–1958*, pp. 17–31.

73. Herkenhoff, "Lygia Clark," p. 37. See also Herkenhoff, "A aventura planar de Lygia Clark — de caracóis, escadas e caminhando" in *Lygia Clark*, exh. cat. (São Paulo: Museu de Arte Moderna de São Paulo, 1999), and Suely Rolnik, "Entrevista com Paulo Herkenhoff," in *Lygia Clark: Da obra ao acontecimento, somos o molde, a você cabe o sopro,* exh. cat. (São Paulo: Pinacoteca do Estado, 2006), pp. 81–87.

74. Lygia Clark, "Meu contato com Burle Marx" in "Carta de Lygia em 6 pontos," 1980, Archives of the Associação Cultural "O Mundo de Lygia Clark," ID 6840. According to Clark, Burle Marx first introduced her to major figures of European modernism such as Pablo Picasso, Piet Mondrian, and Henri Matisse. She notes, however, that her interest in the "sensitive" and "animal" character of life preexisted her time under his tutelage.

75. Alfred Barr, *Cubism and Abstract Art*, exh. cat. (New York: Museum of Modern

Art, 1936), p. 19. The term "biomorphic" was coined by Geoffrey Grigson in "Comment on England," *Axis* (January 1935), p. 8.

76. Max Bill, "O inteligente iconoclasta, entrevista de Flavio d'Aquina em 'Manchete,'" *Habitat: Arquitetura e Artes no Brasil* 12 (September 1953), pp. 34–35. Bill further criticized Brazilian architects for their use of "free form, organic form, [and] free plan" in "O arquiteto, a arquitetura, a sociedade," *Habitat: Arquitetura e Artes no Brasil* 14 (January–February 1954), pp. A–B.

77. See Oliver Botar, "Defining Biocentrism," in Oliver Botar and Isabel Wünsche, eds., *Biocentrism and Modernism* (Burlington: Ashgate, 2011), pp. 15–45.

78. As Roger Caillois put it in an essay on Burle Marx, "The garden installs within a crude space a neatly arranged minigeography, gently dislocated from nature." Caillois, "Jardins Possíveis" (1975), in Jacques Leenhardt, ed., *Nos jardins de Burle Marx* (São Paulo: Perspectiva, 1994), p. 2.

79. Mindlin, *Modern Architecture in Brazil*, p. 240. See also Lauro Cavalcanti and Farès el-Dahdah, eds., *Roberto Burle Marx, 100 anos: A permanência do instável*, exh. cat. (Rio de Janeiro: Editora Rocco, 2009). The designs for this garden were also exhibited at the Second São Paulo Bienal, in which Clark also participated. Jacques Leenhardt has also commented on this "double register" of displacement in "O jardim: Jogos de artifícios," in Leenhardt, ed., *Nos Jardins de Burle Marx*, pp. 6–42.

80. As William Howard Adams has noted, such sharply defined lines were a "consistent element of [Burle Marx's] design strategy," one that required "the most intense skills of execution and maintenance, defying nature to rebut the artist's argument." Adams, *Roberto Burle Marx: The Unnatural Art of the Garden*, exh. cat. (New York: Museum of Modern Art, 1991), p. 22.

81. Isabela Ono and Julio Ono, interview with author, Escritório de Paisagem Roberto Burle Marx, October 20, 2017, Rio de Janeiro. The *cinto* (belt) or *divisor da canteiro* (plant bed divider) would typically be set 20 to 30 centimeters deep.

82. Tim Ingold, *The Life of Lines* (London: Routledge, 2015).

83. Alfred Barr, *Painting and Sculpture in the Museum of Modern Art* (New York: Museum of Modern Art, 1948), p. 175. This volume was in Pedrosa's library.

84. Mário Pedrosa, "Dentro e fora da Bienal" (1954), in Mário Pedrosa, *Dos murais de Portinari aos espaços de Brasília*, ed. Aracy Amaral (São Paulo: Perspectiva, 1981), pp. 47–54.

85. On shifting approaches to the construct of the wall and exhibition design in Brazil in this period, see Anagnost, *Spatial Orders, Social Forms*, particularly Chapters 3 and 4.

86. Ferreira Gullar, *Lygia Clark: Uma experiência radical, 1954–1958*, exh. cat. (Rio de Janeiro: Departamento de Imprensa Nacional, 1958), n.p.

87. Tomás Maldonado, *El arte concreto y el problema de lo ilimitado: Notas para un estudio teórico, Zürich 1948* (Buenos Aires: Ramona, 2003), n.p.

88. On the progression of these experiments, see Juan N. Melé, *La vanguardia del 40: Memorias de un artista concreto* (Buenos Aires: Ediciones Cinco S.A., 1999), and Pino Monkes, "Argentine Concrete Art, the First Decade: Between Material and Formal Tradition and Innovation," in Gilbert et al., eds, *Purity Is a Myth*, pp. 236–51.

89. Melé, *La vanguardia del 40*, p. 99. Melé further noted that works were realized on these moveable, but stable grounds in light of "the impossibility of approaching an integral art (a plastic art tightly linked to architecture)" (p. 239).

90. Maldonado notes in *El arte concreto y el problema de lo ilimitado: Notas para un estudio teórico*, that the notion of creation of pictures with transportable structures (the "muro portátil") was a "grave error." See also Alexander Alberro, *Abstraction in Reverse: The Reconfigured Spectator in Mid-Twentieth-Century Latin American Art* (Chicago: University of Chicago Press, 2017). Maldonado's approach resonates with practitioners such as László Moholy-Nagy, who described the importance of a holistic, totalizing approach to design in *Vision in Motion* (Chicago: Theobald, 1947).

91. See Raúl Lozza, "El Perceptismo," in Nelly Perazzo, *El arte concreto en la Argentina en la década del 40* (Buenos Aires: Ediciones de Arte Gaglianone, 1983), pp. 109–20, and Mario H. Gradowczyk and Nelly Perazzo, *Abstract Art from the Río de la Plata: Buenos Aires and Montevideo, 1933–1953* (New York: Americas Society, 2001). Although Lozza created a complex system of color tables and equations to advance the aims of *cualimetría*, scholars have yet to identify the systematicity of this system, and it appears that intuition, in the end, was as much a guiding force as anything else. Significantly, Lozza himself noted that Perceptismo structures were not strictly mathematical or geometric, but organic in "La nueva estructura de la pintura perceptista," *Perceptismo: Teórico y polémico* 3 (November 1951), pp. 2–3 and 8.

92. See, for example, Raúl Lozza, "El color en el arte: Resumen y fragmentos de un libro en prensa," *Perceptismo: Teórico y polémica* 1 (October 1950), pp. 3 and 6–8.

93. Gabriel Pérez-Barreiro, "The Argentine Avant-Garde 1944–1950," PhD diss., University of Essex, 1996, p. 273.

94. Abraham Haber, "Pintura y arquitectura," *Perceptismo: Teórico y polémica* 2 (August 1951), n.p.

95. In her review of an exhibition at Galería Van Riel, Blanca Stábile likewise notes the contradictory status of Lozza's reliefs vis-à-vis literal and pictorial space, in this case calling attention to the shadows cast by Lozza's forms upon the wall. For Stábile, this three-dimensionality—and the intrusion of the shadows that results—destroys the notion of a neutral ground. Stábile, "Artistas no figurativos," *Ver y Estimar: Cuadernos de Crítica Artística* 3.14–15 (November 1949), n.p.

96. This architectural feature is known as a "reveal" in English and *rodapé invertido* in Portuguese. Other terms used by Latin American architects for a recessed molding include *canteria*, *dilatación*, and *zócalo rehundido*. "Reveal" already appears in English in art and architectural dictionaries in the mid-twentieth century, where it refers primarily to vertical recesses around door or window frames, a classical precedent of which was the *scotia* (from the Greek *skotos*, or darkness), which was a decorative element used to create shadow lines. See Charles Dagobert D. Runes and Harry G. Schrickel, *Encyclopedia of the Arts* (New York: Philosophical Library, 1946), and Henry H. Saylor, *Dictionary of Architecture* (New York: Wiley, 1952). For more contemporary definitions, see Howard Walker, *Theory of Mouldings* (New York: W. W. Norton, 2007), John F. Pile. *Dictionary of 20th-Century Design* (New York: Facts on File, 1990), and Allen Edward and Patrick J. Rand, *Architectural Detailing: Function, Constructability, Aesthetics* (New York: Wiley and Sons, 2016). My thanks to Julian Rose for his assistance and generative conversations about this architectural element.

97. The retrospective appears to retain both possibilities of this edging element: as a physical distinction along the horizontal edge and as a painted one along the vertical.

98. Isabel Plante, "Printing Invention: Artwork, Project, or Device," in Gilbert et al., eds., *Purity Is a Myth*, pp. 181–99. Here, Plante also argues compellingly for the philosophical valence of the artwork as device for artists associated with Concrete art.

99. See, for example, Alfred Barr's catalogues *Modern Architecture, International Exhibition, New York February 10 to March 23, 1932*, exh. cat. (New York: Museum of Modern Art, 1932), and *De Stijl, 1917–1928*, exh. cat. (New York: Museum of Modern Art, 1952), in which he notes that Theo van Doesburg and J. J .P. Oud abolished moldings around doors to purge thickness and weight. Fellow De Stijl members such as Vilmos Huszar likewise suppressed the distinction between walls and doors in order to intensify the spatiality of color. See Nancy Troy, *The De Stijl Environment* (Cambridge, MA: MIT Press, 1983). On the reemergence of joining itself as an ornament expressed on the surface, see Hughes, *The Architecture of Error*, and Beatriz Colomina, *Privacy and Publicity: Modern Architecture as Mass Media* (Cambridge, MA: MIT Press, 1996).

100. Such partitions appear in the influential work of Herbert Bayer in the 1930s and in Lina Bo Bardi's numerous experiments with museum and pavilion architecture of the 1950s. See Alexander Dorner, *The Way Beyond "Art": The Work of Herbert Bayer* (New York: Wittenborn, Schultz, 1947), as well as Bo Bardi's designs of the unrealized Museum at the Seashore. They were likewise used in numerous exhibitions in the years around Clark's discovery of the organic line, including at a 1952 exhibition of Roberto Burle Marx's work hosted by the Museu de Arte de São Paulo.

101. The feature appears in installation images of both Bienal venues, at the Pavilhão dos Estados (now Pavilhão das Culturas Brasileiras), as well as in the famed Pablo Picasso exhibition and upper galleries at the Pavilhão das Nações (now Museu Afro Brasil), both of which had been newly constructed in the Parque Ibirapuera. Floor plans for the exhibition indicate that the feature was a detail of the permanent walls. The biennial's exhibition designers also used numerous freestanding partitions.

102. Georg Simmel, "Bridge and Door," trans. Mark Ritter, *Theory, Culture & Society* 11.1 (1994), p. 7.

103. See Yve-Alain Bois, "Mondrian and the Theory of Architecture," *Assemblage* 4 (October 1987), pp. 102–30, and Theo van Doesburg, "Towards a Plastic Architecture" (1924), in Hans L. C. Jaffe, ed., *De Stijl* (New York: H. N. Abrams, 1971), p. 186.

104. In his review of the Second Grupo Frente exhibition, Antônio Bento notes that Clark first looked to the tradition of Neoplasticism, but found it insufficient in terms of the integration of painting and architecture. Bento, "Lígia Clark," *Modulo* 1.5 (September 1956), pp. 38–39.

105. Herkenhoff, "A aventura planar de Lygia Clark," p. 17.

106. Teixeira, "Una esperienza brasiliana."

107. The intersecting and overlapping bands recall certain of Léger's abstract works from the 1920s, which Clark may have encountered while studying with him in France between 1950 and 1952.

108. On the relation between pictoriality and architecture, see, for example, Beatriz Colomina, "Where Are We?," in Eve Blau and Nancy Troy, eds., *Architecture and Cubism* (Cambridge, MA: MIT Press), pp. 158–66, and Hubert Damisch, "The Slightest Difference: Mies van der Rohe and the Reconstruction of the Barcelona Pavilion," in Damisch, *Noah's Art: Essays on Architecture* (Cambridge, MA: MIT Press, 2016), pp. 213–28.

109. Claude, "A mulher na arte moderna, p. 46.

110. "A quebra da moldura: Entrevista de Lygia Clark a Luciano Figueiredo e Matinas

Suzuki Jr.," *Folhetim de Folha de São Paulo*, March 2 1986, p. 4. See also Cunha, "Ligia Clark busca na pintura a expressão do proprio espácio," in which Clark differentiates between organic and mechanistic approaches to seriality.

111. Mark Wigley, "Whatever Happened to Total Design?," *Harvard Design Magazine* 5 (Summer 1998), http://www.harvarddesignmagazine.org/issues/5/whatever-happened-to-total-design.

112. Siegert, "Door Logic, or, The Materiality of the Symbolic," in *Cultural Techniques*, p. 193 and Gottfried Semper, *Style in the Technical and Tectonic Arts, or, Practical Aesthetics* (1860–1862; Los Angeles: Getty Publications, 2004).

113. Simmel, "Bridge and Door," p. 8.

114. Siegert, "Door Logic, or, The Materiality of the Symbolic," p. 194.

115. Sergio Delgado Moya, "Lygia Clark, at Home with Objects," in Delgado Moya, *Delirious Consumption: Aesthetics and Consumer Capitalism in Mexico and Brazil* (Austin: University of Texas Press, 2017), pp. 153–92.

116. Clark, "Lecture at the Escola Nacional de Arquitetura, Belo Horizonte, Fall 1956," p. 55, translation emended.

117. A 1944 letter from Clark's father to her husband, Aluízio Clark-Ribeiro, a civil engineer for the mining industry, following an argument between the couple, entreated Aluízio not to abandon the marriage, despite Lygia's "many defects," and to reinstate the true "value" of home and family. "Carta de Jair Lins, pai de Lygia Clark, para Aluízio marido de Lygia Clark, August 4 1944," Archives of the Associação Cultural "O Mundo de Lygia Clark," ID 10622. The title of Antonio Belucco's 1961 article likewise suggests the patriarchal attitude of Clark's father: "Pai de Lygia Clark queria a filha lavando panelas" (Lygia Clark's father wanted his daughter washing pots), *Revista Binomio* (September 18, 1961) Archives of the Associação Cultural "O Mundo de Lygia Clark," ID 5557. Clark and Aluízio separated shortly after Clark's return to Rio from Paris in August 1952.

118. Nelson, "On Gender and Surface in Lygia Clark's Early Abstraction," p. 63. Nelson notes that Clark declared, "Art does not have a gender" in the 1957 interview "A mulher na arte moderna," but suggests that the artist's use of industrial materials, as prominently displayed in her profile in the women's magazine *Querida*, constituted a challenge to gender stereotypes (p. 71).

119. Siegert writes, "As long as doors functioned as operators of difference between inside and outside, they also helped to create, in line with the public-private distinction, an asymmetry of knowledge. Doors produce an information gap." They "are crucial

actors in the distribution and circulation of knowledge." "Door Logic, or, The Materiality of the Symbolic," p. 201.

120. "Un armario multiple," *Nuestra Arquitectura* 22.254 (July 1951), pp. 276–79. The unit was designed by the Italian architect P. A. Chessa.

121. As indicated here, Le Corbusier's original French is in fact not *machine à vivre*, but he always translated the phrase as "machine for living."

122. Le Corbusier, fourth lecture, "A Dwelling at Human Scale," Thursday, October 10, 1929, Faculty of Exact Sciences, in *Precisions*, p. 87.

123. Ibid., p. 87.

124. Ibid. Hans Arp and Vicente Huidobro may have parodied Le Corbusier's various articulations of such cells for living in their 1931 "posthistorical novella" when they wrote of man being replaced by a "hermaphrometallic globule," a "perfectly standardized" commodity whose "living space is never more than 25 cubic centimeters. Arp and Huidobro, "Save Your Eyes," from "Three Exemplary Novellas," in *Arp on Arp: Poems, Essays, Memories*, ed. Marcel Jean, trans. Joachim Neugroschel (New York: Viking, 1972), p. 51.

125. In this parable of creative insight, Columbus, who has been told that his discovery of the Americas was inevitable, challenges his detractors to make an egg stand on its tip. When they can't, he taps the egg slightly on the table, flattening its tip, and thus allowing it to stand on end.

126. Le Corbusier, *Precisions*, p. 88.

127. Ibid.

128. Ibid., p. 90, emphasis in the original.

129. Ibid., pp. 64 and 66.

130. Anne Anlin Cheng, *Second Skin: Josephine Baker and the Modern Surface* (Oxford: Oxford University Press, 2011), p. 13.

131. Fabiola López-Durán, "Picturing Evolution: Le Corbusier and the Remaking of Man," in López-Durán, *Eugenics in the Garden: Transatlantic Architecture and the Crafting of Modernity* (Austin: University of Texas Press, 2018), pp. 144–92.

132. Le Corbusier, "Commentaires relatifs à Moscou et à la 'Ville Verte'" (1930), in Jean-Louis Cohen, *Le Corbusier et la mystique de l'USSR: Théories et projets pour Moscou, 1928–1936* (Brussels: Éditions Mardaga, 1987), quoted in López-Durán, p. 176. Le Corbusier also discusses his visits to the *favelas* of Rio de Janeiro in *Precisions*, where he speaks in admiring, though highly patronizing tones, of their inhabitants.

133. See Jean-Claude Baker and Chris Chase, *Josephine: The Hungry Heart* (New York: Random House, 1993), p. 164.

134. Cheng, *Second Skin*, p. 95.

135. Le Corbusier, *Precisions*, p. 87.

136. Cheng, *Second Skin*, p. 77. On Loos's Baker house, see Beatriz Colomina, "The Split Wall: Domestic Voyeurism," in Beatriz Colomina, ed., *Sexuality and Space* (New York: Princeton Architectural Press, 1992), pp. 73–80; Darell Wayne Fields, "House for Josephine Baker (Parody Series)" (2003), in *HarlemWorld: Metropolis as Metaphor*, exh. cat. (New York: Studio Museum in Harlem, 2004); Ines Weizman, "Tuning into the Void: The Aurality of Adolf Loos's Architecture," *Harvard Design Magazine* 38 (Spring–Summer 2014), http://www.harvarddesignmagazine.org/issues/38/tuning-into-the-void-the-aurality-of-adolf-looss-architecture; and Mario Gooden, *Dark Space: Architecture, Representation, Black Identity* (New York: Columbia Books in Architecture and the City, 2016). Le Corbusier proposed building an orphanage for Baker in 1936, although this project was never realized or designed. Le Corbusier's letters to his mother discuss Josephine Baker; Baker's own letters note that Le Corbusier dressed as her in blackface.

137. See "Lígia Clark — Prêmio 'Diário de Notícias' na IV Bienal."

138. Ingold, *The Life of Lines*, p. 24.

139. See Semper, *Style in the Technical and Tectonic Arts*.

140. Colomina, "The Split Wall: Domestic Voyeurism."

141. One exception to the absence of specific claims to function occurs in Pedrosa's "Integration of the Arts," which captions an illustration of one of the maquettes "Interior of a Living Room" (pp. 60–61).

142. Simmel, "Bridge and Door," p. 5.

143. In 1953, Clark designed sets for a play, gaining notice for an unusual solution to the problem of transforming one backdrop into another. "Festival do Rio," *Diário de Notícias*, November 15, 1953, section 1, p. 8. Clark likewise designed an interior office for the Museu de Arte Moderna at its construction site and a vitrine for the museum to be installed in the Brazilian Ministry of Tourism as part of a UNESCO campaign in 1956, suggesting an awareness of architecture as solicitation and display. See "Iniciada ontem a construção do Museu de Arte Moderna do Rio," *Correio da Manhã*, December 10, 1954, p. 1, and "Vitrine de Lygia Clark para o museu," *Correio da Manhã*, October 14, 1956, p. 18.

144. Mondrian's set designs were for Seuphor's 1926 play *L'éphémère est eternal*. Clark likewise would have been familiar with Mondrian's experiments with dispersing colored

panels across the walls of his studio, illustrated in *L'art abstrait* and reproduced in Brazil in Michel Seuphor, "A integração das artes é possível?," *Suplemento Dominical do Jornal do Brasil*, October 18, 1956, section 2, p. 5.

145. Spyros Papapetros, *On the Animation of the Inorganic: Art, Architecture, and the Extension of Life* (Chicago: University of Chicago Press, 2012).

146. Sandro Mezzadra and Brett Neilson, *Border as Method, or, The Multiplication of Labor* (Durham: Duke University Press, 2013), p. viii, and Étienne Balibar, "What Is a Border?," in Balibar, *Politics and the Other Scene* (London: Verso, 2002), pp. 75–86.

147. Mezzadra and Neilson, *Border as Method*, p. 251.

148. Ibid. See also Matthew Hart, "Threshold to the Kingdom: The Airport Is a Border and the Border Is a Volume," *Criticism* 57.2 (Spring 2015), pp. 173–89, who observes how the two-dimensionality of the border swells into a three-dimensional volume in extraterritorial zones such as airports.

149. Mezzadra and Neilson, *Border as Method*, p. 166.

150. Wendy Brown, *Walled States, Waning Sovereignty* (New York: Zone Books, 2010), p. 65.

151. Ibid., p. 143.

152. Kalindi Vora, *Life Support: Biocapital and the New History of Outsourced Labor* (Minneapolis: University of Minnesota Press, 2015).

153. Ibid., pp. 32 and 5.

154. Ibid., p. 14.

155. On the relationship between these two regimes of capitalism, see Husan L. Hsu, "Mika Rottenberg's Productive Bodies," in *Mika Rottenberg*, exh. cat. (Amsterdam: Appel Arts Center, 2011), pp. 94–115.

156. As Rottenberg explains, "I wanted viewers to respond physically, so this expansion and contraction of space will also happen in viewers' bodies, kind of like ASMR triggers. I tried to play with two cinematic logics, one more linear logic of special connections and synthetic continuity, making disconnected locations appear linked, and then the other is more of a structuralist film logic, where the cut from A to B creates new meaning." Rottenberg in Margot Norton, ed., *Mika Rottenberg: Easy Pieces*, exh. cat. (New York: New Museum, 2019), p. 23.

157. Clark, "1957 — Entrevista para o jornal de Campinas." Sergei Eisenstein tellingly described the ideogrammatic principle of filmic montage as "copulative," fusing the two inflections of the organic. Eisenstein, "The Cinematographic Principle and the

Ideogram" (1929), in Jay Leyda, ed. and trans., *Film Form: Essays in Film Theory* (New York: Harcourt Brace Jovanovich, 1977), p. 29. The literature on the cinematic interval is vast. I note here in particular Dziga Vertov's 1923 manifesto, "Kinoks: A Revolution," in Vertov, *Kino-Eye: The Writings of Dziga Vertov,* trans. Kevin O'Brien (Berkeley: University of California Press, 1984), pp. 11–20, and Trinh T. Minh-ha, *Cinema Interval* (New York: Routledge, 1999).

158. Online Etymology Dictionary, s.v. "Symbol," https://www.etymonline.com/word/symbol which notes that "symbol" combines *syn-,* "together," and *bole,* "a throwing, a casting, the stroke of a missile, bolt, beam."

159. Aristotle, *Categories; On Interpretation; Prior Analytics,* trans. H. P. Cooke and Hugh Tredennick (Cambridge, MA: Loeb Classical Library, 1938), p. 115. On the *symbolon* and Aristotle's philosophy of language, see Ömer Ayugün, *The Middle Included: Logos in Aristotle* (Evanston: Northwestern University Press, 2017), particularly Chapter 6, "Speech (Logos in the Politics)," pp. 159–66. See also Roy Harris, "Derrida's Saussure," in Harris, *Saussure and His Interpreters* (Edinburgh: Edinburgh University Press, 2003), pp. 171–88.

160. Borders, symbolic and otherwise, play a particularly generative — and fraught — role in the relationships between guests and hosts embodied in the Greek concept of *xenia,* or hospitality. On this relation, see, for example, Anne Carson, *Economy of the Unlost: Reading Simonides of Keos with Paul Celan* (Princeton: Princeton University Press, 1999), and Tomaz Grusovnik, Eduardo Mendieta, and Lenart Skof, eds., *Borders and Debordering: Topologies, Praxes, Hospitableness* (New York: Lexington Books, 2018).

161. Carson, "Alienation," in *Economy of the Unlost,* pp. 10–44, and David Graeber, *Debt: The First 5,000 Years* (Brooklyn: Melville House, 2011), pp. 298–305.

162. Carson, "Alienation," p. 18.

163. Peta Carlin, *On Surface and Place: Between Architecture, Textiles and Photography* (New York: Routledge, 2018), p. 69.

164. Louis Sullivan, "Kindergarten Chats" (1900), quoted in Sigfried Giedion, *Space, Time and Architecture: The Growth of a New Tradition* (Cambridge, MA: Harvard University Press, 2009), p. 874; see also Wright, *The Future of Architecture.*

165. Siegert, "Door Logic, or, The Materiality of the Symbolic," p. 193.

166. Ibid.

167. On this viral metaphor, see Ricardo Basbaum, "The Production of the Artist as Collective Conversation," lecture, Simon Fraser University, 2014, https://youtu.be/EpyKioofN8M. This metaphor was particularly resonant with the politicized rhetoric

around AIDS and viral transmission at the time. See, for example, Gregg Bordowitz, *General Idea: Imagevirus* (London: Afterall Books, 2010).

168. Basbaum recalled that he first learned of Lewin through Vito Acconci's descriptions of his early work. See Basbaum, "From 'love songs' to Other Rhythms," in *Ricardo Basbaum: Diagrams, 1994—Ongoing* (Berlin: Errant Bodies Press, 2016), pp. 125–44.

169. Kurt Lewin, *Principles of Topological Psychology*, trans. Fritz Heider (New York: McGraw Hill, 1936).

170. Pedrosa had copies of Lewin's *Principles of Topological Psychology* (1936); *A Dynamic Theory of Personality: Selected Papers* (1935); *Resolving Social Conflicts: Selected Papers on Group Dynamics* (1948); and *Field Theory in Social Science: Selected Theoretical Papers* (1951/1952), the latter of which contains the diagram "The life spaces of a husband and a wife and the social field containing them both."

171. Humberto Maturana, introduction to *Autopoiesis and Cognition: The Realization of the Living* (London: D. Reidel, 1980), p. xxix. Basbaum recalls that the first diagram pertaining to this relationship dates to 1993 and remains private. The 1994 diagram reproduced here is his first public diagram, which dispensed with names in favor of the generic shifters "me" and "you."

172. "The Phrases We Keep Repeating: A Conversation Between Ricardo Basbaum, Adeline Lépine and Tanja Baudoin" (2020), unpublished text.

CODA: OF MUTANT COORDINATES AND LIVING THINGS

The epigraphs are from Félix Guattari, *Chaosmosis: An Ethico-Aesthetic Paradigm*, trans. Paul Bains and Julian Pefanis (Bloomington: Indiana University Press, 1995), p. 106, and Humberto Maturana and Francisco Varela, *The Tree of Knowledge: The Biological Roots of Human Understanding* (Boston: Shambala Press, 1987), p. 245.

1. Kazimir Malevich, *The Non-Objective World*, trans. Howard Dearstyne (1927; Chicago: Paul Theobald, 1959), p. 14.

2. Ibid., p. 26.

3. Malevich, "Introduction to the Theory of the Additional Element in Painting," in *The Non-Objective World*, pp. 10–65. See also Mark Cheetham, *Abstract Art against Autonomy: Infection, Resistance, and Cure Since the 1960s* (Cambridge: Cambridge University Press, 2006), who suggests that Malevich's vision poses a model of impure abstraction that "overturns any claim to aesthetic autonomy." (p. 2)

4. Lygia Clark, "1957—Entrevista para o jornal de Campinas," diário 4, Archives of the Associação Cultural "O Mundo de Lygia Clark," ID 61701.

5. Varela notes that the term "autopoiesis" first appeared in his notes in May 1971 and that he and Maturana had produced the complete English text of "Autopoiesis: The Organization of the Living" by December of that year. The text was first published in Spanish as *De máquinas y seres vivos: Una teoría de la organización biológica* (Santiago: Editorial Universitaria, 1973). The original English version did not appear until 1980 as *Autopoiesis and Cognition: The Realization of the Living* (London: D. Reidel, 1980). Francisco Varela, "The Early Days of Autopoiesis," in Bruce Clarke and Mark B. N. Hansen, eds., *Emergence and Embodiment: New Essays on Second-Order Systems Theory* (Durham: Duke University Press, 2009), pp. 62–76.

6. Humberto Maturana, "Introduction," in *Autopoiesis and Cognition*, p. xv, my emphasis.

7. Guattari, *Chaosmosis*, p. 106.

8. Ibid., p. 28.

9. Quoted in Tina Kukielski, "Fade Through Black," in Michael Riedel, *Michael Riedel: Poster-Painting-Presentation* (New York: David Zwirner Books, 2016), p. 7. See also Niklas Luhmann, *Art as a Social System*, trans. Eva Knodt (Stanford: Stanford University Press, 2000).

10. Kukielski, "Fade Through Black," p. 8.

11. Michael Riedel, quoted in Eva Linhart, "Grafik als Kunst," in *Michael Riedel: Grafik also Ereignis, 9. Juni-14. October 2018, Texte zur Austellung*, exh. cat. (Frankfurt: Museum Angewandte Kunst, Frankfurt am Main, 2018), p. 89 and p. 101 n. 12.

12. Carl Schmitt, *The Nomos of the Earth in the International Law of the Jus Publicum Europeaum* (1950; Candor: Telos Press, 2006), see Chapter 1, note 16.

13. Riedel, quoted in Kukielski, "Fade Through Black," p. 9.

14. In *Chaosmosis*, Guattari explores this possibility by emphasizing ontological heterogeneity, transversality, and emergence, rather than operational closure. See also Mark B. N. Hansen's discussion of the philosopher Cornelius Castoriadis (himself a friend of Varela's) in "System-Environment Hybrids," in Clarke and Hansen, eds., *Emergence and Embodiment*, pp. 113–42.

15. See Cameron Rowland, *91020000*, exhibition pamphlet (New York: Artists Space, 2016), n.p, https://texts.artistsspace.org/uwccıtpk.

16. Maturana and Varela, *Autopoiesis and Cognition*, pp. 70–71.

17. Maturana, introduction to *Autopoiesis and Cognition*, p. xvi. Maturana further describes the term "autopoiesis" as a "word without history" and thus capable of inaugurating a new understanding of living systems (p. xvii).

18. Ibid., p. xxviii.

19. Francisco Varela, "Reflections on the Chilean Civil War," *Lindisfarne Letter* 8 (Winter 1979), pp. 13–19. See also John Protevi, "Beyond Autopoiesis: Inflections of Emergence and Politics in Francisco Varela," in Clarke and Hansen, eds., *Emergence and Embodiment*, pp. 94–112.

20. Maturana, introduction to *Autopoiesis and Cognition*, p. xxix. More recently, Maturana indicated that he subsequently preferred to remain within the biological interpretation of autopoiesis, even as he recognized that the concept allowed for new interpretations of its applicability. Conversation with the author, Santiago de Chile, September 11, 2015.

21. Fred Moten, *Black and Blur*, vol. 1 of *consent not to be a single being* (Durham: Duke University Press, 2017). Moten borrows the phrase from Édouard Glissant.

22. Maturana, introduction to *Autopoiesis and Cognition*, pp. xxvii–xviii.

23. Humberto Maturana, "Biology of Cognition" (1970), in *Autopoiesis and Cognition*, pp. 28–29 and 51.

24. Sylvia Wynter and Katherine McKittrick, "Unparalleled Catastrophe for Our Species?," in McKittrick, ed., *Sylvia Wynter: On Being Human as Praxis* (Durham: Duke University Press, 2015), pp. 9–89. See also Sylvia Wynter, "Unsettling the Coloniality of Being/Power/Truth/Freedom: Towards the Human, After Man, Its Overrepresentation—An Argument,'" *CR: The New Centennial Review* 3.3 (Fall 2003), pp. 257–337, and "The Ceremony Found: Towards the Autopoietic Turn/Overturn, Its Autonomy of Human Agency and Extraterritoriality of (Self-)Cognition," in Jason R. Ambroise and Sabine Broeck, eds., *Black Knowledge / Black Struggles: Essays in Critical Epistemology* (Liverpool: Liverpool University Press, 2015), pp. 184–252.

25. Wynter, "Unparalleled Catastrophe for Our Species?" Wynter's phrase "hybridly human" refers to Frantz Fanon's imperative to take sociogeny into account alongside phylogeny and ontogeny, which also anticipates and critically differences the more recent "epigenetic turn" associated with the philosopher Catherine Malabou. See Malabou, in Alexander Miller, et. al, "On Epigenesis," *October* 175 (Winter 2021), pp. 109–44.

26. Wynter, "Unsettling the Coloniality of Being/Power/Truth/Freedom."

27. Considering that the *passe-partout* refers both to a framing mat and a master

key, it is significant that Guattari notes that the spatial interval between a lock and key is the alterity that transforms discrete parts into an autopoietic machine. *Chaosmosis*, pp. 43–45.

28. I have discussed the implications of this approach to medium apropos Niklas Luhmann's and Fritz Heider's medium/form distinctions and the importance of the observer in "Medium Aspecificity / Autopoietic Form," in Alexander Dumbadze and Suzanne Hudson, eds., *Contemporary Art: 1989–Present* (London: Wiley Blackwell, 2013), pp. 117–25.

29. Significantly, this work likewise recasts Clark's characterization of individualist expression or invention as a form of "vomiting" into a collective action.

30. As David Summers observes, this epistemology inheres etymologically in such concepts as "explanation," "explication," and "display." Summers, *Real Spaces: World Art History and the Rise of Western Modernism* (London: Phaidon, 2003), pp. 349–50.

31. As Ricardo Nascimento Fabbrini observes, the organic line subverts the fixity of definitions and the presumption that "every plane is flat, without gaps . . . a square is a quadrilateral, each of whose sides are equal." In this sense, the organic line is "the retentive trace of a loss — a sign of disappearance." Fabbrini, *O espaço de Lygia Clark* (São Paulo: Editora Atlas, 1994), p. 41.

32. Avrum Stroll, *Surfaces* (Minneapolis: University of Minnesota Press, 1988), p. 20.

33. Quoted in "Entrevista Lygia Clark," in Fernando Cocchiarale and Anna Bella Geiger, eds., *Abstracionismo geométrico e informal: A vanguarda brasileira nos anos cinqüenta* (Rio de Janeiro: FUNARTE, 1987), p. 148.

34. Variations of this phrase appear in multiple texts written singly or jointly by Maturana and Varela, including in Maturana's 1970 text "Biology of Cognition," which sparked the theorization of autopoiesis.

35. The emphasis on observation was particularly galvanizing for second-order cybernetics and later systems theorists such as Luhmann. In her work on the Venezuelan artist Gego, Mónica Amor has appealed to Luhmann's thought as a way of articulating the contingency of modernity, aesthetic canons, and the role of the viewer. See Amor, "On the Contingency of Modernity and the Persistence of Canons," in Terry Smith, Okwui Enwezor, and Nancy Condee, eds., *Antinomies of Art and Culture: Modernity, Postmodernity, Contemporaneity* (Durham: Duke University Press, 2008), pp. 81–96, and "Edge," in *Gego: Weaving the Space in Between* (New Haven: Yale University Press, 2023), pp. 1–13.

36. See Katherine McKittrick, "Yours in the Intellectual Struggle: Sylvia Wynter and the Realization of the Living," and Wynter and McKittrick, "Unparalleled Catastrophe for Our Species?," in McKittrick, ed., *Sylvia Wynter*, pp. 1–8 and 9–89.

37. See Francisco Varela, "A Calculus for Self-Reference," *International Journal of General Systems* 2.1 (1975), pp. 5–24.

38. George Spencer-Brown, *Laws of Form* (1969; New York: Julian Press, 1972), p. v.

39. Ibid., p. 3.

Index

ABSTRACTION: Arabic calligraphy and
ancient Iraqi art, 41; and avant-garde, 192;
and Cage, 217; Clark's work as radical
proclamation of, 123; vs. Concretism,
171–72; and *Descoberta da linha orgânica*,
125; and figuration, 73; Latin American,
65; MoMA's chart of (1936), 36, 37;
and organic line, 249; possibilities of,
blasted open by modern art, 10; and
representation, 77, 149, 272; and subject
misrecognized as object, 151; vanguard,
179; violence of, 127.

Abstractions (group show), 192.

Abyssal line, 86, 133.

Acconci, Vito, 324.

Açotex (Brazilian company), *240*, 241–43, 255.

Adorno, Theodor, 313.

Affect, 50, 69–70, 164, 266, 292–93, 298, 301, 326,
340; and viewer, 419 n.170.

Africa: African art, 131, 151; African diaspora,
97; Marinetti on, 391 n.122; rectangular
shipping cartons for export from, 246.
See also Anti-Blackness; Black art; Race/
racialization.

Agamben, Giorgio, 53; *The Signature of All
Things*, 26.

Alberro, Alexander, 385 n.78.

Albers, Josef, 229; *Homage to the Square*, 231;
Structural Constellations, 229, 231.

Alberti, Leon Battista, 263; *De pictura*, 60.

Alchemy, 139, 393–94 n.147.

Alexander VI, Pope, 86.

Allais, Alphonse, *Album primo-avrilesque*, 93, 94.

Allende, Salvador, 41, 337.

Alvarez, Mariola, 357 n.12.

Americas, invention of, 86–87.

Amor, Mónica, 369 n.103, 407 n.78, 443 n.35.

Anagnost, Adrian, 53, 431 n.85.

Anand, Mulk Raj, 43.

Andre, Carl, 35, 40–41.

Anti-Blackness, 98, 129; echoed in Malevich's
Black Square, 129, 131, 145, 149. *See also*
Race/racialization.

Anzieu, Didier, 234.

Architecture: anonymity of, 259; and art, 259–
65, 274, 282, 286; baseboard molding, 164,
165, 279–80, 282, 432 n.96, 433 n.99; built
environment, 257, 262, 283, 310; Clark's
architectural experiments, 249, *250*, 251,
261, 287; Clark's architectural maquettes,
74, 160, *250*, 254, 257, *258*, 260–61, 274, 282–
83, *284*, 285, 287, 297–300, 305, 310, 312–13, 315,
316; Clark's carpentry apprenticeship, 160,
257, 298; Clark's enthusiasm for, 251, 423
n.18; Clark's lecture at architecture school
in Belo Horizonte, 68, 255, 261–62, 286–87,
298, 312, 424 n.25; domestic space, 164, 278,
286–87, 290, 292, 298; and eugenics, 293; as
immersive pictoriality, 285; integrative
design, 259; and labor, 292, 297; modern
architecture, 246, 259, 264–65, 280, 293;
modular armoire wall unit, 287, *288*, 289;
and modulation, 249, 251; mutability of
constructed elements, 270, 298; organic,
263–66, 298, 312; organic line as core of
Clark's architectural investigations, 261;

and painting, 259, 261–63, 272, 278, 285;
as social construction, 298; and standardization, 246; and subject, 299; total
design, 112, 277, 285; viewers and artworks
shielded from, 272, *273*, 274; and wall,
279–80, 282, 287.

Aristotle, 264, 310.

Arp, Hans, 42, 90, 157, 180, 182–84, 192–94, 197,
435 n.124; Clark's reference for Concretism,
53, 169; on Concretism, 171–73; exhibition
at Venice Biennale, *180*; *Horloge* (Clock),
180, *181*, 182–83, 191; *Die Kunstismen / Les
ismes de l'art / The Isms of Art*, 90, 92, 104,
116, 118–19; works illustrated in *L'art
abstrait*, *171*.

Art/artwork: affective boundaries of, 70;
affective nature of form in, 69; architectural matter of, 154; and architecture,
259–65, 274, 282, 286; artistic intentionality
vs. viewer response, 419 n.170; and autopoiesis, 75, 328–30; Black art, 42; capacity
to invent mutant coordinates, 75, 325, 329;
and capitalism, 330–31; Clark abandoned
art for therapy, 28, 234; and frame, 123, 183,
187–88, 190–91, 274; and gender, 435; and
globalization, 75; importance of diffusion
of, to general population, 426 n.44; interactive ecologies of, 330; as investigation by
which the human emerges, 71; and its
environment, 75, 112; line-limit between
frame and, 22; and making, 157; of mentally ill, 164, 166; mosaics, 270, *271*; murals,
259, 272; necessary to burst rectangle, 137;
psychological origins of, 164; and race,
burden of representation, 149; and referentiality, 113; rethink autonomy of, 64;
seam allows acknowledgment of composite elements, 12; should express its own
reality entirely, 104, 130, 135, 172; and
subject, 115; surface as screen of activity
between viewer and, 201; synthesis of,
259–65; as technique, 12; total work of, 259;
and viewer, 198–99, 237, 266; and wall,
35, 272, *273*, 274, 277–79; and woman, Clark
on, 136; "the work is always more intelligent than the artist," 370 n.113.

Art therapy, 73–74, 162, 164, 166, 192, 394 n.147.

Artaud, Antonin, 164.

Arte Madí, *108*, 274, *281*, 384 n.60, 403 n.55.

Artists Space, 334–35.

Arturo: Revista de artes abstractas (journal),
103–104, 107.

Ashton, Dore, 40–41.

Asociación Arte Concreto-Invención, 107, 113,
274, 384 n.60, 403 n.53.

Ateliê (Studio), 155.

Author: abstract vs. embodied, 213; authorial
withdrawal, 74, 179, 192, 195, 200, 213, 216–
17, 222, 238; birth metaphor as alternative
model of, 62, 71, 139; construction vs., 186;
and influence, 12; and mark, 158. *See also*
Human; Subject.

Autopoiesis, 329, 336–39, 345–46, 440 n.5;
and artwork, 75, 328–30; living beings
defined as autopoietic, 326, 328; and
organic line, 339.

Avant-garde: and abstraction, 192; age of
exploration metabolized by, 87; and anti-
Blackness, 145; Clark influenced by, 32;
lay bare the device, 12, 24; narratives
of modernist intervention, 26; shaped by
story of modernism, 90; Soviet avant-
garde, 87–88, 90, 93, 97, 108, 186, 386 n.89.

BABA ANTROPOFÁGICA (Anthropophagic
slobber), 340, *343*.

Baker, Josephine, 241; and Le Corbusier,
293, 295–96, *297*, 303.

Bakhtin, Mikhail, 12.

Balibar, Étienne, 300.

Ball, Hugo, 147.

Baraka, Amiri, 219; *Black Dada Nihilismus*, 147.

Bardi, Lina Bo, 433 n.100.

Barr, Alfred, 90, 267, 272, 363 n.60, 365 n.71;
*Painting and Sculpture in the Museum
of Modern Art*, 116.

Barros, Geraldo, 409 n.88.

Basbaum, Ricardo, 10, 75, 126, 191; *love songs*,
320, *321*; *NBP* (New Bases for Personality),
317, 319–22, *323*, 324; *Would you like to
participate in an artistic experience?*, 317,
318, 319–22, 324.

Bayer, Herbert, 433 n.100.

Bebop, 210, 212–13.

Bergson, Henri, 264.

Bernardes, Sergio, 426 n.42.

Berrada, Omar, 151.

Bessa, Sergio, 254.

Best, Susan, 372 n.131.

Bichos (Critters), *28, 39,* 157, 340, 401 n.42.

Bilhaud, Paul, 95.

Bill, Max, 36, 53, 114–15, 169, 172, 180, 267, 386 n.83, 401 n.44; *Tripartite Unity, 50, 51.*

Binyon, Laurence, 416 n.141.

Birth/ovulation/pregnancy/reproduction: Clark's artistic practice as, 142–43, 337; Eugenics, 293, 295; metaphors of, 62–64, 66–67, 71–72, 135–37, 139, 144, 168.

Black art, 42; artists of color and burden of representation, 149; negation as representation of Blackness, 129; Where are the Blacks?, 127, *128,* 129, 131. *See also* Africa; Brazilian art; Race/racialization.

Black Dada, 77, 147, *148,* 149, *150,* 151, 338; and organic line, 149, 151.

Black, Hannah, 129.

Black music, 219, 221.

Blaszko, Martín, 113, 280; works at São Paulo Bienal, *281.*

Bloom, Harold, 27, 368 n.91; as model of influence, 50, 54, 367 n.85.

Body: *Breviário sobre o corpo* (Breviary of the body), 143–44, 154, 156; *A casa é o corpo* (The house is a body), 251, *252–53;* embodied nature of marks and representation, 154; and improvisation, 211; and labor, 301–302, 304; and making, 154; organic line, corporeality of, 144; organic line reminds us painting is a body, 126; and representation, 246; surface as limit of, 198; and therapeutic practice, 235, 237; virgin's mutating body in fairytale, 254.

Bois, Yve-Alain, 50, 192–93, 195, 360–61 n.38, 366 n.84, 381 n.55, 408 n.86, 410 n.94, n.97.

Borders proliferate, 300–301.

Braque, Georges, 10.

Brazil: construction of new modern society, 262, 266, 272; contemporary art was predominantly representational and ideologically nationalist, 272; marginal context of, 27–28; military dictatorship in, 41, 237; modular units unfurling across, 242–43, *244–45,* 290; myth of racial democracy, 42, 127; as periphery, 62; redemocratization,

317; standardization and modernity in, 242–43; tariffs on artists' paints, 24.

Brazilian art, 9–10, 42, 50, 69–70, 114–15, 151, 154, 164, *175, 176,* 233, 317, 363 n.59, 367 n.87, 369 n.106, 385 n.82, 401 n.43, 418 n.168.

Brett, Guy, 27, *28,* 360 n.38.

Breviário sobre o corpo (Breviary of the body), 143–44, 154, 156.

Brito, Ronaldo, 233.

Brown, Wendy, 301.

Bruyn, Eric de, 13, 376 n.16..

Built environment, 257, 262, 283, 310.

Burle Marx, Roberto, 154, 160, 172, 257, *268,* 430 n.74, 433 n.100; and gardens, 267, *269, 270, 272;* influence on Clark, 266–67.

CABANÃS, KAIRA, 164, 166, 234, 237.

Cabeça coletivo (Collective head), 254.

Cage, John, 157, 192, 217; and Eastman, 213, 215–19, 221, 227, 238, 416 n.140; 4'33", 74, 200, 202, *203–205,* 207–208, *209,* 210–13, 216, 221, 233; *Silence,* 200–201; *Silent Prayer,* 208, 212; *Theater Piece #1,* 200.

Caminhando (Walking), 50, *52, 53,* 340.

Campos, Augusto de, 414 n.130.

Campos, Haroldo de, 54.

Canvas: burst open spatial enclosure of, 120; burst rectangle of, 137; and edge, 197; and frame, 80–81, 190; history of art and rectangular canvas, 113; to introduce a real door into, 133; irregularly shaped, 36, 104, *105–106,* 107–108, *109,* 110, 115, 280; organic line as space between frame and, 78, 139, 160, 183–84; pictorial elemements disobey boundary of, 137; rotating canvases multiplies spatial possibilities, 103; space engenders relation between frame and, 125; wall assumes optical function of, 107–108. *See also* Frame; Painting.

Capitalism: and art, 330–31; and coloniality, 75; global capitalism, 75, 300–304, 308; racial capitalism, 335; and slave labor, 217.

Cardboard, 65, 69, 81, *109,* 137, 158, 160, 162, 184, 186, 227, 229, 231–32, 237, 300, 339, *346,* 388 n.99, 410 n.97.

Cardoso, Rafael, 359 n.32.

Carlin, Peta, 310.

Carson, Anne, 310.

A Casa é o corpo (The House is a body), 251, 252–53.

Center: "bracketing the center," 32; Clark's muted reception despite exhibitions in artistic centers, 27; Europe as, 260; inclusion/exclusion, local/universal, derivative/original, 86–87; and influence, 32; and periphery, 29, 32, 45; possibility of disruption by peripheral practices, 32; rectangular shipping cartons for export from Africa to, 246; weak links and contemporary history of modern art refuse subsumption in, 44–45.

Cercle et Carré, 104.

Cézanne, Paul, 36.

Chance, 192–94, 207, 210, 212.

Cheng, Anne Anlin, 293, 295–97.

Chéret, Jules, *Les Zoulous, Tous les Soirs, 96.*

Chile, 43; military dictatorship, 337.

Chinese railway, 305.

Chromonormativity, 371 n.115.

Circling the square, 139, 151.

Ciudad Universitária in Caracas, 259–60.

Clark, Lygia: accounts of artistic evolution, 64–65; archive of documents, 355; artistic career launched after solo exhibition in Rio, 169, 193; artistic practice as pregnancy, 142–43; avant-garde influence on, 32, 169; beginning of art making for, 158; carpentry apprenticeship, 160, 257, 298; Catholic upbringing, 139; childhood traumas, 254; children of, 222, *223–26,* 227, *228,* 229; circle of artists around, 32, 113, 115–16, 166, 192, 360 n.37; circling the square, 139, 151; on Concretism, *114;* on edge of an abyss, 168; epigraph, 241; exteriority to major language of modernism, 62, 64; "far too elegant for a painter," 213; and feminism, 71; and Gullar, *313;* in her studio in Rio, *170;* "I am the before and the after," 67, 77, 134; irregular recurrence of forms in series by, 231–32; lecture at architecture school in Belo Horizonte, 68, 255, 261–62, 286–87, 298, 312, 424 n.25; loneliness of, 32, 369 n.106; and Maldonado, 113–14; Malevich cited in work by, 84, 98, 113, 118–20, 122–23, 125, 133–34; "Minas Gerais Painter (Lygia Clark) Discovers New Organic Lines in

Plastic Arts" (newspaper headline), 255; Oiticica on importance of work by, 36; painting-object as radical intervention, 24; period of uncertainty, 255; photographed with *Quebra da moldura, 18,* 19; postpartum psychosis of, 142, 158; set aside institutional affiliation with art in later years, 28, 234; and Stella, 39, 41, 44; with studies for modulated surfaces, *163;* topological form, introduction to, 50; two types of painting by, 173, 183; as woman from marginal context of Brazil, 27–28; writings by, 370 n.111. *See also* Exhibitions; Organic line.

Clark, T. J., 381 n.54.

Clark-Ribeiro, Aluízio, 434 n.117.

Clay, Jean, 27.

Clayton, Jace, 339.

Cleave, 222, 310.

Cocchiarale, Fernando, 251.

Coelho, Frederico, 363 n.59.

Coleridge, Samuel Taylor, 264.

Colomina, Beatriz, 299.

Coloniality: and capitalism, 75; colonization of space, 144; and conquest of New World, 86; and contemporary art, 333; countless visual tropes within colonial imaginary, 95, *96;* decolonial articulation of modernism, 44; decolonial discovery looks to artistic practice, 151; fog of whiteness that blinds people produced by, 146; Futurism and colonialism, 130; and human, 346; and modernity, 24–25, 66, 87, 247; outsourcing labor in global capitalism has a precursor in colonial networks, 301–302; rectangular shipping cartons for export from Africa, 246–47, 293, 300; Russian definition of savage, 130; and wall, 292–93, 297.

Columbus, Christopher, 86–88, 290, 435 n.125.

Commentari (journal), 283.

Composição (Composition), *174, 175,* 183, 186.

Composition, 186, 188, 193–94, 229; absenting self from, 200; anticompositional operations, 192–95, 197; composing with space, 231–32; noncompositional strategies, 74, 157, 194; and organic line, 192.

Conceptual art, 147, 149.

Concrete art/Concretism, 36, 50, 53, 90, 113–15, 169, 180, 262; vs. abstraction, 171–72; and architecture, 262; Clark's explanation of, *114*; Clark's reference for, *53*.

Constructivism, 28, 88.

Contemporary: global contemporary, 67; history of modern art, central task of, 44–45, 75, 151; as paradigm of discovery against invention, 73.

Contemporary art: and African art, 131; in Brazil, 272; and coloniality, 333; contemporary history of modern art, 44–45, 75, 151; frame as problem in, 104, 107, 115, 274; and line, 363 n.59; and modern art, 10, 66–67, 66–68, 371 n.119; and possibilities of resistance, 303. *See also Names of individual artists and critics.*

Corcraft, 334–35, *336*.

Cordeiro, Waldemar, 115.

Correio da Manhã (newspaper), 261–62.

Costa, Lúcio, 262, 265, 426 n.36.

Creationismo, 104.

Crockett, Vivian, 414 n.130.

Cubism, 36, 67, 130–31, 171.

Cultural technique, 313–15; grid as, 12, 242, 249.

Cut/cutting, 17, 104, 158, 160, 162, 166, 168, 179, 182–83, 232–33, 305, 344, 347.

DAVID ZWIRNER GALLERY, 332.

De Stijl, 259, 282.

"Death of the Plane, The" (text), 49, 135, 137, 142.

Deductive structure, 35, 363 n.54.

Delaunay, Robert, 26, 36; *Simultaneous Windows onto the City*, 20, 21, *22*.

Delaunay, Sonia, 259, 425 n.34.

Deleuze, Gilles, 27, 55, 147; *A Thousand Plateaus*, 13, 15.

Delgado Moya, Sergio, 286.

Deligny, Fernand, 15.

Derrida, Jacques, 139, 187–88.

Descoberta da linha orgânica (Discovery of the organic line), 73, 78, *79*, *81*, 84, 98, 113–15, *114–15*, 118–20, 122–27, 133–34, 160, 188, 326, 338, 375 n.7, 388 n.99; citation of *Black Square*, 98, 113, 118–20, 133; compositional emphasis on corner of, 122; decisiveness of, 78; deliriously heterogeneous materiality of, 125; materiality external to canvas as representational conceit, 123; mathematical vectors of relationality in, 120, 123, *124*, 125–27; painting within a painting, 119, 122–23, *124*, 125, 133; rotation of, 134. *See also* Organic line.

Di Cavalcanti, Emiliano, 272.

Dimock, Wai Chee, 49–50.

Diniz, Fernando, 164, 166, 235; untitled paintings, *165*, *167*.

Discovery: Clark's work as paradigm of, 84; decolonial discovery looks to artistic practice, 151; vs. invention, 77–78, 84, 86–88; of organic line, 45, 53, 64, 68–69, 84, 137, 144, 146, 158, 160, 162, 173, 175, 184, 186, 188, 197, 255, 257, 261, 267, 339.

Dobrinsky, Isaac, 169.

Doesburg, Theo Van, 282, 386 n.85, 402 n.45.

Domestic: labor, 286, 289, 292, 298–99, 302; space, 164, 278, 286–87, 290, 292, 298.

Drawing, 153, 156–58, 160, 257; embodied nature of, 154; rendering of form in, transformed perception into naming, 13; of stairs, 134, *152*, 153–54, *157*, 257, 266.

DuBois, W. E. B., 147.

Duchamp, Marcel, 10, 27, 157, 194, 199–200, 217, 409 n.91, 411 n.103, 422 n.8..

Duve, Thierry de, 199.

EASTMAN, GERRY, 227.

Eastman, Julius, 74, 147, 153, *214*, 227, 339; *Buddha*, 418 n.159; and Cage, 213, 215–19, 221, 227, 238, 416 n.140; *Gay Guerrilla*, 415 n.132; *Nigger Series*, 217, *218*, 219, *220*, 221–22; *Solo for Voice 8*, 213, 215–17.

Edge: as activation of interface with environment, 232; and canvas, 197; and frame, 172–73; and mark, 195; and self-referentiality, 197–98; and surface, 190; and topology, 68.

Eichhorn, Maria, *Maria Eichhorn Public Limited Company*, 330, *331*, 332.

Engelstein, Stefani, 227.

Engenho de Dentro, 74, 162, 166, 192, 234–35, 394 n.147, 398 n.21, 399 nn.

Erber, Pedro, *Breaching the Frame*, 29, 32, 357 n.2.

Escadas (Stairs), *152*.

Espaços modulados (Modulated spaces), 340.

Espada, Heloisa, 401 n.42.

Estruturação do Self (Structuring of the Self), 158, *159*, 234–35, *236*, 237, 240, 340, 420 n.177.

Estudo para Quebra da moldura (Study for Breaking the frame), 8.

Eugenics, 293, 295.

Exhibitions (Lygia Clark's): artistic career launched after solo exhibition in Rio, 169, 193; *Bichos*, *28*, 39; at Ciudad Universitária, 260; Clark with *Quebra da moldura*, *18*, 19; at Exposição Nacional de Arte Abstrata/Concreto, 386 n.84; first exhibition of architectural maquettes, 260, 274; first organic line paintings sent to Venice Biennale, 60; first solo show, 41, 409 n.89; Grupo Frente exhibtion, 404 n.58; at L'Institut Endoplastique, 169; at Museu de Arte Moderna de São Paulo, 386 n.84; at Museu de Arte Moderna do Rio de Janeiro, 160, 162, 164, 257, 260, 386 n.84, 401 n.42; muted reception despite exhibitions in artistic centers, 27; pamphlet for, suggests encounter with Malevich, 118; *Quadro objeto* at Salão Preto e Branco, 22, *23*, 24, 60, *175*; retrospective at Museum of Modern Art, 10, 388 n.101; at São Paulo Bienal, 160; at Signals Gallery, 360 n.38; at Venice Biennale, 24, 60, 160, 173, *175*, *176*, 183–84, 186. *See also* Clark, Lygia.

Exposition internationale d'art psycho-pathologique, 166.

FABBRINI, RICARDO NASCIMENTO, 65, 190, 231, 360 n.36, 375 n.6.

Família (Family), 222, *223–25*, *226*.

Fasani, Antoine, 263.

Fédida, Pierre, 234.

Feminism, 62; and Clark, 71; female principle in *Geometria amorosa*, 137, 139; politics and performance of, 287. *See also* Gender; Woman.

Fer, Briony, 99.

Ferko, Frank, *218*.

Ferreira, Gina, 235, 237.

Figueiredo, Luciano, 388 n.99, 397 n.9.

Figure: and abstraction, 73; and ground, 108, 110, 112, 118, 129, 133, 149, 173, 175, 180, 274, 409 n.91.

Fluxus, 202.

Focillon, Henri, 153–54, 157.

Fontana, Lucio, 180, 182–83; *Buchi* (Holes) series, 178–79, 406 n.64; *Concetto spaziale* (Spatial concept), *178*; *Tagli* (Cuts), 17, 19, *179*, 405 n.62.

Forma (magazine), 146.

Foster, Hal, 25.

Foucault, Michel, 26; *The Order of Things*, 144.

Frame: and artwork, 123, 183, 187–88, 190–91, 274; "break the frame," 9, 134, 162; burst open spatial enclosure of canvas to run beyond, 120; burst rectangle of, 137; and canvas, 80–81, 190; Derrida on, 187; dissolution of, 21; and ground, 123; irregularly shaped frames, 36, 104, *105–106*, *107–108*, *109*, 110, 115, 172, 179; line-limit between artwork and, 22; *marco recortado* (cut-out or broken frame), 104, 107, 112–13, 122, 134, 172–73, 179, 192, 280, 383 n.63, 386 n.89; mural means painting will lose frame, 259; organic line as space between canvas and, 78, 139, 160, 183–84; *passe-partout* (framing mat), 9, 68, 139, 186–88, 190, 339; pictorial elemements disobey boundary of, 137; as problem in contemporary art, 104, 107, 115, 274; as protective security for artwork, 282; and *Quebra da moldura (p x b) versão 1*, 45, *46–47*; relation between pictorial motif and framing edge, 35; space engenders relation between canvas and, 125; Western music requires a frame, 216. *See also* Canvas; Painting.

Freeman, Elizabeth, 71.

French railway line, 246–48, 293.

Frente 3 de Fevereiro, 73, 127, *128*; Where are the Blacks?, 127, *128*, 129, 131.

Fried, Michael, 35, 122.

Futurism, 130.

GAINES, MALIK, 221.

Gann, Kyle, 202.

Gaps: between canvas and frame suppressed, 35; between images, long tradition in Western art, 13; and networks, 149. *See also* Space.

García, María Amalia, 110.

Garden, 267, 269–70.

Geiger, Anna Bella, 251.

Gender, 227; and art, 435 n.118; disembodied
female hand in advertisement, 314;
domestic labor, 286, 289, 292, 298–99, 302;
female difference, 71; gendered divisions
of space, 312, 319, *320*; gendered terms in
Geometria amorosa, 137, 139; and global
capitalism, 302; politics and performance
of, 287; and structure of psyche, 234;
and wall, 301. *See also* Feminism; Woman.

Geometria amorosa (Amorous geometry),
137, *138*, 139, *140–41*, 142, 144, 234–35, 337,
346, 347; circling the square, 139.

Gestalt theory, 69–70, 112, 115, 118, 231, 319,
324, 347, 386 n.86.

Giani, Giampiero, 179–80.

Giedion, Sigfried, 265, 310.

Gilbert, Zanna, 418 n.159.

Gilliam, Sam, 41.

Giunta, Andrea, 104, 375 n.11..

Globalization: and artwork, 75; flattened
image of the global, 68; global capitalism,
75, 300–304, 308; global contemporary,
67; globalism before, 43; history of art
is more global than canonical, 41; and
regulation of space by grid, 242–43;
and standardized shipping cartons, 248,
293, 300.

Goethe, Johann Wolfgang von, 54, 264.

Golan, Romy, 259.

Gottschaller, Pia, 179, 407 n.76.

Graeber, David, 310.

Granovetter, Mark, 38.

Greenberg, Clement, 201, 259.

Grid, 195, 197, 242–43; as cultural technique, 12,
242, 249; and human, 315; of standardized
shipping cartons, 246–48; surface as, 61.

Ground: and figure, 108, 110, 112, 118, 129,
133, 149, 173, 175, 180, 274, 409 n.91; and
frame, 123.

Groupe Espace, 260, 263.

Groys, Boris, 371 n.119.

Grupo Frente, 175, 257, 260, 274, 312, *313*; exhibition with Clark, 404 n.58.

Guattari, Félix, 27, 55, 75, 320, 325, 329, 331;
mutant coordinates, 75, 325, 329, 338;
A Thousand Plateaus, 13, 15.

Gullar, Ferreira, 29, 67, 69–70, 78, 80–84, 90,
115–16, 118, 274, 312, *313*, 375 n.8, 381 n.51,
386 n.88, 388 n.91, 388 n.101, 399 n.30,
405 n.62; *Lygia Clark: Uma experiência
radical, 1954–1958, 80, 163.*

Guston, Philip, 41.

HAACKE, HANS, 41.

Haber, Abraham, 277–79.

Habitat (magazine), *314*.

Hamoudi, Jamil, 41–42, 169; *Meditation, 42.*

Hand, 154, 156–57, 229; touch, 312, 314.

Happenings, 202.

Haynes, Roy, *211*.

Hepworth, Barbara, 42.

Herkenhoff, Paulo, 29, 65, 69, 134–35, 266, 282.

Herrera, Carmen, 42.

Hesse, Eva, 41.

History of art: artistic intervention held dear,
12, 24; Black Dada as alter archaeology
of, 151; and chimeras of invention, 26;
Clark's work in, 65; and coloniality, 25;
composition, notion of, exhausted and
overdetermined, 192; contemporary
history of modern art, 44–45, 75, 151; geopolitics of, 29, 43–44; and line, 347; the
major produces canon of, 27–28, 72–73;
more global than canonical, 41; multitude
of paths not taken, 44; nonnormative
global complexity of, 43; and organic line,
10, 13, 15, 27, 36, 66, 69, 72, 345; and rectangular canvas, 113; strong misreadings of
influence and intervention, 27; structured
by patrilineal drive for origins, 63; vertical relationships of antagonism pervade,
227; and weak links, 53.

Hlito, Alfredo, 107, 274.

Hughes, Francesca, 246.

Hughes, Gordon, 21.

Huidobro, Vicente, 104, 172, 435 n.124.

Human: and architecture, 299; birth/ovula-
tion/pregnancy/reproduction, 62–64,
66–67, 71–72, 136, 142–44, 168, 337; Black
humanity, 129; and built environment,
310; and coloniality, 346; composition
predicated upon coherent notion of, 192;
and cultural techniques, 314; dissolution
of man's mimetic projection of himself,

135; dream of reciprocity between man and environment, 251; as emergent, non a priori category, 70–71, 239; and eugenics, 293, 295; and grid, 315; hands as primary signal of, 154; liberal notion of universal human subject, 129; lines contain developmental history of, 157; man as locus of transformed subjectivity, 136; man as recent invention, 144; and modulation, 251; mutability of human life, 312; racialized conception of, 129, 338; synthesis of arts as human imperative, 259, 262. *See also* Author; Subject.

Hurufiyya movement, 41.

IDENTITY, 71.

Ikemoto, Wendy, 13.

Improvisation, 210–12.

India Triennale, 40–41, 43.

Indigenous peoples: American indigenous culture, 374 n.4; in colonial imaginary, 95; colonial seizure of territory from, 86; exhibitions of, 378 n.29.

Influence: and authorship, 12; and center, 32; and geopolitics of art history, 29; plagiotropic deflects overdetermination of, 54–55; strong misreadings of influence and intervention, 27; and weak links, 53.

Infrathin, 184, 199, 217, 389 n.112.

Ingold, Tim, 143, 270.

International Art Exhibition for Palestine, 43, *44.*

Invencionistas, 77, 90.

Invention: of Americas, 86–87; art's capacity to invent mutant coordinates, 75, 325, 329, 338; authorial model of, 192; battle for, 90; burgeoning language of Brazilian Concretism indebted to discourse of, 114; the contemporary as paradigm of discovery against, 73; vs. discovery, 77–78, 84, 86–88, 376 n.12, 413 n.124; Malevich distanced from, 116; man as recent invention, 144; modern art history's language of, 10, 26; modernist invention and anti-Black racism, 98; Western trope of, dismissed and inverted by Clark, 63.

Irigaray, Luce, 72, 369 n.107.

JACKSON, GEORGE, 15.

Jackson, Matthew Jesse, 379–80 n.42.

Jackson, Zakiyyah Iman, 129.

Jazz, 145, 208, 210, *211,* 212–13, 227.

Jeffries, James, 95.

Johns, Jasper, 27.

Johnson, Jack, 95; advertisement for, *96.*

Joseph, Brandon, 27, 201–202.

Judd, Donald, 28.

Jung, Carl, 164, 234, 394 n.147.

KAHN, DOUGLAS, 208, 212.

Kandinsky, Wassily, 36.

Kapur, Geeta, 365 n.73.

Kattas, Janet, 218.

Katz, Jonathan, 415 n.132, n.136.

Kelly, Ellsworth, 42, 74, 157, 192–94, 410 n.97; *Cité,* 195; *Colors for a Large Wall, 195, 196, 197; La combe II,* 194; noncompositional paintings, *194, 195; Window, Museum of Modern Art,* 194.

Klee, Paul, 15; *Pedagogic Sketchbooks,* 16.

Klein, Melanie, 234.

Köhler, Wolfgang, 319.

Kosice, Gyula, 113.

Kotik, Petr, *214.*

Kotz, Liz, 202.

Krauss, Rosalind, 385 n.79.

Kubler, George, 66.

LA BORDE CLINIC, 234.

Labor: and architecture, 292, 297; and body, 301–302, 304; cheap, 300; and commodity, 304; domestic labor, 289, 292, 298–99, 302; and network, 297, 300; outsourcing labor in global capitalism has a precursor in colonial networks, 301–302; prison labor, 334–36; servant labor on ocean liner, 290–93, 296–97, 305; slave labor, 217; slavery, 302, 334–35.

Lacan, Jacques, 53.

Laneri, Roberto, *214.*

Le Blanc, Aleca, 404 n.55.

Le Corbusier, 241, 302, 324; in blackface, 296–97; "dwelling machines" (modular units) unfurling across South America, *242–43, 244–45,* 290; and eugenics, 293, 295; and Jospehine Baker, 293, 295–96, 297, 303;

"machine for living," 251, 289–90, 293, 297; *The Modulor*, 74, 246, *247*, 248–49, 263, *264*, 293, 297, 301; *Precisions on the Present State of Architecture and City Planning*, 289, *291*, 294, 295; and servant labor on ocean liner, 290–93, 296–97, 305; *The Sleeping Josephine Baker*, 295; standardized shipping containers, 246–48, 293, 300, 314–15; on unifying force of architecture, 259; voyage from Paris to Buenos Aires, 243, 289–90, *291*, 292–93, 295–300.

Léger, Fernand, 169, 259, 400 n.37, 425 n.32.

Leonardo da Vinci, 144, 198–99, 410 n.98.

Lepecki, André, 372 n.130.

Levi, Rino, 262.

Lewin, Kurt, 319, 324; *Field Theory in Social Science*, 319, *320*; *Principles of Topological Psychology*, 319.

Lewis, George, 210–11.

LeWitt, Sol, 41; *Incomplete Open Cubes*, 147.

Line: abyssal line, 86, 133; to "break the frame," 9, 134; and contemporary art, 363 n.59; cross-medial applicability of, 262; developmental history of human contained in, 157; and differentiation, 13; French railway line, 246–48, 293; and hands, 156; and history of art, 347; Klee on, 15; Le Corbusier's ocean liner voyage, 243, 289–90, *291*, 292–93, 295–99; light line, 134; line-limit between artwork and frame, 22; "lines of flight," 15, 238; as minimal condition to establish figure against ground, 13; and organic line, 197–98, 255, 257, 263; and organic line, distinction between, 15, 249; organic line unlike any other line in history of art, 13; plagiotropic points to relations between lines, 55; and plane, 279; and space, 60–61; of space, 187; and standardization, 243, 246; and surface, 64; thickness of, 56; as vector of force, 13; and viewer, 198, 233. *See also* Organic line.

Lins, Sonia, 168–69, 194, 400 n.37, 409 n.89.

Lissitzky, El, 73, 88, 108, 118, 125; *About Two Squares*, 88, 90, *102*, 103–104, 120, 134; *Die Kunstismen / Les ismes de l'art / The Isms of Art*, 90, *92*, 104, 116, 118–19; *PROUNs*, 103, 120, 134.

Loos, Adolf, 297, 299.

López-Durán, Fabiola, 293.

Love, 320, 337.

Lozza, Raúl, 107, 110, 113, 274, 280; compositions differentiated with wooden dividers, 277, *278*; illustration of artwork by, *279*; *Pintura no. 171*, 276, *277*; works at São Paulo Bienal, *281*, 282.

Lozza, Rembrandt, 277.

Luhmann, Niklas, 332, 369 n.103, 442 n.28, 442 n.35.

Lurçat, Jean, 60, 426 n.37.

MACEL, CHRISTINE, 234.

Major, and minor, 27–28.

Making: and art, 157; and body, 154; Clark's beginning of, 158; and hands, 156; and human being, 71; not making, 197, 232, 239; and subjectivity, 158; and viewing, 32.

Maldonado, Tomás, 36, 73, 90, 103–104, 112–15, 118–20, 169, 172, 179–80, 274, 277, 374 n.4, 388 n.59; "El arte concreto," *111*; and Clark, 113–14; *Pintura*, 106; *Sin título*, 90, 108, *109*, 110, 173.

Malevich, Kazimir, 32, 36, 77, 89, 95, *101*, 136, 144, 326, 329, 338, 345; *Analytical Chart*, *327*; anti-Blackness echoed in, 129, 131, 144–45, 149; "The Art of the Savage and Its Principles," 130, 146; *Black Square*, 10, 73, 84, *85*, 88, 97–100, 113, 115–16, 118–20, 122, 125, 127, 129–30, 133–34, 145; Brazilian Portuguese name for *Black Square*, 145; cited in Clark's work, 84, 98, 113, 118–20, 122–23, 125, 133–34; *From Cubism and Futurism to Suprematism*, 130; inscription on *Black Square*, 73, 93, 97–99, 127, 129–31, 146, 149, 338; Latin American influence, 103–104, 107–108, 110, 115–16; *The Non-Objective World*, 115–16, *117*, 123, 325; *Painterly Realism of Boy with Knapsack*, 90, *91*, 104, 120, 381 n.56, 382 n.59; research on, *93*, 97–98; set design for *Victory over the Sun*, 98, *99*, 122–23, 131; on square, 135; on Suprematism, 75, 136; translated in Brazil, 116, 375 n.9.

Mãos (Hands), 156.

Maquette do interior para armário embutido (Maquette of the interior for a built-in closet), 255.

Maquette para interior (Maquette for interior), *250, 258, 316.*

Marco recortado (cut-out or broken frame), 104, 107, 112–13, 122, 134, 172–73, 179, 192, 280, 383 n.63, 386 n.89.

Margins: Clark as woman from marginal context of Brazil, 27–28; and weak links, 38.

Marinetti, Filippo, 130, 145, 391 n.122.

Mark: and author, 158; *Black Square* as marked form on unmarked support, 100; and delimitation of painterly plane in Stella's painting, 35; and edge, 195; gallery as operation of marked and unmarked spaces, 35; and hands, 156; how can a mark not be made?, 158; mark-making in Pape's woodblock prints, 32; marked and unmarked as foundational act of distinction, 347; and modernism, 73; not making marks, 232; and organic line, 198; organic line devoid of mark, 15, 17, 179, 229, 248; puncturing the plane, 179; and representation, embodied nature of, 154; in Rottenberg's work, 308.

Markov, Vladimir, 131; *Iskusstvo negrov* (Negro art), 131, *132.*

Martelotte, Luiza, 237–38.

Martin, Patricia, *218.*

Martins, Sérgio, 414 n.130, 419 n.171.

Marx, Karl, 304.

Mathematics, 45, *48*, 49, 120, *121*, 122–23, *124*, 126, 169, 265, 346; *cualimetría, 277.*

Matisse, Henri, 42, 430 n.74.

Maturana, Humberto, 75, 320, 325–26, 328–29, 332, 337–38, 345–47.

Maurício, Jayme, 116, 118.

Mavignier, Almir, 162, 166, 192.

Mayakovsky, Vladimir, 97, 377 n.22.

McKay, Claude, *97,* 97, 391–92 n.130.

McVey, Sam, 95.

Medalla, David, 27, *28.*

Medium specificity, 35, 201, 207.

Meister, Anna-Maria, 243.

Melé, Juan, 107, 274, 276, 277, 382 n.59; portfolio, *275.*

Mel'nikov, Konstantin, 87–88; lighthouse dedicated to Christopher Columbus, *87.*

Mentally ill, 164, 166.

Mercer, Kobena, 149.

Meu doce rio (My sweet river), 254, 304.

Meyerhold, Vsevolod, 97.

Mezzadra, Sandro, 300–301.

Mies van der Rohe, 263.

Mignolo, Walter, 144.

Milliet, Maria Alice, 65.

Mindlin, Henrique, 242, 261, 265, 269.

Mingus, Charles, *211.*

Minimalism, 29, 35.

Ministério da Educação e Saúde, 266, 269–70.

Minor: and major, 27–28, 361 n.39; and weak links, 38.

Mitchell, Juliet, 222, 227.

Mitter, Partha, 62.

Möbius strip, 50, 53.

Modern art/modernism/modernity: affinity for rhetoric of origins, 84; and anti-Black racism, 98; artistic intervention held dear, 12, 24; avant-garde proposes to lay bare the device, 12, 24; battle for authentically modern art, 90; Black Dada as blindspot of, 151; Clark's ample exposure to, 169; Clark's exteriority, 27–28, 62, 64; and coloniality, 24–25, 66, 87, 247; composition, notion of, exhausted and overdetermined, 192; constituted by interstices, 62; construction of new modern society in Brazil, 262; and contemporary art, 10, 66–68, 371 n.119; contemporary history of modern art, 44–45, 75, 151; deformations of, 49–50; geopolitics of, 43–44; inclusion/exclusion, local/universal, derivative/original, 86–87; language of European modernism, 25–27; modern architecture, 246, 259, 264–65, 280, 293; multiple modernisms, 10, 49, 359 n.33; nonnormative histories of, 43; organic line reconfigures (as topology), 9, 45, 61, 84; pictorial surface revolutionized by, 10; plagiotropic relations reveal lacunae in, 66; political vision of international modern art from South, 41; and psychological origins of art, 164; radical gestures of, 157; rectangular shipping cartons for export from Africa, 246–47, 293; representation, modernist rupture with, 73, 122; to show, not to tell, 77; and standardization, 242; viewed from the present, 346; weak link of organic line as method for rethinking modernism, 39, 345.

Modulation: and architecture, 249, 251; beginning of modulated surfaces, 234; dream of modularity, 251; and human, 251; modular armoire wall unit, 287, *288*, 289; modular coordination, 242; modular products, 241–42, 265; modular units for Montevideo and São Paulo, 242–43, *244–45*; modulated surface defined, 232; modulated surface partitions volume and captures subjectivity, 242; modulated surfaces, 68, 262, 265–66, 285; modulated surfaces relocate representation to viewer, 233; mutation of modernist architectural modularity, 254–55; and networks, 243; organic could enliven modularity, 266; spatiality in terms of, 419 n.169.

Molenberg, Alberto, 107, 274.

Mondrian, Piet, 26, 32, 36, 259, 282, 300, 409 n.91, 430 n.74; *Broadway Boogie Woogie*, 57; *Design for the Salon of Ida Bienert*, 260; and surface, 56, 60; *Victory Boogie Woogie*, 145; works at São Paulo Bienal, 27, 56, 368 n.95, 425 n.34.

Monk, Thelonius, 211.

Monteiro, Odette, 267; residence of, *269*.

Moreira, Jorge Machado, 261.

Morellet, Françoise, 192.

Morris, Robert, 29.

Mosaics, 270, *271*.

Moscow School of Painting, Sculpture, and Architecture, 95.

Moten, Fred, 145, 337, 373 n.137, 413 n.125..

Murals, 259, 272.

Museo de Arte Moderno de Buenos Aires, 279.

Museo de la Solidaridad Salvador Allende (Santiago de Chile), 39–40, 41, 43–44.

Museu de Arte de São Paulo, 171, 386 n.84, 433 n.100.

Museu de Arte Moderna do Rio de Janeiro, 60, 113, 160, 164, 261, 266, 272, *273*, 386 n.84, 426 n.37; Groupe Espace exhibition on synthesis of art and architecture, 260.

Museu de Arte Negra, 42–43.

Museum of Modern Art (New York): chart of abstraction, 36, *37*; Clark's 2014 retrospective at, 10; organic furniture design, 264–65.

Music: Black music, 219, 221; experimental music, 213, 215, 217; improvisation, 210–12; jazz, 145, 208, 210, *211*, 212–13, 227; Muzak company, 208; Western music, 216, 219, 221; Western music requires a frame, 216. *See also Names of individual musicians.*

Mutant coordinates, 75, 325, 329, 338.

Muzak company, 208.

NADAL MORA, VICENTE, *Técnica gráfica del dibujo geométrico*, 120, *121*.

Nascimento, Abdias, 42–43, 365 n.69.

Neilson, Brett, 300–301.

Nelson, Adele, 287, 398 n.14.

Neoconretism, 28–29, 50, 65, 169, 233; organic line as irruption of real space that led to, 69–70.

Nesselrode Moncada, Sean, 110, 383 n.63.

Network: attempts at generating transnational network outside of West, 43; and gaps, 149; global capitalism, 300–304; and human labor, 297, 300; organic line knits viewer into artwork in spatial network, 237, 285; outsourcing labor in global capitalism has a precursor in colonial networks, 301–302; of standardized modular units, 243; of standardized shipping crates, 246–48, 293, 300, 314–15; stretches beyond work in space to viewer, 199; and subjectivity, 74–75, 298; and weak links, 38, 43–44.

Neufert, Ernst, 243, 248.

New World, Old World, 86, 88.

Niemeyer, Oscar, 261–62, 267.

Nuestra Arquitectura (journal), 287, *288*.

OBRAS MOLES (Soft works), 50, 340, 341.

O'Gorman, Edmundo, 87.

Ogura, Tadao, 41.

Oiticica, Hélio, 29, 36, 53, 115, 166, 317, 345, 386 n.89, 414 n.130.

Old World, New World, 86, 88.

Ono, Yoko, 216.

Onobrakpeya, Bruce, 41.

Organic: defined, 263–65, 267; developing notion of, 180; organic character of subject must be transmuted to environment, 266; as ten-fingered grasp on reality, 310.

Organic form, 53, 182, 218–19.

Organic line: and actuality of encounter, 66; analytic potential of, 127, 344–45; appearance of, at Venice Biennale, 24, 60, 175; beginning of Clark's research on, 64, 68–69; biocentric conception of, 267; and Black Dada, 149, 151; and blackness, 145; as bridge between heterogeneous surfaces of built environment, 262–63; and composition, 192; corporeality of, 144; defined, 17; as device for registering misregistration of content and form, 191; devoid of mark, 15, 17, 179, 229, 248; discovery of, 45, 53, 64, 68–69, 84, 137, 144, 146, 158, 160, 162, 173, 175, 184, 186, 188, 197, 255, 257, 261, 267, 339; encourages conception of artwork's relations with its environment, 75; escapes integration into Concretism, 114; excavation of, 233; as fugitive entity, 340, 344; and history of art, 10, 13, 15, 27, 36, 66, 69, 72, 345; interstitial character of, 26, 36, 65, 186, 270, 326, 340, 347; and line, 197–98, 255, 257, 263; and line, distinction between, 15, 249; modern art reconfigured (as topology) by, 9, 45, 61, 68, 84; naming of, 9, 13, 69, 137, 184, 257, 261, 326; negativity of, 233, 239, 344, 347; as new artistic paradigm, 115; objects and mediums are not self-evident facts, as demonstrated by, 36; organizes, 153, 235, 237; and Orozco's shoebox, 19, 21; between painting and frame of Stella's works, 35; and *Quebra da moldura (p x b) versão 1*, 45; as realm alongside making, 157; resemblance to modern artistic techniques, 12; as space between canvas and frame, 78, 139, 160, 183–84; as space of conversion where incommensurate realities meet and are transformed, 126, 133; and spatial interval, 13, 32, 186; textiles as model for, 60; as third term, 118, 127, 149; and topology, 127, 191; uniqueness of, 13, 15; and viewer, 19, 305; as weak link, 36, 38; and weak link as method for rethinking modernism, 39; within and beyond relations between

lines, 55. *See also Descoberta da linha orgânica.*

Origins, 146; chimeras of, 26; inclusion/exclusion, local/universal, derivative/original, 86–87; modern art's affinity for rhetoric of, 84; patrilineal drive for, 63; psychological origins of art, 164.

Orozco, Gabriel, *Empty Shoe Box, 19, 21.*

Oshtoff, Simone, 367 n.87.

Otolith Group, 339.

Ovo linear (Linear egg), 134, *135,* 340, 406 n.69, 418 n.159.

Ozenfant, Amédée, 263.

PAINTING: and architecture, 259, 261–63, 272, 278, 285; artistic merits of *Black Square* questioned, 100; "break the frame," 9, 134, 162; burst open spatial enclosure of canvas, 120; burst rectangle of, 137; crisis of easel picture, 259; to destroy pictorial illusion, 107; dissolution of orientation, 135; experiments with painterly plane, 160; irregularly shaped paintings, 36, 104, *105–106,* 107–108, *109,* 110, 115; modernist manifesto on, 77–78; mural means painting will lose frame, 259; organic line reminds us painting is a body, 126; organic line sunders and sutures painterly plane, 78; orientation as pictorial illusion, 119; painterly surface as topology, 56; pictorial space, abolish all residues of, 274; pictorial space, disappearance of, 80–81; referentiality innate to historicity of, 115; rotating canvases multiplies spatial possibilities, 103; and sculpture, *Bichos* sprung from interrogation of, 28; space beyond, 179; of stairs, 193–94, 285; Suprematism's influence on, 116; surface isolated as nucleus of, 81; transformed conception of, 133; two types of painting by Clark, 173, 183; and wall, 261; what a painting should be, 107; and woman, 213. *See also* Canvas; Frame.

Palestine, International Art Exhibition for, 43, *44.*

Pan-American Union, 87–88.

Paneth-Pollack, Tessa, 402–403 n.52.

Papapetros, Spyros, 300.

Pape, Lygia: and Stella, 29, 32, 35; *Untitled* (woodcut), *30, 33.*

Parker, Charlie, *211.*

Participation, 157; *Would you like to participate in an artistic experience?* (Basbaum), 317, *318,* 319–22, 324.

Passage, 133, 139, 142–44, 157, 186, 235, 249, 278, 337, 347.

Passe-partout (framing mat), 9, 68, 139, 186–88, 190, 339, 442 n.27.

Pedra e ar (Stone and air), 340, *342,* 419 n.173.

Pedrosa, Mário, 12, 40, 63, 164, 176, 182, 261, 263, 266, 272, 319, 324, 337, 360 n.37, 363 n.60, 406 n.70, 419 n.169; and Clark's recourse to topological thinking, 53; idea for museum, 41, 43–44; and Malevich, 115–16.

Pendleton, Adam, 73, 77; *Black Dada,* 146–47, *148,* 149, 151, 338; *Black Dada Reader,* 149, *150,* 151; *That Which Is Fundamental,* 339.

Perceptismo, 277, *278,* 279–80.

Pérez-Barreiro, Gabriel, 110, 277, 367 n.85, 382 n.59.

Pérez-Oramas, Luis, 10, 119, 126, 419 n.172.

Péri, László, 104.

Periphery: and center, 29, 32, 45; Clark's exteriority to major language of modernism, 62; inclusion/exclusion, local/universal, derivative/original, 86–87; paradigm of delay and derivation endemic to, 84; and Soviet avant-garde, 88; and Western modernity, 10.

Phenomenology, 69–70, 285, 305, 310, 326, 340, 344, 387 n.89.

Photocopy, 147, *148,* 149.

Piaget, Jean, 53.

Picasso, Pablo, 10, 26–27, 42, 156, 409 n.91, 430 n.74.

Piotrowski, Piotr, 29.

Piper, Adrian, 147.

Plagiotropic, 54–56, 346, 368 n.91; and autopoietic living systems, 328; and Basbaum, 324; defined, 54; deflects overdetermination of influence, 54–55; illustrated, *54;* relations reveal lacunae in modern art, 66.

Plane: aesthetic space extends beyond, 179; as background, 278; Clark's critique of, 120; concept of, 136; "contagion" of world by, 134; death of, 49, 135, 137, 142; defined by facingness, 122; to disintegrate continuity of, 107; experiments with, 160; and line, 279; materiality of, 175; overturning of rectilinearity of, 135; pictorial illusion of, 123; and psychic recuperation, 162, 166; real plane, 238; and space, 115; as textile, topological, 56; thickness of, 298; unrealized potential of painterly plane, 120.

Planos em superfície modulada no. 3 (Planes in modulated surface no. 3), *58.*

Planos em superfície modulada (Planes in modulated surface), 162, *163,* 229, *230,* 231, 326.

Plante, Isabel, 279, 382 n.59.

Police, 127, 129.

Pollock, Griselda, 62.

Portinari, Candido, 272.

Prati, Lidy, 104, 113, 118–20; *Concreto,* 110, *112.*

Preciado, Paul, 71.

Pregnancy. *See* Birth.

Prison labor, 334–36.

Pseudomorphism, 29, 36, 98, 380 n.46.

Psyche, 234; psychological life space, 319.

Puni, Ivan, 100.

QUADRO OBJETO (Painting object), 22, *23, 24, 175,* 358 n.28, 403–404 n.54.

Quebra da moldura (Breaking the frame), 11, *18, 19,* 78, 81, 134, 137, 160, 175, 186, 188, 191, 283, 388 n.99, 407 n.81, 410 n.97; Clark photographed with, *18, 19.*

Quebra da moldura composição no. 5 (Breaking the frame composition no. 5), 81, 119, 183–84, *185,* 186, 197, 404 n.55.

Quebra da moldura composição no. 4 (Breaking the frame composition no. 4), 81, *82,* 119, 183.

Quebra da moldura (p x b) versão 1 (Breaking the frame [b x w] version 1), 45, *46–47,* 81, 190–91, 231, 326, 388 n.99.

Quebra da moldura versão 1 (Breaking the frame version 1), 81, *83.*

Quijano, Aníbal, 25.

Quiles, Daniel R., 409 n.88.

Quin, Carmelo Arden, 383 n.60, 385 n.80, 403 n.53.

RACE/RACIALIZATION: "A Fight of Negroes at Night" gag banner, 95;

anti-Blackness echoed in Malevich's *Black Square*, 129, 131, 145, 149; artists of color and burden of representation, 149; "Battle of negroes" inscription on Malevich painting, 73, 93, 97–99, 127, 129–31, 146, 149, 338; b(B)lackness, 73, 100, 129, 131, 145–46; "The Black [Negro] from the inside" article, 146; capitalism and slave labor, 217; countless visual tropes within colonial imaginary, 95, 96; eugenics, 293, 295; and experimental music, 213, 215, 217; Futurism and racism, 130; history of human cloaked in, 157; human conceived racially, 338; Le Corbusier in blackface, 296–97; modern art and anti-Black racism, 98; and modern coloniality, 25; myth of racial democracy in Brazil, 42, 127; negation as representation of Blackness, 129; "Negro problem" as question of world revolution, 95, 97; prison labor, 334–36; racial capitalism, 335; racial ontologies, 73, 338; racism, 98, 130, 215, 227, 335, 391 n.122; slave labor, 217; slavery, 302, 334–35; violence of, 127, 129; Where are the Blacks? (F3F), 127, *128*, 129, 131.
Rainer, Yvonne, 212.
Ramos, Guerreiro, 42, 146, 147, 365 n.69.
Rauschenberg, Robert: *Erased de Kooning Drawing*, 157; *White Paintings*, 200, *201*, 202, *206*, *207–208*, 210.
Referentiality, 113–15; *mise en abyme* of representational, 120; self-, 197, 346–47.
Reidy, Affonso Eduardo, 261.
Reinhardt, Ad, 145.
Relational Objects (Clark), 235, 237, 254, 286.
Representation: and abstraction, 77, 149, 272; battle against, 179, 386 n.89; and body, 246; to break with fiction of, 107; burden of, 149; and *Descoberta da linha orgânica*, 125; endurance of, 110; and mark, embodied nature of, 154; materiality external to canvas as, 123; metaphor and materiality at core of modernist rupture with, 122; as mimetic impulse of savage, 131, 146; modernist banishment of, 77–78, 90; modulated surfaces relocate representation to viewer, 233; and organic line, 198; oscillation between abstraction and figuration at core of modernist rupture with, 73; and

space, 197; and Suprematism, 130; and viewer, 126.
Rhizome, 55.
Riedel, Michael, 332–33; *The quick brown fox jumps over the lazy dog*, 332, *333*.
Río de la Plata, 173, 179.
Rivera, Tania, 53.
Robinson, Julia, 412 n.111, 413 n.120.
Rodchenko, Aleksandr, 13; *Line, No. 128*, 14.
Rolnik, Suely, 10, 71, 234, 237, 370 n.111, 420 n.174.
Romero Brest, Jorge, 22, 113; *La pinture europea contemporánea*, 116.
Rothfuss, Rhod, 172; "El marco," 104, *105*, 107.
Rottenberg, Mika, 75, 303–305, 308; *Bowls Balls Souls Holes*, 308, *309*; *Cosmic Generator*, 305, *306*; *Mary's Cherries*, 305, *307*; *NoNoseKnows*, 305; *Squeeze*, 303.
Rowland, Cameron, 334–36; *New York State Unified Court System*, 336; *91020000* (exhibition), 334, 335–36.
Russia: Blackness in, 95, 96, 97–98; Russian definition of savage, 130; Soviet avant-garde, 87–88, 90, 93, 97, 108, 186, 386 n.89.
Ryman, Robert, 41.

SALÃO PRETO E BRANCO, 23, 24, 60, 175, 404 n.55.
Salgado, Zélia Ferreira, 154, 160, 257.
Salon des Réalités Nouvelles (Paris), 42, 107, *108*, 113, 192, 385 n.80, 403 n.53, 408 n.86, 409 n.90.
Sant'Ana, Flavio, 127.
Santos, Boaventura de Sousa, 86, 133.
São Paulo Bienal, 21, *22*, 26, 113, 160, 171, 280, *281*, 282, 405 n.62, 408 n.86; Clark exhibits at, 160; Mondrian works at, 27, 56, 425 n.34.
Schmitt, Carl, *The Nomos of the Eart*, 86, 333.
Scorpion, 63, 71.
Sedgwick, Eve, 71.
Self, 71; absenting the self from compositional processes, 200; self-identity, myth of, 88; self-referentiality, 197, 346–47; strategies to absent rational self, 192–93.
S.E.M. ensemble, 213, *214*.
Semper, Gottfried, 12, 286, 300; grid as surface, 61.

Serpa, Ivan, 175–76, 182–84, 360 n.37; *Colagem sob calor e pressão, 177.*

Serra, Richard, 41.

Seuphor, Michel, 104, 182, 197; *L'art abstrait*, 116, *171*, 300, 385 n.80, 401 n.42, 402 n.45, 403 n.53.

Sex, 136, 295; Eastman's overt sexuality, 415 n.132; erotic charge between Le Corbusier and Baker, 295–96; sexism, 227.

Sexton, Jared, 129.

Shadows, 193–94, 197.

Shatskikh, Aleksandra, 98.

Shipping: containers, 246–48, 293, 300, 314–15; revolution, 74.

Shklovsky, Viktor, 12.

Siegert, Bernhard, 242–43, 286, 301, 313–14.

Silence, 200, 202, 207–208, 212, 233.

Silveira, Nise da, 162, 164, 166, 192, 234–35, 394 n.147.

Simmel, Georg, 282, 286, 299–300.

Slavery, 302, 334–35; slave labor, 217.

Snead, James, 219.

Snoep, Nanette Jacomijn, 95.

Solução para painel (Solution for a panel), 255.

Souza, Francis Newton, *Black Paintings*, 151.

Soviet avant-garde, 87–88, 90, 93, 97, 108, 186, 386 n.89.

Space: aesthetic space extends beyond plane, 179; architecture as spatial protagonist, 300; borders proliferate, 300–301; burst open spatial enclosure of canvas, 120; colonization of, 144; composing with, 231–32; domestic, 164, 278, 286–87, 292, 298; emergence of, as material element in Clark's work, 175; gendered divisions of space, 312, 319, *320*; grid, 242–43; "I am afraid of space, but I rebuild myself from it," 168; irruption of, by organic line led to Neoconcretism, 69–70; irruption of, within and beyond plane, 179; juridical order of, as template for colonial conquest, 86; and line, 60–61; line of, 187; modulated space, 60; network stretches beyond work in, to viewer, 199; organic line and spatial interval, 13, 32; organic line as space between canvas and frame, 78, 139; organic line as space of conversion where incommensurate realities meet and are transformed, 126; organic line as space within work and beyond it, 114, 339; and pictorial plane, 115; psychological life space, 319; relation between canvas and frame engendered within, 125; and representation, 197; rotating canvases multiplies spatial possibilities, 103; segmentation of, 241–42; between shipping cartons, 248, 293, 315; spatial interval, 12; spatial interval necessary for material assembly, 248; standardization in architecture to combat variability of matter in, 246; thickness of, 56, 183; unleashed from breaking of frame, 162.

Spencer-Brown, George, *Laws of Form*, 346–47.

Spillers, Hortense, 129.

Spinoza, Baruch, 264.

Stairs: drawings, 134, *152*, 153–54, *157*, 257, 266; Kelly's, 193–94; paintings, 285.

Standardization, 74, 242–43, 246–47, 265; and architecture, 265–66; blind spots of, 315; and line, 243, 246; and modular units, 265; and organic line, 312; and organic quality of matter, 265; resistance to, 312.

State Tretyakov Gallery, *93, 97*, 131.

Stein, Gertrude, 147.

Stella, Frank, *31*; and Clark, 39, 41, 44; *Isfahan III, 39*; *Kingsbury Run, 34*; and Pape, 29, 32, 35.

Stroll, Avrum, 344, 410 n.98.

Subject/subjectivity: abstract vs. embodied, 213; abstraction and subject misrecognized as object, 151; and architecture, 299; and artwork, 115; and built environment, 310; captured by surface divided, 242; colonial subjects, 95; composition predicated upon coherent notion of, 192; embodied and porous, 10, 142, 168, 238; embodied nature of marks and representation, 154; and global capitalist networks, 74–75, 302; human subject as non a priori category, 70–71, 239; liberal notion of universal human subject, 129; and mark, 158; as monadic unit of sensation, 136; negation as representation of, 129; and network, 74–75, 298; organic character of, must be transmuted to environment, 266; and organic

line, 234–35, 238, 249, 298; as porous sur-
face, 74; precarity of, 372 n.131; reproduction of female subjectivity, 289, 292; sound
as freedom from, 200; subjective emergence, 237; and surface, 296; and wall, 299.
See also Author; Human.
Sullivan, Edward, 364 n.68.
Sullivan, Louis, 310.
Sullivan, Megan, 358 n.21.
Summers, David, 154, 157, 238.
Sun Ra, 147.
Superfícies moduladas (Modulated surfaces),
160, *161*, 242, 255, 256, 257, 282–83, *284*,
398 n.13.
Suprematism, 75, 84, 88, 90, 95, 100, 103–104,
116, 123, 136, 325–26; ontologized plasticity
of anti-Blackness echoed in, 129, 131;
and representation, 130; *Suprematism:
34 Drawings* (pamphlet), 88, *89*, 99, 122.
Surface: composing with space is what Clark
called "modulated surface," 232; as composite of heterogeneous units, 60; concept
of, 136; and edge, 190; false vs. true surfaces, 292, 295, 297; as grid, 61; ground of
Black Square destroys illusion of, 118;
inverted by Clark, 56, 60; isolation of, as
nucleus of painting, 81; as limit of body,
198; and line, 64; materiality of, *173*; modulated surfaces, 68, 262, 265–66, 285; and
Mondrian, 56, 60; organic line as bridge
between heterogeneous surfaces of built
environment, 262–63; organic line entails
unraveling of a priori existence of, 344;
organic line reveals corporeal investments viewers bring to, 126; porositry of,
60; as screen of activity between work
and viewer, 201; and standardization, 246;
and subject, 296; subjectivity captured
by division of, 242.
Symbolon (symbol), 308, 310, 312–13, 315.
Systems theory, 332, 347.
Szeemann, Harald, 41.
Szenes, Árpád, 169.

TAEUBER-ARP, SOPHIE, 36, 193, 259,
425 n.34.
Tatlin, Vladimir, 27, 36, 115.
Teatro Experimental do Negro, 42.

Teixeira, Lucy, 283; on shared pictoriality of
Clark's paintings and maquettes, *284*.
Textile: as model for organic line, 60;
plane understood as, 56.
Therapy: art therapy, 73–74, 162, 164, 166, 192,
394 n.147; Clark abandoned art for, 234;
cutting as therapeutic function, 233;
Estruturação do Self (Structuring of
the Self), 158, *159*, 234–35, *236*, 237, 240;
relational objects of therapeutic practice,
235, *236*, 237–38; therapeutic practice, 71,
73–74, 158, 168, 234–35.
Thickness: of borders, 301; of boundaries, and
coloniality, 293; of matter and space, 154;
of organic line, 199–200, 335; of plane, 298;
of space, 56, 183; of space between shipping cartons, 248, 293, 315; of void, 17, 217.
Thom, René, 49, 328.
Thomas, Frederick Bruce, 95.
Topography, 266, 269–70.
Topology, 347, 367 n.87, 371 n.119; and biology,
328–29; birth/ovulation/pregnancy/
reproduction as, 62–64, 66–67, 139; Clark's
introduction to, 50; in Clark's work,
53; complicates notions of inside and
out, 45; and edge, 68; modernity troubled
by analogy with, 49; and organic line,
127, 191; organic line reconfigures modern
art as, 9, 45, 61, 68; painterly surface
as, 56; topological transformations, *48*.
Torres-García, Joaquín, 104, 374 n.4,
382 n.60.
Total design, 112, 277, 285.
Touch, 312, 314.
Translation, 54.
Treaty of Tordesillas, 86.
Tregulova, Zelfira, *93*.
Tretyakov Gallery, *93*, 97, 131.
Trotsky, Leon, 97.
Tudor, David, 207.

UNDERCOMMONS, 73, 373 n.137.
Unidades (units), 56, 59, 340.
Universalismo Constructivo, 104.
Untitled (Studio), *193*.

VAKAR, IRINA, *93*, 98.
Valentim, Ruben, 151.

Varela, Francisco, 75, 325–26, 328–29, 332, 337, 345–47.

Velde, Henry van de, 157.

Veloso, Caetano, 158.

Venice Biennale, 178–79, 404 n.55; Brazilian representation at, *176*; Clark participates in, 24, 60, 160, 173, *175*, *176*, 183–84, 186; Hans Arp exhibition, *180*; Orozco's shoebox in, 19.

Viewer/viewing: affective boundaries of, 70; and art, 198–99, 237, 266; artistic intentionality vs. viewer response, 419 n.170; Clark more interested in viewer than artist, 198; and corner of *Descoberta da linha orgânica*, 122; "everything said is said by an observer," 345; inescapable presence of, 112; and line, 198, 233; and making, 32; modern banishment of representation as freedom for, 90; and modulated surfaces, 266; network stretches beyond work in space to, 199; and organic line, 19, 305, 358 n.21; organic line as perceptual phenomenon, 249; organic line depends upon, 19; organic line knits viewer into artwork in spatial network, 237, 285; and passage into participation, 157; and phenomenology, 69–70; and representation, 126; surface as screen of activity between artwork and, 201; viewing modernism from the present, 346.

Villanueva, Carlos Raúl, 259.

Vipax advertisement, *314*, *315*.

Void, 36, 60, 71–72, 125, 129, 133–34, 153, 168, 179–80, 182–83, 190–91, 198, 229, 232–35, 237, 242, 248; in Asian aesthetics, 12–13, 357 n.12; thickness of, 17, 217.

Vora, Kalindi, 301–304.

Voronina, Yekaterina, 93.

WALL: and architecture, 279–80, 282, 287; and art, 35, 272, *273*, *274*, 277–79; borders proliferate, 300–301; and coloniality, 292–93, 297; and gender, 301; irregularly framed works unable to extend beyond canvas or, 115; modular armoire wall unit, 287, *288*, 289; and mural, 259, 272; optical function of canvas assumed by, 107–108; and organic line, 298; and painting, 261; painting's interior space makes contact with, 134; portable wall, 277, 282; and subjectivity, 299; traditional function of, 280.

Wanderley, Lula, 153, 235, 237, 420 n.177.

Weak links, 151, 173, 192, 346; and influence, 53; missed connections have ability to reshape modernism, 50; and networks, 38, 43–44; ongoing community of, 324; organic line as, 36, 38, 345; organic line as method for rethinking modernism, 39; and plane as textile, 56; "The Strength of Weak Ties" (Granovetter), *38*.

Weakness, 49–50, 339, 345.

Wertheimer, Max, 319.

West: attempts to generate transnational networks outside of, 43; and coloniality, 25; framed picture, Western tradition of, 21; inclusion/exclusion, local/universal, derivative/original, 86–87; language of European modernism, 25–27; long tradition of anti-Blackness in, 131; long tradition of gaps between images in Western art, 13; modernity complicated as Western notion, 10; myth of self-identity, 88; racialized conception of human, 338; representation as mimetic impulse of savage, 131, 146; trope of invention dismissed and inverted by Clark, 63; Western music, 216, 219, 221.

Wigley, Mark, 285.

Williams, Jan, *214*.

Winnicott, Donald, 234, 372 n.131.

Woman: Clark and feminism, 71; Clark as woman in marginal context of Brazil, 27–28; Clark on woman and artwork, 136; Clark's position as, 27, 62, 345; does not exist yet, 72; domestic labor, 289, 292, 298–99, 302; female scorpion birthing process, 63, 71; gendered terms in *Geometria amorosa*, 137, 139; law of the mother, 222, 227; and painting, 213; reproduction of female subjectivity, 289. *See also Feminism; Gender.*

Wright, Frank Lloyd, 263, 310, *311*.

Wynter, Sylvia, 25, 71, 75, 144, 338, 346.

ZEGHER, CATHERINE DE, 13.

Zevi, Bruno, 310.

Zone Books series design by Bruce Mau
Image placement and production by Julie Fry
Typesetting by Meighan Gale
Printed and bound by Studley Press